The Windows 98 Textbook

Extended Edition

Stewart Venit

California State University, Los Angeles

Scott/Jones, Inc., Publishers
P. O. Box 696, El Granada, CA 94018
E-mail: scotjones2@aol.com
(650) 726-2436 *or* Fax: (650) 726-4693
http://www.scottjonespub.com

The Windows 98 Textbook: Extended Edition
Stewart Venit

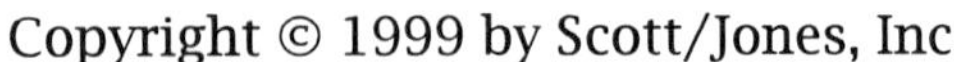

ISBN 1-57676-025-1   0 9 8   X Y Z

Text Design and Composition: Stewart Venit
Book Manufacturing: Malloy Lithographing, Inc.
Sponsoring Editorial Group: Richard Jones, Cathy Glenn
Production Management: Heather Bennett
Marketing & Sales: Barbara Masek, Lynne McCormick, Hazel Dunlap, Donna Cross
Business Operations: Chuck Paetzke, Michelle Robelet, Cathy Glenn
Publisher: Richard Jones

Other Windows 98 Titles from Stewart Venit and Scott/Jones

The Windows 98 Textbook: Standard Edition

Introduction

Chapter 1 The Basics of Using Windows 98

Chapter 2 Working with Applications and Documents

Chapter 3 Managing Files, Folders, and Disks

Chapter 4 Using Windows Efficiently

Chapter 5 Customizing Windows with Control Panel

Chapter 6 Windows and the Internet
(Does not include "Creating Your Own Web Pages")

Chapter 7 Word Processing with WordPad

Chapter 8 Creating Graphics with Paint

Chapter 9 Using Other Windows Accessories

Appendixes
(General Shortcut Keys, Running DOS Programs, Answers to Exercises)

A Short Course in Windows 98

Introduction

Chapter 1 The Basics of Using Windows 98

Chapter 2 Working with Applications and Documents

Chapter 3 Managing Files, Folders, and Disks

Chapter 4 Customizing Windows with Control Panel

Chapter 5 Windows and the Internet
(Does not include "Creating Your Own Web Pages")

Chapter 6 Additional Topics
(Tricks with the Taskbar, The Windows Find Utility, More on WordPad, An Introduction to Paint, Additional Accessories)

Appendix
(Using DOS with Windows 98)

The Windows 98 Textbook: Extended Edition

Contents in Brief

Contents

Preface

The Windows 98 Textbook: Extended Edition is intended for use in a variety of courses on the Windows 98 operating system. It is expected that some readers will have had little or no experience with computers, whereas others will be familiar, to various degrees, with the workings of DOS or another version of Windows. With this in mind, we have written this text for the novice user, but in such a way that those with more experience can easily skip over or quickly review the material with which they are familiar. For example, almost all the general information about computers has been placed in the Introduction. Other aids to quickly locating and moving through familiar topics are described under *Features of the Text*, later in this preface.

Organization of the Text

We have organized this text to provide flexibility in choosing topics and the order in which they are presented. A pictorial representation of the text's organization is shown in the Chapter Dependency Flowchart on the next page. Here is a more detailed description:

- An Introduction provides general information about computer hardware and software. It is intended primarily for those students who have little or no experience with computers, but may also be useful reading for others.

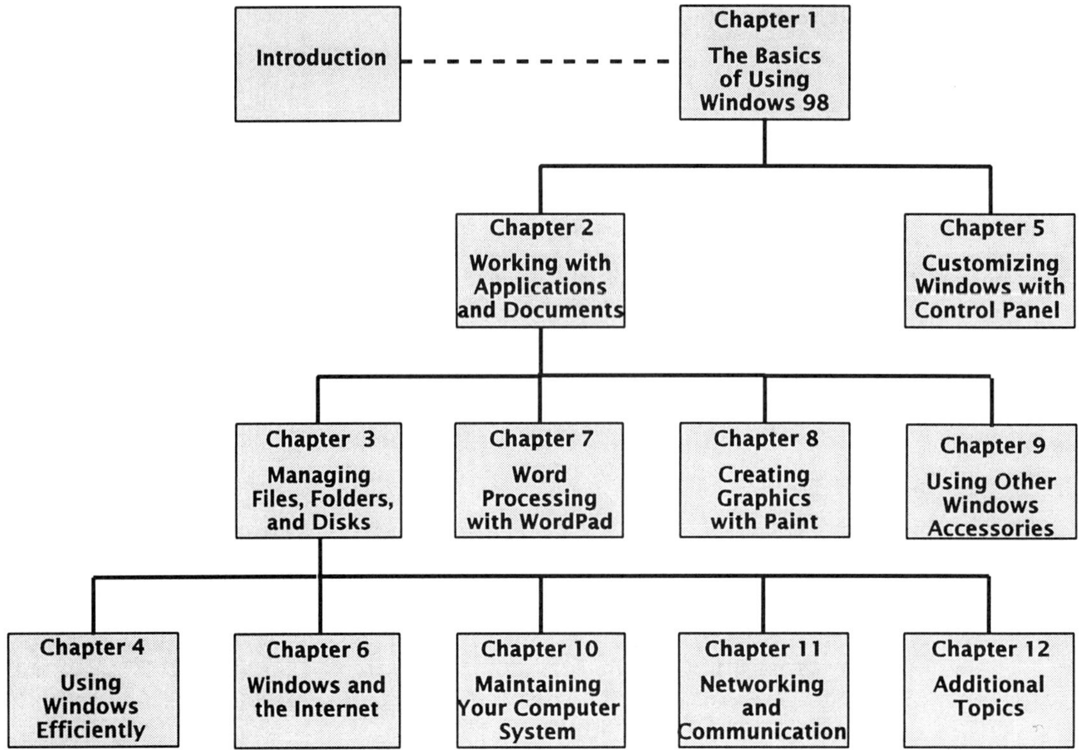

Chapter Dependency Flowchart

- Chapter 1, which covers the basics of using Windows 98, is the normal jumping-off point for those who have some familiarity with computers, but not with Windows 95 or 98. Be aware that the terminology and techniques discussed in Chapter 1 are used throughout the text.
- Chapter 2 presents some fundamental material on working with applications and documents, and would typically be covered next. However, those instructors who want to follow a more gentle path can instead jump to Chapter 5, which deals with some of the ways to customize Windows 98.
- After completing Chapter 2, Chapter 3, 5, 7, 8, or 9 could be covered next. Chapter 3 is the most difficult of these, but also contains the most important material.
- After completing Chapter 3, all the remaining chapters are accessible to the reader.

- Chapters 4, 9, 10, and 12 deal with an assortment of related, but mostly independent topics. In each of these chapters, individual sections can usually be omitted, if so desired. Moreover, the first two sections in Chapters 4 and 9 and the first section of Chapter 12 cover relatively straightforward material that does not require the Chapter 3 prerequisite stated in the flowchart above.

Features of the Text

End-of-section Tutorials

1. Certainly, the best way to learn Windows 98 is to use Windows 98. With this in mind, we have written the text in a way that encourages students to follow along at the computer. Moreover, almost all sections end with a brief Tutorial that reviews the material by leading the student through a hands-on exercise.

No delay in starting up

2. The text introduces Windows' terminology and techniques immediately; we start up Windows on the first page of the first chapter. However, for those courses that require it, the Introduction provides general information about personal computers.

Objectives and summaries

3. We have tried to integrate the material in each chapter as much as possible, so that it forms a cohesive whole. To help in this regard, every chapter (and the Introduction, as well) begins with a brief overview and list of objectives, and ends with a fairly comprehensive summary.

Chapter exercises

4. The text contains three types of exercises at the end of every chapter:
   - Review Exercises (containing completion, true/false, and multiple-choice questions) test the students' knowledge of facts presented in the chapter. Answers to the odd-numbered exercises are provided in Appendix C.
   - The last Review Exercise in each chapter asks the student to "Build Your Own Glossary" — to provide definitions for a given list of important terms introduced in that chapter, (To make this task a little easier, the listed terms are boldfaced when they first appear within the chapter.)
   - Lab Exercises require students to perform the kinds of tasks they will encounter in using Windows on an everyday basis.

If You Want to Learn More ...

5. For those students who want something extra, the very end of each chapter contains a section entitled "If You Want to Learn More ...". This section consists of a series of notes that delve more deeply into the chapter material and refer, when possible, to future sections in the text that expand on this material.

TIPs

6. TIPs appear periodically throughout the text. These short notes provide insight into, or specialized knowledge about, the topic at hand. A fact or technique may be called a TIP because it is especially important or because it is interesting or unusual.

WARNINGs

7. Other specialized notes are designated as WARNINGs. They caution the reader against taking certain actions, which in some circumstances could lead to extreme regret.

Troubleshooting

8. Troubleshooting tips appear, when appropriate, throughout the text. They try to anticipate situations in which something may go wrong and tell the student what can be done about it.

Margin notes

9. Occasional brief phrases in the left margin of the text make it easy for the reader to locate subtopics and important procedures.

Supplements

10. The following ancillary material is available for this textbook:
    - A *Student Disk*, containing the files referenced in the Tutorials and Lab Exercises, accompanies the text.
    - An *Instructor's Resource Manual*, which contains a test bank of additional short-answer questions keyed to the material in the text and the answers to *all* Review Exercises and Lab Exercises, is available directly from the publisher.*

A Few Words about Homework

This text, through its end-of-chapter exercises, provides an ample supply of homework problems. The Review Exercises can usually be answered with a single word (or letter, in the case of the multiple-choice problems), and the Lab Exercises contain frequent questions that require a brief answer or explanation. (The Lab Exercises also occasionally call for an optional screen capture.)

In a computer course, it is desirable to provide students, as quickly as possible, with the ability to use the computer for printing solutions to their homework problems. For this reason, we introduce, relatively early in the text, the basics of WordPad (Section 2.2) and the techniques for capturing windows and screens (Section 2.3). Once this material has been completed, students will be able to hand in computer-printed homework.

*The mail address, Web address, phone, and fax numbers for the publisher appear on the title page and back cover of this text.

Acknowledgments

I would like to thank the many people who helped bring this project to fruition. A textbook always benefits from varied points of view and I was lucky to have the following experienced instructors offer helpful suggestions for the developing manuscript:

Valerie Evans
Cuesta College

Art Freeman
Los Angeles City College

Chuck Fuchs
Portland CC, Mt. Hood College, Clark College, Clackamas CC

Janos T. Fustos
Metropolitan State College of Denver

Tony Gaddis
Haywood Community College

Carol Grim
Palm Beach Community College

Dee Harrington
Brazosport College

Laura Hunt
Tulsa Junior College

Nancy Lanning
Western Iowa Tech Community College

Patricia Rausch
Lake-Sumter Community College

Marian Sedlacek
Metropolitan Community College

Bill Smith
Sinclair Community College

Wayne Snelling
South Plains College

Nancy Webb
City College of San Francisco

Wesley Scruggs of Brazosport College and Jen Chen of Cal State, L. A. created the test bank for the *Instructor's Resource Manual* . Professor Chen also worked all the Lab Exercises and provided the answers found in the IRC.

A special thanks to my publisher, Richard Jones, who gave enthusiastic and unwavering support for this text, and managed, as usual, to make criticism sound like praise. I would like to thank my wife, Corinne, and my daughter, Tamara, for understanding that a project of this sort requires the author to spend countless hours glued to a computer monitor. Finally, special mention should be made of my dogs, Maggie and Abby, who often kept me company, sleeping peacefully next to the humming computer.

Introduction

Overview

We are living in a world that is becoming increasingly dependent on the electronic computer. Computers help run our businesses and institutions, design and build manufactured products, provide instantaneous worldwide communication, publish our newspapers, magazines, and books, and supply all sorts of educational and recreational activities. Many forms of employment now require some kind of **computer literacy** — an understanding of how to use a computer effectively.

In this introduction, we will describe, in general terms, the computer's *hardware* and *software* — the components and programs that make it work. Although this material is not essential for an understanding of Windows 98, it may help with certain topics and will probably increase your computer literacy. More specifically, you will learn about:

1. Computers in general and personal computers in particular.
2. The components of a computer: its central processing unit, internal memory, mass storage, and input and output devices.
3. Types of computer applications.
4. The function of an operating system.
5. Microsoft Windows — what it is and why it's important.
6. The history of the personal computer.

Personal Computers

Everyone who uses a computer on a daily basis becomes accustomed to dealing with special computer-related terminology. Yet, to a beginner, many of these terms can be confusing and even intimidating. There are floppy disks and hard disks, kilobytes and megabytes, mice and monitors, and much, much more. In this section, we will try to take some of the mystery out of computer terminology.

What is a Computer?

As with any evolving technology, precisely defining the term *computer* is not easy. Computers can take many different forms and their capabilities are constantly expanding. Yet, all computers do the same basic things. Every **computer** can input, store, manipulate, and output vast quantities of data at very high speed. Moreover, all computers are *programmable* — they can follow a list of instructions (a **program**) and act upon intermediate results without human intervention.

A **personal computer**, or **PC**, is a relatively small type of computer intended for use by one person at a time. (Larger machines — known as *minicomputers*, *mainframes*, and *supercomputers*, in order of increasing size and power — can be simultaneously shared by many users, connected to the computer by cables or telephone lines.) All personal computers are small enough to fit on a desktop; portable PCs are even smaller — usually no larger than a looseleaf binder. A drawing of a typical PC is shown in Figure 1.

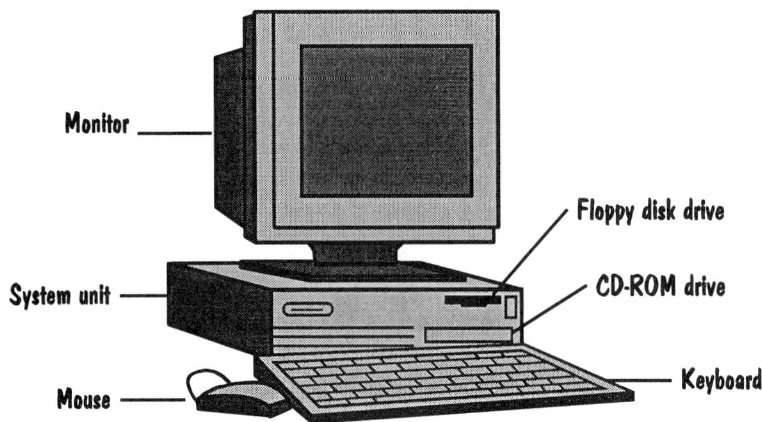

Figure 1 A Typical Personal Computer

Components of a computer

As the definition implies, a computer must have the ability to input, store, manipulate, and output data. These functions are carried out by the five main components of a computer system:

1. The central processing unit (or CPU)
2. Internal memory (consisting of RAM and ROM)
3. Mass storage devices (such as floppy and hard disk drives)
4. Input devices (such as a keyboard or mouse)
5. Output devices (such as a monitor or printer)

In a personal computer, the first two of these components (and usually the third as well) are located in the **system unit** (see Figure 1). The input and output devices are housed in their own enclosures and are connected to the system unit by cables. Components like these, that are used by a computer but located outside the system unit, are sometimes referred to as **peripherals**. All the physical equipment that makes up the computer system is known as **hardware**.

The Central Processing Unit

The **central processing unit** (also called the **processor** or **CPU**) is the brain of the computer. It receives all program instructions, performs the arithmetic and logical operations necessary to execute them, and controls all the other computer components. In a personal computer, the processor consists of millions of transistors residing on a single *chip* about the size of a postage stamp, and plugged into the computer's main circuit board, the **motherboard**.

More than any other component, the CPU distinguishes one computer from another. In the kind of computer you will be using, which is known as **IBM-compatible**, the processor is probably made by Intel Corporation and is some version of a *486* (pronounced "four-86") or *Pentium* chip.

The power of a processor is determined largely by two factors: its speed, measured in *megahertz* (MHz), and the amount of data — the number of *bits* — it can process at a time. (A **bit** is the smallest piece of information a computer can manipulate; its value is represented by either a 0 or 1.) For example, the Pentium is a 64-bit chip that is produced in variations that run at speeds from 60 MHz to (as of this writing) 450 MHz. To use Windows 98, you need a computer with at least a 32-bit chip, and the more speed the better.

Internal Memory

A computer uses its **internal memory** to store the instructions and data to be processed by the CPU. In a personal computer, memory resides on a series of chips either plugged directly into the motherboard or into one or more smaller circuit boards connected to the motherboard.

ROM and RAM

Internal memory is divided into two types: ROM and RAM. **ROM** stands for *Read-Only Memory*. It contains an unalterable set of instructions that the computer consults during its start-up process and during certain other basic operations. **RAM** (*Random-Access Memory*), on the other hand, can be both read from and written to. (Think of ROM as a reference sheet, while RAM is a scratchpad — a very large scratchpad.) RAM is used by the computer to hold program instructions and data. Whereas ROM is a permanent form of memory storage, all the information stored in RAM is lost when the computer is turned off.

Memory is usually measured in *kilobytes* and *megabytes*; one **byte** consists of eight bits and is the amount of memory used to store one character of information. (Loosely speaking, a *character* is any symbol you can type, such as a letter, a digit, or a punctuation mark.) One **kilobyte**, abbreviated *KB*, is 1,024 (= 2^{10}) bytes and one **megabyte** (*MB*) is 1,024 kilobytes. For example, a computer with 32 megabytes of RAM, a typical amount nowadays, can store 33,554,432 (= 32 × 1,024 × 1,024) characters of information.

Mass Storage Devices

In addition to ROM and RAM, a computer needs **mass storage**, another form of memory, which stores programs and data semi-permanently. (They remain in mass storage until you decide to erase them.) However, to make use of any information stored on a mass storage device, the computer must first *load* (copy) that information into RAM.

Hard and floppy disk drives

On personal computers, the primary type of mass storage device is the **disk drive**. Most PCs contain a *hard disk drive* and a *floppy disk drive* housed within the system unit. The latter drive is accessible from the outside (see Figure 1) so that disks can be inserted and removed from it. To store information, the hard disk drive makes use of a constantly spinning magnetic platter — the **hard disk** — which is sealed within the drive. **Floppy disks** (or **diskettes**), on the other hand, are stored away from the computer and, when needed, are inserted into the diskette drive.

Modern personal computers use floppy disks that are 3½ inches in diameter (see Figure 2) and store 1.44 megabytes of data. (You may encounter diskettes of other sizes and/or capacities on older, less powerful PCs.) Hard drives hold much more data than floppies. Modern personal computers are equipped with hard drives that exceed 1,024 megabytes — one **gigabyte** (GB) — of storage capacity.

Write-protect switch

Figure 2 Floppy Disk

Write-protecting a diskette

If you want to prevent the accidental erasure of data on a floppy disk, you can *write-protect* it. A write-protected diskette can be read from, but not written to or erased. To write-protect a 3½-inch diskette, throw its write-protect switch so that the hole under it is exposed (see Figure 2).

You may be wondering why computers contain both hard and floppy drives. Typically, the hard drive is used to store most of the programs and data to be used by a PC. Floppy drives, which are much slower in operation, are typically used in the following ways:

- To transfer newly purchased programs from the distribution disks to the computer's hard disk.
- For *backup* purposes — to make copies of valuable hard disk data in the event that the hard disk becomes damaged.
- To help transfer information from one computer to another.
- For *archival* purposes — to move information from the hard disk to floppies when it is unlikely to be needed in the foreseeable future.

CD-ROM drives

Virtually all PCs sold today are equipped with another type of mass storage device, the **CD-ROM drive**. These drives use disks that are similar to audio compact discs (hence the "CD" in the name). Like floppies, CD-ROMs are removable and portable, but, unlike floppies, they hold large amounts of information — about 600 MB each. Because CD-ROM drives are read-only devices (hence the "ROM" in the name), they are used primarily:

- To distribute large applications to the computer user (instead of using dozens of floppies).
- To run applications that require an unusually large amount of storage space, such as encyclopedias and graphics-intensive games.

However, even CD-ROMs do not have the capacity needed to run certain modern computer applications, such as those that use large amounts of video and sound. For this reason, the *digital versatile disk*, or DVD, was developed. A DVD has more than seven times the storage capacity of a CD-ROM. **DVD drives**, which can also read CD-ROMs, are slowly replacing the latter in computer systems.

Other mass storage devices

Floppy disk drives and CD-ROM drives are referred to generically as *removable media* devices because, unlike hard drives, their disks are inserted into the drive before use and removed from it afterwards. Other types of removable media drives have recently become popular; they have large storage capacities, yet preserve the floppy's ability to *write* data to the disk. The most common of these is the *Zip* drive made by Iomega Corporation, which holds 100 megabytes of information. Other drives of this type can store as much as two *gigabytes* of data.

Another fairly common mass storage devices is the **tape drive**, which uses media that resemble audio cassettes. It can be used to copy (back up) the entire contents of a hard disk onto a magnetic tape. Should the information on the hard disk become inaccessible for any reason, the data could then be retrieved from the backup tape. A tape drive works slowly, but this isn't too important considering its intended role.

Input Devices

The computer uses its **input devices** to receive data from the outside world. For this purpose, every computer includes a typewriter-like **keyboard** (see Figure 3). To enter information into the computer, you simply type it at the keyboard in the same way you would using an ordinary typewriter. The characters you type will simultaneously appear on the computer's display screen.

Special keys

Computer keyboards contain quite a few keys not found on a typewriter. (Figure 3 shows a common keyboard layout for IBM-compatible machines.) These "extra" keys include:

- Twelve *function keys* labeled F1 through F12 are arrayed across the top of the keyboard. They perform special tasks that vary from program to program.
- Just to the right of the large block of typewriter-like keys are ten *cursor control keys*: the four *Arrow keys* (↑, ↓, ←, and →) plus Insert, Home, etc. These keys allow you to move the *cursor*, which indicates the current typing position, around the screen.

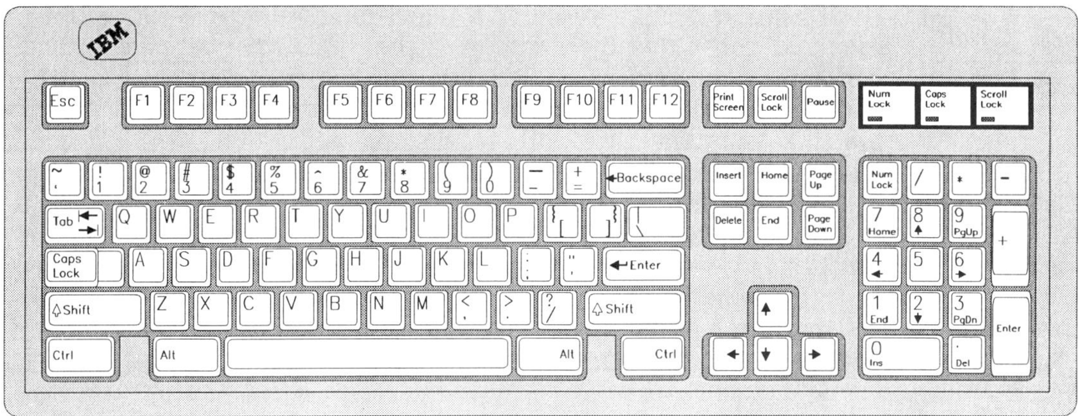

Figure 3 A Typical Keyboard Layout

- A *numeric keypad*, at the far right of the keyboard, allows you to enter numbers quickly. If the *Num Lock* light (above the keypad) is off, pressing one of these keys doesn't input a number; it performs the secondary function indicated on the key (for example, Home or ↑). To turn the Num Lock light on or off, press the Num Lock key.

You may notice a few other special keys (such as Esc and Print Screen) here and there on the keyboard. We will explain their function at the appropriate times, later in the text.

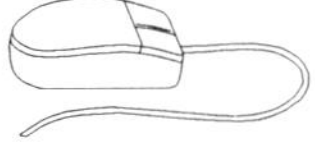

Another standard input device is the **mouse**, a hand-held object containing two or three buttons, which (together with the cable that connects it to the computer) vaguely resembles a long-tailed rodent. When you roll the mouse around on the desk top, a pointer moves correspondingly on the screen. For example, if you roll the mouse to the left, the pointer moves left. Once the pointer is positioned appropriately on the screen, pressing a mouse button (*clicking the mouse*) performs a program function. The mouse can speed up many Windows operations, but it lacks the versatility of the keyboard.

Output Devices

Whereas input devices allow us to communicate with the computer, **output devices** make it possible for the computer to "talk" to us. The most common output devices are *monitors* and *printers*.

A **monitor** is a high resolution television-like screen enclosed in a case and controlled by circuitry — the *video adapter* — within the computer. (The screens on portable computers use an entirely different technology; they are usually *LCD* — liquid crystal display — *panels.*) As is the case with televisions, monitor size is measured along the screen's diagonal. The most common screen sizes for desktop computers are 15 and 17 inches, but other sizes are also available. Another characteristic that affects the quality and cost of a monitor is its *resolution* — the number of *pixels* (tiny dots of light) it uses to create images. Nowadays, screen resolutions of 1024 × 768 — 768 horizontal rows, each containing 1,024 pixels — are becoming commonplace. This kind of resolution puts even the finest of televisions to shame.

Unfortunately, output to the screen is both impermanent (it disappears when the power is turned off) and not terribly portable (you'd need a pretty long extension cord to take your screen output home from school). If you want to make a permanent copy (a *hard copy*) of a program's output on paper, you need to use a **printer.**

The text and pictures produced by virtually all printers are composed of tiny dots of ink or an ink-like substance. The size of these dots and how closely they are packed together determine the quality of the output. Currently, two types of printers dominate the market:

- **Laser printers** have become the standard for business use. They produce excellent-looking black-and-white text and graphics at a high rate of speed, and are remarkably reliable. Laser prices start at about $400, but they cost relatively little to run and maintain. *Color* laser printers are not as common as their monochrome brethren, mainly because of their considerable cost.
- **Ink jet printers** spray incredibly tiny drops of ink on the paper creating surprisingly clear images. Most ink jets produce relatively good color output as well. Although, generally speaking, ink jet printers cost less to buy than lasers, they are slower and have a higher cost of operation. For these reasons, ink jets are more common in the home than in the office.

Software, Operating Systems, and Windows

The most powerful hardware cannot accomplish anything by itself. It needs **software** — computer programs — to bring it to life. Software provides instructions for the central processing unit and, in so doing, allows the computer user to write letters, calculate loan balances, draw pictures, play games, and perform countless other tasks.

Applications Software

Software can be divided into two general categories: applications software and system software. **Applications** are programs you use to enhance your productivity, solve problems, supply information, or provide recreation. To be able to run programs like these is the reason one learns to use a computer.

Here are some of the more popular kinds of applications:

Types of applications

- *Word processors* help you create, edit, and print documents such as letters, reports, memos, and so on.
- *Database managers* allow you to enter, access, and modify large quantities of data. You might use a database program to create a personal phone directory. A business can use this kind of application to maintain customer lists and employee records.
- *Spreadsheet programs* simplify the manipulation and calculation of large amounts of tabular data (spreadsheets). These programs are often used by businesses to try to foresee the effect of different strategies on their bottom line.
- *Painting programs* allow one to use the computer to draw pictures (*graphics*) on the screen and print them on paper.
- *Multimedia applications* make extensive use of sophisticated graphics, sound, and sometimes video images to provide information or entertainment.

Applications are developed and published by many different companies and are sold by retail stores and mail order firms. Each software package consists of a *user's guide* together with one or more diskettes or CDs that contain the application *files* — the programs, data, and documents needed by the application. Before you can use a software package, it must be *installed* — the computer must copy files from the floppies or CDs to the hard disk and supply certain information about the application to the operating system.

The Operating System

The second general software type is **system software**, the programs used by the computer to control and maintain its hardware and to communicate with the user. The most important piece of system software is the **operating system** — the computer's master control program. The operating system has two general functions:

1. It helps the application you are using to communicate with the computer hardware. Applications are written to run under a specific operating system, which supplies easy ways for the programmers to access the computer's disk drives, memory, and so on.
2. It provides an *interface* — a link — between you and the computer that allows you to install and start up applications, manipulate disk files, and perform other very basic tasks.

DOS The central processing unit may be the brain of the computer, but the operating system gives the machine its personality. For years, the most common operating system for IBM-compatible computers was **DOS** (for *disk operating system*), which was developed by Microsoft Corporation for the original IBM Personal Computer introduced in 1981. Although major changes have been made to it over the years, DOS retains much of the awkwardness of its distant past, and as a result, its popularity has waned considerably in the 1990s.

An immediate clue to an operating system's personality is its *start-up screen*, the one you see after you turn on the computer and it has gone through its preliminary functions. With pure, unadorned DOS, you are presented with a few lines of mysterious-looking text ending with the *DOS prompt* (most likely, `C:\>`) followed by a blinking underline (the *cursor*). This is DOS' way of asking you to enter a command. For example, if you want to start up your word processor, you might type the following two lines (pressing the Enter key at the end of each):

```
CD \WP51\DATA
\WP51\WP
```

This kind of **command line interface** is classic DOS. In order to direct DOS to perform a function, the computer user must memorize (or have a handy list of) a large number of arcane commands. This is certainly not a *user-friendly* system.

GUIs A vast improvement in user-friendliness is the **graphical user interface** (**GUI**, pronounced "gooey") popularized by the Apple Macintosh line of computers. In a GUI, the start-up screen contains a collection of small stylized pictures called **icons** (see Figure 4) together with a set of **menus** that supplies available options. (The menus in Figure 4 are entitled *File*, *Options*, *Window*, and *Help*.) With a graphical user interface, you can start up applications and perform other operating system functions as easily as moving the mouse pointer to the corresponding icon or menu item and pressing a mouse button. The keyboard can also be employed to carry out functions, but using a GUI is much easier with a mouse.

Microsoft Windows

Windows is a very sophisticated piece of software, originally developed in 1985 by Microsoft Corporation, that employs a graphical user interface to help make IBM-compatible computers easier to use. Although Windows sold slowly at first, version 3.0 (introduced in 1990) and especially **Windows 3.1** (1992) were wildly popular. The latter version established Windows as the standard operating environment for IBM-compatible computers. (Figure 4 shows its start-up screen.)

Benefits of Windows

Windows provides many benefits for its users:

- Its graphical user interface is much easier to use than a command line interface like that of DOS.
- Windows has *multitasking* capabilities — you can run more than

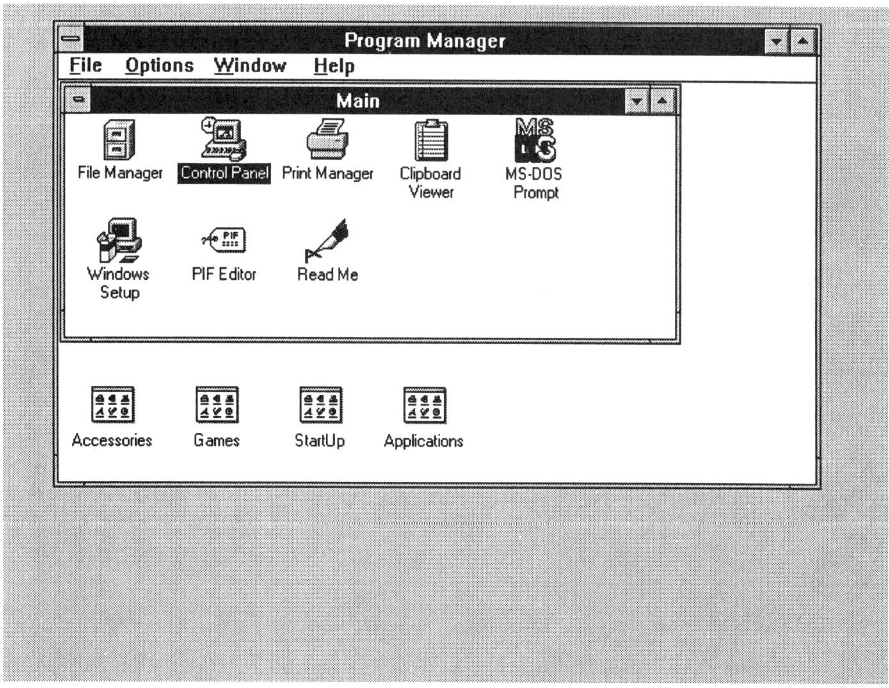

Figure 4 A Typical Windows 3.1 Start-up Screen

one application at a time, each occupying its own area on the screen. For example, you can start up a paint program to draw a picture without closing down the word processor that is already running.

- You can easily transfer data from one application to another. For example, the picture you've just completed in the paint program can be inserted by Windows into your word processing document.
- Windows provides uniform standards for the look and feel of applications developed to run under it. (Such programs are called *Windows applications*; those not designed specifically for Windows are called *DOS applications*.) This is of great benefit to the computer user, making it easier to learn and use new applications.
- The Windows user interface is highly customizable; you are given a great amount of control over the way that it looks and acts. For example, you can design your own start-up screen, choose your own screen colors, and position and size the areas on the screen in which your applications are running.
- Windows supplies a large number of useful small and medium-sized applications. These include an on-screen calculator, a word processor, a paint program, an easy-to-use file manager, and even a couple of games.
- Windows provides modules that control a wide assortment of different monitors, printers, mice, and other peripherals. As a result, applications programmers don't have to worry about writing their own software to communicate with the huge variety of available input and output devices.

Windows 98 Windows 3.1 was not an operating system in the true sense of the term; it could not run unless DOS was present in RAM. This limitation, in turn, led to certain problems and inefficiencies in its use. To remedy this situation, in the summer of 1995, Microsoft brought the long-awaited Windows 4.0 to market. Officially known as **Windows 95**, this new version no longer required DOS in order to run; it was a true operating system. Then, in June 1998, Microsoft released an upgrade to Windows 95, appropriately known as **Windows 98**. Windows 98 is the operating system you will learn about in this text. A typical start-up screen (which is virtually identical to that of Windows 95) is shown in Figure 5.

Windows 98 is very similar to Windows 95 in most respects. It has the same basic interface as the latter, and anyone who is already familiar with Windows 95 will have little trouble in quickly adapting to this newer version. Nevertheless, as upgrades must, Windows 98 did introduce some new features:

- Windows 98 provides closer integration with the Internet's *World Wide Web* than any previous version of Windows. Using its Active Desktop and folder customization features, you can have Windows 98 take on the look and feel of the Web. Other features make it easier to send and receive e-mail, incorporate Web-based information in your everyday work, and even create your own Web page.
- Windows 98 allows you to install and maintain the latest hardware devices, such as DVD drives and TV-tuner adapters. It includes an advanced form of *Plug and Play* to facilitate the installation of hardware and a suite of hardware maintenance tools to help keep it working properly. Portable computer users benefit from improved power management features.
- The Windows Help system has been revamped. In addition to extensive "local" help with Windows 98 and its applications, you now can easily access the Microsoft Web site, if need be, for additional help and updates.

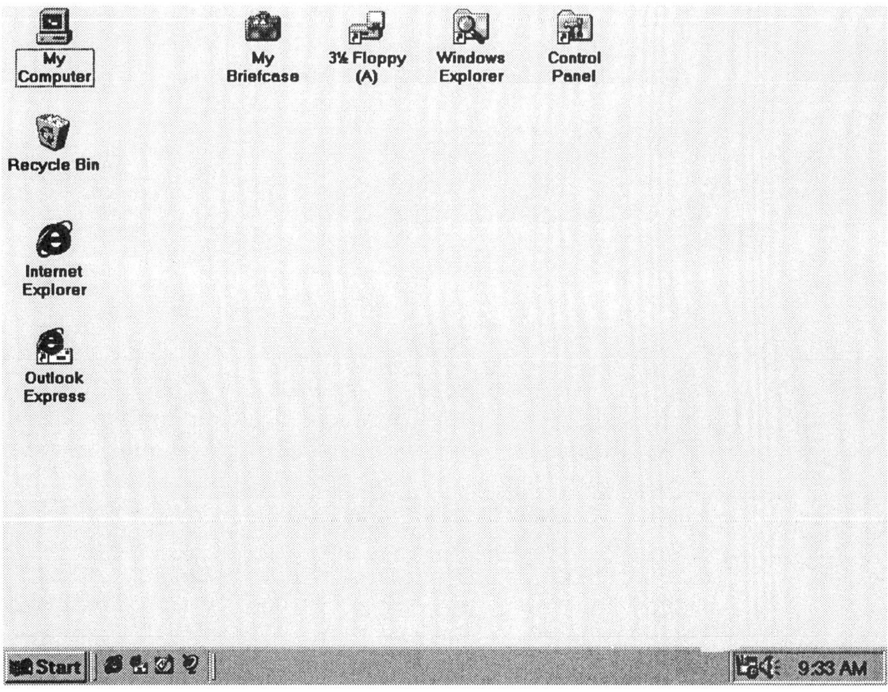

Figure 5 A Windows 98 Start-up Screen

Although many of the features we have just discussed may make little sense to you now, you will learn much more about them as you progress through this textbook.

A Brief History of the Personal Computer

In this section, we will briefly describe the development of the personal computer, beginning with a look at its much larger ancestors and continuing on to the present day.

Prelude to the Personal Computer

The origins of electronic computers

The electronic computer is a relatively recent invention; the first fully-operable computer was developed little more than 50 years ago, at the end of World War II, by a team at the University of Pennsylvania's Moore School of Engineering. This team was headed by John Mauchly and J. Presper Eckert, who named the new machine *ENIAC*, for Electronic Numerical Integrator and Calculator. ENIAC was hardly a *personal* computer, occupying a large room and weighing about 33 tons. By today's standards, ENIAC was also extremely slow, unreliable, and expensive to operate. In 1945, on the other hand, it was considered a marvel.

Over the next 30 years, computers became smaller, faster, and less expensive. Nevertheless, most of these machines were kept isolated in their own air-conditioned rooms, tended by specially trained personnel. By 1975, computers were in great demand at universities, government agencies, and large businesses, but relatively few people had ever come face-to-face with an actual computer. This all began to change in the late 1970s.

To understand why, let's take a closer look at the early computers. ENIAC and its immediate successors were large, slow, and unreliable primarily because they used thousands of large, slow, and unreliable *vacuum tubes* in their electronic circuits. Vacuum tubes were glass cylinders, a few inches high and an inch or so in diameter, which generated a lot of heat and consequently couldn't be placed very close together. But, in 1947 at Bell Labs, William Shockley, John Bardeen, and Walter Brattain announced the invention of the *transistor*, one of the most important inventions of the twentieth century. Only about an inch long and a quarter inch across, a transistor did the same job as a vacuum tube, but produced very little heat.

The downsizing of computers began in the 1950s as transistors replaced vacuum tubes, and continued into the 1960s with the introduction of the *integrated circuit* (IC) — an ice cube-sized package containing hundreds of transistors. By the late 1960s, **microchips** (or *chips*), consisting of thousands of electronic components residing on a piece of silicon the size of a postage stamp, had begun to replace ICs. At this time, a new breed of **minicomputers** appeared, costing less than $25,000 and occupying a space no larger than a small filing cabinet. Then, in 1970, Ted Hoff, Jr., working at Intel Corporation, invented the **microprocessor**, a central processing unit on a chip. The technological world was now ready for the personal computer.

The personal computer

The first personal computer to be successfully marketed to the public was built in 1974. It was designed by Micro Instrumentation and Telemetry Systems (MITS), a small electronics firm located in New Mexico, which named it the Altair 8800. The Altair was a very primitive machine, about the size of a bread box. It contained 256 bytes (not kilobytes) of RAM, had no ROM, and its input and output devices consisted of rows of toggle switches and lights, respectively. The Altair was also quite inexpensive — $395 in kit form. Sales of this machine took off after an article about it appeared in the January, 1975 issue of *Popular Electronics* magazine.

Although add-on products for the Altair 8800 (such as memory boards and paper tape readers) gradually appeared over the next couple of years, few people did any useful work with this machine. Nevertheless, the Altair is of major historical significance because it inspired thousands of computer hobbyists and professionals to become interested in personal computers.

Two of the hobbyists inspired by the Altair were Paul Allen and Bill Gates, both about twenty years old at the time. They joined together to write and sell a version of the BASIC programming language for the new computer. With the easy-to-use BASIC now available, Altair owners no longer had to write programs in low-level, mind-numbing machine language. Soon thereafter, Gates and Allen formed Microsoft Corporation, which is now the world's largest software company (and the publisher of Windows).

Another Altair aficionado was Stephen Wozniak, who joined forces with his friend and fellow Californian, Steven Jobs, to form Apple Computer, Inc. In 1977, they brought the now legendary Apple II personal computer to market. The Apple II was an instant hit and for the next few years, Apple was the fastest growing company in the United States.

The Personal Computer Comes of Age

The IBM PC

By 1980, there were dozens of companies manufacturing personal computers, but the major producers of the larger minicomputers and mainframes had not yet entered the fray. This changed dramatically in 1981, when IBM brought out its first personal computer, which was (not so imaginatively) named the *IBM Personal Computer*) Although it wasn't much more powerful than most other personal computers of the time, the IBM PC (Figure 6) was a milestone in the history of personal computers for two basic reasons:

1. For many businesses, especially the larger ones, it "legitimized" personal computers. If IBM was selling them, the reasoning went, then maybe PCs really could be useful business tools. As a result, the IBM PC became wildly popular; IBM could not produce them fast enough to keep up with the demand.
2. It was built with generic parts and used the PC-DOS operating system, which was developed by Microsoft and was virtually identical to MS-DOS, a Microsoft product. The IBM PC also used *open architecture* — IBM published detailed specifications so that anyone could build circuit boards for it to expand its capabilities. These features enabled some enterprising companies to "clone" the PC — to build their own IBM-compatible personal computers.

The Apple Macintosh

Over the next few years, the personal computer industry slowly evolved as a few IBM clones and dozens of non-IBM-compatible PCs were brought to market. Then, in 1984, Apple introduced the Macintosh (Figure 6), which it advertised, with a decidedly anti-IBM slant,

Figure 6 Two Historic Computers

as "the computer for the rest of us". With its small size and integral screen, the Mac certainly *looked* different, but what really made it stand out was its easy-to-use, mouse-driven, graphical user interface. (This GUI is similar, broadly speaking, to the Windows interface developed later by Microsoft. Both interfaces, and the mouse as well, trace their roots back to work done about 1980 at Xerox Corporation's Palo Alto Research Center.) The Apple Macintosh was not at all compatible with the IBM PC. Nevertheless, after a slow start, it became increasingly popular. Today, descendants of the original Macintosh are the only remaining popular alternative to IBM-compatible personal computers.

From this point on, the increased competition for the PC buyer's dollar brought forth new and more powerful computers at an ever-accelerating rate. This boom was fueled by Intel Corporation, which introduced a new generation of microprocessor every few years — the 386 in 1986, the 486 in 1989, the Pentium in 1992, and variations of the latter every couple of years after that. With each advance in the microprocessor, personal computer manufacturers quickly brought out machines designed around the new chip and software developers used the greater speed to create more sophisticated applications.

Windows Microsoft Windows was one of the major beneficiaries of the more powerful computers. When it was first introduced in 1985, Windows ran sluggishly on the existing hardware (because graphics-intensive programs require relatively fast computers), and it did not have much success. However, by the time the much improved version 3.0 was brought to market in 1990, hardware had caught up with the demands of the software, and this version of Windows was an immediate hit. Then, when an even better Windows 3.1 was introduced in 1992 in the midst of a computer price war that made top-of-the-line machines affordable, Windows became the standard operating environment for IBM-compatible microcomputers. The next version of Windows, Windows 95, was rolled out in August, 1995 with the most publicized (and most costly) introduction for any computer product ever. It is estimated that more than 80% of the world's computers now use either this operating system or its successor, Windows 98, which was introduced in June 1998.

The Internet Despite all the recent advances in hardware and software, the most significant computer-related development in the 1990s was the phenomenal rise in popularity of the Internet. The **Internet** is a world-wide collection of *networks*, interlinked computers that are able to share resources and data via cables or phone lines. The Internet has roots that date back to a United States Defense Department project in the mid-1960s. Over the last three decades, the

Internet has grown from a small collection of mainframe computers used by universities and the military to a smorgasbord of mullions of computers, whose users range from grade-school students to billion-dollar corporations.

The two main attractions of the Internet are e-mail and the World Wide Web. **E-mail**, which is short for *electronic mail*, allows anyone with access to the Internet to use his or her computer to exchange messages — almost instantaneously and at little or no cost — with any other Internet user anywhere in the world. The **World Wide Web**, which originated in 1989, is a vast collection of linked documents (*Web pages*) created by Internet users and stored on thousands of Internet-connected computers. Although accessing (or *browsing*) the polyglot of information available on the Web can often be frustrating, its potential seems boundless. Some computer visionaries believe that the Internet, and especially e-mail and the World Wide Web, will ultimately play a more important role in our everyday lives than any other aspect of computer technology.

Summary

Components of a Computer	Central processing unit (CPU)	Receives and executes program instructions; controls other computer components.
	Internal memory (RAM and ROM)	Stores instructions and data to be processed by the CPU; contents of RAM are lost when the computer's power is turned off.
	Mass storage devices	Store all applications and data used by the computer. Examples are hard and floppy disk drives, and CD-ROM and tape drives.
	Input devices	Transmit information from the user to the computer. Examples are the keyboard and mouse.
	Output devices	Transmit information from the computer to the user. Examples are monitors and printers.
Types of Software	Applications	Include word processors, database managers, spreadsheet programs, painting programs, and multimedia applications.
	System software	Includes the computer's operating system (for example, DOS or Windows 98).

Microsoft Windows	Benefits of using Windows	Customizable graphical user interface (GUI), multitasking, easy transfer of data between programs, software tools and uniform standards for application development, and built-in applications.
	New features of Windows 98	Strong Web integration with the operating system, improved hardware support, and more extensive help.
History of the Personal Computer	1945	The first fully-operable electronic computer, ENIAC, is built.
	1947	The transistor is invented
	1970	The microprocessor, a CPU on a chip, is invented.
	1974	The first widely-marketed personal computer, the Altair 8800, is built.
	1977	The Apple II makes its debut.
	1981	The IBM PC is introduced.
	1984	The Apple Macintosh, with a user-friendly GUI, hits the market.
	1985	Microsoft rolls out the first version of Windows.
	1986	Intel introduces the 32-bit 386 processor.
	1989	The World Wide Web is born.
	1992	Windows 3.1 is brought to market.
	1992	The original Pentium processor is introduced.
	1995	Windows 95 is launched.
	1998	Windows 98 is introduced.

Review Exercises

Personal Computers

1. The physical components of a computer system are referred to as its ___________.
2. A computer's main circuit board is called its ___________.
3. One byte of memory consists of ___________ bits.
4. One kilobyte is equal to ___________ bytes.
5. Some examples of mass storage devices are floppy disk drives, hard disk drives, and ___________ drives.

6. Of the various types of printers, the highest quality output is produced by a ____________ printer.
7. True or false: Computer components housed outside the system unit are called peripherals.
8. True or false: A bit can be represented by a 0 or a 1.
9. True or false: The contents of a computer's ROM are lost when the power is turned off.
10. True or false: Floppy disk drives access data more slowly than hard disk drives.
11. True or false: A CD-ROM drive can be used for backup purposes.
12. True or false: Computer keyboards contain fewer keys than a standard typewriter.
13. True or false: Inexpensive laser printers are especially good at producing color output.
14. Which of the following components is *not* contained within the system unit of a typical PC?
    a. The motherboard
    b. A floppy disk drive
    c. Random access memory (RAM)
    d. None of the above answers is correct.
15. The computer's central processing unit
    a. Processes program instructions.
    b. Performs arithmetic and logical operations.
    c. Controls the other components of the computer.
    d. Performs all the above functions.
16. Which of the following is an input device?
    a. A monitor
    b. A keyboard
    c. A printer
    d. Read-only memory (ROM)
17. One advantage of a floppy disk over a hard disk is that
    a. It can be used to transfer data between computers.
    b. It holds more data.
    c. Data can be retrieved from it more quickly.
    d. None of the above answers is correct.

Software and Operating Systems

18. Software is divided into two broad categories: ____________ soft ware and system software.

19. The master control program that oversees the computer's operations is called its ___________.

20. The generic name for the operating system used by virtually all IBM-compatible computers before the advent of Windows 95 is ___________.

21. Windows makes use of a GUI, which stands for ___________.

22. True or false: Computer programs are also known as software.

23. True or false: Most computer users find it easier to use a command line interface than a graphical user interface.

24. True or false: One of the advantages of Windows over DOS is the speed with which it runs applications.

25. True or false: Unlike Windows 3.1, Windows 95/98 is a true operating system.

26. Which of the following is an example of system software?

    a. The computer's RAM
    b. The computer's operating system
    c. A computer game
    d. A word processor

27. One advantage of DOS over Windows is that

    a. It can run several programs at once.
    b. It is easier to learn to use.
    c. It requires less powerful hardware.
    d. All of the above are correct.

28. Windows 98

    a. Requires DOS to be running before it can be started up.
    b. Can run most programs that were written for DOS and Windows 3.1.
    c. Runs on both IBM-compatibles and the Apple Macintosh.
    d. Was the first operating system to use a graphical user interface.

History of the Personal Computer

29. The first fully-operable electronic computer was known by the acronym ___________.

30. The ___________, a CPU residing on a single computer chip, was invented in 1970.

31. The first personal computer received national attention in the year ___________.

32. The first microcomputer built by International Business Machines Corporation was called the ___________.

33. The first widely-used computer to make use of a graphical user interface was the ____________.

34. True or false: The invention of the transistor led to smaller, cheaper, more reliable computers.

35. True or false: The first personal computer was manufactured by Apple Computer, Inc.

36. True or false: The Apple Macintosh makes use of the Windows 98 operating system.

37. True or false: Computers have not increased appreciably in speed and power in the last ten years.

38. True or false: The primary reasons that people use the Internet are to exchange e-mail messages and browse the World Wide Web.

39. The first *personal* computer was

    a. ENIAC.
    b. The Altair 8800.
    c. The Apple II.
    d. The IBM Personal Computer.

40. Microsoft Corporation was founded by

    a. Stephen Wozniak and Steven Jobs.
    b. Richard Rodgers and Oscar Hammerstein.
    c. J. Presper Eckert and John Mauchly.
    d. Paul Allen and William Gates.

41. In the 1970s,

    a. The World Wide Web was born.
    b. The first personal computer was sold.
    c. Microsoft Corporation brought DOS to market.
    d. None of the above is correct.

42. In the 1990s,

    a. Intel Corporation introduced its first computer chip.
    b. Microsoft Corporation brought out Windows.
    c. Apple Computer, Inc. introduced the Macintosh computer.
    d. None of the above is correct.

Build Your Own Glossary

43. The following words and phrases are important terms that were presented in this Introduction. (They appear within the text in boldface type.) Write a definition for each term. After you learn to use WordPad (in Section 2.2), you should enter these definitions into the Glossary file on the Student Disk.

Application
Bit
Byte
CD-ROM drive
Central processing unit (CPU)
Command line interface
Computer
Computer literacy
Disk drive
Diskette
DOS
DVD drive
E-mail
Floppy disk
Gigabyte (GB)
Graphical user interface (GUI)
Hard disk
Hardware
IBM-compatible computer
Icon
Ink jet printer
Input device
Internal memory
Internet
Keyboard
Kilobyte (KB)
Laser printer
Mass storage
Megabyte (MB)
Menu
Microchip
Microprocessor
Monitor
Motherboard
Mouse
Operating system
Output device
Peripheral
Personal computer (PC)
Printer
Processor
Program
Random access memory (RAM)
Read-only memory (ROM)
Software
System software
System unit
Tape drive
Windows
Windows 3.1
Windows 95
Windows 98
World Wide Web

CHAPTER 1

The Basics of Using Windows 98

Overview

In the introduction to this text, we discussed the *what* and *why* of Windows 98. Recall that the primary goal of this powerful operating system is to make computers easier to use. In this chapter, you will begin to see some of the things that Windows can do and how easily they are done. More specifically, you will learn to:

1. Recognize the elements on the Windows 98 Desktop.
2. Use the mouse to perform basic Windows operations.
3. Choose items from menus.
4. Select and activate icons in a window or on the Desktop.
5. Move, resize, minimize, maximize, and close windows.
6. Scroll through the contents of a window.
7. Use dialog boxes to indicate preferences.
8. Shut down Windows 98.

1.1 The Windows 98 Desktop

If Windows 98 is installed on your computer, when you turn on the machine:

1. You will probably see some text on the screen that supplies information about your computer system, followed by the Windows 98 logo, and then possibly some more text.
2. After a short while, a *dialog box* entitled "Enter Network Password" may be displayed. If so, either
   - Type your user name, press the Tab key, then type your password, and press the Enter key. (If you don't know your user name or password, check with your instructor or lab coordinator.)

   or
   - Press the Escape (Esc) key.

The Windows startup screen will then be displayed. A typical opening screen is shown in Figure 1. Depending on how your computer has been set up, its opening screen may look quite different from the one pictured here.

Every once in a while, the computer will "hang up" before the startup process is complete. If this happens, the screen image will freeze and the hard disk will stop chattering. In this case, try pressing the Reset button on the system unit. The startup process will begin again and may proceed this time without a hitch. If the computer hangs up on the restart, consult your instructor or lab coordinator. After you become a more experienced Windows user, you might be able to fix the problem yourself with the aid of the material in Section 12.3.

The entire screen area is referred to as the Windows **Desktop.** Just like a regular desk top, it's the place on which you will do your work. Currently (in Figure 1), there are only a few objects on the Desktop. After we begin working with a program or two, however, most of the Desktop will be covered by *windows* of various sorts and the objects you see here (except the Taskbar) will usually become obscured.

Items on the Desktop

The **Start button**, located in the lower left corner of the screen in Figure 1, is the jumping off point for a typical Windows session. It not only provides access to all the applications (programs) installed on your computer, but also allows you to customize Windows, to obtain help in using Windows, and to end your Windows session.

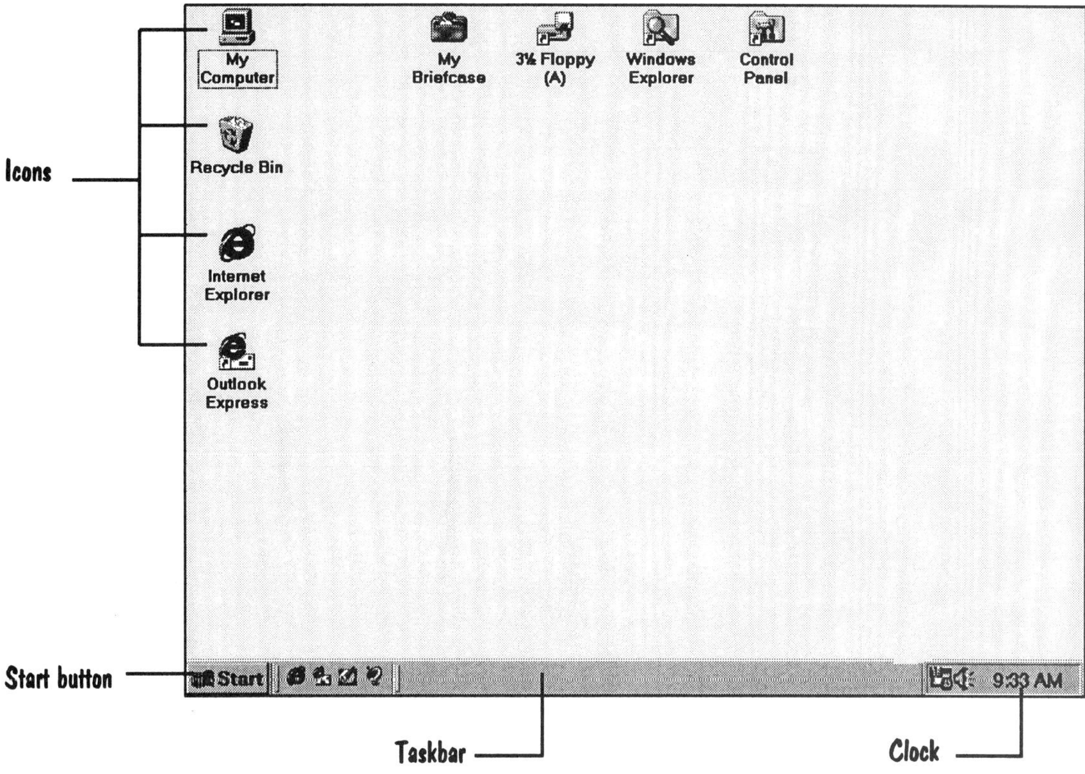

Figure 1 The Windows 98 Desktop

The labeled pictures along the left side of the screen are called **icons.** These icons (and others like them throughout the Windows environment) represent Windows 98 objects, such as applications or groups of files, and provide easy access to them. For example, as you will see in Chapter 3, activating the icon labeled "My Computer" allows you to work with virtually every piece of hardware and software that is part of your computer system.

The **Taskbar** displays (among other things) the applications and documents that you are currently using. The Taskbar in Figure 1 contains several icons and the Clock utility, which not only provides the time of day but, as you will see later, can also be used to display the date and a month-by-month calendar.

1.2 Of Mice and Menus

As you know, one of the primary advantages of working with Windows is that it is easy to use. It accomplishes this, in part, by the extensive use of the mouse and menus.

Using the Mouse

When a mouse is moved around on a flat surface, its pointer moves in a corresponding way on the screen. The shape of the mouse pointer depends on the application that is running and the use to which it is being put. The pointer may look like an arrow, a double-headed arrow, an I-beam, or a hand, among other things.

In Windows and its applications, the mouse can be used to select items displayed on the screen, initiate actions, and move and resize certain objects. Before we illustrate these uses, let's discuss some important mouse terminology.

Mouse terminology

- To *point at* an object means to move the mouse so that its on-screen pointer is positioned over the specified object and held in place for a few moments.
- To *click* the mouse means to press and release the left mouse button. To *right-click* is to press and release the right mouse button. To click (or right-click) *on* an object means to point at the object and then click (or right-click).
- To *double-click* on an object means to point at the object and click the left mouse button twice in rapid succession.
- To *drag* an object with the mouse means to point at the object, press (but not release) the left mouse button, move the mouse pointer to a new location, and then release the button. To *right-drag* an object is to perform the same actions using the right mouse button instead of the left.

If the functions of your left and right mouse buttons seem to be reversed, they can easily be restored to their "normal" settings. Either ask your lab coordinator to do this for you or see Section 5.4. (If you want to try switching the buttons yourself, it would be a good idea to first finish reading Chapter 1.)

To illustrate the mouse operations, let's return to the computer screen shown in Figure 1. If we double-click on the My Computer icon, the **window** — the boxed-in area on the screen — shown in Figure 2 will be displayed. (Your My Computer window may look quite different from the one pictured here. Don't worry; for the purposes of the current discussion, it does not matter.)

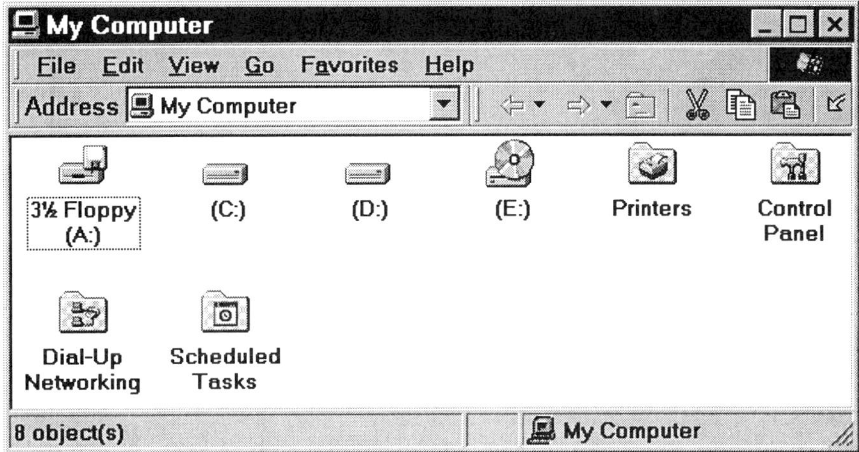

Figure 2 The My Computer Window

If you double-click on an object and it doesn't initiate an action, you may have moved the mouse slightly between clicks or perhaps you didn't follow the first click by the second quickly enough. Try double-clicking again.

Using Menus

The top line of the My Computer window (in Figure 2, it's the one containing the words "My Computer") is called its **title bar**; it contains the name of the window together with some symbols that we'll discuss in Section 1.3. Below the title bar is the My Computer **menu bar**:

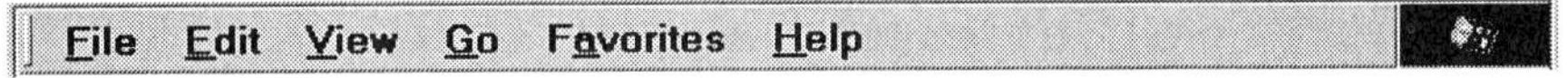

Opening a menu The words listed on the menu bar are the names of **menus** — lists of commands — that can be used to manipulate the contents of the My

Computer window. To *open* (display) a menu, simply click on its name. For example, if you click on the word *View*, the menu pictured in Figure 3 appears. (Because this kind of menu looks as if it were pulled down, like a window shade unrolling from the word View, it is called a **pull-down menu.**)

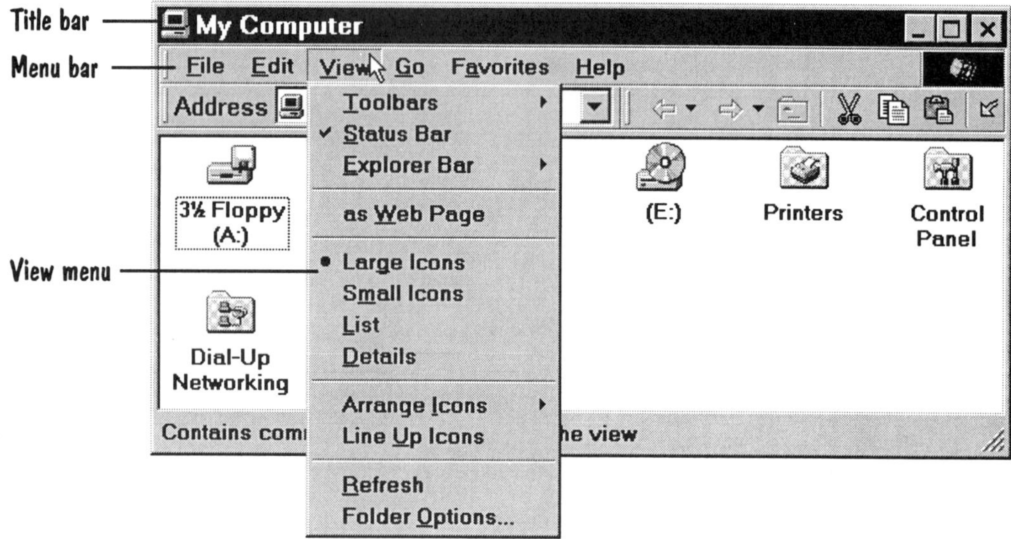

Figure 3 A Typical Pull-down Menu

Selecting a menu option

Once a menu has been opened, you can choose one of the options listed by clicking on that item. (Doing so will also close the menu.) For example, to choose the "Line up Icons" option from the View menu in Figure 3, move the mouse pointer straight down until it is positioned over this item, which will become highlighted, and click the left button.

NOTE

If you prefer, the options listed on a pull-down menu can be accessed using the keyboard. Notice that each name on the menu bar has one letter underlined; for example, the *V* in View. To display a pull-down menu, hold down either Alt key, press the key corresponding to the underlined letter, and then release the Alt key. (We will write this sequence of actions as — if the underlined letter is V — "press Alt+V".) Then, to select an option on that menu, either:

- Press the key corresponding to the underlined letter in the desired option.

or

- Press the Down Arrow key (↓) until the desired option is highlighted and then press the Enter key.

For example, to display the View menu as in Figure 3, hold down the Alt key, press the key labeled V, and release Alt. Then, to select the Line up Icons option, *either* press the E key *or* press the Down Arrow key several times until the option is highlighted and then press the Enter key.

Canceling a menu If you want to close a menu without selecting any of the options, just click on any other part of the screen. As an alternative, press the Escape key.

Types of Menu Items

Let's take a closer look at the View menu that is displayed in Figure 3. Notice that some options on this menu are preceded or followed by a special symbol, such as a check mark or bullet (see Figure 4).

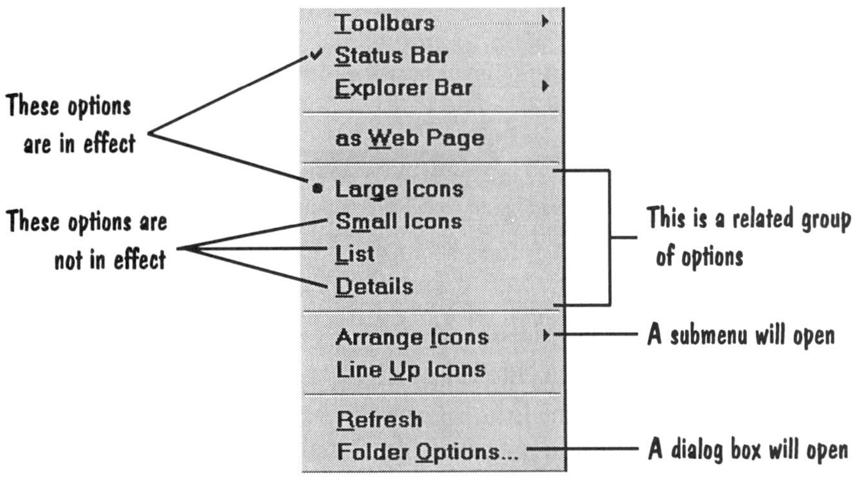

Figure 4 Special Symbols for Menu Options

These symbols have a consistent meaning in Windows and its applications. (We will describe the *function* of most of the items on the View menu later in the text; here, we will just discuss the meaning of the symbols attached to some of these items.)

Menu symbols

- If a *check mark* (✔) appears next to a menu option, it indicates that this item or characteristic is currently in effect. For example, in Figure 4, the check mark next to Status Bar indicates that this object is displayed in the My Computer window. If you click on Status Bar, the menu will close and the status bar will disappear from the window. (Try it!) Then, the next time you pull down the My Computer View menu, you'll notice that the check mark next to Status Bar has disappeared as well — this option is no longer in effect. To get it back, choose Status Bar again. We call this kind of option a *toggle*: if the Status Bar *is* currently displayed, choosing the menu option toggles (turns) it off; if it is *not* displayed, choosing the option toggles it on.
- A *bullet* (•) next to a menu option not only means that this option is in effect, but also indicates that the rest of a group of related items are *not* in effect. (The horizontal lines within a menu — see Figure 4 — divide it into these groups.) For example, the bullet on the Large Icons option in Figure 4 describes the contents of the My Computer window (see Figure 3). This window does *not* contain Small Icons, a List, or Details. Only one bulleted item within its group can be in effect at any given time.
- A *triangle symbol* (▸) next to a menu item indicates that a *submenu* of additional options will appear if you "point at" this item. For example, if you move the mouse pointer over the Arrange Icons option in Figure 4 and hold it steady for a few moments, the following submenu is displayed at its right:

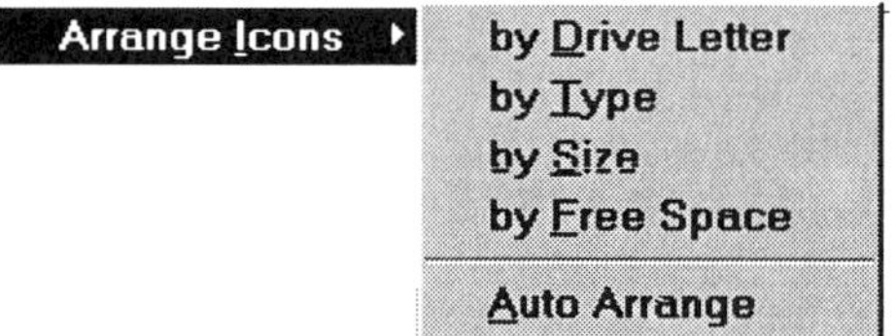

- If you choose a menu item that is followed by an *ellipsis* (three consecutive periods), a *dialog box* will appear requesting additional information. (Dialog boxes are discussed in Section 1.4.) For example, choosing the Folder Options item from the View menu of Figure 4 displays a dialog box presenting the available options. (If you open this dialog box, you can close it, removing it from the screen, by pressing the Escape key.)

To illustrate a few additional points about menus, let's pull down My Computer's Edit menu (by clicking on the word Edit on the menu bar). This menu is shown in Figure 5.

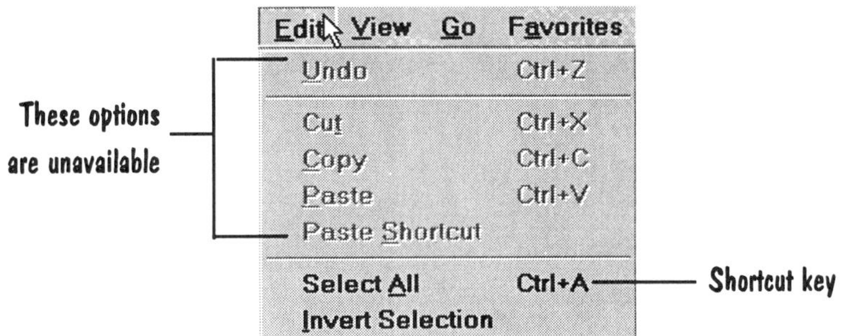

Figure 5 The My Computer Edit Menu

In Figure 5, notice that:

- The first five options are *dimmed* — they appear to be "faded out". This indicates that these options are temporarily not available. If you click on one of these items, nothing will happen!
- Keystrokes (such as Ctrl+A) appear next to several menu items. These keystrokes are called **shortcut keys**. They provide a quick way of choosing the corresponding menu option *without displaying the menu itself.* For example, to select all the objects in the My Computer window without displaying the Edit menu, just press Ctrl+A; that is, hold down the Ctrl (Control) key, type A, and then release Ctrl.

Classic Style Mode versus Web Style Mode

In the last few pages, we introduced My Computer's View and Edit menus to help describe the *types* of menu items that appear on Windows menus. The *function* of most of the options on the Edit and View menus will be discussed later in the text. However, we will look more closely at one of these menu items now, with the goal of eliminating a possible source of confusion concerning some basic Windows operations.

Windows' two selection modes

The Folder Options item on the View menu lets you choose (among other things) the way in which icons in windows and on the Desktop are selected or activated. You have the following two choices:

1. Under the **Classic style** setting, icons react to the mouse as they have in all previous versions of Windows:
   - To *select* (highlight) an icon, click on it.

- To *open* (activate) the object represented by an icon, double-click on it.

For example, in Classic style mode, if we click on the My Computer icon, it will become highlighted, as shown at the right. If we double-click on it, the My Computer window will open.

2. Under the **Web style** setting, which is new to Windows 98, the icons look the same, but their titles are now underlined. ("Web" refers to the Internet's World Wide Web, which we will discuss in Chapter 6.) With the Web style setting in effect:

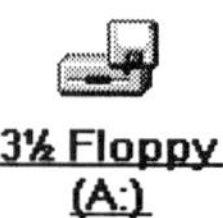

- To *select* (highlight) an icon, just point at it — position the mouse pointer over it and hold the pointer steady for a few moments. The pointer will change to a hand shape (as shown at the right) and the icon will become highlighted.

- To *open* the object represented by an icon, just click (once) on it.

NOTE

Because the way you activate an icon to open the associated object differs between the two icon settings, we will use the word **choose** to describe this action. For example, the phrase "choose the My Computer icon ..." means:

- Double-click on the My Computer icon if the Classic style setting is in effect.
- Click on the My Computer icon if the Web style setting is in effect. (Double-clicking will work in this case as well.)

Similarly, the words "**select** an icon" will mean either *click on it* if you're in Classic style mode or *point at it* when in Web style mode.

To determine which mode is currently in effect, just look at any icon in a window or on the Desktop. If its title is underlined, the Web style setting is being used; otherwise, the Classic style setting is in effect. (We will use the Classic style mode for all screen shots in this text unless we are specifically illustrating the Web style case.)

Switching between settings

To switch between Classic style and Web style settings:

1. Choose the My Computer icon to open its window.
2. Select the Folder Options item from the View menu. The Folder Options dialog box will open.
3. Toward the bottom of this dialog box (which is shown below),

click on the words *Web style* or *Classic style*, depending on which setting you want to put into effect. (We will discuss the third option, *Custom*, in Chapter 6, which also contains information about the general concept of Web-integration in Windows 98.)

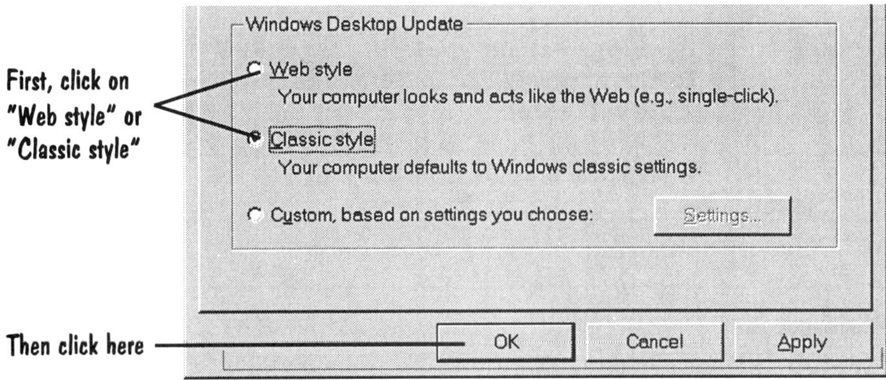

4. Click on the button labeled OK.

Before closing this section, we will mention some of the other items on My Computer's View menu. If your My Computer window looks like the one pictured below, you can return it to the way it looks in Figure 2 by choosing the *as Web Page* item from the View menu. This item is a toggle, so choosing it again will change the window back to the way it was.

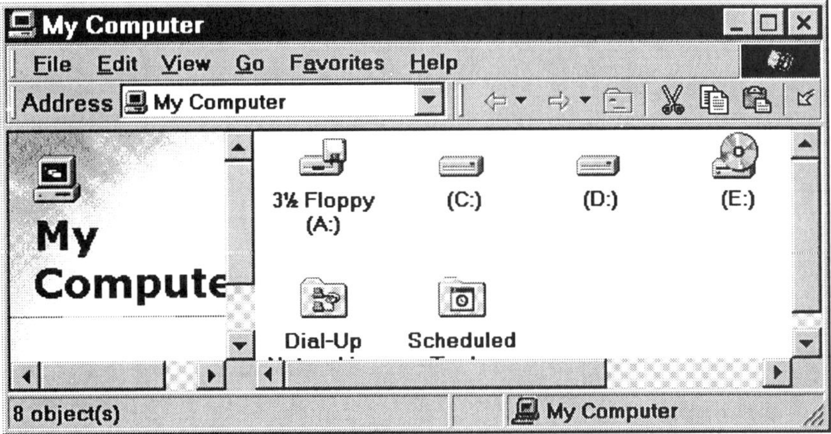

Choosing the Large Icons, Small Icons, List, or Details item will also alter the appearance of the window. (Try each to see the resulting effect!) The My Computer window pictured above (and in Figure 2) has Large Icons in effect.

NOTE

If you have been following along at the computer and you now want to close the My Computer window, click on the little box marked with an **X** in the upper-right corner of this window. To shut down Windows 98, which is wise to do before turning off your computer, follow the instructions in Section 1.5.

TUTORIAL

Try the following exercise on your own.

1. Turn on your computer (if it's not already on) to start Windows 98. If the My Computer window is not open, display it by positioning the mouse pointer over the My Computer icon and *double-clicking* (tapping the left mouse button twice in rapid succession).
2. In the My Computer window, open (display) the View menu by *clicking* (tapping the left mouse button) on the word View that appears on the *menu bar* toward the top of the window.
3. There will be a *bullet* (a filled circle) next to one of the options in the group of items on the View menu beginning with "Large Icons". Click on one of the other three items in this group. The View menu will close. Notice the change in the My Computer window.
4. Open the View menu and *point at* Arrange Icons by moving the mouse pointer over these words and holding it still for a few moments. A *submenu* will appear. Note whether or not the option Auto Arrange is checked on this submenu.
5. Now click on the Auto Arrange option. The two menus will close. Reopen the View menu and the Arrange Icons submenu. If Auto Arrange had originally been "checked", it should now be "unchecked", and vice-versa.
6. Close the My Computer window by clicking on the box marked with an **X** in the upper-right corner of this window.
7. *Drag* the My Computer icon to another location on the Desktop. To do so, position the mouse pointer over the icon, press (but do not release), the left mouse button, move the pointer to a new location on the screen, and release the mouse button.

8. Drag the My Computer icon back to its original location.
9. Position the mouse pointer over an empty part of the Desktop and *right-click* (tap the right mouse button). A menu will open. Close this menu by pressing the Cancel key.
10. If you want to quit, to shut down Windows 98 see the NOTE that precedes this tutorial.

1.3 Windows within Windows

While working at your desk (say, doing homework), you might have several documents open at once — perhaps a textbook, a reference book, and your notebook. This is often the case on the Windows Desktop as well. Here, the documents and other related objects are contained in *windows*. Depending on what you're doing at the moment, you might want to move some of these windows around, make one of them bigger, or perhaps take some of them off the Desktop. In this section, we will describe how to perform these actions —how to move, resize, and close windows.

Operations on Windows

Before we explain *how* to move or resize a window, let's look at a few reasons *why* you might want to perform these operations. For one thing, it's usually much easier to use the contents of a window when it occupies the entire screen; you can view more information and, in some cases, see more detail as well. Often, however, when a window opens, it just occupies part of the Desktop. In such a case, you might want to increase the size of the window, perhaps **maximizing** it so that it uses as much screen real estate as possible.

The disadvantage of maximizing a window is that it then might obscure everything else on the Desktop. Even when not maximized, a window might cover vital information in another window or on the Desktop itself. Thus, at times you will want to reduce the size of a window or even **close** it, which takes it off the Desktop. Instead of closing a window, it is sometimes possible to **minimize** it, which also removes it from the screen. The difference between closing and minimizing a window is a subtle one:

- *Closing a window* removes its contents from the computer's internal memory, RAM (see the Introduction to this text).

- *Minimizing a window* keeps its contents in RAM and reduces the window to a button on the Taskbar, allowing you to restore the window quickly and easily.

To illustrate the different ways in which we can manipulate a typical window, let's open the My Computer window by double-clicking on the My Computer icon, as we did in Section 1.2. Figure 6 shows the parts of the title bar that are involved in moving, minimizing, maximizing, and closing a window.

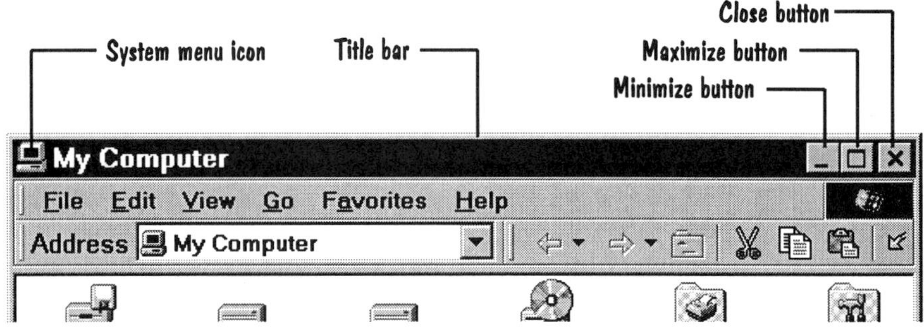

Figure 6 Parts of the Title Bar

Moving a Window To *move* a window, just drag its title bar to the new location. More specifically, position the mouse pointer over the title bar, press (but don't release) the left mouse button, and move the mouse in the direction you want the window to move.

Resizing a Window To *resize* a window, drag its border or corner to a new position. For example, to increase the height of a window, position the mouse pointer on the bottom border (it becomes a two-headed arrow, as pictured at the right) and drag the border down. When the window is the desired height, release the mouse button. (If you drag a window *corner*, both sides attached to that corner move at once.)

If you change your mind during the process of moving or resizing a window and want to cancel the operation, press the Escape key before releasing the mouse button.

Minimizing, Maximizing, or Closing a Window To *minimize*, *maximize*, or *close* a window, click on the **minimize button**, **maximize button**, or **close button**, respectively (on the right end of the title bar).

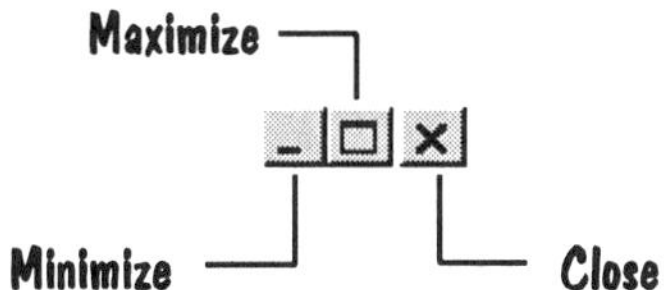

Note that:

- When a window is minimized, it is removed from the screen but its name and icon continue to appear on a button on the Taskbar. To reopen a minimized window, click on its Taskbar button.
- When a window is maximized, it expands to its largest possible size and the maximize button is replaced by a **restore button**. Clicking on the latter, **restores** the window, returning it to its previous position and size.
- When a window is closed, it disappears from the screen.
- If you forget the function of one of these buttons, just position the mouse pointer over it. A **tool tip** will pop-up (as shown at the right), indicating the function of that button.

You can also *maximize* a window by double-clicking on its title bar. Once a window is maximized, the same operation — double-clicking on the title bar — restores it. A window can also be *closed* by double-clicking on its System Menu icon (see Figure 6), but since every Windows 98 window has a close button, this fact is useful for little more than impressing your friends, and it's not likely to do even that.

Although using the mouse is easier, Windows 98 does allow you to use the keyboard to carry out the move, resize, maximize, minimize, and close operations on a window. These operations (when available)

are listed on the window's **System menu**. To open the System menu using the keyboard, press Alt+Spacebar or Alt+Hyphen, whichever works. (Remember: The notation "Alt+*keystroke*" means "hold down the Alt key, type the keystroke, and then release the Alt key.) You can also open its System menu by right-clicking on the window's title bar or by clicking on its System menu icon — see Figure 6 — if the window has one.

The System menu will appear in the upper left corner of the window, as shown in the figure at the right. Choosing the Minimize, Maximize, Close, or Restore option performs the indicated task. Choosing Move or Size requires some maneuvering with the Arrow keys to complete the task; for these two operations, it's *a lot* easier to use the mouse!

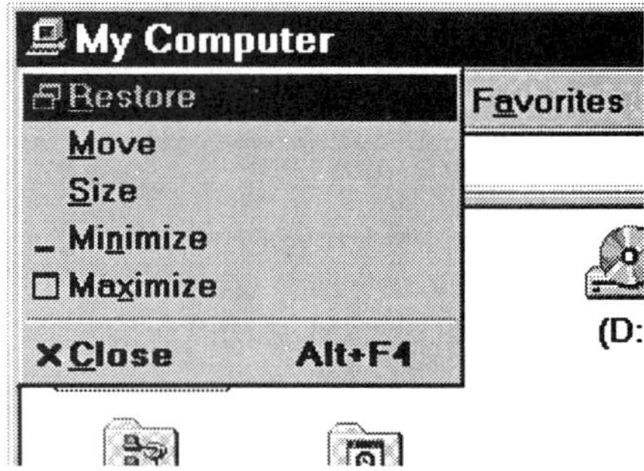

Scroll Bars

When a window is not large enough to view all its contents at once, one or two **scroll bars** will be displayed to allow you to move through the contents without increasing the size of the window. For example, if we decrease the size of the My Computer window shown in Figure 6 so that the icons are partially or completely covered, the resulting window will look similar to the one in Figure 7.

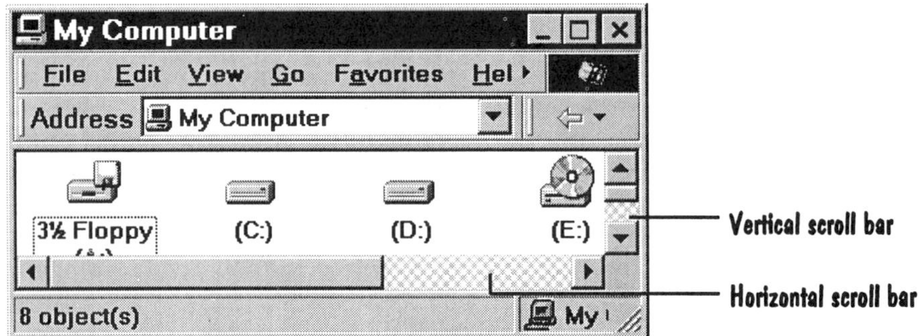

Figure 7 Scroll Bars Visible in a Window

Scrolling in a window

If the contents of a window — let's call it a *document*, even if it's just a collection of icons — is only partly visible, you have to **scroll** to see the rest of it. To understand how this works, imagine that the entire document is lying on the Desktop, but the window acts like a "cutout", allowing us to see only part of it. To see more (without increasing the window's size), we have to move the cutout around. For example, when you *scroll down*, imagine the cutout moving in a downward direction so that a lower part of the document comes into view. (In actuality, the window stays fixed on the screen and, figuratively speaking, the document itself moves around.)

You can use the mouse to scroll through the contents of a window by clicking on various parts of a scroll bar (see Figure 7): the *horizontal* scroll bar scrolls the window left or right; the *vertical* scroll bar scrolls it up or down. Let's take a closer look at a vertical scroll bar:

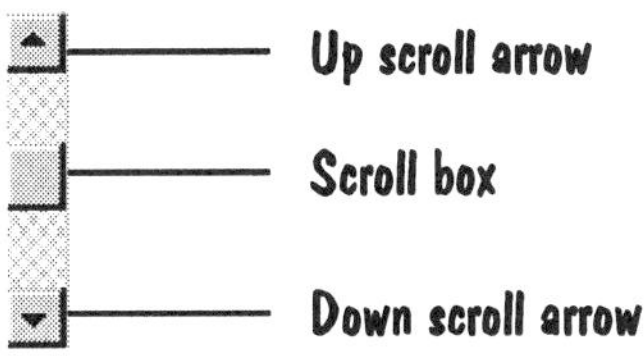

Here's how this scroll bar is used. (A horizontal scroll bar works in an analogous way.)

- Clicking the up or down scroll arrow scrolls the window up or down one "step". Holding down the mouse button while pointing at the up or down scroll arrow scrolls the window continuously in that direction until you release the button.
- Clicking on the scroll bar above or below the scroll box scrolls up or down one window's worth of information.
- Dragging the scroll box up or down scrolls the window proportionally within the document. For example, if you drag the scroll box to the middle of the scroll bar, the window will scroll about halfway through the document.

NOTE

Horizontal and vertical scroll bars also give visual clues to the size of the document in the window and your current location within it:

- The *length* of a scroll box is proportional to the amount of the document you are viewing. For example, the horizontal scroll box in Figure 7 is roughly two-thirds of the length of the corresponding scroll bar; we can deduce from this that we are seeing about two-thirds of the width of the underlying "document". The vertical scroll box in Figure 7 is about half the length of its scroll bar; we are viewing about half the height of the document.

- The *position* of a scroll box along its scroll bar gives your relative location in the document. For example, in Figure 7, the horizontal scroll box is positioned at the left of its bar and the vertical scroll box is positioned at the top of its bar; we conclude that we are viewing the upper-left part of the underlying "document".

Try the following exercise on your own.

1. Start up your computer (if necessary) and open the My Computer window by choosing its Desktop icon.
2. If the My Computer window is maximized (occupies the entire screen above the Taskbar), restore it by double-clicking on the title bar.
3. Minimize this window by clicking on its minimize button, toward the right end of the title bar. The title *My Computer* and its icon continue to appear on a button on the Taskbar.

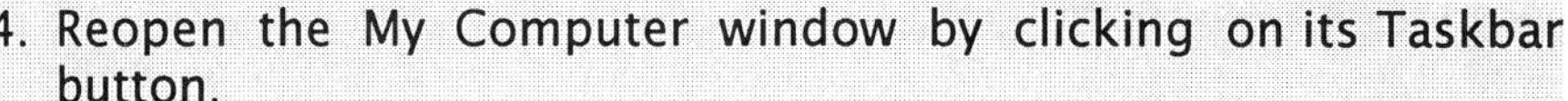

4. Reopen the My Computer window by clicking on its Taskbar button.
5. Move the My Computer window to the upper-left corner of the screen by positioning the mouse pointer on the title bar and dragging it to the appropriate place.
6. Make the window as small as possible in the horizontal direction. To do so, position the mouse pointer over the right window border (the pointer is placed properly when it turns into a "double arrow") and drag the border to the left as far as it will go. The horizontal scroll bar (and possibly the vertical one, as well) should appear.
7. Scroll across the window by positioning the mouse pointer over the right scroll arrow and holding down the left mouse button until the scroll box reaches the right end of the scroll bar. Now scroll back the other way by dragging the scroll box to the left end of the scroll bar. Increase the window to its former size.
8. Maximize the My Computer window by clicking on the maximize button, toward the right end of the title bar.
9. Pull down the System menu by clicking on the System menu icon (which looks like a computer) on the left end of the title bar (or by pressing Alt+Spacebar). Notice that the Maximize option is dimmed.

10. Restore the My Computer window by clicking on the Restore option on the System menu.
11. Close the My Computer window by clicking on the close button on the right end of the title bar. (Should you now want to shut down your computer, see Section 1.5.)

1.4 Conversing with Dialog Boxes

As you may recall, choosing a menu item followed by an ellipsis (...) displays a dialog box. A **dialog box** is a special type of window that presents various options from which you can make selections and initiate actions. As you work with Windows 98 and its applications, you will encounter a seemingly infinite variety of dialog boxes. Yet, all dialog boxes have certain things in common. In this section, we will discuss these common features.

A Typical Dialog Box

To illustrate the features of a dialog box, let's take a look at a very interesting one. (Although we will discuss the types of objects in this dialog box here, a description of its capabilities will come later, in Chapter 5.) If you right-click — click the right mouse button — on an empty area of the Desktop, the following menu will pop-up next to the mouse pointer.

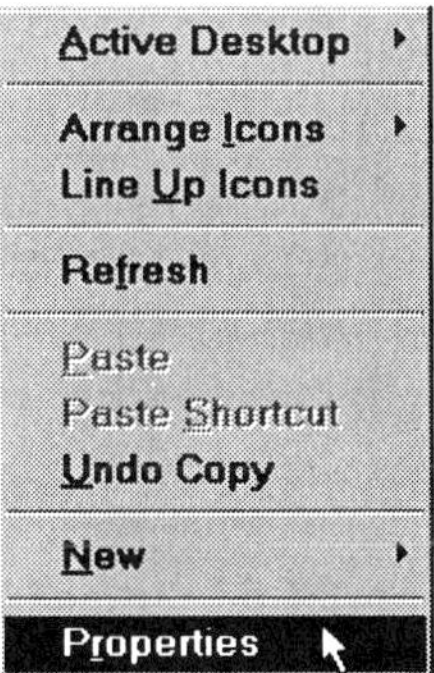

Choosing the Properties option from this menu opens the Display Properties dialog box shown in Figure 8.

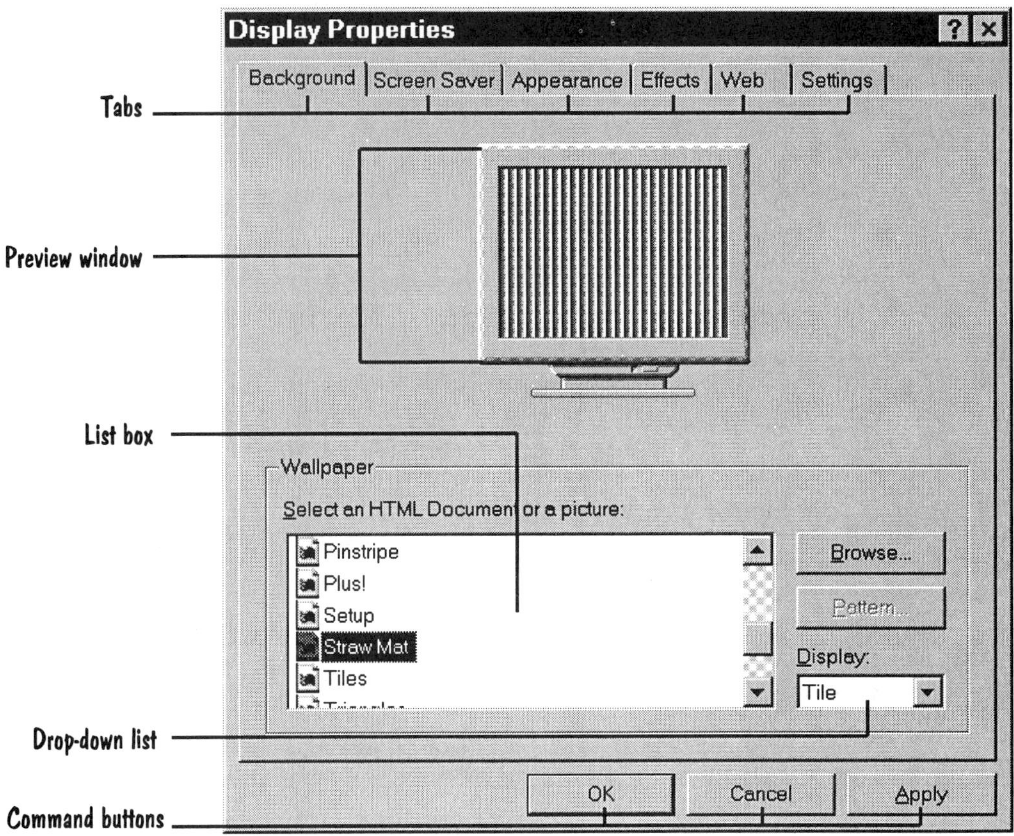

Figure 8 A Typical Dialog Box

At the top of this dialog box is the familiar title bar, which supplies the name of the window. It also contains a close button (marked with an **X**) and a help button (marked with a **?**), but not a minimize or maximize button. In general, dialog boxes cannot be resized in any way; in particular, they cannot be minimized or maximized. A dialog box *can* be moved about the screen (by dragging its title bar).

Most objects in a dialog box allow the user (that's you!) to specify preferences or execute commands. These objects (for example, the command buttons, tabs, and list box of Figure 8) are arranged in related groups and associated with easily recognized symbols. Each symbol indicates a different function, as described below.

OK

Command buttons are represented by large labeled rectangles. When you click on a command button (when you *choose* that button), it initiates an action. For example, choosing the Browse button in Figure 8 opens another dialog box. (Notice the ellipsis following the word *Browse*.) Here are a few special features of command buttons:

- Usually, one command button in a dialog box is enclosed in a heavy outline. (In Figure 8, it's the OK button.) We say that this is "the default button". As you select options in a dialog box, the default button may change, but the button that is currently the default can always be activated by pressing the Enter key.
- Almost all dialog boxes have a button labeled "OK" or "Close". When this button is activated, the dialog box closes and the options you have selected go into effect.
- Some dialog boxes contain an "Apply" button. When this button is chosen, the options you have selected go into effect, but the dialog box remains open.
- The Cancel button allows you to close a dialog box without putting any of your new selections into effect. (Pressing the Escape key or clicking on the title bar's close button has the same effect as choosing the Cancel button.)
- If the label on a command button is dimmed (for example, the Pattern button in Figure 8), that option is not presently available.

A **list box** contains a list of items from which you can choose. To select an item, click on its name. If the list is too long to fit in the box, a scroll bar will be displayed so that you can scroll through the list. The currently selected item in the list is highlighted. For example, in Figure 8, the selected item in the Wallpaper box is "Straw Mat".

A **drop-down list box** is a special type of list box. Here, only one of the listed items (the current value) is initially visible. To display the rest of the list, click on the downward-facing triangle at the right end of the box. Then, to select an item from the list, click on that item. The list will close and the new item will become the current value.

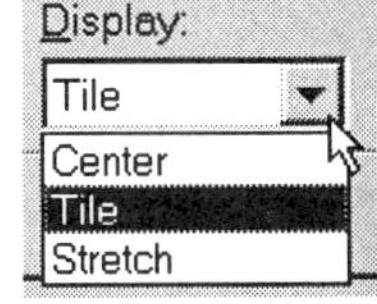

Background

Tabs, which resemble file folder tabs, appear at the top of a dialog box (if they appear at all). The currently selected tab (which is "Back ground" in Figure 8) appears to be in front of the others. The name on the tab provides a short description of the group of options currently visible in the dialog box. To select another tab, click on it; a new *page* of options will become available. For example, clicking on the Screen Saver tab in the Display Properties dialog box displays the page shown in Figure 9.

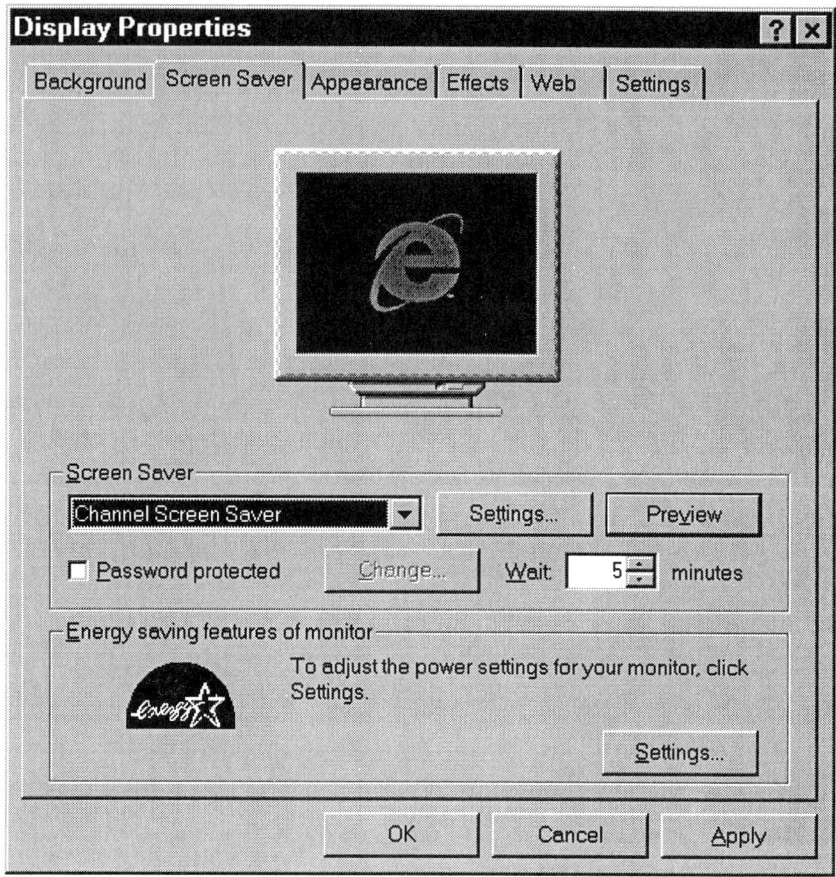

Figure 9 A New Page of the Display Properties Dialog Box

NOTE

Some dialog boxes also display written or pictorial information for the user. For example, the dialog box in Figure 8 contains a *preview area* that shows the effect your selections will have on the Windows Desktop should you choose the OK or Apply command button.

Additional Dialog Box Features

If we select Channels Screen Saver from the drop-down list in Figure 9 and then choose the Settings command button, the Screen Saver Properties dialog box opens. Figure 10 shows a portion of this dialog box. We will use it to illustrate additional features of a dialog box.

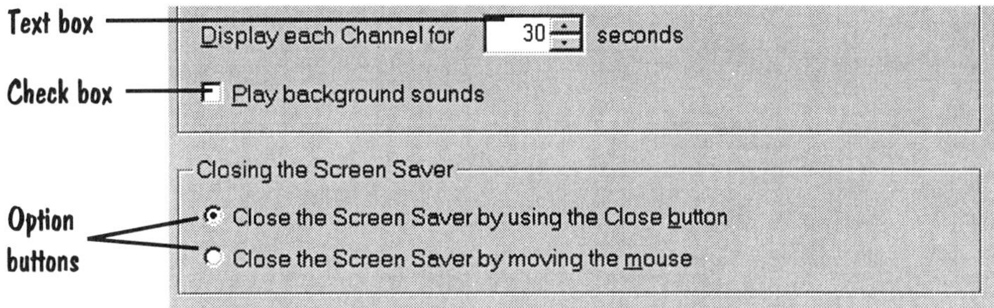

Figure 10 Additional Features of a Dialog Box

A **check box** is represented by a small square, which may or may not contain a check mark. When the check mark is present, we say that the check box is *selected*, and the stated option is in effect; when the check mark does not appear, the check box is *deselected* and this option is not in effect. For example, the deselected check box in Figure 10 indicates that "background sounds" will not be played. A check box is a toggle:

- If you click on it when it's deselected, then it becomes selected.
- If you click on it when it's selected, then it becomes deselected.

A **text box** allows you to input a name or number into a dialog box. It is symbolized by a rectangle that may contain the current value for that option — the name or number that is used if you don't change it. (In Figure 10, the current value is 30.) To enter data into a text box, click inside it, erase the current value (if necessary) by pressing the Backspace key, and then type the desired letters or digits. Do not press the Enter key after typing unless you want to activate the default command button!

Option buttons are represented by small circles. These buttons are sometimes called *radio buttons* because they work like the station selection push buttons on a radio — when you click on one of them, it is *selected* (turned on) and the others are automatically *deselected* (turned off). For this reason, in a group of these buttons, exactly one of the corresponding options is selected at any given time. The currently selected option button is indicated by a *bullet*. For example, in Figure 10, the "by using the Close button" option is currently selected (and is in effect). If you click on the "by moving the mouse" option button, it will acquire the bullet (and this option will go into effect when you choose the OK command button).

TUTORIAL

Try the following exercise on your own.

1. Start up your computer (if necessary) and/or close any open windows by clicking on their close buttons.
2. Open the Display Properties dialog box by right-clicking on (an empty area of) the Desktop and then selecting Properties from the resulting menu.
3. In the Wallpaper text box, select the Straw Mat wallpaper. To do so, scroll down the list of wallpapers until Straw Mat appears and then click on this item.
4. Click on the Screen Saver tab to view this page of the Display Properties dialog box.
5. Select 3D Flower Box from the Screen Saver drop-down list by clicking on the downward-facing triangle to open the list, scrolling down until this item is visible, and then clicking on it.
6. Click inside the check box to the left of the words *Password protected*. If a check mark were there prior to clicking, it has now disappeared, indicating that this option has been deselected (is no longer in effect). If the box were empty prior to clicking, it now contains a check mark — it has been selected. Click again in this check box to return it to its original status.
7. Change the time in the Wait text box to 2 minutes by clicking on this box, pressing the Delete key to erase the current value, and typing the number 2. Alternatively, you could have clicked on the Wait box and then on its up or down arrow until "2" appeared in this text box.
8. Click on (*choose*) the Settings command button to open the 3D Flower Box Setup dialog box.
9. Note that one of the Coloring option buttons is selected (has a bullet within the circle next to it). Now, select one of the other options by clicking on its button and notice that it has acquired the bullet.
10. Click on the close button on the title bar to close the 3D Flower Box Setup dialog box.
11. In the Display Properties dialog box, elect to cancel all changes by clicking on the Cancel command button or by pressing the Escape key. (Had you wanted to put the changes into effect, you would have chosen the OK command button.) If you now want to shut down your computer, follow the instructions provided in Section 1.5.

1.5 Shutting Down Windows 98

All good things (in fact, all things in general) must come to an end. At some point, you're going to want to quit working with Windows 98 and turn off your computer. To do so, you should:

1. Close all applications that are currently running. If an application's window is open on the Desktop, click on its close button (see Section 1.3); if the application has been minimized, right-click on its Taskbar button and then choose Close from the resulting menu. If you have used an application to modify a document and have not saved these changes to disk, Windows will display a message warning you of this fact. (We will discuss closing applications and saving documents in Section 2.2.)

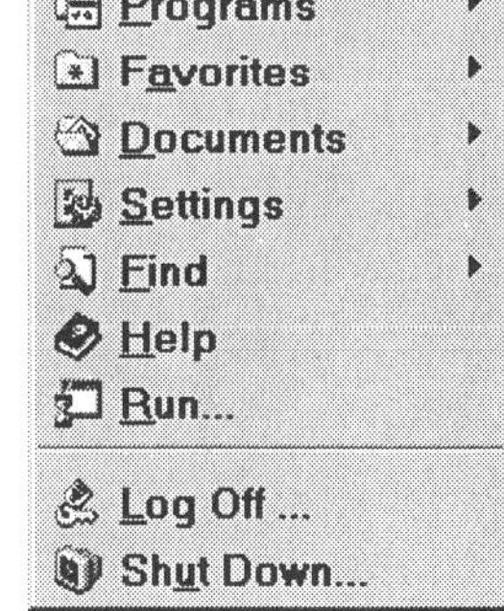

2. Click on the Start button, which can normally be found in the lower-left corner of the Desktop. This action opens the **Start menu**, which is pictured at the right.

TIP

If the Start button is not visible anywhere on the Desktop, you can open the Start menu by pressing Ctrl+Esc; that is, hold down the Ctrl (Control) key, press the Esc (Escape) key, and then release Ctrl.

3. Click on the Shut Down option on the Start menu. The Shut Down Windows dialog box, shown in Figure 11, will open.

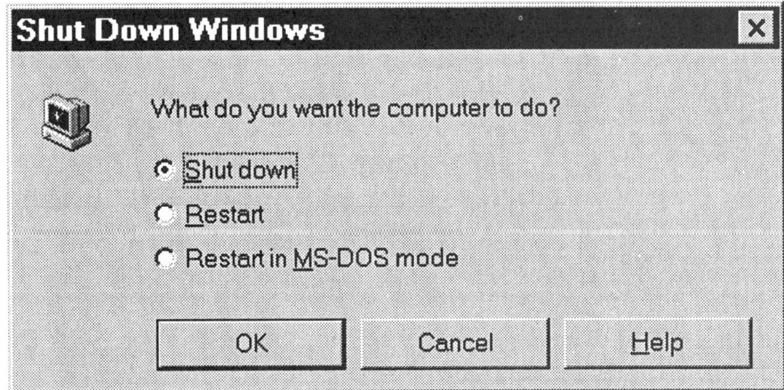

Figure 11 The Shut Down Windows Dialog Box

4. Now select an option* by clicking, if necessary, on the appropriate option button and choosing the OK command button. Or, close this dialog box and return to Windows 98 by choosing Cancel (or by pressing the Escape key).

   - The "Shut down" option should be selected when you want to turn off your computer. Activating this option eventually brings up the message: "It's now safe to turn off your computer."

If you want to turn off your computer, you should first shut down Windows 98. Doing so ensures that all open files will be properly closed. As a result, you are much less likely to inadvertently lose data or your preferred Windows settings.

   - Activating the option, "Restart", restarts Windows 98, reinitializing all its settings. This option is usually used after a program *crashes* (terminates abruptly) and/or Windows itself does not seem to be responding properly to your commands.

   - The last option, "Restart in MS-DOS mode", shuts down Windows 98 and starts **DOS**, Microsoft's plain vanilla operating system (see the Introduction). Once in DOS, you can safely turn off the computer when you see the DOS prompt (probably, `C:\WINDOWS>`). You can also restart Windows at the DOS prompt by typing `WIN` and pressing the Enter key.

Here are a couple of shortcuts for shutting down Windows:

- You can display the Shut Down Windows dialog box after closing all applications by pressing the Alt+F4 keystroke combination.
- You can activate the "Shut down" option in the Shut Down Windows dialog box even if there are applications running. In this case, Windows will attempt to close these applications and, if successful, shut down your computer. (If you try this approach, you may see a message prompting you to save changes in a document or requesting that you close certain applications yourself.)

---

*Figure 11 depicts a typical Shut Down Windows dialog box. The options shown here are available on all machines, but additional options, if any, vary from computer to computer.

- Another shut down option, Log Off, appears on the Start menu itself. If you select this option and choose Yes in the resulting message box, an Enter Password dialog box will be displayed on the screen. You. or someone else, can then log on to Windows by typing a user name and password and choosing the OK button, or by just pressing the Escape key. In either case, the Windows 98 opening screen will then be displayed.

TUTORIAL

Try the following exercise on your own.

1. Turn on your computer, if necessary, to start Windows 98. If Windows is already running, close all windows by clicking on their close buttons.
2. Restart Windows 98: Open the Start menu by clicking on the Start button (if you can't find this button, press Ctrl+Esc to open the Start menu); choose Shut Down from the menu; select the "Restart" option button in the resulting dialog box; and choose the OK command button.
3. After Windows 98 starts again, press Alt+F4 to open the Shut Down Windows dialog box. This time, select the "Restart in MS-DOS mode" option button and choose OK. After a few seconds, you will see a mostly blank screen displaying the DOS prompt, probably `C:\WINDOWS>`.
4. Type `WIN` and press the Enter key to start Windows 98.
5. This time, open the Shut Down Windows dialog box, select the "Shut down" option button, and choose OK. When the message "It's now safe to turn off your computer." appears, do just that.

Chapter Summary

Objects on the Desktop

Icons	Small stylized pictures representing Windows' objects
Start button	Opens the Start menu when clicked
Taskbar	Contains the Clock and buttons for applications that are currently running
Windows	Boxed-in areas of the screen that contain applications, documents, dialog boxes, and other items

Mouse Terminology	Point at an object	Move the mouse so that its pointer is positioned over the object.
	Click	Press and release the left mouse button.
	Right-click	Press and release the right mouse button.
	Click/right-click *on* an object	Point at the object and click the left/right mouse button.
	Drag/right-drag an object	Point at the object, press (but don't release) the left/right mouse button, move the pointer to another position, and release the button.
Working with Menus	To open a menu	Click on its name (or press Alt+*underlined letter*).
	To choose an item from a menu	Click on it or, if ▸ is present, point at the item (*or*, in either case, type the letter that is underlined in the item's name).
Classic style and Web style modes	Switching between these settings	Start My Computer, choose the Folder Options item from the View menu, select the desired option button in the resulting dialog box, and choose the OK button.
	Selecting an icon	Under the Classic style setting, click on it; under the Web style setting, point at it.
	Activating (choosing) an icon	Under the Classic style setting, double-click on it; under Web style setting, click on it.
Working with Windows	To move a window	Drag its title bar to a new location.
	To resize a window	Drag a border or corner to a new location.
	To maximize/minimize/restore a window	Click the appropriate button at the right end of the title bar; for maximize or restore, double-click on the title bar.
	To close a window	Click on its close button.
	To scroll in a window	Click on the scroll bar arrows; drag the scroll box; *or* click on the scroll bar between an arrow and the box.
	To open a window's System menu	Click on the System Menu icon; right-click on the title bar; *or* press Alt+Spacebar or Alt+Hyphen.

Parts of a Dialog Box	Command buttons	Initiate actions such as close, cancel, etc.
	Option (radio) buttons	Allow one of several related options to be selected
	List boxes and drop-down list boxes	Allow an item to be selected from a list
	Tabs	Display a "page" of related options
	Check boxes	Turn a particular option on or off
	Text boxes	Allow text or numbers to be input by the user
Shutting Down Windows 98	To open the Start menu	Click on the Start button *or* press Ctrl+Esc.
	To open the Shut Down Windows dialog box	Close all running applications, and choose Shut Down from the Start menu *or* press Alt+F4.
	To choose a shut down option	Select the corresponding option button in the Shut Down Windows dialog box and activate the OK command button. (Activating the Cancel button closes the dialog box and returns you to Windows.)

Review Exercises

Section 1.1

1. A(n) ____________ is a small stylized picture used to represent a Windows 98 object.
2. The ____________ button is positioned to the left of the Taskbar.
3. True or false: To start Windows 98, you must type the proper command after turning on your computer.
4. The Windows *Desktop* refers to:
   a. The area occupied by your computer, keyboard, and mouse.
   b. The windows that are currently open.
   c. The application that is currently running, including its menus, toolbars, and so on.
   d. None of the above is the Windows Desktop.

Section 1.2

5. To click on an object on the screen, move the mouse pointer over that object and press the ____________.

6. To open an application's View menu, you can click on the word ____________ on the menu bar.
7. If the name of a menu item is followed by an ellipsis (...), then choosing that menu item opens a(n) ____________.
8. To switch between the Classic style and Web style icon settings, open the My Computer window and choose the Folder Options item from the ____________ menu.
9. True or false: When double-clicking the mouse, you should pause for a second or two between clicks.
10. True or false: To use a shortcut key to perform a task, open the menu that lists that task, and then press the shortcut key.
11. True or false: To right-drag an object, move the mouse pointer over it and click the right button.
12. True or false: When the Classic style setting is in effect, to select an icon, just point at the icon.
13. When you position the mouse pointer over an object, hold down the left button, and move the pointer to a new location, it is called
    a. Clicking on the object.
    b. Double-clicking on the object.
    c. Dragging the object.
    d. Pointing at the object.
14. If an item on a menu is dimmed, clicking on that item
    a. Opens a dialog box.
    b. Opens a submenu.
    c. Closes the menu.
    d. Does nothing at all.

Section 1.3

15. To move a window, drag its ____________ to the desired location on the screen.
16. Clicking on a window's ___________ increases the window's size as much as possible.
17. To increase the width of a window without increasing its height, drag its ____________ to the right or its ____________ to the left.
18. True or false: You can close a window by clicking on its menu bar.
19. True or false: When a window is minimized, the window disappears from the screen.

20. True or false: When a window opens, horizontal and vertical scroll bars are always displayed.
21. Which part of a window contains its maximize, minimize, and close buttons?
    a. Its title bar.
    b. Its menu bar.
    c. Its toolbar.
    d. Its status bar.
22. If an application is maximized, from its System menu, you can never
    a. Open the application's window.
    b. Close the application's window.
    c. Minimize the application's window.
    d. Restore the application's window.

In Exercises 23 and 24, identify the indicated parts of the window shown in Figure 12. Your answers should come from the following list:

Close button	System menu icon
Horizontal scroll bar	Maximize button
Menu bar	Minimize button
Title bar	Vertical scroll bar

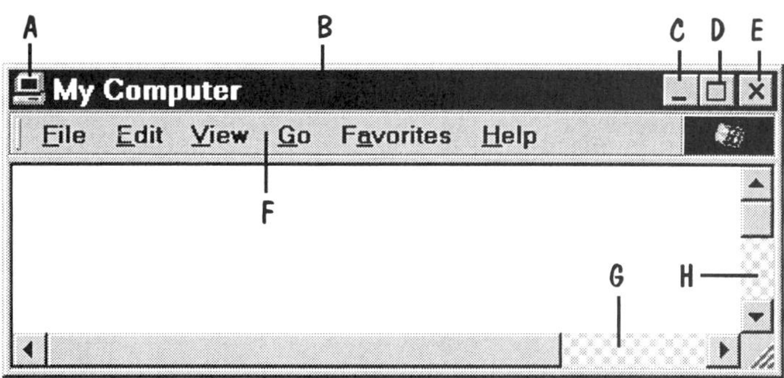

Figure 12 Window for Exercises 23 and 24

23. Identify the components of the window in Figure 12 that are marked A, B, C, and D.
24. Identify the components of the window in Figure 12 that are marked E, F, G, and H.

Section 1.4

25. When you click on the command button labeled ____________ in a dialog box, the box closes and the selected options go into effect.
26. In a dialog box, instead of clicking on the Cancel button, you can press the ____________ key.
27. In a dialog box, a ____________ allows the user to turn an option on or off without affecting other options.
28. True or false: Dialog boxes can be moved around the screen.
29. True or false: A drop-down list box only displays a single item until you click on the appropriate symbol to display the list.
30. True or false: In a group of related option buttons, only one button can be selected at any given time.
31. Which of the following objects appears on the title bar of a dialog box?

    a. A minimize button
    b. A maximize button
    c. A close button
    d. A System menu icon

32. Dialog boxes never contain

    a. Command buttons.
    b. Restore buttons.
    c. Option buttons.
    d. Tabs.

Section 1.5

33. The Shut Down menu item, which allows us to shut down Windows 98, appears on the ____________ menu.
34. The Shut Down Windows dialog box gives us the option of shutting down or ____________ Windows 98.
35. True or false: It is a good idea to shut down Windows 98 before turning off your computer.
36. True or false: To display the Start menu, even if the Start button is not visible on the screen, press Ctrl+Esc.
37. You can display the Shut Down Windows dialog box after closing all applications by pressing the keystroke combination

    a. Alt+Spacebar.
    b. Alt+Hyphen.
    c. Alt+F4.
    d. None of these keystrokes works.

Build Your Own Glossary

38. The following words and phrases are important terms that were introduced in this chapter. (They appear within the text in bold-

face type.) Write a definition for each term. After you learn to use WordPad (in Section 2.2), you should enter these definitions into the Glossary file on the Student Disk.

Check box
Choose an icon
Classic style mode
Close a window
Close button
Command button
Desktop
Dialog box
Drop-down list box
Icon
List box
Maximize a window
Maximize button
Menu
Menu bar
Minimize a window
Minimize button
Option button
Pull-down menu
Restore a window
Restore button
Scroll
Scroll bar
Shortcut key
Start button
Start menu
System menu
System menu icon
Tab (in a dialog box)
Taskbar
Title bar
Tool tip
Web style mode
Window

Lab Exercises

Work each of the following exercises at your computer. Begin by turning the machine on (if necessary) to start Windows 98. Then, close all open windows by clicking on the button labeled with an **X** on the title bar of each window. To shut down the computer after completing an exercise, follow the instructions in Section 1.5.

Lab Exercise 1 (Section 1.2)

a. *Right*-click (click with the right mouse button) on an empty part of the Desktop. On the resulting menu:

   Which options (if any) are dimmed?
   Which options (if any) will open a dialog box when selected?
   Does a bullet appear next to any option?

b. Point at the Arrange Icons option to open its submenu. Notice that there is an Auto Arrange item on the submenu. (Don't click on this item!) The Auto Arrange item is a toggle. Is it selected? How do you know?

c. Point at the New option on the original menu. In the submenu that appears, click on Folder. What is the name of the new icon that has appeared on the Desktop?

d. Click on an empty part of the Desktop. Then *right*-drag the new icon to another part of the Desktop. How many items are listed on the menu that appears when you release the mouse button?

e. Select the Copy Here option. How many copies of the new icon now appear on the Desktop?

f. Drag each copy of the new icon on top of the Recycle Bin icon. (Release the mouse button when the words *Recycle Bin* become highlighted.) What happens each time?

Lab Exercise 2 (Section 1.2)

a. Double-click on the Recycle Bin icon to open its window. List the names of the menus that appear on the menu bar.

b. Open the Edit menu. What is the shortcut key for the Cut option? Is this option dimmed?

c. Press Ctrl+A, the shortcut key for the Select All option. Why didn't anything happen?

d. Cancel the Edit menu (close it without choosing any item). What mouse action or keystroke did you use?

e. Open the View menu. How many items have bullets next to them? How many items have submenus?

f. The Status Bar menu item is a toggle; is there a check mark next to it? Choose the Status Bar item. The View menu will close. What else happened?

g. Reopen the View menu. Is the Status Bar menu item "checked" now?

h. *Right*-click (click with the right button) on the Folder Options item. What, if anything, happened?

i. Click on the word *View* to close this menu. Then, click on the button labeled with an X in the upper-right corner of the Recycle Bin window to close it.

Lab Exercise 3 (Section 1.2)

a. Open the My Computer window by double-clicking on its icon.

b. Display the View menu. Which menu item has a bullet next to it?

c. Choose the Folder Options item from the View menu to open the Folder Options dialog box. Select the Web style setting and click on the button labeled "OK" to close the dialog box. Are the titles of the icons in the My Computer window underlined?

d. Point at the "(C:)" icon in the My Computer window. What, if anything, happened?

e. Click on the "(C:)" icon. What, if anything, happened?

f. Close all open windows by clicking on the button labeled with an X in each window's upper-right corner.

g. Reopen the My Computer window and then display the Folder Options dialog box. In the latter, select the Classic style setting and then click on the OK button. Are the titles of the icons in the My Computer window underlined?

h. Repeat steps *d*, *e*, and *f* of this exercise, answering the questions posed in steps *d* and *e*.

Lab Exercise 4 (Section 1.3)

a. Click on an empty part of the Desktop, then press the F3 function key to open the Find window. Does this window have a System menu icon on its title bar?

b. If the Find window is maximized, restore it. Then, decrease its width as much as possible. Is the entire window title visible now? Did any scroll bars appear?

c. Try to increase or decrease the height of this window. Was it possible to do either?

d. Maximize the Find window. Does it occupy the entire screen?

e. Right-click the title bar to display the System menu. List the items on this menu that are not dimmed. Choose the Restore item from the System menu.

f. Move the window downward. Is it possible to move part of it off the screen?

g. Minimize the window to a button on the Taskbar; then restore it to a window. Is it the same size as it was before being minimized?

h. Resize and reposition the Find window to the approximate size and location it had when you began this exercise. Close the Find window.

Lab Exercise 5 (Section 1.3)

a. Right-click on an empty part of the Desktop; then select Properties from the resulting menu to open the Display Properties window.

b. Notice that this window (a *dialog box*) does not contain a minimize or maximize button, or a System menu icon. Try to maximize the window by double-clicking on its title bar. Did this work?

c. Can this dialog box be: Moved? Resized? Minimized?

d. Open the window's System menu. What mouse action or keystroke combination did you use? What items are listed on the System menu? Cancel this menu.

e. In the small window entitled *Wallpaper*, use the vertical scroll bar to scroll to the bottom of the list. What name appears there? Why isn't a *horizontal* scroll bar displayed?

f. Try closing the Display Properties window by pressing Alt+F4. Did it work? If not, close it by clicking on the close button.

Lab Exercise 6 (Section 1.4)

a. Double-click on the Clock on the Taskbar to open the Date/Time Properties dialog box. (If the Taskbar is not on the screen, press Ctrl+Esc to display it.)

b. Erase the year displayed in the Date text box and try to type in a new year. Were you able to do this?

c. Using the up and down arrows in the Date text box, determine the allowable range of years. What is it?

d. Click on the Time Zone tab to change to this set of options.

e. Open the drop-down list and scroll to the bottom. What places are given for the "GMT+12:00" entry? Close the drop-down list.

f. Click on the **?** button on the title bar; then click on the text to the right of the check box. What happened?

g. Close this dialog box by clicking on the Cancel button or by pressing the Escape key.

Lab Exercise 7 (Section 1.4)

a. Click on an empty part of the Desktop; then press the F3 function key to open the Find window. What features does the Find window have that are not present in a dialog box?

b. Deselect the *Include subfolders* check box. Did the text in the *Look in* drop-down list box change?

c. Click on the Date tab. Notice that the *All files* option button is selected.

d. Select the *Find all files* option button. What happened to the *All files* button?

e. Select one of the *previous* option buttons. Try to enter the number 0 in the corresponding text box. Were you able to do this?

f. Click on the Advanced tab and open the *Of type* drop-down list. Why is a vertical scroll bar necessary here? What name is at the bottom of the list?

g. Close the Find window by clicking on its close button.

Lab Exercise 8 (Section 1.5)

a. Open the Shut Down Windows dialog box; then close it without shutting down or restarting the computer. How did you do this?

b. Reopen the Shut Down Windows dialog box and activate the "Restart in MS-DOS mode" option. What text eventually appears on the screen?

c. Insert the Student Disk that accompanies this text into its drive; then type `a:dosprog` and press the Enter key. Does the application you just started appear in a *window*?

d. Follow the on-screen instructions to exit this application. What did you do to exit?

e. Restart Windows 98 by typing `win` and pressing the Enter key. Was the Windows 98 logo displayed before Windows started?

f. Open the Shut Down Windows dialog box and activate the "Shut down" option. Was any message displayed prior to "It's now safe to turn off your computer"?

g. Turn off your computer.

If You Want to Learn More ...

This section, and others like it throughout the text, present some notes that allow you to delve more deeply into the material in the current chapter. Most of the notes found here deal with esoteric or advanced topics, so there is no need for you to spend much time reading them now. On the other hand, you may find some of these comments interesting and, on occasion, they may help you work through a potentially frustrating situation.

More on the Taskbar Clock

The Taskbar Clock gives not only the time but also the current day and date. To view the latter, position the mouse pointer over the clock and hold it steady for a few moments. Here are a couple of more tips on using the Clock:

- If the Clock does not appear on the Taskbar, right-click on an empty part of the Taskbar, and choose the Properties option from the pop-up menu. Then select the Show Clock check box in the resulting dialog box and choose the OK command button.

- If the Clock is not showing the correct time or date, double-click on it. The Date/Time Properties dialog box will open, and the date and time can be adjusted, as described in Section 5.5.

Quicker restarts

To decrease the amount of time it takes the computer to restart (see Section 1.5), proceed as follows:

1. Open the Shut Down Windows dialog box from the Start menu and select the Restart option button.
2. Hold down the Shift key as you click on the OK button.

Windows will shortcut part of the usual restart process, and the Desktop will reappear considerably more quickly.

Navigating with the keyboard

Certainly, the easiest way to select items on the Desktop or in a dialog box is to use the mouse. But Windows supplies keyboard alternatives for most mouse operations, and these are no exception. For example:

- To select a particular Desktop icon (when no windows are open), press the appropriate Arrow keys until the icon is highlighted. (If nothing happens when you press an Arrow key, repeatedly press the Tab key until one of the Desktop icons becomes highlighted or "boxed-in".) Once an icon is highlighted, pressing the Enter key chooses that icon, opening the object it represents.
- You can move the *focus*, a "dotted" rectangular box, from one item to another in an active dialog box by pressing the Tab key. To cycle through a set of option buttons when one of them has the focus, repeatedly press an Arrow key. To select or deselect the check box that has the focus, press the Spacebar.

For a more complete list of keyboard alternatives, see Appendix A.

The "Standby" shut-down option

In Section 1.5, we discussed the three options that always appear in the Shut Down Windows dialog box: Shut down, Restart, and Restart in MS-DOS mode. Depending on a system's configuration, other options may also be present. The most common of these is "Stand by". If you select this option button and then choose the OK command button, the computer system will go into *standby mode* — it will shut down certain components (for example, the monitor and hard disk) so as to consume less electricity. To resume working after you have placed the computer on standby, either press a key or click or move the mouse.

Displaying an off-screen title bar

If part of a window is located beyond the screen boundary, you can usually move the entire window on-screen by dragging its title bar. However, this technique does not work if the title bar itself is "off the screen".

When a window's title bar is located off-screen, there are two basic ways to get it back. First, click on any part of the window to make it the active window. Now, either press Alt+Spacebar to open the window's System menu or right-click on the window's Taskbar button to open a pop-up menu. Then, you can:

- Maximize the window (if it *can* be maximized) by choosing the Maximize command from either of these two menus.

or

- Choose the Move command from either of these two menus and then use the Arrow keys to move the window in the appropriate direction. When the window is positioned where you want it, press the Enter key to complete the process.

Where to go from here

Here's where to find more information about some of the topics discussed in this chapter.

- Adding and removing Desktop icons (*shortcuts*) — Section 3.4
- Changing the Desktop background — Section 5.2
- Using the Taskbar — Sections 2.3 and 4.1
- Using the other Start menu options:

  Programs, Documents, and Run — Section 2.1
  Favorites — Section 6.2
  Settings — Sections 4.1, 4.2, 4.5, and 5.1
  Find — Section 4.3
  Help — Section 2.5

- Changing the appearance of various Desktop and window elements (such as the title bar color or icon text) — Section 5.3
- Web integration features of Windows 98 — Section 6.6

CHAPTER 2

Working with Applications and Documents

Overview

In Chapter 1 we discussed the structure and general use of some basic Windows 98 objects — the Desktop, menus, windows, and dialog boxes. In this chapter, we will concentrate on how to use Windows 98 to run your **applications** (programs) and manipulate your **documents** (the work created by an application). To be more specific, you will learn:

1. Various ways to start and close applications.
2. How to use the WordPad application to create simple word processing documents.
3. How to open, save, print, and close documents.
4. How to switch among the applications that are running.
5. How to transfer information from one document to another.
6. How to "capture" windows and screens.
7. How to install new applications and Windows components.
8. How to use the online Windows 98 Help system to locate information about a desired topic.
9. How to obtain online context-sensitive help.

After completing this chapter, you should be able to use Windows 98 to print a copy of your homework!

2.1 Starting and Closing Applications

Windows 98 supplies a myriad of ways to start (or *open*) and exit (or *close*) applications. In this section we will describe most of these techniques.

Starting an Application

Typically, Windows 98 provides a variety of ways of performing just about any task, and opening applications is no exception. In this section, we will describe several simple techniques for starting programs; others will be presented later in the text.

The easiest way

If an icon representing an application or document appears on the Desktop, just choose that icon to open that application or document. (In the latter case, Windows will first start the application that created the document and then display the document within it.) Remember (from Section 1.2) that to *choose* an icon, you

- Double-click on the icon if the Classic style setting is in effect (the icon is not underlined).
- Click on the icon if the Web style setting is in effect (the icon is underlined).

If an application or document that you use frequently is not represented by an icon on the Desktop, you should create one for it. We will discuss how to create these icons (*shortcuts*) in Section 3.4.

Using the Start menu

Start

Recall that if you click on the Start button to the left of the Taskbar, the Windows 98 Start menu opens (Figure 1). In Section 1.5, we discussed how to use the last item on this menu to shut down or restart Windows. Here, we will describe how to use the Start menu to open the applications installed on your computer.

The Programs option

Often the most straightforward way to open a program is to select the **Programs option** from the Start menu. When you point at this item (holding the arrow-shaped mouse pointer steady for a moment or two), a submenu listing specific applications and groups of applications will be displayed, as shown in Figure 2. (Your list of programs will undoubtedly be different from these.)

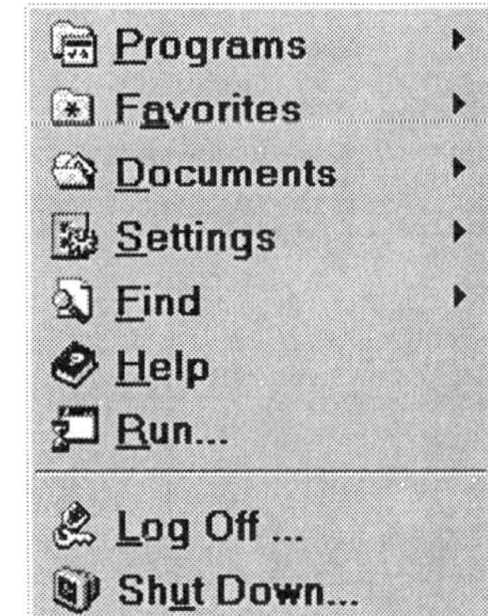

Figure 1
The Start Menu

Figure 2
Pointing at the Programs Option on the Start Menu

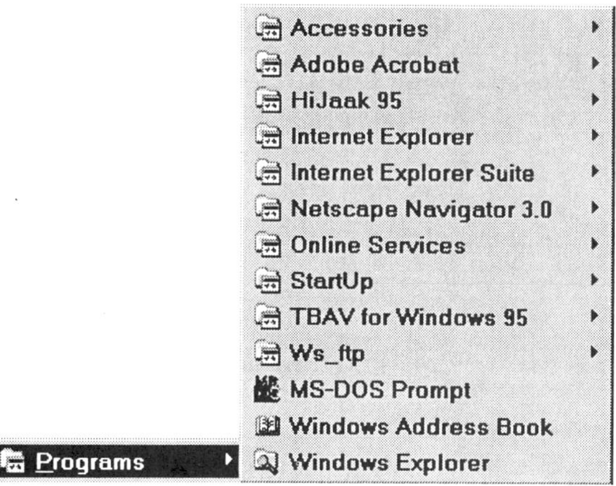

On the submenu, the items followed by a right-facing triangle (such as Accessories, at the top in Figure 2) represent *groups* of applications; if you point at one of these items, another submenu will open, presenting further applications and possibly groups of applications. A submenu item that is not followed by a right triangle (such as Windows Explorer at the bottom of the list) represents a program. To start a program, just click on it! The Start menu will close and the program will begin running.

For example, suppose you want to open WordPad, a word processor that is included with the Windows 98 software package. To do so, click on the Start button to open the Start menu and point at the Programs option to open its submenu (Figure 2). Then, point at the Accessories option, which opens another submenu, and finally click on the WordPad item at the bottom of the latter. After a few moments, the WordPad opening screen will be displayed.

The Documents option

Using the **Documents option** on the Start menu can sometimes be a real time-saver. Pointing at this item (see Figure 3) displays a submenu containing a list of documents that have recently been saved to disk. (We will discuss saving documents in Section 2.2.) Clicking on one of the listed documents starts the application that created it and also displays (*opens*) the designated document within it.

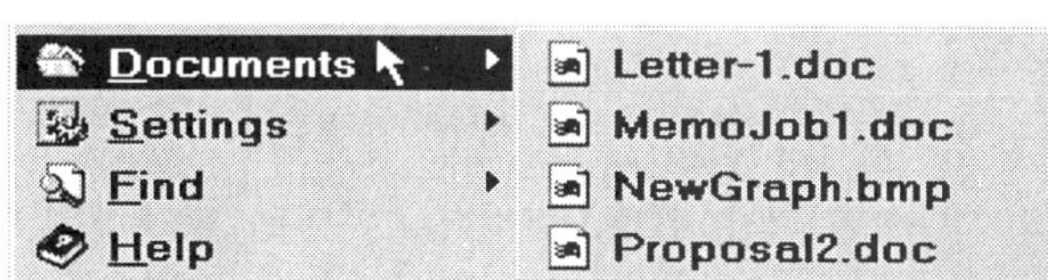

Figure 3 Pointing at the Documents Option

This simple technique may not always work as planned. When you select an item from the Documents submenu (or choose a document's icon on the Desktop), Windows sometimes starts an application other than the one that created the specified document.

For example, on our Documents submenu, there is a file named "Letter-1.doc". This document was created by WordPad, But, when we click on Letter-1.doc in the list of documents, Windows might start the Microsoft Word word processor instead. (The reason why this could happen is discussed in Section 4.4.) The workaround for this problem is simple — just start WordPad first and then open the desired document from within it as described in Section 2.2.

The Run option

The techniques we have just described for starting an application are quick and easy, but require that the program, or a document created by it, appear on one of the Start button submenus. The **Run option**, which appears near the bottom of the Start menu, can be used to open *any* application on your hard or floppy disks.

When you click on the Run command, the following dialog box is displayed:

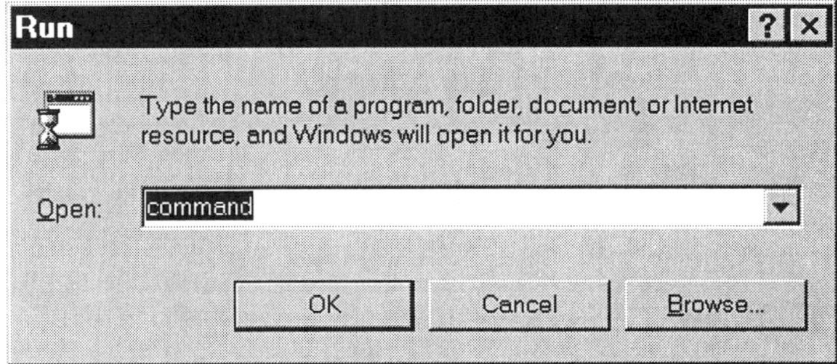

To start a program from this dialog box, you must know its file name, and possibly the folder in which that file is located — this is the major drawback of using the Run option. (We will discuss files and folders in Section 3.1.) If you have this required information, you can open the desired application by performing any of the following actions:

- Type the appropriate folder and file names (the program's *path name*) in the Open text box. (If a highlighted name already appears there, just type over it!) Then, click on the OK button or press the Enter key.
- If you have previously started the desired application from the

Run dialog box, its name may appear on the Open drop-down list. Display this list (by clicking on the down-triangle), select the program's file name, and activate the OK button.

- Click on the Browse command button to open the Browse dialog box and use it to help you locate the program's file name; then activate the OK button. (This technique requires some familiarity with the Windows 98 folder system, which we will discuss in Chapter 3.)

In any case, the Run dialog box will close and the program will start.

As you can see, using the Run option is usually not the easiest way to start a program. However, there is one case in which Run is especially useful: when the program you want to start is on a floppy disk (diskette). To start a program from a floppy:

1. Insert the diskette in its drive.
2. Select the Run option from the Start menu.
3. Type the characters a: (assuming that the diskette is in this drive) followed by the program's file name in the text box; for example, a:big-game.
4. Press the Enter key or click on the OK button. The Run dialog box will close and the program will start.

NOTE

We will discuss additional ways to start applications later in the text. These techniques make use of Windows Explorer (Section 3.2), My Computer (Section 3.5), or the Windows Find utility (Section 4.3).

Closing an Application

If you read Chapter 1 carefully (or worked its tutorials), you already know how to close a Windows-based application — just close its window. As usual, this task can be done in several ways. The following techniques are listed (more or less) in order of likely use; take your pick:

Ways to close Windows-based applications

- Click on the application window's close button (on the right end of the title bar). 
- Choose Exit from the application's File menu.
- Right-click on the application's Taskbar button and choose Close from the resulting menu.

- Press Alt+F4 (hold down the Alt key, tap the F4 key, and release Alt).
- Double-click on the application's System menu icon (on the left end of the title bar).
- Open the application's System menu by clicking on its System menu icon (right-clicking the title bar may also work) and choose the Close option.

NOTE

If you have used the application to make changes to a document and did not subsequently save the document to disk, Windows will display a warning message before closing the application. We will discuss this further in Section 2.2.

Closing DOS applications

As we mentioned in the Introduction, Windows 98 not only runs applications specifically designed for itself and previous versions of Windows, but it also runs *DOS applications.* Although some DOS applications can be closed by selecting Exit from their File menus (if they have one!), none of the other techniques listed above is likely to work. If you try one of them, you'll probably get a message that "Windows cannot shut down this program automatically."

Unfortunately, DOS applications, especially older ones, are notorious for performing common tasks in their own peculiar ways. So, you'll just have to learn the keystrokes or mouse clicks necessary to exit each DOS application you use. After exiting the program, its window may still remain on the screen, with the word *Finished* displayed at the left end of the title bar. To close the window, use any of the usual techniques (such as clicking on the close button).

There is another way to exit *any* application, but it should only be used in an emergency; for example, if the application has "locked up", and no longer responds to the keyboard or mouse. In this case, press Ctrl+Alt+Del; that is, hold down the Ctrl and Alt keys, tap the Del key, and then release Ctrl and Alt. A dialog box will open, listing all programs that are currently running. The offending application should be highlighted in this list. (If it isn't, click on it.) Now activate the End Task command button and follow the on-screen instructions. Using this procedure, you will probably lose all unsaved work in the application that has locked up, but other open programs should survive unscathed.

TUTORIAL

Try the following exercise on your own.

1. Turn on your computer, if necessary, to start up Windows 98.
2. Open the WordPad application from the Start menu, as follows:
   - Click on the Start button to open the Start menu.
   - Point at the Programs option (and keep the mouse pointer stationary for a few moments) to open this submenu.
   - Now, point at the Accessories item at the top, to display another submenu.
   - Finally, click on the WordPad item to start this application.
3. Close the WordPad application by clicking on its close button.
4. Open the Start menu and point at the Documents option to open this submenu.
5. If any documents are listed, click on one of them, which should open that document within the application that created it. Close this application by choosing the Exit item from its File menu.
6. Place the Student Disk in its drive.
7. Start the DOSPROG application on this diskette, as follows:
   - Open the Start menu and click on the Run option to open the Run dialog box.
   - Type `a:dosprog` in the Open text box and press the Enter key. The Run dialog box will close and the program will start.
8. Exit the DOSPROG application by following the on-screen instructions. If the application window remains on the screen, close it by pressing Alt+F4.

2.2 An Introduction to WordPad; Documents

In Windows, the word *document* is used to refer to any collection of data that is created by an application. Thus, a document could be a letter written using a word processor, a picture created by a painting program, or a collection of numbers produced by a spreadsheet program. Nevertheless, there are certain operations that are common to almost all documents: they must be created, saved, opened, printed, and closed. The way in which a document is created *does* vary considerably from application to application. However, all Windows documents are opened, saved, printed, and closed in a uniform way. (This is one of the beauties of using Windows!) In this section, we will use the WordPad application to illustrate these operations.

An Introduction to WordPad

WordPad is one of the small applications (sometimes called *applets* or *accessories*) that are included as part of the Windows 98 package. WordPad is a *word processor* — an application used to create text-based documents such as memos, letters, reports, and so on. In this section, we will be viewing WordPad as an example of a typical Windows 98 application, but in the process you will learn enough to use it to produce very simple documents. WordPad's features will be discussed in more detail in Chapter 7.

To start WordPad, select Programs from the Start menu and Accessories from the resulting submenu. Then, click on the WordPad item on the Accessories submenu. This action starts WordPad and opens a window similar to the one in Figure 4. (The toolbar, format bar, ruler, and status bar may or may not be displayed.)

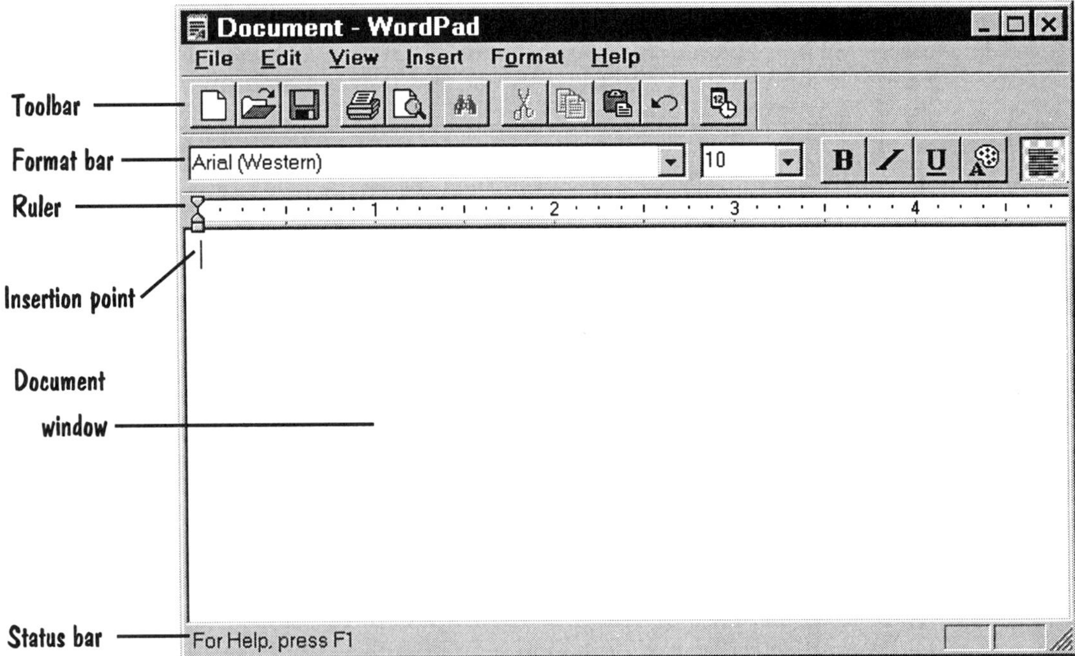

Figure 4 The WordPad Window

Entering text Once you have started WordPad, type whatever you want at the keyboard; the corresponding text will appear in the *document window* and be stored in the computer's internal memory, RAM. The *insertion point*, the blinking vertical bar, indicates where the next character you type will appear on the screen.

When you reach the end of a line, just keep typing; WordPad's *word wrap* feature will automatically continue the text at the beginning of the next line. To start a new line manually, press the Enter key and the insertion point will move to the beginning of the next line. To skip a line, press Enter again. (When you reach the bottom of the window, moving to the next line will scroll the window down.)

For example, if you type your name, your class, and the date, pressing the Enter key after your name and class, the three entries will appear on separate lines. Moreover, if you press Enter *twice* after the date and then type Homework 1, the screen will look like the one shown in Figure 5.

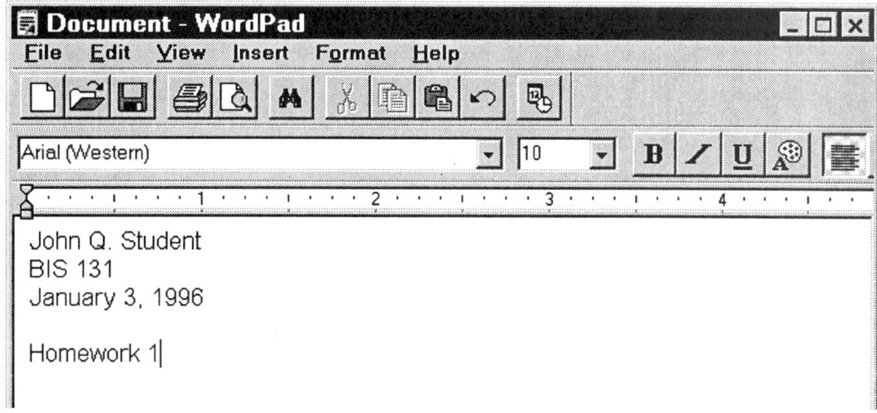

Figure 5 Entering Text into the WordPad Window

Correcting mistakes It is very easy to correct typing errors. To erase the character just to the *left* of the insertion point, press the Backspace key (which may be labeled ←); to delete the character just to the *right* of the insertion point, press the Delete (Del) key. Holding down either key erases a succession of characters.

You can use the mouse or the keyboard to move the insertion point to a mistake anywhere in the document:

- To use the mouse, scroll the document window (see Section 1.3), if necessary, until the desired location is visible on the screen. Then, click on this location to move the insertion point there.

- You can also use the Arrow keys (←, →. ↑, ↓) to move the insertion point left, right, up, or down and to scroll the window (by pressing the appropriate Arrow key when the insertion point is at an edge of the window).

For example, suppose your screen looks like the one in Figure 5, and you realize you've made a mistake: your middle initial is "X", not "Q". To correct the error:

1. Move the insertion point just before the Q by either mouse-clicking on this location or pressing the Up Arrow key four times and the Left Arrow key six times.
2. Press the Delete key to erase the Q.
3. Type an X.

Saving a Document

The short document we just created (Figure 5) is not only displayed on the screen, but also stored in RAM. If we start a new document, close WordPad, or shut down Windows, the document will be removed from both the screen and RAM. Thus, if we want to retrieve this document in the future, we must store a copy of it on a more permanent medium — we must **save** the document to disk! The save operation, with your help, also provides a name for the document. In this section, we will only discuss how to save a document to a floppy disk (diskette), but once you learn to navigate the Windows 98 folder system (Chapter 3), you will see how to save it to a specified location on a hard disk.

The Save command

To save the document that is currently displayed to a floppy disk:

1. Insert the diskette into its drive.
2. Choose Save from the File menu.
   - If this document has been saved before, the current version will be saved under the same name, *replacing the former version on disk.* The File menu will close and you will be returned to the document window.
   - If this document has *not* been saved before, the Save As dialog box (Figure 6) will open and you must carry out all the remaining steps of this procedure.

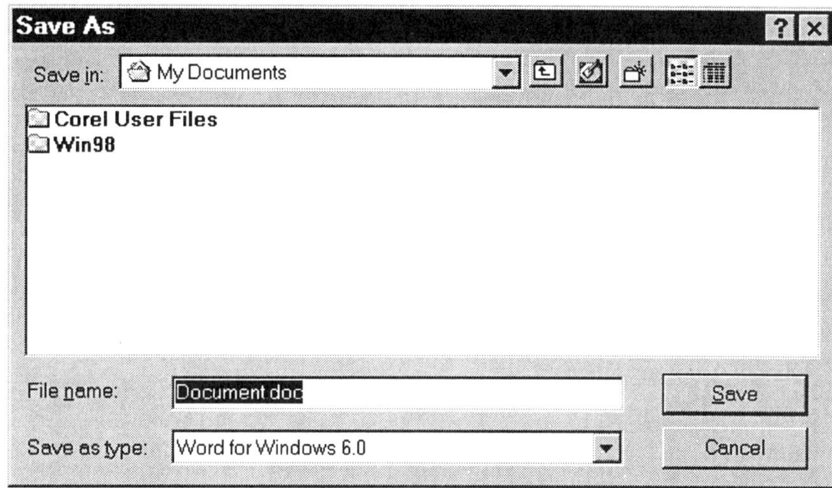

Figure 6 The Save As Dialog Box

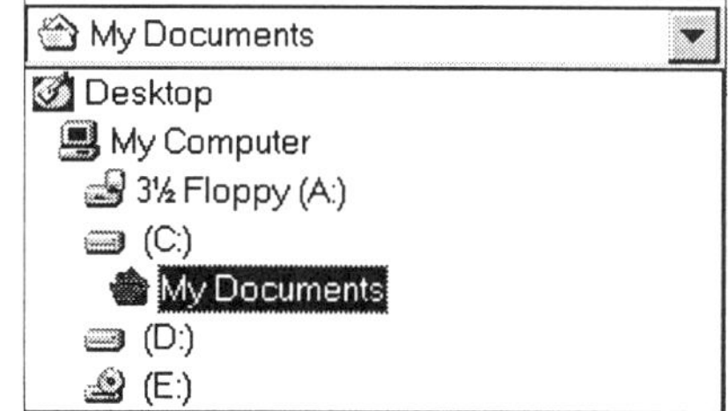

3. If the *Save in* box does not contain "3½ Floppy", then display its drop-down list (like the one at the right) by clicking on the down-triangle. Now select the appropriate floppy drive by clicking on it.
4. Erase the name in the File name text box (click in the box and then use the Delete or Backspace key) and type a name* for the document. For example, in saving the document displayed in Figure 5, we might use the name Homework 1.
5. To complete the save operation (and close the dialog box), press the Enter key or click on the Save command button.

NOTE

A simpler way to save a document in WordPad and many other Windows 98 applications is to use its **toolbar**, which sits just under the menu bar, as shown in Figure 4. (If the toolbar is not visible on the screen, choose the Toolbar item from the View menu to display

*If you're using WordPad or another application designed to run under Windows 95 or 98, you may choose almost any name up to 255 characters in length. If you're using any other application, the name should be no longer than 8 characters and there are restrictions on the characters you can use. (See Section 3.1 for more information.)

it.) The icons on the toolbar provide quick access to certain menu commands. When you mouse-point at one of the icons, a *tool tip* appears, indicating the icon's function:

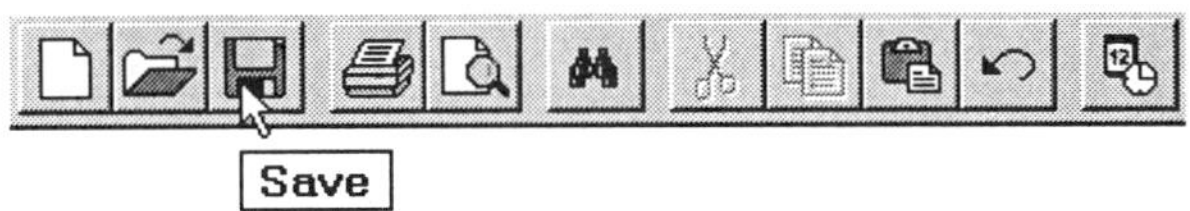

To activate a toolbar function, just click on it. For example, clicking on the floppy disk icon has the same effect as choosing Save from the File menu!

The Save As command

On occasion, you may make changes to a document, but want to keep both the old and new versions. In this case, you cannot use the Save command; it will automatically erase the old version while saving the new one. Instead, you should choose the Save As item from the File menu, which displays the Save As dialog box (Figure 6) even though the current document has been previously saved. Now, just save the new (current) version under a name different from the old one, and both versions are safely stored on disk.

Closing a Document

To **close** a document means to remove it from both the screen and RAM. When you exit a Windows application, any open documents are closed automatically. You may, however, wish to close a document before exiting your application, perhaps to begin working on another document. To accomplish this in WordPad:

1. Choose New from the File menu or click on the New icon on the toolbar. The New dialog box will be displayed.

2. Activate the OK command button to accept the default document type. If you have not saved the latest changes to this document, a message similar to the one at the right will appear.

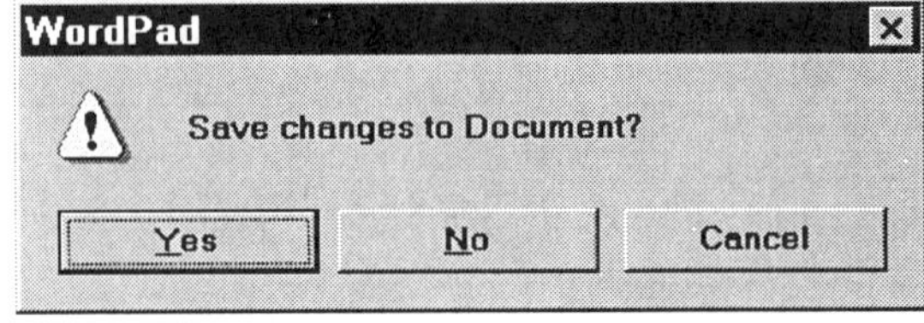

3. Choose the Yes command button and Windows will give you the opportunity to save your changes; choose No and the document will close, but your changes will not be saved to disk. Clicking on the Cancel button (or pressing the Escape key) returns you to the document; it will not close.

NOTE

WordPad only allows one document window to be open at any time. Certain other Windows applications allow multiple open document windows. Choosing New in such a case does not close the current document; it just clears it from the screen. To close a document when multiple open windows are allowed, choose Close from the File menu.

Opening a Document

When you save a document, it is stored on disk under the name you have chosen for it. Saving it does not remove it from the screen or the computer's RAM, so you *can* continue to work on it. However, after the document has been closed, to work on it again you must have Windows copy it from disk into RAM and display it on the screen. In other words, you must **open** the document. Just as there are many ways to open an application, Windows 98 provides many ways to open a document.

The Open command

To open a document within an application that is already running, one normally uses the Open command. We will demonstrate here how to use this command to open a document that is stored on a floppy disk, but once you learn to navigate the Windows 98 folder system, it will be just as easy to open any document. To open a document stored on a diskette:

1. Start (if necessary) the application that created the document.
2. Insert the diskette containing the document into its drive.
3. Choose Open from the File menu or click on the Open icon on the toolbar. The Open dialog box, like the one in Figure 7 (on the next page), will be displayed. If the floppy drive does not appear in the *Look in* text box, click on the down-triangle and select the floppy drive from the drop-down list.

4. If the name of the document you want to open isn't listed, display the *Files of type* drop-down list and select the entry labeled "All Documents (*.*)". A new, probably longer, list of names will

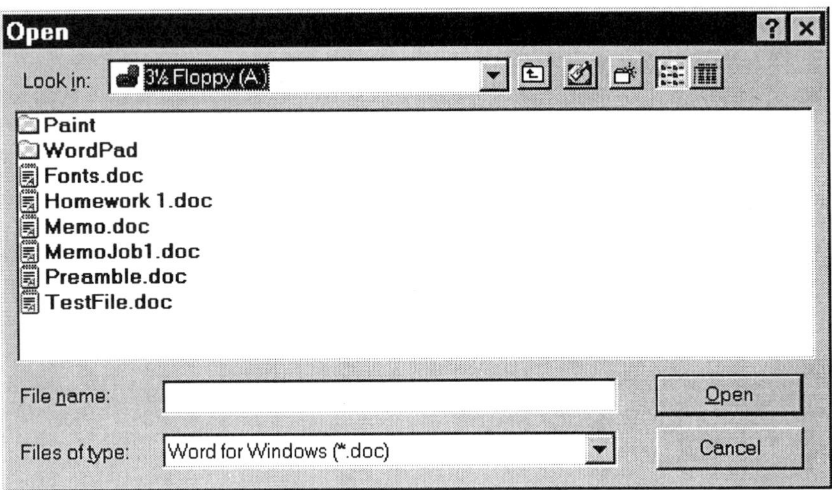

Figure 7 The Open Dialog Box

be displayed and the document you are seeking may be one of them.

5. Select the document you want to open from the list. It will become highlighted.
6. Choose the Open command button. The dialog box will close and the specified document will open.

Open programs and documents simultaneously

To use the Open command, the relevant application must be running. If it isn't, recall from Section 2.1 that you can sometimes open a document and the application that created it at the same time using one of the following simple techniques:

- If the desired document is represented by an icon on the Desktop, choose this icon.
- If the desired document is listed on the Start menu's Documents submenu, click on its name.

Printing a Document

When you **print** a document, you send a copy of it to a printer. Here is the most straightforward way to print a document:

1. Open the document if it is not already on screen.

2. Choose the Print command from the File menu. The Print dialog box will open, as shown in Figure 8.

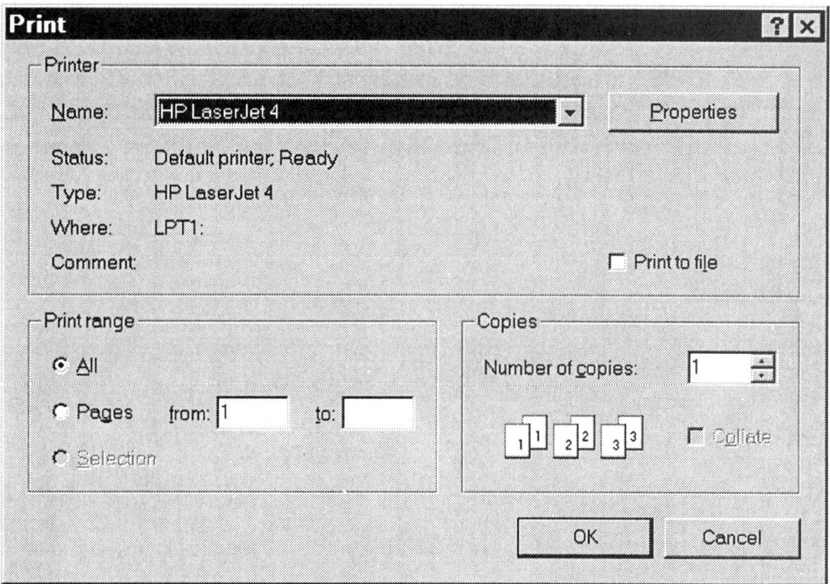

Figure 8 The Print Dialog Box

3. Make the desired selections from this dialog box:
   - If your computer is connected to more than one printer, you can select the one you want to use from the Printer Name drop-down list.
   - If you don't want to print the entire document (indicated by the *All* option button), you can print a range of pages by clicking on the *Pages* option button and then filling in the *from* and *to* text boxes. You can also *select* a portion of your document (as described in Section 2.3) prior to opening the Print dialog box and then print just the selected text by clicking on the Selection option button.
   - If you want to print more than one copy, change the number that appears in the *Number of copies* text box. To collate (sort) the copies, select this check box.
4. Make sure that the selected printer is ready to receive information.

5. Choose the OK command button. The document (or the selected portion of the document) will be printed.

If you want to print a document using the default information in the Print dialog box (for example, all pages and one copy), you need not open it. Just click on the Print icon on the toolbar. The dialog box will not be displayed and the print process will begin immediately.

Try the following exercise on your own.

1. Turn on your computer (if necessary) to start up Windows 98.
2. Start the WordPad word processor: Click on the Start button, point at Programs to open this submenu, point at Accessories to open a second submenu, and click on WordPad on the latter.
3. Insert the Student Disk in its drive and open the Homework 1 document that is stored on it: Choose the Open command from the File menu, select the floppy drive from the *Look in* drop-down list, click on the name "Homework 1", and activate the Open command button.
4. Edit the Homework 1 document so that it gives *your* name and class and the current date. To do so:
   - Repeatedly press the Delete key until the current name is erased.
   - Type in your name.
   - Click the mouse pointer (an "I-beam" symbol) at the beginning of the next line (or press the Right Arrow key once) to move the insertion point to this location.
   - Repeat these steps to correct the class and date.
5. Save the new document under the new name My Homework 1: Choose the Save As command from the File menu, select the floppy drive from the *Save in* drop-down list, type the new name in the *File name* text box, and choose the Save command button.
6. Print the current document by either choosing Print from the File menu and activating the OK button or clicking on the printer icon on the toolbar. (If the latter is currently not visible, choose Toolbar from the View menu to display it.)
7. Clear the current document from the screen: Select New from the File menu (or click on the "page" icon on the toolbar) and then activate the OK command button in the dialog box.

8. Exit WordPad: Choose Exit from its File menu or click on the close button on the title bar.

2.3 Running Several Applications at Once

As you know, Windows allows you to run several applications at the same time, each of which is instantly available. To see how this can be useful, suppose that you are using the WordPad word processor to write a report and you realize that a picture will illustrate your point better than the proverbial thousand words. To create the picture, you start Paint, the painting program supplied with Windows 98 and which (like WordPad) is found on the Accessories submenu of the Start menu's Programs option.

Starting Paint does not close WordPad, so these two applications are now both running at the same time (see Figure 9). After completing your picture, you switch back to WordPad, copy the picture into the

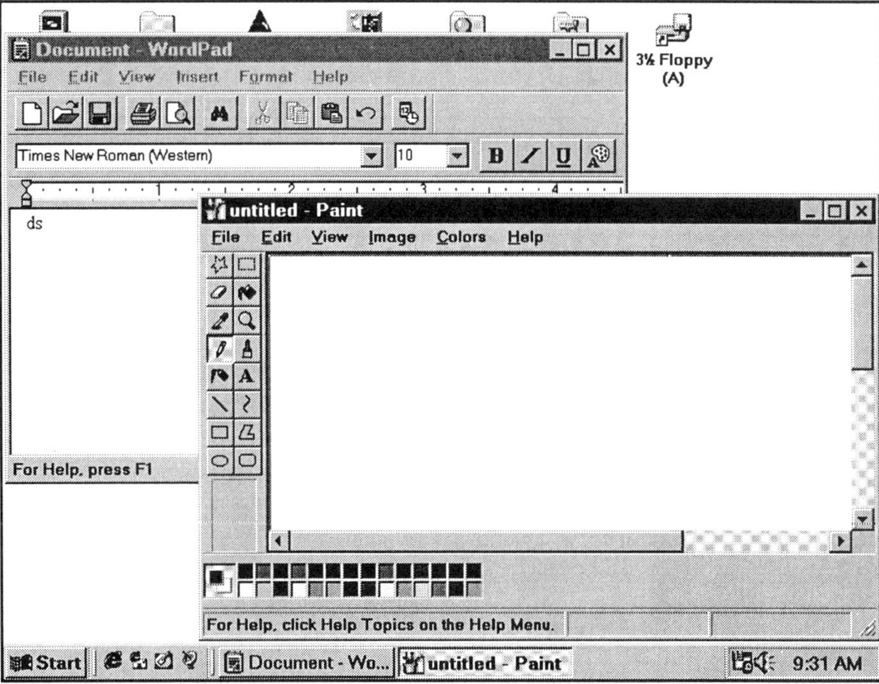

Figure 9 WordPad and Paint Open on the Desktop

word processing document, and continue writing. Before you finish this Windows session, you might use other applications as well, perhaps to make a backup copy of your documents or just to take a break with a computer game.

To make use of the kind of flexibility illustrated in this scenario, you have to be able to quickly and easily switch among several running applications and to transfer information between them. We will discuss these techniques in the remainder of this section.

Switching Among Applications

Each application that is currently running is represented by a button on the Taskbar. The program in which you are currently working is called the **active application**. Its Taskbar button appears to be "brighter" than the others and its title bar is highlighted (see the Paint button and title bar in Figure 9).

Ways to switch applications

To switch from the active application to an inactive one, perform any of the following actions:

- If any portion of the inactive program's window is visible, just click within that window. It becomes the active one and moves to the front.
- Click on the inactive program's Taskbar button. (Remember: If the Taskbar is not visible on the screen, it can be displayed by pressing the Ctrl+Esc keystroke combination.) This application becomes the active one and its window is displayed on the screen.
- Hold down the Alt key and press the Tab key. A window similar to the following one will appear on the screen:

In this window, each icon represents a currently running program. The application corresponding to the "boxed in" icon has its name displayed on the line below. To cycle through your running applications, continue to hold down the Alt key, and repeatedly press the Tab key; the "box" will move from icon to icon. When the name of the desired application appears in the window, release the Alt key. Windows makes this application the active one and displays it on the screen.

Transferring Information between Documents

The process of transferring information — for example, a block of text or a picture — from one document (the *source*) to another (the *target*) usually involves the following steps:

1. In the source document, *select the information* to be transferred. Here's how to select a *block of text* while running any Windows application. Either

   - Position the mouse pointer in front of the first character in the desired block of text and drag the insertion point to the end of the block.

   or

   - Position the insertion point in front of the first character in the desired block of text, hold down the Shift key, move the insertion point to the end of the block (for example, using the Arrow keys), and then release Shift.

   In either case, the selected text will be highlighted. (If you want to *deselect* the text, just click the mouse anywhere else in the document or press an Arrow key.)

2. *Cut* or *copy* the selected information to the Windows **Clipboard**, a temporary storage location in RAM set aside for this purpose. When information is **cut**, it is deleted from the source document and moved to the Clipboard; when information is **copied**, it is also transferred to the Clipboard, but the source document remains unchanged. To perform the cut or copy operation, choose the Cut or Copy command from the source application's Edit menu.

The Clipboard can only hold one block of information at a time. Thus, when you cut or copy something to the Clipboard, Windows automatically erases the previous contents (if any). No warning message will be issued!

You can examine the current contents of the Clipboard by opening the **Clipboard Viewer** utility. (Some configurations of Windows 98 contain **Clip*book* Viewer** instead.) To start Clipboard Viewer, choose this item from the System Tools submenu of the Start button's Accessories menu. The current Clipboard contents will be displayed in the Clipboard Viewer window. (Clipbook Viewer is also started from the Accessories submenu, but the contents of the Clipboard are not displayed automatically; you have to choose the Clipboard command from the Window menu.)

3. Start, or switch to, the target application (unless the source and target are the same) and open the target document, if necessary.
4. In the target document, position the cursor where you want to insert the information.
5. **Paste** (insert) the information on the Clipboard into the target document at the cursor position by choosing the Paste command from the target application's Edit menu.

   Pictorially, the process looks like this:

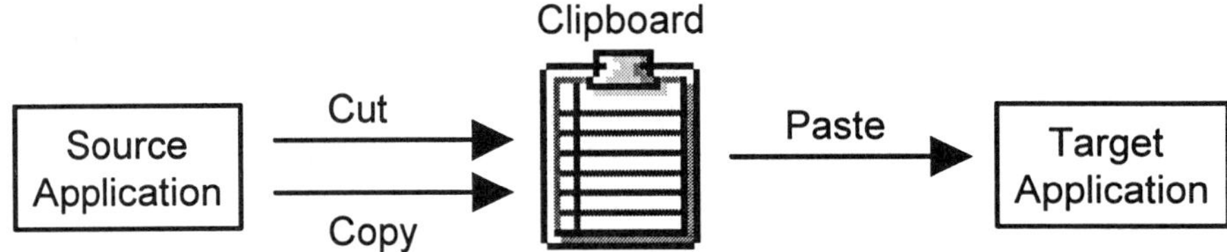

Here are a couple of other ways to issue the cut/copy or paste commands that work with many Windows applications. After selecting the text to be transferred to the Clipboard, you can *cut or copy* it by either

- Pressing Ctrl+X for cut or Ctrl+C for copy.

or

- Positioning the mouse pointer over the selected text, right-clicking, and choosing Cut or Copy from the resulting menu.

To *paste* text from the Clipboard, position the cursor where you want to insert the text and then, either press Ctrl+V or right-click the mouse and choose Paste from the resulting menu.

NOTE

If you want to copy the *entire current screen* to the Clipboard, press the Print Screen key. To copy the *active window* to the Clipboard, press Alt+Print Screen. In both cases, you can paste these graphics into the target document in the usual way, as described in steps 4 and 5 of the procedure given above.

An Example

Now let's take a look at a specific example of the cut/copy and paste process. We will copy some text from a WordPad document into a Notepad document. (Notepad is a very simple word processor, a *text editor*, supplied with Windows 98.) First we start WordPad and open the Homework 1 document, which can be found on the Student Disk. The resulting WordPad window is shown in Figure 10.

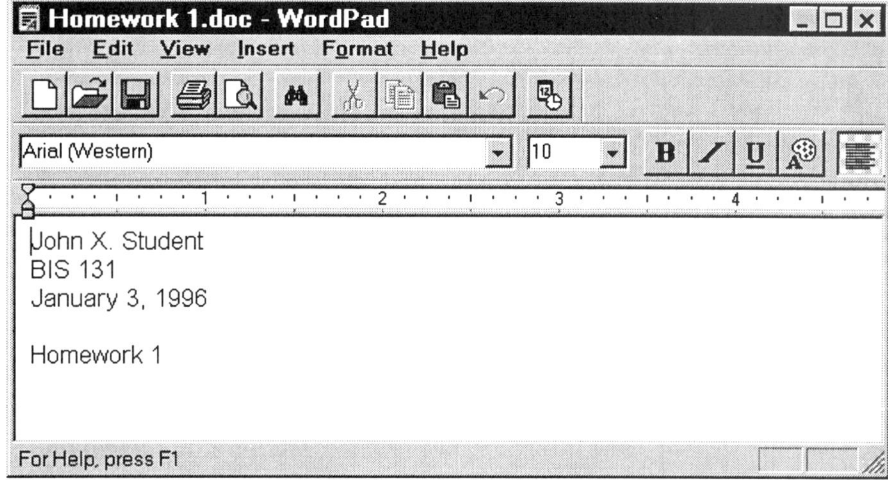

Figure 10 The Text to be Copied

Suppose we want to copy the first three lines (the student's name, his class, and the date). To do so, we must first select the text. Notice that the insertion point in Figure 10 is already positioned at the beginning of this block of text. So, all we need do to select it is

- Hold down the Shift key, tap the Down Arrow key three times, and release Shift.

or

- Position the mouse pointer at the insertion point and drag it down until the first three lines are highlighted.

In either case, the text in the window will look like this:

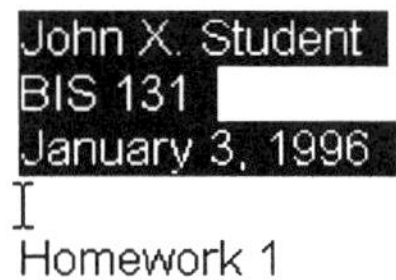

Now, we copy the selected text to the Clipboard by choosing the Copy command from WordPad's Edit menu.

To paste the contents of the Clipboard into Notepad, we start this application by clicking on its name on the Accessories submenu of the Start menu's Programs option. (Or, if Notepad is already running, we switch to it by clicking on its Taskbar button.) Then, we choose the Paste command from Notepad's Edit menu. The selected text will be transferred to the beginning of the Notepad document, as pictured in Figure 11. (Notice that the pasted text has a somewhat different appearance from the original because Notepad changes the *font*, or typeface, to its default setting.)

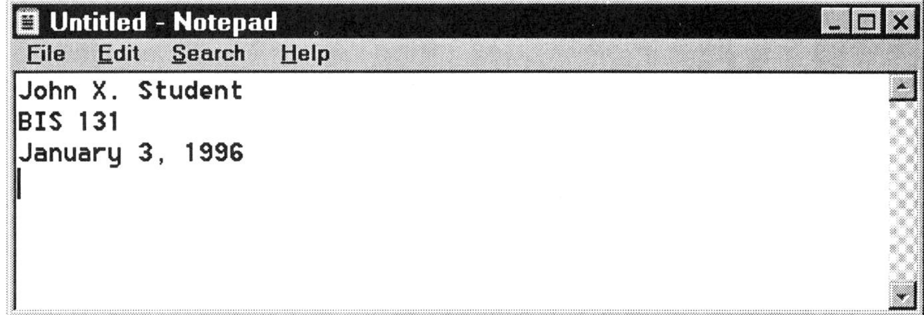

Figure 11 The Original Text Pasted into Notepad

Try the following exercise on your own.

1. Turn on your computer (if it's not already on) to start up Windows 98. Close any open windows.
2. Start the WordPad word processor (from the Accessories submenu of the Start menu's Programs option).
3. Type the text: `This is a test.`
4. Select this block of text by either:
   - Dragging the insertion point to the beginning of the sentence.

   or
   - Holding down the Shift key, tapping the Left Arrow key until the insertion point is at the beginning of the sentence, and releasing Shift.

   In either case, the sentence should now be highlighted.

5. *Cut* the selected text to the Clipboard by choosing Cut from WordPad's Edit menu or by pressing Ctrl+X.
6. Start the Notepad application by clicking on its name on the Accessories submenu of the Start menu's Programs option.
7. *Paste* the text from the Clipboard into Notepad by choosing Paste from its Edit menu or by pressing Ctrl+V.
8. Switch to WordPad by clicking on its Taskbar button. (If the Taskbar isn't visible, press Ctrl+Esc to display it.)
9. Paste the sentence into the WordPad document by right-clicking the mouse and selecting Paste from the resulting menu.
10. Close WordPad and then close Notepad, answering No to the "Save changes?" warning message in both cases.

2.4 Installing and Removing Applications

From time to time, you will probably want to use software that is not yet installed on your system. In this section, we will discuss how to install and remove applications and also describe the process of adding Windows components, such as games and accessories, to your system from the Windows 98 CD-ROM.

Installing Applications

When you buy software for use on your computer, it comes on a CD-ROM or a set of floppy disks. Before you can use an application, it must be **installed** on your hard disk. The installation process copies files from the distribution disks to the hard disk, creates icons and folders (sets of files), and supplies Windows with information about how the program operates. The mechanics of the process differ somewhat from application to application depending on the media (floppy disk or CD-ROM) used and the operating system under which the software was designed to run.

Windows CD-ROMs If your new application is designed for Windows 98 (or Windows 95) and comes on a CD-ROM, the installation process may be very simple. Here's how it may proceed:

1. Start Windows and insert the new CD in its drive. Normally, the

application's "setup screen" will be displayed. Alternatively, a dialog box, entitled "Install New Program Wizard", will open. If nothing seems to happen when the CD is inserted, skip the rest of the steps in this procedure and proceed to the instructions listed under "Installing other applications" that are given below.

2. You will then be presented with a sequence of screens and/or dialog boxes that provide information or ask you to state your preferences concerning various aspects of the installation process. (To move to the next screen, you may have to choose a Next or OK command button.)
3. When the process is complete, you may have to choose a Finish command button or close a final window.

Installing other applications

For applications that come on floppy disks or those for which the process just described does not work, the installation process is usually almost as easy. With Windows running:

1. Insert the floppy disk labeled "Install" or "Setup", or the application's CD-ROM, in its drive.

2. Click on the Start button, point at the Settings option on the Start menu, and choose Control Panel from the resulting submenu.
3. In the Control Panel window, choose the Add/Remove Programs icon to open the Add/Remove Programs Properties dialog box (Figure 12).
4. Choose the Install command button. The Install Program dialog box will appear.
5. Choose the Next command button. Windows will automatically search the floppy disk or CD for an installation program and, if found, display its name.

If Windows is unable to locate the installation program, or does not seem to have found the correct one, consult the documentation that came with the application to determine the appropriate file name. Then, type this name in the text box.

6. Choose the Finish command button. The new application's installation program will then begin to run.
7. Respond to any on-screen queries until installation is complete.

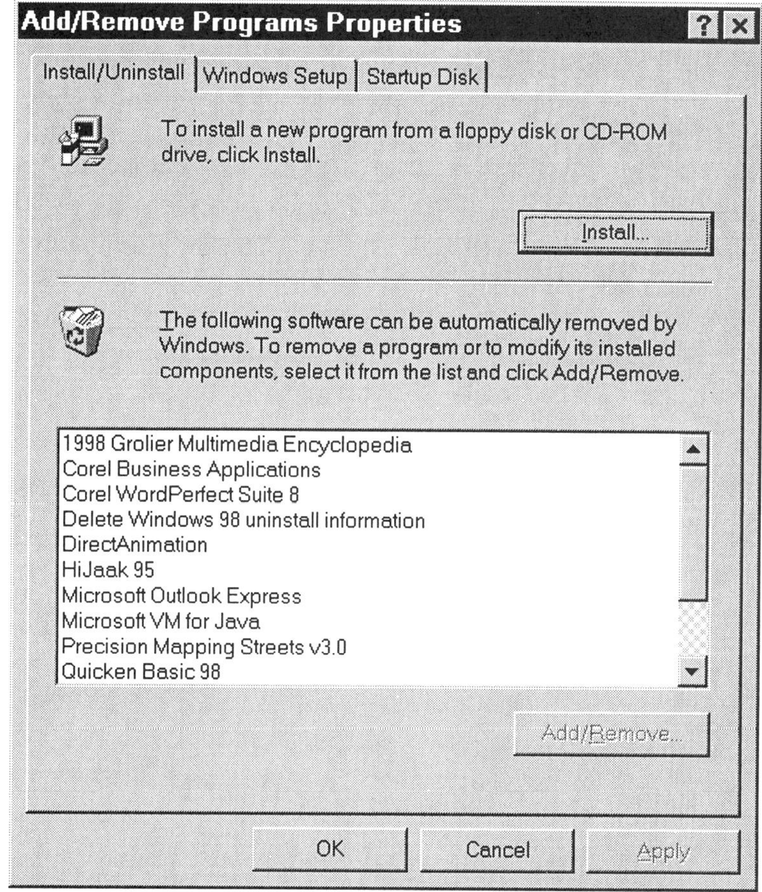

Figure 12 Add/Remove Programs Properties Dialog Box

Regardless of how the installation process works, once it is complete you may have to close a window or two left on the screen and/or restart Windows. A menu item for the new application should now appear on one of the submenus of the Start button's Programs option (or on the Start menu itself). If you want to create a Desktop icon (*shortcut*) for the new application, see Section 3.4.

Uninstalling Applications

If you no longer use a certain application, you might want to remove (or **uninstall**) it from your hard disk. This process entails deleting all of its program files, as well as removing any references to the application in Windows itself (such as the menu item that opens the program from the Start menu). Although deleting most of the program files is not difficult once you understand how to navigate the Windows folder system (see Chapter 3), manually removing *all* files and references to the program is next to impossible.

Fortunately, for most programs designed to run under Windows 98 (or Windows 95), you can use the Add/Remove Programs utility to perform this task. To uninstall such an application:

1. Start Control Panel from the Settings option of the Start menu, as described earlier in this section.
2. Choose the Add/Remove Programs icon in the Control Panel window to open the corresponding dialog box (Figure 12).
3. Click on the desired application in the list box. It will become highlighted. (If the program you want to remove does not appear on the list, it cannot be removed automatically by Windows.)
4. Click on the Add/Remove command button. A dialog box will open asking if you really want to remove this program.
5. Click on the Yes command button.

Adding Windows Components

When Windows was set up on your computer, some of the *components* (programs and other files) contained on the Windows CD-ROM were not installed on your hard disk. As a result, as you read this text, you might occasionally see a reference to a feature that is not present on your system. To install such a Windows component:

1. Start Control Panel from the Settings option of the Start menu, as described earlier in this section.
2. Choose the Add/Remove Programs icon in the Control Panel window and click on the Windows Setup tab in the resulting dialog box to display the page shown in Figure 13.

   The types of components you can add are displayed in the Components list box. The check box to the left of a component type indicates whether or not components of that type are already installed on your hard disk.

   - If a check mark appears against a white background (for example, Accessibility in Figure 13), then all the components of this type are installed.

5. Insert the Windows 98 CD-ROM into its drive and choose the OK command button twice. Windows will copy the selected components to your hard disk.
6. Close the Windows 98 CD-ROM and Control Panel windows.

NOTE

The Add/Remove Programs Properties dialog box also allows you to create an emergency startup disk, which can be used to start your system should the hard disk, or key information on it, become inaccessible. To create a startup disk:

1. Place the Windows 98 CD-ROM and a blank (formatted) diskette in their respective drives.
2. Display the Startup Disk page of the Add/Remove Programs Properties dialog box.
3. Choose the Create Disk command button.
4. When the process is complete, remove the disks from their drives and label the floppy "Windows 98 Startup Disk".

TUTORIAL

Try the following exercise on your own.

1. Turn on your computer (if it's not already on) to start Windows 98.
2. Open the Control Panel window: Point at the Settings option on the Start menu and then click on the Control Panel item on the resulting submenu.
3. Display the Add/Remove Programs Properties dialog box by choosing the corresponding icon in the Control Panel window.
4. Insert the Student Disk in its drive. We will simulate installing an application from this disk:
   - Choose the Install command button in the Add/Remove Programs Properties dialog box. A new dialog box will open.
   - Choose the Next command button to display the next page of this dialog box. Type the text A:\SETUP in the text box.
   - Choose the Finish command button. A message will appear stating that a:setup cannot be found. Click on OK and then on the Cancel button in the dialog box to abort the process.

   If this were an actual program installation, the process would proceed automatically, displaying information and occasionally requesting that you answer questions.

5. Display the Windows Setup page of the Add/Remove Programs Properties dialog box.
6. Read the instructions at the top of this dialog box. Then, select each item listed in the Components list box and read its description at the bottom of the box.
7. Choose the Cancel button to close the Add/Remove Programs Properties dialog box.
8. Close the Control Panel window and remove the diskette from its drive.

2.5 Getting On-screen Help

No matter how experienced you become at using Windows and its applications, there will be times when you'll need some help in performing a particular task. At such a time, you might find the answer to your questions in this book, but it may be more convenient to use the Windows 98 **on-screen help** system. This powerful feature provides immediate on-screen information about Windows itself or the Windows application that is currently active on your Desktop.

Accessing On-screen Help

Types of help available

The Windows 98 Help system provides access to several kinds of on-screen help:

1. Extensive help is available for Windows itself and can be accessed at any time in two different ways:
   - *Local help* resides on the computer's hard disk. It includes general information about using Windows, procedures for performing specific tasks, and troubleshooting advice.
   - *Web-based help* is located at the Microsoft Web site. It provides access to technical support for Windows 98 and other Microsoft products.
2. Each built-in Windows 98 application, such as WordPad, provides the two types of help described above. Most other Windows-based applications also supply on-screen help of one sort or another. Application-specific help can be accessed while the application is running.

3. *Context-sensitive* help provides help with the task at hand. It is available for Windows 98 itself and for most Windows-based applications.

Starting the Help system

How you obtain on-screen help depends on the kind of help you need:

- To access help with Windows 98 itself, click on the Start button and then click on the Help option on the Start menu. The window shown in Figure 14 will open.
- Help for the active Windows application can be accessed by displaying that program's Help menu and choosing the option entitled Help Topics or Help Contents. For Windows 98 built-in applications, a window like the one in Figure 14 will open; for other Windows-based applications, a Help window or dialog box will open, but it may look considerably different from the one in Figure 14.
- There are a couple of ways to access context-sensitive help. We will discuss them at the end of this section.

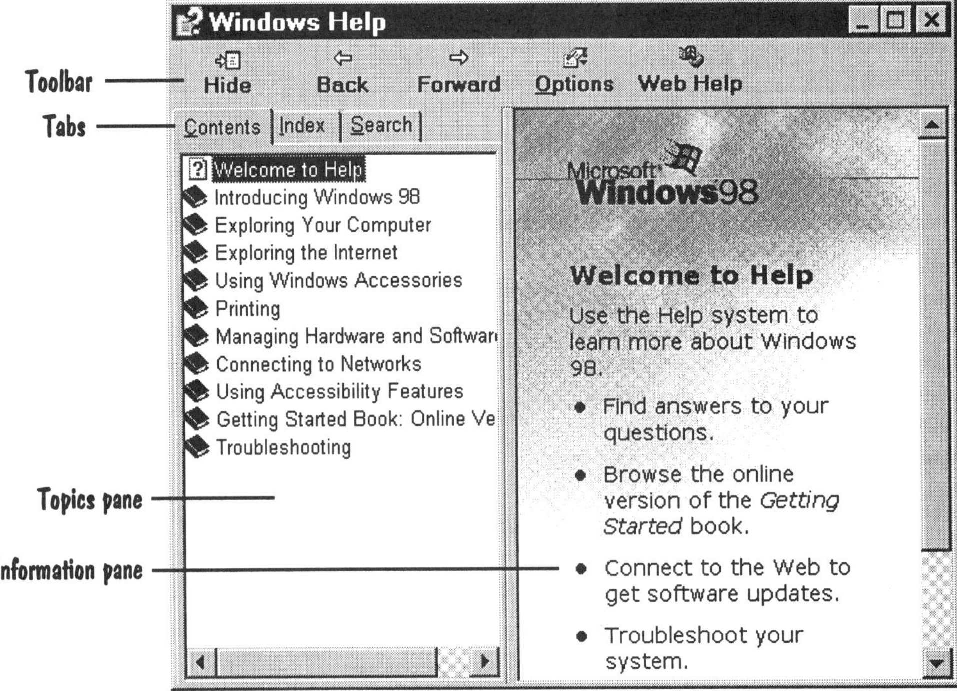

Figure 14 The Windows Help Window

Locating the Information You Need

You can use the Help window displayed in Figure 14 to obtain either local or Web-based help.

Web-based help

Accessing Web-based help is only possible if your computer has an Internet connection. If so, to obtain help from Microsoft's online support Web pages:

1. Click on the Web Help toolbar button, shown at the right.

2. The right pane of the Help Window will change to one displaying information about Microsoft's Web-based technical support. Scroll to the bottom of this pane and click on the words *Support Online*. If your computer has access to the Internet, the online support page of Microsoft's Web site will be displayed.

To begin your search, go to Support Online.

3. Follow the on-screen instructions to locate the information you need.

NOTE

We discuss using Internet Explorer and browsing the World Wide Web in Chapter 6. If you want to make use of Web-based support, the material in this chapter, especially that of Section 6.2, might come in handy.

Local help

Since it is usually easier to locate information about a specific topic using the local help system, you should view Web-based help as a last resort. Locating a particular help topic in the local help system is relatively straightforward.

Notice that the Help window in Figure 14 has three tabs: Contents, Index, and Search. The pages corresponding to these tabs occupy the left pane of the window and provide different ways to locate the information you need. Generally speaking:

- The Contents page (like the table of contents in a book) contains just a few relatively broad topics. This option is useful if you want to browse through general information.
- The Index page (like the index of a book) contains a much more detailed list of topics. This is usually the first place you would go for help with a specific task.
- The Search page searches the local help files for a specified key word and then displays a list of topics containing that word.

The Contents Page Clicking on the Contents tab provides access to information of a general nature. For example, as you can see in Figure 14 (which shows this page), the listed topics include an introduction to Windows 98 and some of its major features, as well as help with troubleshooting.

If a topic in the left (Topics) pane on the Contents page is preceded by a book icon (such as *Exploring the Internet* in Figure 15), clicking on this topic will "open the book" and display a list of subtopics. If a topic is preceded by a question mark icon (such as *Welcome to Help* in Figure 15), then clicking on this topic will display information about it in the right (Information) pane of the window. For example, Figure 15 shows the Help window after clicking on Using Accessibility Features and then on Install Accessibility Options.

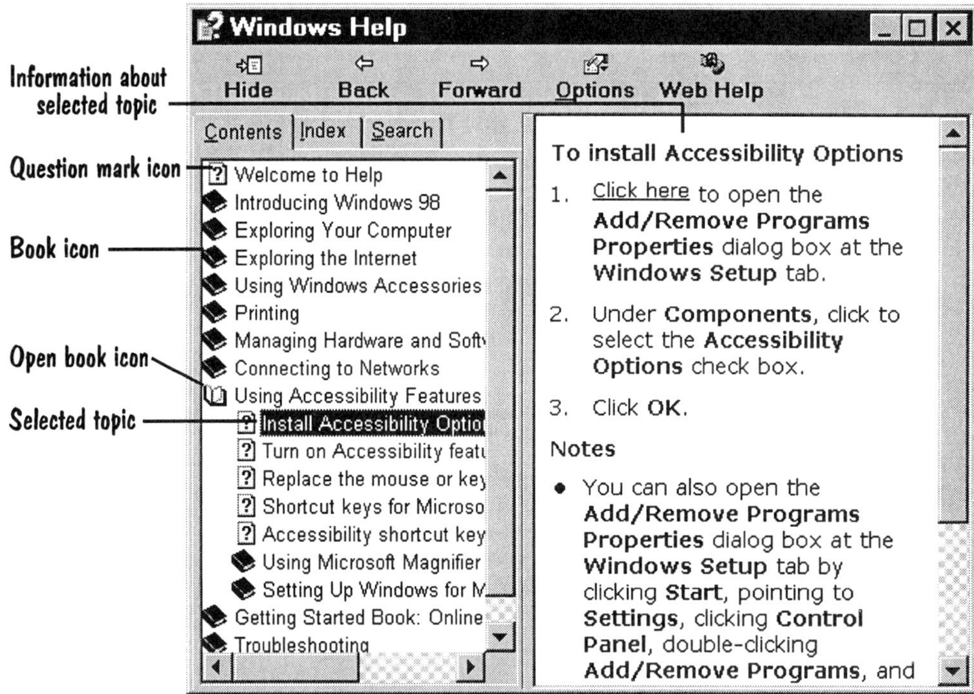

Figure 15 Using the Contents Page of the Help Window

NOTE

Whether Classic style or Web style mode is in effect (see Section 1.2), when you move the mouse pointer over a topic in the Contents list, the pointer will turn into a hand shape and the topic will acquire an underline. To select that topic (displaying its subtopics if it's preceded by a book icon or information about it if it's preceded by a question mark icon), click once on the topic.

The Index Page Clicking on the Index tab of the Help window displays a much more detailed list of items in the Topics pane (see Figure 16).

To use the Index to display information about a particular topic:

1. Double-click on the desired topic, or click on it and then click on the Display command button.

   To move more quickly through the list of topics, type the first few letters of the item you're seeking in the text box; the first topic beginning with these letters is highlighted. For example, Figure 16 shows the result of typing *Cal* in the text box.

2. If there is more than one topic associated with the item you have chosen in step 1, a Topics Found dialog box will open, displaying a list of subtopics. Double-click on the desired topic (or click on it and then on the Display button).

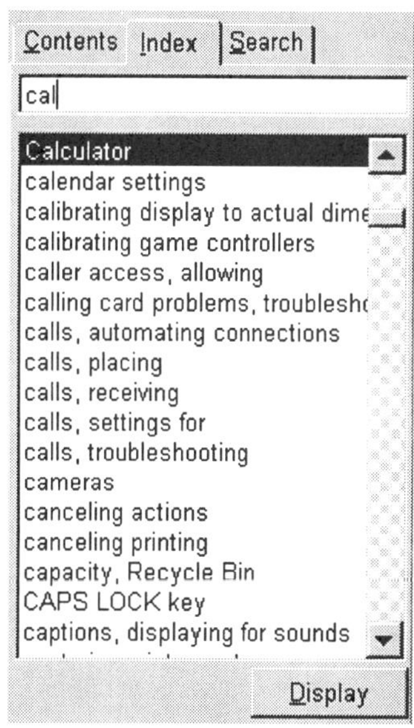

Figure 16
The Index Page

The Search Page Windows 98 Help and most Windows applications contain a *Find utility* that enables you to search the Help files for a specific word or phrase. To use this utility, click on the Search tab in the Help window to open the corresponding page in the Topics pane (see Figure 17, on the next page) and carry out the following steps:

1. Type a word or phrase (a *keyword*) in the text box at the top of the Search page. For example, if you are trying to determine how to use your modem with Windows to place a phone call, you might type *phone.*

2. Choose the List Topics command button. A list of topics in the Help files that contain text which matches your keyword will appear in the Topics pane.

3. Click on the desired topic and choose the Display command button (or double-click on the topic) to display its contents in the Information pane. Each occurrence of your keyword will be highlighted there. For example, the result of double-clicking on the topic *Using Phone Dialer to dial from your computer* displays the information shown in Figure 17.

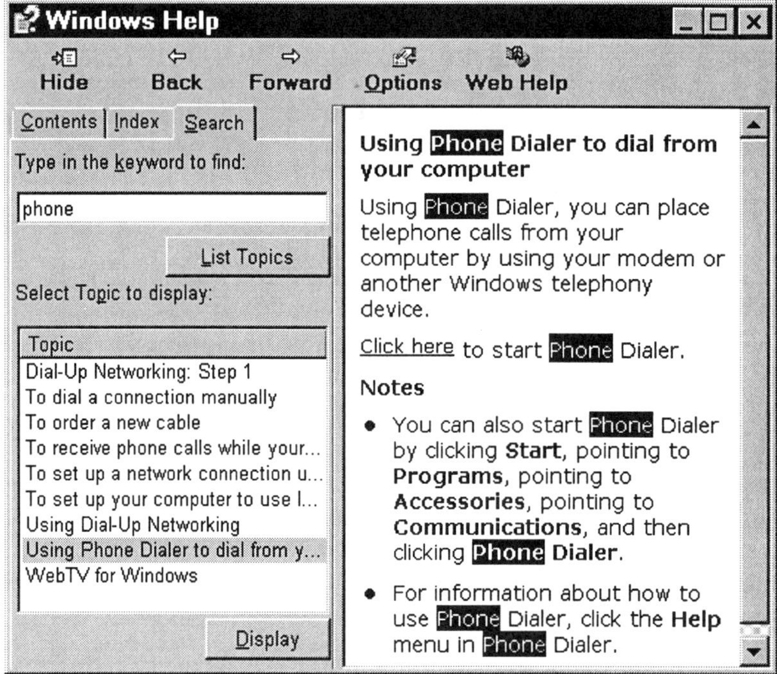

Figure 17 Using the Search Page

NOTE

Whether Classic style or Web style mode is in effect (see Section 1.2), to *select* a topic on the Index or Search pages of the Help window, you must click on it. To *choose* a topic, displaying information about it in the right pane of the window, either select it and then click on the Display command button, or just double-click on it.

Features of the Help Window

After you have located the desired topic using the Topics pane of the Help window and displayed its contents in the Information pane:

- You can hide the Topics pane so that the Information pane fills the entire Help window by clicking on the toolbar's Hide button (see Figure 17). The Hide button will then be replaced by a Show button; click on it to redisplay the Topics pane.
- You can return to the help topic displayed prior to the current one by clicking on the toolbar's Back button.
- You can return to the help topic displayed just after the current one (assuming you've returned to the latter) by clicking on the toolbar's Forward button.
- Click on the toolbar's Options button to open a menu of additional options. (Most of these menu items duplicate the functions of the other toolbar buttons or offer Web-based options.) The most important menu item is Print. Choosing this command displays the Print dialog box, and clicking on its OK button prints the current help topic.
- You can copy all or part of the contents of the Information pane to the Clipboard by selecting the desired text (as described in Section 2.3), right-clicking on this text, and choosing Copy from the resulting pop-up menu. To print selected text, right-click on it and choose Print from the pop-up menu.

Some topics contain **links** (or **hot spots**) that allow you to display related information or start a related application. A link in the Information pane is represented by underlined text. If you mouse-point at a link, the pointer becomes a hand icon. Clicking on a link displays a definition, a new help topic, or in some cases, starts an application. For example, in the Help Window shown in Figure 17, the words *Click here* represent a link; clicking on this hot spot starts the built-in Phone Dialer application.

Click here to
Notes

Context-Sensitive Help

Context-sensitive help provides information about some aspect of the task at hand. For example, suppose you've opened the Run dialog box (see Section 2.1) but have forgotten the purpose of the Browse button. You can use Windows 98 context-sensitive help to explain its function without bringing up the entire Help system. Context-sensitive help, when it's available, can be accessed in several ways:

- If the active window contains a question-mark button on the title bar, click on this button. The cursor will become an arrow with the question-mark attached, as shown at the right. Now click on the item for which you want help, and a small window will pop up, displaying information about this object. For example, if you click on the question-mark icon in the Run dialog box and then click on the Browse command button, the following pop-up window will appear.

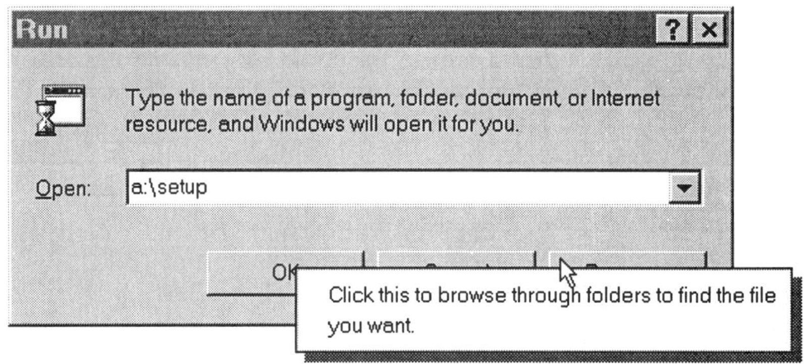

To close the pop up window, click anywhere on the screen.

- With Windows 98 and most Windows applications, you can right-click on an object to access context-sensitive help. Right-clicking displays a one-item *What's This?* menu:

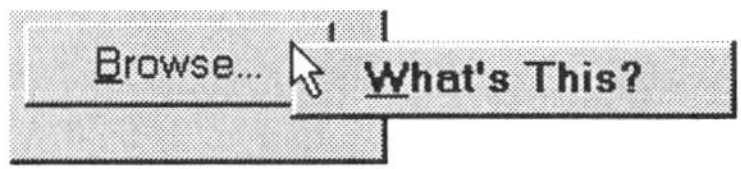

Click on this command to open an explanatory pop-up window.

- When using an older Windows application, you may not see a question-mark button and right-clicking on an object may not work either. However, the application's dialog boxes may contain a Help command that gives information about using that dialog box. If not, try pressing the Shift+F1 keystroke combination or just the F1 function key to get help with the dialog box.

Try the following exercise on your own.

1. Turn on your computer (if it's not already on) to start Windows 98.

2. Start Windows 98 Help by clicking on the Start button and then clicking on the Start menu's Help option. The Windows Help window will open.
3. Let's locate information about the Calculator application that is supplied with Windows 98:
   - Click on the Index tab to display the Index page.
   - Type the word *calculator* in the text box in the left (Topics) pane of the Help window.
   - In the box listing the available topics, double-click on the word *Calculator*.

   The right (Information) pane of the Help window will display the topic called "Using Calculator".
4. In the Information pane of the Help window, click on the underlined words *Click here*. This is a *hot spot* (or *link*) that starts the Calculator application. The Calculator window will appear on the screen.
5. Now let's get some general information about Calculator:
   - Choose Help Topics from the Help menu. The Calculator Help window will open.
   - Click on the Contents tab (if necessary) to display this page.
   - Display (if necessary) the list of subtopics under *Performing Calculations* by double-clicking on its "book" icon. Now, click on *Performing a simple calculation* and then choose the Display command button. Information about this topic will be displayed in the right pane of the window.
6. Click on the Options toolbar button to display the Options menu and successively choose each option to see what, if anything, it does.
7. Click on its close button to close the Calculator Help window.
8. Notice that one of the calculator keys is labeled *Backspace*. To determine the function of this key:
   - Right-click on it. The one-item *What's This?* menu will be displayed.
   - Click on the *What's This?* command. A window will pop up explaining the function of the Backspace key. Click anywhere within the Calculator window to close the pop-up window.
9. Exit the Calculator application and close the Windows Help window.

Chapter Summary

Starting an Application	From the Start menu	Click on the Start button (or press Ctrl+Esc) to open the Start menu and then use either the Programs, Documents, or Run option.
	From the Desktop	Choose the application's icon.
	From Explorer, My Computer, or the Find utility	See Section 3.2, 3.5, or 4.3.
Closing an Application	To close a Windows application, take any of these actions	Click on its close button; *or* select Exit from its File menu; *or* press Alt+F4; *or* right-click on its Taskbar button and choose Close from the resulting submenu.
	To close a DOS application	Use the procedure appropriate for that application and then close its window (if necessary) by clicking on the close button.
Basic WordPad Operations	To start WordPad	Open the Start menu and click on WordPad on the Accessories submenu of the Programs option.
	To enter text	Type it at the keyboard.
	To delete text	Move the insertion point to the desired place using the mouse or Arrow keys, then press the Delete (or Backspace) key to delete the character in front of (or behind) the insertion point.
Operations on Documents	To open a document	Point at the Documents option on the Start menu and click on the desired document; *or* start the application that created the document and choose Open from its File menu.
	To save a document	Choose Save or Save As from the File menu.
	To print a document	Choose Print from the File menu.
	To close a document without closing the application	Choose New from the File menu (or, if the application allows multiple open document windows, choose Close from the File menu).
Running Several Applications at Once	To switch to another running application	Click on any part of its window; *or* click on its Taskbar button; *or* hold down the Alt key while repeatedly pressing Tab until the name of the desired application appears, then release both keys.

	To select a block of text in a document	Position the insertion point at the beginning of the block and then either: mouse-drag it to the end of the block; *or* hold down the Shift key and move the insertion point to the end of the block.
	To cut/copy selected information to the Clipboard	Choose Cut/Copy from the Edit menu; *or* right-click and select Cut/Copy from the resulting menu.
	To paste information from the Clipboard	Position the cursor in the proper place and select Paste from either the Edit menu or the right-click menu.
	To copy the entire screen/active window to the Clipboard	Press Print Screen/Alt+Print Screen.
Installing Applications	To open the Add/ Remove Programs Properties dialog box	Click on the Start button, point at Settings on the Start menu, choose Control Panel from the resulting submenu, and double-click on the Add/Remove Programs icon.
	To install an application	Insert the disk containing the program into its drive. In the Add/Remove Programs Properties dialog box, choose the Install button and follow the on-screen instructions.
	To uninstall an application	In the Add/Remove Programs Properties dialog box, select the application from the list box, choose the Add/Remove button, and follow the instructions.
	To add a Windows component	Insert the Windows 98 CD-ROM in its drive. In the Add/Remove Programs Properties dialog box, click on the Windows Setup tab, select the component type from the list box, choose the Details button, select the components to be added, and choose OK.
Using Help	To start Help	Choose Help from the Start menu for help with Windows; *or* choose Help Topics from an application's Help menu.
	To locate information	Click on the Web Help button and then on the Support Online link for Web-based help; *or* Use the Contents, Index, or Search pages of the Help window to locate and display the desired local help topic.

Features of a Help window	Click on the Hide button to hide the left pane of the window; click on the Back or Forward button to return to a previous topic; click on the Options button to print the contents of the current topic.
To obtain context-sensitive help	Click on the question-mark button on the title bar and then click on the desired item; *or* right-click on the desired item and then on the *What's This?* command.

Review Exercises

Section 2.1

1. You can open the Start menu by clicking on the Start button or by pressing the ____________ keystroke combination.
2. Resting the mouse pointer on the ____________ item on the Start menu displays a menu of programs and groups of programs.
3. You can close an application, by choosing ____________ from the File menu.
4. True or false: You can start an application that is represented by an icon on the Desktop by choosing that icon.
5. True or false: To start a program named MyProg that is located on the floppy disk in the A: drive, choose Run from the Start menu, type A:MyProg in the dialog box, and press the Enter key.
6. True or false: All DOS applications are exited in the same way as a Windows application.
7. Which of the following items on the Start menu cannot be used to open an application?
   a. Programs
   b. Documents
   c. Shut Down
   d. Run
8. Which of the following will not close a Windows application?
   a. Clicking on its close button.
   b. Clicking on its minimize button.
   c. Right-clicking on its Taskbar button and choosing Close from the resulting menu.
   d. Pressing the Alt+F4 keystroke combination.

Section 2.2

9. WordPad is listed on the ___________ submenu, which contains a group of small applications built into Windows 98.
10. To ___________ a document means to copy it from the computer's RAM onto disk.
11. To ___________ a document means to copy it from disk into RAM and simultaneously display it on the screen.
12. The ___________ option on the Start menu displays a list of recently-saved documents.
13. True or false: Choosing New from WordPad's File menu closes the current document and clears the document window.
14. True or false: If you create but never save a document, you will not be able to open it once it has been closed.
15. True or false: You can open, close, save, and print a WordPad document by using its toolbar.
16. True or false: If you click on the print icon on the WordPad toolbar, one copy of the entire on-screen document will be printed.
17. WordPad's File menu contains two different commands for
    a. Saving a document.
    b. Opening a document.
    c. Printing a document.
    d. Exiting the application.
18. To save a document that is not yet named:
    a. You can use the Open command.
    b. You can use the Save command.
    c. You can use the New command.
    d. None of the above commands can do the job.

Section 2.3

19. To switch to an inactive application, you can click on its button located on the ___________.
20. You can select a block of text by positioning the insertion point at the beginning of the block and holding down the ___________ key as you move the insertion point to the end of the block.
21. When information is cut or copied from a document, it is transferred to the Windows ___________.
22. True or false: Windows 98 allows you to have more than one application window open on the screen.
23. True or false: When information is transferred to the Clipboard, its previous contents (if any) are erased.

24. True or false: Pressing the Print Screen key copies the entire screen to the Clipboard.

25. Which of the following techniques cannot be used to switch to an inactive application?

    a. Click on the inactive application's window.
    b. Click on the inactive application's Taskbar button.
    c. Press the Ctrl+Esc keystroke combination.
    d. Press the Alt+Tab keystroke combination.

26. To transfer selected information to the Clipboard and simultaneously delete it from a document:

    a. Choose Cut from the application's Edit menu.
    b. Choose Copy from the application's Edit menu.
    c. Choose Paste from the application's Edit menu.
    d. Choose Delete from the application's Edit menu.

Section 2.4

27. To ____________ an application means to copy its files from the distribution disks to the computer's hard disk and set up the application for use in Windows.

28. To add Windows components, such as Accessories or Games, use Control Panel's ____________ utility.

29. True or false: Some applications that are distributed on CD-ROMs can be installed without starting Control Panel.

30. True or false: The Add/Remove Programs uninstall utility can be used to uninstall *any* application.

31. To start Control Panel, from the Start menu, choose the

    a. Programs option.
    b. Documents option.
    c. Settings option.
    d. Run option.

32. Using the Add/Remove Programs utility in Control Panel

    a. You can install applications to your hard disk.
    b. You can uninstall applications present on your hard disk.
    c. You can add Windows components to your hard disk.
    d. You can perform all the above tasks.

Section 2.5

33. To obtain on-screen help for Windows itself, click on the Help item on the ____________ menu.

34. To obtain on-screen help for the active application, click on Help Topics on the ____________ menu.

35. If a topic on the Contents page of the Windows Help window is

preceded by a ____________ icon, it contains a list of subtopics.

36. If you want to print text in the Information pane of a Help window, begin by clicking on the ____________ toolbar button.

37. True or false: If a window has a question-mark button on the title bar, you can click on this button to access context-sensitive help.

38. True or false: Clicking on a hot spot (link) in a Help window displays a new topic or definition, or starts an application.

39. True or false: If you can't locate the topic you're seeking in the Windows Help Index, you should try the Search page.

40. Which of the following is not a tab in a Help window:

    a. Contents
    b. Glossary
    c. Index
    d. Search

41. The Options menu in a Help window allows you to

    a. Hide the left (Topics) pane of the window.
    b. Return to a previously-displayed topic.
    c. Print the contents of the window.
    d. Change the size of the Help window.

42. To obtain context-sensitive help in a Windows 98 dialog box:

    a. Click on an object in the box.
    b Double-click on an object in the box.
    c. Right-click on an object in the box.
    d. Drag the *What's This?* button onto an object.

Build Your Own Glossary

43. The following words and phrases are important terms that were introduced in this chapter. (They appear within the text in boldface type.) Use WordPad (see Section 2.2) to enter a definition for each term, preserving alphabetical order, into the Glossary file on the Student Disk.

Active application
Application
Clipboard
Clipboard Viewer
Clipbook Viewer
Close a document
Context-sensitive help
Copy to Clipboard
Cut to Clipboard
Document
Documents option (on Start menu)
Help window
Hot spot
Install application
Link
On-screen help
Open a document
Paste from Clipboard
Print a document
Programs option (on Start menu)
Run option (on Start menu)
Save a document
Toolbar
Uninstall application
WordPad

Lab Exercises

Work each of the following exercises at your computer. Begin by turning the machine on (if necessary) to start Windows 98. Then, close all open windows.

Lab Exercise 1 (Section 2.1)

a. Start MS-DOS Prompt, which is a DOS application that appears on the Programs submenu of the Start menu. If, once MS-DOS Prompt is open, you don't see a title bar, press Alt+Enter to run MS-DOS Prompt in a window.

b. Try to close MS-DOS Prompt by pressing Alt+F4. Does this work? If not, try to close its window by clicking on the close button. If this doesn't work, type Exit and press the Enter key.

c. Insert the Student Disk in its drive and start the Dosprog program on this disk by using the Start menu's Run command. What did you type in the text box to get Dosprog to open?

d. If Dosprog is not running in a window, press Alt+Enter. Try to close this application by clicking on its close button. What does the resulting dialog box tell you? (Click on the No button.)

e. Exit Dosprog by pressing the Enter key. Notice that its window remains on the screen, but the title bar has changed. What word now appears on it?

f. Click on the close button again to close the Dosprog window, and remove the Student Disk from its drive.

g. Repeatedly open and close the Windows Explorer application, which can be found on the Programs submenu of the Start menu. Try the following methods for closing it:

   - Click on its close button.
   - Right-click on its Taskbar button and choose Close from the resulting menu, if one appears.
   - Press Alt+F4.
   - Right-click the title bar and choose Close from the resulting menu, if one appears.

   Which techniques worked?

Lab Exercise 2 (Section 2.2)

a. Start the WordPad word processor.

b. Type your name, your class, and the date on separate lines. Then, skip a line and type: Chapter 2, Lab Exercise 2

c. Insert the Student Disk in its drive.

d. Save the document to this diskette; use the name Ch 2, LabEx 2. What name appears on the title bar?

e. Print the document.

f. Type the current time on the same line as the date.

g. Save the revised document using the Save command on the File menu. Did the name on the title bar change?

h. Print the revised document.

i. Exit WordPad and remove the diskette from its drive.

Lab Exercise 3 (Section 2.2)

a. Start WordPad and insert the Student Disk in its drive.

b. Open the document named Memo on this diskette.

c. Change the date to the current date, the *From* entry to your name, and the *Re* entry to Windows 98.

d. Move the insertion point to the end of the document (two lines below *Re*) and type a short description of Windows 98.

e. Save the document to the floppy disk under the new name Win98 Memo (using the Save *As* command).

f. Print the revised document.

g. Exit WordPad and remove the diskette from its drive.

Lab Exercise 4 (Section 2.3)

a. Start the WordPad word processor and insert the Student Disk in its drive.

b. Open the document named Preamble on this diskette.

c. Select all the text in this document except for the title.

d. Copy the selected text to the Clipboard.

e. Move the insertion point to the end of the document (deselecting the block of text in the process) and then move the insertion point down two lines by pressing the Enter key twice.

f. Paste the contents of the Clipboard into the document.

g. Repeat steps *e* and *f*. (The Preamble now appears three times.)

h. Print the current document.

i. Exit WordPad, answering No to the "Save changes" message, and remove the diskette from its drive.

Lab Exercise 5 (Section 2.3)

a. Start the WordPad word processor and then start the Calculator application by clicking on Calculator on the Accessories submenu of the Start menu's Programs option.

b. Open Calculator's View menu. If Standard is not checked, choose this item; otherwise, press the Escape key to close the View menu.

c. Click successively on the 1, 2, and 3 calculator keys (which enters the number 123 into the calculator's "display").

d. Copy the contents of the display to the Clipboard by choosing Copy from the Edit menu. (Notice that in the Calculator application, you need not select the number before copying it.)

e. Switch to WordPad and paste the Clipboard contents into the document.

f. Switch back to Calculator and copy its window to the Clipboard (using *Alt*+Print Screen, not Print Screen).

g. Exit Calculator, which makes WordPad active.

h. Skip a couple of lines and paste the contents of the Clipboard (the captured window) into the WordPad document.

i. Print the document and exit WordPad (saving the document to a floppy disk if you want).

Lab Exercise 6 (Section 2.4)

a. Open the Control Panel window. What steps did you take to accomplish this?

b. Choose the Add/Remove Programs icon to open the corresponding dialog box. How many applications are displayed in the list box? Is Windows 98 one of them?

c. Choose the Install command button. What is the name of the new dialog box?

d. Choose the Next button and insert the Student Disk in its drive. Then, type `a:setup` and choose Finish. What happened?

e. Close windows until you return to the Add/Remove Programs Properties dialog box, and remove the diskette from its drive.

f. Click on the Windows Setup tab to display this page of the Add/Remove Programs Properties dialog box. Which item in the Components list box is selected?

g. Select the Accessories component and then the Details command button. How do you know which Accessories are not installed and which are only partly installed?

h. Choose the Cancel button and then close the Add/Remove Programs Properties dialog box.

Lab Exercise 7 (Section 2.5)

a. Right-click on an empty part of the Desktop and choose Properties from the pop-up menu to open the Display Properties dialog box.

b. Right-click inside the preview window. According to context-sensitive help, what is the purpose of the preview window? Close the pop-up help window.

c. Click on the question-mark button on the title bar; then on the word Display. Does help explain the meaning of all three items on the Display drop-down list (Tile, Center, and Stretch)? Close the pop-up window and the Display Properties dialog box.

d. Start Windows 98 Help by choosing Help from the Start menu (which opens the Windows Help window). If the Contents page is not displayed, click on its tab. What is the title of the topic displayed in the right pane of the window?

e. Display the subtopics of "Printing". How many are there?

f. Click on the topic called *Change printer settings*. How many hot spots are there in the right pane?

g. Click on the *Related topics* hot spot and choose the *Change the paper size* item from the resulting pop-up menu. Which Start menu option is used to change the paper size setting?

h. Click on the Back toolbar button? Which topic is displayed now?

i. Close the Help window to exit Help.

Lab Exercise 8 (Section 2.5)

a. Start WordPad and choose Help Topics from the Help menu to open the WordPad Help window.

b. Let's try to determine the function of the WordPad Ruler. Click on the Index tab (if this page is currently not displayed).

c. Type *ruler* in the text box. What is the name of the topic that is highlighted?

d. Choose the Display command button. What is the name of the resulting dialog box?

e. Display the topic called "To show or hide the ruler". According to Help, what WordPad menu is used to show or hide the ruler?

f. Click on the Search tab.

g. Type *ruler* in the text box and choose the List Topics button. How many topics are listed?

h. Display the topic entitled "To set or remove tab stops in paragraphs". Scroll to the bottom of the right pane How are tabs deleted?

i. Choose the Tabs command from WordPad's Format menu. The Tabs dialog box will open. Now, using either the WordPad Help window or context-sensitive help in the Tabs dialog box, answer the following questions:

   - What is the difference between the Clear and Clear All commands?
   - What is the purpose of the Set command button in the Tabs dialog box?

j. Close the Help window and exit WordPad.

If You Want to Learn More ...

The notes presented here allow you to delve more deeply into some of the topics covered in this chapter.

Redisplaying the Taskbar

As you know, if the Taskbar is hidden from view, you can temporarily redisplay it by pressing Ctrl+Esc. To permanently redisplay the Taskbar:

1. Choose the Taskbar & Start Menu item from the Settings submenu of the Start menu. The Taskbar Properties dialog box will be displayed.
2. Select the *Always on top* check box and deselect the *Auto hide* check box.
3. Choose the OK command button.

(To hide the Taskbar, select the *Auto hide* option in the Taskbar Properties dialog box.)

Accessing the Taskbar from the keyboard

If you are a confirmed mouse-hater, here's a way (albeit an awkward one) to access the Taskbar buttons using the keyboard:

1. Press Ctrl+Esc to open the Start menu (and display the Taskbar, if it's hidden).

2. Press the Esc key to close the Start menu and place the "focus" on the Start button.
3. Press the Tab key to move the focus to the Taskbar.

You can now cycle through the Taskbar buttons by repeatedly pressing the Arrow keys. To activate the selected button, press the Enter key.

Having problems with WordPad?

TROUBLESHOOTING

In using WordPad, you may encounter some difficulties simply because we did not discuss it in very much detail in Section 2.2. Here's how to handle a few common problems:

- If word wrap is not in effect (the insertion point doesn't move to a new line unless you press the Enter key), choose the Options item from the View menu, select the *Wrap to ruler* option button in the resulting dialog box, and choose the OK command button.
- If, when you print a document, the page margins are not to your liking, choose the Page Setup command from the File menu, enter the desired margins in the resulting dialog box, and choose the OK command button.
- If, when you print a document, the text runs parallel to the long side of the page, choose the Page Setup command from the File menu, select the *Portrait* option button in the resulting dialog box, and choose the OK command button.

For a complete discussion of WordPad, see Chapter 7.

Getting help with troubleshooting

As you know, if you need help with a *specific* topic, the Contents page of the Windows Help system is usually not very useful. Nevertheless, when you have some time free, you might enjoy browsing through some of the topics found there. The Contents page also provides access to built-in Windows 98 "troubleshooters" that can help you resolve many software and hardware problems. To use one of these troubleshooters:

TROUBLESHOOTING

1. Start Windows 98 Help and click on the Contents tab (if necessary) to display this page of the window.
2. Click on the Troubleshooting icon in the Topics pane and then on the Windows 98 Troubleshooters icon to display the list of available troubleshooters.
3. Click on the specific troubleshooter in which you're interested. This troubleshooter will start and pose a basic question concerning your problem in the Information pane of the Help window.

4. Select the option button that best answers this question and then choose the Next command button.
5. A new pane will appear in which the troubleshooter will either ask additional questions or suggest possible solutions (or both). Answer the questions and/or try the solutions.
6. This process will continue until you indicate (via the Yes option button) that your problem has been solved.

Web-based help If you access Web-based Help (as described at the beginning of this section), the Internet Explorer browser (see Section 6.2) starts and connects you to Microsoft's Web site. Here's a general description of how to use this site.

The first time you request Web-based help, you may be asked to register with Microsoft. If so, the title bar will display "Microsoft Technical Support Online Registration" and you will be required to fill out an electronic registration form. After completing this form (and clicking on the Next command button), you will be transferred to the online help Web site.

In future sessions, the registration screen will be skipped and you will immediately access Web-based help. The initial screen for Web-based help will be entitled *Basic View* (which is shown in Figure 18) or *Advanced View*. To move from one to the other, click on the appropriate words (*link*).

In either of these views, you can access certain areas of the Web site, such as *Popular Topics* or *Frequently Asked Questions* by clicking on the corresponding links (see Figure 18) or search the site for help with a specific problem. To accomplish the latter:

1. Select *Windows 98* from the *My search is about* drop-down list.
2. Enter key words (for example "Copying disks") in the *My question is* text box. (The Advanced View will provide you with additional options for refining the search. See Section 6.3 for tips on using a search routine.)
3. Click on the *Find* link button.

Internet Explorer will then display a list of topics that match your search criteria. Each match will include a short description of the corresponding "article". To access the entire article, click on the underlined text. If there are more than 25 matches, a command button will appear at the bottom of the list that allows you to access the next 25 matches.

To exit Web-based help, just exit the Internet Explorer application.

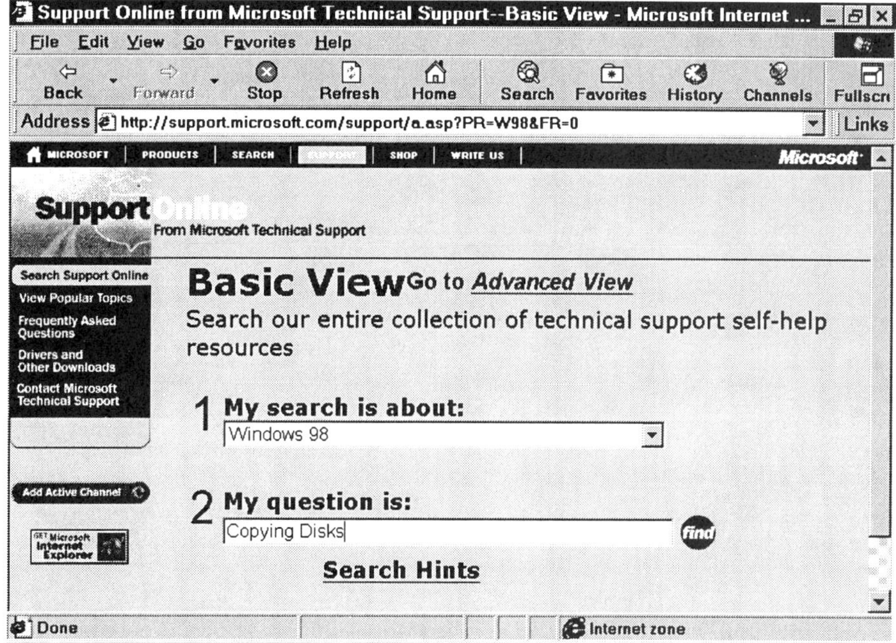

Figure 18 Web-based Help — Basic View

Where to go from here

Here's where to find more information about some of the topics discussed in this chapter.

- Starting applications — Sections 3.2 (using Explorer) and 4.3 (using the Find utility)
- Adding and removing items from the Programs option submenus — Section 4.2
- Associating document types with applications — Section 4.4
- Using WordPad — Chapter 7
- Changing printer settings — Section 4.5
- Transferring information between applications — Sections 7.4, 8.3, and 12.5

CHAPTER 3

Managing Files, Folders, and Disks

Overview

In Chapter 2 we discussed, in a general way, how to use applications (programs) and documents. Both applications and documents are stored in files, which in turn are located in folders on a disk. This chapter describes how to use Windows Explorer and My Computer to perform basic operations on files, folders, and disks. To be more specific, you will learn:

1. How files and folders are organized under Windows.
2. The rules for creating valid file and folder names.
3. How to start Explorer and change views of its contents.
4. How to select files and folders in Explorer.
5. How to use Explorer to
   - Move or copy files and folders.
   - Create, rename, and delete files and folders.
   - Create shortcuts.
6. How to use My Computer to locate and manipulate files and folders.
7. How to use Explorer or My Computer to format and copy floppy disks.

3.1 Files and Folders

Computer disks are capable of storing a lot of information — both data and programs. In order to facilitate access to this information, Windows, with your help, organizes it into files and folders. In this section, we will provide some useful information about these concepts.

What are Files and Folders?

Files A **file** is a collection of information that has been generated by the computer and stored (saved) on disk. A file may contain an application, in which case it's called a *program file*, or data created by an application, which is a *data file*. For example, recall that when you save a document for the first time in the WordPad word processor (itself a collection of files stored on your hard disk), you choose a name for that document. When you issue the Save (or Save As) command, Windows creates a file by copying the document from internal memory (RAM) to disk and assigning the name you chose to it.

Folders Since a hard disk can contain thousands of files, it is necessary to organize them into **folders** (or **directories**[*]). Each folder is a collection of related files that you (or a program) have grouped together and given a name. For example, you might place all the letters you've written in one folder called Letters and all your reports in another folder (uncreatively) called Reports.

Sometimes it makes sense to place a related group of folders within a larger folder. In this case, the bigger folder is called the **parent folder** and each of the folders within it is a **subfolder** (or *child folder*) of the parent. For example, your disk might have several folders that contain word processing data files: Letters, Reports, and so on. To better organize the disk, you could place all of these in a (parent) folder called, say, Word Processing. (A parent folder can contain files as well as subfolders. For example, on a hard disk, the Word Processing folder might hold the *program* files for your word processing application.)

The folders on a disk form a tree-like structure with subfolders branching out from their parents, which in turn may be subfolders

[*]The Windows 98 documentation, like that of Windows 95, uses the term *folder* instead of *directory*. If you are familiar with DOS or Windows 3.1, just think *directory* whenever you see *folder*. Don't worry; you'll soon get used to the new terminology.

themselves. On each disk there is one folder, called the **root folder**, that contains all the others. Figure 1 shows a *folder tree* — a graphical way of representing the folder structure of a disk. It may take a little imagination to see this structure as a tree; in particular, notice that the root is at the top!

In Figure 1, the root folder is designated as "3½ Floppy (A:)" and its three subfolders (Drawing Files, Word Processing, and Zingers) are connected to it by dotted lines. Notice that the Drawing Files and Word Processing folders have subfolders of their own (each connected to its parent by dotted lines), and one of these subfolders (Letters) also has subfolders. Each folder, including the root, may contain files as well.

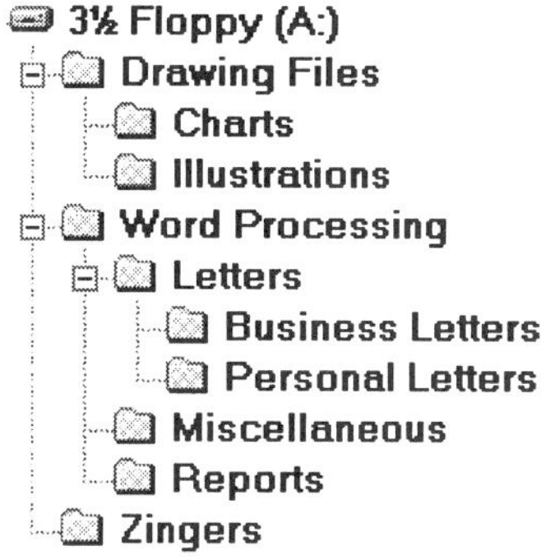

Figure 1 A Folder Tree

Naming Files and Folders

Disk drive designations

Every drive, folder, and file used by your computer must have a name. Drive designations (for hard and floppy disk drives, CD-ROM drives, network drives, and the like) are assigned by the operating system. They consist of a single letter followed by a colon; for example, A: and B: are reserved for the computer's floppy drives; its primary hard disk is designated C:, even if there is only one floppy drive. Other drives (D:, E:, etc.) may be present as well.

DOS file names

Naming files can get complicated. There are different rules for what constitutes a valid file name depending on whether the program that created the file was designed to run under DOS or Windows 3.1 on the one hand, or under Windows 95 or Windows 98 on the other. If the program that created the file is a DOS or Windows 3.1 application, the resulting name is known as a **DOS file name**, and must follow these rules:

- The name may consist of two parts: A required *filename* containing from one to eight characters, possibly followed by an *extension* consisting of up to three characters. If the extension is present, it must be separated from the filename by a period (.). For example, for the file Joe.Ltr, Joe is the filename and Ltr is the extension.
- The filename and extension may contain any characters *except*

period (.)	comma (,)	colon (:)
semicolon (;)	quotation mark (")	brackets ([ ])
slash (/)	backslash (\)	equals sign (=)
vertical bar (|)	question mark (?)	asterisk (*)

Moreover, *no spaces* are permitted in a DOS file name.

- Lowercase letters are not distinguished from uppercase letters. So, the names MyFile, myfile, and MYFILE are considered identical.

For example, the following names are all valid:

Ch1   Ch1.Txt   Ch-1.{   history.rpt   X   1(#$%).n1

However, the following names are *invalid* DOS file names:

inventory.dat	(Filename is too long.)
Top Gun	(Spaces are not allowed.)
File:1	(The colon is an illegal character.)

Windows 98 file and folder names

Windows 98 frees us from many of the restrictions imposed by DOS file names. Most importantly, in naming a file created by a Windows 98-based application or *any* folder, you may use up to 255 characters, including spaces. (For this reason, these names are called **long file names.**) Moreover, all punctuation marks *except* for the following ones are permitted in long file names:

colon (:)	vertical bar (|)	quotation mark (")
slash (/)	backslash (\)	question mark (?)
asterisk (*)		

As a result, the following names are valid for a folder or for a file created by an application designed to run under Windows 98:

J. Gomez - Letter 1	(but *not* J. Gomez: Letter 1)
BIS HW #7 1-5-98	(but *not* BIS HW #7 1/5/98)
Annual Report - 1997	(but *not* "Annual Report - 1997")

Long file names may have extensions, but they are usually assigned by Windows, not the user.

NOTE

Long file names can only be created and used by Windows 98 and Windows 95 and their applications. So, when you are running a DOS or Windows 3.1 program, you have to follow the stricter rules for DOS file names.

This situation raises an interesting question: What happens if you try to open a document with a long file name in an application that doesn't support long file names? In this case, Windows 98 supplies a "DOS alias", a related DOS file name, for use in this application. To form the alias, Windows truncates the original file name to six characters and inserts two special symbols followed by the file's extension. In addition, any blank spaces are deleted and illegal characters are replaced by underscores. For example, suppose you create documents named `Assignment #5`, `Assignment #6`, and `Asg [7]` in WordPad and then open each of these documents in a Windows 3.1-based word processor. Here, the document file names become `assign~1.doc`, `assign~2.doc`, and `asg_7_~1.doc`.

Path Names

When you start an application, Windows automatically specifies a certain folder as the current (or default) folder for that application. (To see which folder is the current one, just open the Save As or Open dialog box; it will be displayed in the *Save in* or *Look in* text box.) If you want to refer to any file in the current folder, you need only give its file name. For example, if you save a file, naming it Sam.doc, it is automatically placed in the current folder.

To refer to a file that is not in the current folder, you must change folders or give the file's **path name**, a kind of road map that tells Windows how to find the file. The path name for a file begins with the drive designation (for example, C:), followed by the names of the root folder (which is \, a backslash) and all subfolders (from largest to smallest) that contain the file, and ends with the name of the file itself. All subfolder names must be followed by backslashes. Thus, the complete path name for a file called Sam.doc in the Personal Letters folder in the folder tree shown in Figure 1 is:

A:\Word Processing\Letters\Personal Letters\Sam.doc

3.2 An Introduction to Windows Explorer

When you use Windows on a regular basis, you will frequently find it convenient to delete, move, copy, or rename files and folders. Windows' primary tool for performing these kinds of operations is the **Explorer** application. In this section, we will provide some basic information about Explorer; its capabilities will be discussed in more detail in Sections 3.3 and 3.4.

The Explorer Window

To start Explorer, click on the Start button (or press Ctrl+Esc) to open the Start menu. Then, point at the Programs option and click on Windows Explorer on the resulting submenu. When you do, a window similar to the one in Figure 2 will open.

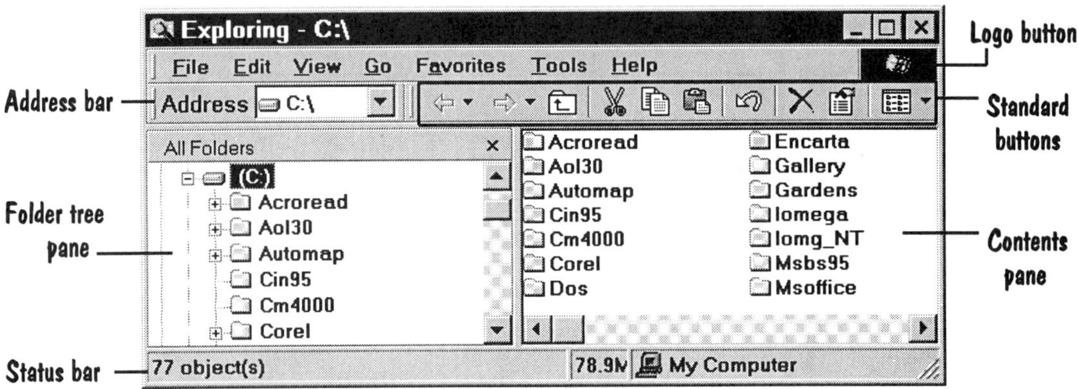

Figure 2 The Explorer Window

Parts of the Explorer window

The Explorer window has a title bar, menu bar, and toolbar at the top and a status bar at the bottom. The **status bar** displays various messages depending on which item is currently selected. For example, if you select a folder, the status bar displays its size. The status bar can be hidden (if currently displayed) or displayed (if currently hidden) by choosing the Status Bar item from the View menu.

The **toolbar** consists of two parts: an *address bar* on the left and *standard buttons* on the right. Here are a few things that are useful to know about manipulating the parts of the toolbar. (We will discuss the *functions* of the address bar and various standard buttons at the appropriate times later in this chapter.)

- The address bar or the set of standard buttons can be displayed or hidden. To do so:
    1. Either open the View menu and point at the Toolbars command, or right-click on the Windows logo button.
    2. Choose Address Bar or Standard Buttons from the resulting

submenu. A check mark next to the item indicates that it is currently displayed.

- If you move the mouse pointer over a standard button, a *tool tip* (top figure at the right) pops up to inform you of that button's function. If you would like the button's name to be always visible (bottom right), point at the Toolbars item on the View menu (or right-click on the logo button) and choose Text Labels from the submenu. To hide these labels, click on this menu item again.

- The set of standard buttons can be moved up, down, left, or right by positioning the mouse pointer over the toolbar's *handle* (the pointer will become a double-arrow, as shown at the right) and dragging the handle in the desired direction.

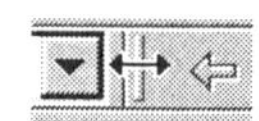

In Figure 2, the rest of the Explorer window is divided into two large subwindows or *panes*: the **folder tree pane** on the left and the **contents pane** on the right. If your Explorer window does not contain a folder tree pane, point at the Explorer Bar command on the View menu and choose the All Folders item from the resulting submenu. If your *contents pane* displays the name and icon of the highlighted folder in large type (as shown at the right), you can turn this off by choosing the as Web Page command from the View menu.

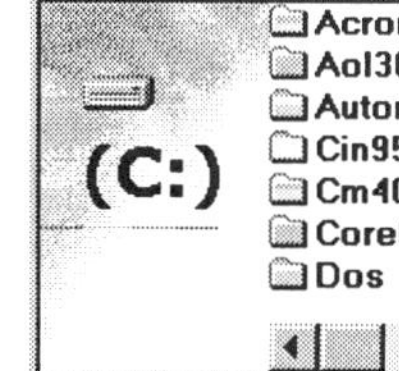

The Folder Tree Pane

The *folder tree pane* lists all folders on all drives connected to your computer and also provides access to other objects on the Desktop, such as My Computer and the Recycle Bin.

When you start Explorer, the root directory on the C: drive is normally the *current* (or *open*) folder — the folder tree pane displays its immediate (*child*) subfolders in alphabetical order. Moreover, the *contents* of the root directory — its files and subfolders — are shown in the contents pane. If you want to view the contents of another object in the folder tree pane, just scroll the folder tree up or down until that object is visible and click on it. Its name will become highlighted and, if it is represented by a folder icon, that icon will "open", as shown at the right.

Opening a folder displays an up-to-the-moment list of its contents, even if they have changed in the current session. You should be aware, however, that there are several reasons why the contents pane may not accurately reflect the contents of the open folder.

- If you change the disk in a floppy drive when its folder is open, Windows will continue to display the contents of the previous disk. To view the contents of the new disk, either click again on the floppy drive icon in the folder tree pane or choose the Refresh command from the View menu.
- Explorer can be configured to prevent certain files or the extensions of certain files from being displayed in the contents pane. To see all files and/or all extensions, choose the Folder Options item from the View menu and click on the View tab in the resulting dialog box. Then, select the *Show all files* option button and/or deselect the *Hide file extensions for known file types* check box, and choose the OK command button. (Notice that the other check boxes allow you to make additional changes in the look of the Explorer window.)

Expanding the folder tree

To display subfolders in the folder tree pane that are hidden from view (even after scrolling), you have to *expand* a branch of the folder tree. When a folder contains hidden subfolders, its icon is preceded by a plus (+) symbol (see, for example, the Corel folder in Figure 2). To view these subfolders, expand this branch of the folder tree; either

- Click on the plus symbol.

or

- Double-click on the folder name or icon.

In either case, the subfolders will be displayed and the plus symbol will become a minus (-) symbol. (If you double-click on the folder's name, that folder also becomes the current folder and its contents are displayed in the contents pane.) Clicking on the minus symbol *collapses* the branch, hiding the subfolders.

For example, if we click on the plus symbol next to the Corel folder icon, a list of subfolders will be displayed, as shown at the right. Notice that there is a plus symbol attached to two of these subfolders, indicating that they have subfolders of their own. Now, if we click on the minus sign preceding Corel, this branch collapses, returning the folder tree to its original look, as in Figure 2.

Corel
Office7
Suite8
Versions

Moving quickly between folders

Explorer includes several menu items (and corresponding toolbar buttons) that can help you, on occasion, move quickly from folder to folder. These items — Back, Forward, and Up One Level — are located on the Go menu. Their functions are as follows:

- Choosing the *Back* command opens the folder that was open prior to the current one. (When you start Explorer, this item is dimmed because there is no previously-open folder.)
- Choosing the *Forward* command opens the folder, if any, that had been opened after the current one. (The Forward item is dimmed unless you have reopened some folder.)
- Choosing the *Up One Level* command opens the parent folder of the current one. For example, if the Suite8 folder in the figure on the previous page were currently open, choosing Up One Level from the Go menu would open the Corel folder, displaying its contents in the contents pane.

These features can also be accessed using Explorer's toolbar. To do so, click on one of the buttons shown below:

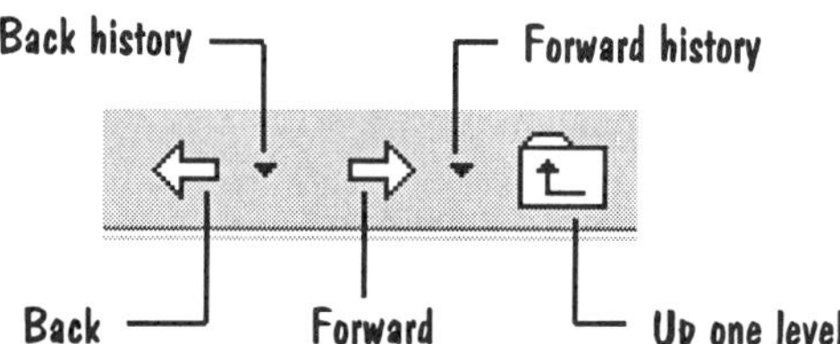

The toolbar also contains two "history" buttons represented by downward-facing triangles. Clicking on the down-triangle to the right of the Back button displays a list of all folders that were opened (since Explorer was started) prior to the current one. Clicking on the down-triangle to the right of the Forward button displays a list of all folders that were opened after the current one. To open any of the listed folders, click on it. (A list of previously-opened folders also appears on the File menu.)

The address bar can also help you to move between folders. It is more useful in My Computer than in Explorer, and will be discussed in Section 3.5.

If you make use of the contents of a particular folder frequently, you should place an icon representing it (a *shortcut* to it) on the Desktop (as described in Section 3.4). Then, to open that folder, just choose its Desktop icon; you need not start Explorer.

Another way to make a particular folder more easily accessible is to add it to your "favorites list". These folders will then be listed on the Start menu's Favorites option and on the Favorites menu in Explorer and many other Windows applications. To open a favorite folder, just choose it from one of these menus. To place a folder on your favorites list:

1. Select the desired folder in the Explorer window.
2. Choose the Add to Favorites item from the Favorites menu, which opens the corresponding dialog box.
3. Choose the OK command button.

The Contents Pane

As you know, the *contents pane* of the Explorer window lists all folders and files contained in the current folder. The word *folder* in this context refers to any folder, drive, or other object (such as My Computer) that can be accessed through Explorer.

As in most windows, the way you *select* an object in the contents pane, highlighting its icon and name, depends on whether Windows is in Web style or Classic style mode (see Section 1.2). In Web style mode, point at the object to select it; in Classic style mode, click on the object to select it. (We will have more to say about selecting objects in Section 3.3.)

To *choose* an object in the contents pane, click on it in Web style mode or double-click on it in Classic style mode. When you choose an object, what happens next depends on the nature of that object:

Choosing an object in the contents pane

- Choosing a folder icon opens that folder, displaying its contents in the contents pane. (In other words, choosing a folder icon in the contents pane has the same effect as clicking on the corresponding icon in the folder tree pane.)

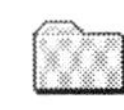

- Choosing a program file icon starts the corresponding application. This technique provides an effective way to start any application on your hard or floppy disks.

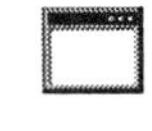

- Choosing a document file that is associated with an application starts that application and opens the given document within it.

- Choosing other kinds of file icons displays the Open With dialog box. This dialog box allows you to select an application to be used with the given file. Choosing the OK command button starts that application and opens the file within it.

On a well-used hard disk, there may be hundreds of folders, containing thousands of files. It's not surprising that finding a particular file or folder may be difficult. To help you in this regard, Explorer provides easy access to the Windows Find utility. You can open this utility by pointing at the Find item on the Tools menu and then choosing Files and Folders from the submenu. (We will discuss Find in Section 4.3.)

Contents Pane View Options

Explorer displays the files and folders in the contents pane using one of four available "views": Large Icons, Small Icons, List, and Details. These options are described below. To select one of them, choose the corresponding item from the View menu or use the toolbar as described at the end of this section.

The Large Icons and Small Icons View Options Here, each object in the contents pane is represented by an icon (either large or small) labeled with the name of the object (Figures 3 and 4). You can move these icons to any position in the window by dragging them with the mouse. To be more specific:

Moving icons

1. Select the icon that you want to move.
2. Position the mouse pointer over this icon, hold down the left mouse button, move the pointer to the icon's new location, and release the button.

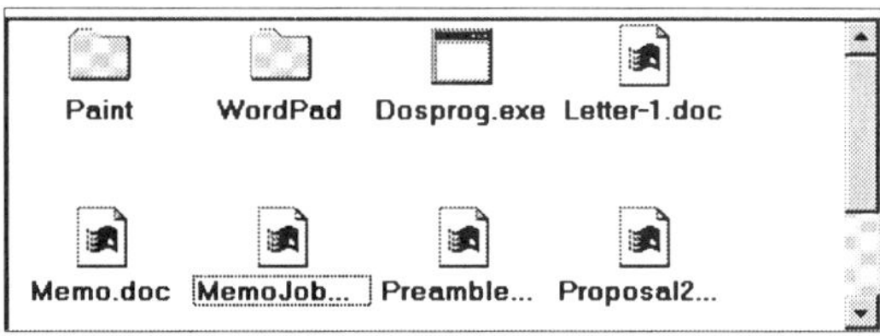

Figure 3 Contents Pane — Large Icons

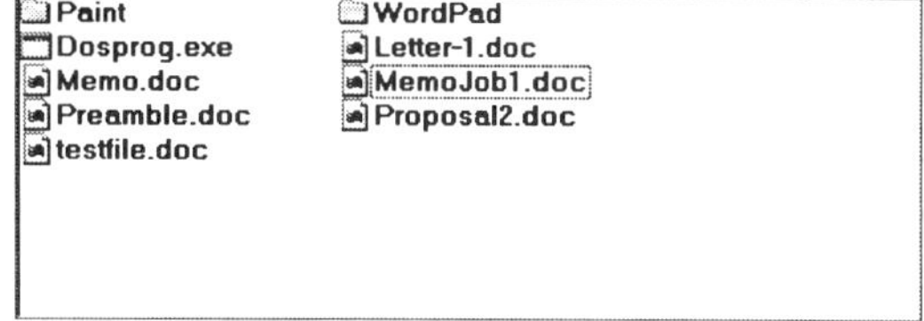

Figure 4 Contents Pane — Small Icons

Lining up the icons

To display the icons in neatly ordered rows and columns (as illustrated in Figures 3 and 4), choose Line Up Icons from the View menu. Or, to have Windows automatically line up the icons whenever they are moved, turn on the Auto Arrange option from the Arrange Icons submenu of the View menu.

The List and Details View Options Choosing the List option (Figure 5) from the View menu displays the icons and names in the contents pane in a way similar to that of the Small Icons option. But, with the List option, the icons are displayed in columns instead of rows and cannot be individually moved about. The Details option (Figure 6) lists the objects in the contents pane, one per line, together with the information specified on the buttons at the top of this pane:

- *Size* refers to the size of a file in kilobytes (KB) or megabytes (MB).
- *Type* refers to the kind of object; for a file, Windows determines its type (for example, *application*) from the file name extension.
- *Modified* provides the most recent date and time that a file was saved; for folders, it is when it was created.

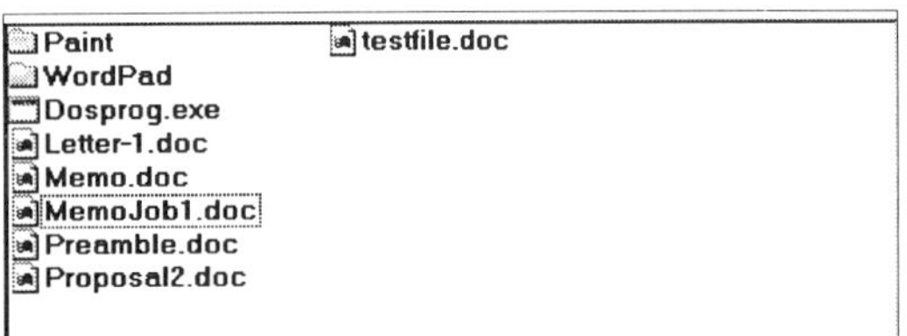

Figure 5 Contents Pane — List Option

Name	Size	Type	Modified
Paint		File Folder	11/27/95
WordPad		File Folder	11/27/95
Dosprog.exe	5KB	Application	10/13/93
Letter-1.doc	5KB	Microsoft Word ...	10/23/95
Memo.doc	5KB	Microsoft Word ...	11/12/95
MemoJob1.doc	5KB	Microsoft Word ...	10/23/95
Preamble.doc	5KB	Microsoft Word ...	11/16/95

Figure 6 Contents Pane — Details

Ordering files in the Details view

By default, the Details view displays the files and folders in the contents pane in alphabetical order by name. (Folders are always listed first.) You can display the files in other orders, as well. To do so, click on the appropriate button at the top of the contents pane; that is:

- Click on the Size button to list files in order of increasing size; click again on this button to list them in decreasing size order.
- Click on the Type button to list files in alphabetical order by type; click again on this button to list them in reverse alphabetical order by type.
- Click on the Modified button to list files in order of their last modification date; most recently modified files are listed first. Clicking again on this button lists recently modified files last.
- Click on the Name button to restore alphabetical order by name; clicking again on this button lists files in reverse alphabetical order.

The icons in *all* the view options (Large Icons, Small Icons, List, and Details) can be ordered by either name, file size, type, or modification date. Just choose the appropriate item from the Arrange Icons submenu of the View menu. However, "reverse orders" are not possible using the Arrange Icons submenu. For example, selecting *by Size* from this menu lists the icons in order of increasing file size; icons cannot be listed in order of *decreasing* size using the Arrange Icons menu.

by Name
by Type
by Size
by Date
Auto Arrange

You can use Explorer's toolbar to quickly select a different contents pane view option. To do so, either

- Click repeatedly on the Views button (shown at the right) until the desired view appears.

or

- Click on the downward-facing triangle to the right of the Views button, which opens a menu listing the four views, and then click on the one desired.

In any view, you may want to make the contents pane somewhat larger. To do so, first maximize the Explorer window. Then, move the mouse pointer over the vertical bar separating the folder tree and contents panes (the pointer becomes a double-headed arrow, as pictured at the right). Now, drag the bar to the left, and the contents pane will expand accordingly.

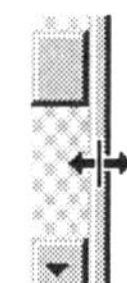

Try the following exercise on your own.

1. Turn on your computer, if necessary, to start up Windows 98 and close any open windows.
2. Start Explorer: Click on the Start button, then point at the Programs option on the Start menu, and finally click on Windows Explorer on the resulting submenu. The Explorer window will open. Maximize this window.
3. Insert the Student Disk in its drive and select this drive in the folder tree (left) pane of the Explorer window. For example, if the Student Disk is in the A: drive, scroll the folder tree pane up until the "3½ Floppy (A:)" folder appears; then, click on this item. The files and folders in the root folder of the disk will be displayed in the contents (right) pane of the window.

4. Expand the "3½ Floppy (A:)" branch of the folder tree by clicking on the plus symbol to the left of this item. (You can also do this by double-clicking on the name "3½ Floppy (A:)".)
5. Choose the Large Icons option from the View menu. Now, drag the Paint folder icon to a new position in the contents pane: Position the mouse pointer over it, then hold down the left mouse button while moving the pointer (and icon) to a new location in the contents pane, and finally release the mouse button.
6. Arrange the icons in the contents pane neatly by choosing Line Up Icons from the View menu.
7. Point at the Arrange Icons item on the View menu and then choose *by Size* from the submenu to sort the files in order of increasing size. Take note of the other sorting options available on the submenu.

8. If no toolbar buttons appear on or below the menu bar, point at the Toolbars item on the View menu and choose Standard Buttons from the submenu. If the Views button is not visible, drag the "handle" (see the figure at the right) to the left until that button appears.
9. Successively click on the Views button to display the Small Icons, List, and Details views. To verify which view is active at any time, click on the downward-facing triangle to the right of the Views button and note which item on the pop-up menu has the bullet.
10. With the Details view in effect, sort the files in order of the last date they were saved. To do so, click on the button labeled *Modified* at the top of the contents pane. Click on this button again to reverse the order. Also try the other buttons (Name, Size, and Type) to see their effect.
11. In the folder tree pane, click on the Paint icon to open its folder.
12. Reopen the previous folder (the root directory of the floppy disk) by clicking on the toolbar's Back button. (You can determine the name of a button by pointing at it and reading the resultant tool tip.)

    Note that you could have reopened the previous folder by choosing the Back item from the Go menu; or, since the previous folder is the parent of the current one, by clicking on the Up One Level toolbar button or Go menu item.
13. Exit Explorer (as you would any application) and remove the Student Disk from its drive.

3.3 *Moving and Copying Files and Folders*

An application such as WordPad allows you to modify the content of *files*; Explorer, on the other hand, allows you to manipulate the contents of *folders*. Using Explorer, you can move, copy, rename, delete, and create files and folders. In Sections 3.3 and 3.4, we will describe how to accomplish each of these tasks.

Selecting Files and Folders

The first step in using Explorer to manipulate a file, a folder, or a group of files or folders is to identify or *select* the objects* in which you are interested. A selected object is displayed with a highlighted name and icon, as illustrated below.

Memo.doc	Memo.doc
Selected object	Object not selected

How to select an object

To select an object from the *folder tree pane*:

1. If necessary, scroll the pane or expand the tree (see Section 3.2) until the name of the object appears.
2. Click on the object to select it. (The selected folder will open, displaying its contents in the contents pane.)

To select an object from the *contents pane*.

1. Scroll the pane, if necessary, until the name of the object appears.
2.
   - If Windows is in Web style mode (if the icons are underlined — see Section 1.2), point at the object to select it.
   - If Windows is in Classic style mode, click on the object to select it.

Selecting multiple objects

To save time in performing operations on files and folders, it is often useful to manipulate several of them at once. For example, if you want to delete ten files from disk, it is faster to select all ten and then perform the delete operation than to select and delete them one at a time. Selecting *multiple* (more than one) objects can only be done

*Recall that, in this context, an *object* is any item listed in Explorer's folder tree or contents pane. Any Explorer object (including My Computer, a floppy drive, and the Desktop itself!) that is not a file is considered to be a *folder*.

in the contents pane, but it can be done in several ways:

- Select one of the objects; then, hold down the Ctrl key and select each of the others; finally, release Ctrl.
- If the objects to be selected are *in consecutive order*: select the first object; then, hold down the Shift key and select the last object in the group; finally, release Shift.
- If the objects to be selected are *adjacent to one another*, so that they can be "boxed-in", as illustrated at the right, position the mouse pointer to the upper left of these objects, hold down the left mouse button, move the pointer to the lower right of the desired objects, and release the button.

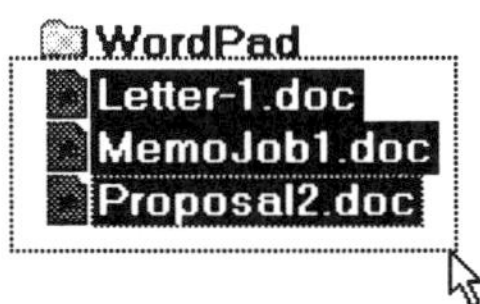

- To select *all* objects in the contents pane, choose Select All from Explorer's Edit menu. To select *almost all* the objects in the contents pane, select those objects you do *not* want and choose Invert Selection from the Edit menu.

As an example of the selection process, here's one way to select the objects shown highlighted in Figure 7:

1. The files Memo.doc, MemoJob1.doc, and Preamble.doc are in consecutive order, so we select the first (by either pointing at it or clicking on it, depending on whether Web style or Classic style mode is in effect), hold down the Shift key, select the last, and release Shift.
2. To select the remaining files, Dosprog.exe and testfile.doc, we hold down the Ctrl key, select each file, and release Ctrl.

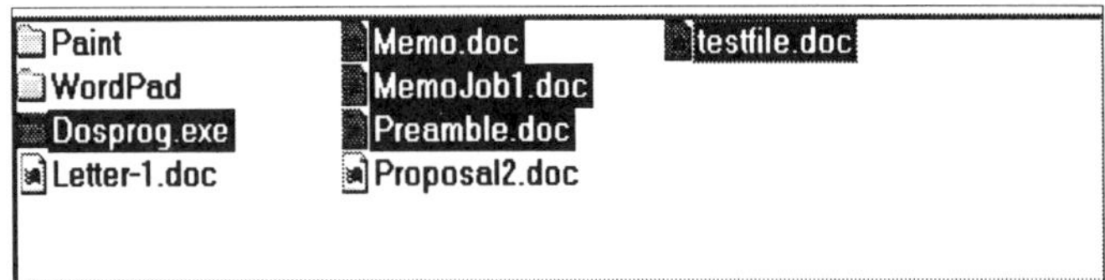

Figure 7 Selection Process Example

To select additional objects after at least one has been selected, be sure to hold down the Ctrl key while clicking. If you forget to press this key, all previously selected objects will be deselected!

To *deselect* all selected objects, click on any empty place in the contents pane. To deselect an object after some have been selected, hold down the Ctrl key while selecting that object. Here, too, don't forget to hold down Ctrl. Otherwise, all objects *except* the one you point at/click on will be deselected!

Initially, you may find multiple selection operations to be somewhat difficult to perform while in Web style mode. If so, see Section 1.2 for information about switching modes.

Moving and Copying Objects

When you **move** an object, it is deleted from its original location and placed in a new location. When you **copy** an object, a duplicate of that object is placed in the new location, but it is not deleted from the original. If the object being moved or copied is a folder, then it and all its contents (files and subfolders alike) are moved or copied to the new location. With one exception (which we will mention later), the move and copy operations are performed in analogous ways, so we will discuss them together.

You can move or copy an object from one folder (the *source*) to another (the *destination*) in two basic ways:

- Drag the object from the source and drop it onto the destination.
- Cut or copy the object from the source and paste it into the destination.

Drag-and-Drop Move or Copy To move or copy objects using the **drag-and-drop** method sometimes takes a little preparation, but the actual operation is very simple. It involves the following steps:

1. Select the objects to be moved or copied.
2. Arrange the Explorer window so that at least one of the selected objects as well as the destination folder are both visible. To do this, you may have to scroll or expand the folder tree to display the destination folder.
3. Position the mouse pointer over any selected object and:
   - If you want to *move* the object, hold down the Shift key and drag the pointer to the destination.
   - If you want to *copy* the object, hold down the Ctrl key and drag the pointer to the destination.

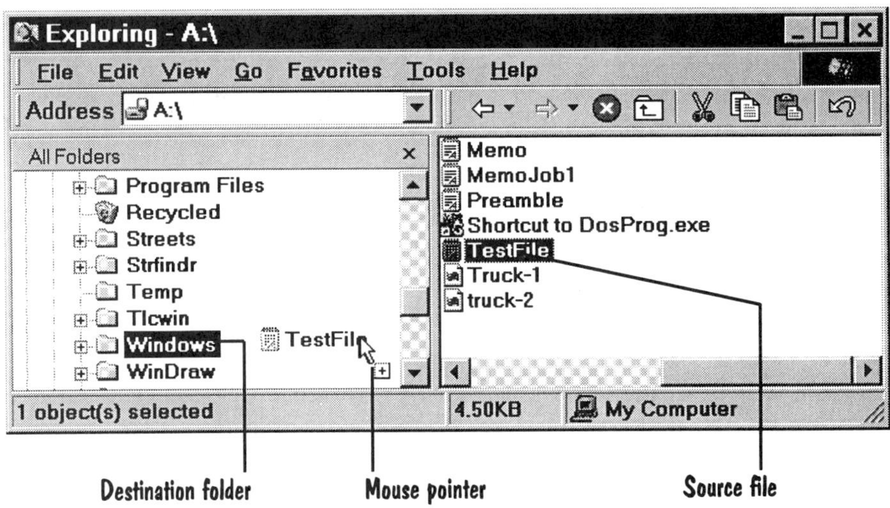

Figure 8 Drag-and-Drop Copying

As you drag the mouse pointer, it seems to pull the objects' icons and names with it (see Figure 8). The plus symbol below the pointer arrow in Figure 8 indicates that this is a copy operation. When *moving* objects, the plus symbol will not appear.

4. As the mouse pointer approaches the destination folder, the latter will become highlighted (see the Windows folder in Figure 8) to let you know that you're on target. Now, release the mouse button (and the Ctrl or Shift key) and the *Moving...* or *Copying...* animated dialog box will appear, confirming that the operation is taking place. (If you change your mind and want to abort the process, press the Escape key before releasing the mouse button.)

If you try to move or copy an object into a folder that already contains an object with the same name, the Confirm File Replace (or Confirm Folder Replace) dialog box (Figure 9) will appear. Choose the Yes command button if you want the source file to replace the destination file in this folder, *deleting the destination file* in the process. Otherwise, click on the No button. (If you are moving or copying multiple objects, this dialog box will also contain Yes to All and Cancel buttons. Choosing Yes to All indicates that you want to replace *all* destination files that have the same name as a source file; choosing Cancel aborts the Move or Copy operation.)

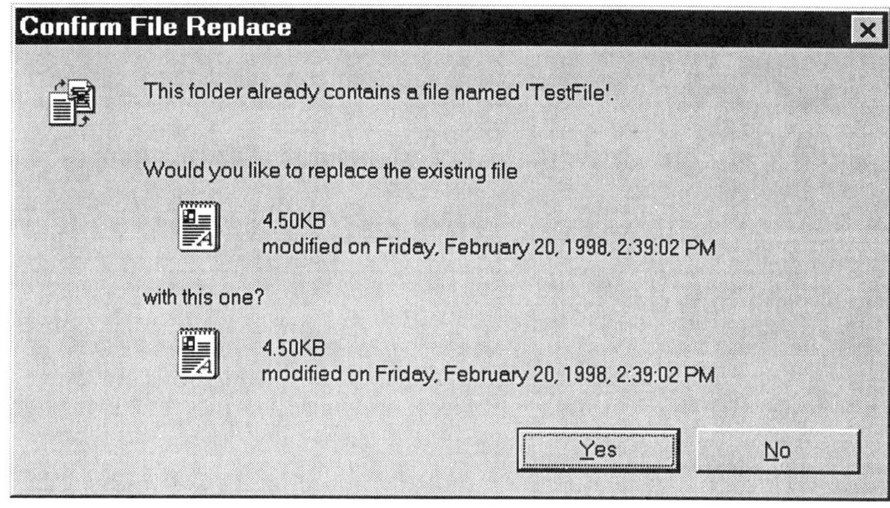

Figure 9 The Confirm File Replace Dialog Box

When *moving* objects between folders on the *same drive*, you do not have to hold down the Shift key while performing the drag-and-drop. When *copying* objects between folders on *different drives*, you do not have to hold down the Ctrl key.

If you don't want to memorize the Shift/Ctrl rules, Windows provides an alternative: just *right-drag* a selected object from the source to the destination. In this case, when you release the mouse button, the menu shown here will appear. To *move* the file to the destination, choose the Move Here command; to *copy* the file, choose the Copy Here command.

Both the left-drag and right-drag techniques work when the destination is an icon on the Desktop or the Desktop itself. For example, to copy a file to the My Computer folder, select the file in Explorer and either

- Drag it onto the My Computer icon on the Desktop (you need not hold down the Ctrl key).

or

- Right-drag it onto the My Computer icon and choose Copy Here from the menu that pops up when you release the mouse button.

Cut/Copy and Paste Move or Copy The second basic method for moving or copying objects resembles the process for transferring information from one document to another (see Section 2.3). It involves the following steps:

1. Select the objects to be moved or copied.
2. Choose Cut (if you're moving the objects) or Copy (if you're copying the objects) from any of the following:
   - Explorer's Edit menu.
   - The buttons on Explorer's toolbar (as shown at the left).
   - The menu (pictured at the right) that pops up when you right-click on one of the selected files.

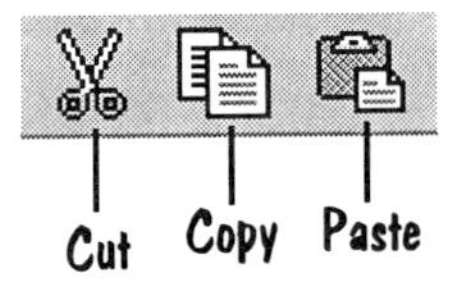

3. Select the destination folder in the folder tree pane.
4. Choose Paste from Explorer's Edit menu, toolbar, or the menu that pops up when you right-click the destination folder.

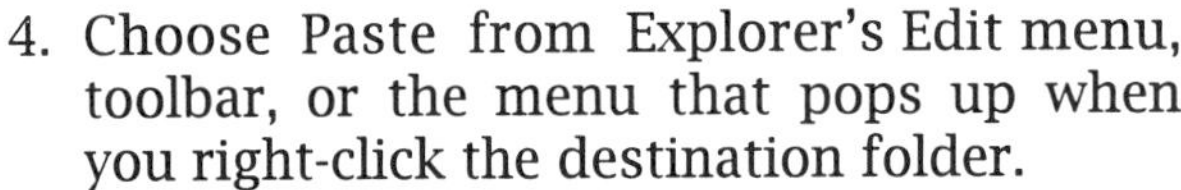

If there is an object in the destination folder with the same name as one of the objects being moved or copied, a Confirm File Replace or Confirm Folder Replace dialog box will be displayed (see Figure 9). Choose the Yes or No command button, as you wish.

Suppose you move or copy an object (using any method) and then decide that this wasn't such a good idea. You could move the object back to the source folder or delete it from the destination, but there is an easier way. Windows supplies an Undo command that cancels the last move or copy. This command is located on Explorer's Edit menu. It can also be executed by clicking on the toolbar's Undo button (shown at the right).

The Send To Command

Perhaps the most common use of the copy operation in Windows is to copy a file or group of files to a floppy disk. This action is usually taken for one of two reasons:

- To *back up* files on the hard disk (to make copies in case the hard disk becomes damaged or its files cannot be accessed for some other reason).

- To transfer files to another computer.

Windows makes it very easy to copy files or entire folders to a floppy disk. To do so:

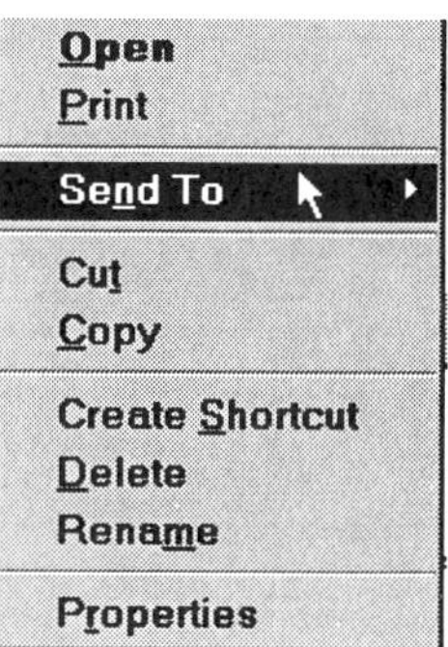

1. Select the objects you want to copy.
2. Right-click on one of them, which opens the menu shown at the right.
3. Point at the Send To command on this menu.
4. Choose the appropriate floppy disk drive from the resulting submenu.

TUTORIAL

Try the following exercise on your own.

1. Turn on your computer, if necessary, to start up Windows 98 and close any open windows.
2. Start Explorer, maximize its window, and select the List view option from the View menu or toolbar.
3. Insert the Student Disk in its drive and select this drive (for example, "3½ Floppy (A:)") in the folder tree pane.
4. Select the last five (consecutive) files listed by selecting the first of them, then holding down the Shift key while selecting the last. (Remember: To select an object in Web style or Classic style mode, point at it or click on it, respectively.)
5. Deselect the selected files by clicking on an empty part of the contents pane.
6. Select the files Fonts, Preamble, and Testfile by selecting the first of these, then holding down the Ctrl key as you select the other two, one at a time.
7. Deselect the Fonts file by holding down the Ctrl key while pointing at it or clicking on it, as appropriate..
8. Move the two remaining selected files to the Paint subfolder using the (right-) drag-and-drop method:
   - Move the mouse pointer over either file name and press, but do not release, the *right* mouse button.
   - Reposition the pointer so that the Paint folder name and icon become highlighted and release the mouse button.

- Choose Move Here from the resulting pop-up menu.

9. Move the Testfile and Preamble files back to the root folder of the Student Disk using the cut and paste method:
   - Open the Paint folder by choosing its icon (clicking on it or double-clicking on it in Web style or Classic style mode, respectively) in the contents pane.
   - Select Testfile and Preamble.
   - Choose Cut from Explorer's Edit menu or click on the Cut toolbar button.
   - Open the diskette's root folder by clicking on its drive icon (for example, "3½ Floppy (A:)") in the folder tree pane.
   - Choose Paste from Explorer's Edit menu or click on the Paste toolbar button.
10. Copy the Fonts file from the root folder to the Paint subfolder using (left-) drag-and-drop:
    - Select the Fonts file.
    - Position the mouse pointer over the selected file name, hold down the left mouse button and the Ctrl key (Ctrl is for *copy*, Shift is for *move*).
    - Reposition the pointer so that the Paint folder name and icon become highlighted, and release the mouse button and Ctrl key.
11. Undo the last copy operation by choosing Undo Copy from the Edit menu or clicking on the Undo toolbar button.

12. Exit Explorer and remove the Student Disk from its drive.

3.4 Other Operations on Files and Folders

In Section 3.3, we described how to select, move, and copy objects (files and folders). In this section we will continue this discussion, describing how to use Explorer to delete, rename, and create files and folders. We will also discuss how to create a *shortcut*.

Deleting Files and Folders

Deleting objects from disk is a common operation, often used to create additional free disk space or just to reduce clutter. In the usual sense of the word, to **delete** a file or folder means to remove it and all its contents from disk. When you use Explorer to delete an object, however, that object is normally (but not necessarily always) just copied to a special folder called the **Recycle Bin**. To remove the object from disk, you then have to delete it from the Recycle Bin.

Ways to delete objects

To delete files or folders, start Explorer and select the objects to be deleted (see Section 3.3). Then, perform any of the following actions:

- Press the Delete (Del) key.
- Drag any of the selected objects onto the Recycle Bin icon on the Desktop.

- Click on the Delete button (shown at the right) on Explorer's toolbar.

- Choose the Delete command from Explorer's File menu.
- Right-click on any of the selected objects and choose the Delete command from the resulting pop-up menu.

After performing one of these actions, the Confirm File Delete (or Confirm Folder Delete) dialog box shown in Figure 10 may appear. Choose the Yes or No command button, as appropriate.

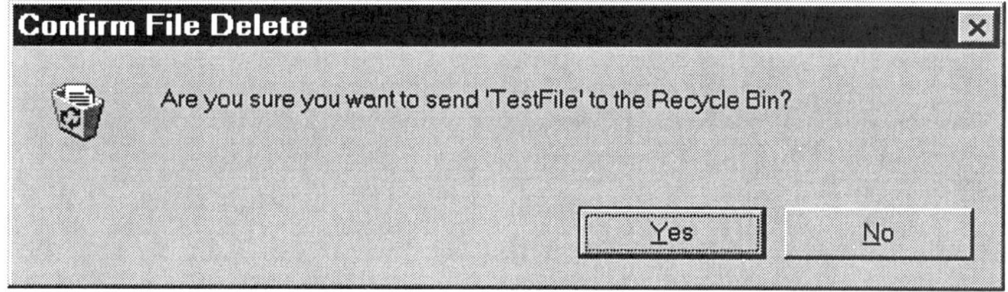

Figure 10 The Confirm File Delete Dialog Box

WARNING

By default, Windows 98 does not send files deleted from floppy disks to the Recycle Bin. In this case, the message in the Confirm Delete dialog box will read "Are you sure you want to delete ..." and, if you activate the Yes button, the selected objects will immediately be removed from disk. If one of these objects is a folder, all its contents — files and subfolders alike — will be removed from disk. So, before you give the command to delete files or folders, think about what you are doing and whether you really want to do it!

The Recycle Bin The Recycle Bin is simply a Windows 98 folder. When files or folders are "deleted" by sending them to the Recycle Bin, these objects still take up disk space and can still be retrieved (or *restored*). If you are sure you no longer need an object in the Recycle Bin, you should delete that object to increase your free disk space. The safest way to accomplish this is to:

1. Open the Recycle Bin by choosing its Desktop icon. The Recycle Bin window will be displayed (Figure 11).

Recycle Bin

File Edit View Go Favorites Help

Address Recycle Bin

Name	Original Location	Date Deleted	Type
TestFile	C:\WINDOWS	5/29/1998 1:02 PM	WordPad
True BASIC	C:\WINDOWS\Desktop	5/27/1998 9:27 AM	Shortcut
Study Skills Template	C:\WINDOWS\Desktop	5/25/1998 6:31 PM	Shortcut
DISPPROP	C:\Corel\Suite8\WP...	5/15/1998 5:38 PM	HiJaak Im
folderoptions	C:\Corel\Suite8\WP...	5/15/1998 5:38 PM	HiJaak Im
MyCompWeb	C:\Corel\Suite8\WP...	5/15/1998 5:38 PM	HiJaak Im
CHNLBAR	C:\Corel\Suite8\WP...	5/15/1998 5:35 PM	HiJaak Im
CHNLBTN	C:\Corel\Suite8\WP...	5/15/1998 5:35 PM	HiJaak Im

80 object(s) 11.2MB

Figure 11 The Recycle Bin Window (Details View)

2. Select the objects you want to delete.
3. Delete the selected objects: Press the Delete key, or choose Delete from the File menu, or click on the toolbar's Delete button, or right-click on a selected object and choose Delete from the pop-up menu.
4. If a Confirm Delete dialog box appears, asking whether you're sure you want to delete the objects, choose the Yes button (unless you've changed your mind). The selected objects are now removed from disk.

NOTE

As you can see in Figure 11, the Recycle Bin window strongly resembles the Explorer window. In fact, the Recycle Bin window is just Explorer's view of a folder called *Recycled* without the folder tree pane. There are, however, two menu options available for the Recycle Bin that are not available for a typical folder:

1. You can choose Empty Recycle Bin from the File menu to delete *all* objects in the Recycle Bin. (You can also accomplish this task by right-clicking on the Recycle Bin's Desktop icon and then choosing Empty Recycle Bin from the pop-up menu.)
2. You can choose Restore from the File menu to move selected objects back to their original location.

Renaming Files and Folders

To **rename** (change the name of) a file or folder:

1. Start Explorer and select the object to be renamed.
2. Perform any of the following actions:
   - Choose Rename from Explorer's File menu.
   - Right-click on the selected object and choose Rename from the pop-up menu.
   - In Classic style mode, click on the selected object.

   In any case, Windows places a box around the selected object's name (as shown at the right) to let you know that this object can now be renamed.
3. Type a new name for the object and press the Enter key.

If an object in the current folder has the same name as the one you are trying to assign to the selected object, the following dialog box will be displayed:

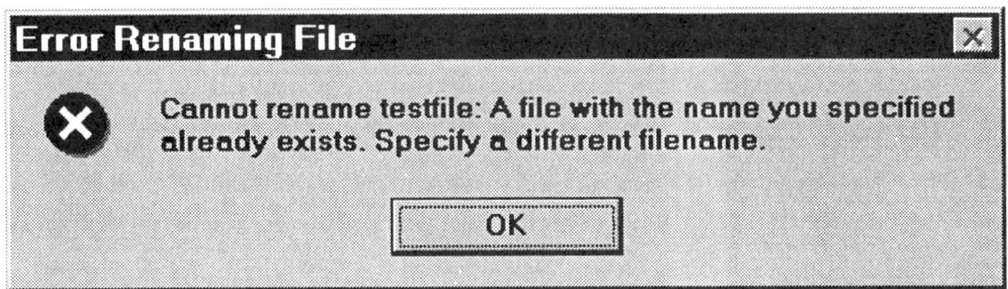

Click on the OK button (or press the Enter key) and this message will be cleared from the screen. If you want to give the selected object the same name as an existing object in that folder, you have to first rename or delete the existing one.

NOTE

You can rename objects represented by Desktop icons in a similar way:

1. Select the icon for the object to be renamed.
2. Right-click on the icon and choose Rename from the pop-up menu (or, in Classic style mode, click on the selected icon). Windows will place a box around the object's name.
3. Type a new name and press the Enter key.

Creating New Files and Folders

Data files (documents) are normally created within a specific application. For example, if you start WordPad, type some text, and save the resulting document (assigning it a name in the process), a file with that name is created on disk. On the other hand, most of the program files and folders on your hard disk were placed there "automatically"— usually when Windows or an application was installed.

You can also use Explorer to create both files and folders. Creating a file this way is not that useful, but creating a new folder — say, to hold certain related documents — is an important operation. To create a file or folder:

1. Start Explorer and select the folder in which you want the new object to reside.
2. Take either of the following actions:
   - Point at the New item on the File menu.

   or
   - Right-click on an empty part of the contents pane and point at the New item on the resulting pop-up menu.

   In either case, a submenu, similar to the one in Figure 12, will be displayed.
3. Choose either the Folder item or one of the file types listed at the bottom of this menu. A new object will appear in the contents pane named, for example, New Folder, New Text Document, or New WordPad Document. The name of the object will be highlighted and boxed-in, ready for renaming.
4. Rename the object whatever you want by typing a new name and pressing the Enter key.

As an example, we will create a new subfolder of the Windows folder and name it Data Files. To do so, we:

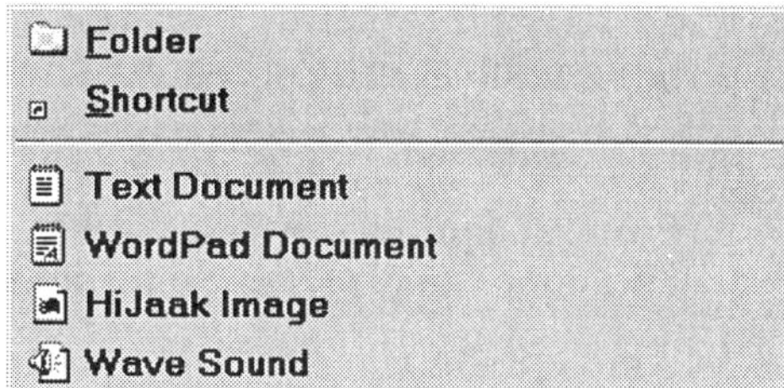

Figure 12 The New Menu

1. Start Explorer.
2. Scroll the folder tree pane until the Windows folder comes into view.
3. Click on the Windows folder to select it. (The word *Windows* becomes highlighted.)
4. Point at the New command on Explorer's File menu and choose Folder from the resulting submenu. (A highlighted object called *New Folder* appears in the contents pane; the "box" around its name indicates that it's ready to be renamed.)
5. To rename the folder, type Data Files and press the Enter key.

Creating Shortcuts

Recall from Section 2.1 that usually the easiest way to start an application is to choose its Desktop icon (click on it in Web style mode or double-click on it in Classic style mode). For this reason, it is convenient to have an icon on the Desktop for each of your favorite programs. As you will see, Windows makes it easy to create such icons.

What's a shortcut?

Most Desktop icons represent **shortcuts** to objects (files or folders); when you choose such an icon, the shortcut provides Windows with the location and name (the path name) of the corresponding object and Windows opens that object. Notice that a shortcut is not a copy of an object, just a small file called a *pointer* (or *link*) that tells Windows where to find the relevant file or folder. For this reason, you can create shortcuts to your heart's content with very little adverse effect on your free disk space.

There are several methods for creating shortcuts. If you want the shortcut to reside on the Desktop, here's the simplest way:

Using the Send To menu

1. Start Explorer and open the folder that contains the object for which you want to create a shortcut.
2. Right-click on the desired object, which opens a pop-up menu.
3. Point at Send To on this menu and then click on the Desktop as Shortcut item on the resulting submenu.

Shortcut "arrow"

An icon representing the shortcut will appear on the Desktop. Icons for shortcuts contain a small arrow in the lower left corner, as shown at the left for the WordPad shortcut icon.

You can also use the drag-and-drop technique (which was described in Section 3.3 for copying and moving files and folders) to create a shortcut. Here's how:

Creating a shortcut by drag-and-drop

1. Start Explorer and open the folder that contains the object for which you want to create a shortcut.
2. Select the desired object and right-drag it to the desired location.
3. When you release the right mouse button, the menu at the right will pop up.
4. Choose Create Shortcut(s) Here from this menu. The shortcut's icon will be displayed.

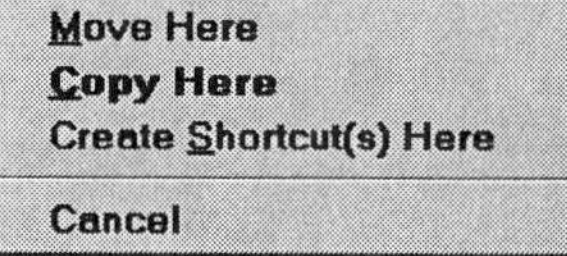

Here's still another technique for creating a shortcut.

1. Start Explorer and open the folder that contains the object for which you want to create a shortcut.
2. Select the desired object and choose the Create Shortcut item from either the File menu or the menu that pops up when you right-click on the selected object. A new object entitled "Shortcut to ..." will appear (highlighted) in the contents pane.
3. To move the new shortcut to the Desktop (if so desired):
   - Drag it there.

   or
   - Cut it to the Clipboard (using the *Cut* Edit menu command or toolbar button) and then paste it onto the Desktop by right-clicking on an empty part of the Desktop and choosing Paste from the pop-up menu.

Once a shortcut has been placed on the Desktop (using any method):

- You can move the shortcut by dragging it with the mouse.
- You can rename the shortcut by right-clicking on it and choosing

the Rename item from the pop-up menu. A "box" will appear around the shortcut's name. Now, type a new name and press the Enter key.

You can also create Desktop shortcuts *without starting up Explorer*. If you want to create a shortcut for an item that is on the Start menu or one of its submenus, the process is very simple:

1. Click on the Start button and open the relevant submenu (if necessary).
2. Drag the desired item onto the Desktop.

If the desired object is not on a Start button menu, you can still create a shortcut without opening Explorer by using the "shortcut wizard", a series of dialog boxes that guides you through the process. To start this wizard:

1. Right-click on an empty part of the Desktop. A menu will pop up.
2. Point at the New item on this menu and then choose the Shortcut option on the resulting submenu.

Now, follow the on-screen instructions. To proceed from the current wizard dialog box to the next one, choose the Next command button and, at the end of the process, choose the Finish button. The "wizard" method, despite the name, is fairly complicated. You will probably only use it if you've forgotten the other techniques and don't want to take the trouble to look one up!

Try the following exercise on your own.

1. Turn on your computer, if necessary, to start up Windows 98, and close any open windows.
2. Start Explorer and select the List view option from the View menu or toolbar.
3. Insert the Student Disk in its drive and select this drive (for example, "3½ Floppy (A:)") in the folder tree pane.
4. Select the file named DeleteFile from the contents pane.
5. Size and move the Explorer window so that the selected file, the Recycle Bin icon, and part of the Desktop are all visible.
6. Create a shortcut for the selected file:
   - Right-drag the file onto an empty part of the Desktop.
   - Choose Create Shortcut(s) Here from the menu that pops up

when you release the mouse button.

- Rename the shortcut icon "DelFile" by right-clicking on it, selecting Rename from the pop-up menu, typing the new name, and pressing the Enter key.

7. Delete the new DelFile icon by dragging it (using the left mouse button) onto the Recycle Bin icon.
8. Restore the DelFile shortcut: Open the Recycle Bin (by choosing its icon), select the DelFile shortcut, and choose the Restore command from the File menu. Now, close the Recycle Bin.
9. Delete the DelFile shortcut again, this time by selecting it and pressing the Del key. Answer *Yes* to the Confirm Delete query.
10. Rename the DeleteFile object in the root folder of the floppy disk by selecting this file in Explorer's contents pane, choosing Rename from the File menu, typing a new name of your choosing, and pressing the Enter key.
11. Delete this newly-renamed file by choosing Delete from Explorer's File menu. Answer *Yes* to the Confirm Delete query.
12. Exit Explorer and remove the Student Disk from its drive.

3.5 My Computer

As you saw in Chapter 1, the Desktop contains an icon called **My Computer** that provides access to virtually all aspects of your computer system. In particular, from the My Computer window you can carry out all the operations on files and folders that we have just discussed. This is not surprising once you realize that the My Computer icon is simply a built-in shortcut that starts Explorer and opens the My Computer folder within it! If you keep this fact in mind, it will be easier to understand the workings of My Computer.

Starting My Computer

My Computer

As you know, you can open the My Computer window (Figure 13) by choosing its Desktop icon. Notice that this window is similar in appearance to the Explorer window, but My Computer lacks a folder tree pane; it uses a single subwindow, a contents pane, to display information. We call a window of this sort a **folder window**. (The Recycle Bin window is another example of a folder window.)

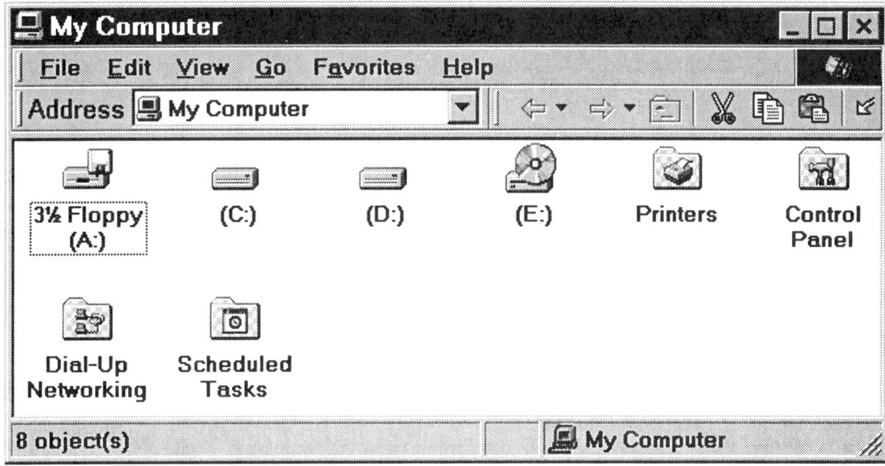

Figure 13 The My Computer Window — Large Icons View

NOTE

You can also start My Computer by right-clicking on its icon and choosing the Open item from the resulting pop-up menu. Interestingly enough, if you choose Explore instead of Open from this menu, Explorer will start and display a dual-pane view of the My Computer folder.

The fact that the My Computer window (or, more generally, any folder window) lacks a folder tree pane results in two basic differences between the way My Computer and Explorer are used to locate and manipulate objects:

1. My Computer provides less flexibility than Explorer in navigating (or **browsing**) the Windows file system. For example, it is often more difficult to locate a particular folder in My Computer.
2. Certain drag-and-drop operations are more difficult to carry out in My Computer than in Explorer. For example, it is sometimes not easy in My Computer to drag a given file onto a particular folder.*

We will now examine the consequences of each of these differences.

*In light of these deficiencies, you might be wondering why Microsoft chose to give My Computer such prominence in the Windows 98 interface. One reason for this approach is to provide easy access, especially for the novice user, to all aspects of the computer system — its drives, files, printers, settings, and so on.

Using My Computer to Browse Folders

Opening a subfolder

Once you have started My Computer, it is easy to access its subfolders: your computer's drives, the Printers folder, and so on (see Figure 13). Just choose the appropriate icon (by clicking on it in Web style mode or double-clicking on it in Classic style mode) to open one of these folders, and its contents will be displayed in a new window. For example, if you choose the "(C:)" icon, a window will open displaying all the files and subfolders in the root folder of the C: drive. A subfolder of *any* folder in any folder window can be opened in the same way — by choosing its icon.

NOTE

When a new one opens, the previous folder window may or may not close. You can control whether or not a separate window opens whenever you change folders using the following procedure:

1. Choose the Folder Options command from My Computer's View menu.
2. Select the *Custom* option button and then choose the Settings command button in the Folder Options dialog box. The Custom Settings dialog box will open.
3. In this dialog box, select the appropriate option button to either browse folders *in the same window* or *in separate windows*.
4. Choose the OK command button in the Custom Settings dialog box and then again in the Folder Options dialog box.

We will discuss this feature again later in this section.

The address bar

Just as in Explorer, the Back, Forward, and Up One Level toolbar buttons or Go menu commands in My Computer (or any folder window) provide ways to quickly move between folders. (For information about these features and about the toolbar in general, see Section 3.2.) Moreover, due to the lack of a folder tree pane, the address bar is especially useful in navigating in My Computer. Figure 14 shows the address bar and the above-mentioned toolbar buttons.

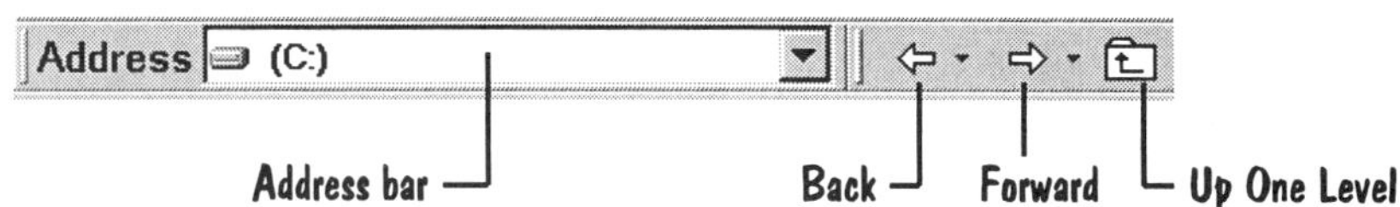

Figure 14 Browsing Features of the Toolbar

The address bar's drop-down list provides a way to change folders quickly in certain situations. When you open this list (by clicking on the down-triangle; see Figure 14), a "mini-tree" is displayed, showing the immediate (child) subfolders of the Desktop and My Computer, as well as the chain of subfolders forming the path to the currently open folder (Figure 15). The current folder, which is Programs in Figure 15, is shown in the text box at the top of the list as well. To display the contents of one of the listed folders, just click on it.

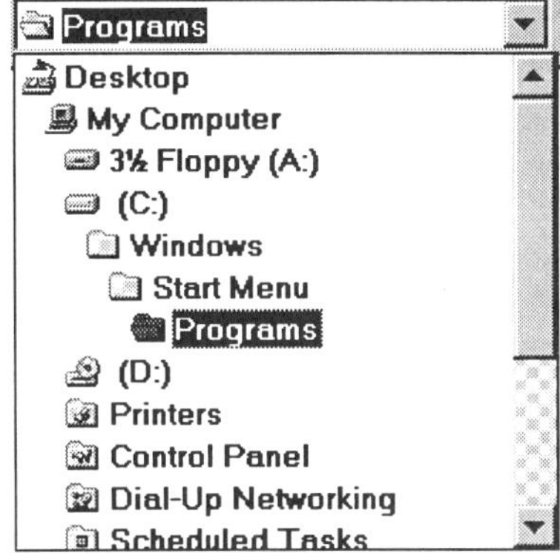

Figure 15 The Address Bar Drop-down List

The address bar drop-down list can be a great time-saving convenience. For example, suppose the current folder is Programs, as in Figure 15. To display the contents of the disk in the A: drive, just open the drop-down list and click on the "3½ Floppy (A:)" object.

The following tips make it easier to use My Computer to browse folders:

- The default view option for My Computer is Large Icons. It's much easier to see what's in the current folder if you use the View menu or the toolbar buttons to switch to the Small Icons or List view option (see Section 3.2).
- Display the *path* of the current folder on its window's title bar (if it is not already displayed there) by choosing the Folder Options command from the View menu, clicking on the View tab in the resulting dialog box, selecting the *Display the full path in title bar* check box, and choosing the OK command button.
- If each change of folder has opened a separate window, you can close all these windows at the same time by holding down the Shift key while clicking on the last window's close button.

NOTE

Some Windows dialog boxes, such as Save As and Open (see Section 2.2) allow you to browse folders as you do in My Computer. For example, when you choose the Open command from the File menu of most Windows applications, a dialog box similar to the one in Figure 16 is displayed. (Save As and Browse dialog boxes are usually very similar to this one.)

- The address bar and Up One Level, List, and Details toolbar buttons work just the way they do in My Computer. Explorer, or any folder window.
- The View Desktop button displays the contents of the Desktop in the dialog box window.
- The Create New Folder button does just that — it creates and displays a new folder, a subfolder of the one shown on the address bar, "boxed-in" and ready for renaming.

However, unlike My Computer, you can restrict the kinds of files displayed by using the dialog box's *Files of type* drop-down list.

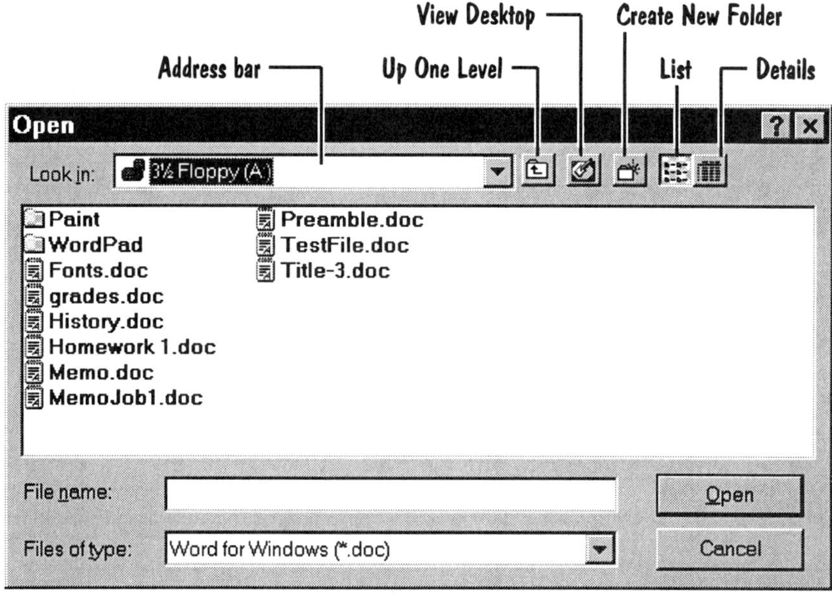

Figure 16 Browsing in an Open Dialog Box

Using My Computer to Operate on Files and Folders

Objects — files, folders and shortcuts — are manipulated from within a My Computer window (or, more generally, any folder window) in essentially the same way as in Explorer (see Sections 3.3 and

3.4). For example, you can copy a file from one folder to another using the Copy and Paste commands, as follows:

1. Open the folder containing the file to be copied.
2. Right-click on the desired file, which selects it and displays a pop-up menu.
3. Choose the Copy command from the pop-up menu.
4. Right-click on the destination folder's name, which displays a pop-up menu.
5. Choose the Paste command from this pop-up menu and the process is complete.

Notice that this procedure could be used without change in Explorer, but there is one subtle difference in its execution here. To carry out steps 1 and 4 in Explorer, you would most likely just scroll and expand the folder tree pane (if necessary) until the name of the desired folder appeared; then click on it. In My Computer, on the other hand, you might have to open several windows in each of steps 1 and 4 before the desired folder became visible!

Drag-and-drop in My Computer

The difference just described causes the greatest trouble if you want to perform a drag-and-drop move or copy (see Section 3.3). The problem here is that the object to be moved or copied *and* the destination folder must be visible at the same time. This is not much of a problem in Explorer, but requires some preparation in My Computer.

The trick to drag-and-drop moving or copying in My Computer is to open both the source and destination folders and arrange them so that both are visible on the screen. For example, suppose we want to copy a file named TestFile from a floppy disk to the Windows folder on the C: drive. To do this using drag-and-drop in My Computer:

1. Insert the floppy disk into its drive and start My Computer.
2. Ensure that a separate window will open for each new folder by proceeding as follows:
   - Choose the Folder Options command from the View menu. The Folder Options dialog box will open.
   - Select the *Custom* option button near the bottom of this dialog box and choose the Settings command button. The Custom Settings dialog box will open.
   - If it's not already selected, select the *Open each folder in its own window* option button in this dialog box. Now, choose the OK command button in this dialog box and the Close command button in the Folder Options dialog box.

3. Back in My Computer, choose the (C:) icon to open the root folder of the C: drive, C:\.
4. Scroll the C:\ window until the Windows folder's name appears.
5. Switch back to the My Computer window by clicking within it or on its Taskbar button.
6. Choose the appropriate floppy drive icon to open its window.
7. Scroll this window (if necessary) until TestFile appears and select this file. The current arrangement of windows is shown in Figure 17.

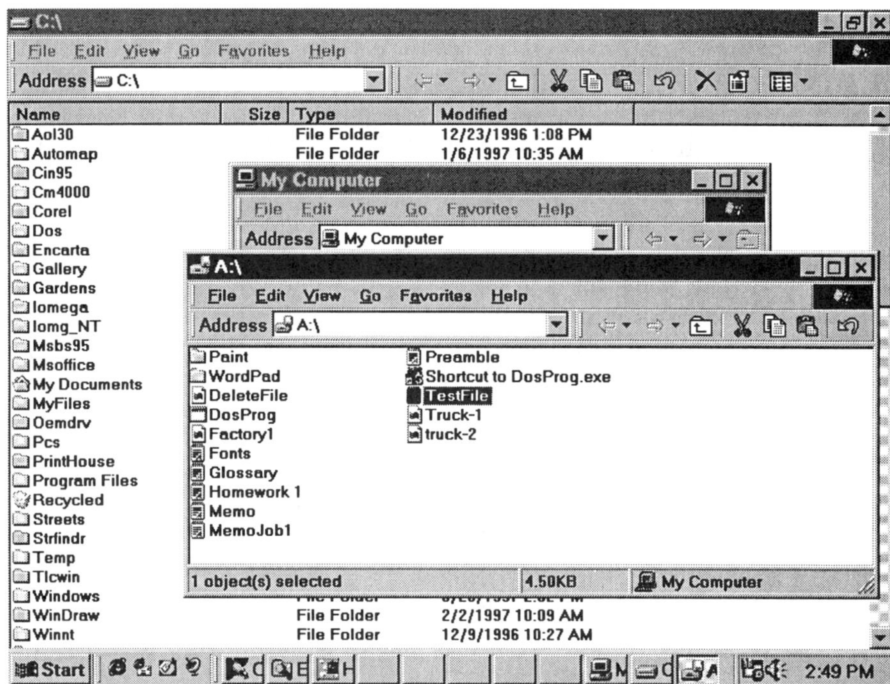

Figure 17 Preparing to Copy with My Computer

8. If necessary, resize or move the floppy drive window and the C:\ window so that the names TestFile and Windows are both visible.
9. Drag the TestFile file onto the Windows folder. The Copying animated dialog box will confirm that the copy operation is taking place.

TUTORIAL

Try the following exercise on your own.

1. Turn on your computer, if necessary, to start up Windows 98, and close any open windows.
2. Start My Computer by choosing its Desktop icon (clicking on it in Web style mode or double-clicking on it in Classic style mode).
3. Elect to use a single My Computer window to display all folders:
   - Choose Folder Options from the View menu to open the Folder Options dialog box.
   - Select the *Custom* option button and then click on the Settings command button. A new dialog box will open.
   - Select the "Open each folder in the same window" option button.
   - Click on the OK button in this dialog box and on the Close command button in the Folder Options dialog box.
4. Insert the Student Disk in its drive and then select this drive (for example, "3½ Floppy (A:)").
5. Choose (click on or double-click on, as appropriate) the WordPad subfolder to open it.
6. Right-click on the Fonts file in the WordPad subfolder and copy it to the Clipboard by choosing the Copy command from the pop-up menu.
7. If the toolbar buttons are not visible in the window, display them by pointing at the Toolbars item on the View menu, then clicking on Standard Buttons on the resulting submenu.
8. Open the root folder on the A: drive (A:\), the parent of the WordPad folder, by either clicking on the Up One Level or Back toolbar button (or by pressing the Backspace key).
9. Paste the Fonts file into the A:\ folder by choosing the Paste command from the Edit menu. If the Confirm File Replace dialog box appears, choose the No command button.
10. Open the root folder on the C: drive in the following way:
    - Display the address bar's drop-down list. (If the address bar is not visible, open the View menu, point at the Toolbars item, and then click on Address Bar on the resulting submenu.)
    - Click on the "(C:)" item on this list.
11. Close the My Computer window and remove the Student Disk from its drive.

3.6 *Formatting and Copying Floppy Disks*

All the procedures we have discussed in this chapter apply to files and folders on floppy disks (diskettes) as well as on hard disks. Two additional operations are useful with floppies: formatting and copying disks. In this section, we will discuss these procedures.

Formatting a Floppy Disk

Before information can be stored on a disk, the disk must be **formatted**. This process prepares the disk to store information, dividing it into sectors and creating a file allocation table on it, and also erases any data that had been stored on the disk prior to formatting. Hard disks are usually formatted by the manufacturer or retailer, and most floppies are also sold already formatted. (In the latter case, the word "formatted" will appear on the box and on each individual disk.) Nevertheless, from time to time, you will have to format a diskette for one of the following reasons:

- To prepare an unformatted diskette for use.
- To reformat a Macintosh disk for use on your Windows computer.
- To quickly erase all files on a disk.

Keep in mind that the format procedure erases all information on the disk being formatted! So, never format a disk unless you are sure there is nothing stored on it or, if there is data on the disk, that you no longer need its contents. Unless the disk is fresh out of the box, it's wise to check its contents before formatting it. To do so, insert the diskette in its drive, start Explorer, and select the appropriate floppy drive in the folder tree pane. If a message is displayed informing you that the disk is not formatted, fine. Otherwise, check each file listed in the contents pane. If you see a file that you're not sure you want erased, open it to view its contents before proceeding.

If you format a disk and then realize you made a mistake — it did contain some information you need — immediately inform your instructor or lab coordinator. It *might* be possible to recover the desired files if you have not yet used the newly-formatted diskette.

To format a floppy disk:

1. Insert the diskette to be formatted in its drive.

2. Start My Computer or Explorer and select this drive.
3. Right-click on the selected drive and choose Format from the resulting pop-up menu (Figure 18). Or, in My Computer, choose Format from the File menu. A Format dialog box, like the one in Figure 19, will be displayed.
4. Select the proper Capacity for the diskette from the drop-down list:
   - For 3.5" disks, select *1.44 Mb* if the disk is a high density one (with an "HD" on its label); select *720 Kb*, otherwise.
   - For 5.25" disks, select *1.2 Mb* if the disk is a high density one (with an "HD" on its label); select *360 Kb*, otherwise.

Figure 18
Floppy Disk Menu

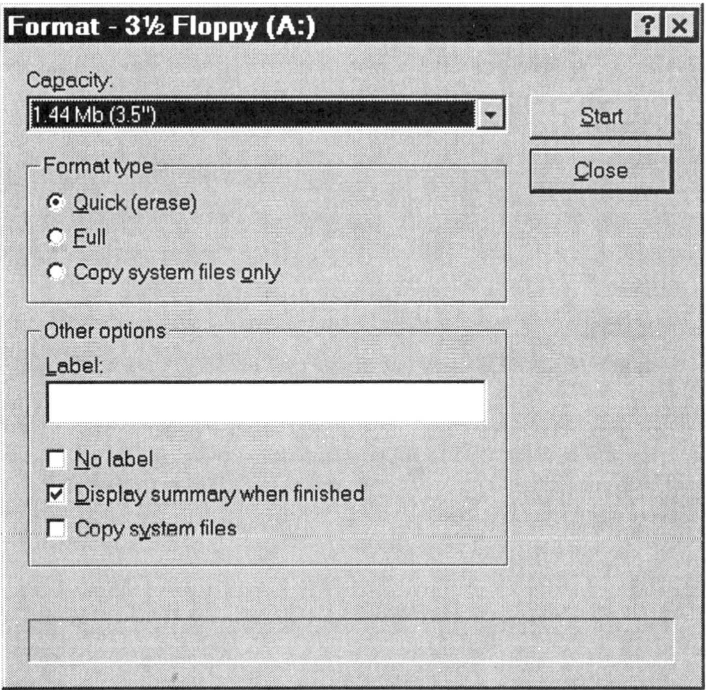

Figure 19 The Format Dialog Box

5. Select a "Format type" option using the option buttons:
   - *Quick (erase)* can only be used with diskettes that have already been formatted. It "erases" all information on the disk (by removing the file allocation table and other system information). This option provides a convenient way to erase old, unneeded disks so they can be used again. Quick format is much faster than the normal (or *full*) format process.
   - *Full* is the option used to format a diskette which has not yet been formatted for a Windows computer.
   - *Copy system files only* is used with formatted diskettes. It creates a *bootable* diskette — if placed in the computer's A: drive at startup, the computer will access the information on this disk, instead of the hard disk, and start DOS. A bootable diskette is useful if your hard disk has become damaged.
6. If you want to associate a name with this diskette, type a name for it in the Label text box. The label (or *volume label*) for a diskette is displayed by certain programs. Select the *No label* check box if you want to delete a previous label for the diskette.
7. Select the *Display summary when finished* check box to display information about the free space on the disk when the formatting process is complete.
8. Select the *Copy system files* check box to create a bootable diskette during the formatting process.
9. Choose the Start command button to begin the formatting process. The message "Formatting" and a bar graph showing the percentage of the process completed will appear at the bottom of the Format dialog box.

Copying an Entire Diskette

If your computer has two floppy disk drives, you can use the cut-and-paste copy procedure, described in Section 3.3, to copy all files from one diskette to another. Windows provides a simpler way to copy an entire diskette, even if your machine only has one floppy disk drive, as long as the diskettes have the *same size and capacity*. Here's how it works:

1. Insert the diskette to be copied (the *source disk*) in its drive. If you have two drives of the same capacity, insert the disk to be copied to (the *destination disk*) in the other drive.

WARNING

When you carry out the copy disk process, all existing information on the destination disk is erased and replaced with a copy of the source disk. Consequently, before beginning the process, be sure that there are no files of any value on the destination disk.

2. Start My Computer or Explorer and select the source drive.
3. Right-click on this drive and choose Copy Disk from the pop-up menu (see Figure 18); or, in My Computer, choose Copy Disk from the File menu. A Copy Disk dialog box, similar to the one in Figure 20, will be displayed.

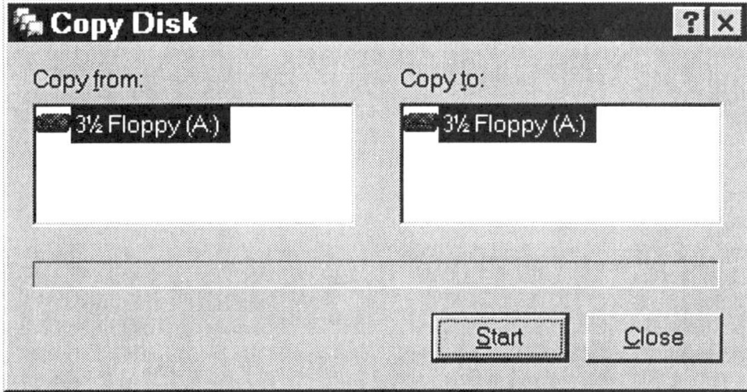

Figure 20 The Copy Disk Dialog Box

4. Choose the Start command button to begin the copying process. Messages and a bar graph at the bottom of the Copy Disk dialog box will indicate the progress of the operation.
5. If you have only one floppy drive, the following dialog box will appear halfway through the copy process:

Insert the destination disk in its drive. Be aware that the copy process will *erase all information* on this disk!

6. When the copy process is complete, a message to this effect will appear at the bottom of the Copy Disk dialog box. When it does, choose the Close command button.

Chapter Summary

File Names	Long file name (for folders and Windows 98 applications)	Maximum length is 255 characters; all characters are allowed *except*: | : " / \ * ?
	DOS file name (for Windows 3.1 and DOS applications)	Consists of a *filename* made up of one to eight characters followed by an optional extension (up to three characters), separated from the filename by a period. Forbidden characters are the space (blank) and: . , : ; " [ ] / \ = | * ?
Basic Operations in Explorer	To start Explorer	Open the Start menu, point at the Programs option, and choose the Windows Explorer item from the submenu.
	To expand a branch of the folder tree	In the folder tree pane, either click on the plus symbol next to the desired folder or double-click on the desired folder's name.
	To open a folder	Click on the folder's name in the folder tree pane or choose the folder in the contents pane.
	To open a file	Choose the file's name in the contents pane.
	To select a view option (Large Icons, Small Icons, etc.)	Click on the appropriate toolbar button or choose the appropriate option from the View menu.
	To sort the objects in the contents pane	Choose the appropriate item from the Arrange Icons submenu of the View menu or, in Details view, click on the appropriate button at the top of the contents pane.
Selecting Files and Folders	A single object	Click on it in Classic style mode or point at it in Web style mode.
	Objects in sequence	Select the first, then hold down the Shift key while selecting the last.

	Additional objects	Hold down the Ctrl key while selecting them.
	All objects in the contents pane	Choose Select All from the Edit menu or press Ctrl+A.
Operations on Files or Folders (in Explorer or My Computer)	To move or copy selected objects	Hold down the Shift (for *move*) or Ctrl (for *copy*) key while dragging the objects onto the target; *or* right-drag the objects onto the target and choose either Move or Copy from the pop-up menu; *or* Cut (for *move*) or Copy the objects to the Clipboard and Paste them onto the target.
	To copy selected objects to a floppy disk	Right-click on one of the objects, point at Send To on the pop-up menu, and choose the floppy drive from the resulting submenu.
	To delete the selected objects	Press the Del key; *or* drag the objects onto the Recycle Bin; *or* choose Delete from the File menu or the right-click menu.
	To rename a selected object	First, choose Rename from the File menu or the right-click menu, *or* press the F2 key. Then, type the new name and press the Enter key.
	To create a new file or folder	Point at the New item on either the File menu or the right-click menu, then choose the appropriate item from the submenu.
	To create a shortcut to a selected object	Right-drag the object to the desired location and choose Create Shortcut(s) Here from the pop-up menu; *or* right-click on the object and choose Create Shortcut from the pop-up menu; *or* right-click on an empty part of the Desktop, point at the New item on the pop-up menu, choose Create Shortcut from the submenu, and follow the instructions in the Create Shortcut wizard.
Operations on Floppy Disks (in Explorer or My Computer)	To format a floppy disk	First, insert the disk in its drive, right-click on that drive's folder icon, and choose Format from the pop-up menu. Then, in the resulting dialog box, select options and choose the Start command button.
	To copy an entire floppy disk	First, insert the disk to be copied in its drive, right-click on that drive's folder icon, and choose Copy Disk from the pop-up

menu. Then, choose the Start command in the resulting dialog box and follow the on-screen instructions.

Review Exercises

Section 3.1

1. A ___________ is a collection of information generated by a program and saved on disk.
2. A ___________ is a collection of files that have been grouped together and given a name.
3. True or false: A folder may contain files and/or subfolders.
4. True or false: If the path name for a file is A:\Paint\Truck.bmp, then it is located in the Paint folder on the disk in the A: drive.
5. Which of the following is a valid DOS file name?
   a. `Homework 1`
   b. `Homework.1`
   c. `HomeworkOne`
   d. All of these names are valid DOS file names.
6. Which of the following is a valid long file name?
   a. `Homework 1`
   b. `Homework.1`
   c. `HomeworkOne`
   d. All of these names are valid long file names.

Section 3.2

7. In the Explorer window, the ___________ pane can contain both files and folders.
8. To see the subfolders of a given folder in Explorer's left pane (if they are not currently displayed), click on the ___________ symbol that precedes the name of the folder.
9. If you want to display the size of a file shown in Explorer's contents pane, click on the ___________ item on the View menu.
10. True or false: Explorer's left pane only shows the folders present on the C: drive.
11. True or false: In Explorer, you can use the toolbar to select one of four view options (Large Icons, Small Icons, List, or Details).
12. True or false: In Small Icons view in Explorer, it is possible to order the icons in alphabetical order by file type.

13. The only Explorer view option in which you can display files in *decreasing* size order is:

    a. Large Icons
    b. Small Icons
    c. List
    d. Details

14. In which of the following view options can file icons be moved, one by one, around Explorer's contents pane?

    a. Large Icons only
    b. Small icons only
    c. Both Large Icons and Small Icons
    d. Neither Large Icons nor Small Icons

Section 3.3

15. To select two nonconsecutive files in Explorer, select the first and hold down the ___________ key while selecting the second.

16. To copy a file from one folder to another on the C: drive, hold down the ___________ key and drag the file to its destination.

17. A simple way to copy a selected file to the disk in the A: drive is to right-click on the file, point at the ___________ command on the pop-up menu, and choose 3½ Floppy (A) from the submenu.

18. True or false: To select a group of objects that are in consecutive order in Explorer's contents pane, select the first and then hold down the Shift key while selecting the last.

19. True or false: When you right-drag an object in Explorer and release the mouse button, the pop-up menu allows you to move *or* copy the object to the new location.

20. True or false: The Cut and Copy buttons on Explorer's toolbar can be used to move text, but not files.

21. If one object in Explorer's contents pane is selected and you select another (without holding down any key), then

    a. The first object is deselected; the second is selected.
    b. The first object remains selected; the second is not selected.
    c. Both objects are selected.
    d. Neither object is selected.

22. To *move* a file from the Windows folder to the disk in the A: drive, you can

    a. Use the Cut and Paste commands on Explorer's Edit menu.
    b. Left-drag the file, dropping it on the A: drive icon.
    c. Use the Send To command.
    d. None of these techniques can be used to move the file.

Section 3.4

23. If you select an object in Explorer and press the Delete key, that object is normally moved to a location called the ___________.
24. To create a subfolder of the Windows folder using Explorer, right-click in the contents pane and point at the ___________ command on the resulting pop-up menu.
25. Windows places a ___________ around an object's name to let you know that this object can now be renamed.
26. True or false: The Empty Recycle Bin command on the Recycle Bin's File menu can be used to remove from disk all items currently in the Recycle Bin.
27. True or false: Shortcuts on the Desktop cannot be renamed.
28. True or false: A shortcut to a file is actually a copy of that file.
29. In Explorer, to delete the currently selected object, you can

    a. Press the Delete key.
    b. Choose the Delete command from the File menu.
    c. Click on the toolbar's Delete button.
    d. Perform any of the above actions.

30. Suppose you have just created a shortcut in Explorer. To place this shortcut on the Desktop, you can

    a. Drag it onto the Desktop.
    b. Cut it to the Clipboard and Paste in onto the Desktop.
    c. Copy it onto the Clipboard and Paste it onto the Desktop.
    d. Perform any of the above actions.

Section 3.5

31. To start My Computer in Classic style mode, ___________ on its Desktop icon.
32. In My Computer, to open the parent folder of the one currently open, press the ___________ key on the keyboard.
33. True or false: In My Computer, you can control whether or not a separate window is displayed when you open a new folder.
34. True or false: You can use My Computer to move, copy, delete, or rename *files*, but not to perform these operations on folders.
35. Suppose My Computer is displaying the contents of the Windows folder, which is a subfolder of the root folder on the C: drive. Opening the address bar's drop-down list, you will see

    a. Every subfolder of the Windows folder.
    b. Every subfolder of the root folder on the A: drive.
    c. Every subfolder of the My Computer folder.
    d. None of the above folders.

36. In My Computer, which view options are available?

    a. Large Icons and Small Icons, but not List or Details
    b. List and Details, but not Large Icons or Small Icons
    c. Large Icons, Small Icons, List, and Details
    d. Only the default view is available.

Section 3.6

37. To format a floppy disk using Explorer, begin by ____________ on the appropriate drive icon in the folder tree pane.

38. The Copy Disk command can only be used with floppy disks of the same ____________ and ____________.

39. True or false: After formatting a disk, you will not be able to access the information that had previously been stored on it.

40. True or false: When you use the Copy Disk command, all information on the source disk is erased.

41. Which option button should you select in the Format dialog box to format an unformatted diskette?

    a. Quick
    b. Full
    c. Copy system files only
    d. None of these options will format an unformatted diskette.

42. To create a bootable diskette without erasing the data on it, in the Format dialog box

    a. Select the *Quick* option button.
    b. Select the *Full* option button.
    c. Select the *Copy system files only* option button.
    d. Select the *Copy system files* check box.

Build Your Own Glossary

43. The following words and phrases are important terms that were introduced in this chapter. (They appear within the text in boldface type.) Use WordPad (see Section 2.2) to enter a definition for each term, preserving alphabetical order, into the Glossary file on the Student Disk.

Browse folders
Contents pane
Copy file or folder
Delete file or folder
Directory
DOS file name
Drag-and-drop
Explorer
File
Folder
Folder tree pane
Folder window
Format a diskette
Long file name
Move file or folder
My Computer
Parent folder
Path name
Recycle Bin
Rename file or folder
Root folder
Shortcut
Status bar
Subfolder
Toolbar

Lab Exercises

Work each of the following exercises at your computer. Begin by turning the machine on (if necessary) to start Windows 98. If you want to produce a written record of your answers, review the material on WordPad and capturing screens in Sections 2.2 and 2.3.

Lab Exercise 1 (Section 3.2)

a. Start Windows Explorer and maximize its window.

b. Insert the Student Disk in its drive and select this drive in the folder tree pane.

c. Display, *in the folder tree pane*, the subfolders of the floppy disk drive's (root) folder. How did you do this?

d. Select the Details view option from the View menu. In what year was the Dosprog application created?

e. Sort the files by modification date. Which *object* is at the top of the list? Which *file* is highest on the list?

f. Select the Large Icons view.

g. Interchange the positions of the Paint and Memo icons. Use the View menu to line up the icons. Did the icons return to their original positions?

h. Restore the Explorer window and resize it so that the Paint and Memo icons are visible, but the window is as small as possible. Which scroll bars appeared? *Optional*: Capture this Explorer window (see Section 2.3).

i. Close Explorer and remove the diskette from its drive.

Lab Exercise 2 (Section 3.2)

a. Start Explorer and maximize its window. Is the Classic style or Web style setting in effect? How do you know?

b. If the toolbar's address bar and all its standard buttons are not visible, display them. Which Explorer menu did you use (or would you have used) to display the address bar?

c. Insert the Student Disk in its drive and select this drive in the folder tree pane.

d. Perform each of the following actions in sequence. If possible, use the address bar or a standard button to carry out the task. For each action: Can it be accomplished using the address bar? Can it be accomplished using a standard button? If neither is true, how did you carry out that task?

- Display the contents of the Paint subfolder.
- Display the contents of the root folder.
- Redisplay the contents of the Paint subfolder.
- Switch from the current view to another one.

e. Reposition the standard buttons so that only the Back button is now visible. How did you accomplish this?

f. Enlarge the contents pane (reducing the size of the folder tree pane in the process) until it is as large as possible? How did you do this? Return the contents pane to its former size.

g. Close Explorer and remove the diskette from its drive.

Lab Exercise 3 (Section 3.3)

a. Start Explorer and maximize its window.

b. Insert the Student Disk in its drive and select this drive in the folder tree pane.

c. Select Small Icons view. In what order are the files listed?

d. Select all files (but no folders). How did you do this?

e. *Copy* the selected files to the Paint folder on the floppy disk by (left-) dragging them onto the Paint icon. Is it *necessary*, in this situation, to hold down the Ctrl key while dragging the files?

f. Open the Paint folder and select the Details view option. How many of the listed files are *not* of the "Bitmap Image" type?

g. *Move* (by left-drag-and-drop) the copied files back to the root folder of the floppy disk. (Answer "Yes to All" to the Confirm Replace message.) Is it *necessary*, in this situation, to hold down the Shift key while dragging the files?

h. Close Explorer and remove the diskette from its drive.

Lab Exercise 4 (Section 3.3)

a. Start Explorer, maximize its window, and select the Small Icons view option.

b. Insert the Student Disk in its drive and select this drive in the folder tree pane.

c. Select the file MemoJob1 and *cut* it to the Clipboard. Then, select the file Memo and *copy* it to the Clipboard. Was either file deleted from the contents pane?

d. Minimize Explorer and any other open windows.

e. Right-click on the Desktop and choose Paste from the pop-up menu. Which file has appeared on the Desktop?

f. Restore the Explorer window and resize and move it so that the copied file is visible on the Desktop. Now, using the right-drag technique, *move* the file back to the contents pane. (Answer "Yes" to the Confirm File Replace message.) Where in the contents pane were the file name and icon placed?

g. Close Explorer and remove the diskette from its drive.

Lab Exercise 5 (Section 3.4)

a. Start Explorer, maximize its window, and select the Small Icons view option.

b. Insert the Student Disk in its drive and select this drive in the folder tree pane.

c. Create a new subfolder of the (root) floppy drive folder. It appears highlighted in the contents pane. What is it called?

d. Rename the new folder My Folder. How did you accomplish this?

e. Size the Explorer window so that an empty part of the Desktop is visible. Then, right-drag My Folder to the Desktop, release the mouse button, and choose Create Shortcut(s) Here from the pop-up menu. How would one know, just by looking at the *icon*, that it represents a shortcut?

f. Open My Folder by choosing its Desktop shortcut. If you were in Classic style mode, would you click or double-click on it to open it? Does the My Folder window have both a left and right pane? *Optional*: Reduce this window to a small size and capture it.

g. Delete the My Folder *folder* from the floppy drive. Did the My Folder *window* close when the folder was deleted?

h. Close the My Folder window, if necessary, and delete its shortcut.

i. Open the Recycle Bin and delete any references to My Folder. Was a Confirm Delete message displayed?

j. Close Explorer and remove the diskette from its drive.

Lab Exercise 6 (Section 3.5)

a. Start My Computer, maximize its window, and select the List view option.

b. Choose the Folder Options command from the View menu. In the Folder Options dialog box, select the *Custom* option button and choose the Settings button. What is the name of the resulting dialog box?

c. In the new dialog box, select the lower of the two *Browse folders* option buttons and choose the OK button. What is the selected option called? Choose OK in the Folder Options dialog box.

d. In the My Computer window choose the icon of the drive that contains the Windows folder. Try C: first, then others. On which drive is the Windows folder located?

e. Open the Windows folder. How many subfolders does it have?

f. Successively open the following folders: Start Menu, Programs, and Accessories. What are the subfolders of Accessories?

g. Display the address bar's drop-down list. Are all the folders you have opened in this exercise listed there?

h. Select Recycle Bin from the drop-down list. In the new window, open the address bar's list again. Is the Accessories folder still listed there?

i. Close the Recycle Bin window.

Lab Exercise 7 (Section 3.5) Repeat Exercise 3, replacing every occurrence of *Explorer* by *My Computer* and *folder tree pane* by *My Computer window.*

Lab Exercise 8 (Section 3.6) [This exercise requires a blank floppy disk.]

a. Start Windows Explorer and insert a blank diskette in its drive.

b. Check the contents of the diskette by selecting the appropriate drive from the folder tree. What is displayed in the contents pane?

c. If the diskette contains any files or folders, do *not* continue this exercise! Otherwise, format the diskette, selecting the *Full* option and deselecting all check boxes in the Format dialog box. When you choose the Start command button, what message appears at the bottom of the dialog box?

d. Again use Explorer to check the contents of the diskette. Are any files or folders listed now?

e. Open the Format dialog box again. This time, select the *Copy system files only* option button (*not* the check box), and choose Start. What message is displayed in the dialog box?

f. One more time, check the diskette's contents. What are they?

g. Close Explorer and remove the diskette from its drive.

If You Want to Learn More ...

The notes presented here allow you to delve more deeply into some of the topics covered in this chapter.

Other ways to start Explorer

When you start Explorer from the Start menu's Programs submenu, this action also usually opens the root folder of the C: drive. You can also start Explorer in the following ways:

- Right-click on the Start button and then choose Explore from the pop-up menu. In this case, the Start Menu subfolder of the Windows folder will be opened.
- Right-click on the My Computer icon (or any folder icon) and then choose Explore from the pop-up menu. Here, the My Computer window (or the folder's window) will be opened.

Of course, you can also put a shortcut to Explorer on the Desktop and start Explorer by choosing this icon. An even better idea is to put several Explorer shortcuts on the Desktop and configure them to automatically open your favorite folders. Here's how:

1. Create a shortcut to Explorer as described in Section 3.4. (The easiest way is to drag the Windows Explorer item from the Start menu's Programs submenu onto the Desktop.)
2. Right-click on the Explorer shortcut's icon and choose Properties from the pop-up menu.
3. Click on the Shortcut tab in the Properties dialog box.
4. In the Target text box, type C:\EXPLORER.EXE /E, immediately followed by the path name for the folder you want to be opened when Explorer starts. For example, to automatically open the Windows folder, type: C:\EXPLORER.EXE /E,C:\WINDOWS
5. Choose the OK command button.
6. Rename the shortcut appropriately.

Starting up with Explorer running

If Explorer, My Computer, or any folder window is open when you shut down Windows, that window will open automatically the next time Windows is started. If you do not want the window to open in this situation, hold down the Shift key when you hear the "start-up sound" — just as the Desktop icons begin to appear on the screen. Holding down the Shift key also causes Windows to ignore the applications present in your StartUp folder (see Section 4.2); they, too, will not open when Windows starts.

Repositioning the menu bar and toolbar

In Section 3.2, we mentioned that the set of standard buttons in Explorer can be moved left, right, up, or down by dragging its "position button". This trick will also work in My Computer or any folder window. It is also possible to reposition the menu and address bars by dragging their position buttons, which are located just to the left of these objects (as shown at the right), to a new location. For example, in the figure below, the address bar and menu bar have been dragged toward the top and bottom of the screen, respectively, to create the arrangement shown here.

File

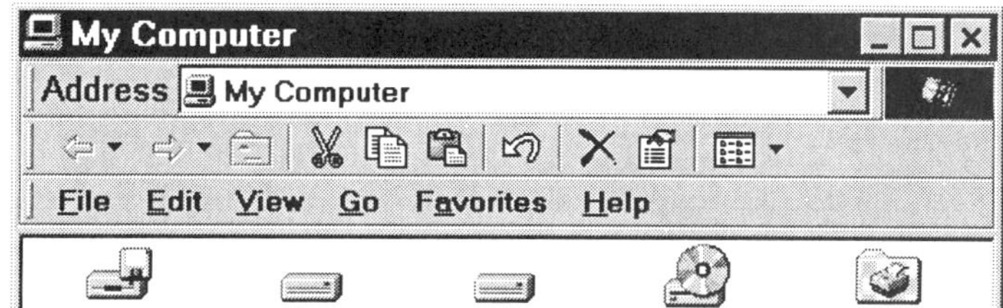

Keyboard alternatives in Explorer

There are many keyboard shortcuts that work with Explorer (most also work in any folder window). Here are a few that you might find useful:

- Asterisk (on the numeric keypad) expands all folders in the folder tree pane.
- Backspace opens the parent of the current folder.
- Ctrl+A selects all objects in the contents pane.
- Ctrl+C or Ctrl+X copies or cuts, respectively, all selected objects to the Clipboard; Ctrl+V pastes objects from the Clipboard.
- Home or End selects the object at the top or bottom of the active pane (folder tree or contents).
- Plus or Minus (on the numeric keypad) expands or collapses, respectively, the folder selected in the folder tree pane.
- Shift+Del deletes the selected objects without sending them to the Recycle Bin.

For a complete list of shortcut keys, see Appendix A.

Recycle Bin properties

As you know, when you "delete" a file, folder, or shortcut that resides on a hard drive or the Desktop, it is normally sent to the Recycle Bin after you respond Yes to a confirmation message. (Objects deleted from floppy disks or cut to the Clipboard are not placed in the Recycle Bin; they are immediately deleted.) To change the way the Recycle Bin works:

- Right-click on the Recycle Bin icon and choose Properties from the resulting pop-up menu. The Recycle Bin Properties dialog box will be displayed.
- If you want objects removed from disk immediately as you delete them, select the *Do not send files to the Recycle Bin* check box.
- If you don't want a confirmation message displayed when you delete objects, deselect the *Display delete confirmation dialog box* check box.

The Recycle Bin Properties dialog box offers additional options that you might want to explore on your own.

More on choosing files and folders

As you know, when you *choose* a file or folder (click on it in Web style mode or double-click on it in Classic style mode) in Explorer, My Computer, or any folder window, that object opens. Here are a couple of other things you should know about this concept (still more will be said in Section 4.4):

- If you want to open several objects at once, select them and hold down the Ctrl key while choosing one of them. (If you don't hold down the Ctrl key, then, even though several objects may be selected, only the one you choose will open.)
- In My Computer or any folder window, choosing a folder icon opens a folder window with a single-pane view of its contents. If you want an Explorer-like, dual-pane view instead, right-click on the folder icon and choose Explore from the pop-up menu.

Windows Explorer and the Web

Compared to previous versions of Windows, Windows 98 has added some Internet-related features and improved on others, and integrated the Internet (and its World Wide Web) more closely into the operating system. (The Internet and Web integration will be discussed in Chapter 6.) In Windows 98, you can:

- Configure icons to look and act like "Web links" as described in Section 1.2.
- Start the Internet Explorer Web browser from within:

  Windows Explorer by clicking on *The Internet* object in the folder tree pane;

Windows Explorer, My Computer, or any folder window by clicking on *The Internet* object in the address bar's drop-down list or on the Windows logo button on the menu bar.

- Access a particular Web site from within Windows Explorer, My Computer, or any folder window by typing the address in the address bar's text box and pressing Enter.
- Provide a "Web view" of My Computer or any folder window by choosing the corresponding item from the View menu.
- Make any folder window resemble a Web page by choosing the Customize this Folder item from the View menu.
- Provide easy access to certain Web pages from within Windows Explorer, My Computer, or any folder window by using the Explorer Bar command on the View menu.

More on folder view options

As you have seen, the View menu in Explorer, My Computer, or any folder window provides a lot of flexibility as to how the contents of a folder are displayed. You can fine-tune these settings by using the View page of the Folder Options dialog box. Recall that this dialog box can be opened by choosing the Folder Options item from the View menu. It can also be opened by clicking on the Start button, pointing at the Settings option, and choosing Folder Options from the resulting submenu.

In Section 3.5, we discussed a few of the "Advanced settings" available on the View page. You can determine the function of each of the other options by right-clicking on it, which pops up a one-item *What's This?* menu, and then clicking on this item. To close the explanatory pop-up window, click anywhere in the dialog box.

The View page also contains three command buttons that can save you a lot of time in creating a consistent look for all your folder windows.

- Choosing the *Like Current Folder* button applies the View menu settings for the active folder window (except for those that refer to the toolbars) to all folder windows. (This button is dimmed if you open the Folder Options dialog box from the Start menu.)
- Choosing the *Reset All Folders* button returns the View menu settings of all folder windows to their defaults — the settings that were in effect after installation of Windows 98.
- Choosing the *Restore Defaults* button returns the "Advanced" settings to the ones in effect after installation of Windows 98.

Where to go from here

Here's where to find more information about some of the topics discussed in this chapter.

- Copying, moving, deleting, and renaming files and folders using the Windows Find utility — Section 4.3
- Creating shortcuts:

  On the Start menu and Programs option submenus — Section 4.2
  Using the Find utility — Section 4.3
- The Folder Options dialog box, File Types page — Section 4.4
- Properties of shortcuts — Section 4.6
- The Web-related aspects of Explorer, My Computer, and folder windows — Section 6.6

CHAPTER 4

Using Windows Efficiently

Overview

In Chapters 2 and 3, we presented basic information about working with applications, documents, files, folders, and disks. You will probably make use of some of this material every time you use Windows. In this chapter, we present additional information about these topics. Although none of this new material is critical, it should help you to use Windows more productively. You will learn:

1. To move the Taskbar to another location, increase its size, hide it from view, and add toolbars to it.
2. To rearrange (tile or cascade) open application windows, or minimize them all at once, if so desired.
3. To customize the Start button menus by adding or deleting items from them.
4. To use the Windows Find utility to search for files and folders on your hard disk and, once found, to manipulate (for example, move or copy) these files and folders.
5. To associate a file type (extension) with a specific application.
6. To change printer settings and manage print jobs.
7. To add a new printer to your system.
8. To display the property sheet for a file, folder, or shortcut, and interpret the information found there.

4.1 Tricks with the Taskbar

The **Taskbar** (Figure 1) is a key element in the Windows 98 interface. As you know, the Taskbar contains the Start button, which provides access to the Start menu, and a button for each open application. By default, it also contains a digital clock, a toolbar, and a few other icons. In this section, we will discuss the kinds of things you can do with the Taskbar.

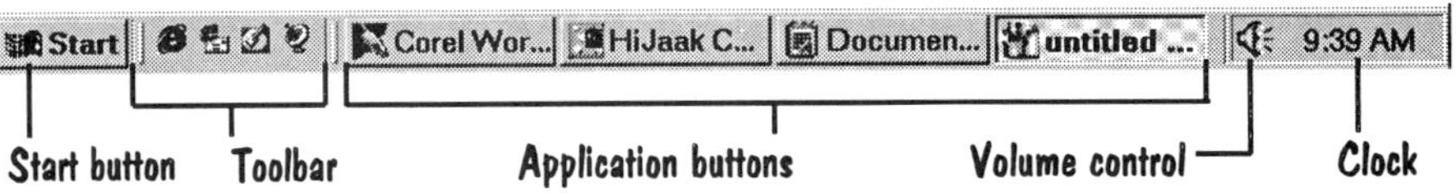

Figure 1 A Typical Taskbar

Changing the Way the Taskbar is Displayed

By default, the Taskbar is positioned at the bottom of the screen and is always visible, even when application windows are maximized. If you wish, you can:

- Increase the size of the Taskbar, reposition it along another edge of the screen, or hide it from view.
- Remove the clock and/or other icons from the Taskbar.

We will now describe how to perform these tasks.

Increasing the Size of the Taskbar The standard one-row Taskbar provides enough space for the default toolbar and a few application buttons. If you like to run a lot of applications at the same time or want to make use of additional toolbars (as described later in this section), you may wish to increase the size of the Taskbar. To do so:

1. Move the mouse cursor over the top edge of the Taskbar. It will become a double-headed arrow when positioned properly.
2. Drag the cursor upward until the Taskbar is the desired height. The Taskbar objects will be repositioned (and some will be resized) when you release the mouse button.

Here is a two-row high Taskbar:

If the meaning of a Taskbar button or icon is not clear to you, just point at it; a *tool tip* will display its full name.

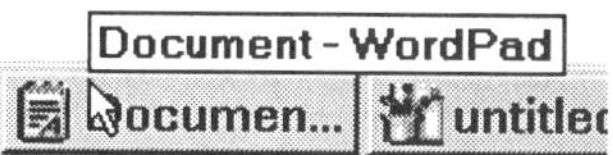

Repositioning the Taskbar The Taskbar can be positioned at any of the four edges of the screen. To move the Taskbar from its current location to another edge of the screen:

1. Position the mouse cursor over an empty part of the Taskbar.
2. Hold down the left mouse button and drag the cursor toward one of the other screen edges. As you approach this edge, the Taskbar will reposition itself there.
3. Release the mouse button to complete the procedure. The figure below shows the Taskbar at the left edge of the screen.

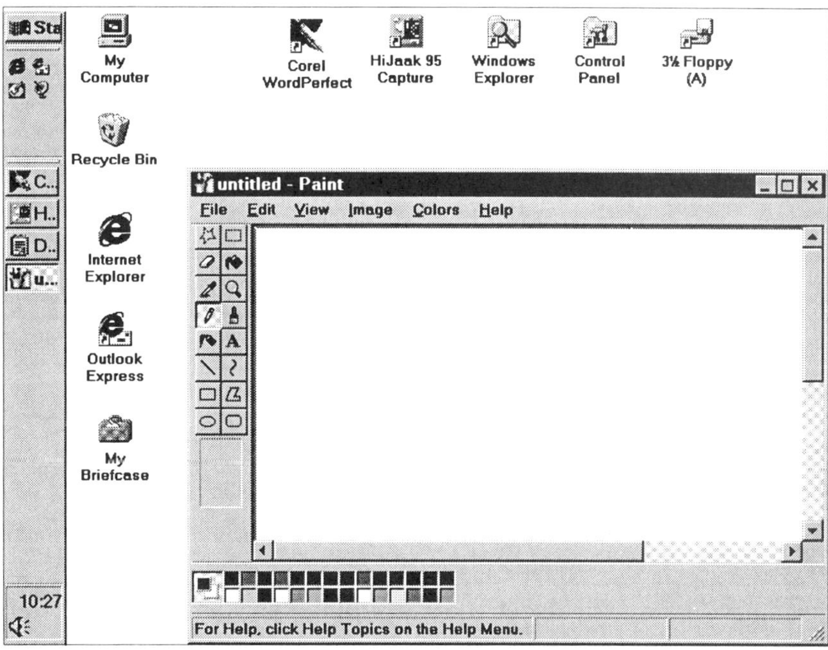

Hiding the Taskbar The Taskbar is convenient to have around, but it does take up space on the Desktop. At times, you may want to hide the Taskbar so that application windows can use the entire screen. To hide the Taskbar (or redisplay it if it is currently hidden):

1. Click on the Start button to open the Start menu, point at the Settings option, and choose the Taskbar & Start Menu item on the resulting submenu. The Taskbar Properties dialog box, shown in Figure 2, will be displayed. (You can also open this dialog box by right-clicking on an empty part of the Taskbar and choosing Properties from the resulting pop-up menu.)

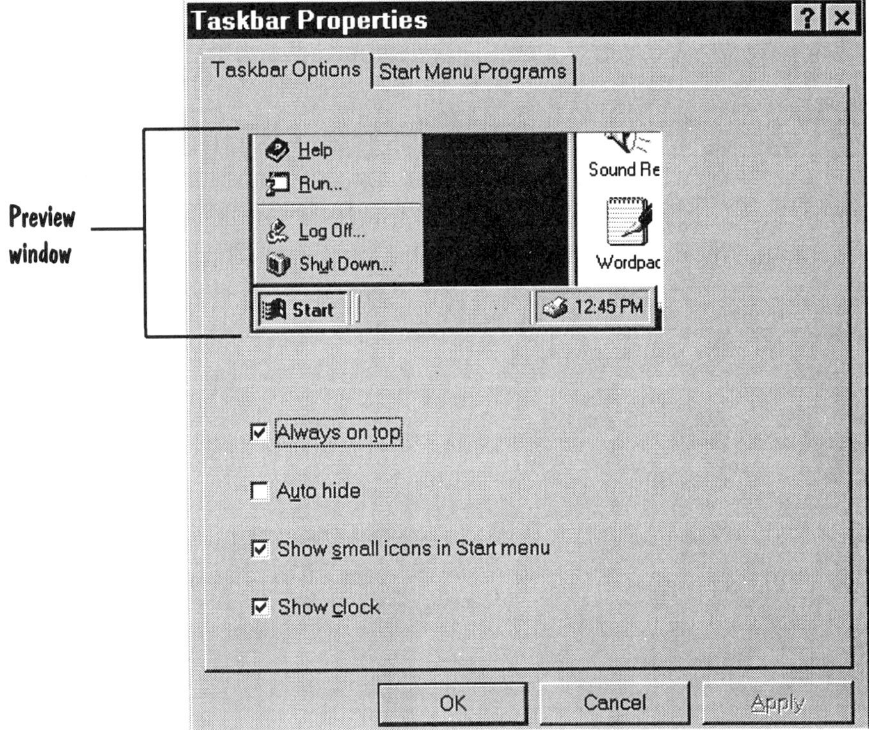

Figure 2 The Taskbar Properties Dialog Box

2. Select the *Always on top* check box to prevent the Taskbar from being obscured by windows that might otherwise cover it.
3. Select the *Auto hide* check box to hide the Taskbar. When Auto hide is selected, the Taskbar is reduced to a thin line at the edge

of the screen. To temporarily redisplay the Taskbar, point the mouse at this thin line. Moving the mouse pointer away from that edge of the screen will cause the Taskbar to disappear again.

4. Choose the OK command button to put your changes into effect and close the dialog box, or choose the Apply button to put your changes into effect without closing the dialog box.

Selecting the "auto hide" feature is a convenient way to increase the amount of screen real estate available to your running applications. Be aware, however, that if *Always on top* is not selected and an application is running full-screen, pointing at the Taskbar "line" will not display the Taskbar; it will still be obscured by the application window! Also keep in mind that you can *always* display the Taskbar (and simultaneously open the Start menu) by pressing the Ctrl+Esc keystroke combination.

Hiding the Clock To hide the Taskbar clock (which provides a little more room for application buttons):

1. Open the Taskbar Properties dialog box (Figure 2), as described above.
2. Deselect the *Show Clock* check box. (Reselecting this check box will, of course, redisplay the clock if it is currently hidden.)
3. Choose the OK command button.

Placing Toolbars on the Taskbar

Windows 98 allows you to place certain kinds of *toolbars* on the Taskbar. These toolbars can help you access commonly used applications, folders, shortcuts, and even the Internet.

To place a toolbar on the Taskbar:

1. Right-click on an empty part of the Taskbar.
2. Point at the Toolbars item on the resulting pop-up menu, which opens the submenu shown at the right.

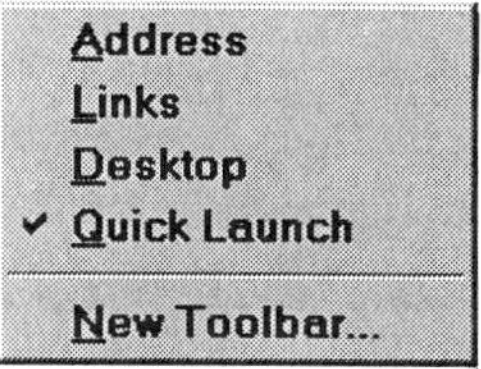

3. Click on one of the top four options, to place the corresponding *standard* toolbar on the Taskbar (or remove it from the

Taskbar if it's already there) or click on New Toolbar, which allows you to place the contents of a folder of your choice on the Taskbar.

Here's is a description of each item on the Toolbars submenu.

- *Address* places an address bar, like the one in Windows Explorer, on the Taskbar. You can use this toolbar to open a folder (by typing its path name) or access a Web site (by typing its URL — see Section 6.2).
- *Links* places Internet Explorer's Links toolbar on the Taskbar, which allows you to quickly access a few specific Web sites.
- *Desktop* places copies of all Desktop icons on the Taskbar.
- *Quick Launch* places a Show Desktop icon on the Taskbar together with icons that can be used to open (launch) certain Internet-related applications (see Chapter 6). Clicking on the Show Desktop icon minimizes all open windows; clicking on it again restores these windows.

Custom toolbars

- *New Toolbar* allows you to place the contents of a specified folder on the Taskbar. This, in turn, enables you to add *any* set of icons to the Taskbar. To do so, just create a new folder (Section 3.4), copy the desired objects into it (Section 3.3), and then use the New Toolbar option to place that folder's contents on the Taskbar.

NOTE

If the Taskbar is not big enough to display all the contents of a toolbar, left and right scroll arrows are displayed (as shown for the Desktop toolbar below) so that you can scroll through the various icons.

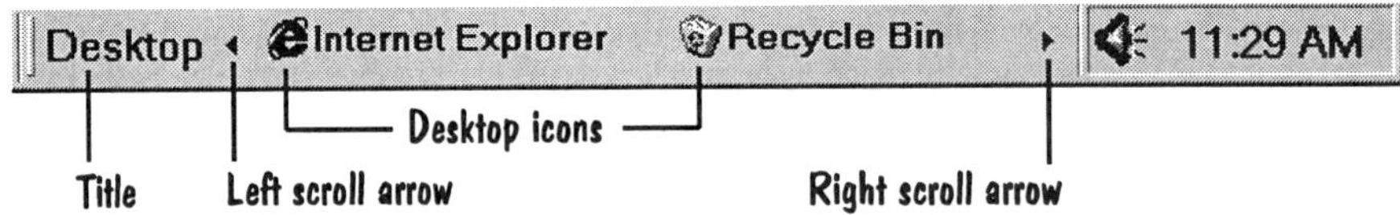

TIP

If a Taskbar toolbar has a large number of icons, you can ensure that it takes up a minimal amount of space in the following way. First, right-click on an empty part of that toolbar to pop up the menu shown on the right of Figure 3. (If you right-click on the Taskbar outside of a toolbar, the menu on the left of Figure 3 pops up.) Then:

- Point at the View item and then choose Small to display small icons for that toolbar.
- If a check mark appears next to the Show Text item, choose this option to hide the names of all icons in the affected toolbar.
- If a check mark appears next to the Show Title item, choose this option to hide the name of the toolbar itself.

Another way to deal with this situation is to increase the size of the Taskbar as described earlier in this section and then reposition the toolbar by dragging its position button to the desired location.

Figure 3 Taskbar Pop-up Menus

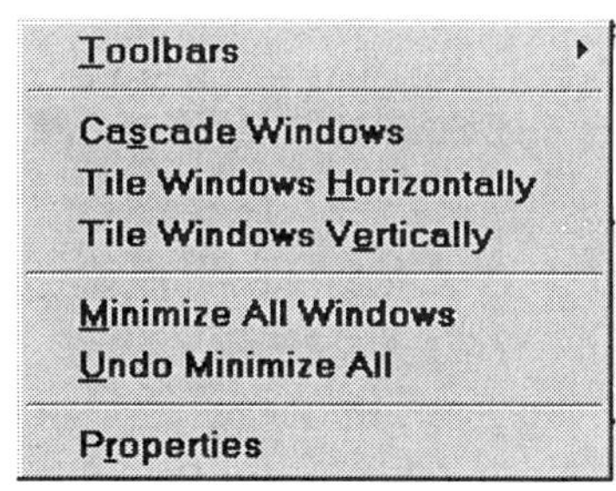

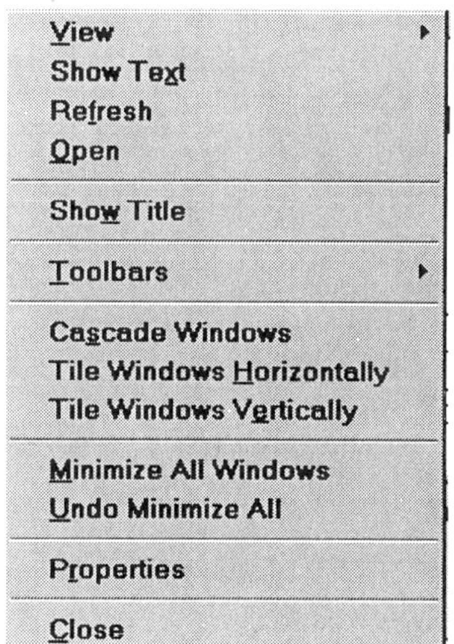

Manipulating Application Windows

Right-clicking on the Taskbar pops up one of the menus shown in Figure 3 (depending on where you click). Using either menu, you can:

- Rearrange windows by **cascading** or **tiling** them on the Desktop.

- Minimize all open windows simultaneously, or restore all windows that have been minimized.

Arranging Windows on the Desktop Three items on the Taskbar pop-up menus shown in Figure 3 affect the way open application windows are grouped on the Desktop:

- Choosing the Cascade Windows command overlaps the windows in such a way that little more than the title bars of the back windows are visible (Figure 4).
- Choosing the Tile Windows Horizontally command arranges the windows in a non-overlapping fashion, one above the other. The effect is shown in Figure 5.
- Choosing the Tile Windows Vertically command arranges the windows side-by-side in a non-overlapping fashion. See Figure 6.

NOTE

The Cascade and Tile commands only apply to the windows that are open when the command is issued. If another window is opened or restored later on, it will not be included in the grouping. However, if you maximize or minimize one of the grouped windows and then restore it, the original cascading or tiling will also be restored.

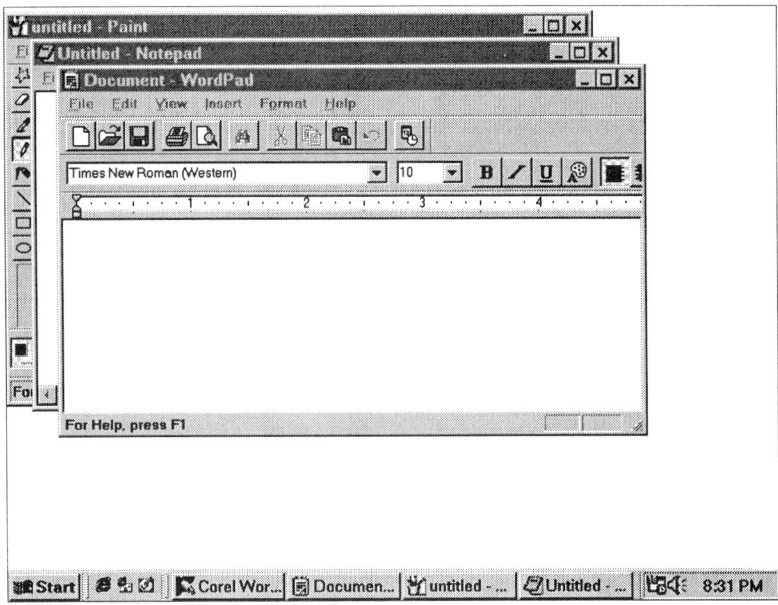

Figure 4 Cascading Windows

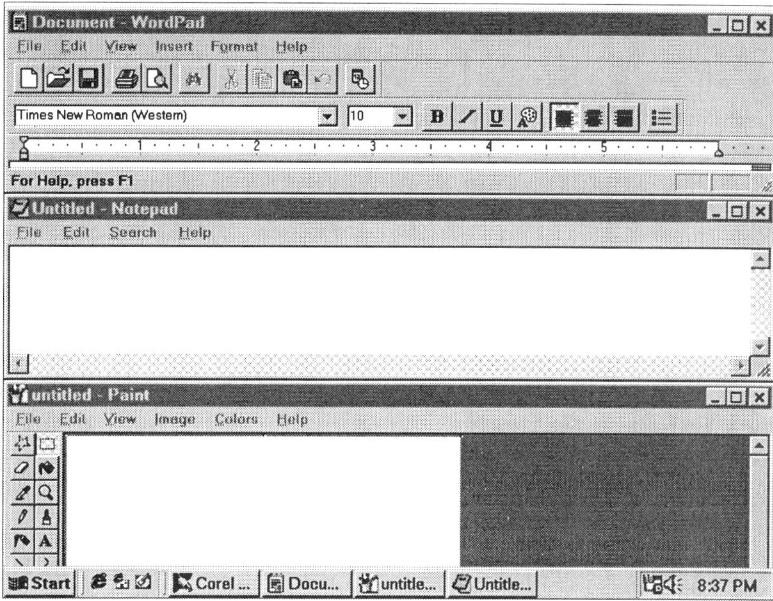

Figure 5 Windows Tiled Horizontally

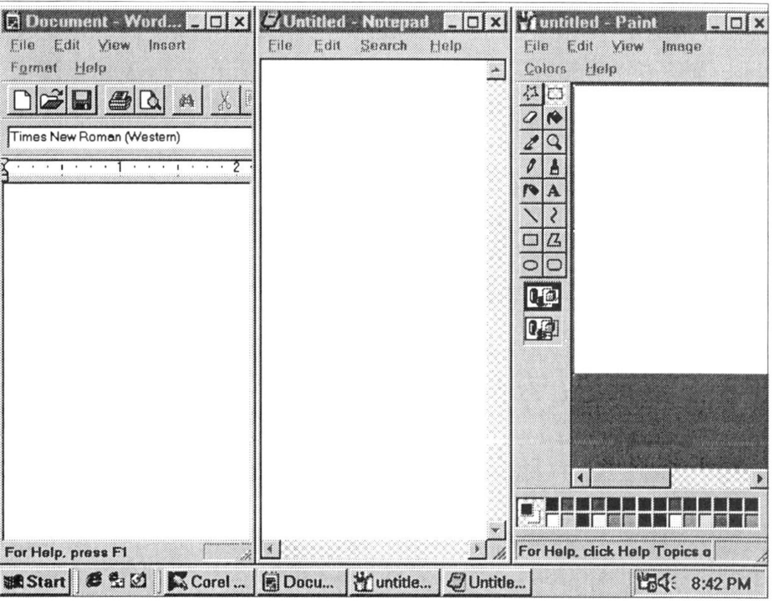

Figure 6 Windows Tiled Vertically

Minimizing All Open Windows The Minimize All Windows command on the pop-up Taskbar menu does just that — it minimizes all open windows. It has the same effect as clicking on the Show Desktop icon described earlier in this section. When you reopen the pop-up Taskbar menu after issuing this command or clicking on the Show Desktop icon, you will notice another available option — Undo Minimize All. As you might guess, choosing this menu item restores all windows that had been reduced to Taskbar buttons by either technique.

TUTORIAL

Try the following exercise on your own.

1. Turn on your computer, if necessary, to start Windows 98 and close any open windows.
2. If the Taskbar is not visible on the screen, press Ctrl+Esc to display it and the Start menu; then press Esc to close the latter.
3. Reposition the Taskbar at another edge of the screen by dragging it there; that is, mouse-point at an empty part of the Taskbar, press (and hold down) the mouse button, move the pointer to the desired edge of the screen, and release the button.
4. Position the Taskbar at the bottom edge of the screen.
5. Change the size of the Taskbar: Position the mouse pointer over the top edge of the Taskbar (the pointer will become a double-headed arrow), drag the pointer upward (the Taskbar will grow in size), and release the mouse button. Now, return the Taskbar to its former size by a similar process.
6. Open the Taskbar Properties dialog box by clicking on the Start button, pointing at the Settings option, and choosing the Taskbar & Start Menu command from the resulting submenu.
7. Select the *Auto-hide* check box and choose the Apply command button. The Taskbar will disappear from the screen. To redisplay it, move the mouse pointer past the bottom edge of the screen. Move the pointer away from the bottom edge of the screen, and the Taskbar will disappear again.
8. Deselect Auto-hide and choose the OK command button to close the dialog box.
9. Open the WordPad application (from the Accessories submenu of the Start menu's Programs option) and maximize it. Then, open the Paint application (also on the Accessories submenu) and maximize it.

10. Right-click on an empty part of the Taskbar, successively choose each of the following commands from the resulting pop-up menu, and notice the effect. (You will have to reopen this menu before issuing a new command.)
    - Cascade Windows
    - Tile Windows Horizontally
    - Tile Windows Vertically
    - Minimize All Windows
    - Undo Minimize All
11. Right-click on an empty part of the Taskbar, point at the Toolbars item, and, if there is no check mark next to it, choose the Quick Launch item from the resulting submenu. There should now be a toolbar consisting of four icons on the Taskbar.
12. Point at each icon and use the tool tip to identify it. Click on the Show Desktop icon to minimize the application windows.
13. Click again on the Show Desktop icon to restore the windows.
14. Close all open windows.

4.2 *Customizing the Start Button Menus*

When Windows 98 is installed on a computer, it automatically creates the Start menu and several submenus, and places certain items on them. Moreover, whenever Windows applications are installed, additional menu items are created. In this section, we will demonstrate how you can "manually" add items to, or remove them from, the Start menu or one of its Programs option's submenus. (For simplicity's sake, we will refer to these menus collectively as the **Start button menus.**)

Location of the menu shortcuts

Each item on a Start button menu is actually a *shortcut* (see Section 3.4) to a file or folder. These shortcuts are small files stored in various related folders. The shortcuts on the Start menu itself are located in the Start Menu subfolder of the Windows folder, and those in the Programs option submenu are located in the Programs subfolder of the Start Menu folder. Similarly, each submenu of the Programs option corresponds to a subfolder of the Programs folder. Part of the folder tree is shown at the right.

Choosing a menu item

The shortcuts on the Start button menus may represent applications, documents, or folders. In fact, any file or folder listed in Explorer can be placed on these menus. Clicking on a menu item (shortcut) opens the corresponding file or folder. To be more specific, clicking on

- A shortcut to a program file starts the corresponding application.
- A shortcut to a document starts the application associated with it and then opens the document within that application.
- A shortcut to a folder opens the corresponding folder, displaying its contents in a window.

Thus, the Start button menus can be configured to provide easy access to your most-used applications, documents, and folders. The Start menu itself is an especially convenient location for shortcuts to your favorite things. Although Desktop icons can be used for the same purpose, they are often buried beneath an open window or two. The Start menu, on the other hand, is always a mouse click (or, at worst, the Ctrl+Esc keystroke) away from the task at hand.

The Easiest Way to Add or Remove Items

The easiest way to add an item to a Start button menu is by dragging the relevant file or folder (or a shortcut to it) onto the Start button or the desired submenu of the Start menu. To be more specific:

1. Start Windows Explorer or My Computer and locate and select the file or folder that you want to add — as a shortcut — to a Start button menu. (The easiest way to locate a particular item is by using the Windows Find utility, which is discussed in Section 4.3.)
2. To add the item to the top of the Start menu, drag it onto the Start button and release the mouse button.

   To add the item to a submenu of the Start menu:

   - Drag the item on top of the Start button, but don't release the mouse button. The Start menu will open.
   - Continuing to hold down the mouse button, point at the appropriate menu names until the submenu to which you want to add the selected item is open.
   - Position the mouse pointer (an arrow and thick horizontal line) on this submenu at the location where you would like the selected item to be listed. Release the mouse button, and the item will appear at that location.

You can also use drag-and-drop (or cut-and-paste) to move a shortcut from one Start button menu to another. Here's how it works.

1. Click on the Start button and open the submenu (if necessary) on which the shortcut is located.
2. Select (highlight) the item that you want to move by pointing at it.
3. Either
   - Hold down the mouse button, drag the cursor to the desired Start button submenu, and release the mouse button.

   or
   - Right-click on the selected item and choose Cut from the pop-up menu. Then, select the Start button group to which you want to add the item, right-click on it, and choose Paste from the pop-up menu.

In either case, the shortcut will be moved to that submenu. For example, to move an item from the top of the Start menu to the Accessories submenu of the Program's option, highlight it and either

- Drag it onto the Accessories submenu (*not* onto the Accessories *item* on the Programs submenu).

or
- Right-click on it, choose Cut from the pop-up menu, point at the Accessories *item* on the Programs menu, right-click on it, and choose Paste from the pop-up menu.

NOTE

After adding a shortcut to a Start button menu, you may want to rename it. Unfortunately, this takes some work. To rename the new shortcut, start Explorer or My Computer and open the folder in which all Start button menu shortcuts are stored — the Start Menu subfolder of the Windows folder. Locate the desired shortcut in that folder (or one of its subfolders) and rename it using one of the techniques described in Section 3.4.

Removing menu items

To remove an item (shortcut) from a Start button menu, just:

1. Select (highlight) the item by pointing at it.
2. Right-click on the selected item.
3. Choose the Delete command from the pop-up menu. A "confirm delete" dialog box will open.
4. Choose the Yes command button in this dialog box.

Other Ways to Add and Remove Menu Items

You can also add or remove items from a Start button menu by working with the Start Menu folder or one of its subfolders. The desired folder can be accessed indirectly with the aid of the Taskbar Properties dialog box or directly by suing Windows Explorer.

Using the Taskbar Properties Dialog Box To add or remove a menu item using the Taskbar Properties dialog box:

1. Open this dialog box by either:
   - Pointing at the Settings option on the Start menu and choosing Taskbar & Start Menu from the resulting submenu.

   or
   - Right-clicking on an empty part of the Taskbar and choosing Properties from the resulting pop-up menu.
2. Display the Start Menu Programs page (Figure 7).

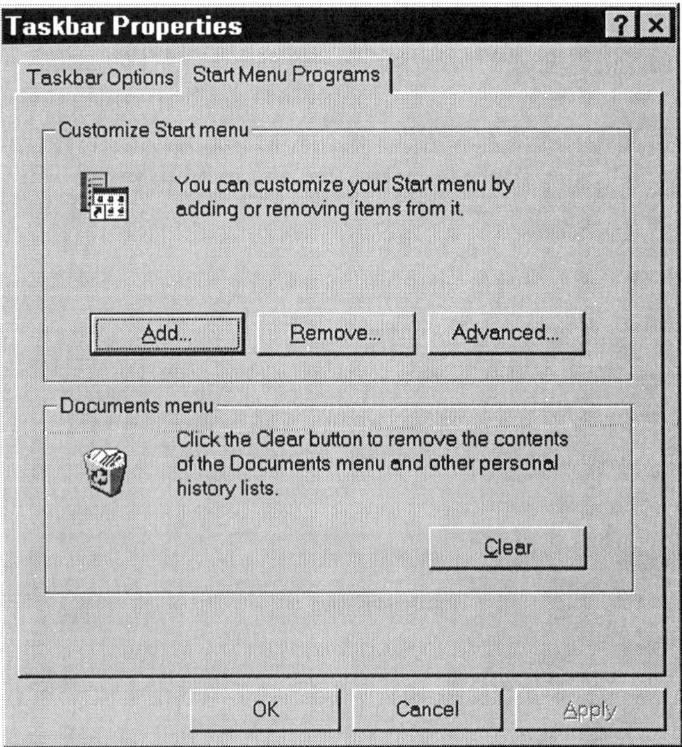

Figure 7 Clicking on the Start Menu Programs Tab

3. Choose the Add command button. This action starts a Create Shortcut "wizard" and opens the corresponding dialog box.
4. If you know the path name (see Section 3.1) of the file or folder for which you want to create a menu item, type it in the Command line text box. Otherwise, choose the Browse command button, which opens a Browse dialog box to help you locate the file or folder. (Browsing folders is discussed in Section 3.5.)
5. Click on the Next command button. The Select Program Folder dialog box will open (Figure 8) and display a folder tree showing the Start Menu folder (which contains the shortcuts on the Start menu) and its subfolders (which correspond to the Programs option menu and its submenus).

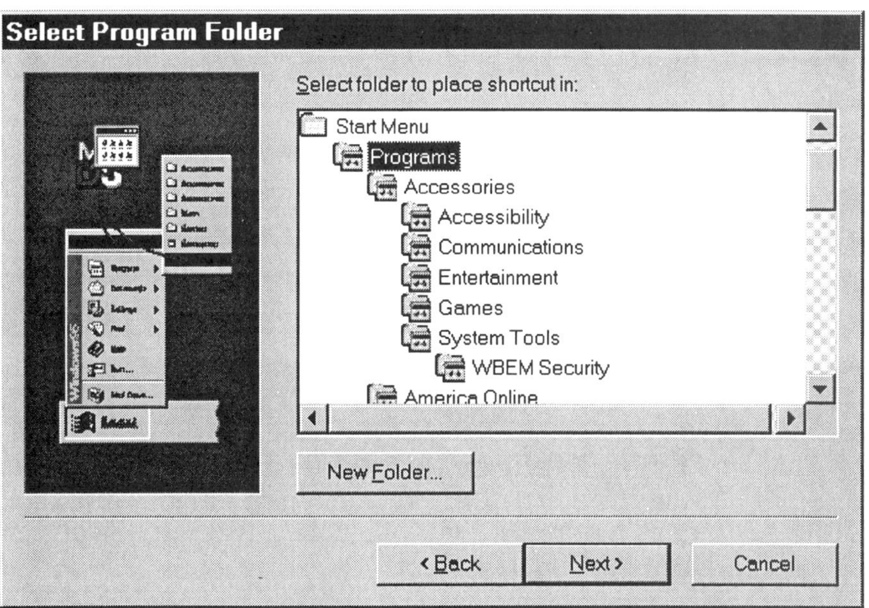

Figure 8 The Select Program Folder Dialog Box

6. If you want to create a new submenu, select the folder corresponding to the menu on which you want your new submenu to appear, and choose the New Folder command button. (At the right, we show the result of selecting Accessories and then choosing New Folder.) A new subfolder will be displayed. To rename it, just type a new name.

7. Select (click on) the folder that corresponds to the menu in which you want the new shortcut to appear.
8. Choose the Next command button. A new dialog box will appear allowing you to select a name for the new shortcut. If you don't want to use the default name, type a new name in the text box.
10. Choose the Finish command button, which returns you to the Taskbar Properties dialog box.
11. Choose the OK command button to close this dialog box.

The Windows\Start Menu\Programs folder contains a special subfolder called StartUp. Each application, document, and folder contained in the StartUp folder automatically opens every time you start Windows. Thus, if you run certain applications whenever you use Windows, you might consider adding their shortcuts to the StartUp folder.

NOTE

The Remove command button

You can also use the Taskbar Properties dialog box to remove a Start button menu item. To do so, choose the Remove command button on the Start Menu Programs page. This action opens a dialog box that allows you select the items you want to remove. It is easier, however, to remove a menu item by just right-clicking on it (on its Start button menu) and choosing Delete from the resulting pop-up menu, as described earlier in this section.

Using Explorer to Add/Remove Menu Items If you examine the Start Menu Programs page of the Taskbar Properties dialog box (Figure 7), you will notice two additional command buttons: Advanced and Clear.

The Advanced command button

Choosing the Advanced button starts Explorer, displaying a folder tree with the Start Menu folder at its root. Then, using the techniques described in Sections 3.3 and 3.4, you can:

- Place a shortcut in the Start Menu folder or any of its subfolders. This action adds an item to the corresponding menu.
- Delete an existing shortcut from a folder, which removes the corresponding item from its menu.
- Move or copy a shortcut from one folder to another, thus moving or copying the corresponding item from one menu to another.

If you are comfortable with Explorer, you may find that using the

Advanced button is preferable to the other methods for customizing the Start button menus.

NOTE

Since the Advanced button does nothing more than start Explorer, the techniques just described for adding, removing, or moving menu items can be accomplished without opening the Taskbar Properties dialog box. Just start Explorer in the usual way or, better yet, right-click on the Start button and choose Explore from the pop-up menu, which starts Explorer and opens the Start Menu folder.

The Clear command button

Choosing the Clear command button in the Taskbar Properties dialog box removes all items from the Documents submenu of the Start menu. No warning message is given.

If you would like to remove a *single* item from the Documents menu, right-click on it and choose Delete from the pop-up menu. As an alternative, you can start Explorer, open the Recent subfolder of the Windows folder (which contains the shortcuts on the Documents submenu), and delete the appropriate shortcut from this subfolder.

TUTORIAL

Try the following exercise on your own.

1. Turn on your computer, if necessary, to start Windows 98 and close any open windows.
2. Start Explorer (from the Programs submenu of the Start menu) and open the Accessories subfolder of the Program Files folder.
3. Add a shortcut for the WordPad application to the Start menu by dragging the Wordpad file name from the contents pane onto the Start button. (If you now click on the latter, you will see "Wordpad" listed toward the top of the Start menu.)
4. Now, use another technique to add a shortcut for the Paint application to the Programs option submenu of the Start menu:
   - Open the Taskbar Properties dialog box by right-clicking on an empty part of the Taskbar and choosing Properties from the resulting submenu.
   - Click on the Start Menu Programs tab in this dialog box.
   - Choose the Add command button, which starts the Create Shortcut wizard.

- Now enter the path name for Paint in the *Command line* text box by choosing the Browse command button, opening the Accessories subfolder of the Program Files folder, selecting "Mspaint", and pressing the Enter key.
- Choose the Next command button, which opens the Select Program Folder dialog box.
- To tell Windows that you want the shortcut on the Programs submenu, select the Programs folder in the tree and choose the Next command button, which opens another dialog box.
- Finally, select a name for the new menu item: Type *Paint* in the text box and choose the Finish command button. (You can check, if you want, that a Paint item now appears on the Programs submenu of the Start menu.)

5. Remove the Paint item from the Programs submenu by right-clicking on it and choosing Delete from the pop-up menu.
6. Remove the Wordpad item from the Start menu in another way:
   - On the Start Menu Programs page of the Taskbar Properties dialog box, choose the Remove command button.
   - In the resulting folder tree, select Wordpad (which is listed as a subfolder of Start Menu, toward the bottom of the tree).
   - Choose the Remove command button; then choose Close.
7. Close all open windows.

4.3 The Windows Find Utility

A typical hard disk contains thousands of files spread across dozens of folders. As a result, locating a particular file or folder (say, to create a shortcut for it) can be a daunting task. Fortunately, Windows provides a powerful utility, called **Find**, that helps you with the search. In this section, we will discuss how to use Find to locate files and folders. (If you can access the Internet from your computer, Find can also help you search for information and even for people!)

The Find Utility Window

There are several ways to start the Find utility:

- Click on the Start button, point at the Find option, and choose Files or Folders from the resulting submenu.

- Right-click on the Start button, the My Computer icon, or any folder icon, and choose the Find item from the pop-up menu.
- Click on an empty part of the Desktop and then press the F3 function key.
- In Explorer, either press the F3 function key, or point at the Find command on the Tools menu and choose Files or Folders from the resulting submenu.

In any case, the Find window (Figure 9) will open.

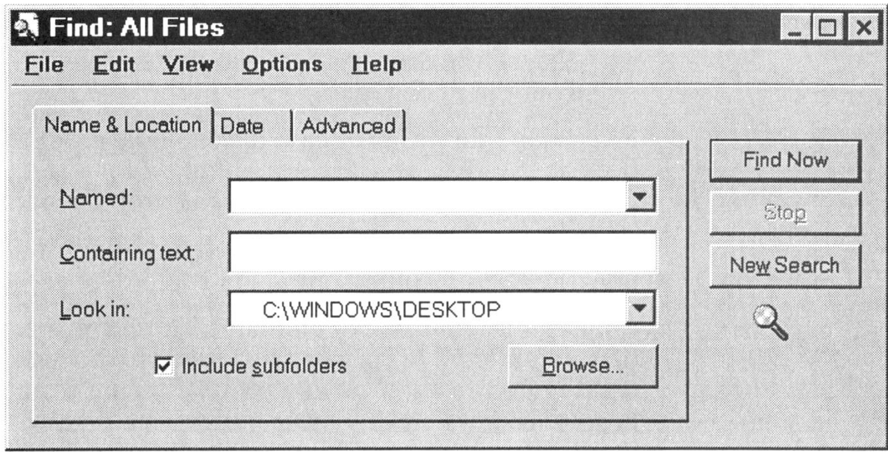

Figure 9 The Find Window

Since Find is an application, its window can be resized, minimized, or maximized. Notice (in Figure 9) that the Find window contains both pull-down menus and tabs. The menus provide capabilities that are similar to those of Explorer; the tabs supply options that help narrow the search for a particular file or folder.

Performing Simple Searches

Typically, we use the Find utility to locate a file or folder because:

- We have forgotten its name.

or

- We don't know in which folder it is located.

If you know the name of the file or folder ...

If you know the name (or at least part of the name) of the file or folder you are seeking, proceed as follows:

1. Start the Find utility, as described above.
2. Type the name (or partial name) of the file or folder in the *Named* text box. (The *Named* drop-down list contains the entries for recent searches.)
3. If you know the folder that contains the object you are seeking, enter that folder in the *Look in* text box. As an alternative, you can either

   - Select the folder from the *Look in* drop-down list.

   or

   - Choose the Browse button and then select the desired folder from the folder tree.

   If you don't know in which folder to look, enter the drive designation of the disk you are searching — for example, C: — in the *Look in* text box or select it from the drop-down list.
4. Select the *Include subfolders* check box if you want to search, not only the *Look in* folder, but all its subfolders as well.
5. Choose the Find Now command button to start the search. All files and folders in the specified folders whose names contain the text entered in the *Named* text box will be displayed in a Search Results window in the lower part of the Find window; the status bar indicates the number of files found (Figure 10).

You can use *wildcards* in the *Named* text box to narrow the search. A **wildcard** is a symbol that represents one or more characters of any kind. Windows uses two wildcards:

- The symbol * represents any number of consecutive characters.
- The symbol ? represents any single character.

For example, in the *Named* text box, entering

.	displays all files and folders.
*.exe	displays all files with extension *exe*.
start??.*	displays all files with names that contain *start*, followed by two characters and any extension.
?s?	displays all files and folders with *s* somewhere in the name from the second to the next-to-last character.
?s?.*	displays all files with a three-letter name and *s* as the second letter.

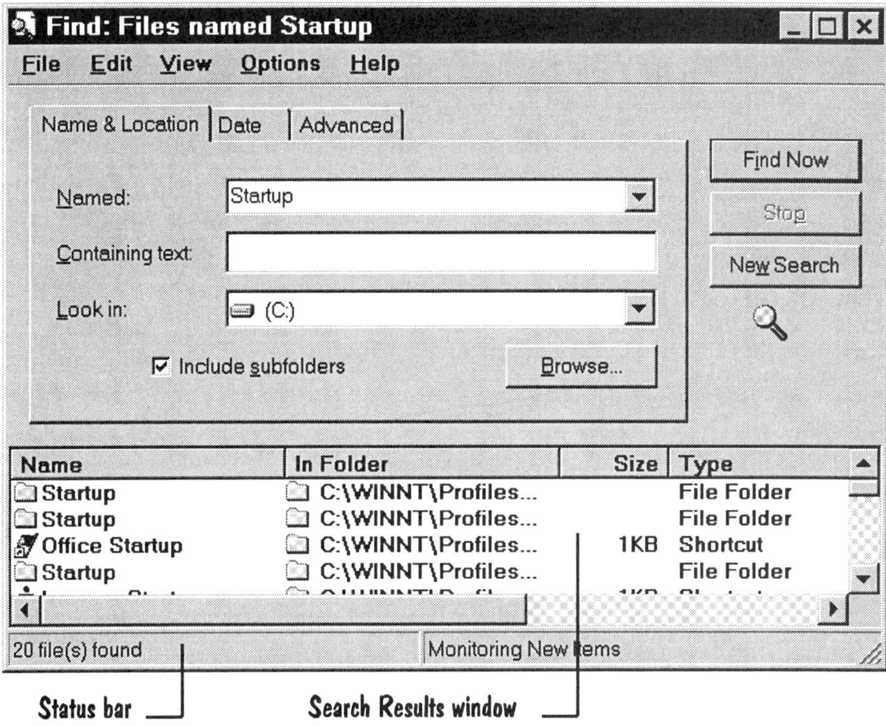

Figure 10 The Find Window After a Search

If the file you're seeking contains distinctive text

If you are looking for a document (such as a letter or report) that contains distinctive text (such as a person's name), then follow the search procedure just given, but:

- Leave the *Named* text box empty.
- Enter the distinctive text in the *Containing text* text box before choosing the Find Now command button.

For example, if you're trying to locate a letter you wrote to Al Lopez that is stored somewhere on your C: drive, follow these steps:

1. Open the Find window as described above.
2. Type *Lopez* in the *Containing text* text box.
3. Enter C: in the *Look in* text box and make sure the *Include subfolders* check box is selected.
4. Choose the Find Now command button.

Refining the Search Criteria

If you do not know the name of the file you are seeking or some distinctive text within it, or you just want to narrow the search (so that fewer files will be found), use the Date and/or Advanced pages of the Find window.

The Find windows's Date tab

The Date page is most useful in locating a file if

- You know the approximate date that this file was created, last modified, or last accessed.

or

- The file was created, modified, or accessed recently.

To start a search in one of these cases:

1. Start the Find utility, if it's not already running.
2. Fill in information on the Name & Location page, as described earlier in this section. If you do not know certain information, leave the corresponding text box blank.
3. Click on the Date tab to display the options shown in Figure 11.
4. Select the *Find all files* option button.
5. Select *Modified*, *Created*, or *Last accessed* from the drop-down list depending on which of these dates you can best estimate.
6. If you can "bracket" the actual date (for example, you know the file was created between 6/5/97 and 9/3/97), select the *between* option button and, in the two text boxes, enter these dates.

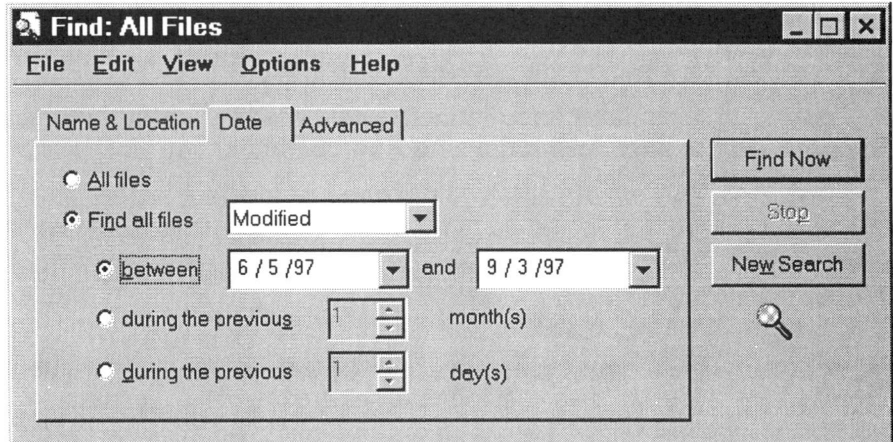

Figure 11 The Date Page of the Find Window

If the file was modified, created, or accessed recently, you could select either the *during the previous day(s)* or the *during the previous month(s)* option button; then enter an appropriate number in the corresponding text box.

7. Begin the search by choosing the Find Now button. All files that match the search criteria will be displayed in the Search Results window, as shown in Figure 10.

The Find window's Advanced tab

The Advanced page of the Find window allows you to refine a search even further. After providing as much information as possible on the Name & Location and Date pages, click on the Advanced tab to display the options shown in Figure 12. Then:

- You can restrict the search to files of a specified type by selecting it from the *Of type* drop-down list. This is especially useful if you're looking for a document created by a particular application, say, the WordPad word processor.
- You can specify the minimum or maximum sizes for the files to be included in the search by using the *Size is* drop-down list and text box.

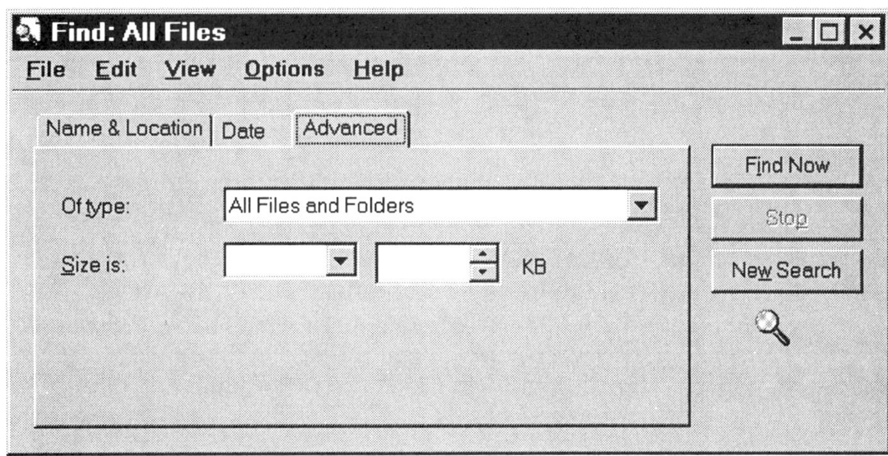

Figure 12 The Advanced Page of the Find Window

NOTE

In addition to the Find Now button, there are two other command buttons in the Find window:

- While a search is taking place, choosing the Stop button discontinues the search.

- Choosing the New Search button resets all search criteria to their defaults and clears all files and folders (if any) from the Search Results window.

Using the Results of a Search

As you know, when a search is complete, the files and folders found are displayed in the Search Results window at the bottom of the Find window (see Figure 10). For all practical purposes, this window can be used as if it were a My Computer (or any folder) window, or the contents pane of an Explorer window. To be more specific:

- You can display the files in the Search Results window in different ways by choosing Large Icons, Small Icons, List, or Details from the View menu. The advantages of each view option are discussed in Section 3.2.
- You can select objects in the Search Results window using the techniques described in Section 3.3.
- Selected objects can be cut or copied to the Clipboard (so they can be pasted into other folders or onto the Desktop) by choosing Cut or Copy from the Edit menu, or by right-clicking on a selected object and choosing Cut or Copy from the pop-up menu.
- You can drag-and-drop objects from the Search Results window to another folder, onto the Desktop, or onto the Recycle Bin.
- You can create a shortcut for an object in the Search Results window using the techniques described in Section 3.4.
- You can delete, rename, or open a selected object by choosing the corresponding command from either the File menu or the menu that pops up when you right-click on the object. (An object can also be opened by clicking on it in Web style mode or double-clicking on it in Classic style mode.)
- You can print selected documents by choosing Print from the File menu or the right-click pop-up menu.

TUTORIAL

Try the following exercise on your own.

1. Turn on your computer, if necessary, to start Windows 98 and close any open windows.
2. Start the Find utility by clicking on the Start button, pointing at the Find command, and clicking on Files or Folders.

3. Try to find the file that starts the Paint application. It is located somewhere on the drive that contains the Windows folder.
   - Enter this drive (for example, C:) in the *Look in* text box and type `Paint` in the *Named* text box.
   - Select (if necessary) the *Include subfolders* check box.
   - Choose the Find Now command button. After a few moments a list of files will appear in the lower part of the Find window, all of which include "paint" as part of their names. The file that you are seeking is called `Mspaint` and is of type "Application".
4. Start Paint by choosing its file name from the Search Results window. (Other operations, such as move and copy, can also be performed on any file listed in the Find window.) Now, close the Paint application.
5. Determine if there is a document on the Student Disk that contains the word *people*.
   - In the Find window, choose the New Search command button to reset the search parameters. (Click on OK when the warning message appears.)
   - Insert the Student Disk in its drive.
   - Click on the Name & Location tab and enter the appropriate drive designation (for example, A:) in the *Look in* text box.
   - Type the word `people` in the *Containing text* box.
   - Choose the Find Now command button. After the search, the file Preamble should be displayed (twice) in the Find window.
6. Close the Find utility as you would any application.
7. Start Find again, this time by right-clicking on the Start button and choosing the Find command from the resulting pop-up menu.
8. Determine if any files were saved to the C: drive today:
   - Enter `C:` in the *Look in* text box, click on the Date tab, and select the *Find all files* option button.
   - Select *Modified* from the drop-down list.
   - Click on the *between* option button and enter today's date in both of the corresponding text boxes.
   - Choose the Find Now command button. All files saved today to the C: drive will be listed at the bottom of the Find window.
9. Remove the Student Disk from its drive and close the Find utility window.

4.4 Associating File Types with Applications

To a certain extent, Windows 98 is a document-oriented operating system. For example, as you know, you can open certain documents by choosing their icons from the Desktop (or in Explorer, My Computer, or any folder window). When you choose such an icon, the associated application starts and the document opens within it. In this section, we will discuss how a document becomes associated with an application and how you can create or modify the association.

File Types

Windows assigns a **file type**, based on the file's extension, to every file stored on your disks. File types are displayed in the Type column of Details view in Explorer or any folder window (see Figure 13).

- If the file extension is *registered* (as described below), and is thus recognized by Windows, the corresponding file type is displayed (see, for example, "HiJaak Image" in Figure 13).
- If the file has an extension but it is not registered, its type is the extension itself (see "LOG File" in Figure 13).
- If the file has no extension, then it is typed as simply "File".

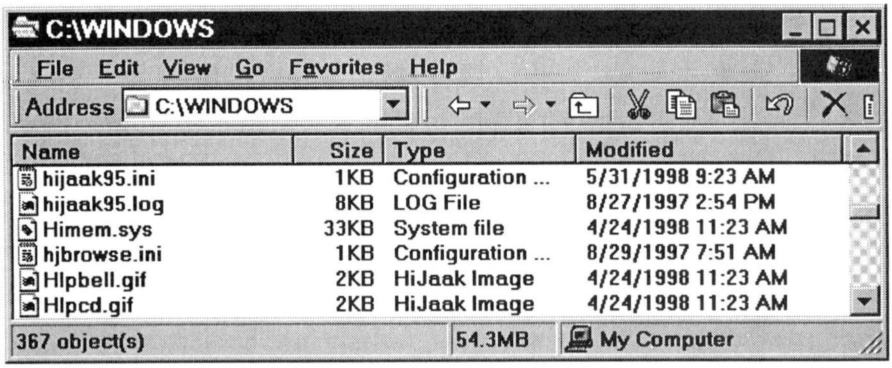

C:\WINDOWS

File Edit View Go Favorites Help

Address C:\WINDOWS

Name	Size	Type	Modified
hijaak95.ini	1KB	Configuration ...	5/31/1998 9:23 AM
hijaak95.log	8KB	LOG File	8/27/1997 2:54 PM
Himem.sys	33KB	System file	4/24/1998 11:23 AM
hjbrowse.ini	1KB	Configuration ...	8/29/1997 7:51 AM
Hlpbell.gif	2KB	HiJaak Image	4/24/1998 11:23 AM
Hlpcd.gif	2KB	HiJaak Image	4/24/1998 11:23 AM

367 object(s) 54.3MB My Computer

Figure 13 Some File Types

How extensions are registered

When a file extension is **registered** with Windows, it is associated with a particular application. These associations can occur in several ways:

- When Windows 98 is installed, it sets up certain associations; for example, the extensions BMP and TXT are normally associated with Paint and Notepad, respectively. (The corresponding file type descriptions are "Bitmap Image" and "Text Document".) Moreover, if a previous version of Windows is present on the machine at the time Windows 98 is installed, any existing associations are carried over to Windows 98.
- Many Windows applications register at least one extension as part of their installation process.
- You can "manually" register an extension to associate it with a particular application. We will discuss how to carry out this process, and how to modify or remove existing associations, later in this section.

NOTE

When an extension is registered, it is normally associated with a distinctive icon, often the icon of the corresponding application. All documents with that extension inherit this icon, which makes them easy to spot in Explorer and My Computer windows, especially in Large Icons view. In the figure below, the files `hijaak95.ini` and `Himem.sys` have registered extensions, whereas `hijaak95.log` does not; the latter has a generic icon.

hijaak95.ini hijaak95.log Himem.sys

Why register an extension?

Once an extension is registered with Windows, all documents with that extension become associated with a particular application. As a result, you can perform certain operations directly on these documents. For example, choosing the document's icon (normally) opens the associated application, as well as the document. Moreover, additional actions become available on the menu that pops up when you right-click on the document's icon. From the right-click menu, you might be able to:

- Open the document within another specified application.
- View the document without opening its application.
- Print the document.
- Play the document, if it represents a sound file.

As you will see, some of the options that are available on a particular right-click menu depend on how the association between the file extension and the application was set up.

NOTE

The extension of a file having a registered file type may or may not be displayed as part of its file name in Explorer or a folder window. For example, since bmp is a registered extension, the file Arcade.bmp may be listed in the \Windows folder as `Arcade.bmp` or simply as `Arcade`. To display registered extensions (or hide them if they're currently displayed), choose Folder Options from the View menu and click on the View tab in the resulting dialog box. Then, either select or deselect the *Hide file extensions for known file types* check box.

Creating a New Registered File Type

Windows allows you to create new file types by registering extensions that are currently unregistered. In doing so, you associate an extension with a particular application and also define some of the options that will be available on the menu that pops up when you right-click on a file with that extension. Here's how it's done:

1. Start Explorer or My Computer.
2. Choose the Folder Options item from the View menu and click on the File Types tab in the resulting dialog box. A list of registered file types is displayed, as shown in Figure 14.

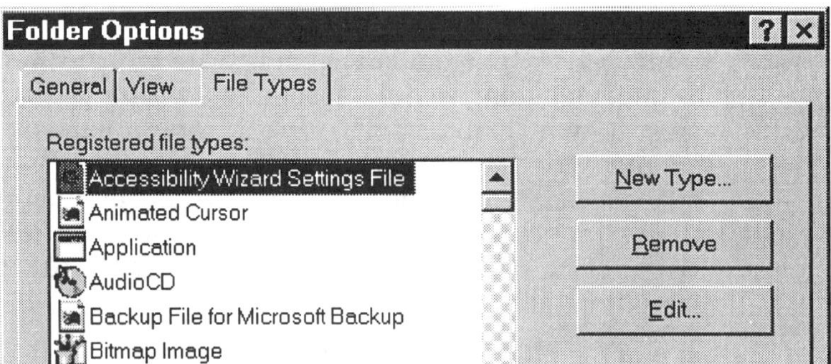

Figure 14 File Types Page of Folder Options Dialog Box

3. Choose the New Type command button to display the Add New File Type dialog box, which is shown in Figure 15.

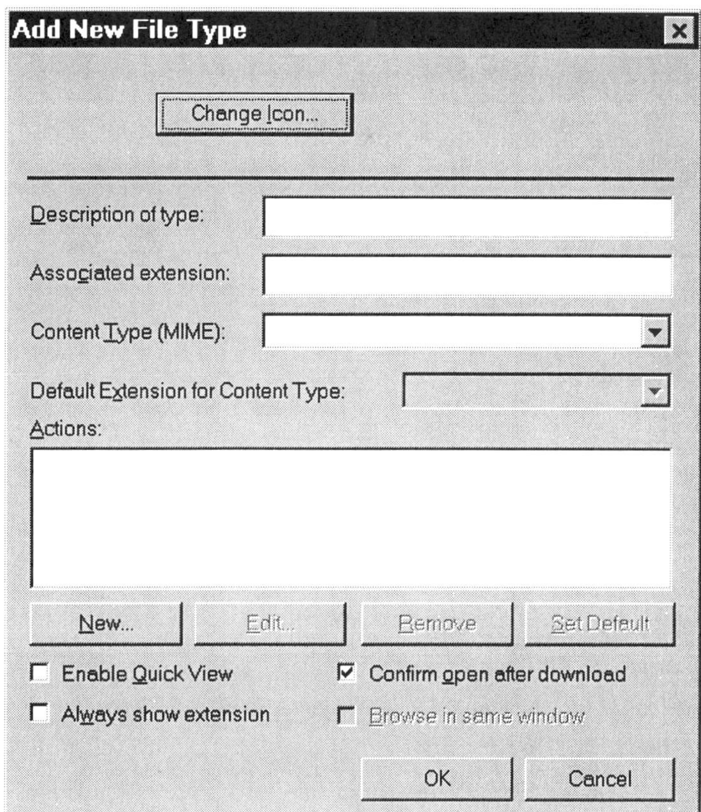

Figure 15 The Add New File Type Dialog Box

4. Type a description for the new file type in the *Description of type* text box. For example, if you use the extension LTR for all letters you write using Corel WordPerfect, you might use *Letters in WP* for the description of this extension. The description will appear in the Type column of a folder's Details view.
5. Type the extension you wish to register in the *Associated extension* text box. Using the example of step 4, you would type LTR here.
6. Either leave the *Content type* text box empty, or enter an appropriate expression here, such as *text* or *image* or select a type from the drop-down list that fits your file type.
7. Now, you can define *actions* (such as Open or Print) for this association. These actions will appear on the menu that pops up

when you right-click on a file with the specified extension. To specify an action, choose the New command button, which opens the New Action dialog box (Figure 16).

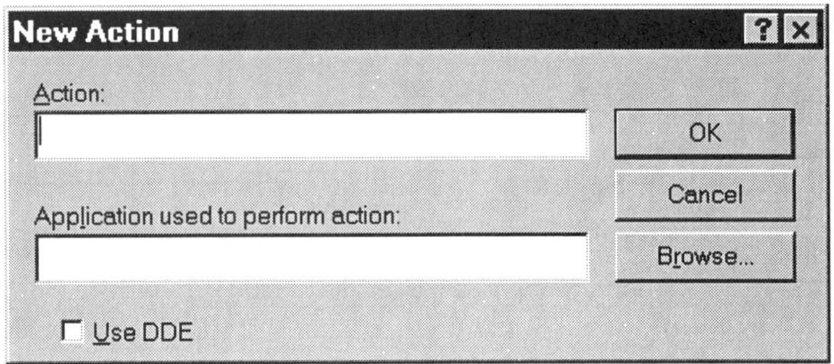

Figure 16 The New Action Dialog Box

Defining an action

8. In the *Action* text box, type a name for the action. This name will appear on the right-click pop-up menu. For example, if you want to be able to open the document from the right-click menu, use "Open" or, continuing the example of steps 4 and 5, "Open with WP".

9. Now type the command that will perform the action specified in step 8 in the *Application used to perform action* text box. If you want to *open* the application, give the appropriate program file's path name (which can usually be found in the application's documentation); for example, C:\Corel\Suite8\Programs\WPWin8.exe. If you can't determine the appropriate path name, choose the Browse command button, and then try to track down the relevant exe file.

   If you want to perform an action other than opening the file, you'll have to check the application's documentation for the appropriate start up command.

10. Choose the OK button to return to the Add New File Type dialog box; the description of the action you have just defined appears in the *Actions* box.

11. If you want to define another action for the current file type, click on the New command button and repeat steps 8 through 10.

Selecting other options for the association

12. Select the *Enable Quick View* check box (when this option is available) if you want to be able to view the contents of a document without starting its associated application. (A Quick View

item will appear on the right-click pop-up menu.)

13. Select the *Always show extension* check box if you want the extension for files of this type to be displayed when they are listed in Explorer or a folder window, regardless of whether or not other registered extensions are hidden.

14. Choose the OK command button to complete the file type creation process. The Add New File Type dialog box will close and you will be returned to the Folder Options dialog box. Your new file type will be highlighted in the latter's list box and information about the file type will appear at the bottom of the dialog box as shown below:

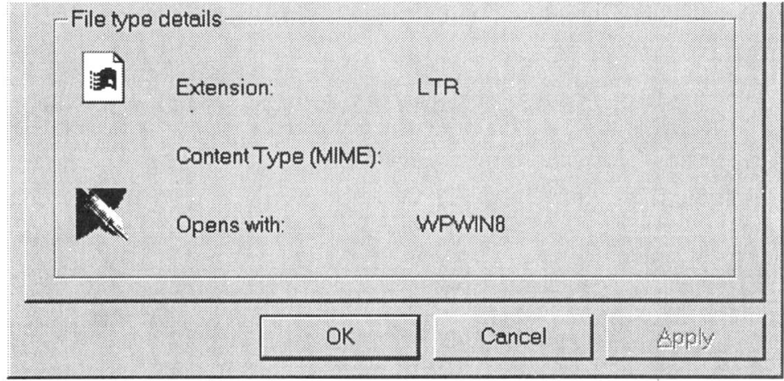

15. Choose the OK command button in the Folder Options dialog box to complete the process.

The right-click pop-up menu

When you right-click on a file name that has an extension you have registered, a menu will pop up listing (among other standard items) the actions you defined when that file type was created. The menu item displayed in bold type (which is "Open with WP" in the menu shown at the right) is thc *default* action; choosing the file's icon (say, in Explorer) causes the default action to be executed; there is no need to right-click and then select this item.

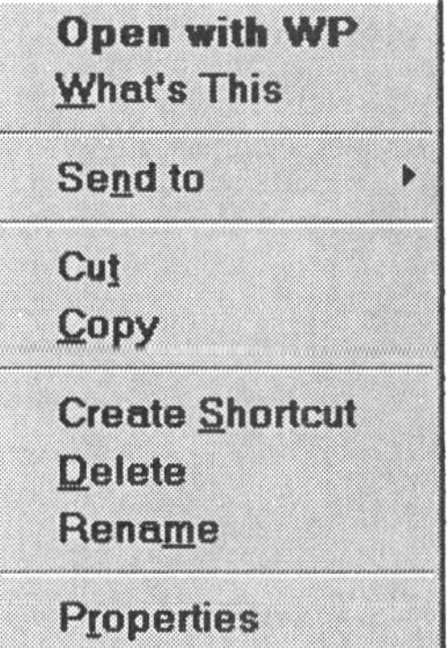

Here is a quick way to register a file type if the only action you want to associate with this type is opening the file:

1. Start Explorer or My Computer and right-click on any file having the extension you want to register.
2. Choose the Open With command from the resulting pop-up menu. The Open With dialog box, shown below, will be displayed.

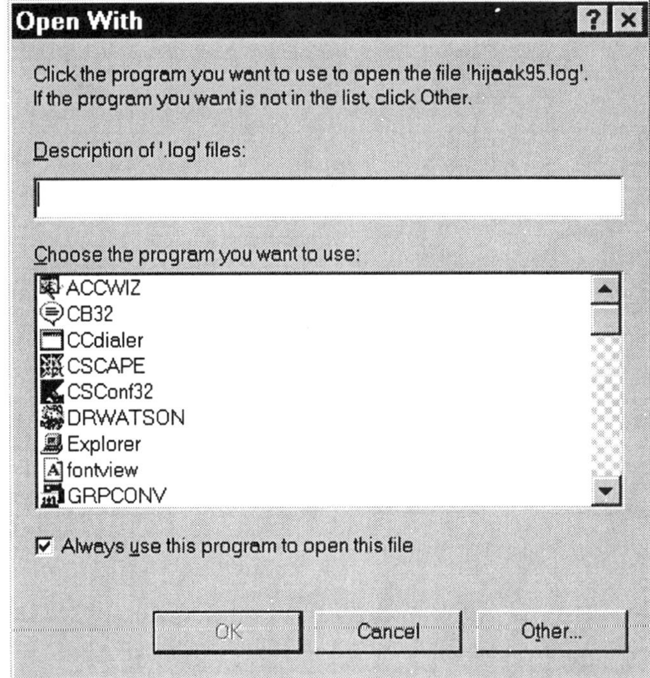

3. In the text box, provide a description of the file type; it will appear in the Type column of the Details view in Explorer or any folder window.
4. Select, from the list, the application you want to use to open files that have this extension, or choose the Other command button to browse for the desired application.
5. Be sure that the *Always use this program to open this file* check box is selected.
6. Choose the OK command button. (The selected application will start and the selected file will open within it.) The creation of the new file type is now complete.

Note that you can define additional actions for a file type registered using this technique by modifying the file type as described in the next subsection.

Modifying a Registered File Type

Windows allows you to modify or remove an existing registered file type; you can, for example, change the application associated with it or add a new action to its right-click menu. To modify or remove an existing registered file type:

1. Start Explorer or My Computer.
2. Choose the Folder Options item from the View menu and click on the File Types tab in the resulting dialog box. The dialog box page shown in Figure 14 (on page 176) will be displayed.
3. In the list of registered file types, select the one with which you want to work; it will become highlighted.
4. If you want to remove the registration of the highlighted file type (ending the association between the corresponding extension and application):
   - Choose the Remove command button.
   - Choose the Yes button in the resulting warning message box.
   - Choose the OK command button.
5. If you want to modify the properties of the highlighted file type, choose the Edit command button (which opens an Edit File Type dialog box, like the one shown in Figure 17 on the next page), and follow the rest of the steps of this procedure.
6. To change the icon for all files of this type:
   - Choose the Change Icon command button. The Change Icon dialog box will open.
   - Choose the Browse button to locate a file that contains icons. By default, the resulting dialog box will only display files that are registered as "Icon Files" to make your task easier. (The file \Windows\System\Shell32.dll contains an extensive collection of icons.)
   - Click on the icon you want and choose the OK button.

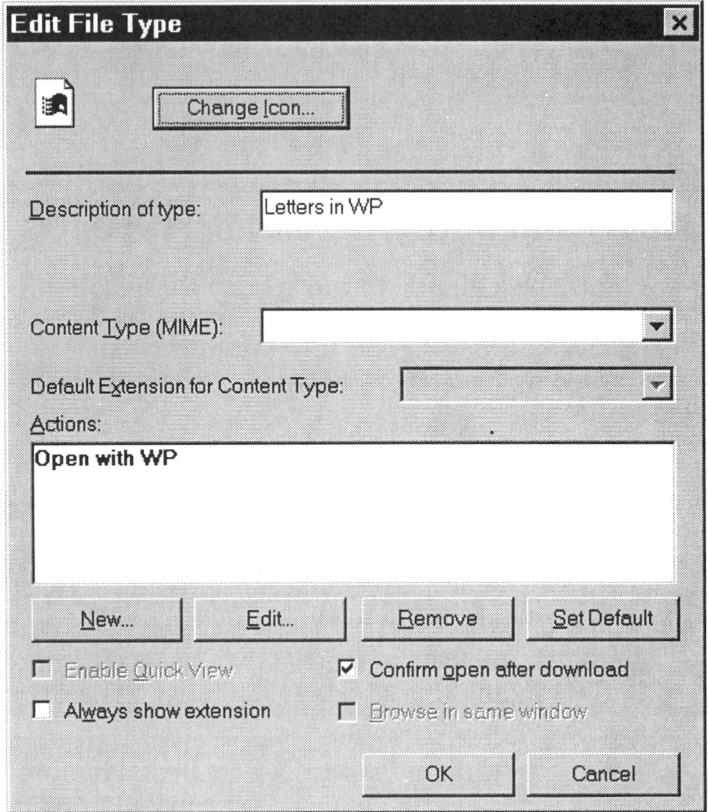

Figure 17 The Edit File Type Dialog Box

7. To add an action to the right-click menu for this type, choose the New command button and proceed as described earlier in this section, under the heading "Creating a New Registered File Type".
8. To edit an existing action, select it and choose the Edit command button. Then, proceed as you would for a "new" action.
9. To remove an action from the right-click menu for this type, select the desired action and choose the Remove command button.
10. To return the set of actions to the default list for this file type, choose the Set Default command button.
11. Choose the OK command button when you're done with your modifications, and you will be returned to the Folder Options dialog box.

TUTORIAL

Try the following exercise on your own.

1. Turn on your computer, if necessary, to start Windows 98 and close any open windows.
2. Start Explorer, choose the Folder Options command on the View menu, and click on the File Types tab.
3. Associate the extension NOT with the Notepad application:
   - Choose the New Type command button, which opens the Add New File Type dialog box.
   - In the *Description of type* text box, enter Notepad Document; in the *Associated extension* text box, enter NOT.
   - Select the *Enable Quick View* check box (if available) so that a Quick View item will appear on the menu that pops up when you right-click on a file name with extension NOT.
   - Choose the New command button, which opens the New Action dialog box.
   - In the *Action* text box, type `Open with Notepad`; in the *Application used to perform action* text box, type the path name for Notepad: `C:\windows\notepad.exe` Now, if you choose the icon of a file with extension NOT (or right-click on that icon and choose Open with Notepad from the pop-up menu), Notepad will start and automatically open the file within it.
   - Choose the OK command button to close the New Action dialog box; then choose the Close command button to exit the Add New File Type dialog box.
4. In the Folder Options dialog box, choose the Edit command button to open the Edit File Type dialog box.
5. Change the current icon for the Notepad Document file type:
   - Choose the Change Icon command button, which opens the Change Icon dialog box.
   - Select another icon from the *Current icon* box and choose the OK command button.
6. In the Edit File Type dialog box, choose the Close command button to return to the Folder Options dialog box.
7. Remove the association of the extension NOT with the Notepad application: With the Notepad Document file type still highlighted, choose the Remove command button and answer Yes to the query.
8. Close the Folder Options dialog box and then close Explorer.

4.5 Managing Printers

In Section 2.2, we discussed how to print a document from within a Windows-based application. Recall that choosing Print from the File menu opens a Print dialog box, which allows you to select various print options, such as which pages to print and the number of copies of each. Using the Windows **Printers folder**, you can exert even more control over the printing process, changing the printer setup, managing active print jobs, and adding a new printer.

The Printers Folder

The quickest way to open the Printers folder window is to:

1. Click on the Start button to display the Start menu.
2. Point at the Settings option and then choose the Printers item from the resulting submenu.

The Printers folder window, shown in Figure 18 will open. (Your Printers folder may look quite different from the one pictured here.)

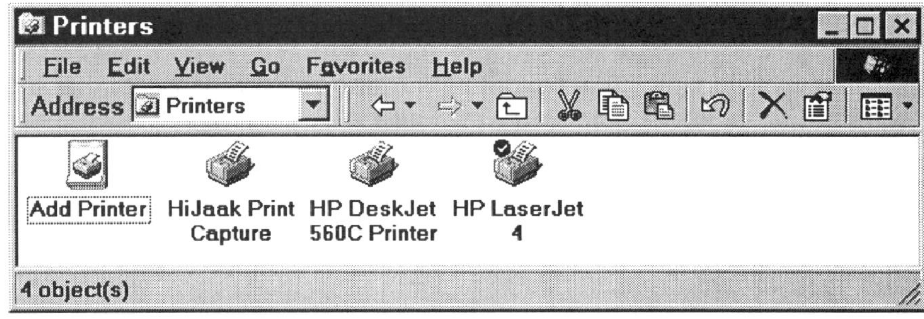

Figure 18 The Printers Folder Window

You can also open the Printers folder window in the following ways:

- Start My Computer and choose the Printers icon from the My Computer window (see Section 3.5).
- Start Explorer and open the Printers folder — near the bottom of the folder tree pane (see Section 3.2).
- Start Control Panel from the Start menu's Settings option and choose the Printers icon from the Control Panel window.

Changing the Printer Setup

From time to time, you may want to change certain printer settings, such as the print quality (resolution) or page orientation. In Windows 98, printer settings are changed from within the Printer Properties dialog box. To display this dialog box:

1. Open the Printers folder, as described earlier in this section.
2. Right-click on the desired printer icon.
3. Choose the Properties item from the resulting pop-up menu.

The content of the Printer Properties dialog box varies considerably from printer to printer. A typical one is shown in Figure 19.

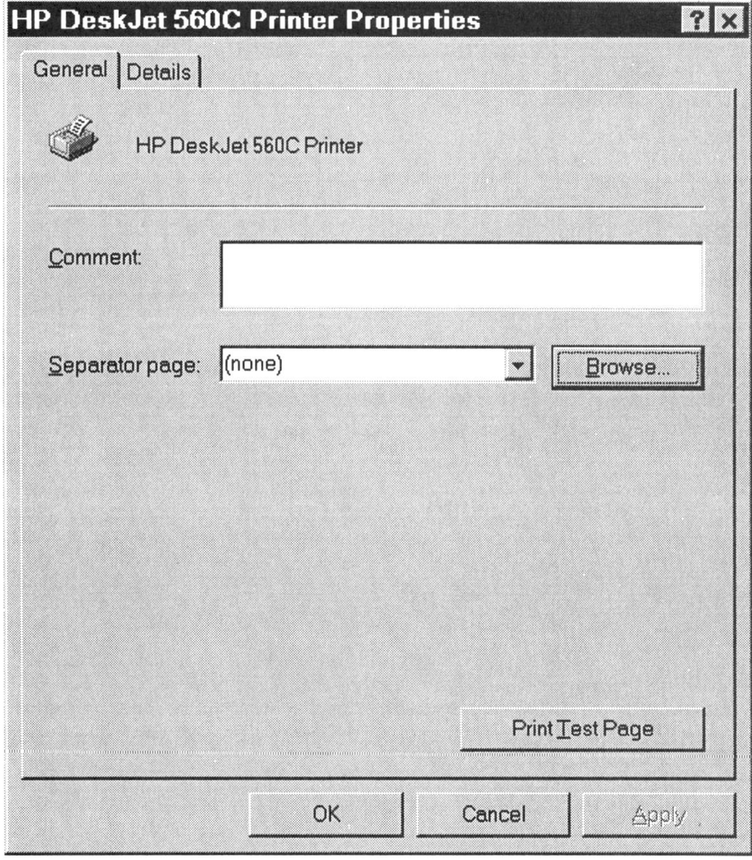

Figure 19 Printer Properties Dialog Box — *General* Page

The first page (the General page) of this dialog box gives the name of the printer and allows you to:

- Define a "comment" for this printer. This comment will appear in the Details view of the Printers folder.
- Specify a "separator page" — a page that will automatically be inserted between print jobs. It can be blank or be printed from a specified file.
- Print a "Test Page" to check that the printer is working properly.

The Details page (and other pages, if present) allows you to change the way the printer is configured. For example, clicking on the Details tab for the HP DeskJet 560C printer displays the page shown in Figure 20.

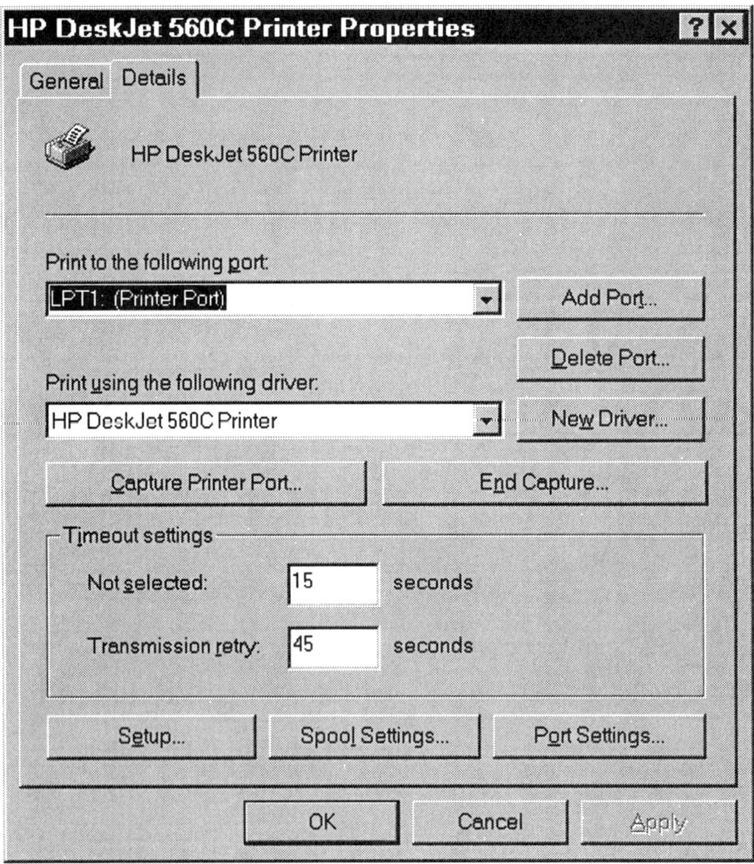

Figure 20 Printer Properties Dialog Box — *Details* Page

Much of the information on the Details page is fairly technical. Here is a quick rundown of the various options:

- The *Port* drop-down list and command buttons can be used to change settings that reflect how your computer is physically or logically (for a network printer) connected to the printer.
- The *Driver* drop-down-list and command button are used to install a different **printer driver** — a program that translates a document's text, graphics, and special codes into a language that the printer can understand.
- The *Capture* command buttons are used in *mapping* (or removing the mapping of) a port to a network drive.
- The *Timeout* text boxes determine the amount of time Windows will wait for the printer to come online (*Not selected*) or to be ready to print (*Transmission retry*) before reporting an error.

Spooling print jobs

- The *Spool Settings* command button is used to change the manner in which a document is sent from the application to the printer. When a print job is **spooled**, it is temporarily stored on the hard disk (which is a rapid process) and then transferred to the printer at the leisurely pace required by these devices. With spooling in effect, you can use the computer for other tasks once the document has been sent to disk, instead of having to wait until the print job is complete. (You might want to turn spooling *off* if you have little free disk space or if you are encountering certain printing problems.)
- The *Setup* command button opens a dialog box with additional options. (For some printers, additional pages in the Properties dialog box take the place of the Setup button.)

Setup options

Although the Setup options (or additional dialog box pages) vary from printer to printer, a few are common to virtually all printers. To illustrate these features, consider the Setup options for an HP DeskJet printer, which are shown in Figure 21, on the next page.

Almost all printers allow you to adjust:

- *Print Quality* In the dialog box of Figure 21, the available print quality choices are labeled *Normal* (medium resolution), *Presentation* (high resolution), and *Fast* (low resolution). The higher the resolution, the nicer text and graphics will look on the page. Some printers refer to these settings using different terms, such as *Draft*, instead of low resolution. Others (including laser printers) use *dots per inch* (dpi) to describe resolution — the higher the dpi number, the better-looking the output.

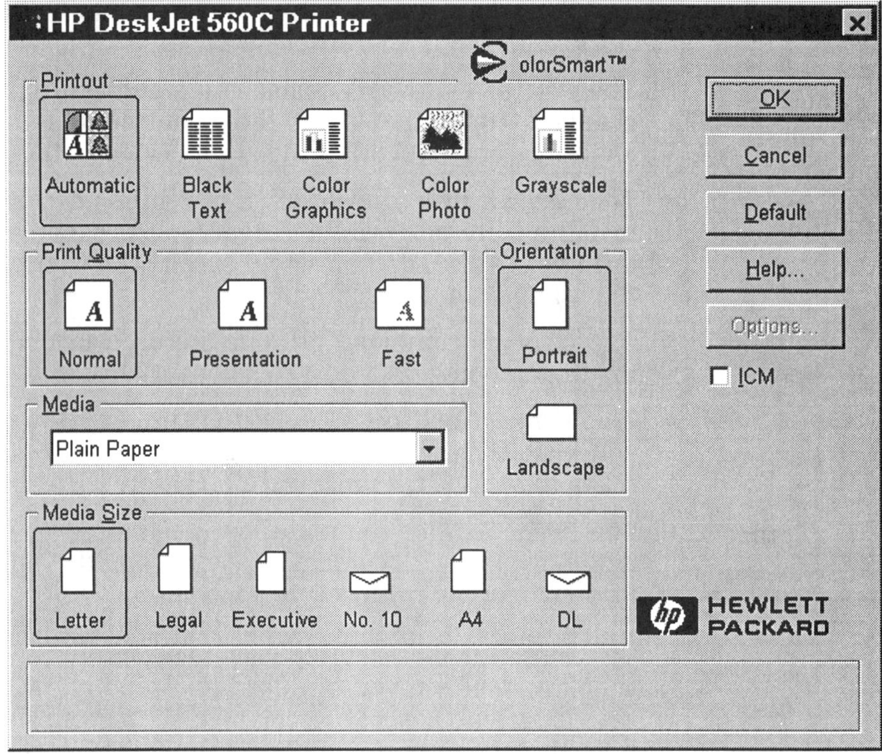

Figure 21 The Result of Choosing the Setup Command Button

- *Paper Orientation* The term *Portrait* means that printing takes place parallel to the short side of the paper; the page you are reading is in portrait orientation. *Landscape* means that printing takes place parallel to the long side of the paper; for example, certificates and diplomas are usually printed in landscape orientation.
- *Media Size* The common 8½" by 11" paper is referred to as *letter size.* If you are about to print on a different size paper or on an envelope, you should let the printer know this by selecting the appropriate paper size.

NOTE

You can usually access some printer properties from within an application. For example, in WordPad, choosing Page Setup from the File menu opens a dialog box that contains options for paper size and orientation. Moreover, choosing the Printer command button and then the Properties button in the resulting dialog box provides access to additional setup options. In many other applications, you access printer properties by choosing Printer Setup from the File menu or by choosing the Properties command button in the Print dialog box.

Managing Print Jobs

If print spooling is in effect (see above), you can control various aspects of your print jobs while they are running or waiting to be printed. To do so, either:

- Open the Printers folder (as described earlier in this section) and choose the appropriate printer icon.

or

- While a document is printing, double-click on the printer icon to the left of the clock on the Taskbar.

In either case, a print manager window, like the one in Figure 22, will open*. The list of documents displayed in this window is called the **print queue**. The window in Figure 22 was captured during the printing process; it shows two documents in the queue. If you open the print manager window when the printer is idle, the queue will be empty.

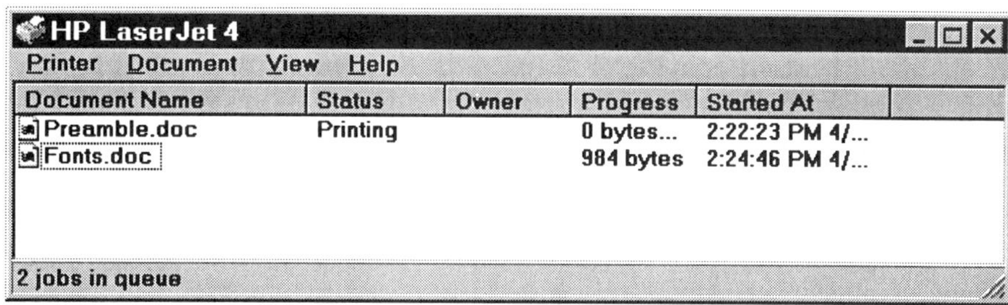

Figure 22 The "Print Manager" Window

Here's how to use the print manager window:

- To cancel printing of a document, select the desired document in the queue and choose Cancel Printing from the Document menu.

*This window, which has no official name, takes the place of the Windows 3.1 Print Manager. Most people still refer to it as "the print manager window".

- To cancel all print jobs listed in the queue, choose Purge Print Documents from the Printer menu. All documents will be removed from the queue.
- To pause the printing of a particular document, select the desired document in the print queue and choose Pause Printing from the Document menu. (A check mark will appear next to this menu item and the word *Paused* will appear next to the document name in the Status column.) To restart a paused print job, select the document and choose Pause Printing from the Document menu.
- To pause all print jobs, choose Pause Printing from the Printer menu. (A check mark will appear next to this menu item and the word *Paused* will appear on the title bar.) To restart a paused printer, choose Pause Printing from the Printer menu.
- To change the order of the documents in the print queue, select the document you want to move and drag it to the desired position in the queue.

Adding a New Printer

If you want to use a new printer with your computer, you must first establish a physical connection between the two (say, via a cable) and also provide Windows with some information about the printer. Windows then installs and configures the appropriate printer driver for that printer and sets up the proper pathway between computer and printer.

To add* a new printer:

1. Open the Printers folder, as described earlier in this section.
2. Choose the Add Printer icon (see Figure 18). The Add Printer Wizard will start, displaying an informational page.
3. Click the Next button. If you are connected to a network, you'll then be asked whether you want to install a local or network printer. To install a local printer (one that is directly connected to

*In Windows parlance, to "add" a piece of hardware (such as a printer) to your system usually means to install and configure the appropriate driver for it. Of course, before you can make use of the new hardware, it also has to be physically connected to your system, but Windows does not concern itself with such mundane matters.

your computer), select Local and choose the Next button, which displays the dialog box shown in Figure 23.

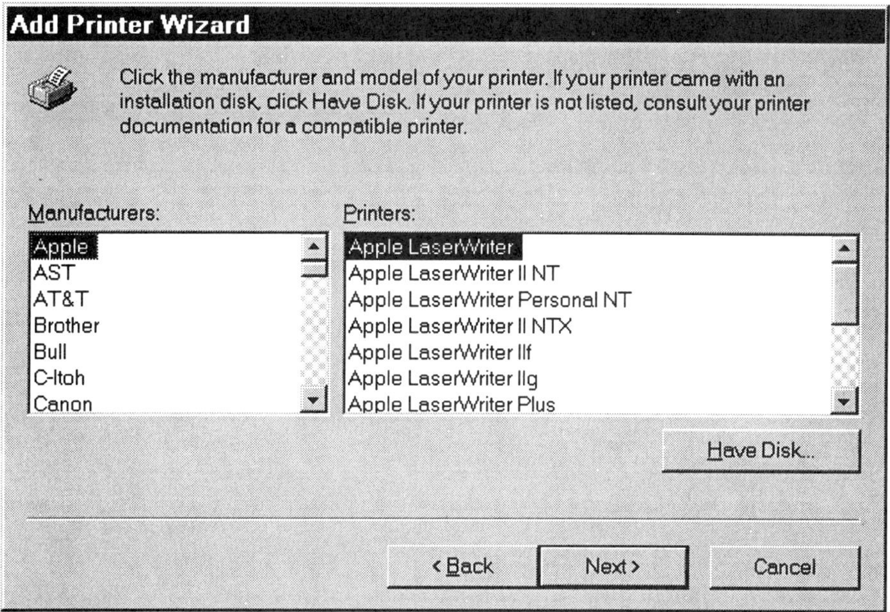

Figure 23 Choosing the Manufacturer and Model of Printer

4. Select the manufacturer and then the model of the new printer from their respective text boxes. If the manufacturer has supplied a printer driver on disk, insert this disk in its drive, choose the Have Disk command button, enter the appropriate drive in the resulting dialog box, and choose the OK button.

5. Choose the Next button. The Add Printer Wizard page shown in Figure 24 (on the next page) will be displayed.

6. Check the printer's documentation to determine if it's a parallel or serial printer. In the former case, select "LPT1"; in the latter case, select "COM1" if no other device is attached to the computer's primary serial port, otherwise select "COM2".

   If the printer is of the serial variety, you may have to configure its port. In this case, choose the Configure Port command button, enter the requested information (as specified in the printer manual), and choose the OK button.

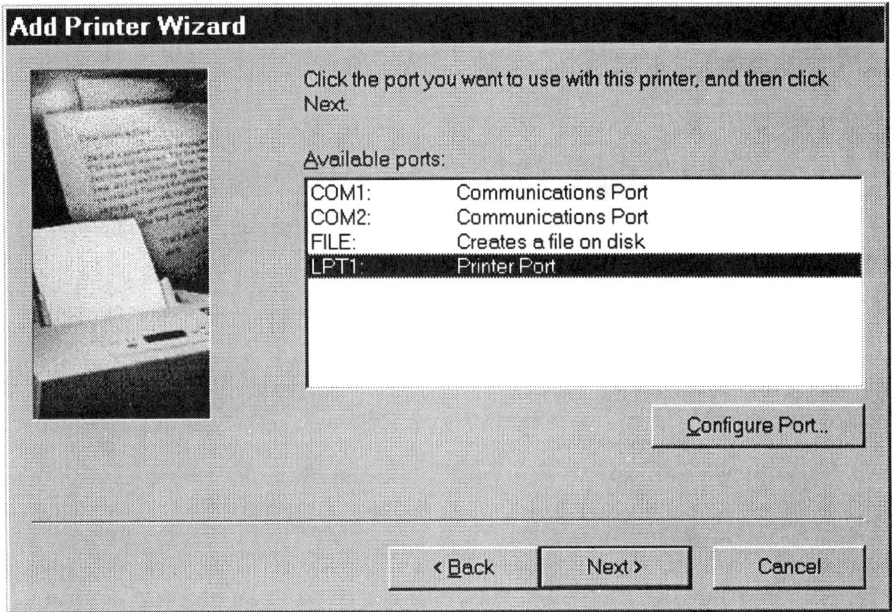

Figure 24 Choosing a Printer Port for the New Printer

Select the *FILE* option if the new printer cannot be accessed directly from your computer, but you would occasionally like to print files on it. In this case, when this printer is selected, the print job will be stored on disk and can be copied at a later time to the desired printer (via a computer connected to it).

7. Choose the Next button. The resulting dialog box allows you to select a name for the new printer (which will appear in the Printers folder window). You can also make this printer the default printer, in which case it will automatically be used to print a document unless you specify otherwise at the time of printing.
8. Choose the Next button one more time. You are now asked if you want to print a test page. This is not necessary, but it is a good idea to check if the new printer is working properly.
9. Choose the Finish button. You may now be prompted to insert a diskette or CD-ROM in its drive. If so, insert it and choose the OK button. The appropriate printer driver files will be copied to the computer's hard disk and, if you requested that a test page be printed, printing will begin.
10. If the test page looks okay, choose the Yes button in the dialog

box, and the process is complete. The new printer will now be listed in the Printers folder window.

After the test page prints, a dialog box will open, asking if the page has printed correctly. If it hasn't, choose the No command button. This will start the Printer Troubleshooter. Answer the questions posed by it, and you will be led through some troubleshooting procedures that will hopefully cure the problem.

Try the following exercise on your own.

1. Turn on the computer (if necessary) to start Windows 98, and close any open windows.
2. Open the Printers folder: Click on the Start button, point at the Settings option, and choose Printers from the submenu.
3. Right-click on the icon of one of the available printers and then choose Properties from the pop-up menu.
4. In the Properties dialog box, click on the Details tab, choose the Spool Settings command button, then select the *Spool print jobs so that program finishes printing faster* option button (if it's not already selected), and choose the OK button.
5. Check out the function of the various options in the Printer Properties dialog box: Click on the question-mark button on the title bar and then click on the desired item. (To close the resulting window, click anywhere within the dialog box.)
6. Close the Properties dialog box.
7. In the Printers folder window, choose the icon of the selected printer. This opens the "print manager" window.
8. Pause the printer by choosing the Pause Printing command on the Printer menu. (Notice that the word *Paused* appears on the title bar.)
9. Insert the Student Disk in its drive and start WordPad by clicking on the WordPad Item on the Accessories submenu of the Start menu's Programs option.
10. Open (from the File menu) the Fonts document on the Student Disk and send it to the printer (choose Print from the File menu and then choose OK in the resulting dialog box). Do the same for the Preamble document on the diskette.

11. Switch to the print manager window. The two print jobs will be listed in the "print queue" with the Fonts document first.
12. Change the order of the print jobs (so that Preamble will be printed first) by dragging the Fonts document to the bottom of the queue.
13. Cancel the Preamble print job: Select it and choose Cancel Printing from the Document menu.
14. Cancel the remaining print job by choosing Purge Print Documents from the Printer menu.
15. "Unpause" the printer by choosing Pause Printing from the Printer menu. (The word *Paused* will disappear from the title bar.)
16. Close the print manager window, the Printers folder, and WordPad, and remove the diskette from its drive.

4.6 Property Sheets

Just about everything in Windows, or that interacts with Windows, has "properties" — files, folders, disks, and even, as we saw in Section 4.5, hardware. When you right-click on an icon representing one of these objects, the last item listed on the resulting pop-up menu is Properties. Choosing this menu item opens the object's Properties dialog box, also known as its **property sheet**. In this section, we will discuss property sheets for files, folders, and shortcuts.

The Property Sheet for a File or Folder

Figure 25 shows a typical file (or folder) property sheet. This particular dialog box was displayed by right-clicking in Explorer on the file name Internet.txt, and then choosing Properties from the pop-up menu.

The contents of a property sheet varies depending on the type of object it represents, but always includes general information about the object. The property sheets for files and folders also allow you to change their **attributes** (see Figure 25). A check mark next to an attribute indicates that the attribute is *set* — it is currently in effect; otherwise, we say that the attribute is *clear* — it is not in effect.

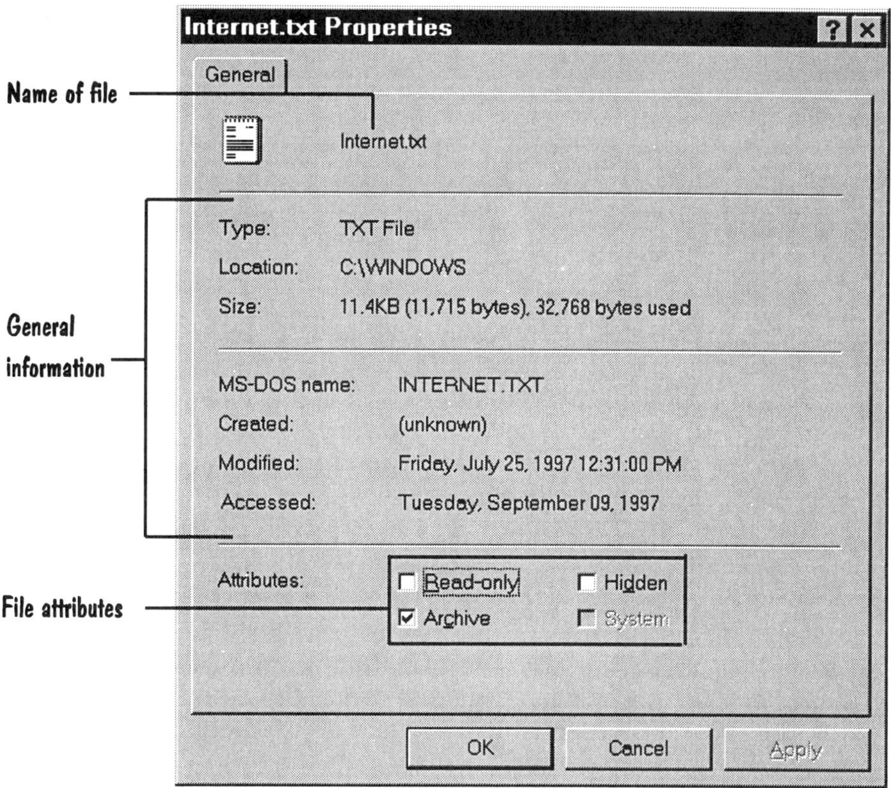

Figure 25 A Typical Property Sheet

File attributes

- Putting the *Read-only* attribute into effect makes it harder to accidentally erase or modify the file. Setting this attribute for a file is analogous to write-protecting a floppy disk (see the Introduction); it reduces the likelihood of accidental erasure or modification of the contents.
- The *Archive* bit is used in conjunction with backup software (see Section 10.2). The Archive bit is usually set automatically for a file that has never been backed up or that has been modified since the last backup.
- When the *Hidden* attribute is set, the given file's name is not normally displayed in Explorer or a folder window.
- Windows attaches the *System* attribute to certain files, called *system files*, that it uses to perform basic functions. This attribute cannot normally be set or cleared by the user. (Notice that *System*

is dimmed in Figure 25, indicating that this option is not available.)

Some Properties dialog boxes have more than one tab, providing additional pages of information and possibly additional available options. For example, documents created in the Microsoft Word 97 word processor have property sheets with five tabs: General, Summary, Statistics, Contents, and Custom.

The Property Sheet for a Shortcut

As you know, a shortcut is a small file that tells Windows where to find the associated (or *target*) object. When you right-click on a shortcut to a file or folder and choose Properties from the resulting pop-up menu, the property sheet for the shortcut (not for the target object) is displayed.

The property sheet for a shortcut normally contains two pages. The first page, which is displayed by clicking on the *General* tab, supplies information about the file in which the shortcut is defined; it provides the same information as the page shown in Figure 25. The second page, triggered from the *Shortcut* tab, supplies additional information and options. For example, if we display the Properties dialog box for a shortcut to the WordPad word processor and then click on the Shortcut tab, the resulting dialog box looks like the one in Figure 26.

The shortcut's name and icon are displayed at the top of the Shortcut page, followed by the target's type and the folder in which it resides. The text boxes and drop-down list on this page allow the user to alter certain properties of the shortcut. To be more specific:

Shortcut properties

- The *Target* text box contains the full path name for the target. The path is defined at the time the shortcut is created and would normally only need to be changed if the target file or folder were subsequently moved to another location. In this case, you would want to supply the new path name in this text box so that the shortcut would continue to work.
- The *Start in* text box shows the folder that will be opened by default after the shortcut is used to start an application. Then, for example, if you choose Open from the File menu, the Open dialog box will display the folder specified in the *Start in* text box (unless this feature is overridden by the application).

Shortcut keys

- The *Shortcut key* text box allows you to define a keystroke combination to open the file or folder. The shortcut keystrokes must

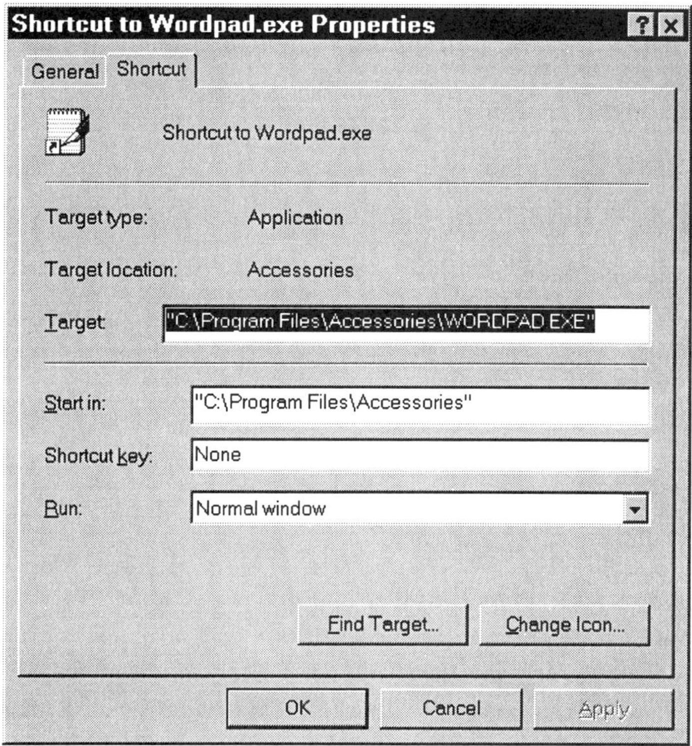

Figure 26 The Shortcut Page of a Property Sheet

begin with Ctrl+Alt and be followed by a single character. For example, to define the shortcut key Ctrl+Alt+W to start WordPad:

1. Display the property sheet for a WordPad shortcut and click on the Shortcut tab (see Figure 26).
2. Click in the Shortcut key text box.
3. Press the W key (Windows automatically inserts Ctrl+Alt in front of the W).
4. Choose the OK command button.

Now, when you press Ctrl+Alt+W from anywhere within Windows or one of its applications, WordPad will start.

- The *Run* drop-down list supplies three options for displaying the file or folder window when you use this shortcut to open it:
  1. *Normal* means that the initial window will be the same size it was when the target file or folder was last closed.

2. *Maximized* means that the target file or folder window will automatically be maximized when it is opened.
3. *Minimized* means that the target file or folder, when opened, will automatically be reduced to a button on the Taskbar.

NOTE

The Shortcut page also contains two command buttons:

- Clicking on Find Target opens the folder window that contains the target and highlights the latter.
- Clicking on Change Icon opens the Change Icon dialog box. (See Section 4.4 for information about changing an icon.)

Chapter Summary

Customizing the Taskbar	To reposition the Taskbar	Drag it to any other edge of the screen.
	To change the size of the Taskbar	Drag its inner edge away from the edge of the screen.
	To open the Taskbar Properties dialog box	Point at the Settings option on the Start menu and choose Taskbar & Start Menu from the submenu; *or* right-click on an empty part of the Taskbar and choose Properties from the pop-up menu.
	To turn on or off the Always on top, Auto hide, or Show Clock Taskbar options	Open the Taskbar Properties dialog box, select or deselect the appropriate check box, and choose OK.
Manipulating Windows from the Taskbar	To place a toolbar of icons on the Taskbar	Right-click on the Taskbar, point at Toolbars on the pop-up menu, and choose Address, Links, Desktop, Quick Launch, or New Toolbar from the resulting submenu.
	To tile or cascade application windows	Right-click on the Taskbar and choose Cascade, Tile Horizontally, or Tile Vertically from the pop-up menu.
	To minimize all open application windows	Right-click on the Taskbar and choose Minimize All Windows from the pop-up menu.

Customizing the Start Button Menus	To add an item using drag-and-drop	Drag a file, folder, or shortcut onto the Start button to add the item to the Start menu or drag it onto a Start button submenu to add it to that submenu.
	To move a menu item using drag-and-drop	Drag the item from its current Start button menu location to another menu location.
	To display the Start Menu Programs page of the Taskbar Properties dialog box	Open the Taskbar Properties dialog box and click on the Start Menu Programs tab.
	To add items to a Start button menu using this dialog box	Choose the Add or Advanced command button on the Start Menu Programs page.
	To delete items from a Start button menu	Right-click on the item to be deleted and choose Delete from the pop-up menu; *or* choose the Remove or Advanced command button on the Start Menu Programs page.
	To remove all items from the Documents submenu	Choose the Clear command button on the Start Menu Programs page.
Using the Find Utility	To start Find	Point at the Find option on the Start menu and choose Files or Folders from the sub-menu; *or* right-click on the Start button, My Computer icon, or any folder icon and choose Find; *or* in Explorer, point at Find on the Tools menu and choose Files or Folders.
	Selecting the search criteria	In the Find window: use the Name & Location page to enter files, folders, or distinctive text; use the Date page to limit the search to certain dates; use the Advanced page to search for files of a certain size or type.
	Using the Search Results window	In the Search Results window, files or folders can be selected, cut, copied, deleted, renamed, opened, or printed.
File Types	To create, remove, or modify a file type	In Explorer or My Computer, choose Folder Options from the View menu and click on the File Types tab in the resulting dialog box.
	To create a new registered file type	On the File Types page, choose the New Type button; then specify the extension to

		be registered and its description, and define the actions to be associated with this type.
	To remove an existing registered file type	On the File Types page, select the file type and choose the Remove button.
	To modify an existing registered file type	On the File Types page, select the file type and choose the Edit button.
Managing Printers	To open the Printers folder	Choose Printers from the Start menu's Settings option; *or* choose the Printers icon from the My Computer window.
	To change a printer's settings	Open the Printers folder, right-click on the desired printer, and choose Properties from the pop-up menu; then, enter changes in the resulting dialog box.
	To manage print jobs	Open the Printers folder, choose the desired printer icon, and use the resulting "print manager" window to manipulate print jobs.
	To add a new printer	Open the Printers folder, choose the Add Printer icon, and use the resulting Add Printer Wizard.
Property Sheets	To display an object's property sheet	Right-click on the object's icon and choose Properties from the pop-up menu.
	Shortcut property sheets	Allow the user to change, for the target application, its path name, default folder, shortcut key, and initial window type.
File Attributes	Read-only	When set, the file cannot be modified or deleted.
	Archive	When set, the file needs to be backed up.
	Hidden	When set, the file's name is not normally displayed in Explorer or a folder window.
	System	When set, indicates a system file.

Review Exercises

Section 4.1

1. To increase the size of the Taskbar when it is located at the bottom of the screen, position the mouse pointer over the Taskbar's

___________ edge and drag it in an upward direction.

2. You can open the Taskbar Properties dialog box by right-clicking on the Taskbar and choosing ___________ from the pop-up menu.
3. When three windows are ___________ on the screen, each window occupies one-third of the available space.
4. True or false: When the auto-hide feature is in effect, the only way to display the Taskbar is to press Ctrl+Esc.
5. True or false: The Taskbar can be repositioned along any of the four edges of the screen.
6. True or false: To minimize all application windows simultaneously, right-click on the Taskbar and choose the Properties command.
7. True or false: To place all the Desktop icons on the Taskbar, choose the Desktop item from the Start menu.
8. To place the Show Desktop icon on the Taskbar, open the Taskbar pop-up menu, point at the Toolbars item, and, on the resulting submenu, choose

   a. Desktop.
   b. Quick Launch.
   c. New Toolbar.
   d. Links.

9. Which of the following tasks cannot be accomplished using the Taskbar Properties dialog box?

   a. Ensuring that the Taskbar is "always on top".
   b. Hiding the Taskbar from view.
   c. Removing the Clock from the Taskbar.
   d. Repositioning the Taskbar at another edge of the screen.

10. Which of the following tasks cannot be accomplished by right-clicking on the Taskbar and choosing a command from the pop-up menu?

    a. Cascading the open application windows.
    b, Tiling the open application windows.
    c. Maximizing all open application windows.
    d. Minimizing all open application windows.

Section 4.2

11. The Windows Explorer item on the Programs submenu of the Start menu is actually a ___________ to a program file.
12. If you drag a file onto the Start button, a corresponding item is added to the ___________.

13. You can add items to the Programs submenu of the Start menu using the ____________ page of the Taskbar Properties dialog box.

14. True or false: Choosing the Advanced command button in the Taskbar Properties dialog box starts Explorer.

15. True or false: The Clear command button in the Taskbar Properties dialog box removes all items from the Programs submenu.

16. True or false: If the \Windows\Start Menu\Programs\StartUp folder contains a shortcut to an application, that application will open when Windows is started.

17. To add an item to the Programs submenu of the Start menu:

    a. Drop its shortcut onto the Start button.
    b. Drop its shortcut into the \Windows folder.
    c. Copy its shortcut into the \Windows\Start Menu folder.
    d. Copy its shortcut into the \Windows\Start Menu\Programs folder.

18. To delete one of the items on the Documents submenu of the Start menu:

    a. Choose the Remove command button in the Taskbar Properties dialog box.
    b. Choose the Clear command button in the Taskbar Properties dialog box.
    c. Open the Recent subfolder of the Windows folder and delete the item from it.
    d. Open the StartUp subfolder of the \Windows\Start Menu\Programs folder and delete the item from it.

Section 4.3

19. To use the Windows Find utility to locate a file, type its name in the ____________ text box on the Name & Location page.

20. After the Find utility completes a search, all files and folders found are displayed in the ____________ subwindow.

21. If the Classic style setting is in effect, to open a folder located in a Find search, ____________ on its name in the Find window.

22. True or false: The Find utility can be used to locate all files and folders whose names contain the word *start*.

23. True or false: If the *Look in* text box contains C: and the *Include subfolders* check box is selected, the Find utility will search the entire C: drive for the specified file or folder.

24. True or false: You can copy a file from Find's Search Results window to the Clipboard by highlighting its name and choosing Copy from the Edit menu.

25. If you have forgotten a file's name but you know it contains the text "Dear Bob", you should enter this information on

    a. The Advanced page of the Find window.
    b. The Date page of the Find window.
    c. The Name & Location page of the Find window.
    d. The Text page of the Find window.

26. If you have forgotten a file's name but you know that it was created in the last three days, enter this information on

    a. The Name & Location page of the Find window.
    b. The Date page of the Find window.
    c. The Advanced page of the Find window.
    d. The Recent page of the Find window.

Section 4.4

27. If double-clicking on a file's icon opens the file, then the corresponding file type is ___________ with Windows.

28. To associate an extension with an application, begin by choosing the ___________ command from Explorer's View menu.

29. True or false: An application cannot be associated with two different extensions.

30. True or false: The menu that pops up when you right-click on a file icon always contains a Print command.

31. The File Types page of the Folder Options dialog box allows you to

    a. Create a new registered file type.
    b. Remove an existing registered file type.
    c. Edit an existing registered file type.
    d. Perform all of the above tasks.

32. Which characteristic of a file type registration cannot be changed in the Edit File Type dialog box?

    a. The icon associated with this file type.
    b. The extension associated with this file type.
    c. The actions associated with this file type.
    d. Whether or not Quick View is enabled for this file type.

Section 4.5

33. To ___________ a print job means to have it temporarily stored on the hard disk before it is transferred to the printer.

34. A ___________ is a program that translates your document's text, graphics, and special codes into a language that the printer can understand.

35. The "print manager" window displays the current print jobs in a list that is known as the print ___________.

36. To start the Add Printer Wizard, choose the ___________ icon in the Printers folder window.
37. True or false: The Printers folder can be opened from the Start menu's Settings option.
38. True or false: A separator page is a page that Windows automatically inserts between print jobs.
39. True or false: If a document is printed in portrait orientation, its text runs parallel to the long side of the page.
40. True or false: To interchange the order in which the first two jobs in the print queue will be printed, drag the first document's name and icon just below that of the second document.
41. If a printer is "paused", as indicated on the title bar of the print manager window, you can restart it by choosing
    a. Pause Printing from the Printer window.
    b. Unpause Printing from the Printer menu.
    c. Pause Printing from the Document menu.
    d. Unpause Printing from the Document menu.
42. The computer's primary parallel port is referred to as
    a. COM1
    b. COM2
    c. LPT1
    d. File

Section 4.6

43. The Properties dialog box for an object is commonly known as its property ___________.
44. To open the Properties dialog box for an object, right-click on its icon and choose ___________ from the pop-up menu.
45. True or false: When a file's read-only attribute is set, that file cannot be modified.
46. True or false: The shortcut key assigned to a shortcut must begin with the Ctrl+Alt keystroke combination.
47. Which file attribute is cleared when the file is backed up using backup software?
    a. Archive
    b. Backup
    c. Hidden
    d. System
48. On the Shortcut page of the Properties dialog box for a shortcut to a folder, the word *target* refers to

a. The folder in which the shortcut resides.
b. The folder that opens when you choose the shortcut.
c. The file that defines the shortcut.
d. None of the above is the target for a shortcut.

Build Your Own Glossary

49. The following words and phrases are important terms that were introduced in this chapter. (They appear within the text in boldface type.) Use WordPad (see Section 2.2) to enter a definition for each term, preserving alphabetical order, into the Glossary file on the Student Disk.

Attributes for a file or folder	Printer driver	Spool print jobs
Cascade windows	Printers folder	Start button menu
File types	Print queue	Taskbar
Find utility	Property sheet	Tile windows
	Registered file type	Wildcard

Lab Exercises

Work each of the following exercises at your computer. Begin by turning the machine on (if necessary) to start Windows 98 and closing any open windows. If you want to produce a written record of your answers, review the material on WordPad and capturing screens in Sections 2.2 and 2.3.

Lab Exercise 1 (Section 4.1)

a. If the Taskbar is hidden, display it. Position the Taskbar at the left edge of the screen. Is the Start button at its top or bottom?

b. Increase the size of the Taskbar as much as possible. What percentage (roughly) of the entire screen does it occupy?

c. Remove the Clock from the Taskbar or, if it's currently hidden, redisplay it. Also, ensure that the *Always on top* check box is selected. What dialog box did you open to accomplish these tasks?

d. Start My Computer and maximize its window. Does it cover part or all of the Taskbar?

e. Hide the Taskbar. Does the My Computer window expand to fill the entire screen?

f. Temporarily redisplay the Taskbar by moving the mouse pointer to the left edge of the screen. Does the Taskbar cover part of the My Computer window?

g. Close My Computer, "unhide" the Taskbar and Clock (if necessary), and move the Taskbar to the bottom of the screen.

h. If the Quick Launch toolbar is on the Taskbar, remove it; if it's not on the Taskbar, place it there. Which menu and menu item did you use to accomplish this?

i. Return the Quick Launch toolbar to its original state and reduce the Taskbar to its normal size.

Lab Exercise 2 (Section 4.1)

a. Start WordPad and maximize it; then start Paint (which is also on the Accessories submenu of the Start button) and maximize it.

b. Cascade the WordPad and Paint windows. Which one is in front?

c. Tile the two windows horizontally. Which is on top?

d. Tile the windows vertically. Which is on the left?

e. Issue the Minimize All Windows command (from the Taskbar's right-click menu), reducing WordPad and Paint to buttons on the Taskbar. Which button is highlighted?

f. Restore the WordPad window; then close it.

g. Issue the Undo Minimize All command (from the Taskbar's right-click menu). Does the Paint window occupy the entire Desktop?

h. Close the Paint window.

Lab Exercise 3 (Section 4.2)

a. Start Explorer and open the Windows folder.

b. Use drag-and-drop to add Calc and Dialer items to the Start menu. Which item is positioned higher on this menu?

c. Close Explorer.

d. Use the Add command button in the Taskbar Properties dialog box to add a Dialer shortcut to the Programs submenu of the Start menu. Name this shortcut DIALER (all capital letters). Does it appear on the menu in capital letters?

e. Try to use drag-and-drop to move the DIALER shortcut from the Programs submenu to the Start menu. Did Windows allow you to do this? Do both Dialer and DIALER appear on the Start menu?

f. Use right-click pop-up menus to delete the Calc, Dialer, and (if it exists) DIALER items from the Start button menus. Was a warning message displayed at any time?

g. Close any open windows.

Lab Exercise 4 (Section 4.3)

a. Start the Find utility. What steps did you take to do this?

b. Locate all files and folders in the Windows folder, but *not* in any of its subfolders, whose names contain the word *start*. How many are there?

c. Clear the Search Results window without closing Find. How did you accomplish this?

d. Now locate all files and folders in the \Windows\Start Menu folder and its subfolders whose names contain the letters *ter*. How many were found?

e. Create a shortcut for the folder Printers (displayed in the Search Results window) and place it on the Desktop. Can this be done by both copy-and-paste and drag-and-drop?

f. Delete the new shortcut.

g. Open the Printers folder (displayed in the Search Results window). Can this be done by

- Double clicking on it?
- Right-clicking on it and choosing a command from the pop-up menu?
- Choosing the appropriate command from Find's File menu?

h. Close the Find utility.

Lab Exercise 5 (Section 4.3)

a. Insert the Student Disk in its drive and start the Find utility.

b. Use Find to locate all files in the root folder of this disk which satisfy each of the following criteria. (Be sure to clear the Search Results window after each search is complete.)

- Files that were last saved in the year 1997
- Files of type Application
- Files that are at most 10 KB in size

In each case, how many files were found?

c. In the WordPad folder of the Student Disk, locate all documents that contain the word *this*. Which files, if any, were found?

d. Use Find to determine all files on the entire Student Disk that satisfy *all* of the following criteria:

- Their names contain the letters *file*.
- They were saved between 1/1/97 and 12/31/98.
- They are larger than one KB in size.

e. Exit the Find utility and remove the Student Disk from its drive.

Lab Exercise 6 (Section 4.4)

a. Start Explorer and display the File Types page of the Folder Options dialog box. How many tabs are there in this dialog box?

b. Create a new registered file type with extension NOT and description *Notepad Document*. What is the name of the dialog box in which this information is entered?

c. Define the following two actions for the new file type:

   1. Open with Notepad (The path name for the Notepad program file is \Windows\Notepad.exe.)
   2. Print (Add " /p" — without the quotes, but with the space before the slash — after Notepad's path name to define this command.)

d. Choose the OK command button twice to return to the Folder Options dialog box, and close the latter. Were any warning messages issued?

e. Insert the Student Disk in its drive and select this drive in Explorer's folder tree.

f. Check that your printer is ready, right-click on the NoteDoc file, and choose Print from the pop-up menu. Does Notepad close after printing is complete? If not, close Notepad.

g. Use the Folder Options dialog box to remove the registered file type NOT. Were any warning messages issued in the process?

h. Close Explorer and remove the Student Disk from its drive.

Lab Exercise 7 (Section 4.5)

a. Open the Printers folder window. How many printers are listed there?

b. Open the Properties dialog box for the printer that you normally use. What is the name of this printer?

c. Print a test page. Did it print in portrait or landscape format?

d. Click on the Details tab. What is the name of the port to which this printer is connected?

e. By locating the appropriate feature in the Properties dialog box, answer each of the following questions and give the location (for example, "Details page" or "Setup dialog box") of the feature. If a feature cannot be located, answer "Not found".

   - Is paper orientation set to portrait or landscape?
   - What paper size is currently selected?
   - What is the current printing resolution?
   - Are any font cartridges installed?

- How much printer memory is installed?

f. Close the printer's Properties dialog box and the Printers folder.

Lab Exercise 8 (Section 4.5)

Note: You may not be able to do this exercise if you are using a network printer.

a. Open the Printers folder window and select the printer you normally use.

b. Open the "print manager" window for this printer (by choosing that printer's icon). What is the real title of this window?

c. Pause the printer (so that it will accept print jobs, but not print them). How did you accomplish this?

d. Start the WordPad word processor (from the Accessories submenu of the Start menu's Programs option). Type your name, your class, and the date on separate lines.

e. Choose the Print command from the File menu, and in the resulting dialog box, choose the Properties command button. Is portrait or landscape orientation selected?

f. Close the Properties dialog box and choose the OK button in the Print dialog box to send the document to the printer. Was it printed?

g. Insert the Student Disk in its drive and open the Preamble document in WordPad. (Answer "No" to the warning message.) Now, send this document to the printer.

h. Switch to the "print manager" window. How many print jobs are in the queue? What is the first job called? *Optional*: Size the window so that it has no extra "white space" and capture it.

i. Cancel all print jobs and restart ("unpause") the printer. How did you accomplish these tasks?

j. Close the print manager window, the Printers folder, and WordPad, and remove the diskette from its drive.

Lab Exercise 9 (Section 4.6)

a. Insert the Student Disk in its drive.

b. Start Explorer and open the root folder of this drive.

c. Display the property sheet for the Shortcut to WordPad file. How did you accomplish this?

d. Set the Read-only attribute for this file. Is the System attribute available (can it be set)?

e. Try to delete the Shortcut to WordPad file. What message is displayed?

f. Using the Shortcut page of this property sheet:

- Set the default folder ("Start in") to A:\.
- Set the shortcut key to Ctrl+Alt+W.
- Set the Run type to Minimized.

g. Press Ctrl+Alt+W. Does WordPad start? If not, open it.

h. Choose Open from the File menu. What is the current (default) folder in the Open dialog box?

i. Cancel the Open dialog box, close WordPad and Explorer, and remove the Student Disk from its drive.

If You Want to Learn More ...

The notes presented here allow you to delve more deeply into some of the topics covered in this chapter.

More on the Taskbar's toolbars

In Section 4.1, we described how to place a toolbar on the Taskbar. You can also turn such a toolbar into a *floating toolbar* — a window on the Desktop containing the same icons. To do so, drag the position button at the left of the given toolbar onto the Desktop. The toolbar will disappear from the Taskbar and a window will open on the Desktop containing the toolbar's icons. The following figure shows the floating toolbar created from the Desktop toolbar:

After you create a floating toolbar, you can:

- Move or resize it (but not minimize or maximize it).
- Add icons to it (by dragging them into the window) or delete icons from it (by right-clicking on the icon and choosing Delete from the pop-up menu).

- Make the icons large or small by right-clicking on an empty part of the window, pointing at View on the pop-up menu, and then choosing Large or Small from the resulting submenu.
- Display names for the icons by right-clicking on an empty part of the window and choosing Show Text from the pop-up menu.
- Restore it to a toolbar on the Taskbar by dragging its title bar onto the Taskbar.

The floating toolbar feature provides immediate access to the icons in any folder. It also allows you to organize your Desktop icons, perhaps placing groups of related icons on a floating toolbar so that they gain visual coherence. If you are familiar with Windows 3.1, you will recognize this feature as Microsoft's way of paying homage to the Windows 3.1 *Program Manager.*

Putting the Desktop on the Start menu

As you know, if you want to access a Desktop shortcut that is covered by open windows, you could do so by clicking on the Show Desktop icon on the Taskbar (if it's displayed there) or by choosing the Minimize All Windows command from the Taskbar's right-click menu. Here's another way to set up Windows so that you can quickly access the Desktop.

1. Start Explorer or My Computer.
2. Drag the Desktop subfolder of the Windows folder onto the Start button.

The Desktop will now appear as a shortcut on the Start menu. When you click on this menu item, the Desktop folder will open, displaying all the shortcuts you normally see as icons on the actual Desktop. Choose one of these icons to open the corresponding file or folder.

Using wildcards

If you're an experienced DOS user, you have probably used wildcards (Section 4.3) quite a bit in copying, moving, or deleting files, or displaying directory lists. In Windows 98, wildcards can only be used in Open and Save As dialog boxes and in the Find utility (and, there, only in searching for files). However, if you wish to return to your wildcard ways while running Windows 98, there is a work-around: Choose the MS-DOS Prompt item from the Programs option on the Start menu; a window will open displaying the DOS prompt. Within this window, you can issue any available DOS command and include wildcards within it. (For more information about MS-DOS Prompt, see Section 12.1.)

Printer setup

Instead of opening the Printers folder to set printer properties (such as paper size or orientation), you can often specify some settings from within the application you are using. This is typically done by choosing Page Setup from the File menu, which opens a dialog box in which various printer options are available. See Sections 7.3, 8.5, and 9.2 for further information.

Other property sheets

In Sections 4.5 and 4.6, we discussed the property sheets for printers, files, folders, and shortcuts. In fact, just about everything in Windows has "properties"; right-clicking on almost *any* icon displays a pop-up menu whose last item is Properties.

In later sections of the text, we will discuss the property sheets for other objects. These include:

Display properties for the Desktop (Sections 5.2 and5.3)
Keyboard and mouse properties (Section 5.4)
Properties for the computer's clock (Section 5.5)
Sounds properties (Section 5.5)
Multimedia properties (Section 9.3)
Accessibility properties (Section 9.4)
Modem properties (Section 10.5)
Properties for the computer system as a whole (Section 10.5)
Properties for DOS applications (Section 12.2)

CHAPTER 5

Customizing Windows with Control Panel

Overview

People use computers in different ways and for different reasons. With this in mind, the designers of Windows 98 provided many ways to customize its user interface. When this capability is used properly, the result is a more pleasant and productive environment. In Section 3.4, we described one way that Windows can be customized — by placing shortcuts for frequently used applications, documents, and folders right on the Desktop. In this chapter, we will discuss how to use the Control Panel utility to further customize Windows. To be more specific, you will learn:

1. How to start, use, and close Control Panel.
2. How to choose a repeating pattern or wallpaper to decorate the Desktop.
3. How to select a screen saver.
4. How to change the color and size of various objects in the Windows 98 interface.
5. How to change other display settings such as icon size, screen resolution, and the color palette.
6. How to adjust the keyboard repeat rate and delay.
7. How to modify the operation of the mouse.
8. About other Control Panel functions, including setting the computer's clock, viewing fonts, and changing Windows' sounds.

5.1 An Introduction to Control Panel

Control Panel is a collection of small programs (*utilities*) that help you customize the Windows user interface — its colors, sounds, mouse operation, etc. — so that it looks and acts the way you want. In this section, we will provide an overview of the workings of Control Panel.

The Control Panel Window

To open the Control Panel window:

Starting Control Panel

1. Click on the Start button (or press Ctrl+Esc) to open the Start menu.
2. Point at the Settings option and hold the mouse steady for a second or two; the Settings submenu will open.
3. Click on the Control Panel item on this submenu. A window, similar to the one shown in Figure 1, will open.

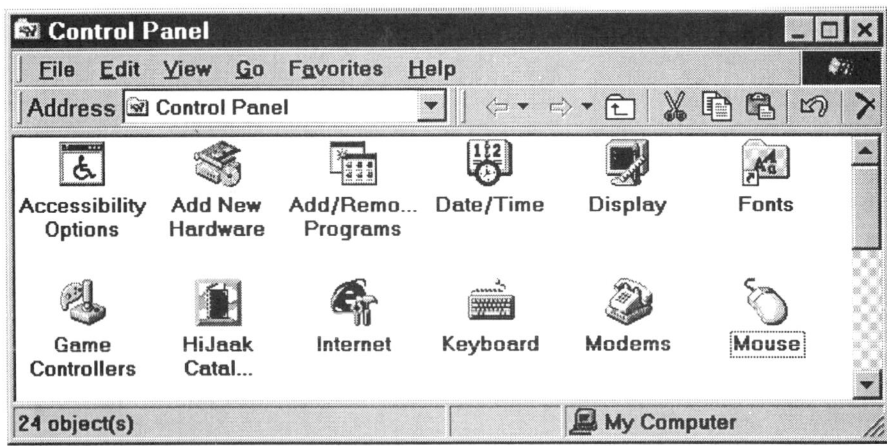

Figure 1 The Control Panel Window

Control Panel view options

The window shown in Figure 1 represents each of the Control Panel functions as a "large icon". If you want, you can display the various functions in several other ways. For example, if we choose the List option from the View menu, the window will look like this:

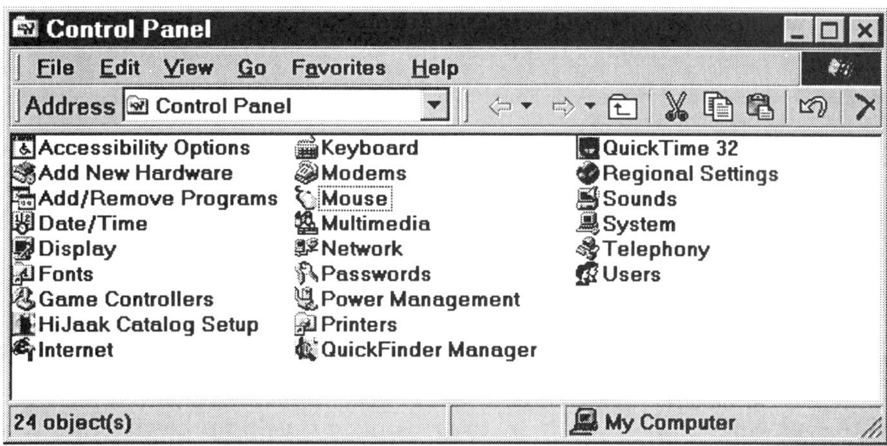

Two other display options are available on the View menu:

- Small Icons view looks similar to List view, but the icons are arranged in a different order.
- Details view lists each Control Panel function on a separate line, which also contains a brief description of that utility.

The *as Web Page* item on the View menu also changes the look of the window. Clicking on this item when *Web page* is in effect turns it off; otherwise, clicking turns it on.

NOTE

The four display options (Large Icons, Small Icons, List, and Details) can also be accessed from the toolbar. To do so, either:

- Click repeatedly on the Views button until the desired view option is displayed.

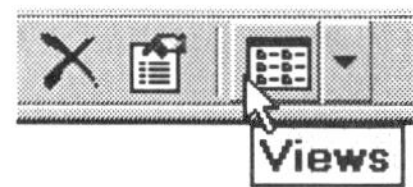

or

- Click on the down-facing triangle next to this button and then choose the desired option from the pop-up menu.

If the toolbar isn't present in your Control Panel window, you can display it by pointing at the Toolbars item on the View menu and choosing Standard Buttons from the submenu. If you forget the function of a toolbar button, point at it with the mouse; a *tool tip* will appear (*Views*, in the figure above) identifying it!

Control Panel Utilities

Each of the icons displayed in the Control Panel window represents a utility that allows you to customize one aspect of Windows. The number, the type, and sometimes even the names of the available Control Panel functions depend on your system's configuration. The following table describes the most common utilities.

Name	Description
Accessibility Options	Changes the way the keyboard, sounds, display, and mouse behave to make Windows more accessible to people with disabilities.
Add New Hardware	Aids you in installing new hardware such as modems, sound boards, and CD-ROM drives on your system.
Add/Remove Programs	Aids you in installing and removing software on your system.
Date/Time	Changes the date and time on your computer's clock.
Display	Changes screen colors, type appearance, the Desktop background, the size of objects, and screen resolution; installs screen savers.
Fonts	Adds, removes, and allows you to view the fonts on your system.
Game Controllers	Configures and tests game controllers, such as joystick devices.
Internet	Changes settings that relate to an Internet connection.
Keyboard	Changes the keyboard type, layout, and repeat rate and delay; changes the cursor blink rate.
Modems	Installs a new modem and changes a modem's properties.
Mouse	Changes the mouse type and allows you to modify aspects of its operation, such as double-click speed and pointer shape and speed.
Multimedia	Changes properties for audio, video, and MIDI (Musical Instrument Digital Interface) devices, and the playing of audio compact discs.
Network	Adds, removes, and configures network connections; aids you in accessing an installed network.
Passwords	Sets up user passwords and preferences (profiles).

Printers	Adds, removes, and changes settings (such as resolution and paper type) for printers.
Power Management	Provides options that decrease electrical power use, such as turning off the monitor or hard disk after a certain period of inactivity.
Regional Settings	Changes international settings such as the format of numbers, currencies, dates, and times.
Sounds	Changes Windows and system sounds, such as the sounds heard when Windows is started and exited.
System	Provides system information and allows you to change settings that affect system performance.
Telephony	Installs and configures drivers for computer-simulated telephone devices, such as answering machines.
Users	Sets up the computer to be used by more than one person.

Choosing a utility

To choose one of the available Control Panel utilities, perform any of the following actions:

- Choose the appropriate icon — click on it in Web style mode or double-click on it in Classic style mode (see Section 1.2).
- Select the desired icon (point at it in Web style mode or click on it in Classic style mode) and choose Open from the File menu.
- Right-click on the appropriate icon, which selects it and pops up a menu, and choose Open from this menu.

When you use a Control Panel utility to modify a setting, the new setting remains in effect every time you use Windows until that setting is changed again.

Closing Control Panel

You can close (or exit) Control Panel in by performing any of the following actions:

- Click on the close button on the right end of the title bar.
- Choose Close from the File menu.
- Press the Alt+F4 keystroke combination.

Try the following exercise on your own.

1. Turn on your computer, if necessary, to start up Windows 98 and close any open windows.
2. Start Control Panel:
   - Click on the Start button (or press Ctrl+Esc) to display the Start menu.
   - Point at the Settings option to open its submenu.
   - Click on the Control Panel item.
3. Maximize the Control Panel window.
4. If the status bar is not visible at the bottom of the Control Panel window, choose Status Bar from the View menu. Then, successively select each item in the window and take note of its function, which is displayed on the status bar.
5. Successively choose each of the four display options (Large Icons, Small Icons, List, and Details) from the View menu and note its effect on the window.
6. Open the Display utility by either choosing its icon or selecting its icon and clicking on the Open command on the File menu. Close this utility by choosing the Cancel command button.
7. Close the Control Panel window by clicking on its close button or choosing the Close command from the File menu.

5.2 *Changing the Desktop Background*

The default Windows 98 Desktop has a solid, dark-colored background. In Section 5.3, we will describe how you can change the background color. This section discusses how to change the look of the Desktop in another way: by decorating it with a picture (graphic) and/or a repeating pattern. We will also describe how to have Windows display an animated image — a *screen saver* — when your system has been idle for a specified period of time.

All the changes just described are accomplished through Control Panel's **Display** utility. To start the Display utility, open Control Panel and choose the Display icon from its window (as described in Section 5.1). The Display Properties dialog box, shown in Figure 2, will then open.

You can also open the Display Properties dialog box without starting Control Panel. To do so, right-click on an empty part of the Desktop and choose the Properties item from the resulting pop-up menu.

Choosing Wallpaper

As you can see in Figure 2, the Display Properties dialog box contains six tabs. The first of these, *Background*, allows you to decorate the Desktop (behind the icons) with a repeating pattern or a graphic image. The latter is commonly known as **wallpaper**. (Yes, using wallpaper to decorate a Desktop does sound a little strange.)

To choose a wallpaper to decorate your Desktop:

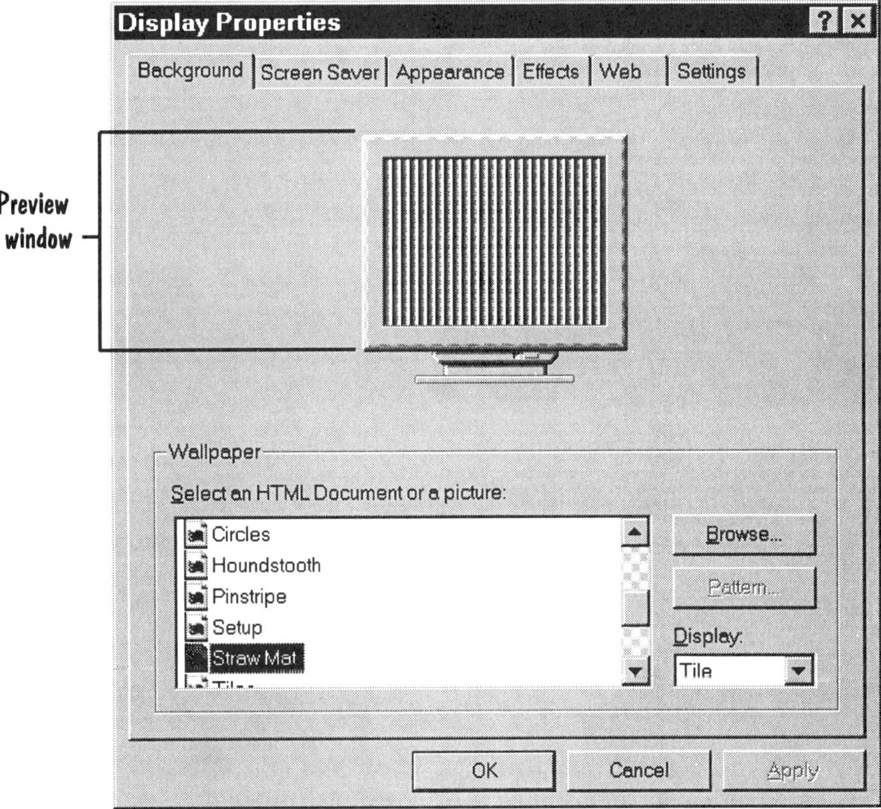

Figure 2 The Display Properties Dialog Box — Background Page

1. Open the Display Properties dialog box as described above.
2. Select a particular wallpaper by clicking on its name in the Wallpaper list box (see Figure 2). If you don't want to use wallpaper, select "(None)" from the top of the list. The preview window shows how the wallpaper will look on your Desktop.
3. From the Display drop-down list, select either Center, Tile, or Stretch.
   - Selecting Center positions the graphic in the center of the screen. If it does not cover the entire screen, the solid or patterned Desktop will be visible around it (see Figure 3a).
   - Selecting Tile repeats the graphic as many times as necessary to cover the entire screen (as in Figure 3b). With small graphics, including most of those supplied with Windows, you will probably want to choose the Tile option.
   - Selecting Stretch expands the graphic to cover the entire Desktop.
4. Choose the OK command button to put the selected wallpaper into effect and close the dialog box, or choose the Apply button to put the wallpaper into effect without closing the dialog box.

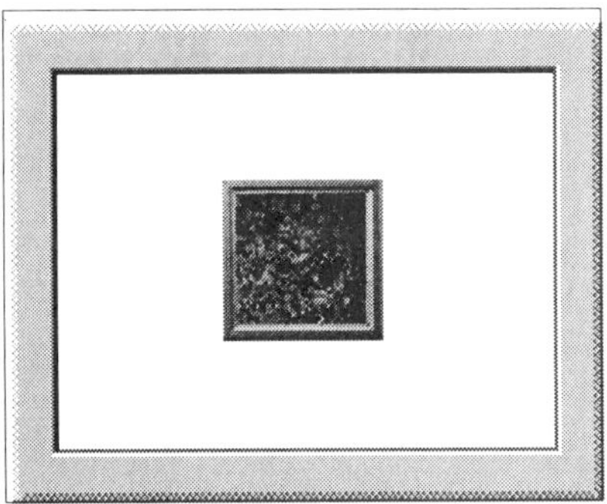

Figure 3a Centered Wallpaper

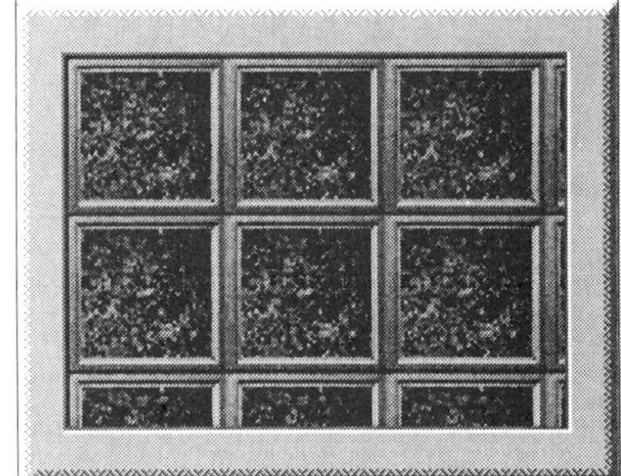

Figure 3b Tiled Wallpaper

Choosing a Desktop Pattern

If wallpaper doesn't cover the entire Desktop, then you can decorate the exposed area with a repeating geometric pattern. To do so:

1. Open the Display Properties dialog box (Figure 2).

2. Choose the Pattern command button. (If wallpaper covers the entire Desktop, this button will be dimmed, indicating that Desktop patterns are unavailable.) The following dialog box will open:

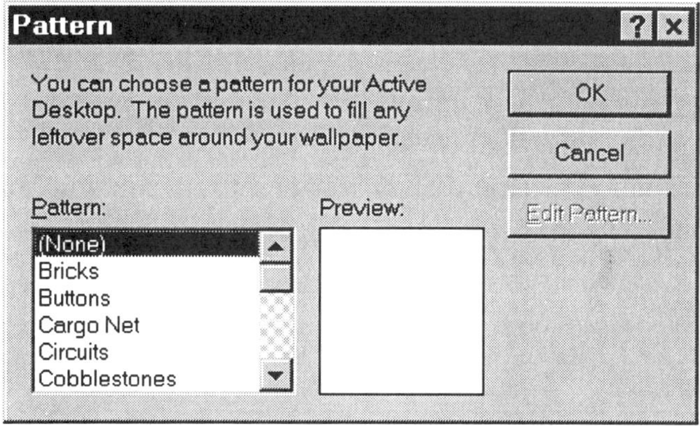

3. Select a pattern by clicking on its name in the Pattern list box. If you don't want to use a Desktop pattern, select "(None)". The Preview window will display a sample of that pattern.
4. Choose the OK command button in the Pattern dialog box; then choose the OK or Apply button in the Display Properties dialog box to put the pattern into effect.

To see the selected pattern in all its glory, close the Display Properties dialog box (if you haven't done so already) and minimize all applications, including Control Panel.

NOTE

You can create Desktop patterns of your own design by selecting an existing pattern as described above and then choosing the Edit Pattern command button. The Pattern Editor dialog box will open, allowing you to change the current pattern or create a new one. The Pattern Editor is fun to play with; if you try it out, click on the close button to close its window when you're done.

Choosing a Screen Saver

When a **screen saver** is in effect and neither the mouse nor the keyboard is used for a specified period of time, the screen will go blank or an animated graphic will be displayed. Screen savers are used just for fun or to deter others from viewing your work while you are away from the computer. They may also prevent damage to the screen from an unchanging image being "burned" into it over time.

Using the Display Properties dialog box, you can choose from among several Windows-supplied screen savers, or choose not to use a screen saver. You can also customize existing screen savers and set the *delay time* — how long the system must be inactive before the screen saver appears.

To select a screen saver:

1. Open the Display Properties dialog box (Figure 2).
2. Click on the Screen Saver tab to display the corresponding page of the dialog box, shown in Figure 4.
3. Select a screen saver by clicking on its name in the Screen Saver drop-down list. Select "(None)" if you don't want to use a screen

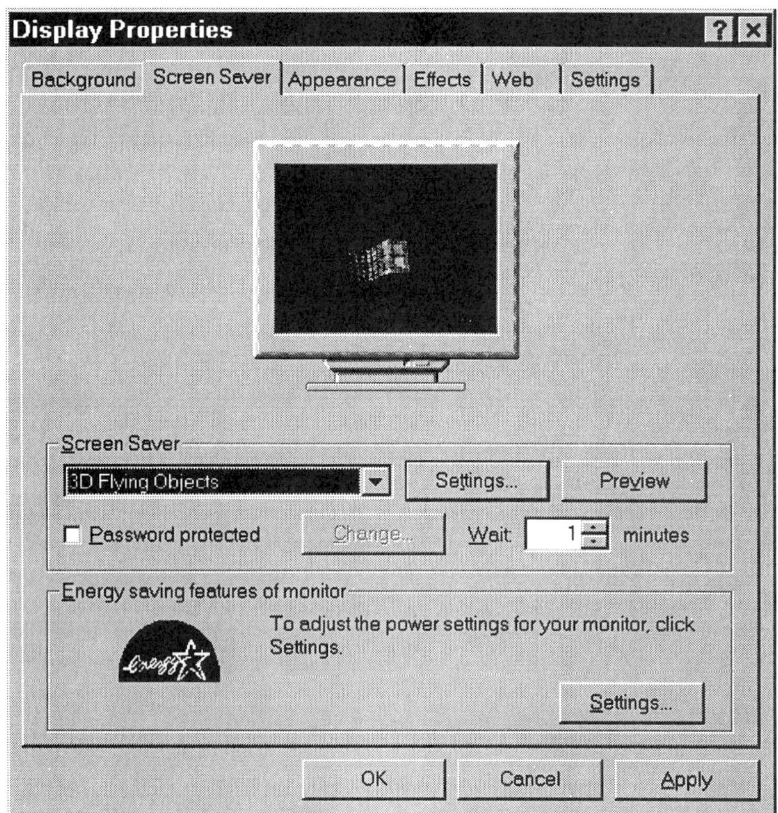

Figure 4 Display Properties — Screen Saver Page

saver. You will then see a simulation of the screen saver in the preview window.

4. To customize the selected screen saver, click on the Settings command button. A dialog box will open allowing you to make changes in the way that screen saver works.
5. To see what the screen saver looks like full-screen, click on the Preview command button. The selected screen saver will be activated for a few seconds. (You may have to click the mouse to deactivate it.)
6. To set the delay time, type a number in the Wait text box (or make use of the up or down arrow in this box to set the time).
7. Choose the OK command button to complete the process and close the dialog box, or choose the Apply button to record your changes without closing the dialog box.

If a screen saver has been selected, it will be activated after the specified delay time. To have the active application reappear on the screen, press any key or move or click the mouse.

You can set up certain screen savers so that a password of your choice must be entered to remove the screen saver's image from the screen once it has been activated. To enable password protection, select the *Password protected* check box (see Figure 4), then choose the Change command button and enter your password in the resulting dialog box. (If password protection is not available for the selected screen saver, this option will be dimmed.)

NOTE

Additional screen savers and wallpaper may be available on the Windows 98 CD-ROM. To install them, open Control Panel's Add/Remove Programs utility, click on the Windows Setup tab, and follow the instructions given in Section 2.4 for adding Windows components. (To locate screen savers and wallpaper, select Accessories in the Components list box and choose the Details button.)

You can access still more wallpaper and screen savers (together with other Desktop enhancements) by choosing the Desktop Themes icon in the Control Panel window. A *Desktop theme* allows you to customize your Desktop using a screen saver, wallpaper, colors, sounds, and other enhancements that follow a specified theme; for example, "Baseball", "Leonardo da Vinci", or "Dangerous Creatures". (If Desktop Themes does not appear in the Control Panel window, use the Add/Remove Programs utility, as described in Section 2.4, to install those themes in which you are interested.)

TUTORIAL

Try the following exercise on your own.

1. Turn on your computer, if necessary, to start up Windows 98 and close any open windows.
2. Start Control Panel and open the Display utility.
3. Select a wallpaper (your choice) from the Wallpaper list box and select Tile from the Display drop-down list. Notice the effect in the preview window. Now, successively select Stretch and Center from the Display drop-down list; notice the change in the preview window.
4. Choose the Pattern command button and then select several successive Desktop patterns from the list in the resulting dialog box. Notice the effect of each of your choices in the Preview box. Choose the OK command button to close the Pattern dialog box.
5. Choose the OK command button in the Display Properties dialog box to put the selected wallpaper and pattern into effect.
6. Close the Control Panel window to see the full effect of the changes you have made.
7. Right-click on the Desktop and choose Properties from the pop-up menu to reopen the Display Properties dialog box.
8. Return the wallpaper and pattern to their original settings.
9. Click on the Screen Saver tab to open a new page of the Display Properties dialog box.
10. Select 3D Flying Objects from the Screen Saver drop-down list and notice the effect on the preview window.
11. Choose the Preview command button to activate the screen saver full-screen. Click the mouse to deactivate it.
12. Choose the Settings command button; then, select Textured Flag from the Style drop-down list in the resulting dialog box and choose the OK button. Notice the effect in the preview window.
13. Click on the Wait text box, erase the current number, type 1, and choose the Apply button. This puts the screen saver into effect without closing the Display Properties dialog box.
14. Do not use the mouse or keyboard for one minute. The screen saver will then be activated. Deactivate it by clicking the mouse or pressing a key.
15. Return the Screen Saver drop-down list and Wait time to their original settings and choose the OK command button to close the Display Properties dialog box.

5.3 Changing Other Display Properties

In Section 5.2, we discussed some of the features found in the Display Properties dialog box: wallpaper, Desktop patterns, and screen savers. In this section, we will describe how to use the Display Properties dialog box to alter the appearance of a window, enable certain visual effects, and change the screen resolution and color palette.

Changing the Window Scheme

Through Control Panel's Display utility, Windows allows you to create a **window scheme** — to choose the color and size of the objects within a window. This feature is not only fun to play with, but can also make for a more pleasant working environment.

Windows supplies you with two basic levels of control in customizing the appearance of a window:

1. You can choose a *predefined* (built-in) window scheme.
2. You can create a *custom* window scheme (one of your own design) by:
   - Choosing a color for each of the window elements.
   - Choosing a size for certain elements, such as title, menu, and scroll bars.
   - Choosing a *font* (a type style and size) for identifying text within the window, such as titles and button captions.

All these operations are carried out from the Appearance Page of the Display Properties dialog box. To open this dialog box, either

- Start Control Panel (if it's not already open) and choose the Display icon from its window, as described in Section 5.1.

or

- Right-click on an empty part of the Desktop and choose the Properties option from the resulting pop-up menu.

Then, to display the Appearance page of this dialog box (Figure 5, on the next page), click on the Appearance tab.

Choosing a Predefined Window Scheme Windows comes with a wide variety of built-in schemes that consist of a combination of colors, sizes, and/or fonts for the various window elements. To select one of these predefined schemes:

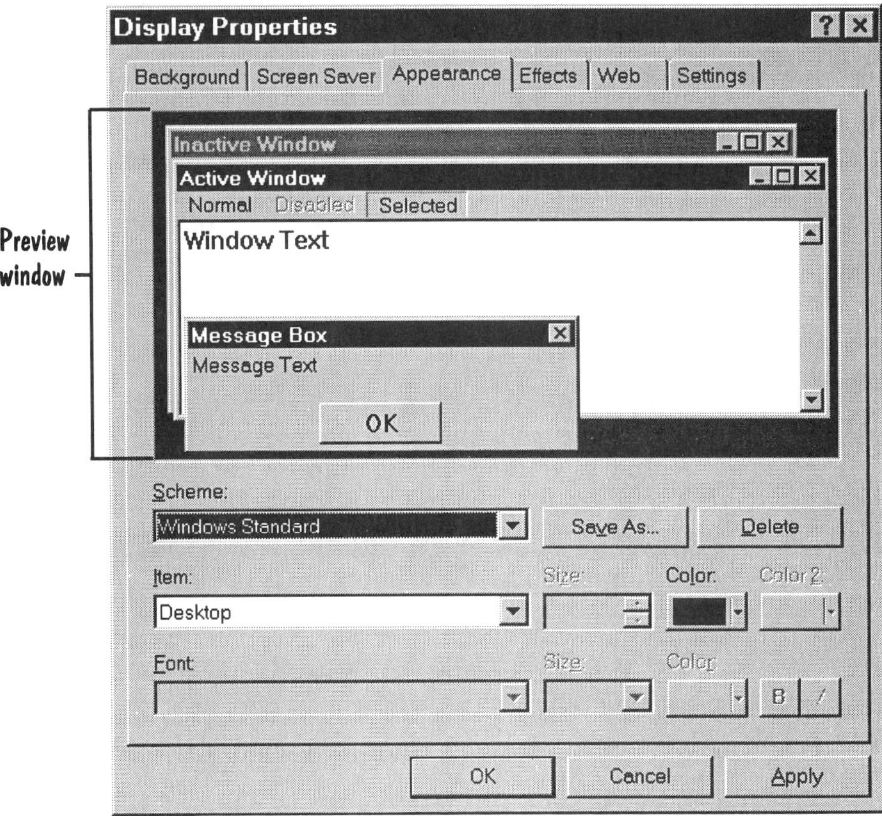

Figure 5 Display Properties Dialog Box — Appearance Page

1. Open the Display Properties dialog box and select the Appearance page as described above.

2. Open the Scheme drop-down list (by clicking on its down triangle). A list of available schemes will be displayed, as shown at the right.

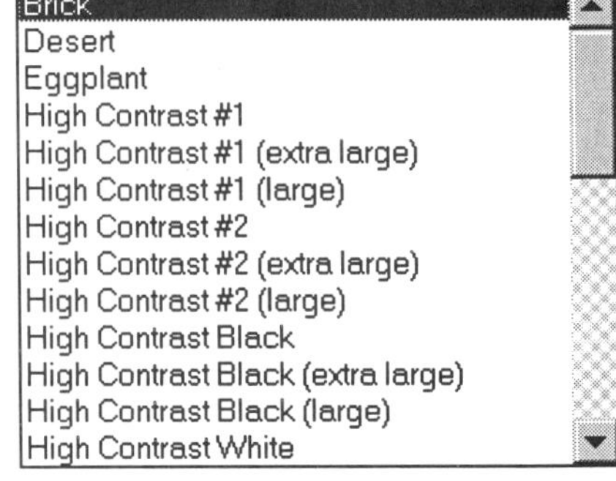

3. Select a scheme from the list. The preview window in the dialog box will show how various screen objects (active and inactive title bars, command buttons, text, and so on) look under this scheme.

4. Choose the OK command button to put the new scheme into effect and close the dialog box, or choose the Apply button to put the scheme into effect without closing the dialog box. (If you'd rather keep the prior scheme, choose the Cancel button.)

Creating a Custom Window Scheme It is likely that you will want to change certain aspects of your favorite predefined window scheme or even create one that is completely different from any built-in scheme. Windows provides you with the tools to fine-tune a scheme as much as you like. Here's how to do it:

1. Open the Display Properties dialog box and select the Appearance page as described at the beginning of this section.
2. Select the predefined scheme that is closest to what you want from the Scheme drop-down list.
3. Select a screen object to be modified by either

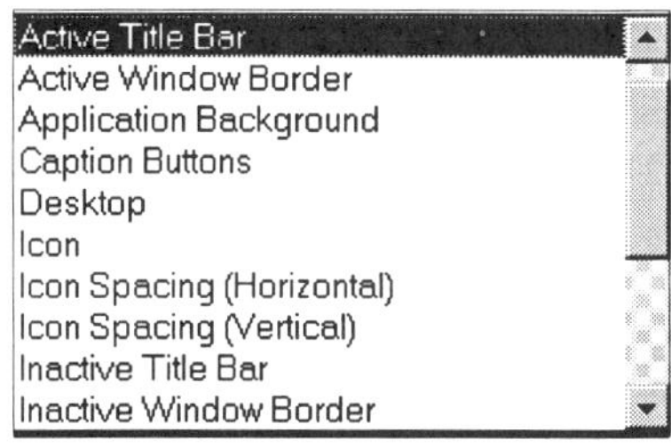

   - Clicking on that object on the Item drop-down list (see Figure 6).

   or

   - Clicking on that object in the preview window area.

   For example, if you want to change the look of the active title bar or the text that appears on it, either select Active Title Bar from the Item drop-down list or click on "Active Window" in the preview window.
4. To choose a size for the selected screen object (if this option is available), click on the Size box next to the Item text box, as

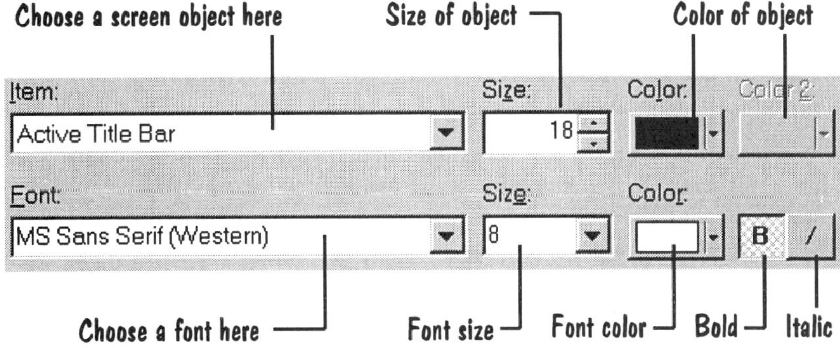

Figure 6 Screen Objects: Size, Color, and Font

shown in Figure 6. The number in the Size box gives the height (or sometimes, width) of the object in *points*. There are 72 points per inch, so the height of the Active Title Bar of Figure 6 is 18/72 of an inch, or 1/4".

5. To choose a color (or colors) for the specified screen object, click on the Color (or Color 2) box to the right of the Item text box (see Figure 6). A palette of 20 colors will be displayed, as shown at the right. Now, just click on the desired color or, if you want to view additional colors, click on the Other command button, which opens a dialog box with more color choices. (This dialog box also allows you to create your own colors.)

6. If the selected screen element contains text, you can choose the *typeface*, *font size*, *font color*, and elect to use *bold* or *italic* attributes for this text. As you make your selections, the text for the given element will change accordingly in the preview window.
   - To select a typeface (the font style), open the Font drop-down list (Figure 6) and select from the available choices.
   - To select a font size, enter a new number in the Size box to the right of the Font text box. The number displayed here represents the height of the font in *points*. (Remember: There are 72 points to the inch.)
   - To select a font color, click on the Color box to the right of the Font text box and select a color from the resulting palette. (See step 5 for more information on selecting a color.)
   - If you want, you can select bold (thicker) or italic (slanted) type for the text by clicking on the appropriate button (see Figure 6).
7. Save your new window scheme, if so desired, by choosing the Save As command button (see Figure 5) and typing a name for the scheme in the resulting dialog box. This scheme will then be added to the schemes appearing on the Scheme drop-down list.

   If you don't save your scheme, but choose OK or Apply in step 8, the scheme will still be put into effect and used in all Windows sessions until another scheme is selected. After that, however, the only way to retrieve the scheme is to recreate it step-by-step.
8. After you have made all the changes you want, choose the OK command button to put them into effect and close the dialog box, or choose the Apply button to put the changes into effect without closing the dialog box.

Modifying certain screen elements also affects other aspects of the Windows interface. For example:

- The settings for the Menu screen element are used for all Windows menus, including the Start menu.
- The font specified for the Icon screen element is also used in the Explorer folder tree and contents panes (see Section 3.2).
- The font specified for the Active Title Bar screen element is also used for the Taskbar.

Customizing the Display in Other Ways

We will now discuss the ways you can customize windows and the Desktop using the Effects, Settings, and Web pages of the Display Properties dialog box. Clicking on the Effects tab displays the page shown in Figure 7.

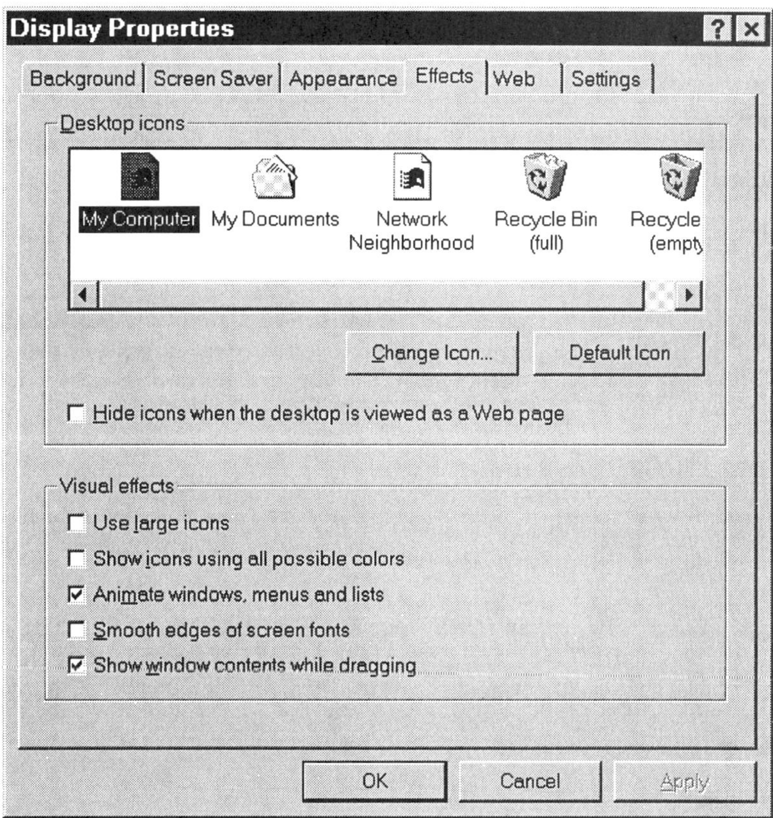

Figure 7 Display Properties Dialog Box — Effects Page

Options on the Effects page

Using the Effects page, you can change certain standard Desktop icons, such as My Computer or the Recycle Bin, to those of your own choosing. To do so:

1. Select (click on) the desired icon in the *Desktop icons* box and choose the Change Icon command button.
2. In the resulting dialog box, select a new icon and choose the OK button.

You can also alter certain visual effects by selecting or deselecting the check boxes located in the bottom portion of the Effects page. Specifically:

- Selecting the *Use large icons* check box increases the size of all icons on the Desktop, and file and folder icons in a window.
- Selecting the *Show icons using all possible colors* check box enables Windows to make use of all colors supported by your display adapter under the current color palette settings. (Changing the Windows color palette is done from the Settings page of the Display Properties dialog box, as described later in this section.)
- Selecting the *Animate windows, menus and lists* check box causes menus and drop-down lists to appear to roll down when opened and windows to appear to collapse into, or expand from, their Taskbar button when minimized or restored.
- If the *Smooth edges of screen fonts* check box is not selected, large screen text may appear to have jagged edges.
- If the *Show window contents while dragging* check box is not selected, when you move or resize a window by dragging its title bar or border, an *outline* of the window will move across the screen. Only when you release the mouse button will the actual window appear in the new location.

After you have chosen new icons and/or selected the desired visual effects, activate the OK or Apply command button in the Display Properties dialog box to put your changes into effect.

Options on the Settings page

The Settings page of the Display Properties dialog box provides ways to *globally* change the size of, and available colors for, objects on the screen; these changes apply to *everything* in the Windows environment. To change these settings:

1. Click on the Settings tab to display the corresponding page of the Display Properties dialog box. (The lower part of this page is shown in Figure 8.)

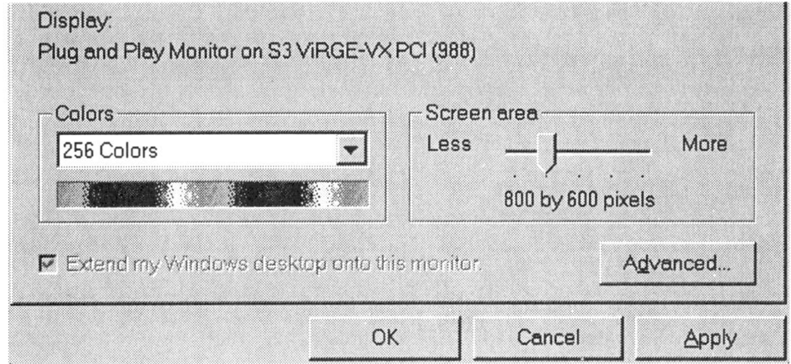

Figure 8 Color Palette and Screen Resolution Settings

2. To change the number of available screen colors (the *color palette*) select one of the options from the Colors drop-down list.

3. To change the size of screen icons, text, and other objects, choose a *screen resolution* by dragging the *Screen area slider* to *Less* or *More*. The text beneath the slider will indicate the new screen resolution, given in *pixels* — the tiny dots of light that make up the screen image. For example, the screen resolution shown in Figure 8 is 800 pixels wide by 600 pixels high. Increasing the resolution decreases the size of objects (including text), seemingly increasing the screen area. Higher resolutions also pack the pixels closer together, providing a less "grainy" image.

4. Choose the OK or Apply command button. (You may have to restart the computer to see the effect of these changes.)

Higher screen resolutions create more "screen area" and nicer looking images, but the resulting text may be too small to read easily. You can, however, sacrifice some screen area for somewhat larger text. To do so, choose the Advanced command button (see Figure 8) and, in the resulting dialog box, select Large Fonts from the Font Size drop-down list and choose the OK button. Large Fonts increases the size of all screen text by 125%. You can opt for an even bigger magnification factor by selecting Other from the Font Size drop-down list and then choosing the percentage desired in a dialog box.

The Web tab Clicking on the Web tab of the Display Properties dialog box provides you with the option of displaying a Web page as background for your Desktop. We will discuss this further in Section 6.6.

TUTORIAL

Try the following exercise on your own.

1. Turn on your computer, if necessary, to start up Windows 98 and close any open windows.
2. Open the Display Properties dialog box: Right-click on an empty part of the Desktop and choose Properties from the pop-up menu.
3. Click on the Appearance tab to open this page of the dialog box.
4. Successively select several window schemes from the Scheme drop-down list and notice their effect on the preview window.
5. Select the Windows Standard scheme.
6. Change the Desktop color to white: Select the Desktop entry in the Item drop-down list, then click on the Color box, and finally, click on the white box in the pop-up palette.
7. Alter the size, color, and text of the active window's title bar:
   - Click on the Active Window title bar *in the preview window.* "Active Title Bar" will appear in the Item text box.
   - Change the height of the title bar to 25 points by clicking on the up-arrow in the Size text box (next to the Item box) until the entry reads "25".
   - Change the color of the active window's title bar to red by clicking on the Color box (to the right of the Item box) and then clicking on the red-colored square in the pop-up palette.
   - Change the active window's title bar font by opening the Font drop-down list and selecting Arial from it.
   - Increase the size of the active window's title bar font to 10 points by clicking on the Size text box (next to the Font box), deleting the current number, and typing 10.
   - Add italics to the active window's title bar text by clicking on the Italic button.
8. Choose the Apply command button to put the new scheme into effect without closing the Display Properties dialog box. (Notice that the font used for the Taskbar buttons has changed.)
9. Select the original window scheme from the Scheme drop-down list (or select Windows Standard, if you're not sure what that scheme was).
10. Click on the Effects tab to open this page of the dialog box.
11. Successively select each check box and choose the Apply button. Try to determine the effect of each selection by trial and error combined with some experimentation.

12. Return the check boxes to their former state.
13. Choose the OK command button to close the Display Properties dialog box.

5.4 Changing the Action of Keyboard and Mouse

In terms of your physical comfort while using a computer, some of the most important factors are the look of the screen display, and the operation of the keyboard and mouse. (Another important factor, the chair you sit on, is beyond our control.) In this section, we will discuss how to alter the operation of the keyboard and mouse so they are easier and more pleasant to use.

Changing the Speed of the Keyboard

Most keys on the keyboard have a *repeat feature*; when you press such a key and hold it down, the character or action corresponding to it is repeated until the key is released. For example, if you press the B key and hold it down for a few seconds, a sequence of Bs will appear on the screen.

The number of times a key repeats in a given period of time depends on two factors:

- The *repeat delay* — how long it takes for a key to start repeating once it is pressed.
- The *repeat rate* — how fast the key repeats after the delay time has elapsed.

To change these parameters:

1. Start Control Panel (if it's not already open) and choose the **Keyboard** icon, as described in Section 5.1. The Keyboard Properties dialog box, shown in Figure 9 on the next page, will be displayed.
2. To decrease the repeat delay, drag the *Repeat delay* slider toward the word *Short* or click to the right of the slider; to increase the delay, drag the slider toward the word *Long* or click to the left of the slider.

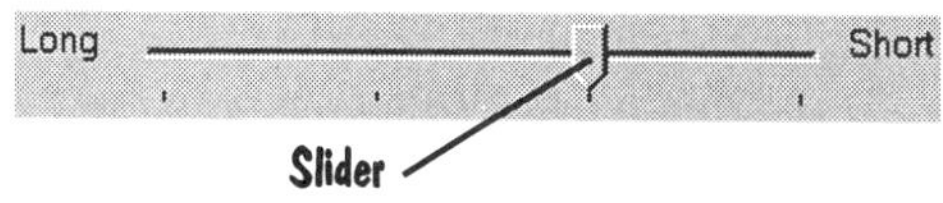

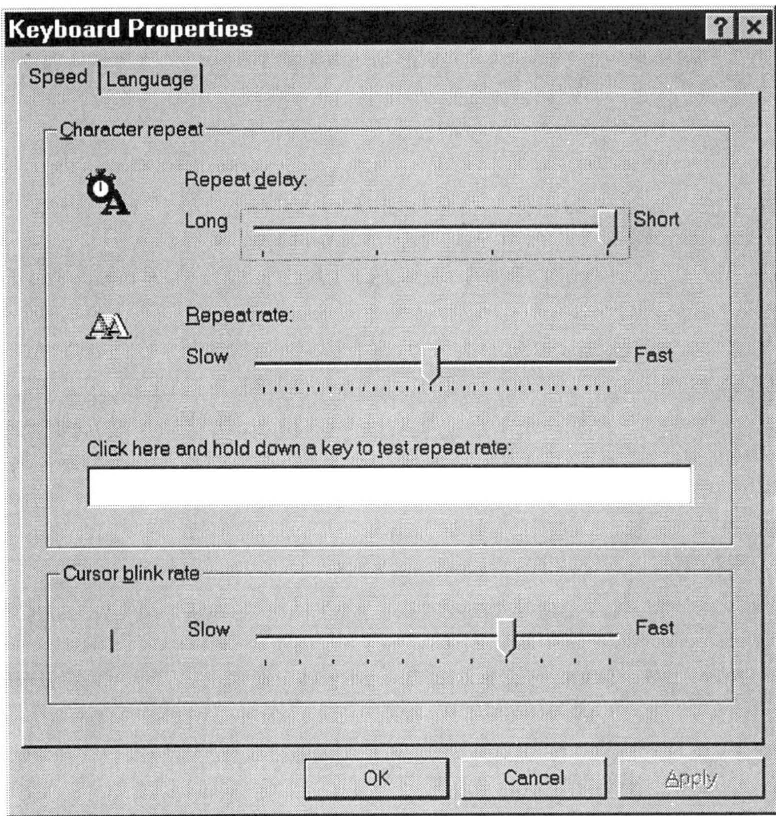

Figure 9 The Keyboard Properties Dialog Box

3. To decrease or increase the repeat rate, drag the *repeat rate* slider toward *Slow* or *Fast*, respectively, or click to the left or right of the slider.
4. To see the effect of your changes without closing the Keyboard Properties dialog box, click in the text box; then, observe what happens when you hold down a character key such as B.
5. Choose the OK or Apply button to put your changes into effect, or choose the Cancel button to leave things as they were.

NOTE

As you can see in Figure 9, the Keyboard Properties dialog box can also be used to adjust the cursor blink rate. To do so, just drag the slider toward the left (*Slow*) or right (*Fast*), or click to the left or right of the slider.

Changing the Action of the Mouse

Different people have different preferences for the way the mouse "feels" when you move or click it. The feel of the mouse affects the ease with which you can choose menu items, double-click icons, move windows, and perform many other tasks.

To change the mouse settings:

1. Start Control Panel (if it's not already open) and choose the **Mouse** icon, as described in Section 5.1. The Mouse Properties dialog box (Figure 10) will be displayed. (With certain types of mice, this dialog box looks considerably different.)
2. On the Buttons page of this dialog box (which is shown in Figure 10), you can:

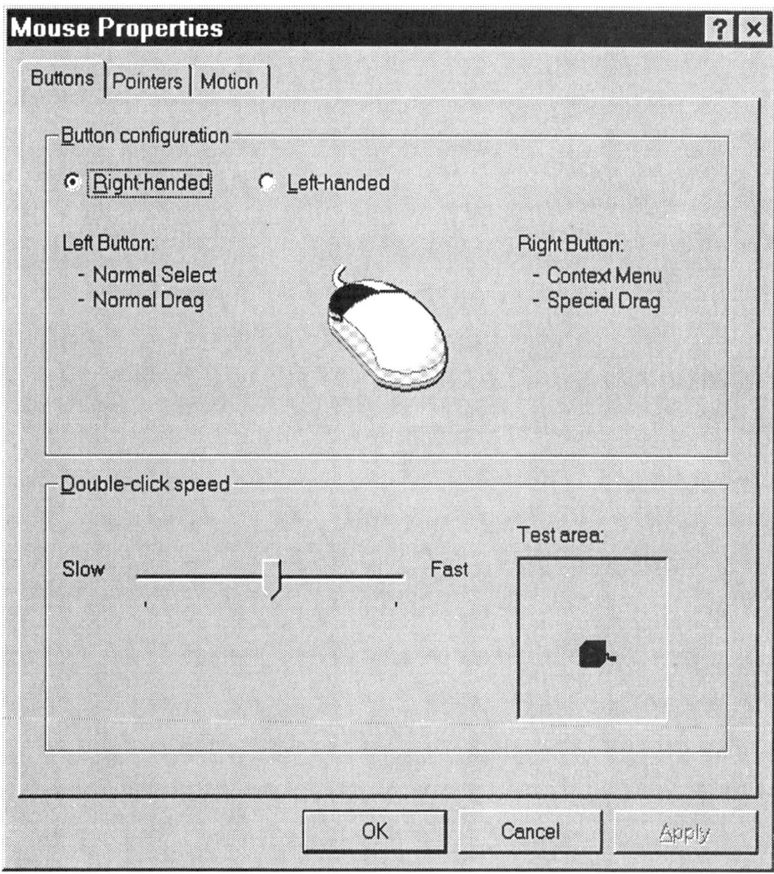

Figure 10 The Mouse Properties Dialog Box

- Swap the functions of the left and right mouse buttons. By default, the left mouse button is the *primary button* — it is used to choose menu items, select icons, and so on; the right button performs the functions we have referred to as right-clicking and right-dragging. If you want to make the right mouse button the primary one, select the *Left-handed* option button (so-named because it usually makes the mouse easier to use for left-handed people). To return to the default configuration, select the *Right-handed* option button.
- Change the double-click speed — the amount of time that elapses before Windows 98 interprets one double-click as two separate clicks. Drag the *slider* to the left (toward *Slow*) or click to the left of the slider to allow yourself more time between the clicks in a double-click. You can test the results by double-clicking on the box in the *Test area*; if Windows interprets your two clicks as a double-click, a "jack-in-the-box" pops out.

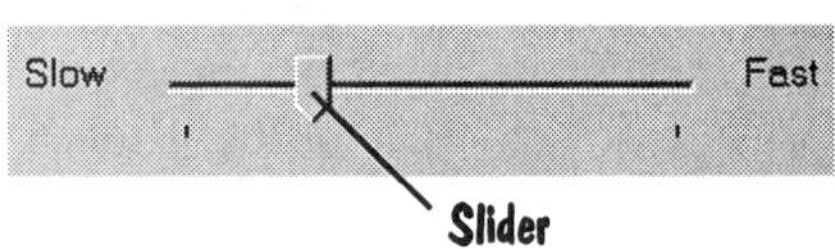

3. Click on the Pointers tab to provide options that allow you to change the shapes (and, in some cases, the colors) of the various Windows pointers.
4. Click on the Motion tab to provide options that:
   - Change the *pointer speed* — the speed with which the pointer moves across the screen when you move the mouse on the desk top. To increase or decrease the speed, drag the slider in the appropriate direction:

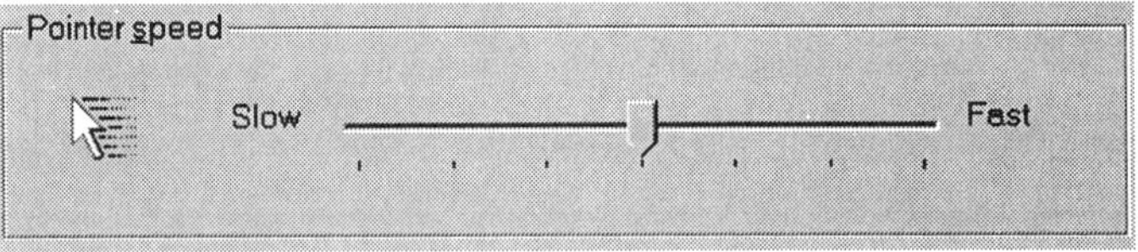

   - Show *mouse trails* — a sequence of pointer icons that follows the path of the mouse across the screen. To turn mouse trails on or off, select or deselect the *Show pointer trails* check box on the Motion page. To increase or decrease the length of the trails, move the slider in the appropriate direction:

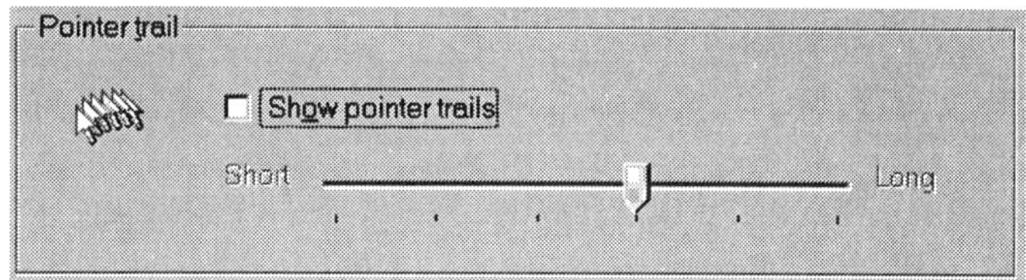

If the *Show pointer trails* check box is selected, moving the mouse pointer in the dialog box demonstrates the effect. (Most people find pointer trails annoying on a regular monitor, but useful on some portable PC's LCD screens.)

5. Choose the OK command button to put your changes into effect and close the Mouse Properties dialog box, or choose the Apply button to put the changes into effect without closing the dialog box.

TUTORIAL

Try the following exercise on your own.

1. Turn on your computer, if necessary, to start up Windows 98 and close any open windows.
2. Start Control Panel from the Settings option on the Start menu.
3. Open the Keyboard Properties dialog box by choosing the Keyboard icon in the Control Panel window.
4. Set the *Repeat delay* to Long and the *Repeat rate* to Fast by dragging the sliders to the far left and far right, respectively. With these settings, a key must be held down "a long time" before it starts to repeat, but then repeats rapidly. Click on the test box and hold down a character key (such as A) to see the effect.
5. Set the *Repeat delay* to Short and the *Repeat rate* to Slow by dragging the sliders to the appropriate positions. Click on the test box and hold down a character key (such as A) to see the effect.
6. Set the *Cursor blink rate* slider to Slow; then set it to Fast. Notice the effect of each on the "insertion point" to the left of the slider.
7. Choose the Cancel command button to close the Keyboard Properties dialog box without putting your changes into effect.
8. Open the Mouse Properties dialog box by choosing the Mouse icon in the Control Panel window.

9. Select the *Left-handed* option button and activate the Apply command button. Now, click the left mouse button on the *Right-handed* option button and notice the result. Then, right-click on the *Right-handed* option button and choose Apply again to return the mouse to "right-handed" use.
10. Set the *Double click speed* slider to Fast and then to Slow. In each case, double-click at a few different speeds on the "jack-in-the-box" to see the effect. Jack will pop up or go down if Windows interprets your two clicks as a double-click.
11. Click on the Motion tab to open the corresponding page.
12. Select the *Show pointer trails* check box and drag its slider from Slow to Fast. Notice the effect on the mouse pointer.
13. Click on the General tab. Note the options available for your mouse and then close this dialog box.
14. Choose the Cancel command button in the Mouse Properties dialog box and then close the Control Panel window.

5.5 Other Control Panel Options

In this section, we will describe a few additional Control Panel functions. (Still others are discussed elsewhere in the text.)

Setting the Computer's Clock

Your computer contains an internal clock powered by a battery that keeps track of the date and time for the computer system. These settings are used by the Taskbar Clock, Explorer, and numerous other applications for various purposes.

The internal clock normally keeps fairly accurate time, but it may need to be adjusted every once in a while. To change the system date and time:

1. Start Control Panel (if it's not already open) and choose the **Date/Time** icon, as described in Section 5.1. The Date/Time Properties dialog box, shown in Figure 11, will be displayed.
2. Change the time with the aid of the digital clock in the lower right part of this dialog box. The hours, minutes, seconds and

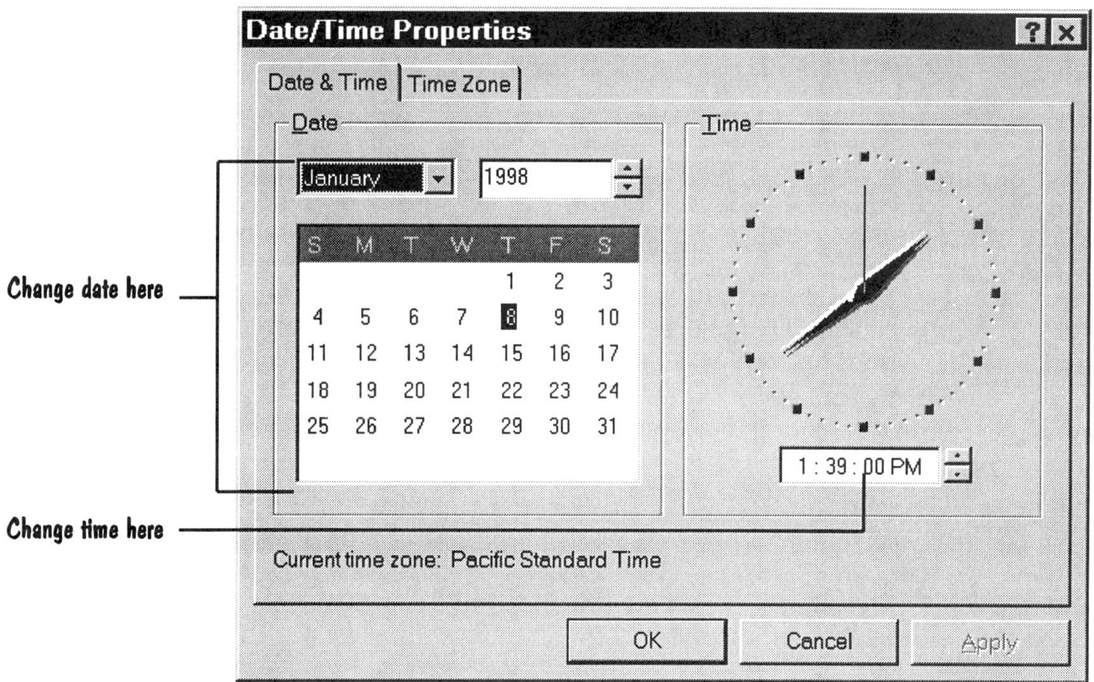

Figure 11 Date/Time Properties Dialog Box

AM/PM areas are set separately. To change any of these areas, click on it, delete the current setting, and type in the new one (or click on the up or down arrow button until the correct setting appears).

3. To change the date, use the left side of the dialog box. Select the correct month from the drop-down list and type in the correct year in the text box (or click on the up or down arrow button until the correct year appears). The correct day is set by clicking on the appropriate number on the calendar.
4. Choose either the OK command button to put your changes into effect and close the Date/Time Properties dialog box, the Apply button to put the changes into effect without closing the dialog box, or the Cancel button to discard all changes.

Here are a couple of easier ways to open the Date/Time Properties dialog box shown in Figure 11:

- Double-click on the Clock on the Taskbar.

or

- Right-click on the Taskbar Clock and choose the Adjust Date/Time command from the resulting pop-up menu.

You can use the Date/Time Properties dialog box to look up dates as you would with a conventional calendar. To do so, select the desired month and year from their respective drop-down lists, and the calendar for that month will be displayed. When you are done, be sure to choose the Cancel command button to close the dialog box. If you click on OK (or press the Enter key), the computer's internal clock will be set to the date highlighted on the calendar!

Viewing Your Fonts

A **font** is a collection of characters — letters, numerals, and other symbols — of a given design, size, and style. Examples of fonts are "12-point Times New Roman" and "10-point Arial bold"; these fonts look like this:

12-point Times New Roman **10-point Arial bold**

The design, or *typeface*, of a font determines the overall look of the characters; the fonts shown above are examples of the Times New Roman and Arial typefaces. The *size* of a font is its height, measured in points; a *point* is 1/72 of an inch. Thus, 12-point type is roughly 1/6-inch high. Fonts are also distinguished by their *attributes*; for example: regular, **bold**, or *italic*.

Some fonts are available in discrete sizes, such as 8-point, 10-point, etc. Others, known as **scalable fonts**, can be used in any size. Times New Roman and Arial are examples of a kind of scalable font called **TrueType**, which is included with the Windows software. TrueType fonts are available from many other sources, as well.

We will show how to make use of fonts in applications in Chapter 7. Here, we describe how to employ Control Panel to view or print samples of the fonts stored on your hard disk. (Control Panel also allows you to add or remove fonts from your disk, but we won't discuss this feature.)

To view or print font samples:

1. Start Control Panel and choose the **Fonts** icon, as described in Section 5.1. The Fonts subfolder of the Windows folder, shown in Figure 12, will open. (The "TT" icon indicates a TrueType font.)

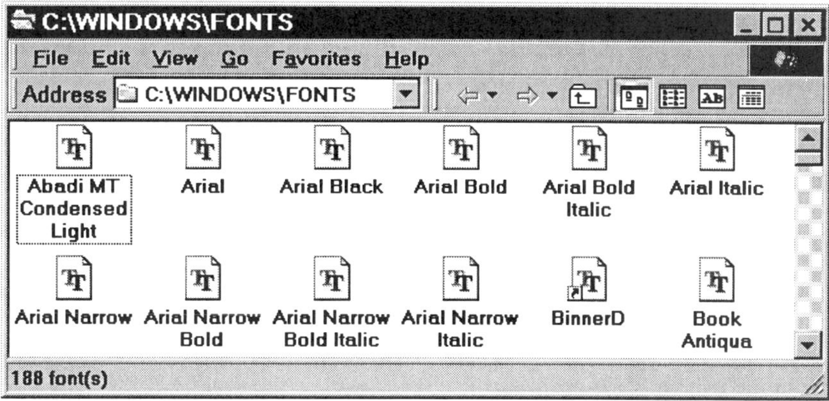

Figure 12 The Fonts Folder (Large Icons View)

2. Select the font in which you are interested.
3. To view a sample of the selected font, either choose its icon or click on the Open command on the File menu. A dialog box, similar to the one in Figure 13, will be displayed.

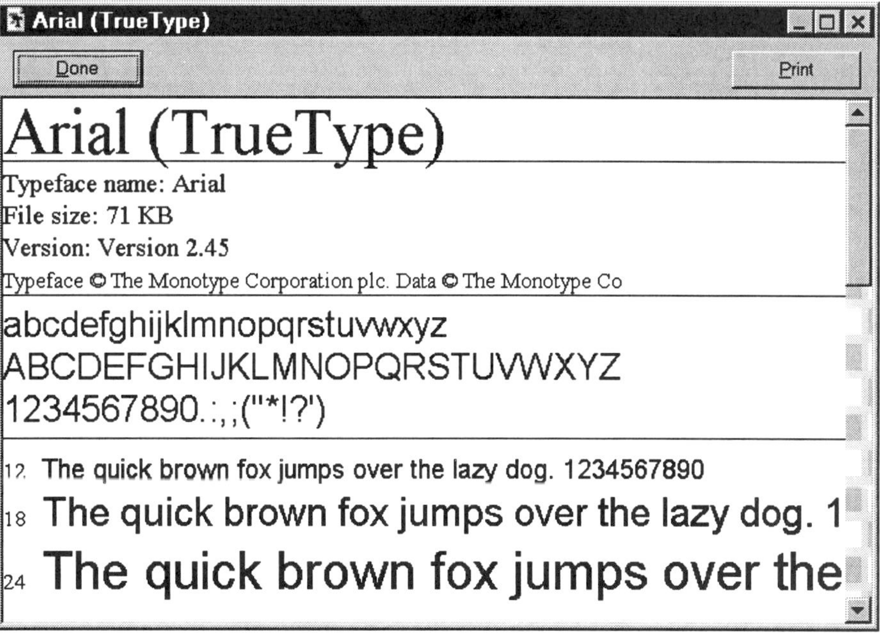

Figure 13 Opening a Selected Font

4. To print the displayed font sample, choose the Print command button in this dialog box and then choose the OK button in the resulting Print dialog box.

   A sample of the selected font can also be printed directly from the Fonts folder window (Figure 12) by choosing the Print command from either the File menu or the right-click pop-up menu.

5. To close the dialog box and return to the Fonts folder window, click on the close button or choose the Done command button.

Figure 12 shows the default "Large Icons" view of the Fonts folder. Even when this window is maximized, it will probably only show a small portion of your available fonts without scrolling. To display more font names and icons:

- Choose the *Hide Variations (Bold, Italic, etc.)* command from the View menu if it's not already checked. Then, instead of seeing (for example) "Arial","Arial Bold", "Arial Bold Italic", and "Arial Italic", only "Arial" will be displayed.
- Choose either List, List Fonts by Similarity, or Details from the View menu, or by clicking a toolbar button as indicated here. (If these buttons are not displayed in the Fonts folder window, point at Toolbars on the View menu and choose Standard Buttons from the resulting pop-up menu.) The List option displays the most font names at once; Similarity lists the fonts and describes their degree of similarity to the selected font; Details provides, for each font, the name, size, and creation date of the file that contains it. You will probably find the List view option to be the most useful.

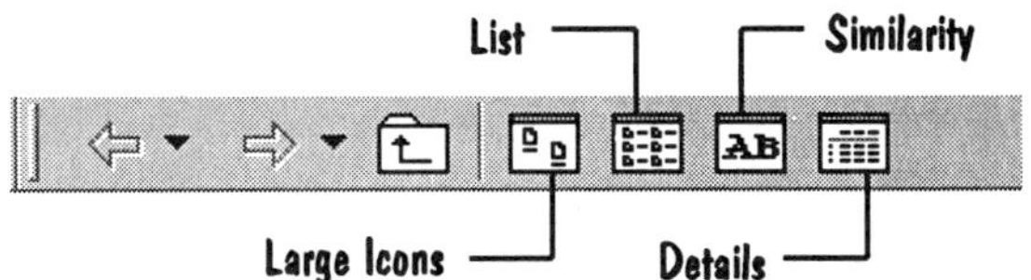

The Sounds Utility

If your computer is equipped with a sound card and speakers, you can specify that certain sounds be played to accompany certain system "events", such as minimizing an application or exiting Windows. The assignment of a sound to a given event is made from within Control Panel's **Sounds utility**.

To start the Sounds utility:

1. Open the Control Panel window and choose the Sounds icon as described in Section 5.1. The Sounds Properties dialog box, shown in Figure 14, will open.

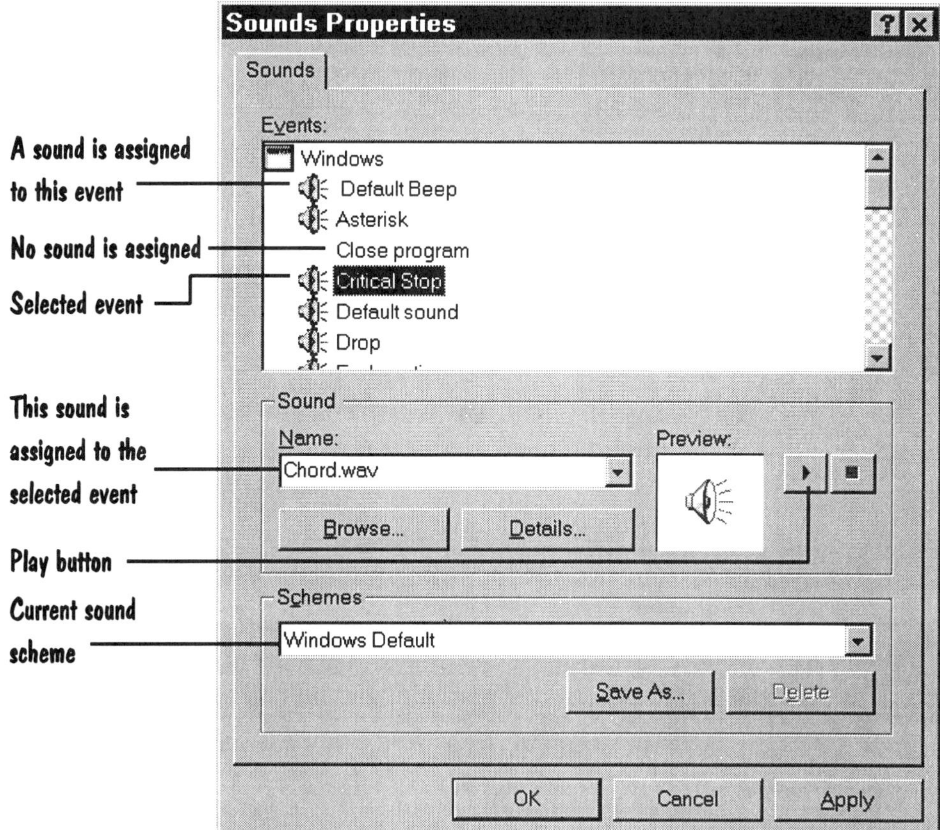

Figure 14 The Sounds Properties Dialog Box

Using the Sounds Properties dialog box, you can:

- Choose a built-in *sound scheme*, consisting of a collection of sounds pre-assigned to system events, or choose not to use sounds at all.
- Create a custom sound scheme by assigning particular sounds to specific events.

Selecting a Built-in Sound Scheme Windows comes equipped with several sound schemes. To select one of them:

1. Open the Sounds Properties dialog box, as described above.
2. Select a sound scheme from the Schemes drop-down list. Select "No Sounds" from the list if you do not want to hear sounds at system events.

Previewing sounds

3. To listen to (*preview*) an assigned sound, select the associated event from the Events list box and click on the Play button. To terminate a sound file before it has finished playing, click on the Stop button.

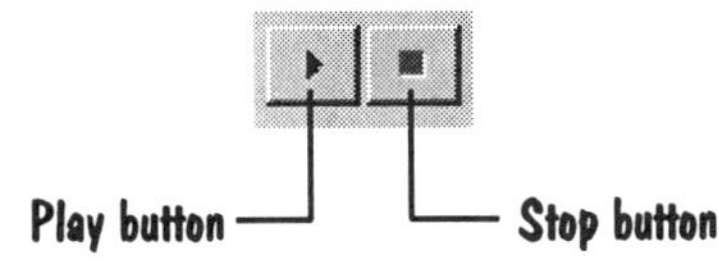

4. Choose the Apply command button, which puts the selected sound scheme into effect without closing the dialog box, or choose the OK button to put the scheme into effect and close the dialog box.

Creating a Custom Sound Scheme If you have the time and inclination, you can assign a sound of your choosing to each individual system event, creating a custom sound scheme. To do so:

1. Select a built-in sound scheme from the Schemes drop-down list that is similar to what you want.
2. Select a system event from the Events list box. (This box displays all events to which you can assign sounds; some events, such as Asterisk and Exclamation refer to dialog boxes of certain types.) The selected event will become highlighted.

   If the selected event is already associated with a sound, it will be preceded by the "speaker" symbol shown at the right, and the name of the corresponding sound file will be displayed in the Name text box. To preview the sound, click on the Play button.

3. To assign a new sound to the selected event, select another sound file from the Name drop-down list. (This list contains all files with extension *wav* in the default folder; to select a sound file from another folder, choose the Browse command button.)
4. Repeat steps 2 and 3 until your sound scheme is complete.
5. If you would like to save your new sound scheme (so that it will be added to the Schemes drop-down list), choose the Save As command button, enter a name for the scheme in the resulting dialog box, and choose the OK button.

6. Choose the Apply command button, which puts the new sound scheme into effect without closing the dialog box, or choose the OK button to put the scheme into effect and close the dialog box. (The Cancel button closes the dialog box and restores the previous scheme.)

And a Few More Utilities ...

To close this chapter, we will briefly discuss a few additional Control Panel utilities. Still others are described in other parts of this text.

The Passwords Utility Using this utility:

- You can change the passwords used for starting Windows and accessing other password-protected services, such as logging onto a network.
- You can set up a user profile for anyone who uses the computer. A *user profile* is a collection of preferences, such as the icons that appear on the Desktop, which is put into effect when one logs onto Windows by entering a username and password in the Enter Password dialog box. (The Users utility, described below, provides a Wizard to help accomplish this task.)

Power Management This utility gives you the opportunity to reduce the power consumption of your computer by turning off certain components (for example, the monitor and hard disk) after a specified period of idleness.

The Regional Settings Utility This utility customizes the way Windows displays numbers, currencies, and times. Its settings affect Windows itself and those Windows applications that make use of them.

The Users Utility This utility allows you to establish and change *multi-user settings* (user profiles) so that the computer can be used efficiently by more than one person. When a user logs onto Windows, his or her username determines which Desktop settings (icons, wallpaper, and so on) are put into effect.

To use this utility to establish a user profile, choose its icon from the Control Panel window, which starts the Multi-user Settings Wizard. Then, enter a username, an optional password, and indicate the type of settings to be affected. When done, click on the Finish button.

Chapter Summary

Control Panel Basics	To start Control Panel	Click on the Start button to open the Start menu, point at the Settings option, and choose Control Panel from the submenu.
	To change views in the Control Panel window	Choose Large Icons, Small Icons, List, or Details from the View menu; *or* click on the appropriate toolbar button.
	To select a Control Panel function (utility)	Choose its icon in the Control Panel window; *or* select its icon and choose Open from the File menu.
Control Panel Utilities and their Functions	Display	Selects and customizes a Desktop pattern (Background page). Selects wallpaper (Background page). Selects or customizes a screen saver (Screen Saver page). Selects a built-in window scheme or modifies an existing one (Appearance page). Changes certain system icons (Effects page). Turns on or off certain visual effects (Effects page). Changes the screen resolution and color palette (Settings page). Allows the Desktop to be viewed as a Web page (Web page).
	Keyboard	Changes the repeat rate and delay. Changes the cursor blink rate.
	Mouse	Selects the primary mouse button (Buttons page). Changes the double-click speed (Buttons page). Changes the mouse pointer icons (Pointers page). Changes pointer speed (Motion page). Shows mouse pointer trails (Motion page).
	Date/Time	Adjusts the internal clock's date and time.
	Sounds	Changes the sounds associated with certain Windows events.
	Fonts	Views and prints font samples. Add or remove fonts.

Review Exercises

Section 5.1

1. To start Control Panel, point at the ____________ option on the Start menu and then click on the Control Panel item.
2. To start a particular Control Panel utility, choose its icon or select it and click on the ____________ command on the File menu or the right-click pop-up menu.
3. True or false: The type and number of Control Panel functions available for your computer system depend on its configuration.
4. True or false: If you change a Control Panel setting, the original setting will be restored the next time you start Windows.
5. Which of the following Control Panel utilities can be used to change the properties of audio devices connected to your system?
   a. Modems
   b. Multimedia
   c. Sounds
   d. Regional Settings
6. Which of the following Control Panel utilities can be used to change settings such as the format of numbers and currencies?
   a. Modems
   b. Multimedia
   c. Regional Settings
   d. System

Section 5.2

7. To place a patterned background on your Desktop, begin by opening Control Panel and choosing the ____________ icon.
8. You can use Control Panel to place ____________, a graphic image (either tiled, centered, or stretched) on the Desktop.
9. A ____________ can be used to cause an animated image to appear on the screen after a specified period of inactivity.
10. True or false: To apply a new Desktop pattern or wallpaper to the Desktop, you must first close the Display Properties dialog box.
11. True or false: When wallpaper is centered (instead of tiled or stretched), it always completely covers the Desktop.
12. True or false: The delay time for a screen saver is how long the mouse and keyboard must be inactive before the screen saver appears.

13. To open the Display Properties dialog box without first opening Control Panel:

    a. Right-click on the Taskbar and then click on Properties.
    b. Right-click on the Desktop and then click on Properties.
    c. Double-click on the Taskbar and then click on Properties.
    d. Double-click on the Desktop and then click on Properties.

14. If your computer has been inactive for a while and a screen saver has been activated, to return to your work you must

    a. Click the mouse.
    b. Move the mouse.
    c. Press a key.
    d. Perform any of the above actions.

Section 5.3

15. To change the colors of various objects in a window, use the ___________ page of the Display Properties dialog box.

16. To select a predefined window scheme, open the ___________ drop-down list in the Display Properties dialog box.

17. True or false: You can modify certain elements of a predefined window scheme by clicking on an object in the Item drop-down list and then making changes.

18. True or false: One-half inch is equivalent to 36 points.

19. True or false: The screen resolution can be changed by using the Settings page of the Display Properties dialog box.

20. From the Appearance page of the Display Properties dialog box, you *cannot* change the size of

    a. Scroll bars.
    b. Title bars.
    c. Menu entries.
    d. The Desktop.

21. From the Appearance page of the Display Properties dialog box, you cannot change the color of

    a. Scroll bars.
    b. Title bars.
    c. Menu entries.
    d. The Desktop.

22. To change the Desktop icon representing the Recycle Bin, use

    a. The Appearance page of the Display Properties dialog box.
    b. The Effects page of the Display Properties dialog box.
    c. The Settings page of the Display Properties dialog box.
    d. The Web page of the Display Properties dialog box.

Section 5.4

23. To change the keyboard repeat rate and delay, begin by choosing the ___________ icon in Control Panel.
24. If it seems as if the functions of the left and right mouse buttons have been interchanged, you can switch them back by using the ___________ utility in Control Panel.
25. True or false: To change the cursor blink rate, use the Cursor utility in Control Panel.
26. True or false: Turning on mouse trails may be useful if you're having trouble following the movement of the mouse pointer.
27. The Mouse Properties dialog box

    a. Cannot be used to change the double-click speed.
    b. Cannot be used to turn mouse pointer trails on or off.
    c. Cannot be used to change the mouse pointer speed.
    d. Can be used to perform all the above tasks.

28. The Keyboard option in Control Panel cannot be used to

    a. Swap the functions of certain keys on the keyboard.
    b. Change the cursor blink rate.
    c. Extend the time delay for repeating keys on the keyboard.
    d. Increase the repeat rate for repeating keys on the keyboard.

Section 5.5

29. If the Taskbar Clock is displaying the wrong time, you can correct it by using Control Panel's ___________ utility.
30. TrueType is a collection of ___________, some of which are included with the Windows software.
31. To change the sounds associated with certain Windows events, use Control Panel's ___________ utility.
32. True or false: The system date and time must be set every time you start Windows.
33. True or false: To listen to the effect of a new sound scheme, you must first exit the Sounds utility.
34. True or false: Every character in an 18-point font is roughly 1/4-inch *wide.*
35. The Fonts utility in Control Panel allows you to

    a. Change the font used for icon titles.
    b. Change the font used in the active application.
    c. Set a default font for your printer.
    d. View the fonts on your hard disk.

36. The Control Panel utility that determines the *format* in which numbers and times are displayed is called

a. Date/Time.
b. Fonts.
c. Regional Settings
d. Passwords.

Build Your Own Glossary

37. The following words and phrases are important terms that were introduced in this chapter. (They appear within the text in boldface type.) Use WordPad (see Section 2.2) to enter a definition for each term, preserving alphabetical order, into the Glossary file on the Student Disk.

Control Panel	Mouse utility	Scalable font
Date/Time utility	Passwords Utility	Screen saver
Display utility	Power Management utility	Sounds utility
Font	Regional Settings utility	TrueType font
Fonts folder		Wallpaper
Keyboard utility		Window scheme

Lab Exercises

Work each of the following exercises at your computer. Begin by turning the machine on (if necessary) to start Windows 98, closing any open windows, and starting Control Panel. If you want to produce a written record of your answers, review the material on WordPad and capturing screens in Sections 2.2 and 2.3.

Lab Exercise 1 (Section 5.2)

a. Start the Display utility from the Control Panel window, which opens the Display Properties dialog box. Which (tab) page of this dialog box is active?

b. If the Pattern command button is dimmed, change the wallpaper to "None". Choose the Pattern button to open the Pattern dialog box. How many items are listed in this dialog box?

c. Select the "Waffle's Revenge" repeating pattern from the Pattern list box. Based on its appearance in the preview window, does this pattern seem to consist of just black and white pixels (dots)?

d. Choose the Edit Pattern command button. How would you answer the question posed in part *c* now?

e. Close the Pattern dialog box and return the Desktop pattern to its original setting.

f. Select the Center item from the Display drop-down list and then select the wallpaper images one-by-one. Which, if any, of the wallpapers cover the entire preview window?

g. Select Tile from the Display drop-down list, select a wallpaper from the list box, and then choose the Apply command button. Does the wallpaper cover the entire visible Desktop?

h. Select Stretch from the drop-down list. How does the effect of Stretch differ from that of Tile?

i. Return the wallpaper to its original setting and close the Display Properties dialog box.

Lab Exercise 2 (Section 5.2)

a. Start the Display utility from the Control Panel window, which opens the Display Properties dialog box. Now, click on the Screen Saver tab. Which, if any, screen saver is in effect?

b. Select the 3D Flying Objects screen saver from the Screen Saver drop-down list. Is this screen saver displayed in the preview window?

c. Set the delay time for ".5" minutes and choose the Preview command button. Click the mouse to end the preview. What time is displayed in the Wait text box after the preview is complete? What conclusion can you draw about the possible delay times?

d. Choose the Settings command button. Try various styles and observe the effect on the preview window. How many styles are available? (You will have to choose OK in the 3D Flying Objects Setup dialog box to see the effect of each change.)

e. In the Display Properties dialog box, choose the Apply button and wait for a minute or two. Did the screen saver become active? If it did, what action did you take to return to the dialog box?

f. Restore the previous screen saver, if any, and close the Display Properties dialog box.

Lab Exercise3 (Section 5.3)

a. Start the Display utility from the Control Panel window, which opens the Display Properties dialog box. Now, click on the Appearance tab. Which, if any, window scheme is named in the Scheme text box?

b. Select the Active Title Bar from the Item list. What font and font size are used for it?

c. Open the Scheme drop-down list. How many schemes are listed?

d. Select, in succession, the "Windows Standard", "Windows Standard (large)", and "Windows Standard (extra large)" schemes. What are the respective font sizes for the Active Title Bar? Is the same font (typeface) used for all three schemes?

e. By selecting, one-by-one, all the available schemes, answer the following questions:
   - Which schemes use no colors other than black and white for the items displayed in the preview window?
   - Which schemes use the Times New Roman font for the Active Title Bar?

f. Select the Windows Standard scheme and 3D Objects (from the Item list). Change the font color to bright red. Which objects in the preview window are affected by the 3D Objects color?

g. Choose the Cancel button to close the Display Properties dialog box.

Lab Exercise 4 (Section 5.3)

a. Start the Display utility from the Control Panel window, which opens the Display Properties dialog box. Now, click on the Appearance tab. Which, if any, window scheme is named in the Scheme text box?

b. Select the High Contrast White scheme and change 3D Objects to light gray. Which objects in the preview window changed color?

c. Change:
   - The Active Title Bar color to dark blue.
   - The Desktop color to teal (blue-green).
   - The Inactive Title Bar color to dark gray and its font color to light gray.
   - Menu items to light gray.

   How does the look of the resulting preview window differ from that of the Windows Standard scheme?

d. *Optional*: Capture the Display Properties window, paste it into WordPad, and print the resulting document. (Try this only if you've already read Sections 2.2 and 2.3.)

e. Choose the Cancel button to close the Display Properties dialog box.

Lab Exercise 5 (Section 5.3)

a. Close the Control Panel window (if it's open). Right-click on an empty part of the Desktop and choose Properties from the pop-up menu to open the Display Properties dialog box.

b. Click on the Effects tab to display this page of the dialog box. Which of the Visual Effects check boxes are currently selected?

c. Select the Visual Effects that are currently not selected and deselect the others. Then, choose the Apply command button. What changes do you notice in the Desktop icons? Return the check boxes to their previous state.

d. Select the My Computer icon in the *Desktop icons* text box and choose the Change Icon command button. What is the title of the resulting dialog box?

e. Select a new icon in the *Current icon* box and choose the OK button. Then, in the Display Properties dialog box, choose the Apply button. Did the My Computer icon change on the Desktop?

f. Choose the Default Icon command button and then the Apply button. Did the My Computer icon change now?

g. Click on the Settings tab of the Display Properties dialog box. How many colors are there in the current palette? What is the current screen resolution (screen area)?

h. Click on the Web tab of the Display Properties dialog box. Is the *View my Active Desktop as a Web Page* check box currently selected?

i. Choose the Cancel command button to close the Display Properties dialog box.

Lab Exercise 6 (Section 5.4)

a. Start the Keyboard utility from the Control Panel window. Where are the *Repeat delay* and *Repeat rate* sliders positioned (relative to the "tick marks" that appear just below each slider)?

b. Set the repeat delay as short as possible and set the repeat rate as fast as possible. Click in the test area and hold down a character key for about one second. How many characters were displayed?

c. Now set the repeat delay as long as possible and the repeat rate as slow as possible. In the test area, hold down a different character key, also for about one second. How many characters are displayed this time?

d. Set the cursor blink rate as slow as possible; then set it at the middle of the scale. In each case, with the aid of a watch with a second hand, determine how many "blinks" take place in ten seconds.

e. Click on the Language tab. What language and layout are used by your keyboard?

f. Choose the Cancel command button to close the Keyboard Properties dialog box.

Lab Exercise 7 (Section 5.4)

a. Start the Mouse utility from the Control Panel window.

b. Switch the button configuration from right-handed to left-handed (or vice-versa). What changes do you see in the dialog box?

c. Set the double-click speed to slow; then to fast. By trying each setting in the Test area, which one requires you to double-click more quickly?

d. Click on the Pointers tab. Make a list of all the available pointer schemes.

e. Click on the Motion tab. What options are available on the Motion page?

f. Set the pointer speed to slow; then, to fast. Do you notice any difference in pointer speed at these two settings?

g. Select the *Show pointer trails* check box (or deselect it, if it's currently selected). Do you notice any change in pointer trails?

h. Choose the Cancel command button to close the Mouse Properties dialog box.

Lab Exercise 8 (Section 5.5)

a. Start the Date/Time utility from the Control Panel window. What is the name of the "current time zone"?

b. By using the up and down arrows, determine the earliest and latest years available for the calendar.

c. Choose the Cancel command button to close this dialog box.

d. Start the Fonts utility from the Control Panel window. How many fonts are available on your system? (Look on the status bar, at the bottom of the Fonts window.)

e. Use the View menu or toolbar to switch to List view. How many columns are displayed?

f. Select the Times New Roman font, view (open) it, and choose the Print command button in the dialog box. (Make sure that the printer connected to your computer is ready before issuing the Print command.)

g. Close the Times New Roman dialog box and the Fonts window.

If You Want to Learn More ...

The notes presented here allow you to delve more deeply into some of the topics covered in this chapter.

Having Control Panel running on Windows startup

If you find that you use the Control Panel utilities frequently, you can arrange to have Control Panel running when you start Windows.

- If Control Panel is minimized when you shut down Windows, it will appear as a Taskbar button the next time you start Windows.
- If the Control Panel window is open when you shut down Windows, it will open automatically on the next startup.

You can also achieve these ends by placing a shortcut to Control Panel in the StartUp folder (see Sections 3.4 and 4.2 for information about shortcuts and the StartUp folder).

Creating your own Desktop patterns

Windows 98 includes a wide variety of Desktop patterns, which are listed in the Pattern dialog box of Control Panel's Display utility (see Section 5.2). By editing these patterns, you can, in effect, create your own Desktop patterns. To do so:

1. From the Background page of the Display utility, choose the Pattern command button to open the Pattern dialog box. (If the button is dimmed, select "None" from the Wallpaper list box.)
2. Select a pattern that is close to the one you want to create and choose the Edit Pattern command button. The Pattern Editor dialog box will open. The figure below shows the result of choosing the Edit Pattern button after selecting the Tile pattern.

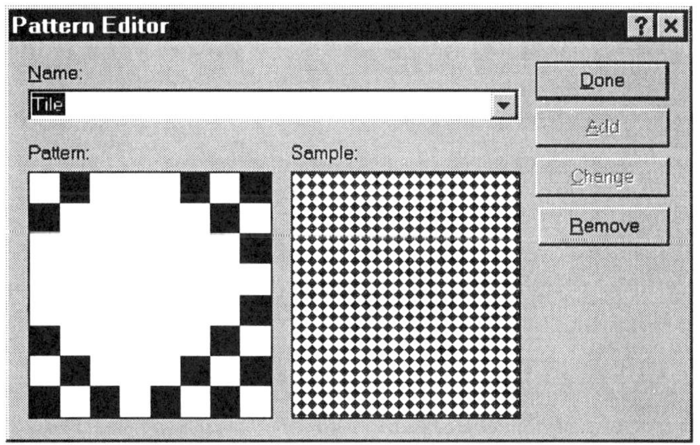

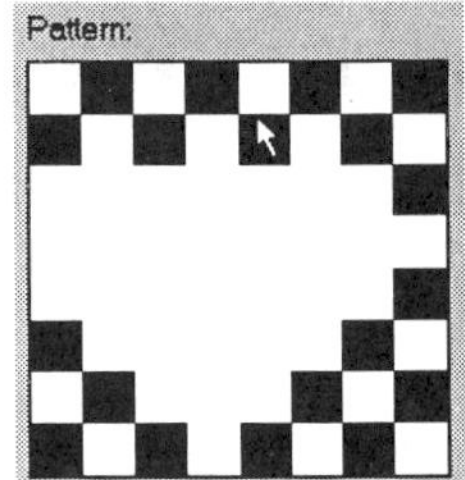

3. Every Desktop pattern is made up of square *blocks* that are eight pixels high and wide. Each pixel is represented by a small black or white square in the Pattern Editor window. When you click on a square, it changes color — if it was originally black, then it becomes white, and vice-versa. For example, to create a checkerboard from the Tile pattern shown on the previous page, we would change some of the white squares to black. The figure at the right show s the result of clicking on three white squares in the first two rows.
4. When you're finished creating your pattern, choose the Done command button. A dialog box will ask if you want to save the changes you've made. Answer Yes, give the pattern a name, and the process is complete.

Creating custom colors

As you have seen in Section 5.3, the color box on the Appearance page of the Display Properties dialog box allows you to choose one of twenty available colors for the selected screen object. To display a broader color palette or define your own custom colors, choose the Other command button in the Color box. The following dialog box will be displayed:

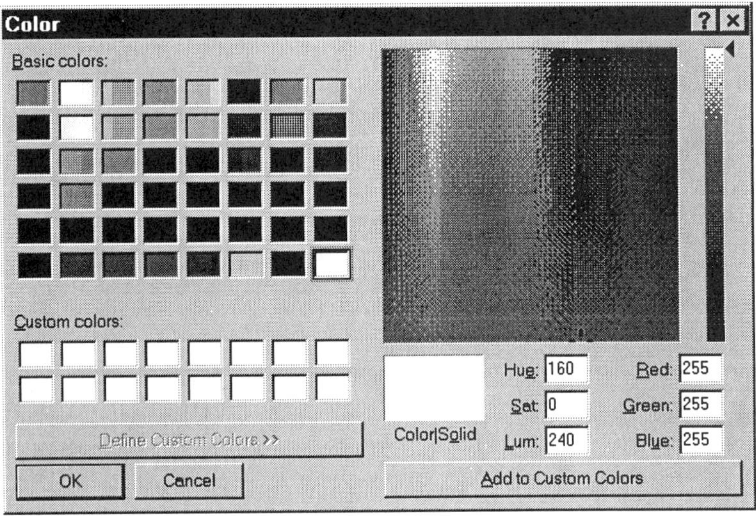

This dialog box provides 48 *basic colors* from which you can choose, or you can create *custom colors* of virtually any shade.

To choose a basic color for the currently selected screen object, just click on that color and then on the OK command button. To create and choose a custom color for the selected screen object:

1. Click on the desired color in the *color spectrum* on the right side of the Color dialog box. The selected color will be displayed in the left half of the Color|Solid box. The right half of this box will display the "solid" (pure) color nearest to the selected one.
2. Make adjustments to the selected color (if you wish) by changing the entries in the Hue, Sat (saturation), Lum (luminosity), Red, Green, and/or Blue text boxes, or by dragging the pointer on the "luminosity bar" (on the far right side of the dialog box) up or down.
3. If you would like to use the nearest pure color to the one selected, click on the right half of the Color|Solid box.
4. If you think that you might want to use your custom color for another screen object at a later time, choose the Add to Custom Colors command button. The color will be displayed in one of the Custom colors boxes.
5. To apply the selected color to the selected screen object (and close the Color dialog box), choose the OK command button.

Icon spacing on the Desktop

After you've used Windows for a while and added a number of shortcuts to the Desktop (see Section 3.4), you'll probably want to arrange them neatly in ordered rows and columns. To accomplish this, right-click on an empty part of the Desktop and, on the resulting pop-up menu:

- Point at Arrange Icons and choose an option from the submenu to order the icons by their names, the types of files they represent, the sizes of these files, or the dates they were created.

or

- Choose Line up Icons, which keeps the icons in the current order but arranges them within an invisible grid of rows and columns.

Each cell in the invisible Desktop grid has a certain default height and width, which determines how far apart the icons are spaced. To change this spacing (perhaps to move the icons closer together):

1. Open the Display utility and click on the Appearance tab.
2. Select *Icon Spacing (Horizontal)* from the Item drop-down list.
3. Enter a smaller figure in the Size text box to move the icons closer together in the horizontal direction, or a larger figure to spread them apart. (The number in the Size box is the width of

each grid cell in *pixels* — the tiny dots of light that make up the screen image.)

4. Select *Icon Spacing (Vertical)* from the Item drop-down list to adjust the vertical spacing of the Desktop icons.
5. Choose the OK or Apply command button to put your changes into effect.

Note that if the icon spacing figures are too small, the reduced size of the grid cell may cut off some of an icon's text and/or picture. You'll probably have to experiment with these settings to get them "right".

Where to go from here

In this chapter, we have described some of the utilities typically supplied by Control Panel. Other utilities are discussed in the following sections of the text:

Accessibility Options — Section 9.4
Add New Hardware — Section 10.1
Add/Remove Programs — Section 2.4
Modems — Section 10.5
Multimedia — Section 9.3
Network — Section 11.1
Printers — Section 4.5
System — Section 10.5

CHAPTER 6

Windows and the Internet

Overview

In this chapter, we will discuss how Windows 98 can help you use the **Internet**, a world-wide network of interlinked computers that joins together thousands of smaller, local networks.

The Internet gives us access — from our homes, schools, and offices — to a wide assortment of information and resources. This chapter explains how to connect to the Internet and how to use Microsoft's Internet Explorer software to access its resources. To be more specific, you will learn:

1. About the capabilities of the Internet.
2. About Internet names and addresses.
3. To use Microsoft's Internet Explorer to browse the Internet.
4. To search for, print, and download information on the Internet.
5. To use Outlook Express to send and receive e-mail and to manage e-mail messages.
6. To use FrontPage Express to create your own Web pages.
7. About the Web-integration features of Windows 98, such as the Active Desktop, Channels, and folder window customization.

6.1 An Overview of the Internet

The Internet is the largest computer network in the world, linking together millions of computers, and it has many powerful capabilities. In a relatively efficient and inexpensive way, the Internet can transmit information (text, graphics, sounds, video, and data) and provide communications for people in virtually every part of the globe.

Internet–related software

The most commonly used method to access the resources of this "information superhighway" is through an application called a **browser**. As the name implies, this software facilitates quick and easy access to many parts of the Internet.

Today's browser applications provide access to a wide variety of services. These include:

- The **World Wide Web** (the *Web*) — An enormous collection of interlinked, multimedia-based documents (**Web pages**) comprising millions of *Web sites.*
- **Usenet** — The structure for the maintenance of *newsgroups*, a system that allows for online discussion and transfer of data among individuals with related interests.
- **E-mail** (electronic mail) — Allows users of computers connected to the Internet to send and receive written messages.
- **FTP**, or File Transfer Protocol — Allows for the transfer of files between computers.

In addition to browsers, other software is used on the Internet for various purposes:

- **Telnet**, a communications application, allows a computer on one network to log onto other networks connected to the Internet.
- **Internet Relay Chat** (IRC), allows for online real-time discussion between users who type their comments and read responses.
- **Internet Phone** is similar to IRC, but users actually talk to others across the Internet connection with the aid of special software and hardware (including a microphone).

A brief history of the Internet

In the mid-1960s, the United States Department of Defense established the *Advanced Research Projects Agency Network* (ARPANET) for the purpose of sharing research information within the scientific community. Another major reason for the government's original interest in this network was that, in case of nuclear attack, the network's multi-point connections guaranteed the continued transmission of information. If one pathway were destroyed, the data could still travel over a different route; communications would not be completely lost.

For the next two decades, universities, government agencies, and government contractors were the primary groups to be connected to this rapidly growing *wide area network.* In 1983, ARPANET was split, creating MILNET to exclusively serve the military. Then, in 1987, the National Science Foundation (NSF) entered the picture, greatly expanding the existing network. A few years later, the World Wide Web was created, which further increased the popularity of this rapidly expanding network of networks.

As the emerging "internet" grew, it became increasingly more common for businesses of all sizes, and even individuals (through a local network), to connect to it. Currently, thousands of new users (primarily attracted by the Web browsing and e-mail features) are added daily to the Internet, which now extends to virtually all parts of the world.

Internet Names and Addresses

Every computer on the Internet has a unique and specific location, called an **Internet address**. This address defines the user, the service provider, and the organization or country hosting the connection. The Internet address of a particular computer (sometimes referred to as a *workstation*) is identified in two ways: with either a word-like *domain name* or a numeric *IP (Internet Protocol) address.* Of course, the name is easier to remember than the numeric address, but both are important to communications on the Internet.

IP Addresses The IP (Internet Protocol) address is usually represented as four numbers separated by periods, sometimes called a *dotted quad.* The ARPANET (the predecessor of today's Internet) originally had the capacity, because of the way each system was addressed, to assign numbers to a maximum of 256 networks. In the early 1980s, when it became clear that requests for numbers would quickly exceed that limit, the dotted quad addressing method was created, making millions of host numbers available for assignment.

Each part of an IP address represents one set of the four sets of numbers that are needed to determine the location of a particular workstation. The first two or three sets of numbers (for instance, 205.228) represent the network, or *subnet,* to which the workstation is connected. For example, all of the computers for one networked site might be in the subnet 205.228. Individual workstations at that site may then have numbers like 205.228.216.10 or 205.228.225.19, with up to 65,000 possible combinations and that many possible workstation locations.

Your computer has either a permanently assigned (static) IP address or a changing (dynamic) IP address assigned by the system each time you connect to the Internet.

Domain Names Names are easier to remember than numbers, and Internet sites can also be referred to by their complete *domain name*. Domain names consist of several parts, separated by periods. For a local network, the name has the following basic components:

- The Internet domain name (such as *www*)
- The service provider or host computer (such as *calstatela*)
- The organization and country codes (such as *edu.us*)

The rightmost component of the domain name is called the top-level domain and identifies the organization and/or country part of the address. (The country code defaults to US if no code is present. Examples of other country codes are FR for France and CA for Canada.) The six main top-level domain names are:

edu — an educational institution
com — a commercial site
net — network resources
gov — government, non-military, organizations
mil — a military site
org — other organizations

The next (middle) component of the domain name indicates the service provider and sometimes the computer host name. The leftmost component, identifying the Internet domain, is usually *www*.

For example, in the Internet address www.amazon.com, *com* represents a commercial domain, *amazon* represents the host computer, and *www* represents the World Wide Web. (We read this address as "amazon dot com".) As another example, the address www.graphics.cc.edu.us, represents a graphics server at a community college, an educational institution in the United States.

NOTE

To refer to an individual user on a particular network for, say, e- mail purposes, the first (leftmost) section of the address is the user's name and is followed by the @ symbol; for example, *CSmith@server.com*. (We will discuss e-mail in Section 6.4.)

When accessing an Internet address, for example www.server.com, the network system for this address is asked if that domain name really exists. Then, *server.com* (the service provider) replies to the network system with the IP address for identification. You, as a user, never see this transaction taking place, and rarely will you need to know the IP address of a site. The network system takes care of that for you!

Connecting to the Internet

Ways to access the Internet

There are three basic ways to connect to the Internet:

- Through a dedicated connection to the Internet via a local network, such as might be established at an educational or government institution.
- Through an **online information service**, such as America Online or the Microsoft Network, which supplies you with a phone number and software to access the Internet via your modem. It also provides specialized newsgroups, “chat rooms”, and non-Internet content, such as personal finance, travel, and entertainment information.
- Through an account with an **Internet Service Provider (ISP)**, which also supplies a phone number and software to access the Internet, but provides no other online services. ISPs operate on both a local and national level.

As there are three ways to access the Internet, the method of establishing a connection differs somewhat from case to case.

- If you can access the Internet via a dedicated connection, the program used to make the connection will have been set up for you. It will appear as an icon on the Desktop or on the Programs submenu of the Start menu. Start that program to connect to the Internet.
- If you are using an online service, that service will send you the necessary software to be installed on your computer. After setting up this software (follow the instructions — the process differs from service to service), an item will appear on the Programs submenu of the Start menu. Start that program to initiate the connection.
- When using an Internet Service Provider, there are several steps that must be completed to configure the connection; here, too, you will have to follow the specific instructions.

6.2 An Introduction to Internet Explorer

Once the connection to the Internet has been established, you will use browser software to interact with the Internet. The software allows users to move from place to place in the Internet environment, much like browsing through books in a library. We will discuss Microsoft's **Internet Explorer** browser in this text; it is supplied as part of the Windows 98 package. (Another popular browser program is Netscape Navigator.)

In Sections 6.2 and 6.3, we will describe some of the features of Internet Explorer. To be more specific, in this section we will discuss how to start Internet Explorer and make use of its toolbars; in the next section we will demonstrate how to search for Web sites, download files, and print the content of a Web page.

The Internet Explorer Window

To start Internet Explorer, perform any of the following actions:

- Choose the Internet Explorer icon on the Desktop. (Double-click on it in Classic style mode or click on it in Web style mode — see Section 1.2.)
- Click on the Start button, point at the Programs option, and choose the Internet Explorer item from the resulting menu.
- Click on the Launch Internet Explorer icon on the Taskbar.

In any case, the Internet Explorer window, which is shown in Figure 1, will open.

NOTE

If this is the first time you have started Internet Explorer, the Internet Connection Wizard will initiate, assisting you in setting up your connection to the Internet.

To access the Internet with Internet Explorer, you work from within the Explorer window. All interaction with the Internet begins with the **Home page**, which is always the first screen you see after opening Internet Explorer. (The Home page is sometimes referred to as the *Start page*.)

Internet Explorer automatically sets the Home page to Microsoft's

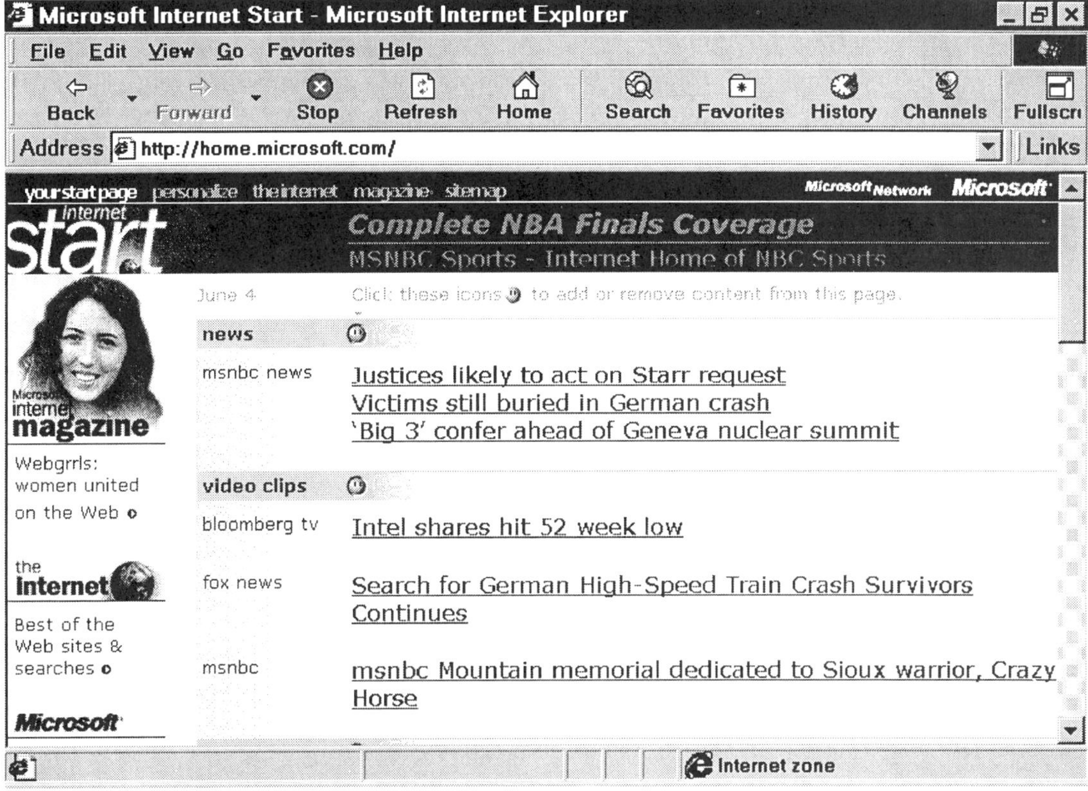

Figure 1 Internet Explorer's Start Page

Internet Start page (see Figure 1). This page lists current information and provides assistance to new users on the Internet. This Home page, like every page on the Internet, displays *links* to other Internet pages.

Links A **link** (or *hyperlink*) on an Internet screen is a connection between pages. Links appear on the screen as one or more words highlighted with color, underlining, or both, in the content area of a page. Images and icons with colored borders also serve as links. When the mouse pointer rests on a link, the pointer appears as a hand and the location of the link is displayed on the status bar at the bottom of the window. Often a *tool tip* — text enclosed in a box with a yellow background describing that link — appears as well.

You can bring the page corresponding to a link (the *linked page*) to the screen by clicking once on the highlighted text, image, or icon. In other words, clicking on a link transfers the content of the corresponding page from the Web server that is storing it onto your computer screen.

An *unfollowed link* is a connection to a page that has not yet been viewed; a *followed link* is one that has been viewed. By default, unfollowed links are shown in blue and followed links in purple.

The Internet Explorer Toolbars

Internet Explorer's (main) toolbar, displayed in Figure 2, provides single-click access to the most frequently used commands. These commands are also found on the Explorer menus, but using the toolbar is quicker.

Figure 2 The Internet Explorer Toolbar

Here are descriptions of the toolbar commands:

Back Returns you to the previously-viewed screen. This button will appear dimmed (ghosted), if no previous pages have been viewed during this session; for example, if you haven't left the Home page.

Forward Moves you to the page that was viewed *after* the current one (assuming that you've returned to the current one during this session).

Stop Stops a request for a new page that is in the process of loading.

Refresh Reloads the current page to the screen; can sometimes push the transmission through a communication bottleneck.

Home Returns you to the Home page.

Search Displays (or hides — it's a toggle) the *Search Explorer bar* — a pane on the left side of the Internet Explorer window that provides access to several popular programs for searching the Web (see Section 6.3).

Favorites Displays (or hides) the *Favorites Explorer bar*, which lists pages you have previously marked as interesting sites. (We will discuss Favorites later in this section.)

History Displays (or hides) the *History Explorer Bar*, which lists pages you have viewed in the current session or during the last 20 days.

Channels Displays (or hides) the *Channels Explorer bar* (see Section 6.6), which lists Web sites (containing news, entertainment, weather, and the like) to which you can *subscribe* — automatically receive updated content.

Fullscreen Displays the Explorer screen with a small toolbar, no status bar, and no Address box, so more of the current Internet page is visible.

Mail Displays a menu that allows you to access your e-mail.

Print Prints the displayed page.

Edit Starts the FrontPage Express Web page editor (see Section 6.5) and opens the current page within it.

If you have already viewed several pages, click on the downward-facing triangle next to the Back button to open a drop-down list from which you can select one of these pages.

The Address Box The **Address box** (Figure 3) identifies the complete Internet location of the currently viewed page. (See the discussion on domain names in Section 6.1.)

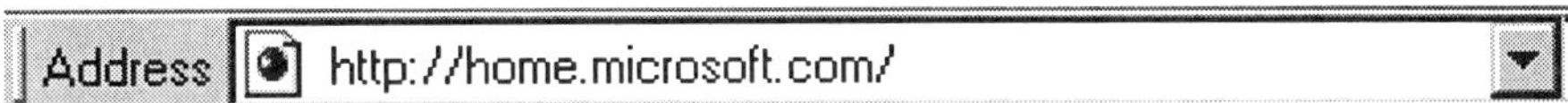

Figure 3 Internet Explorer's Address Box

URLs Web Internet addresses begin with http:// (for *hypertext transmission protocol*) in the **Universal Resource Locator**, which is the address of the page's location, commonly called its **URL**. You can access any Web page by typing its URL in the Address text box and pressing the Enter key.

Be aware that some systems require that URLs be typed exactly as they appear; so case (upper or lower) and punctuation are important. However, using all lowercase letters will suffice in most instances.

The Address box drop-down list displays previously-entered URLs. It provides a quick way to return to a previous site.

Internet Explorer assumes the "http://" part of the URL when you are entering an address in the Address text box, so it is not necessary to type this part of the address.

Using Favorites A **Favorite** is an electronic place-holder, or "bookmark", that identifies your favorite Internet pages. Using Favorites to mark interesting pages on the Internet makes returning to those sites in the future a quick and easy process.

Creating a Favorite

To create a Favorite:

1. Display the desired page.
2. Choose the Add to Favorites item from the Favorites menu. The Add Favorite dialog box will be displayed.
3. Choose the OK command button to accept the suggested name for the Favorite, or type a name of your own and then choose OK. The new Favorite will appear on the Favorites menu and in several other places in Windows 98.

Accessing a Favorite

To go to a Favorite Web site:

1. Click on the Favorites toolbar button to display the Favorites Explorer Bar on the left side of the Internet Explorer window. This pane lists all your current Favorites.
2. Click on the desired name; it is a link to that site.

Deleting a Favorite

Favorites are quick to accumulate, and can become cumbersome to manage. Deleting Favorites that are no longer appealing is important to do from time to time. To delete a Favorite:

1. Choose the Organize Favorites item from the Favorites menu. The Organize Favorites dialog box will be displayed.
2. In this dialog box, highlight the Web page to be deleted.
3. Press the Delete key on the keyboard or choose the Delete command button on the toolbar. Confirm the deletion by choosing

the Yes command button in the "Confirm Delete" dialog box to send the item to the Recycle Bin.

NOTE

Many of the toolbar commands we have just discussed also appear on Internet Explorer menus. Here's a rundown on their location:

- The Go menu lists the commands Back, Forward, Home Page, Channel Guide, Search the Web, and Mail. Each is an alternative to the similarly-named toolbar button. (The Channel Guide and Search the Web commands access specific Web pages found on the Channels Explorer bar and Search Explorer bars, respectively.)
- Pointing at the Explorer Bar item on the View menu pops up a submenu that allows you to display the Search, Favorites, History, or Channels Explorer bar. Note that only one of these bars can be displayed at a time; selecting the None option on the submenu removes the current Explorer bar from the window.
- The items on the Favorites Explorer bar are also listed on the Favorites menu.

The Links Toolbar The Internet Explorer Links toolbar (Figure 4) provides a method of choosing different Internet sites by general topics.

Figure 4 The Links Toolbar

The Links toolbar can be fully displayed by dragging its *handle*, or *position button* (on the left end of the toolbar), to the left. When the Links buttons are all displayed, the Address text box may be temporarily hidden from view. Dragging the Links handle back to the right hides some buttons and redisplays the Address text box.

Dragging the Links toolbar down, just below the Address box, allows both toolbars to be displayed at once, but takes up more space on the screen.

The Links toolbar buttons provide easy access to certain locations in Internet Explorer. Here are the functions of the toolbar buttons:

Best of the Web Lists selected Web sites and their features.

Microsoft Displays the Microsoft Home page.

Product News Provides the latest information on Internet Explorer and other Microsoft products.

Today's Links Today's hot topics.

Web Gallery Provides links to resources for Web page developers.

Status Indicator The Windows logo (on the right end of the menu bar) becomes animated when transfers of data are in progress. Clicking on the logo loads Microsoft's Home page.

NOTE

The progress bar, displayed at the left side of the status bar in the Internet Explorer window, shows the progress of a loading page. When the page finishes loading, the word "Done" is displayed.

TUTORIAL

Try the following exercise on your own.

1. Start Internet Explorer by choosing its Desktop icon. The Home page will be displayed.
2. Scroll down the Home page to locate the first text link on the page. The text will appear in blue, because it is an *unfollowed link*, and may also be underlined.
3. Click once on the text link to display that page.
4. Now, the Back button on the toolbar is available; click on the Back button to return to the previous page. Notice that the link is now purple because it has been used; it is a *followed link*.
5. Now, the Forward button on the toolbar is available. Click on the Forward button to view the previously-accessed page. Notice that the Forward button is now dim because no pages have been viewed after this one.
6. Click in the Address text box to place the text cursor there. The existing address appears highlighted.
7. Type *www.enews.com* in the Address text box.

8. Press the Enter key to display the site. The page displayed will be entitled *The Electronic Newsstand.*
9. Scroll down the page to see what is displayed there. Pass the mouse pointer over any special text or graphic items to determine which are links. Click on one of the Magazines links to display that page.
10. Open the Favorites menu and choose the Add to Favorites item. Then choose the OK command button to accept the creation of a Favorite with the name The Electronic Newsstand.
11. Click on the toolbar's Home button to return to the Home page.
12. Open the Favorites menu and select the newly-listed Favorite from the list to return to The Electronic Newsstand.
13. Drag the Links handle toward the Address text box to display the Links toolbar.
14. Click on the Best of the Web link to display that page. Choose additional links from that page, as desired.
15. Click on the Today's Links link button to view the current topics. Choose additional links, as desired.
16. Click on the Windows logo button (on the menu bar) to go to Microsoft's home page.
17. Exit Internet Explorer.

6.3 Browsing the Internet

In this section we will discuss several aspects of browsing (exploring) the Internet: performing searches, printing Web pages, downloading files, and disconnecting from the Internet.

Performing Searches

Once Internet Explorer is open, you can use search software to locate specific sites and information. There are several ways to search for information that is available on the Internet.

An easy way to display a search screen is to click on the Search button on the Internet Explorer toolbar. This action displays the *Search*

Explorer bar (Figure 5), a pane that opens on the left side of the window. A different search program (a **search engine**) is featured every day. You can use that software or access another search engine by clicking on *Choose a Search Engine*, and then choosing the List of all Search Engines item from the resulting menu.

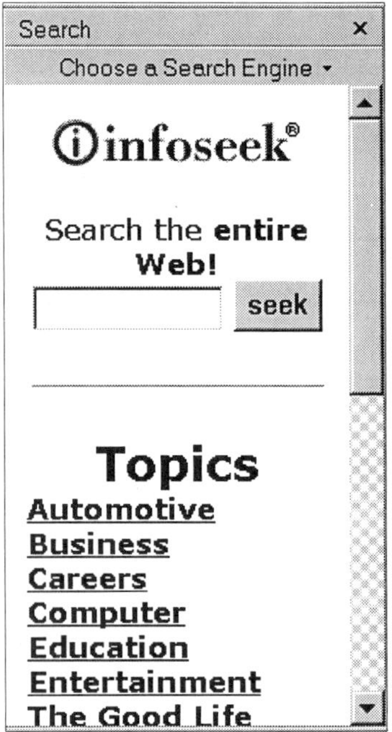

Figure 5 Search Bar

Search engines allow you to look for specific information in many different ways. Some engines search titles or headers of documents on the Internet, others search the documents themselves, and still others search indexes or directories. The type of information you need, and your preferences in requesting it, will help determine which search engine you decide to use. We will describe some of these engines later in this section.

Another way to display one of the search sites is to enter the address of that site in the Address box. We will provide the URLs for some of these Web pages later in this section.

The general search procedure

To perform a search, follow this general procedure:

1. Click on the Search button on the Internet Explorer toolbar to display the Search Explorer bar. Then, choose the List of all Search Engines item from the Choose a Search Engine menu and select a search engine from the resulting screen.

   or

   Type the address of the desired search engine in the Address box and press the Enter key.

   In either case the search engine's home page will be displayed.

2. Click in the text entry search box to place the cursor there and type the search text.
3. Choose the appropriate search command button to perform the search. The results of the search will be displayed on the screen.

Guidelines for the search

Here are some general guidelines for entering search text (step 2 of the previous procedure):

- Capitalize names of people and places, and use a comma to separate lists of names.
- Use lower case letters when case is not a factor.
- To identify a group of words that must appear together in order, use quotation marks around them or hyphenate them; for example, "Abraham Lincoln" or world-wide.

Most search engines provide a list of categories to allow you to search by subject. Each engine also has its own Help program to assist you. Listed below are brief descriptions of some of the available search engines.

Infoseek Infoseek Ultra has one of the largest and most current databases on the Internet. It offers several field-searching options and simplified keyword and phrase searching. Infoseek processes search results quickly and accurately, searching not only the World Wide Web, but also the text of Usenet articles, Web users' FAQs (Frequently Asked Questions), e-mail addresses, current news, and company listings. Each search result is accompanied by a short excerpt from the identified site. The results are presented in order of relevancy to the search criteria. The Infoseek Internet address is www.infoseek.com.

AltaVista AltaVista is a fast search tool, searching millions of pages found on thousands of servers and millions of articles from Usenet newsgroups. AltaVista handles sophisticated searches, offers several field searching options, and returns results quickly. It also provides an Advanced Query Mode for complex searches that prioritizes the results. The AltaVista address is www.altavista.digital.com.

Yahoo! Yahoo! is a searchable, browsable hierarchical index of the Internet. It is primarily a directory, a list of Web sites that users have submitted for listing. If you know exactly what you're looking for, use Yahoo! Select Search, specify a keyword or set of keywords, and Yahoo! will search its entire database to find listings that match the keys you provide. Or choose any of the links on the page to browse through screens by topic or category. Be aware, however, that Yahoo! accepts any site submitted to its database without regard for quality or authority. The Yahoo! location address is www.yahoo.com.

Excite Excite has a unique concept-based navigation technology that can help you find information when you are not sure how to ask for it. The software attempts to determine dominant *themes* (terms) on a given page and then selects the items for the summary that best fit these terms. You can then use the themes as keywords while looking for a site. This process can produce a more accurate summary and keyword relationship than just selecting the first few lines of text from a document, as most other search engines do. Excite is found at www.excite.com.

After the Search The search results screen displays all the *hits,* or links found, on a subject, even if there are hundreds or thousands of them. At the top of the screen is the search engine header, followed by the search criteria that you entered, along with the total number of hits. Below that is usually an advertisement, followed by the first ten links (or more, depending upon the search engine that is being used) to sites found.

To view the next group of hits, choose the text link Next 10 Results (or equivalent) found at the end of the list. Sometimes the search engine will list the results as page numbers at the bottom of the screen, allowing you to "page" back and forth by clicking on the number. The displayed screen will present the next set of results.

A new search link also appears at the bottom of the list that allows you to return to the original, clear search screen. If, however, you want to modify your search, perhaps to narrow it, edit the existing criteria that appear at the bottom of the list and choose the Search command button to search again.

Printing Internet Pages

With all the information that is available on the Internet, it is inevitable that from time to time you will want to make a hard copy of some of it. Fortunately, it is easy to print any Internet page. To do so:

1. Use Internet Explorer to display the desired page.
2. Click on the toolbar's Print button or choose the Print command from the File menu.
3. Choose the OK command button from within the Print dialog box to send the Web page to the printer.

WARNING

Be aware that Internet pages are often copyrighted. Copyright laws apply to information on Internet pages in the same way they apply to conventional printed material.

Downloading Files

Frequently, you may find files on the Internet that you would like to copy to disk. These files might include software updates or fixes, or *shareware* or *freeware*, which is software that is developed by individuals and not available on the mass market. Freeware is, as you might guess, software that does not cost anything to use. Shareware is not free, but you can usually try it before buying it, and the price is generally very reasonable.

The process of copying files from the Internet to a disk is called **downloading**. Copying files *to* the Internet is called **uploading**.

If a site contains software that you can download, there will be links within the page text of that site that pertain to this software. Usually, the linked word *download* will also appear within the related area. Sometimes, just choosing the software link will begin the download process; or, if the linked word *download* appears, choosing it will begin the process of transferring the files to your computer.

To download a file from the Internet:

1. Display the desired Internet page.
2. Choose the link to the software or the linked word *download*, if the latter is displayed.
3. Follow the prompts displayed on the screen. Eventually, you will need to identify the folder on your computer to be the destination for the downloaded file.
4. When the download process begins, a dialog box similar to the one in Figure 6 will be displayed.

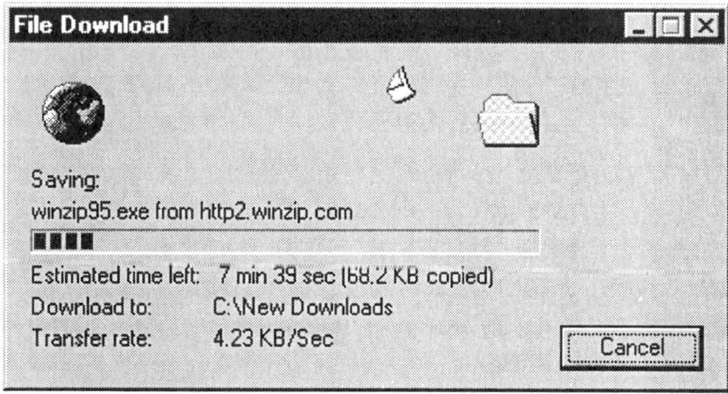

Figure 6 Downloading a File

5. After downloading the file, which is usually in a compressed format, double-click on the file to start the decompression process (if any) and install the software (if applicable). If the software does not automatically install, double-click on the setup or installation file that was downloaded with it.

Disconnecting from the Internet

When finished with your Internet session, you should exit the browser and terminate the connection. Staying online when not using the Internet occupies a connection that someone else could be using, and the Internet is a busy place.

To exit Internet Explorer and disconnect from the Internet:

1. To close Internet Explorer, choose the Exit command from the File menu, click on the close button, or press Alt+F4.
2. To disconnect from the Internet itself:
   - For dedicated network users, exiting Internet Explorer terminates the connection.
   - If you access Internet Explorer from your online service, exiting Internet Explorer returns you to the service's screen. It may then be necessary to execute a log-off procedure (which varies from service to service).
   - For ISP users, terminate the Dial-Up Networking connection by choosing the Disconnect command button in the Connected dialog box.

TUTORIAL

Try the following exercise on your own.

1. Start Internet Explorer, if necessary.
2. Click in the Address text box and type the URL for Infoseek — www.infoseek.com; then press the Enter key to go to this site and display the Infoseek screen.
3. Enter the search word *philharmonic* in the text box. Choose the Seek command button to perform the search. Notice the total number of matches for the search.
4. Scroll down the page to view the "philharmonic" results; then choose the appropriate link to view the Next 10 results.

5. Scroll down the new list and modify the existing search text: Click to place the cursor in the text box and type *philharmonic society*. Choose the Seek command button to perform the search. Notice the difference in total results found; this criterion broadens the search.
6. To narrow the search, modify the existing criteria by typing *"philharmonic society"* (including the quotation marks) and perform the search. Fewer sites are found.
7. Limit the search again. Modify the criteria by typing *New York* in the search text box. Then, click the option button to search only within these pages; perform the search.
8. Display Infoseek's main search screen by choosing it from the Address box drop-down list.
9. Find the Tips link and choose it.
10. Choose the How To Search link to display the How To Search information.
11. Scroll down to the Search Tips link and choose it.
12. Print the Search Tips page, if you wish, by choosing the toolbar's Print button.
13. Choose the toolbar's Home button to return to the Home page.
14. Exit Internet Explorer by clicking on the close button.
15. If you are using an online service or ISP, terminate the connection by exiting from that service.

6.4 E-mail and Outlook Express

E-mail (*electronic mail*) is currently the most heavily-used feature of the Internet. E-mail makes it possible to quickly transmit text messages, pictures, and other types of documents to anyone who has access to the Internet.

E-mail addresses

To ensure that messages are delivered properly, an Internet address is assigned to every e-mail user. An e-mail address, like an Internet address, is made up of several parts; the user name appears first, followed by an @ symbol, then the service provider, and finally the domain designation. For example, in the e-mail address CSmth@ netstuff.com, *CSmith* is the user name, *netstuff* is the service provider, and *com* is the domain designation.

To enable you to send and receive e-mail, Internet Explorer includes the **Outlook Express** application, which is automatically installed with Internet Explorer. If it hasn't yet been done, you can also specify that Outlook Express be the default e-mail program. To do this:

Making Outlook Express the default e-mail program

1. In Internet Explorer, open the Tools menu and choose Options.
2. Click on the General tab and be sure the *Make Outlook Express my default e-mail program* check box is selected.
3. Choose the OK command button.

The Outlook Express Window

Outlook Express can be started in any of the following ways:

Outlook Express

- Choose the Outlook Express icon on the Desktop.
- Click on the Launch Outlook Express icon on the Taskbar.
- From within Internet Explorer, choose the Mail item from the Go menu.

Any of these actions displays the Outlook Express window (Figure 7) and initiates the Connection Manager (if you connect with a modem), which establishes the connection to the Internet.

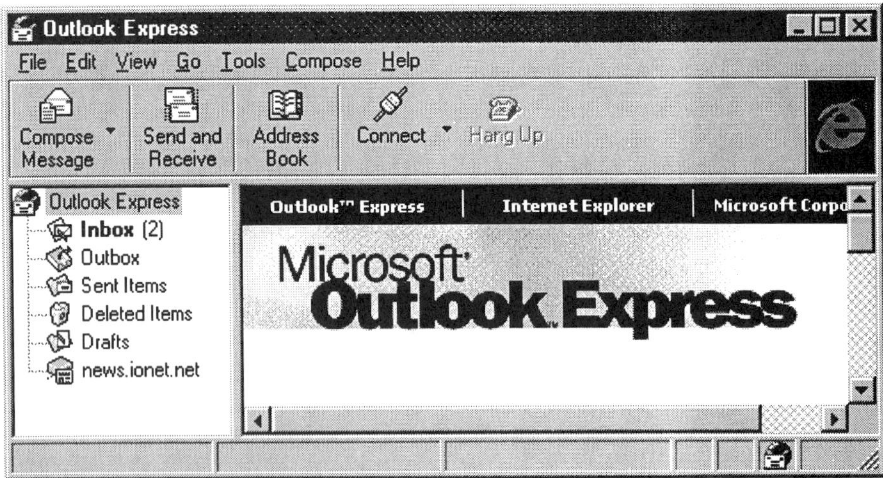

Figure 7 The Outlook Express Window

NOTE

You can connect with a modem at the beginning of the Outlook Express session or, at any time later on, using the toolbar's Connect button or the Connect command on the File menu.

Key parts of the Outlook Express window are:

- The toolbar provides easy, single-click access to the most-used commands in Outlook Express.
- The left pane, the *folders pane*, lists the Outlook Express subfolders. These folders store e-mail messages, as follows:

  The **Inbox** is the folder in which all new messages are delivered. When you start Outlook Express, all new mail is visible in the Inbox. The mail remains there until you delete it or move it to another folder.

  The **Outbox** is the folder in which all messages ready for delivery are placed. Once the messages are delivered, they are removed from the Outbox and placed in the Sent Items folder.

  The **Sent Items** folder holds each message that has been delivered from the Outbox. The messages remain in this folder until you delete them or move them to another folder.
- To open one of the folders in the folders pane, click on it. The right pane, the *contents pane*, will display the contents of the selected folder.

Sending Electronic Mail

E-mail terminology is similar to that used with a traditional paper mailing system. E-mail must be created, addressed, sent, and opened when received.

To create a new e-mail message:

1. From within the Outlook Express window, click on the Compose Message button on the toolbar or choose New Message from the Compose menu. The New Message window will open, as shown in Figure 8 on the next page.
2. In the To text box, type the address of the person(s) to receive the message; to send the message to more than one person, separate the names with semicolons.

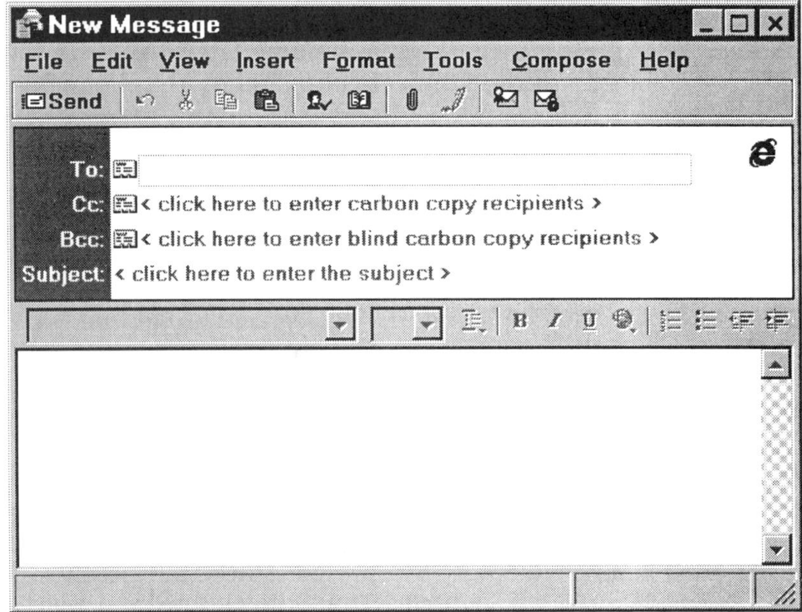

Figure 8 The New Message Window

3. Type the subject of the message in the Subject text box. This information is important, as it will appear in the recipient's Inbox, letting that person know what your message is about.
4. Enter the desired message by typing it in the large text box below the subject line. This text box behaves as a word processing text area, and the text in your message can be formatted with the commands found on the Format menu or on the Formatting toolbar. The Formatting toolbar commands in Outlook Express are similar to those in most word processing programs, including WordPad (see Section 7.3), and they function in the same way. (Outlook Express also includes a spell-check program, found on the Tools menu.)
5. When you have finished entering the message, choose the Send command from the File menu or click on the Send icon on the toolbar to place the message in the Outbox, awaiting delivery. The Outlook Express window will again be displayed; the folders that contain unprocessed information will appear bolded.
6. There are a couple of ways to deliver a message from the Outbox folder:
   - If you are using a LAN system to connect to the Internet, the

network server will periodically check for incoming and outgoing messages, a process called *polling*. However, on most systems, clicking on the Send and Receive toolbar button will initiate a poll, if you want to send messages right away.

- If you connect to the Internet with a modem, either through an online service or an ISP, you will need to choose the toolbar's Send and Receive button to poll the system.

When a message has been delivered, Outlook Express moves that message to the Sent Items folder.

NOTE

If you are using a dial-up connection with a modem, the connection to the Internet will remain established until you exit Outlook Express, at which time Outlook Express will prompt you to terminate the connection with the message box shown below. Click the Yes button to confirm the disconnection.

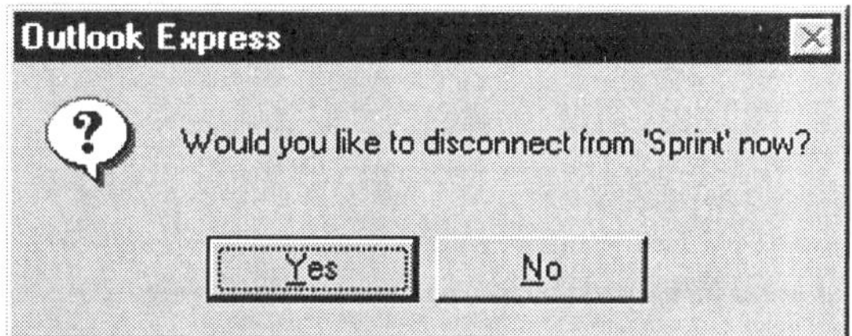

Attachments Files can be sent with an e-mail message to the recipient(s) of that message. In this case, we call the file an **attachment**. For instance, a word processing document or graphic (picture) can be sent as an attachment. When a recipient receives the message, the attached file can then be saved on his or her computer separately from the mail message. It is as if you wrote a note and paper-clipped it to a document before mailing it to someone in the traditional sense.

To attach a file to an e-mail message:

1. When composing the message, click on the Insert File button on the toolbar or choose File Attachment from the Insert menu. The Insert Attachment dialog box will be displayed. This dialog box is similar to the standard Windows Open dialog box (see Section 2.2).
2. Locate the file that you want to attach by browsing the Windows folder system (see Section 3.5). Select the file and choose the

Attach command button. The selected file will display as an icon at the bottom of the mail message.

Continue attaching files as needed.

3. Finish the message and send it. When you send the item, the recipients will see a small paper clip next to the message icon in their Inbox, indicating that there is an attachment.

You can send a file as an e-mail message even if Outlook Express is not open. From any folder window, right-click on the file. Then, point at the Send To item and choose Mail Recipient on the resulting submenu. Outlook Express will open and start a new mail message with the selected file as an attachment.

Receiving Electronic Mail

After the system has been polled for new messages, any new mail is placed in the Inbox. Outlook Express sounds a computer tone and displays any unread messages in bold type in the contents pane of the Inbox.

Opening new mail

To open new mail:

1. Open Outlook Express and display the contents of your Inbox by clicking on the Inbox folder in the folder pane or by choosing the Inbox command from the Go menu.

   The Inbox folder (Figure 9) will appear bolded when new messages are in it and will include the number of unread messages next to the folder icon.

2. Any unread messages will appear in bold within the Inbox contents pane. To display a message, either double-click on it, or select it and press the Enter key.

3. When you are finished reading a message, press the Escape key or click on the window's close button.

The messages you have read will remain in the Inbox until you delete or move them (as described later in this section).

Replying to a Message When a message has been received, it is easy to send a reply to the sender or to the sender and all recipients of the original message.

To reply to a message:

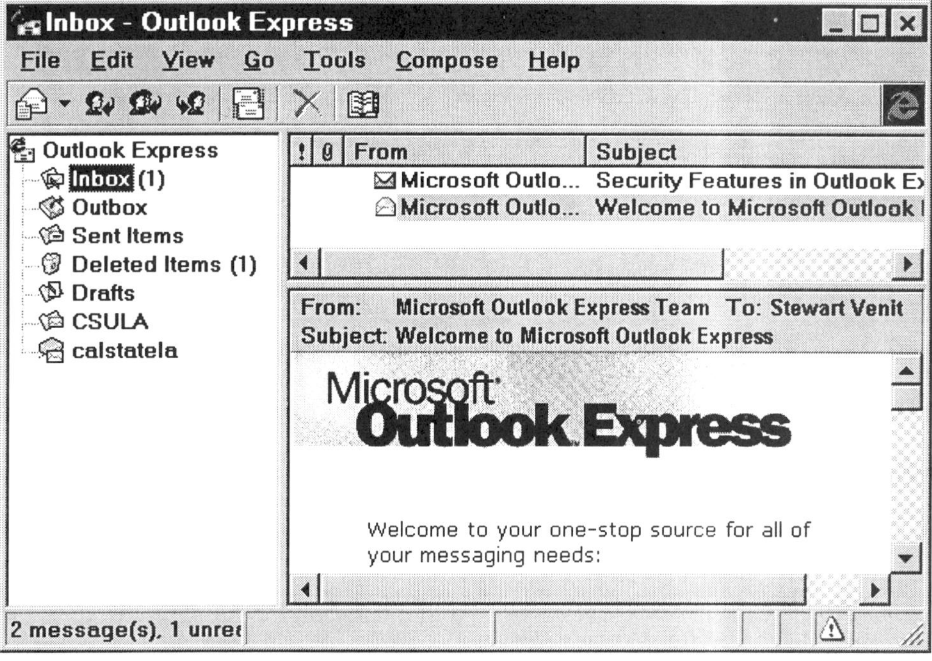

Figure 9 The Inbox Folder Window

1. With the message displayed on the screen or with the message selected in the Inbox folder, click on the Reply to Author button on the toolbar or choose the Reply to Author command from the Compose menu.

   To reply to the sender and all recipients, click on the Reply to All button on the toolbar or choose the Reply to All command from the Compose menu.

2. A new message window opens, and the Subject line now includes RE: in front of the original subject text, indicating that it is a reply.

   The original message appears below the text cursor in the message area, along with the original message information, such as the sender, recipient(s), subject, and date/time sent. Type your response message.

3. Click on the Send button on the toolbar to send the reply to the Outbox, then choose the Send and Receive button (if necessary) to deliver the message.

Forwarding a Message *Forwarding* a message that you have received sends that message to a user (or users) of your choice.

To forward a message:

1. Select or open the message to be forwarded.
2. Click on the Forward Message button on the toolbar or choose the Forward command from the Compose menu.
3. Address the message to the new user(s).

   The subject line will contain FW: in front of the original subject text. The original message also appears within the message field, as it did when replying to a message.
4. Type the current message text and send the message.

Saving an Attachment When receiving a message that has a file attachment, the attached file can be saved on your computer separately from the message.

To save an attachment:

1. Open the message with the attached file.
2. Open the File menu and choose the Save Attachments option. The resulting submenu lists all attachments to the current message. Select the file to be saved. The Save Attachment As dialog box, which is similar to the Save As dialog box discussed in Section 2.2, is displayed.
3. Select the drive and folder in which you want to save the file; then, choose the Save button.

An attached file can also be saved by dragging the icon from the message window and dropping it onto the destination folder.

Managing Mail Messages

Mail messages that you have sent remain in the Sent Items folder and mail messages that you have read remain in the Inbox until you move or delete them. Over time, messages can accumulate in these folders, and mail message management becomes an important task.

Moving Messages Messages can easily be moved by dragging-

and-dropping them into other folders. Initially, the only folders that appear in the folders pane are the default ones. However, Outlook Express gives you the ability to create new folders, providing a logical and easy way to better organize your messages.

Creating a new folder

If you want to store messages in a folder other than a default one, you must first create that folder. To do so:

1. The new folder will be the child (or subfolder) of the currently selected folder, so select the parent folder first.
2. Point at the Folder command on the File menu; then, select the New Folder option from the resulting submenu. The Create Folder dialog box will be displayed (Figure 10).

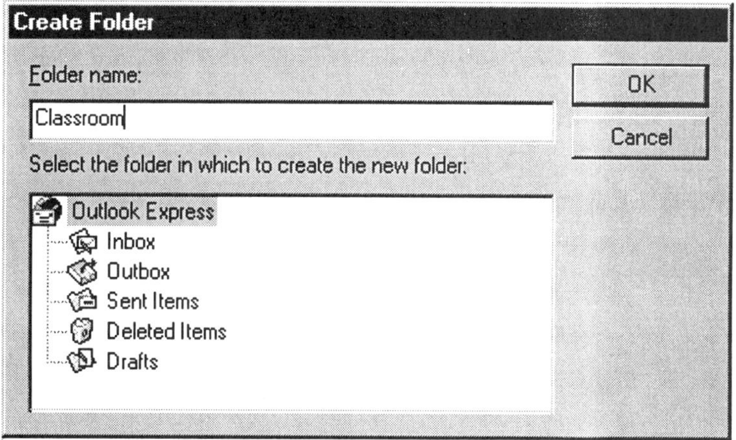

Figure 10 Creating a Folder

3. Type the name of the new folder and choose the OK button. The new folder will appear in the folders pane list.

Moving a message

To move a message into another folder:

1. Select the source folder, the one that contains the message you want to move, to display its contents in the contents pane.
2. Drag that message across the pane divider and drop it onto the destination folder in the folders pane. That message now exists only in the destination folder.

NOTE

If you prefer menu commands to drag-and-drop, the Move to Folder item on the Edit menu achieves the same result. To use this command, select the message to be moved, choose the Move to Folder menu item, select the destination folder in the resulting dialog box, and click on the OK command button. (In a similar way, you can *copy* a message to a new folder by using the Edit menu's Copy to Folder command.)

Deleting Messages If you no longer want to keep a message, you can delete it. Deleting messages that you no longer need, together with moving messages when appropriate, helps to keep your mailbox organized.

To delete a message:

1. If the message is still open, click on the Delete icon on the toolbar to delete that message.

   Otherwise, select the folder that contains the message and click on the message in the contents pane. Then, choose the Delete command from the Edit menu, click on the toolbar's Delete button, *or* press the Delete key on the keyboard.

2. Deleted messages are not removed from disk; they are moved into the **Deleted Items** folder, which allows you to restore a deleted message if you change your mind later. To permanently delete a message, select the Deleted Items folder to view its contents, select the message(s) to be permanently deleted, and choose the Delete command from the Edit menu or press the Delete key. You will be prompted to confirm the deletions; choose Yes to permanently delete the message(s).

WARNING

Folders are deleted using the same steps as messages. However, folders will not be placed in the Deleted Items folder, they are immediately removed from disk.

TUTORIAL

Try the following exercise on your own.

1. Start Outlook Express by choosing its Desktop icon or clicking on the Launch Outlook Express button on the Taskbar. The Outlook Express window will open.
2. Click on the Compose a Message toolbar button to start a new message. The New Message window will be displayed.

3. In the To text box, type the address of the person(s) to receive the message; address the message to someone you know that has an e-mail account or ask your instructor for the address of another student in the class. Include yourself as a recipient, separating the two addresses with a semicolon.
4. Type the subject of the message in the Subject text box; use *Classroom Activity*.
5. Enter a message by typing the text in the large text box below the subject line.
6. When you have finished entering the message, click on the toolbar's Send button to place the message in the Outbox, awaiting delivery. The Outlook Express window will again be displayed.
7. Click on the toolbar's Send and Receive button to send the message.
8. Click on the toolbar's Read New Mail button to view the contents of the Inbox folder. The message you sent to yourself should appear there; if it doesn't, wait a few minutes and then click on the Send and Receive button to check for new mail again. (Sometimes the mail server takes a while to process a message.)
9. Read a new message by double-clicking on it.
10. Click on the Reply to Author toolbar button to send a reply to the original sender.
11. In the message text box, add a comment that is relevant to the original message.
12. Click on the toolbar's Send button to send the reply, then click on the Send and Receive button.
13. Open another new message you have received.
14. Click on the Forward Message button on the toolbar.
15. Address the message to another user in the classroom, someone who is not listed as a recipient of the original message. Add appropriate text to the message area. Send the message.
16. Move this message to the Deleted Items folder by clicking on the Delete toolbar button.
17. Permanently delete the message from disk by selecting the Deleted Items folder in the folders pane, selecting the message in the contents pane, pressing the Delete key, and answering Yes to the resulting query.
18. Exit Outlook Express.

6.5 Creating Your Own Web Pages

The creation of World Wide Web sites is a growing service industry, but individuals are also creating their own Web pages. Many software packages can be utilized for this purpose, but no matter which one you use, it will translate your work into the base language of the Web — **HTML** (Hypertext Markup Language) — so that it can be "read" by a Web browser. In this section, we will discuss the Web page editor software that is built into Windows 98, *FrontPage Express.*

Before you Begin: Some Design Considerations Before starting to develop a Web page, here are a few things that you should consider:

- Visit a wide variety a Web sites to observe what others have done. Take note of the design elements that you find attractive.
- Unless you are confident of your design abilities, create simple, uncluttered pages. For example, use relatively few fonts and graphics, just enough to achieve your objectives.
- If the purpose of your Web page is to entertain as well as inform, sophisticated graphics, sound, and even video will be important. If, however, you are only delivering information, text and simple graphics will suffice.
- Unless you have good reason to do otherwise, you should always design for the "least common denominator"; for example, a resolution of 640 × 480 pixels, with 256 colors. (*Pixels* are the dots that form the image on your monitor; *resolution* is the number of pixels that make up the total screen image.)
- If possible, check your work with different browsers at different resolutions to ensure that your pages look good with the widest variety of browser/system configurations. Unless you keep the page very simple, it probably won't look great with all browsers.

An Introduction to FrontPage Express

There are actually two programs within the FrontPage software to assist in Web page development and maintenance:

- FrontPage Express
- FrontPage Web Publishing Wizard

FrontPage Express is the main program for FrontPage, allowing you to create or edit a Web site. FrontPage Express enables you to create and format a Web page using a WYSIWYG (what you see is what you get) display; it then translates the page into HTML. Most of this section will deal with FrontPage Express.

FrontPage Web Publishing Wizard opens existing Web pages directly from the Web or from a file on your computer or network. It also allows you to save your work directly to the Web.

Starting FrontPage Express

To start FrontPage Express:

1. Click on the Start button and point at the Programs option.
2. Choose the Internet Explorer item from the resulting submenu, Then click on the Microsoft FrontPage Express item. The program window will open, displaying a blank Web page (Figure 11).

The FrontPage Express window consists of elements found in most Windows programs: a title bar, a menu bar, toolbars, and a work area.

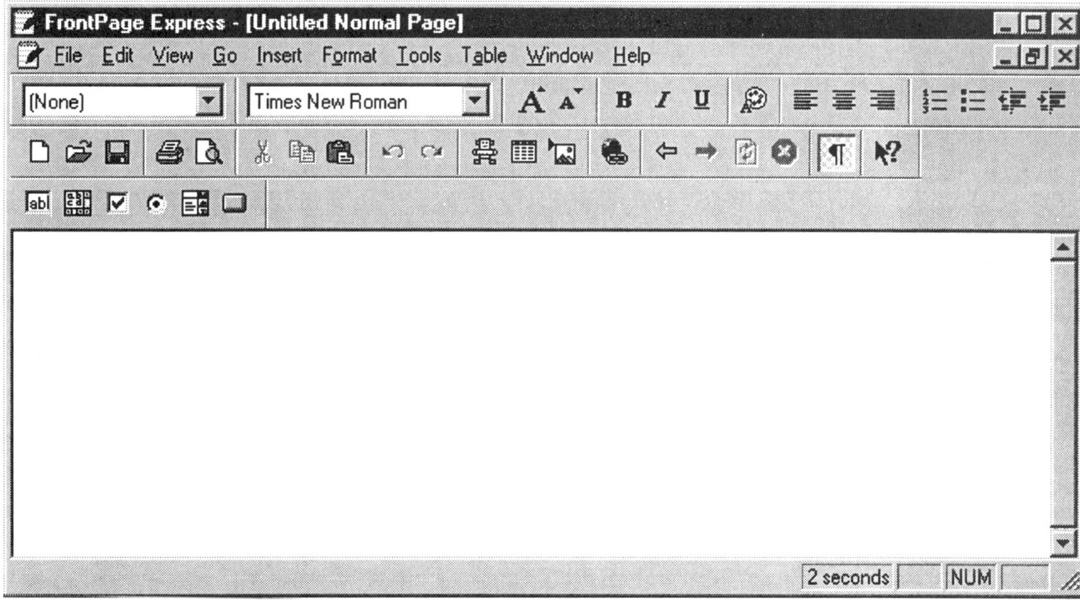

Figure 11 The FrontPage Express Window

As you can see, there are several FrontPage toolbars. (The View menu is used to hide or display any of these toolbars.) Here are their functions:

- The Formatting toolbar (Figure 12), displayed near the top of the FrontPage window, provides single-click access to many of the commands frequently used for changing the look of text on the page. As with most toolbars in the Windows environment, pointing at a toolbar button and holding the mouse steady for a second or two displays a *tool tip* that describes the button's function.

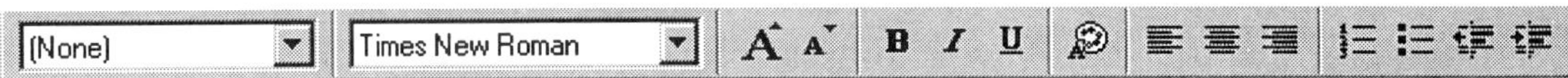

Figure 12 The Formatting Toolbar

- The Standard toolbar (Figure 13) lies under the Formatting toolbar, and displays button commands for working with files and objects on the screen.

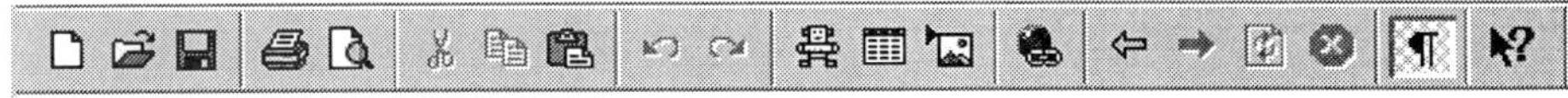

Figure 13 The Standard Toolbar

The Forms toolbar (Figure 14) has buttons for working with check boxes, drop-down lists, and other items to help you create a form.

Figure 14 Forms Toolbar

The Basics of Creating a Web Page

After starting FrontPage Express, the page that is open on the screen is a blank Normal page. A FrontPage Express page can be created from this blank one or from an existing template, which gives you a head start on structure and design.

Using a template

To create a page from a template:

1. Choose the New command from the File menu. The New Page dialog box will be displayed (Figure 15).
2. Select an item from the Template or Wizard list. A description of it is displayed at the bottom of the dialog box.

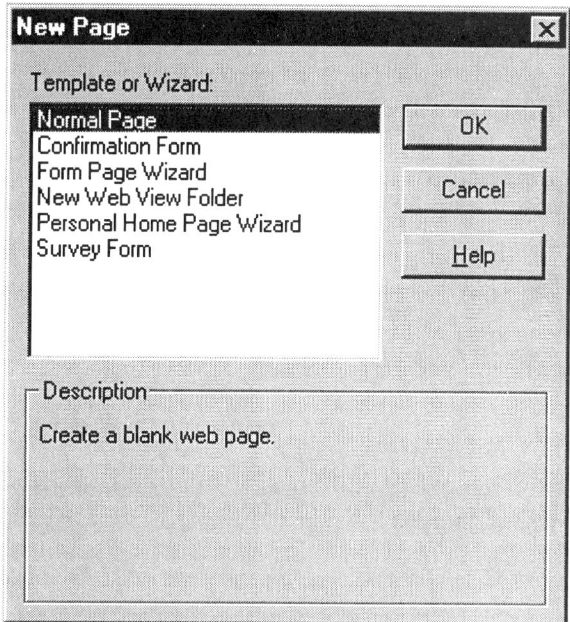

Figure 15 New Page Dialog Box

3. Choose the OK command button. A new page, containing a series of page items that you can customize, is created. If you have selected a wizard, answer the prompts to create the page.

Setting Page Properties You can configure some of the settings for your Web page by choosing the Page Properties command from the File menu. The Page Properties dialog box (Figure 16 on the next page) is displayed.

On the *General* page of this dialog box, you can specify:

- The physical location of your Web page; for example on a server or at an Internet Service Provider (ISP) location.
- The title of your page. The title appears on the browser's title bar when the Web page is viewed.
- A background sound that plays while the page is viewed.

The *Background* page of the dialog box allows you to set properties such as a background image, the text color, and a color for links.

The *Margins* page of the dialog box allows you to set margins for your Web page.

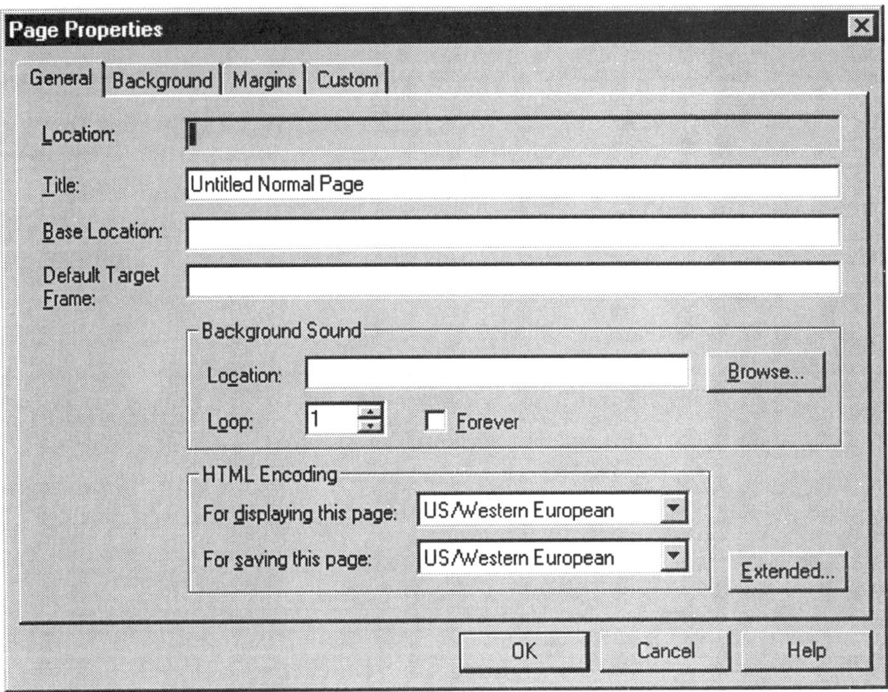

Figure 16 Page Properties Dialog Box

Adding Text to a Page Text is entered onto a Web page in the same way it is inserted in a word processing document (see Section 2.2). After the text is entered, it can be formatted.

To change the text *font* (its typeface, size, and style):

- If you want to change the font of existing text, select it and then choose the desired typeface, style, and/or size from the Formatting toolbar. The font change will apply only to the selected text.
- If you want to change the font for text that you're about to type, first choose the desired typeface, style, and size, and then type the text.

Use care when selecting a font. In order for it to display properly, users viewing your page must have that font present on their computer. It is usually best to stick with standard fonts such as Times New Roman and Arial. If you want to use a specialty font, create a graphic containing the text in a drawing program (such as Paint) and insert the graphic onto your page (as described later in this section).

Changing text color

You can display text in just about any color; choosing appropriate colors will make the text more appealing. To change text color:

1. Select the text.
2. Click on the Text Color button on the toolbar and then select the desired color from the palette.

or

Choose the Font command from the Format menu and select the desired color from the list.

Creating a Hyperlink

A *hyperlink*, (or *link*) is one of the most powerful features of the Internet. **Hyperlinks** are connections to other pages on the World Wide Web, to other pages on your personal Web site, or to a specific place on the current page.

To create a hyperlink:

1. Select the text that will be the link.
2. Choose Hyperlink from the Insert menu. The Create Hyperlink dialog box will be displayed (Figure 17, on the next page).
3. Click on the appropriate tab in the dialog box:
   - Click on *Open Pages* to link to a page you have already created on your Web site. Then select the desired page from the list.
   - Click on *World Wide Web* to link to an existing Web site. Then, type the URL for the site in the text box.
   - Click on *New Page* to link to a page on your Web site that does not yet exist. Then, type a title and URL for the new page in the appropriate text boxes. When creating a new page, you will be asked for a template or wizard name. Select the one you want to use and choose the OK button.
4. Choose the OK command button.

NOTE

Once you have created a hyperlink, to display the linked page:

1. Right-click on the link.
2. Choose Follow Hyperlink from the pop-up menu.

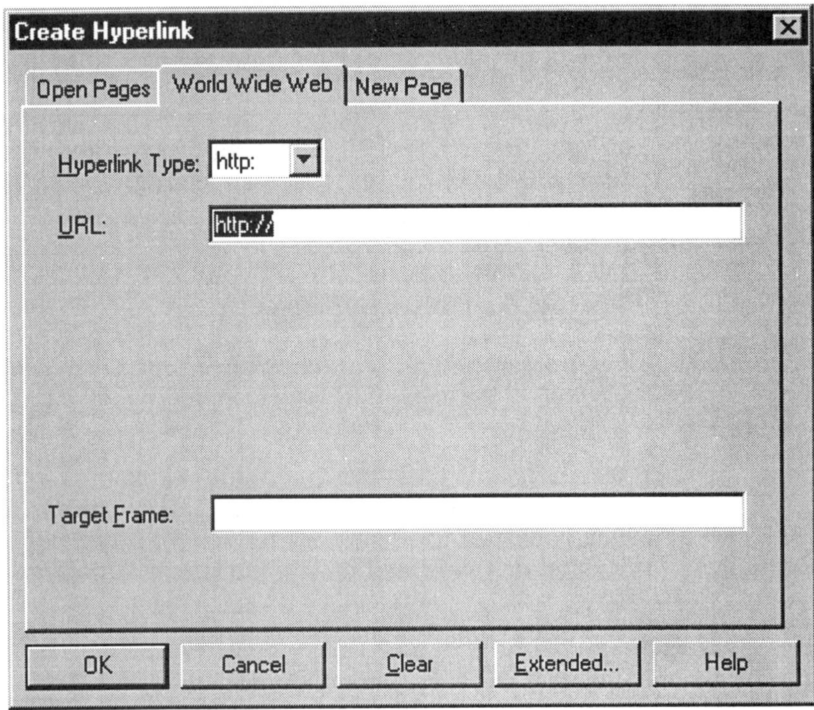

Figure 17 The Create Hyperlink Dialog Box

Working With Images

JPGs and GIFs Image (or graphic) files may be stored in a variety of different formats. While FrontPage Express can import many different formats, every image will ultimately be stored as either a JPG (jay-peg) or GIF (jiff) image. It is important that you understand the benefits and limitations of each.

JPG files JPG images are good for photographs and other graphics that have lots of different colors or contrast in the image. JPGs are usually compressed so that the file size is greatly reduced. However, the greater the compression, the more information that is lost. For that reason, JPG is referred to as a "lossy" format. For some photographs and backgrounds, however, JPG is the only way to go.

GIF files GIF images are also compressed, but not nearly as much as most JPGs. These files compress well when there are large areas of the same color in the picture. For this reason, GIFs generally appear more cartoon-like than JPGs. GIFs have the additional advantage of displaying transparent colors. This allows you to have, among other things, non-rectangular shapes against patterned backgrounds.

GIFs may also be configured to present themselves in "interlaced mode". In Web development, *interlacing* is a term used to describe an image that is presented on the page in "stages" of clarity. You have probably visited pages where the image first has a blocky look, then sharpens as it finishes loading. This is an interlaced GIF.

Ultimately, the decision of whether to use GIF or JPG usually depends on which format will result in the fastest delivery. While maintaining the clarity of the image, JPGs take longer to decompress. Therefore, a GIF image will usually load faster than the same JPG image.

Adding Images to a Page To add an image to your Web page:

1. Position the cursor where the image is to be inserted.
2. Choose the Image item from the Insert menu The Image dialog box will be displayed (Figure 18).

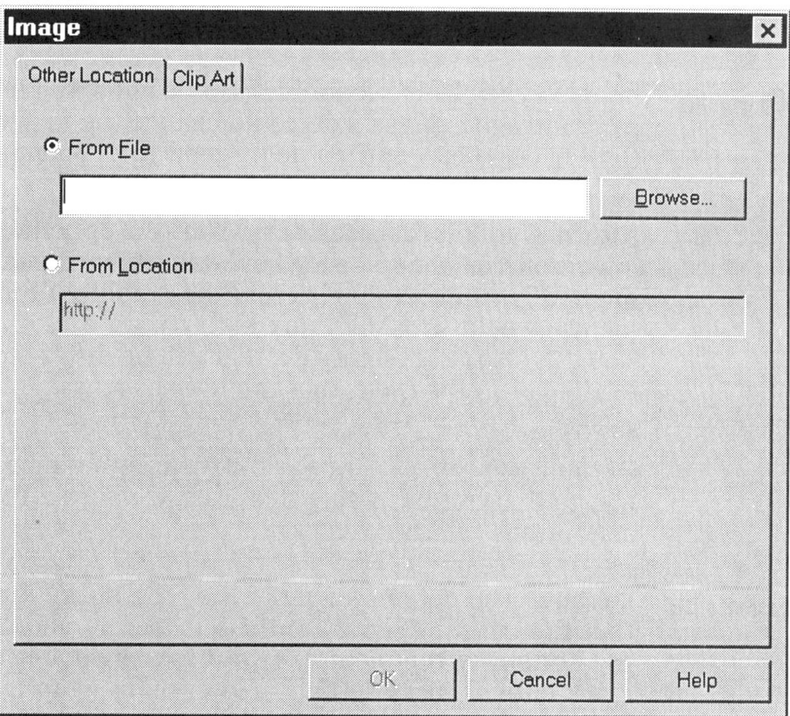

Figure 18 The Image Dialog Box

3. Select the location of the image:
   - On the Other Location page of the dialog box, you can specify an image located on your hard disk (using the *From File* text box) or on the Web (using the *From Location* text box).
   - On the Clip Art page of the dialog box, you can select a graphic that is supplied with FrontPage Express.

Editing Image Properties Once you have inserted an image, you will need to set a few image properties. To do so:

1. Select the image by clicking on it. You will notice eight small squares, or *handles*, that surround the image.
2. Select Image Properties from the Edit menu.
   or
   Right-click on the image and select Image Properties from the pop-up menu.

   The Image Properties dialog box (Figure 19) will open.

Here is a description of some of the contents of the Image Properties dialog box:

General tab

Image Type: This section determines how the image will be treated by FrontPage Express. You could change the image to a different type (JPG or GIF) here, but it's not a good idea. Making a type conversion in a graphics program usually works better.

Alternative Representations: You can optionally specify a second, low-resolution file to send first while this image is transferring. This method is similar to interlacing the graphic, although the alternative picture would probably look better than a blocky interlaced image. You can also enter some text that will be displayed while the image is loading or in the event that the user has disabled the auto-loading of images.

Default Hyperlink: Enter a URL or browse for the page you wish to link to this graphic. Using this feature, you can make your images act as "buttons" on the Web page.

Appearance tab

Layout: The default alignment for the image is *bottom*. This means that the image will shift to the left margin and the text will align at the bottom of the picture. Two other alignment options are *left* and *right*. Both of these settings allow you to wrap text along the side of the graphic, placing it along the left or right margins of the page or table.

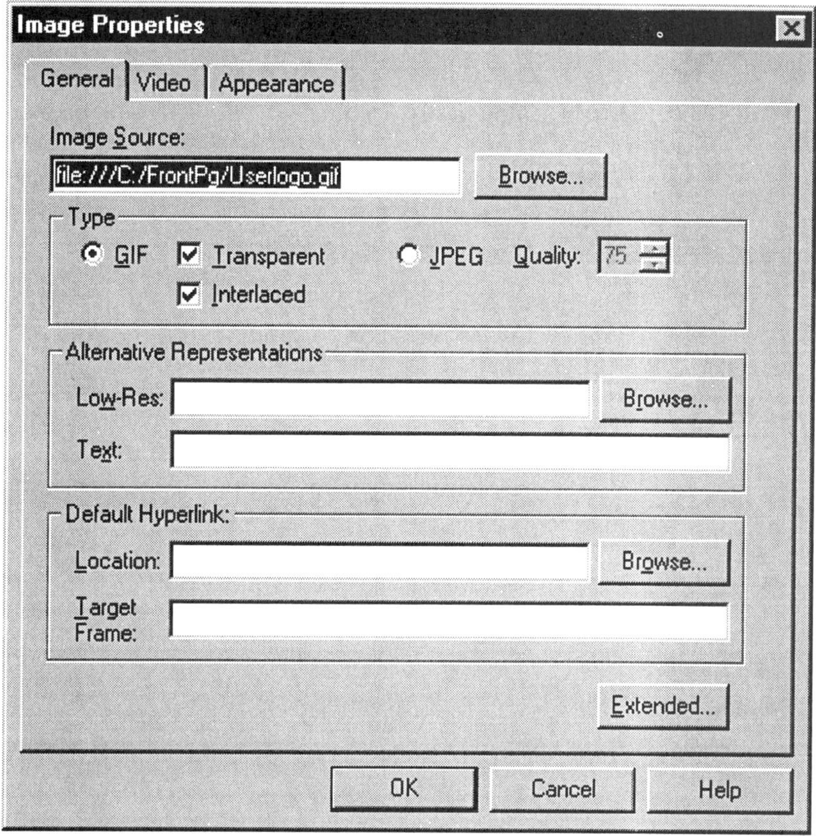

Figure 19 The Image Properties Dialog Box

The *Border Thickness* text box can be used to define a border around the image.

The *Horizontal* and *Vertical Spacing* text boxes allow you to specify how much space should appear between this image and any other text or graphic appearing next to it.

Size: For the image to be displayed properly, it is a good idea to select the Specify Size check box. Netscape Navigator may stretch the image if you do not explicitly specify the size. Moreover, graphics load faster when you check this option. However, the image may not look as good as the original if you change the values in height or width text boxes.

Saving, Viewing, and Publishing Web Pages

Saving a Web Page File Saving a Web page preserves the changes you have made to it; as with word processing documents, the first time a file is saved, it must be named. You can save the page as a file to be transferred to the server later, or as a specific Web page location.

To save a file:

1. Choose the Save command from the File menu or click on the Save button on the Standard toolbar. If this file has not been saved previously, the Save As dialog box (Figure 20) will be displayed.

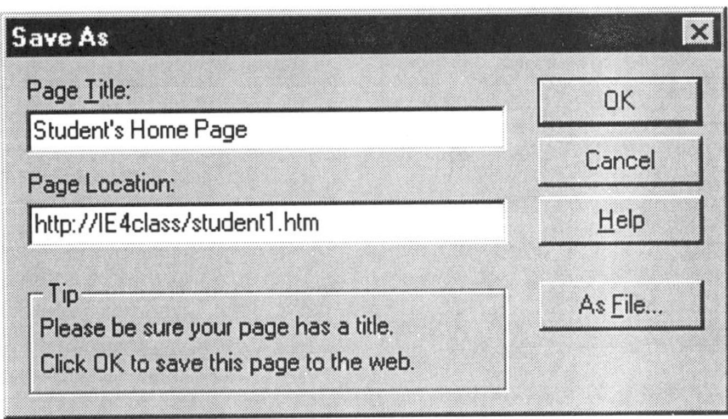

Figure 20 The Save As Dialog Box

2. If you haven't specified a page title yet, type the title in the Page Title text box.
3. Type the location (URL) of your page in the Page Location text box. Or, if you want to store the page on your hard disk, choose the As File command button; then type the path name for the file in the resulting dialog box and choose the OK button.
4. Choose the OK command button in the Save As dialog box.

Viewing Your Pages You can view your Web pages from within Internet Explorer without first transmitting (*posting*) the site on a server. To do so:

1. Start Internet Explorer.

2. Choose the Open command from the File menu.
3. In the URL box, type the name of your domain (or machine) followed by the name of the page you are creating.

Publishing Your Pages To make your site available to anyone on the Internet, you must *publish* your pages; that is, post your site on the Web. To do so, you must transmit the files to a Web server and supply certain setup information. One way to accomplish this is by using the Web Publishing Wizard supplied with FrontPage Express.

To publish from FrontPage Express:

1. Click on the Start button, point at the Programs item, and point at Internet Explorer on the resulting submenu, which opens another submenu.
2. Choose the Web Publishing Wizard from this submenu. The first Wizard window will be displayed.
3. Choose the Next command button. The Wizard window shown in Figure 21 will appear.

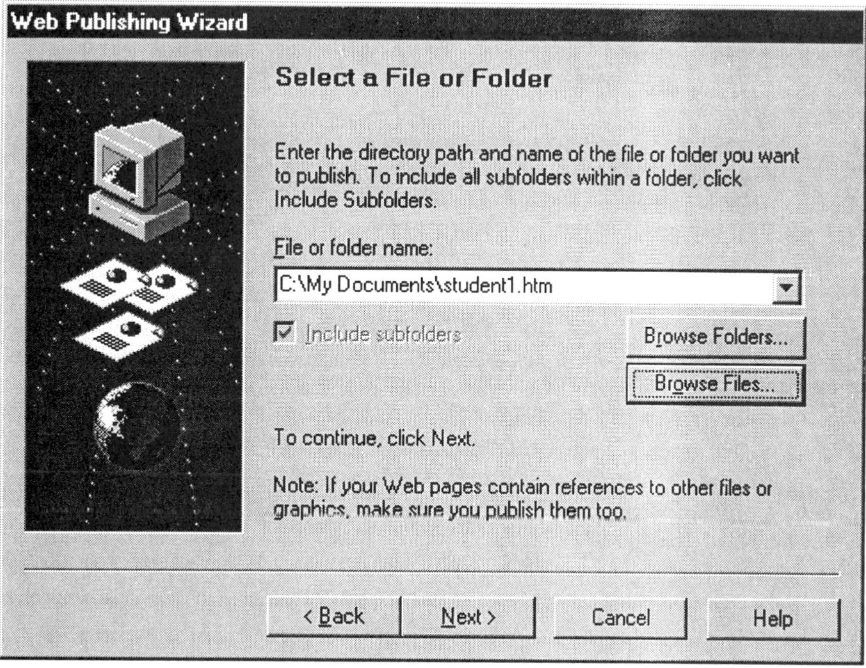

Figure 21 The Web Publishing Wizard

4. Enter or select the name of your Web page. If necessary, choose the Browse Files command button to locate the file on your computer. Choose the Next command button.
5. Enter a descriptive name for the Web server that will house your page. Then, choose the Next button.
6. Specify the URL where the page will be located. The system administrator (for a LAN) or the ISP (for a dial-up connection) can provide this URL. Enter the information and choose the Next button.
7. After all required information is entered, choose the Finish command button. The Web page you created will be transferred and published at the specified site location.

TUTORIAL

Try the following exercise on your own.

1. Start FrontPage Express: Click on the Start button, point at the Programs option, point at Internet Explorer on the resulting submenu, and click on the FrontPage Express item. The program window opens, displaying a blank Web page.
2. Display the New Page dialog box by choosing the New command from the File menu.
3. Select the Personal Home Page Wizard and choose the OK button.
4. Select the check boxes for the following major sections to appear on the page (and deselect the others):

   Hot List: Interesting Web Sites
   Biographical Information
   Personal Interests
   Contact Information

5. Choose the Next button to display the next Wizard screen.
6. In the Page URL text box, type the URL provided by your instructor or use the address designated by your ISP. Then, enter a title for your Web page in the Page Title text box and proceed to the next Wizard screens.
7. On these screens:
   - Accept the default "presentation style".
   - Select the *Personal* format for the Biography section.
   - Enter two or three items in the Personal Interests box and select the *Definitions list* format.

- Enter your "personal contact information" in the appropriate text boxes.
- Accept the given ordering for the sections on your page.

8. Choose the Finish command button. Your Web page will be displayed.
9. Choose the Page Properties command from the File menu and click on the Background tab.
10. Select the Background Image check box and choose the Browse button to open the Select Background Image dialog box.
11. Click on the Other Location tab, enter *file:///C:/WINDOWS/Backgrnd.gif* in the From File text box, and choose the OK command button. A graphic will fill your Web page.
12. Under the Hot List title, select the text Sample Site 1 and type the words *My Favorite Web Page*. Now, select this text, bold it, and change the font to Arial.
13. Make the following changes to the text on the rest of this page:
    - Change the second site text to: *Another choice location*
    - Make up a name for the third sample site text.
    - Delete the comment text beneath the Hot List.
    - Replace the text "Date" under the Biographical Information with a significant date in your life.
    - Replace the Description text beneath the date with text that relates to your specified date.
    - Add another date and explanation, replacing the existing "place holders".
    - Replace the place-holder text in the Personal Interests section with appropriate text.
    - Delete the comment text beneath the Personal Interests list.
14. Select the text *My Favorite Web Page* on the Hot List and make it a hyperlink:
    - Choose Hyperlink from the Insert menu to display the corresponding dialog box.
    - In the URL text box, enter the complete address for your favorite Web site or just enter: *http://www.infoseek.com*
    - Choose the OK button to accept the link information.
15. Save the changes you have made:
    - Choose the Save command from the File menu.
    - In the Save As dialog box, use the file name specified by your instructor and choose the OK command button.
16. Exit FrontPage Express.

6.6 Web Integration in Windows 98

In Windows 98, the operating system and the Internet Explorer browser are linked together in such a way that the Windows Desktop and every folder window becomes a gateway to the Internet and the information it contains. Moreover, as you have already seen in Section 1.2, you can configure Windows so that while you are working with it, it feels as if you are browsing the Web. Microsoft refers to this interconnection between Windows and the Internet as **Web integration**.

Channels and the Active Desktop

Under Windows 98, the Desktop can be transformed into an **Active Desktop**, an interactive window onto the Internet. To create an Active Desktop, Windows makes use of *Internet Channels*.

As you know, you can set up *Favorites* to easily access specific Web pages (see Section 6.2). Windows also provides a similar device, **Channels**, which are special sites on the Internet set up to keep you in touch with rapidly changing information. Enabling an Internet Channel is analogous to subscribing to a newspaper or magazine for the purpose of obtaining up-to-date news, but, in the case of Channels, you subscribe to a Web site to obtain updated information on a regular basis. Channels provide an easy and convenient way to connect to the Internet to retrieve specific content.

When viewing Channel sites, specific information can be placed on your Windows Desktop, making use of its Active Desktop mode. For instance, you may want to constantly display stock exchange quotes or sports scores on the Desktop, periodically updated with the latest information.

Viewing Channels You can select a channel for viewing in several ways. To do so from the Desktop:

Using the Channels toolbar

1. Display the Channels toolbar (Figure 22), if it does not already appear on the Desktop, by right-clicking on the Desktop, pointing at the Active Desktop item on the resulting pop-up menu, and choosing View as Web Page from the submenu.
2. Either select a listed channel by clicking on its toolbar button or click on the Channel Guide button to obtain a list of all active channels on the Web, listed by category.

If the Channels toolbar is not present on the Desktop and choosing View as Web Page from the Desktop right-click menu doesn't display it, do the following:

1. Right-click on the Desktop, point at the Active Desktop item, and choose Customize my Desktop from the submenu.
2. In the resulting dialog box, select the *View my Active Desktop as a web page* and the *Internet Explorer Channel Bar* check boxes.
3. Choose the OK command button.

When you select a toolbar button on the Channels bar, the Internet Explorer browser starts, displays a *Channel Viewer* window in full-screen view, and either connects to the selected site or, if your selection was a category of sites, lists the available sites in this category. For example, Figure 23 (on the next page) shows the result of selecting the "sports" button on the Channel bar.

Figure 22 The Channels Toolbar

Each channel site contains links and commands to customize the viewing of that channel to individual preferences, including subscription information.

The Channel Viewer displays the Channels bar on one side of the window and the channel content on the other. Here are some features of this window:

- The Channel toolbar may "slide" off the screen; to redisplay it, move the mouse pointer to the left edge of the screen.
- To keep the toolbar from sliding off the screen, click on the pushpin on its title bar.
- To view the Windows Taskbar, move the mouse pointer to the bottom edge of the screen.

- To close the Channels bar, click on its close button. To rcopcn it, click on the View Channels toolbar button at the top of the screen.

- To switch from full-screen view to an ordinary Internet Explorer window (or back again), click on the toolbar's Fullscreen button.
- To close the Channel Viewer window, click on its close button.

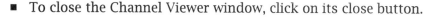

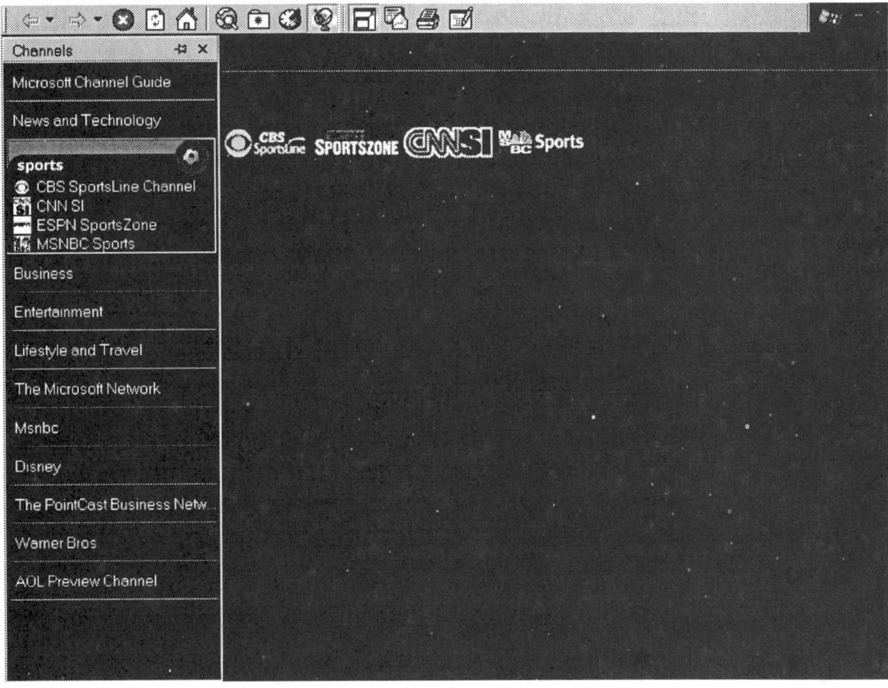

Figure 23 The Channel Viewer Window

You can display the Channel Viewer window and open the Channel Guide within it without making use of the Channels toolbar. To do so, just click on the View Channels Taskbar button.

Subscribing to a Channel Before viewing actual content for a specific channel, you must **subscribe** to that channel. Unlike subscribing to a magazine, subscribing to a channel doesn't cost anything. However, some channel sites do contain offers for extra services or features that are not free of charge.

A channel site will display a subscribe command to let you sign up for that channel. Click the Subscribe link to begin the process. Each site's subscription process will vary somewhat and offer different features, but all channels will request that you choose the method of updating the selected information. A dialog box, similar to the one in Figure 24, will allow you to select the desired method. Then, choose the OK command button.

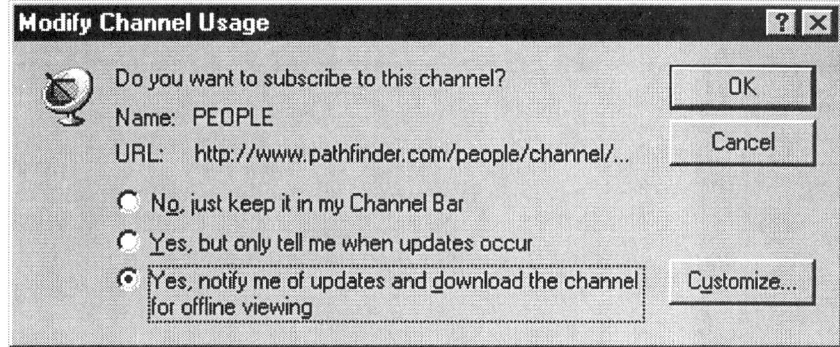

Figure 24 The Methods for Updating a Channel

Placing Channel Content on the Desktop Many channels contain an option to place particular items on the Desktop. The item will be displayed on the background of the Windows Desktop until you close it by clicking on its close button. The updating method you have selected for this channel will determine when and how items are updated to reflect the most current information.

After you have subscribed to a channel, if its content does not appear on the Desktop, to display it:

1. Right-click on the Desktop, point at the Active Desktop item, and choose Customize my Desktop from the resulting submenu. The Display Properties dialog box (see Section 5.2) will open, with the *Web* section visible.
2. If you are not currently using the Active Desktop feature, select the *View my Active Desktop as a web page* check box.
3. Select the check box of a listed channel.
4. Choose the OK command button to accept the changes and display the selected items.

Managing Subscriptions There are various reasons why you may need to *manage* (for example, update or delete) a subscription. For one, information displayed by a channel to which you have subscribed might have to be updated to reflect the most recent changes on the Internet; in this fast-paced information age, keeping current is important.

Updating automatically

Channel subscriptions can be updated automatically or manually. You can choose to update subscriptions automatically during the process of subscribing to a channel, or you can do so afterwards in the following way:

1. In Internet Explorer, choose the Manage Subscription option from the Favorites menu. The Subscriptions window will open, listing all active subscriptions and displaying their status.
2. Select a subscription and choose the Properties command from the File menu or click on the toolbar's Properties button. That subscription's Properties dialog box will open (see Figure 25).

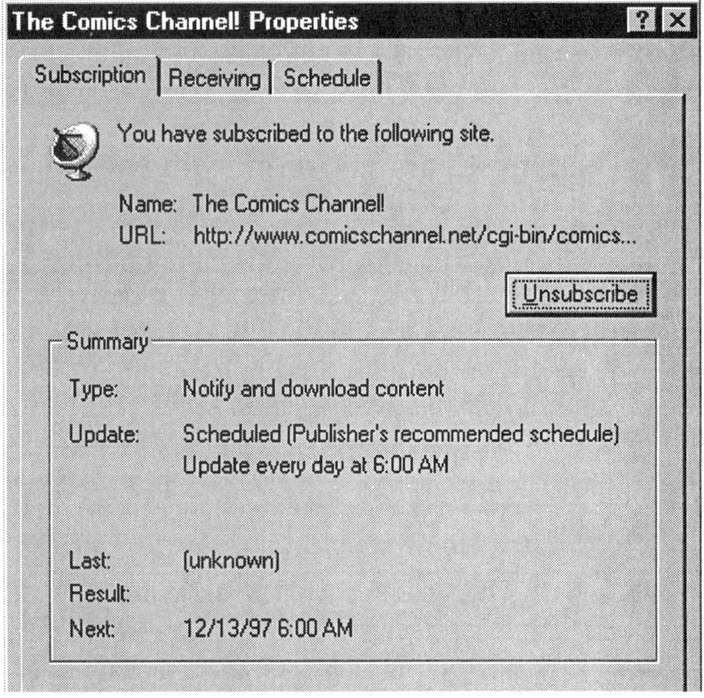

Figure 25 Channel Properties

3. On the Receiving page, specify the type of subscription and whether or not you are to be notified by e-mail when changes have occurred in the subscription information.
4. On the Schedule page, add or modify the update schedule for this channel subscription.
5. Choose the OK command button to accept the changes.

Updating manually

To update subscriptions manually:

1. In Internet Explorer, choose the Update All Subscriptions option from the Favorites menu.
2. Choose the OK button to confirm the action. The most recent information for the subscribed sites will be retrieved from the Internet and downloaded to your computer.

Just as e-mail messages accumulate and become obsolete, so do Channel subscriptions. Some periodic housekeeping may be necessary to keep your Desktop in order.

Deleting a subscription

To delete a subscription:

1. In Internet Explorer, choose the Manage Subscription option from the Favorites menu. The Subscriptions window will open.
2. Select a subscription and choose the Delete command from the File menu or click on the toolbar's Delete button to delete the subscription.

Web Integration in Folder Windows

As you have seen, Channels can link the Desktop to the Internet. Windows 98 also integrates the Internet with folder windows, such as My Computer and Control Panel. You can access the Web from any folder window and have any such window display its contents in a way that resembles a Web page.

Displaying a Folder Window in Web View In Section 1.2, we briefly mentioned that the My Computer window can be viewed as if it were a Web page, complete with single-click access to its subfolders. Here, we will expand on this discussion.

To turn on Web view for a folder window, choose the *as Web Page* item from the View menu. This view is a toggle feature, and a check mark will display next to the command when you are using Web view. Choose *as Web Page* again to display the window in normal view.

Web view (see Figure 26, on the next page) has a more descriptive screen display, with the upper or left part of the window providing the window name and a description of the selected window item. Any HTML (Web) content in the window will display as it would in a Web browser.

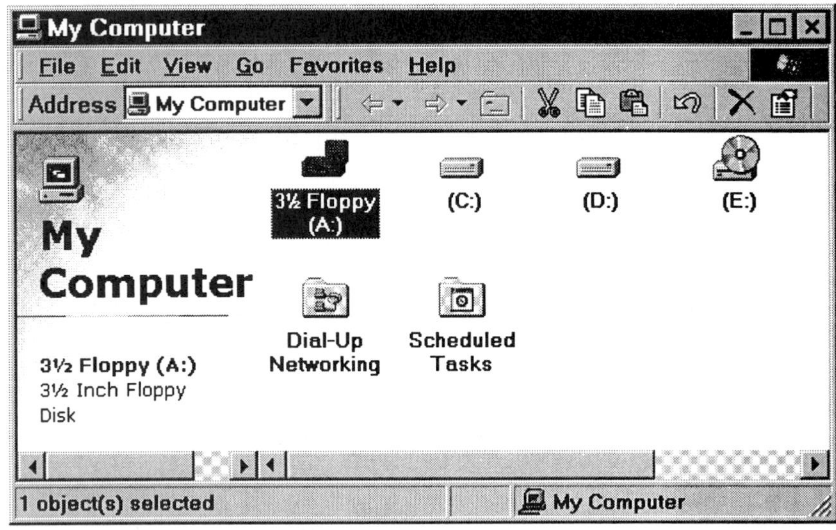

Figure 26 Web View of My Computer

NOTE

Be aware that the Web view setting applies only to the currently displayed window, unless specified otherwise in the Folder Options dialog box (as described later in this section).

The special toolbars typically used on the Internet can be displayed in any folder window.

- The Toolbars item on the View menu can be used to turn on (or turn off) the Address bar and the Links toolbar (see Section 6.2).
- The Explorer Bar item on the View menu can be used to turn on one of the following toolbars: Search, Favorites, History, or Channels (see Section 6.2).

Customizing a Folder Window Any folder window can be customized in certain ways. Most of these customization features are available in the Folder Options dialog box (Figure 27), which is opened by choosing this item from the View menu.

As we explained in Section 1.2:

- Click on the Web style option button to select objects by pointing at them and open objects by single-clicking on them; that is, to treat objects as if they were links on the Web.

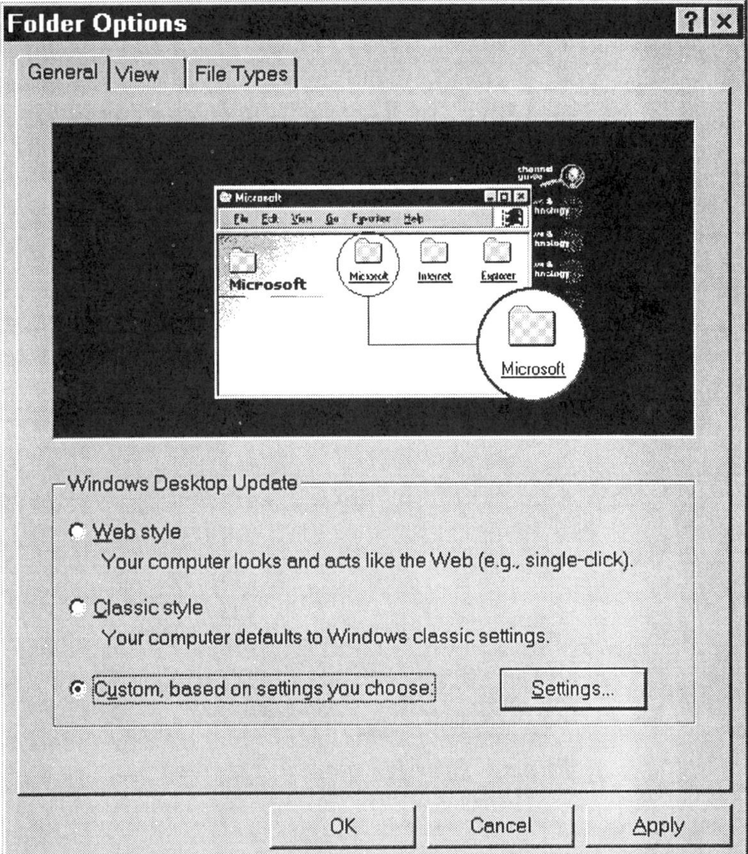

Figure 27 The Folder Options Dialog Box

- Click on the Classic style option button to have Windows 98 behave as in previous versions — single-clicking on an object selects it and double-clicking on an object opens it.

You can create your own settings by selecting the Custom option and then choosing the Settings command button, which opens the Custom Settings dialog box. In this dialog box, you can:

- Turn on or off the Active Desktop.
- Change how folders are opened when browsing, either in separate windows or within the same window.
- Turn on the *View as Web Page* settings for all folder windows.
- Select Classic or Web style click/double-click mode. Moreover, in

Web style mode, the icon underline can be turned off (although it still displays when an icon is pointed at).

To put your changes into effect, choose the OK button in this dialog box and then the Close button in the Folder Options dialog box. The settings will remain in effect until you change them again.

NOTE

You can also customize some folder windows by choosing the Customize this Folder option from the View menu (if it appears there). This action starts the Customize this Folder Wizard which allows you to create your own Web content or specify a background picture for this window. Be aware, however, that doing the former requires knowledge of HTML (Hypertext Markup Language) commands.

If you want *all* your folder windows to have the same View menu settings (except for the toolbar settings), set up one folder window as you would like and then:

1. Choose Folder Options from the View menu.
2. In the Folder Options dialog box, click on the View tab.
3. On the resulting dialog box page, choose the Like Current Folder command button.
4. Choose the OK command button.

Accessing the Internet from a Folder Window You can easily access the Internet from within any folder window. There are several ways to do this:

- Click on the Windows logo in the upper right corner of the window.
- Choose the Home Page or Search the Web item from the Go menu.
- Display the Links toolbar and click on a link.
- Display the Address toolbar and enter a Web address in the text box; then press Enter.
- Choose a favorite Web site from the Favorites menu.

In any case, Internet Explorer starts and displays the requested page within the folder window.

Try the following exercise on your own.

1. Turn on your computer to start Windows 98, if necessary, and close any open windows.
2. If the Channels toolbar is not present on the Desktop, display it: Right-click on the Desktop, point at the Active Desktop item, and choose View as Web Page from the resulting submenu.
3. Move the mouse over the Channels buttons to view the tool tip description of each button.
4. Click on the Entertainment category button to open the Channel Viewer and view its individual channel items.
5. Choose one of the items from the Entertainment list. The corresponding site will display.
6. Choose the Subscribe command. It may appear as a Subscribe link or as an Add as an Active Channel link. Respond to the prompts as necessary to activate the channel. (This process will differ from site to site.)
7. When prompted to set the channel update schedule, select No and choose the OK command button.
8. If there is an option to place an element of this channel on your Desktop, choose that link. While viewing the Desktop as a Web page, that element, along with the Channel toolbar, will be visible.
9. Minimize the Channel Viewer window and view the changes on the Desktop.

10. Restore the Channel Viewer and click on the Fullscreen button on the toolbar to display the Internet Explorer window. Maximize the window, if necessary.
11. Delete the new subscription: Choose Manage Subscriptions from the Favorites menu, select the subscription, and press the Delete key or click on the Delete toolbar button.
12. Close the Internet Explorer window and disconnect from the Internet, if necessary.
13. Open the My Computer window from the Desktop icon. Maximize the window.
14. Choose the *as Web Page* item from the View menu. Notice the change in the My Computer window. Choose this item again to turn off the Web view.
15. Close the My Computer window.

Chapter Summary

	To connect to the Internet	Use a dedicated connection to the Internet via a local network or an educational institution; *or* use an online information service; *or* use an Internet Service Provider (ISP).
Internet Explorer	To start Internet Explorer	Choose the Internet Explorer icon on the Desktop or on the Taskbar; *or* click on the Internet Explorer item on the Start menu's Programs option.
	The Explorer toolbar buttons	*Back* displays the previous page. *Forward* displays the next page. *Stop* halts a page display in progress. *Refresh* reloads a page. *Home* displays the Home page. *Search* displays the Search Explorer bar. *Favorites* lists your favorite Web sites. *History* displays previously visited sites. *Channels* displays custom Web sites. *Fullscreen* switches to full-screen view. *Mail* accesses e-mail functions. *Print* prints the displayed page. *Edit* displays the current page in FrontPage Express.
	Address box	Click in the Address box and type the URL of the Internet page you wish to display, or select a previously viewed address by selecting from the drop-down list. Then, press the Enter key.
	To perform a search	Click on the toolbar's Search button and select a search engine from the Explorer bar; *or* type the address of a search engine in the Address box and press Enter.
	To print a Web page	Display the desired page; then click on the toolbar's Print button, or choose Print from the File menu and choose OK.
	To download a file	Choose the download link or follow screen instructions to initiate the download, identify the folder on your computer to which the file is to be copied, and choose the OK command button. Follow the prompts to complete the process.

	To disconnect from the Internet	For local network users, exit Internet Explorer; for online service users, exit Internet Explorer and the service; for ISP users, exit Internet Explorer and choose the Disconnect button in the Connected dialog box.
Outlook Express	To start Outlook Express	Choose the Outlook Express icon on the Desktop or Taskbar; *or* point at the Internet Explorer item on the Start menu's Programs option and choose Outlook Express from the submenu.
	To send a new message	Click on the toolbar's Compose Message button *or* choose the New Message command from the Compose menu. Then, type the recipient's name, the subject, and the text of the message. Finally, click on the toolbar's Send button (and, if necessary, on the Send and Receive button).
	To receive e-mail	Click on the Send and Receive toolbar button to receive new messages; double-click on any new messages in the Inbox folder to view them.
	To reply to a message	Select or open the message, click on the Reply to Author toolbar button, type the reply, and send the message.
	To forward a message	Select or open the message, click on the Forward Message toolbar button; type any new message text and send it.
	To attach a file to a message	Create a new message; click on the Insert File toolbar button, locate and select the file, and click on the Attach button.
	To move a message	Select the source folder and drag the message onto the destination folder.
	To delete a message	If the message is open, click on the toolbar's Delete button. Otherwise, select the name of the message, then press the Delete key, choose the Delete command from the Edit menu, *or* click on the toolbar's Delete button.
FrontPage Express	To start FrontPage Express	Point at Internet Explorer on the Start menu's Programs option; then choose FrontPage Express from the submenu.

	To use a page template	Choose the File command from the New menu, select the desired template or wizard, and choose OK.
	To save a Web page file	Choose the Save As command from the File menu.
	To create a hyperlink	Select the text that will be the link; choose the Hyperlink command from the Insert menu; select either an existing page or click on the New Page tab to automatically start a new page; and type the new page name and title.
	To add an image to a page	Position the cursor where the image is to be inserted, choose Image from the Insert menu, select the location of the image file, and choose the OK button.
	To view a page in Internet Explorer	Open Internet Explorer and choose the Open File command from the File menu. In the URL box, type the name of your domain (or machine) followed by the name of the page you are creating and press Enter.
Channels	To display the Channels toolbar	Right-click on the Desktop, point at Active Desktop, and select the View as Web Page option from the resulting submenu; *or* click on the View Channels toolbar button.
	To view a channel	Select it from the Channels toolbar; *or* select its category from the toolbar and then select the channel in the Channel viewer window.
	To subscribe to a channel	Click on the Subscribe link at the channel site.
	To update a subscription manually	In Internet Explorer, choose Update All Subscriptions from the Favorites menu and choose OK.
Web Integration in Folder Windows	To display (or turn off) Web view in a folder window	Choose the as Web Page item from the View menu.
	To display (or hide) the special toolbars in a folder window	Point at the Toolbars item on the View menu and choose Address Bar or Links.

To view the Explorer Bar in a folder window	Point at the Explorer Bar item on the View menu and choose Search, Favorites, History, or Channels.
To access the Internet from a folder window	Click on the logo button on the menu bar, *or* choose the Home Page or Search the Web item from the Go menu, *or* choose a link from the Links toolbar, *or* enter a Web address on the Address bar, *or* choose a Web Favorite from the Favorites menu.
To customize a folder window	Choose the Folder Options item from the View menu. Then select the Web style, Classic style, or Custom option. If the last of these, choose the Settings button and select options in the dialog box.

Review Exercises

Section 6.1

1. The three avenues for connecting to the Internet are through a ____________, a ____________, or a ____________.
2. The ____________ is the largest network in the world.
3. The most commonly used method to access information on the Internet is through software called a ____________.
4. True or false: There are established standards for domain names.
5. True or false: The right part of the domain name is the user's name.
6. True or false: The middle part of the domain name usually identifies the service provider.
7. True or false: The *Advanced Research Projects Agency Network* (ARPANET) of the 1960s was a predecessor of today's Internet.
8. Which of the following services is available on the Internet?

   a. FTP
   b. Telnet
   c. Internet Phone
   d. All of the above

9. Every computer on the Internet has a unique location, called

   a. A dynamic address.

b. An Internet connection.
c. A subnet.
d. A dotted quad.

10. If your computer has a permanently-assigned IP address, it is called
    a. A Terminate Stay Resident (TSR) address.
    b. A perpetual address.
    c. A static address.
    d. A dotted quad.

Section 6.2

11. In Internet Explorer, a ___________ is an electronic place holder.
12. By default, an unfollowed link appears ___________ in color.
13. You can access a Web site by typing its URL in Internet Explorer's ___________ and pressing the Enter key.
14. True or false: The Links toolbar can be used to access Microsoft's home page.
15. True or false: A URL always contains the symbol "@".
16. Which Internet Explorer toolbar button reloads a Web page to the screen?
    a. Refresh
    b. Stop
    c. Forward
    d. Back
17. Which toolbar button lists pages you have previously marked as interesting sites?
    a. Refresh
    b. Back
    c. Home
    d. Favorites
18. Which screen is always displayed when you open Internet Explorer?
    a. The Search screen
    b. The Start (or Home) page
    c. The History Explorer bar
    d. The Favorites Explorer bar

Section 6.3

19. A program, like Yahoo!, that is used to search for information on the Internet is called a search ___________.
20. When you copy a file from the Internet to your computer, the process is called ___________ the file.

21. True or false: Choosing the Print command prints every page you have viewed in the current Internet session.

22. True or false: Downloading is the process of copying files from the Internet to a disk.

23. A search engine available on the Internet is:

    a. AltaVista
    b. Excite
    c. Infoseek
    d. All of the above

24. You can access a search engine by

    a. Typing its URL in the Address box and pressing the Enter key.
    b. Choosing it from the History Explorer bar.
    c. Choosing it from the Channels Explorer bar.
    d. All of the above techniques will work.

Section 6.4

25. ___________ consists of electronic messages sent over a network between users in an office environment, or via the Internet or an online service.

26. Existing files to be sent along with an e-mail message are called ___________.

27 The figure at the right is the ___________ button on the Compose Message window toolbar.

28. True or false: In Outlook Express, new messages are delivered to the Sent Items folder

29. True or false: The Outlook Express Outbox is the folder in which all messages ready for delivery are placed.

30. True or false: From within the Outlook Express window, to send a selected message, click on the toolbar's Compose Message icon.

31. Messages can be transferred between folders using the following technique(s):

    a. Dragging and dropping
    b. Cutting and pasting
    c. Copying and pasting
    d. All of the above will work.

32. Which folder does not appear (by default) in the Outlook Express folders pane?

    a. Inbox
    b. Outbox

c. Recycle Bin
d. Sent Items

Section 6.5

33. The figure at the right is the FrontPage Express ____________ toolbar.

34. A ____________, sometimes just called a link, is one of the most powerful features of the Internet.

35. True or false: The base language of the web is HTML (Hypertext Markup Language).

36. True or false: Pages must be coded in the HTML language to be understood by a Web browser.

37. True or false: The FrontPage Web Publishing Wizard allows you to create or open a Web site for editing.

38. True or false: After adding it to a page, a hyperlink can be followed by clicking on it.

39. The image format that is especially good for photographs and other graphics having many different colors or contrast is:

    a. GIF
    b. JPG
    c. PCX
    d. BMP

40. Using the Page Properties dialog box, you can specify

    a. The title of your page.
    b. The hyperlinks on your page.
    c. The text font for your page.
    d. None of the above properties can be specified.

Section 6.6

41. A ____________ is a special Web site designed to keep its users in touch with rapidly changing information.

42. If the Channels toolbar is not present on the Desktop, to display it: right-click on the Desktop, point at the Active Desktop item, and choose ____________ from the resulting submenu.

43. To delete a subscription, begin by choosing the ____________ item from Internet Explorer's Favorites menu.

44. To select the Web style or Classic style mode, you must open the ____________ dialog box.

45. True or false: Subscribing to an Internet Channel always costs money.

46. True or false: Channel subscriptions can only be updated automatically.

47. True or false: The Internet can be accessed from within any folder window.

48. True or false: Using the Custom folder option, you can enable Web style mode, yet have icons appear without an underline.

49. To display the Channels toolbar from within a folder window
    a. Click on the Windows logo button.
    b. Use the View menu's Toolbars submenu.
    c. Choose the View menu's *as Web Page* command.
    d. Use the Go menu.

50. To update subscriptions manually, choose Update All Subscriptions from Internet Explorer's
    a. File menu.
    b. Tools menu.
    c. Favorites menu.
    d. Go menu.

51. Which of the following is *not* a way to access the Internet from within any folder window?
    a. Display the Address toolbar, type a Web address in the text box, and press the Enter key.
    b. Choose a Web Favorite from the Favorites menu.
    c. Click on the Windows logo in the upper right corner of the window.
    d. Click on the Internet Explorer icon on the status bar.

52. From within the Folder Options dialog box, to make icons behave like links that can be opened with a single click, select the
    a. Classic style option button.
    b. Web style option button.
    c. Explorer style option button.
    d. None of the above.

Build Your Own Glossary

53. The following words and phrases are important terms that were introduced in this chapter. (They appear within the text in boldface type.) Use WordPad (see Section 2.2) to enter a definition for each term, preserving alphabetical order, into the Glossary file on the Student Disk.

Active Desktop
Address (on Internet)
Address box
Attachment
Browser
Channel
Deleted Items folder
Download a file
E-mail
Favorite
FrontPage Express
FrontPage Web Publishing Wizard
FTP (File Transfer Protocol)
GIF
Home page
HTML

Hyperlink
Inbox
Internet
Internet Explorer
Internet Phone
Internet Relay Chat (IRC)
Internet Service Provider (ISP)
JPG
Link
Outbox
Outlook Express
Search engine
Sent Items folder
Subscribe (to a channel)
Telnet
Upload a file
URL (Universal Resource Locator)
Usenet
Web integration
Web page
World Wide Web

Lab Exercises

Work each of the following exercises at your computer. Begin by turning the machine on (if necessary) to start Windows 98 and closing any open windows.

Lab Exercise 1 (Section 6.2)

a. Start Internet Explorer. What is the URL of the page that is displayed?

b. Scroll down the page to locate the first text link. What color is the text for this link?

c. Display the page referred to by this link. How did you do this? What is the URL for this page?

d. Click on the toolbar's Back button. What color is the link of step *b* now.

e. Click on the Forward button. Did a new page load? If so, what page is displayed?

f. Click again on the Forward button. Did a new page load? If so, what page is displayed now?

g. Click on the Back button until it appears dim. What page is displayed?

h. On the current page, scroll up or down to find a new link. Click on that link.

i. Click on the toolbar's Home button. What page is displayed?

j. Use the Address box to access the *www.amazon.com* Web site. did you have to press the Enter key after typing the address or did the site start to load after you typed *com*? What is the title of the displayed page?

k. Try to exit Internet Explorer without returning to the Home page. Were you able to do so? If not, return Home and exit.

Lab Exercise 2 (Section 6.2)

a. Start Internet Explorer, if necessary.

b. Access the *www.kodak.com* Web site. What is the title displayed on this Web page?

c. Add this site to the Favorites list. How did you do this?

d. Use the toolbar to return to the Home page. Which toolbar button did you click on?

e. Open the Favorites menu and select the newly-listed Favorite from the list to return to the Kodak site. Was this site listed at the top of the list, the bottom of the list, or neither?

f. Choose the Favorites option on the Start menu. Is the Kodak site listed there? If so, where on the list (first, second, etc.) does it appear?

g. Delete the Kodak site from the Favorites list.

h. Use the Address box to access *www.toys.com*. How does this site describe itself?

i. Go to *www.si.edu*. What does "si" stand for?

j. Use the Address box drop-down list to return to the Kodak site. Was it at the top of the list?

k. Exit Internet Explorer.

Lab Exercise 3 (Section 6.3)

a. Display the Excite Web site by typing its URL in the Address box and pressing the Enter key. What is its URL?

b. Type *white house* in the Search text box and choose the Search command button. How many "hits" were there?

c. Select all of the *Select words to add to your search* check boxes and choose the Search Again button. Were there fewer or more hits than the first time?

d. Click on the toolbar's Back button until Excite's home page appears. How many times did you have to go Back?

e. Click on the People Finder link and then enter your name (but not city or state) in the text boxes. Were there any hits?

f. Display the Internet Explorer Search bar. What menu could you use to do this?

g. Use this Explorer bar to go to the Alta Vista Web site. How did you do this?

h. Perform a search for *aquatic life*. What is the name of the command button on this site that initiates the search?

i. Click on the first "hit" listed. Can you tell in which country this Web site is located? If so, which one?

j. Exit Internet Explorer.

Lab Exercise 4 (Section 6.3)

a. Start Internet Explorer, if necessary.

b. Go to the WinZip Web site. Its address is www.winzip.com. What are the words at the very top of this Web page?

c. Click on the Download Evaluation Version link. Did any other links on the WinZip home page refer to downloading? If so, what were they?

d. On the resulting page, select the Windows 95 or Windows 98 version to download? What other versions were there?

e. Place a blank disk in the A: drive, select the A: drive as the destination for the file, and choose the Save command button. What dialog box or message appeared?

f. If the file transfer was successful, open Windows Explorer and select the A: drive in the folder tree pane. What are the names of the files that were downloaded?

g. Exit Windows Explorer and Internet Explorer.

Lab Exercise 5 (Section 6.4)

a. Start Outlook Express. How did you do this?

b. Create a message in Outlook Express that is addressed to someone in your class. What is the recipient's address? Address the message to yourself as well. What punctuation mark did you use between the two addresses?

c. Add an attachment to the message using the WordPad file named Preamble on the Student Disk. How did you do this?

d. Send the message. Did you have to click on the toolbar's Send and Receive button or did the Send button suffice?

e. Display the contents of the Sent Items folder. Does the message you just sent appear there?

f. Print the message you just sent. Does the printout include the recipients' names?

g. Check for new mail. Did your message appear in the Inbox?

h. Exit Outlook Express.

Lab Exercise 6 (Section 6.4)

a. Start Outlook Express.

b. Create a new folder in the folder pane using your first name as the folder name. What toolbar button or menu command did you use to do this?

c. Check for any new messages. If you wanted to reply to a message, which toolbar button or menu command would you use?

d. Move the messages from the Inbox into your new folder. How can you do this without using any toolbar button or menu command?

e. Move the messages you have sent from the Sent Items folder into your folder. Use a technique that is different from the one in step *d*. What technique did you use?

f. Delete the messages in your folder, then delete your folder. Is it possible to perform *both* of these operations using the keyboard? If so, what key must you press?

g. Display the contents of the Deleted Items folder. What are they?

h. Delete all of the messages in the Deleted Items folder. List all the ways in which this operation can be accomplished.

i. Exit Outlook Express.

Lab Exercise 7 (Section 6.5)

In FrontPage Express, create a Web page that advertises the class you are taking. Include several appropriate links to other Web sites. Print your Web page. Then, publish it using the Web Publishing Wizard.

Lab Exercise 8 (Section 6.6)

a. Open the My Computer window and choose the Folder Options item from the View menu. How many tabs does the resulting dialog box have?

b. Put the Web style option into effect and point to an icon in the My Computer window. What happened?

c. Click on the C: drive icon. Did a separate window open to display the contents of this drive?

d. Choose the Folder Options item from the View menu and put the Classic style mode into effect.

e. Click on the My Documents folder in the C: drive window. What happened?

f. If the My Documents folder window did not display in step *e*, open it. Did a separate window open to display the contents of this folder?

g. Choose the *as Web Page* item from the View menu. Does this option work with Classic mode in effect?

h. Display the folder options' Custom Settings dialog box. How did you do this?

i. Close all open dialog boxes by clicking on their close buttons. Describe how you would use the Folder Options dialog box to put the current window's settings into effect for all windows.

j. Does the My Documents View menu have a Customize this Folder command? Does the My Computer View menu?

k. Close all open windows.

If You Want to Learn More ...

The notes presented here allow you to delve more deeply into some of the topics covered in this chapter.

Changing the default page in Internet Explorer

In Internet Explorer, you can choose a specific location for the Home page. To do so:

1. Display the page that is to be the new Home page.
2. Choose the Internet Options item from the View menu and select the General page in the resulting dialog box.
3. In the Home Page section, the URL for the displayed page will appear in the Address text box. Choose the Use Current command button. (You can return the Home page to the default URL by choosing the Default command button.)
4. Choose the OK command button to put the changes into effect.

Copy Web page text or graphics

Any text or graphic on an Internet page can be copied to your word processor. Here's how:

1. Display the Web page.

2. If copying text, select the text and then either
   - Right-click on the selected text and choose the Copy item from the pop-up menu.

   or
   - Choose the Copy item from the Edit menu.
3. If copying a graphic, right-click on it and choose the Copy item from the pop-up menu.
4. Open the destination application, such as WordPad.
5. Position the insertion point where you want and choose the Paste item from the Edit menu to insert the copied text or graphic.

Options for Outlook Express

Outlook Express has options that allow you to customize the program to better suit your needs. To change the most commonly used options, open Outlook Express and choose the Options item from the Tools menu. The Options dialog box will open, displaying its General page.

On the General page, select or deselect the appropriate check boxes to enable or disable the indicated feature.

- *Check for new messages every 30 minute(s)* has Outlook Express automatically poll for messages. Change the number of minutes using the up/down arrow buttons.
- *Play sound when new messages arrive* sounds a tone when new mail is received.
- *Empty messages from the 'Deleted Items' folder on exit* automatically deletes them from this folder when you exit Outlook Express. Otherwise, messages remain in the Deleted Items folder until you select and delete them.
- *Automatically put people I reply to in my Address Book* does just that. This is an easy way to build your address book entries.
- *Make Outlook Express my default Simple MAPI client* allows you to use the Send item on the File menu from other programs to send e-mail.

On the Send page:

- Choose the e-mail sending format, either HTML or Plain Text. Some e-mail programs cannot read HTML messages, which may include font changes and formatting. In this case, the message must be sent as Plain Text. The Settings command button contains options for MIME format messages, which is the most common format used by e-mail programs. You can also include a character (the default is >) to display next to the text of the original message when replying. This is a common practice, which minimizes confusion when the recipient reads your reply.

- *Save copy of sent messages in the 'Sent Items' folder* retains each sent message until you delete it.
- *Include message in reply* will display the original message below the reply message as a reference.
- *Send messages immediately* will prompt the server to process your outgoing mail at once. Otherwise, mail will wait in the Outbox until you choose the Send and Receive command.
- *Reply to messages using the format in which they were sent* maintains the sender's format, ensuring that the reply message can be read.
- *Automatically complete e-mail addresses when composing* fills in a user's address when you type the first few letters of the name on the address line.

The Read page sets options for reading newsgroup messages, except for the Fonts button, which lets you change the font of incoming messages.

The Spelling page sets options for using the Spell Check program.

The Security page allows you to specify Security zones, encrypt your e-mail messages, or add a digital signature to your messages, which assures others that you were actually the person who sent the message.

The Dial-Up page sets up the way Outlook Express uses your Dial-Up Networking Connection to send and receive your mail.

The Advanced page has tools for managing newsgroup messages and other options for newsgroups.

CHAPTER 7

Word Processing with WordPad

Overview

Windows supplies two applications whose primary purpose is to help you "process words"; that is, to create text-based documents. **Notepad** is little more than a *text editor*, with virtually no text formatting capability, and we will discuss it in Section 9.2. **WordPad**, which was introduced in Section 2.2, is more powerful and will be considered in depth in this chapter. To be more specific, you will learn:

1. Additional ways to select and edit text in a WordPad document.
2. To change the typeface, font size, and font style of text.
3. To specify page margins and paper orientation for a WordPad document.
4. To format paragraphs by setting tabs and specifying text alignment and indentation.
5. To create a list of items automatically preceded by "bullets".
6. To insert graphics into a WordPad document.
7. To move, copy, resize, and delete graphics.
8. To use WordPad's Find and Replace utility.
9. To preview a document before printing it.
10. About the various file formats that WordPad can recognize.

7.1 WordPad Revisited

Using a word processor to create a document involves several steps. You have to:

1. Enter the text that makes up the document, or open a previously created document.
2. Edit the document to correct errors, modify its content, or improve its style.
3. Format the document; for example, set margins and select fonts.
4. Save the document to disk.
5. Print a copy of the document on paper.

In Section 2.2, we presented an introduction to the WordPad word processor that quickly covered a few of these points. In this section, we will review and expand upon some of this material.

The WordPad Window

To start WordPad:

1. Click on the Start button (or press Ctrl+Esc) to open the Start menu.
2. Point at the Programs option and then at Accessories on the resulting submenu.
3. Click on the WordPad item on the Accessories submenu.

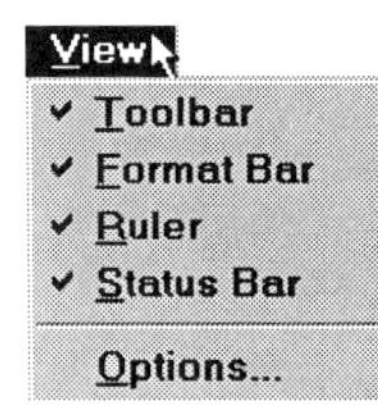

A window, similar to the one in Figure 1, will open. The Toolbar, Format bar, Ruler, and Status bar can all be toggled on or off by selecting or deselecting the corresponding item on the View menu. If you don't use one of these features, you can increase the size of the document window slightly by removing that feature from the screen.

Recall that to create a document, you just begin typing. The text you type will appear in the *document window* and also be stored in the computer's internal memory, RAM. The *insertion point* moves to indicate where the next character you type will appear on the screen. When you reach the end of a line, just keep typing; WordPad automatically *wraps* the text to the beginning of the next line. Press the Enter key to start a new line only if you want to begin a new paragraph or skip a line. When you reach the bottom of the document

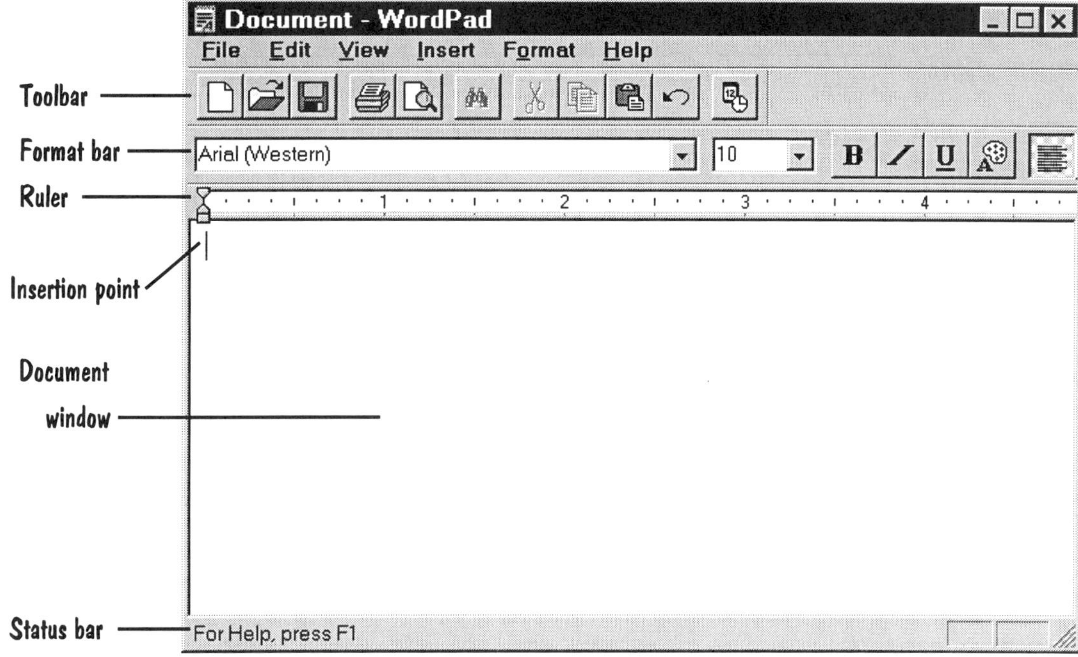

Figure 1 The WordPad Window

window, continue typing; the window will scroll to accommodate the new text.

Editing a Document

It is inevitable that from time to time you will want to modify the content of the text you have typed. Making changes to existing text, for whatever reason, is called **editing** the document. To modify a piece (*block*) of text, you have to:

1. Move the insertion point to the text you are changing.
2. Delete the undesirable text and/or insert the new text.

In Section 2.2, we briefly discussed how to use the mouse or Arrow keys to move the insertion point within the document window or scroll the window. In some situations, you can move the insertion point more quickly to a desired location in the document by using one of the keys or keystroke combinations listed in the following table.

Insertion point movement keys

Key	Moves the insertion point . . .
Home	To the beginning of the current line
End	To the end of the current line
Page Up	One window up
Page Down	One window down
Ctrl + Left Arrow	To the previous word
Ctrl + Right Arrow	To the next word
Ctrl + Home	To the beginning of the document
Ctrl + End	To the end of the document

Deleting and inserting text

Once you have moved the insertion point to the desired spot, you can:

- Delete the character to the *left* of the insertion point by pressing the Backspace key, or delete the character to the *right* of the insertion point by pressing the Delete key. If you want to delete a number of consecutive characters quickly, hold down the Backspace or Delete keys (as appropriate) until the block of text is erased from the screen.
- Insert text at the insertion point by typing it at the keyboard. If the new text just replaces (types over) existing characters, then WordPad is in *overwrite mode*. To return WordPad to the default *insert mode*, press the Insert key.

You can also delete or insert text by moving it from place to place within the document with the aid of the Windows Clipboard. In Section 2.3, we discussed how to select, cut, copy, and paste text. Recall that:

- To *select* a block of text, position the insertion point at the beginning of the block and then either hold down the Shift key while moving the insertion point to the end of the block or mouse-drag the insertion point to the end of the block. In either case, the selected block of text will become highlighted.
- To *cut* a block of text to the Clipboard, deleting it from its current location in the process, choose Cut from the Edit menu or click on the Toolbar's Cut button.

- To *copy* a selected block of text (which does not delete it from its current location), choose Copy from the Edit menu or click on the Toolbar's Copy button.

- To *paste* a block of text at the insertion point, choose Paste from the Edit menu or click on the Toolbar's Paste button.

These techniques work with every Windows-based application. In addition, WordPad provides some shortcuts for these procedures:

Other ways to select text

- To select a word, double-click on any letter in it.
- To select a paragraph, triple-click anywhere within it.

You can also select certain blocks of text by moving the mouse cursor (the I-beam) into the left margin. The cursor will become a right-facing pointer, called the *selection cursor* (see Figure 2). Then:

- To select the line of text at the cursor, click the mouse (see Figure 2). To select several consecutive lines of text, drag the mouse pointer down the left margin until all the desired lines have become highlighted.
- To select the paragraph at the cursor, double-click the mouse.
- To select the entire document, triple-click the mouse. (You can also select the entire document by choosing the Select All command from the Edit menu.)

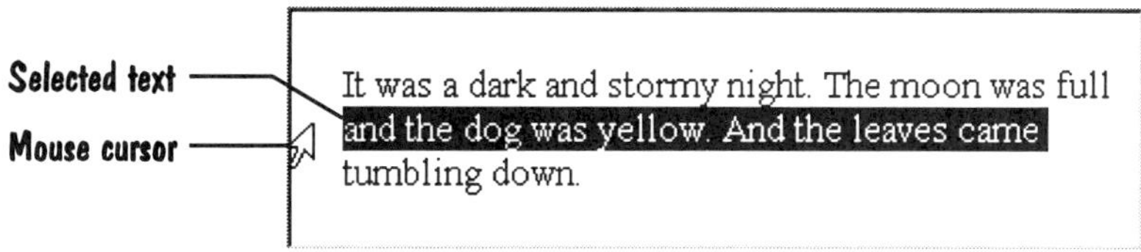

Figure 2 Selecting a Single Line of Text

Deselecting text

To *deselect* a block of text, click the mouse anywhere on the screen or press a cursor movement key, such as an Arrow key. (Do not press any other kind of key while a block of text is selected; the corresponding character will *replace* the selected text!)

Drag-and-drop move or copy

You can also move or copy text from one place in a WordPad document to another using the *drag-and-drop* technique. (In Section 3.3, we used this technique to move and copy files or folders.) Here's the way it works:

1. Select the block of text to be moved or copied.

2. Position the mouse pointer anywhere in the highlighted text (the cursor will become a left-facing pointer).
3. If you want:
   - To *move* the selected text, press (but do not release) the left mouse button and reposition the mouse pointer at the selected text's new location.
   - To *copy* the selected text, hold down the Ctrl key and press the left mouse button as you move the pointer to the selected text's new location. (In this case, the mouse pointer displays a small box containing a plus symbol.)

   The insertion point moves with the mouse cursor and indicates the exact place the text will be positioned (see Figure 3).

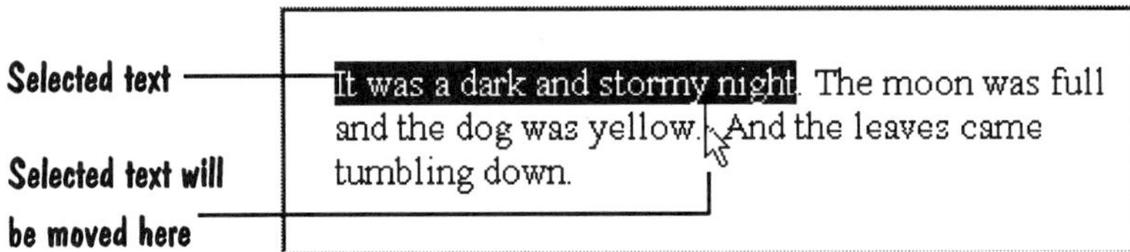

Figure 3 Moving Selected Text by Drag-and-Drop

4. When the insertion point is positioned properly, release the mouse button (and Ctrl key, if copying). The selected text will appear in the new location.

NOTE

Once you have selected a block of text, in addition to moving or copying it, you can:

- Delete the text by pressing the Delete or Backspace key.
- Change the text's font, as described in Section 7.2.

To *undo* your last edit (such as moving or deleting some text), either choose the Undo command from the Edit menu or click on the Toolbar's Undo button.

When using a word processor, you may find it more convenient to perform editing operations using the keyboard rather than by clicking on menu commands or Toolbar buttons. Here are some shortcut keys for the operations discussed in this section:

Ctrl+A selects the entire document.

Ctrl+X cuts a selected block of text to the Clipboard.
Ctrl+C copies a selected block of text to the Clipboard.
Ctrl+V pastes the text on the Clipboard at the insertion point.
Ctrl+Z undoes the last editing operation.

TUTORIAL

Try the following exercise on your own.

1. Turn on the computer (if necessary) to start Windows 98 and open WordPad by clicking on the WordPad item on the Accessories submenu of the Start menu's Programs option.
2. Begin a document by typing the sentences "It was a dark and stormy night. The dogs were barking.", and then pressing the Enter key.
3. Select the first line of this document by moving the mouse cursor into the left margin, where it becomes a right-facing arrow, and clicking. (Because the first line happens to be a paragraph, you can also select it by either double-clicking while the mouse cursor is in the left margin or triple-clicking while the cursor is in the paragraph itself.) The first line of text will become highlighted.
4. *Copy* the selected text to the end of the document by dragging it there: Hold down the Ctrl key (if you forget to do this, the text will be *moved*, not copied), position the mouse cursor within the selected text, press the left mouse button, reposition the cursor (and insertion point) at the end of the document, and release the mouse button and Ctrl key.
5. Select the entire document by either
   - Repositioning the mouse cursor in the left margin and triple-clicking.

   or
   - Choosing Select All from the Edit menu (or pressing Ctrl+A).
6. Copy the selected text to the end of the document: Copy it to the Clipboard (press Ctrl+C), reposition the insertion point at the end of the document (press Ctrl+End), and paste the text there (press Ctrl+V). There should now be four lines of stormy nights and barking dogs.
7. Undo the last action (step 6): Either choose the Undo command from the Edit menu, click on the Undo Toolbar button, or press Ctrl+Z.
8. Close WordPad, responding No to the "save changes?" message.

7.2 Using Fonts in WordPad

In Section 7.1, we discussed some of the basic capabilities of the WordPad word processor. In this section, we will describe how you can control the way text appears on the screen and the printed page.

Fonts Revisited

The fonts you use in a document can greatly affect the impact your words will have on the reader. In this section, we will discuss the nature of fonts and show how they are implemented within a WordPad document.

A **font** is a collection of characters of a given design, size, and style.

- The *design* or **typeface** of a font refers to the general appearance of the characters, independent of their size, thickness, or other attributes. For example, Arial, Courier New, and Times New Roman are three of the typefaces supplied by Windows.
- The *size* of a font refers to its height, measured in **points**. There are 72 points per inch, so 18-point type, for example, is roughly 1/4-inch high on the printed page. Here are some examples of different sizes of the Arial typeface:

  8-point 12-point 18-point

- A font's *style* is dictated by attributes such as **bold** or *italic*.

Some fonts are only supplied in discrete sizes, such as 10-point, 12-point, and so on. Others, called **scalable fonts**, can be scaled to any size. Microsoft includes several scalable typefaces, known as *TrueType fonts*, with the Windows 98 software. These fonts are available for use in any Windows-based application.

WYSIWYG When you type text in WordPad, the corresponding characters appear on the screen in the current font (which is displayed on the Format bar). If you print the document, the fonts that appear on the screen will also be used by the printer. We say that WordPad is a WYSIWYG (What You See Is What You Get, pronounced "whizzywig") word processor. WYSIWYG means that the appearance of the document on the screen, including fonts, graphics, spacing, and so on, previews the way it will appear on the printed page.

Changing the font There are several ways to change the current font in WordPad. With any of these techniques, the font change will apply to either:

- The currently selected block of text, if text is selected when the change is made.

or

- The text you type after the change is made, if no text is selected.

Using the Font Dialog Box

The most flexible way to change the current font is to use the Font dialog box, which allows you to change not only the typeface, style, and size of the font, but also other attributes — underline (underline), strikeout (~~strikeout~~), and color. Here's how to use this dialog box:

1. If you want the new font to apply to existing text, select that block of text. Otherwise, the new font will apply to the text you type after the change is made.
2. Choose the Font command from the Format menu to display the Font dialog box (Figure 4). The current font's typeface, style, and size are shown in the Font, Font style, and Size text boxes, respectively. A sample of this font appears in the Sample box.

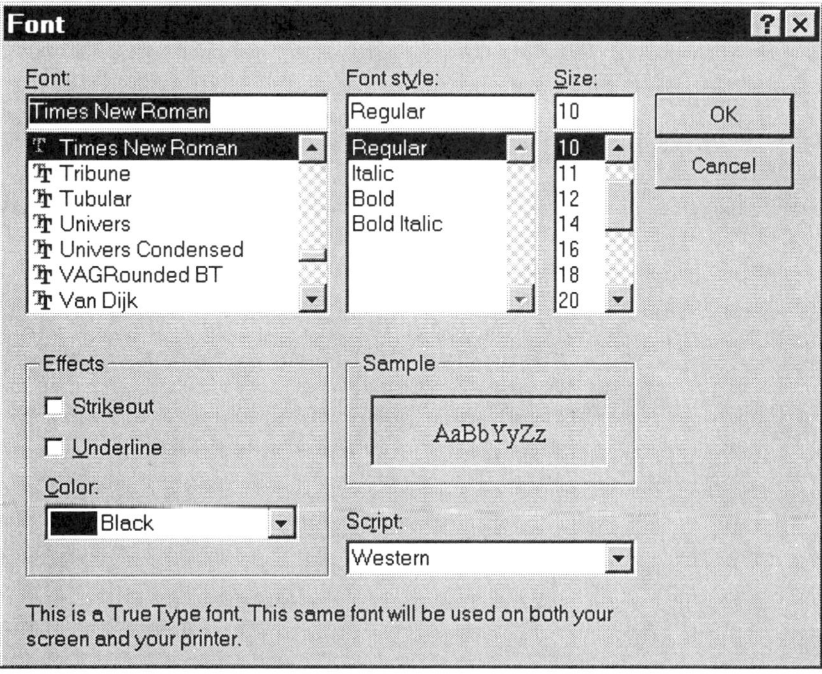

Figure 4 The Font Dialog Box

3. Select a typeface for the new font from the Font list box. Instead of scrolling to the desired name, you might save time by typing its first few letters in the Font text box at the top of the list. For example, to change to Arial, type "ari" in the text box and the Font list box will scroll and highlight the Arial font.
4. Select bold, italic, or bold italic, if you wish, from the Font style list. Selecting Regular turns off (cancels) a current style.
5. Select a font size (in points) from the Size list. You can select any (whole number) size that your printer can print, even if it doesn't appear in this list. Just click on the text box at the top of the Size list and enter the desired size.
6. If you want to add an underline and/or strikeout line to the text, select the appropriate check boxes.
7. You can select a text color from the Color drop-down list. Of course, to print the resulting text in this color, you need to use a color printer. (Some non-color printers print text colors in various shades of gray.)
8. Open the Script drop-down list to select an alternate character set (if desired) for use with a language other than English.
9. To put your font changes into effect, choose the OK command button. To ignore these changes, choose Cancel.

Using the Format Bar

The **Format bar** provides a quicker, though less flexible, way of changing fonts and their attributes. (Remember: If the Format bar is not displayed in your WordPad window, choose the Format Bar item from the View menu to display it.) The functions of the Format bar buttons that alter the current font are identified in Figure 5. Notice that the typeface and font size of the current font are displayed on the Format bar; if the current font has bold, italic, or underline attributes, the corresponding buttons will appear to be "pressed in".

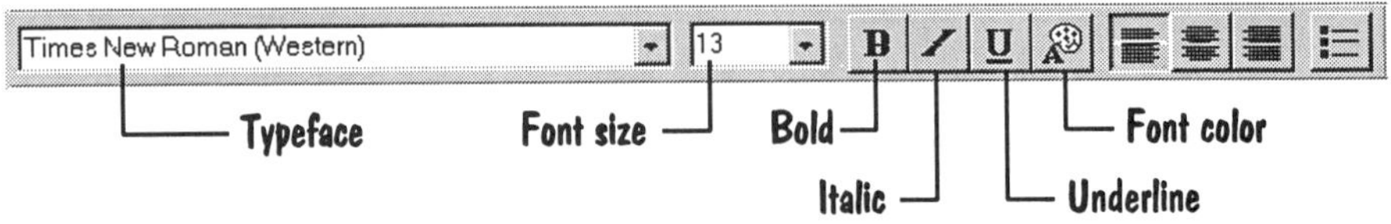

Figure 5 Font Attributes on the Format Bar

To use the Format bar to change the font of selected text or the text that you are about to type:

1. Select a new typeface and/or font size from the appropriate drop-down list.
2. Select or deselect bold, italics, or underline by clicking on the corresponding button.
3. Change the font color by clicking on the Font Color button and selecting the desired color from the drop-down list.

An easy way to turn the bold, italics, or underline attribute on or off is to use the keystroke combinations Ctrl+B, Ctrl+I, or Ctrl+U, respectively. For example, to bold a word you are about to type, press Ctrl+B, type the word, and press Ctrl+B again. Or, to remove italics from a word you have already typed, select the word and press Ctrl+I.

Try the following exercise on your own.

1. Turn on the computer (if necessary) to start Windows 98.
2. Open WordPad and maximize its window.
3. Insert the Student Disk in its drive and open the document named Preamble. (For information on opening documents, see Section 2.2.)
4. If the Format bar is turned off, display it by choosing the Format Bar command from the View menu. Notice (from the Format bar) that 14-point Arial type is used for the title of the document.
5. Change the title's font to 12-point bold italic Times New Roman:
   - Select the title (by, for example, clicking in the left margin).
   - Choose the Font command from the Format menu to open the Font dialog box.
   - In the dialog box, select Times New Roman from the Font list, Bold Italic from the Font style list, and 12 from the Size list.
   - Choose the OK command button.
6. Change the text for the preamble from 12-point Times New Roman to 11-point Arial:
   - Select the text of the preamble (by, for example, double-clicking in the left margin next to this paragraph).
   - Select "Arial (Western)" and "11" from the drop-down lists on the Format bar.

7. Deselect the selected text by clicking in the WordPad window.
8. Italicize the words "United States of America":
   - Select these words.
   - Either press Ctrl+I or click on the Format bar's Italic button to italicize them. 
   - Deselect these words.
9. Add the words THE END at the end of the document in bold type:
   - Reposition the cursor at the end of the document and press the Enter key twice.
   - Turn on boldface by clicking on the Format bar's Bold button (or pressing Ctrl+B).
   - Type the words THE END and turn off boldface by clicking on the Bold button (or pressing Ctrl+B) again.
10. Close WordPad (responding No to the "save changes?" message) and remove the Student Disk from its drive.

7.3 *Formatting Text in WordPad*

Formatting a document changes, in some manner, the way the text in that document is arranged on the page. In this section, we will discuss WordPad's formatting features.

Formatting the Document as a Whole

WordPad provides several formatting features that apply to the entire document. When one of these commands is issued, it doesn't matter where the insertion point is positioned; the command affects all text that has already been typed and will be typed in the current document. These features include:

Document-oriented features

- Placing text on the page in either portrait or landscape orientation.
- Specifying the size of the left, right, top, and bottom page margins.

To access either of these formatting features, choose Page Setup from the File menu. The Page Setup dialog box, shown in Figure 6, will be displayed.

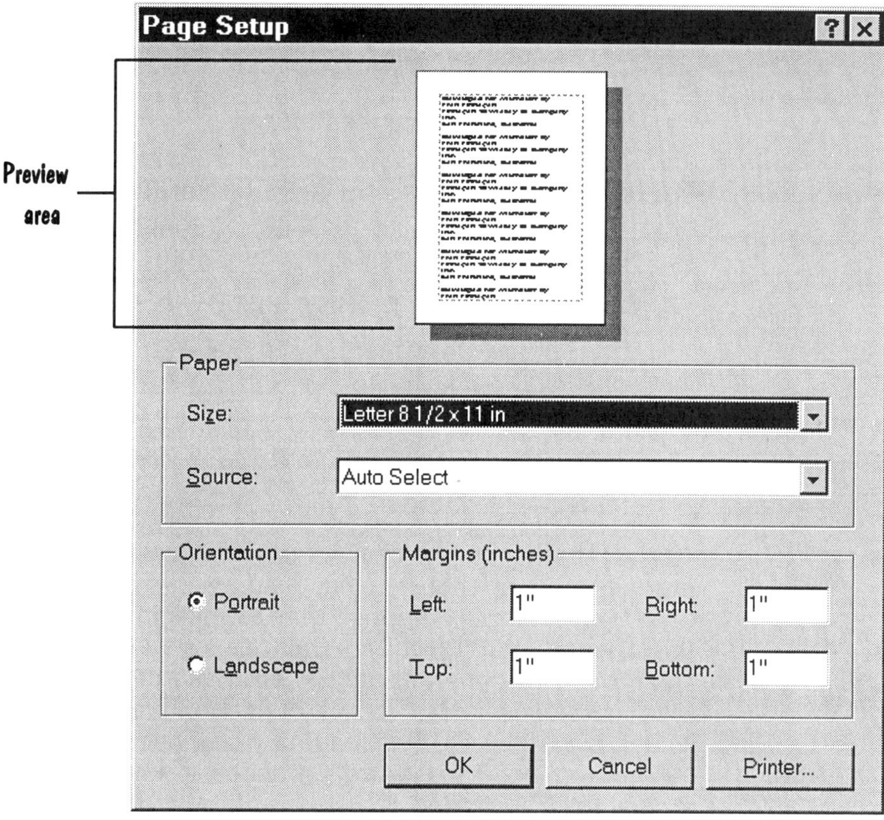

Figure 6 The Page Setup Dialog Box

Specifying Page Orientation You can choose to print your document in either portrait or landscape orientation. In **portrait** orientation, the document's text is printed parallel to the short side of the paper. For example, the page you are now reading is printed this way. In **landscape** orientation, the text is printed parallel to the long side of the paper. Landscape orientation is usually used for certificates and diplomas. The figures at the right further illustrate this concept.

Portrait
Portrait
Portrait
Portrait

Landscape
Landscape
Landscape

To specify page orientation:

1. Open the Page Setup dialog box (Figure 6) from the File menu.

2. Select the Portrait or Landscape option button. (The "page" shown in the preview area will appear in the selected orientation.)
3. Choose the OK command button.

Specifying Margins By default, WordPad leaves the margin settings for a new document the same as they were in the previous one. To specify different margins for the current document:

1. Open the Page Setup dialog box (Figure 6) from the File menu.
2. Enter the desired margins in the Left, Right, Top, and Bottom text boxes. (The "page" shown in the preview area will indicate the new margins.)
3. Choose the OK command button.

NOTE

The width and height of a page's text area depend not only on its margins and orientation, but also on the size of the paper being used. For example, suppose that all margins are set to one inch and the orientation is portrait. Then, on a standard 8½" × 11" ("letter size") piece of paper, all text is enclosed in an imaginary box that is 6½ inches wide and 9 inches high. However, for "legal size" paper (which is 8½" × 14"), our imaginary box becomes 6½ inches wide and 12 inches high. Thus, WordPad needs to know the size of paper you are using. This setting is also specified in the Page Setup dialog box, by selecting the appropriate item on the Paper Size drop-down list.

Formatting Paragraphs

When you press the Enter key while typing text in WordPad, a paragraph marker code, which is not visible on the screen, is placed in the document file. To WordPad, a *paragraph* is the text lying between two paragraph markers, or between a paragraph marker and the beginning or end of the document. In other words, every time you press the Enter key, WordPad interprets it as the beginning of a new paragraph.

WordPad has several formatting features that apply either to the paragraphs containing selected text, or (if no text is selected) to the paragraph that contains the insertion point. These features include:

Paragraph-oriented features

- Centering the text or aligning it with the left or right margin.
- Indenting a paragraph of text from the left and/or right margin,

or the first line of a paragraph from the rest of the paragraph.

- Setting tabs to help create columns of text.
- Automatically placing a "bullet" before each item in a list.

NOTE

When you start typing a new paragraph, it automatically inherits all the formatting characteristics of the previous one. For example, suppose the current paragraph is centered between the margins. If you press the Enter key and start typing, you'll see that the new text is still centered.

Changing Text Alignment WordPad provides three options for aligning (or *justifying*) text relative to the left and right margins:

The text in this paragraph is *left-justified.* All lines in this paragraph align on the left margin.

This text is *centered.* All lines in this paragraph are centered between the margins.

The text in this paragraph is *right-justified.* All lines in this paragraph align on the right margin.

The default alignment option is left-justification. To change text alignment, place the insertion point in the desired paragraph or select the paragraphs to be aligned and:

1. Choose the Paragraph item from the Format menu.
2. Select the desired option (Left, Right, or Center) from the Alignment drop-down list.
3. Choose the OK command button.

It is a little easier to select an alignment option using the Format bar. To do so, place the insertion point in the desired paragraph or select the paragraphs to be aligned and click the appropriate Format bar button, as shown below:

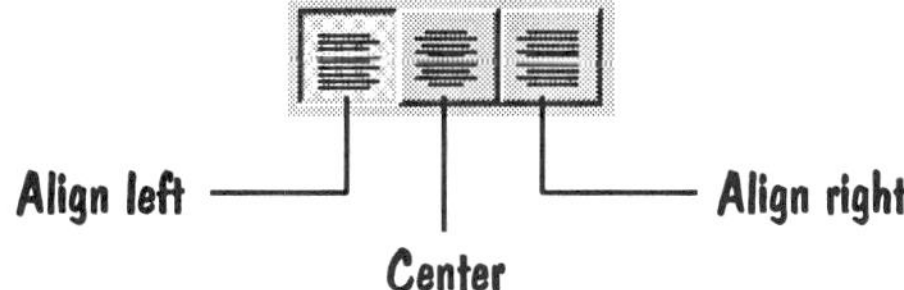

The button that appears to be "pressed in" (*Align left*, in the diagram above) indicates the justification of the current paragraph.

Changing Paragraph Indentation As you know, when you change the margins for a document, that change applies to the entire document. To change the left or right margin for a particular paragraph in WordPad, you change its *indentation* relative to the given margin. The indentation feature also allows you to indent the first line of the paragraph relative to the rest of the paragraph.

For example, in Figure 7:

- The first paragraph is not indented.
- The second paragraph is indented 1 inch on the left, 0.5 inches on the right, and the indent for the first line is 0 inches. As the first line indent is measured relative to the rest of the paragraph, it is indented the same amount as the rest of the paragraph.
- The third paragraph is indented 1 inch on the left, 1.5 inches on the right, and has a first line indent of -0.5 inches. Since the indent for the first line is *negative* and is measured relative to the rest of the paragraph, it starts one-half inch to the *left* of the rest of the paragraph. (*Positive* first line indents start this line to the *right* of the rest of the paragraph.)

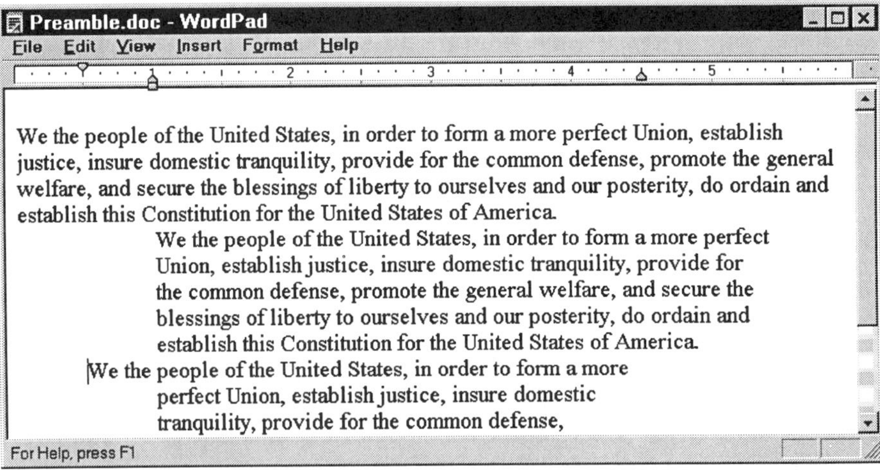

Figure 7 Examples of Indented Paragraphs

To change indentation, place the insertion point in the desired paragraph, or select text in the paragraphs to be changed, and:

1. Choose Paragraph from the Format menu. The Paragraph dialog box, shown in Figure 8, will open.

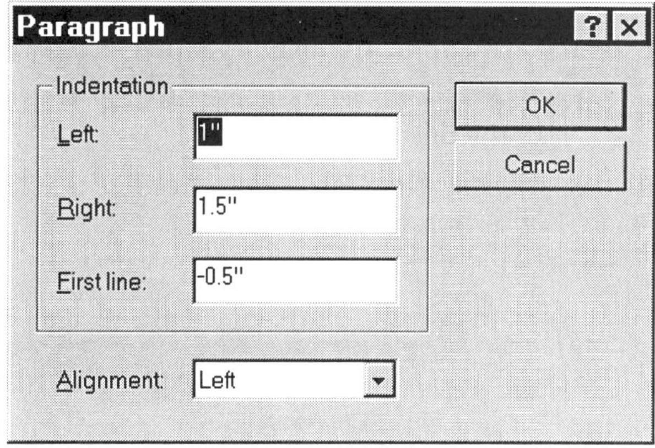

Figure 8 The Paragraph Dialog Box

2. Type the desired numbers in the *Left*, *Right*, and *First line* indentation text boxes.
3. Choose the OK command button.

You can also use the WordPad Ruler to change paragraph indenting. (Remember: If the Ruler is hidden, you can display it by choosing the Ruler item from the View menu.) To change indentation this way:

1. Place the insertion point in the desired paragraph, or select text in the paragraphs to be changed.
2. Use the mouse to drag the left-, right-, and/or first-line-indent markers to the appropriate positions on the Ruler. (Figure 7 shows the markers set for the third paragraph's indentation.)

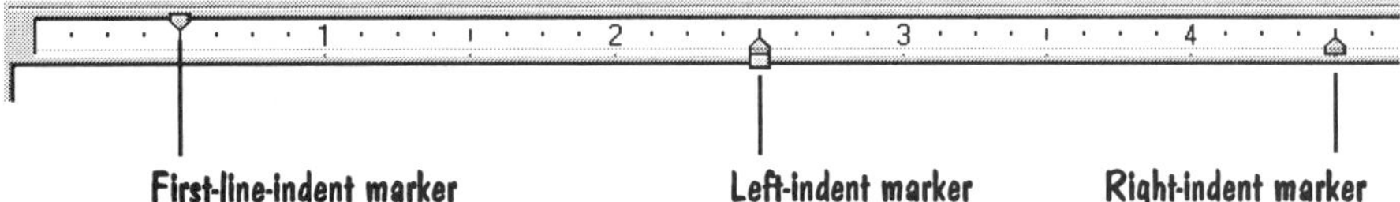

Changing the Tab Settings When you press the Tab key while working in a WordPad document, the insertion point moves to the right and is positioned at the next tab setting (or *tab stop*). By default, the tab stops are set at half-inch intervals, beginning at the left margin. Thus, if you press the Tab key when the insertion point is 2.75" from the left margin (and the default tab stops are in effect), it will move to a position on the same line 3" from the margin.

Tab stops can be very useful in creating columns of text in a document. To add or remove tab stops for a given paragraph:

1. Place the insertion point in the desired paragraph, or select text in the desired paragraph.
2. Choose the Tabs item from the Format menu. The dialog box shown in Figure 9 will open.

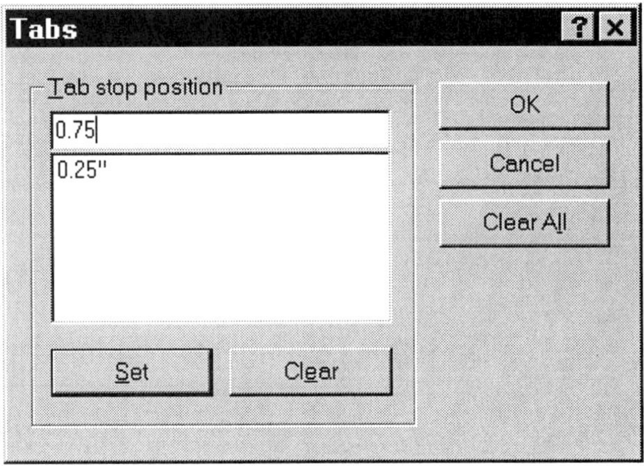

Figure 9 The Tabs Dialog Box

3. To add a new tab stop:
   - Enter its position (relative to the left margin) in the *Tab stop position* text box.
   - Choose the Set command button. The new tab stop will be displayed in the *Tab stop position* list box and all *default* tab stops to its left will be removed. For example, adding a tab setting of 0.75 removes the default tab stop at 0.5.
4. To remove all tab stops displayed in the *Tab stop position* list box, choose the Clear All command button. To remove one of the tab stops displayed in the list box, select it and choose the Clear command button.
5. Choose the OK command button to close the dialog box and put the new settings into effect. If the Ruler is currently displayed in the WordPad window, L symbols will appear on it in the appropriate positions.

The WordPad Ruler provides an easier way to add and remove tab stops. To use the Ruler for these purposes:

1. Position the insertion point (or select text) in the desired paragraph.
2. To add a tab stop, click on the appropriate location on the Ruler. An L symbol will appear there.

3. To remove an existing tab stop, drag the corresponding L symbol off the Ruler.

Creating a Bulleted List If your document contains a list of important points, you can add emphasis by preceding each item on the list by a "bullet". A **bullet** is a small symbol, often round or square, used for this purpose. Here are some examples of typical bullets: ● ■ ○ ☛ ✔

WordPad has a *bullet style* feature that allows you to easily create a bulleted list. When this feature is in effect, new paragraphs will begin with a solid round bullet followed by a tab. To turn the bullet style on, either

- Choose the Bullet Style item from the Format menu.

or

- Click on the Format bar's Bullets button, which is shown at the right.

Once you have completed your list, press the Enter key, moving the insertion point to the next line and inserting a new bullet. Then, either choose Bullet Style from the Format menu (it's a toggle) or click on the Toolbar's Bullets button. The last bullet will disappear.

Here is an example of a bulleted list in WordPad:

- This is the first item.
- This is the second item.
- This is the third item.

The amount a bullet and the corresponding list item are indented is governed by the first-line-indent and left-indent, respectively, for that paragraph. Thus, to change the positions of the bullets and list items relative to the left margin, just change these indentation options (as described earlier in this section) for all lines of the list.

If you want to use another symbol for your bullets, you can do so with the help of the Character Map accessory, which is discussed in Section 9.5. However, with this technique, you will have to manually insert each bullet and then press the Tab key before typing the corresponding list item.

TUTORIAL

Try the following exercise on your own.

1. Turn on the computer (if necessary) to start Windows 98.
2. Open WordPad from the Start button's Accessories submenu and maximize its window.
3. Insert the Student Disk in its drive and open the document named History.
4. Display the Page Setup dialog box, by choosing this item from the File menu, and:
   - Set the margins for the History document to 1.5" on the left and right and 1.25" on the top and bottom by entering these numbers in the appropriate text boxes.
   - Select the Portrait option button (if necessary) so the document's text will print parallel to the short side of the page.

   Choose the OK button to put these changes into effect.
5. Center the title by positioning the insertion point within it and clicking on the appropriate button on the Format bar. In a similar way, right-align the first paragraph of the document. (This step can also be carried out by choosing Paragraph from the Format menu and selecting the proper option from the Alignment drop-down list.)

   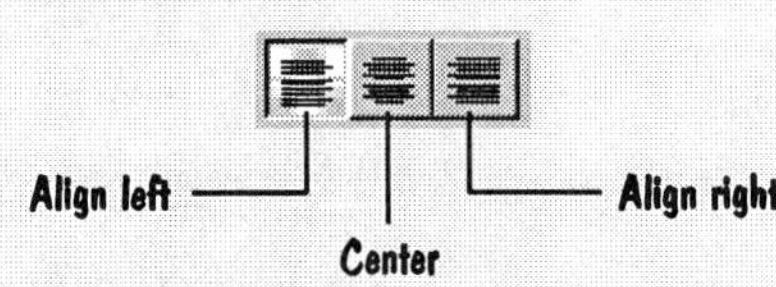

6. Indent the second and third paragraphs 1 inch on the left and right (relative to the margins), with a first-line-indent of 0.5 inches: Select both paragraphs, choose Paragraph from the Format menu, enter these figures in the Indentation text boxes, and choose OK. (These settings can also be made using the Ruler's indent markers; see the TIP on page 343.)
7. Remove all tabs for the second paragraph of the document and set a new tab stop at 2.25 inches for this paragraph:
   - Click the mouse within the second paragraph.
   - Choose Tabs from the Format menu to open this dialog box.

- Choose the Clear All button to remove the existing tabs.
- Enter 2.25 in the *Tab stop position* text box.
- Choose the OK button.

(An existing tab can also be removed by dragging the corresponding **L** symbol off the Ruler; similarly, a new tab can be set by clicking on the appropriate spot on the Ruler.)

8. To see the effect of your new tab stop, position the insertion point in front of the first letter in the second paragraph and press the Tab key.
9. Close WordPad (responding No to the "save changes?" message) and remove the diskette from its drive.

7.4 Using Graphics in a WordPad Document

WordPad lets you do more than just process words. It allows you to insert **graphics** (pictures) into a document and then, if you wish, to move or resize them. In this section, we will describe how to perform these operations.

Inserting a Graphic into a Document

Although WordPad itself cannot be used to create graphics, you can insert (or *import*) a graphic created by another application into a WordPad document. There are two ways to accomplish this task.

Using the Clipboard As we mentioned in Section 2.3, the Windows Clipboard can be used to transfer a graphic from one document to another. Here's the way the process works:

1. Use a graphics program (such as Paint, which is discussed in Chapter 8) to create the picture or to open an existing graphics file.
2. Select the graphic and copy it to the Clipboard.
3. Switch to WordPad.
4. Place the insertion point where you want the graphic to appear.
5. Choose Paste from the Edit menu or click on the Toolbar's Paste button. The graphic will be displayed in your document at the insertion point.

If the graphic does not display satisfactorily in WordPad when you issue the Paste command, delete the graphic (by pressing the Del key), and choose the Paste Special command from the Edit menu. A dialog box will open allowing you to choose from among several image formats. Now, try these one at a time (by selecting a format from the list box and choosing the OK button) to get the most satisfactory image. However, be aware that some formats will not let you edit the graphic (as described later in this section) after it has been imported into WordPad.

Using the Insert Object Command There is another way to import a graphic into a WordPad document. This method works especially well if the graphic is stored on disk, but it does require some familiarity with the Windows 98 file system (Chapter 3). To use this technique:

1. Place the insertion point in the WordPad document where you want the graphic to appear.
2. Choose the Object item from the Insert menu. The Insert Object dialog box, shown in Figure 10, will open.
3. If you want to create the graphic (using another application), select the Object Type corresponding to that application and then choose the OK command button. A box will open (at the insertion point) in the WordPad window, in which you can draw

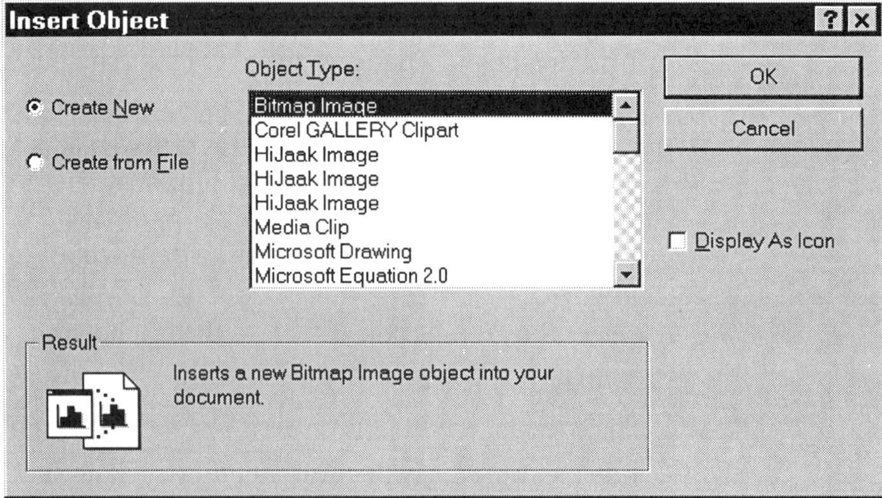

Figure 10 The Insert Object Dialog Box

the graphic using the selected application's tools. When you are done, just click the mouse anywhere outside of the box.

For example, selecting Bitmap Image and choosing OK invokes the Paint application, and the WordPad window looks as pictured in Figure 11. (Although the title bar says "WordPad", the menus and available tools are those of Paint.)

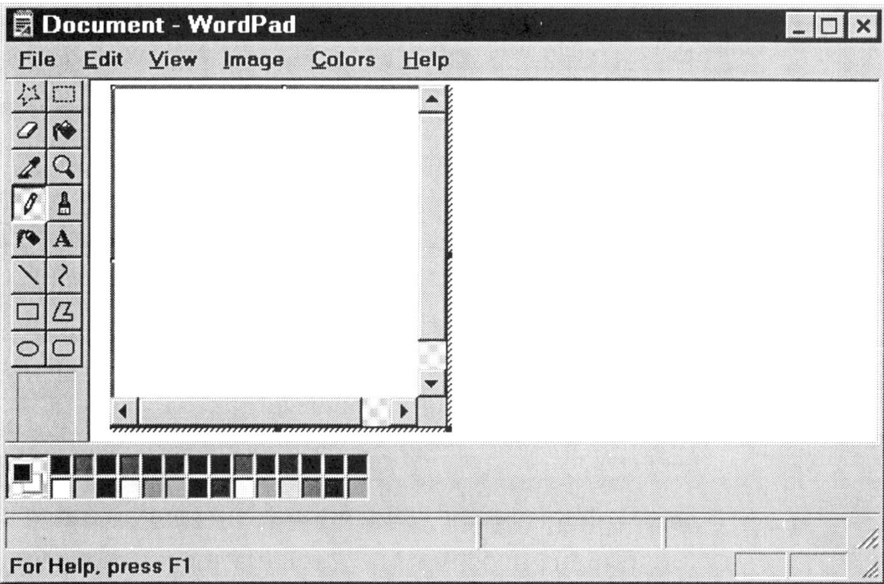

Figure 11 Working with Paint Inside the WordPad Window

4. If, instead of creating a graphic, you want to retrieve one from disk, select the *Create from File* option button. The Object Type list in the Insert Object dialog box will be replaced by the following display:

Now, either type the path name (see Section 3.1) for the desired file in the *File* text box or choose the Browse button to locate the desired file by browsing folders (see Section 3.5). Then, in either case, choose the OK command button in the Insert Object dialog box, and the graphic will be inserted into the WordPad document at the insertion point.

Editing a Graphic

When you *edit* a graphic, you modify the way it looks. WordPad has no graphics editing capabilities of its own. However, you may be able to edit a graphic contained in a WordPad document using a Windows feature known as **Object Linking and Embedding**, or **OLE**.

If the object was pasted or inserted into the document from an application that supports OLE (such as Paint), then it can be edited using that application's tools. To edit such a graphic:

1. Right-click on the graphic and point at the last item on the resulting pop-up menu. (This item has a name of the form *object-type* Object; for example, Bitmap Image Object.)
2. Choose either Edit or Open from the submenu:
   - If you choose Edit, the graphic will be enclosed in a box and the WordPad window will take on the look of the application that is being used to edit the image (see Figure 11).
   - If you choose Open, the application that is being used to edit the graphic will start and the graphic will open within it.

   (Double-clicking on a graphic achieves the same result as right-clicking on it, pointing at the "Object" item, and choosing Edit.)
3. Edit the graphic as you wish using the graphics application's tools.
4. When you are done, to return to WordPad:
   - If you chose Edit to begin the process, just click outside the graphic's box.
   - If you chose Open to begin, now choose Exit & Return to Document from the File menu.

OLE is discussed in more detail in Section 12.5.

Deleting, Moving, and Resizing a Graphic

Although you need to make use of another application to *edit* a graphic, WordPad can be used to delete, move, copy, or resize it.

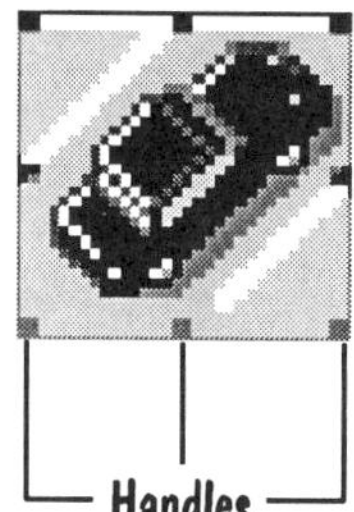

Selecting a Graphic In most cases, before you can delete, move, copy, or resize a graphic, you must first select it. To select a graphic, just click on it. The graphic will become enclosed in a box containing small squares, known as *sizing handles*, at each of its corners and at the midpoint of each side. (See the figure at the right.)

To deselect a graphic just click anywhere else in the document window.

Deleting a Graphic To delete a graphic from a WordPad document, either

- Select the graphic and press the Delete key.

or

- Position the insertion point just before or just after the graphic and press the Delete key or Backspace key, respectively.

Moving or Copying a Graphic To some extent, a graphic acts as if it were a character of text. (For example, as you have just seen, it can be deleted by positioning the insertion point just to the right of it and pressing the Backspace key.) This feature also provides a means for moving a graphic within a document.

Moving a graphic like a piece of text

- The graphic can be left-aligned, centered, or right-aligned (relative to the left and right margins) by selecting it and clicking on the appropriate button on the Format bar:

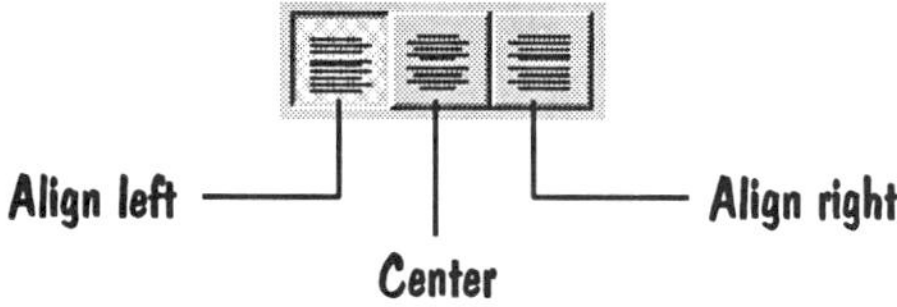

- The graphic can be "pushed" to the right or down the page by positioning the insertion point just to the left of the graphic and pressing the Spacebar, Tab key, or Enter key.
- You can select the graphic, cut or copy it to the Clipboard, and then paste it into another part of the document.

In addition to these text-oriented ways of moving a graphic, you can mouse-drag it to another part of the document. To be more specific:

Using drag-and-drop

1. Select the graphic.
2. Position the mouse pointer over the graphic, press and hold

down the mouse button, and reposition the pointer at the desired place within the document. (If you want to *copy* the graphic, instead of moving it, hold down the Ctrl key during this process.)

3. Release the mouse button (and, if necessary, the Ctrl key). The graphic will be displayed in the new location.

NOTE

If you use drag-and-drop to move or copy a graphic, be aware that the graphic must be dropped at some location *within* the existing document. For example, if the graphic is located at the end of the document and you try to move it down the page, you *will* be able to drag the mouse cursor downward, but when you release the button, the graphic will remain in its original position.

Resizing a Graphic To enlarge or reduce the size of a graphic within a WordPad document:

1. Select the graphic.
2. Position the mouse pointer over one of the eight handles:
   - Use the top side or bottom side midpoint handle to change the height of the graphic without changing its width.
   - Use the left side or right side midpoint handle to change the width of the graphic without changing its height.
   - Use a corner handle to change both height and width at the same time.
3. Drag the handle in the desired direction. An outline of the graphic's box will move with the cursor to indicate the corresponding size, as shown at the right.
4. Release the mouse button when the graphic is the desired size. (To abort the process, press the Escape key before releasing the mouse button.)

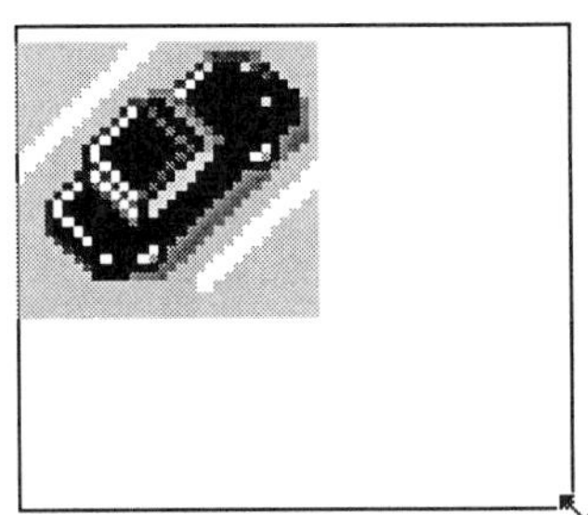

If you are unhappy with the result of an operation, you can undo it: Either press Ctrl+Z, click on the Toolbar's Undo button (shown at the right), or choose the Undo command from the Edit menu.

TUTORIAL

Try the following exercise on your own.

1. Turn on the computer (if necessary) to start Windows 98.
2. Open WordPad from the Start button's Accessories submenu and maximize its window.
3. Insert the Student Disk in its drive.
4. Insert a graphic into the empty WordPad document:
   - Choose Object from the Insert menu.
   - Select the Create from File option button.
   - Erase the text in the *File* box and type: A:\shapes
   - Choose the OK command button. A graphic will be displayed in the document window.
   - Deselect the graphic by clicking elsewhere in the document window. The box around the graphic, together with its eight "sizing handles", will disappear.
5. Press Ctrl+Home to move the insertion point to the beginning of the document, just to the left of the graphic. Press the Enter key twice to "push" the graphic down two lines and then click on the Center Format bar button to center the graphic between the left and right margins.
6. Select the graphic by clicking on it; a box with "handles" will appear around the graphic. Now:
   - Reduce its size: Drag the handle in the lower-right corner of the selection box (the mouse pointer will become a two-headed arrow when it's positioned properly) about half-way toward the upper-left corner.

   - Increase its width without increasing its height: Drag the middle handle on the right side of the box to the right about one inch.
7. Add six blank lines to the bottom of the document by positioning the insertion point at the end of the document and then pressing the Enter key six times.
8. Create a copy of the graphic at the bottom of the document:
   - Select the graphic.
   - Position the mouse pointer over the graphic and hold down the Ctrl key (for *copying*).
   - Drag the cursor to the end of the document, and release the mouse button and Ctrl key.
9. While the copy of the graphic is still selected, delete it by pressing the Delete key.

10. Right-click on the remaining graphic, point at Bitmap Image Object on the resulting submenu, and choose Open. The Paint graphics program will start, allowing you to edit the graphic.
11. Close Paint and WordPad (responding No to the "save changes?" message), and remove the diskette from its drive.

7.5 Other Features of WordPad

In the first four sections of this chapter, we have discussed how to create, edit, format, and add graphics to a WordPad document. In this section, we will introduce a few more assorted features of WordPad.

Find and Replace

Occasionally, you may want to locate an occurrence of a particular word in a given document, perhaps to replace it with another word. You can accomplish this in WordPad using the Find and Replace utility. As its name implies, this utility performs two functions:

- It can be used to locate a particular piece of text within a document.
- It can be used to automatically replace a particular piece of text with something else.

Finding text To locate a desired piece of text:

1. Choose Find from the Edit menu or click on the Toolbar's Find button. The Find dialog box, shown in Figure 12, will open.

2. Type the text you wish to locate in the *Find what* text box, and:

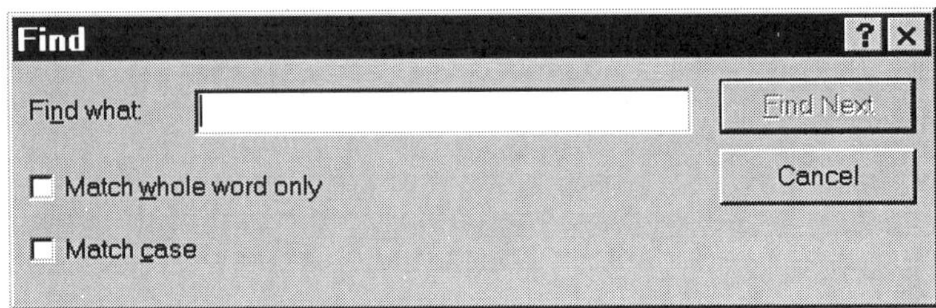

Figure 12 The Find Dialog Box

- Select the *Match whole word only* check box if you do not want the utility to search for longer words that contain the text you've typed. For example, suppose your document contains the words *all*, *small*, and *allow*, and you type *all* in the *Find what* text box. If the *Match whole word only* check box is selected, only the word *all* will be located. If it is not selected, all three words will be found.
- Select the *Match case* check box if you want to locate text that has the same combination of upper- and lower-case letters as the *Find what* text. For example, if this check box is selected and you type *all* in the *Find what* box, then *all* will be searched for, but not *All*; if this check box is not selected, both *all* and *All* (and, for that matter, *ALL*) will be sought.

3. Choose the Find Next command button. The next occurrence of the *Find what* text will be located and highlighted. (The search starts at the insertion point and, if the end of the document is reached before the text is found, the search continues at the beginning of the document.) If the *Find what* text is not found, a message to this effect will appear on the screen.

The Find dialog box will not close when the desired text is found, so that you can locate the next occurrence of the text, if so desired. To close this dialog box, choose the Cancel command button, press the Escape key, or click on the close button.

Replacing text

The Find and Replace utility can also replace the next occurrence of a particular piece of text (or *all* occurrences, if you wish) with text that you specify. To perform this operation:

1. Choose the Replace command from the Edit menu. The Replace dialog box, shown in Figure 13, will be displayed.

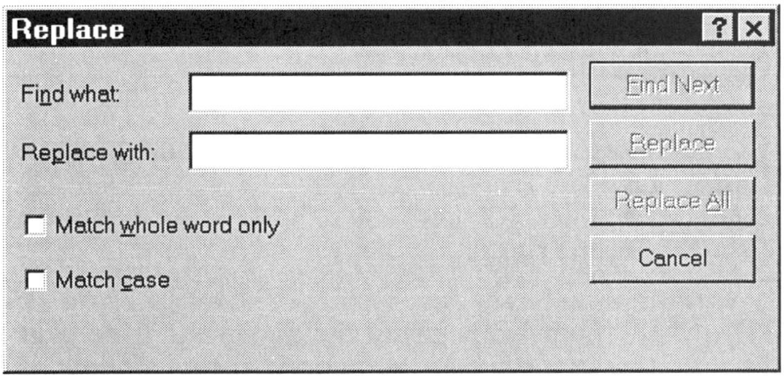

Figure 13 The Replace Dialog Box

2. Type the text you want to change in the *Find what* box and select the *Match whole word only* and/or *Match case* check boxes, if desired (their functions are described above).
3. Type the replacement text in the *Replace with* box.
4. Choose one of the command buttons:
   - Find Next locates the next occurrence of the *Find what* text and highlights it, but does not replace it.
   - Replace automatically replaces the highlighted word (if any) with the *Replace with* text, and then finds the next occurrence of the *Find what* text and highlights it.
   - Replace All automatically replaces every occurrence of the *Find what* text with the *Replace with* text.
   - Cancel terminates the find and replace operation and closes the dialog box.

You can use Find and Replace to speed up the entry of text into a document that has many occurrences of the same long word or phrase. For example, suppose you are writing a report on the Mediterranean region of Italy. Instead of typing the phrase *Mediterranean région of Italy* over and over again, simply type (say) *Med* each time. Then, when you're done, use Find and Replace to automatically replace all occurrences of *Med* with the longer phrase.

Print Preview

WordPad does not show certain formatting features, such as margins and page breaks, in the document window. However, it does provide a *print preview* feature to give you a better idea of what a document will look like when it's printed. This feature can sometimes save lots of time and paper.

To open the print preview window, either

- Choose the Print Preview command from the File menu.

or

- Click on the Toolbar's Print Preview button (as shown at the right).

In either case, the window shown in Figure 14 will open, displaying the first two pages of the document. (The page numbers are given on the status bar at the bottom of the window.) The margins are shown as "white space" outside the dashed lines that enclose the text.

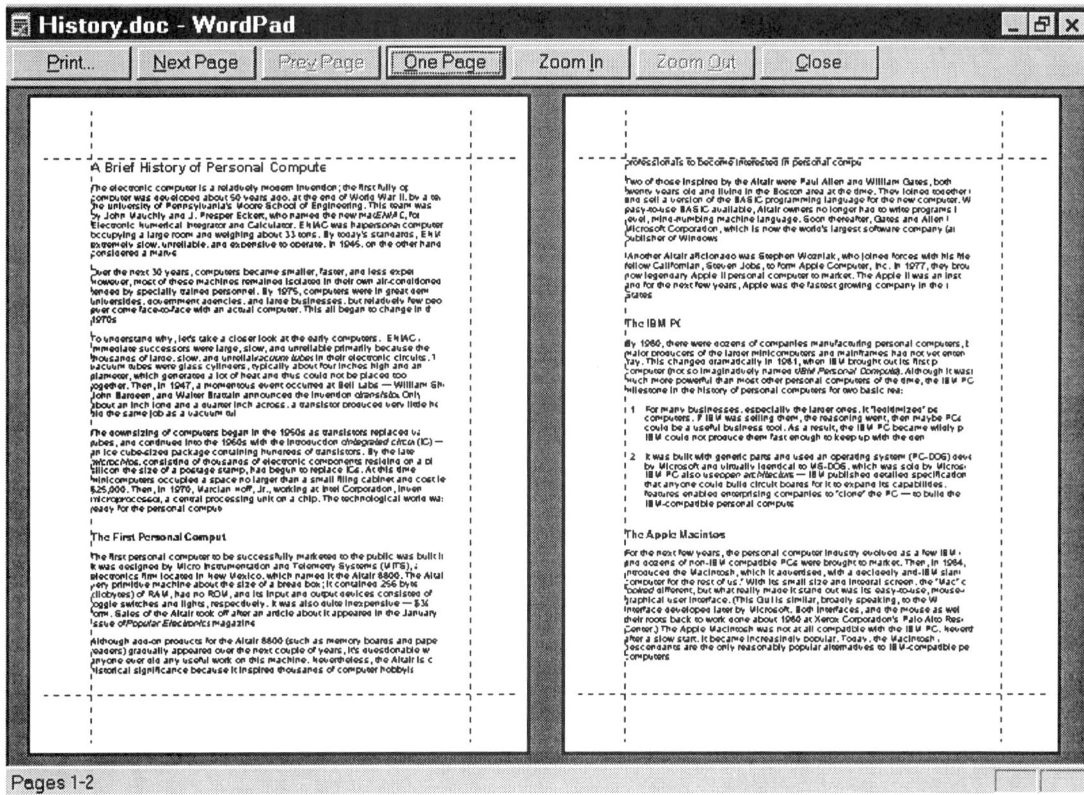

Figure 14 WordPad's Print Preview Window (Two-Page View)

Paging through the document You can get an overall view of the appearance of the entire document by paging through it.

- To display one page at a time click on the One Page button at the top of the window. (It will be relabeled *Two Page*.)
- To display the next page, click on the Next Page button or press the Page Down key (on the keyboard).
- To display the previous page, click on the Prev Page button or press the Page Up kcy.

Zooming in and out As you can see, it is difficult (sometimes, impossible) to read the text displayed in the preview window. (The situation does not improve if you switch to One Page view.) To deal with this problem, WordPad provides three levels of magnification, the default view and two "zoom" modes.

To *zoom in*, so that text appears larger (but with less of it displayed at once), either

- Click on the part of the page that you would like to enlarge. (In the preview window, the mouse cursor takes the shape of a magnifying glass, as shown at the right.)

or

- Click on the Zoom In button (at the top of the window). Then, use the scroll bars to display the desired part of the page.

In either case, the window will switch to One Page view (if necessary) and the text will be displayed in a larger font.

Clicking on the page or the Zoom In button again displays the second Zoom mode, increasing the magnification even more. At this point, the Zoom In button is dimmed, and clicking again on the page will return the display to the default magnification level. While in one of the two Zoom modes, clicking on the Zoom Out button changes the display to the next lower magnification level.

The relative magnification levels are shown below; each figure displays the same amount of screen area.

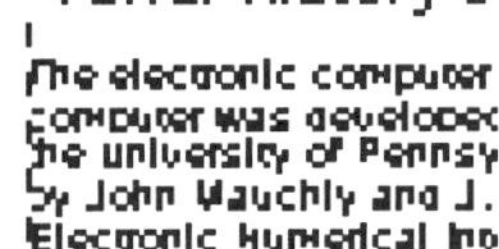

When you are done using the print preview window, either choose the Close button to return to the WordPad document window or choose the Print button to print the document.

Specifying a File Format

When a word processor (or, for that matter, any program) saves a document, it does so using a certain **file format** — a scheme for encoding the document's text, fonts, formatting symbols, and graphics, so that this information can be stored on disk. Unfortunately, every word processor uses a different file format for storing the documents it produces. For this reason, if you want to be able to open a document created by WordPad in another word processor, or vice-versa, you may have to specify a particular file format when it is saved. WordPad recognizes (opens documents in) six different file formats, offers a different default view option for most of them, and also saves files in several formats.

File formats recognized by WordPad

If you want to open a document within WordPad that was created by another word processor:

1. Choose the Open command from the File menu.
2. Display the *Files of type* drop-down list (shown at the right) in the resulting dialog box and select the file format in which the document was saved.
3. Locate the file by browsing the Windows folder system or type its name in the *File name* text box.
4. Choose the Open command button.

Word for Windows (*.doc)
Word for Windows (*.doc)
Windows Write (*.wri)
Rich Text Format (*.rtf)
Text Documents (*.txt)
Text Documents - MS-DOS Format (*.txt)
Unicode Text Documents (*.txt)
All Documents (*.*)

Here is a brief rundown of the available file formats:

- *Word for Windows* Because Word contains a greater number of formatting features than WordPad, some of a document's original formatting may be lost if it was saved in Word and then opened in WordPad.
- *Windows Write* This is the word processor supplied with Windows 3.1 and Windows NT 3.51.
- *Rich Text Format (RTF)* This is a common format, recognized by most word processors. If you are transferring a formatted document from a word processor other than Word for Windows or Write, save it (in that word processor) in RTF.
- *Text Documents* WordPad opens any file whose format it does not recognize as a plain text file, consisting of letters, numbers, punctuation marks, and a few other symbols. If, in fact, the file was saved in a format other than Text, you will see a lot of strange characters on the screen.
- The *MS-DOS* and *Unicode* formats are more sophisticated versions of plain text, which is sometimes referred to as ASCII format. Unicode is useful if the document contains foreign language characters.

File format view options

When WordPad opens a document, it displays the document in a certain way and makes certain "tool bars" available, depending on the format in which the file was saved. For example, by default, text files are displayed in the Courier New typeface with no alignment choices other than left-justification, and the Ruler and Format bar are hidden. You can specify which view option defaults are used for each format in the following way:

1. Choose the Options item from the View menu, which displays the Options dialog box, shown in Figure 15.

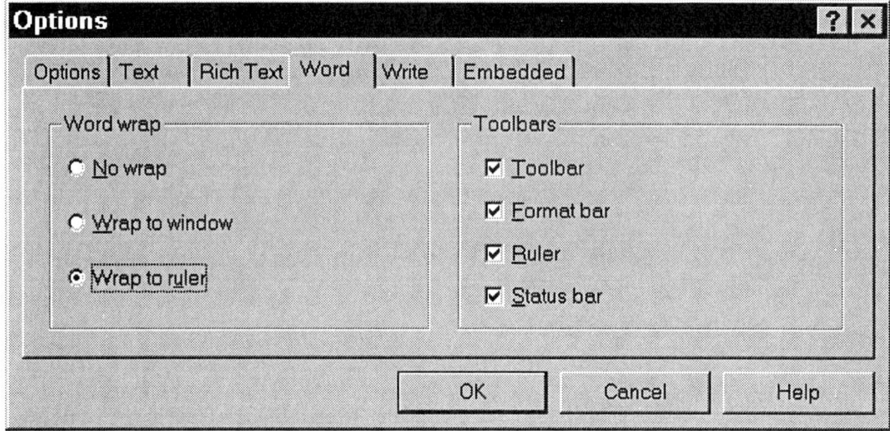

Figure 15 The (View) Options Dialog Box

2. Click on the tab corresponding to the file format for which you wish to set the default view. (The last tab, *Embedded*, is used for text that is exported to another document via Object Linking and Embedding; the first tab, *Options*, applies to all formats and will be discussed later in this section.)
3. Select a *Word wrap* option by clicking on the appropriate button:
   - If you select *No wrap*, the text you type will continue on the same line until you press the Enter key. This option is often used with Text files.
   - *Wrap to window* does just that; it starts a new line when the text reaches the right window border. This option is useful when viewing text in a small document window.
   - *Wrap to ruler* begins a new line as determined by the margins and indents specified for the document and paragraph.

Note that regardless of which word wrap option is in effect, when a document is printed, the specified margins and indents will be used to determine where lines are broken.

4. In the *Toolbars* area, select the check box of each "bar" that you want displayed in the WordPad window.
5. Choose the OK command button to close the dialog box and put the new defaults into effect.

NOTE

When you choose the New command from the File menu, a dialog box opens from which you can select a "document type". The type selected determines the way the document is displayed and the kinds of "bars" available (as specified in the Options dialog box), just as if the document were opened with that file format. It is a good idea to select *Word 6 Document* unless you have a particular reason to do otherwise.

File format save options

WordPad can *save* files in Word for Windows 6.0, RTF, or a Text format, regardless of which one was used to open or view the document. To save a document in one of these formats:

1. With the document displayed in the WordPad window, choose Save As from the File menu. The Save As dialog box will open.
2. Select a file format from the *Save as type* drop-down list.
3. Now, proceed as usual: Type a name for the document in the *File name* box, select a location (disk and folder) for the file, if necessary, and choose the Save command button.

And a Few Frills ...

We will close this section with a look at a few minor (but nice) WordPad features.

Inserting the Date or Time WordPad provides a very easy way to insert the current date or time into a document at the insertion point:

1. Choose the Date and Time item from the Insert menu or click on the Date/Time button, shown at the right, on the Toolbar. The Date and Time dialog box (Figure 16) will open.

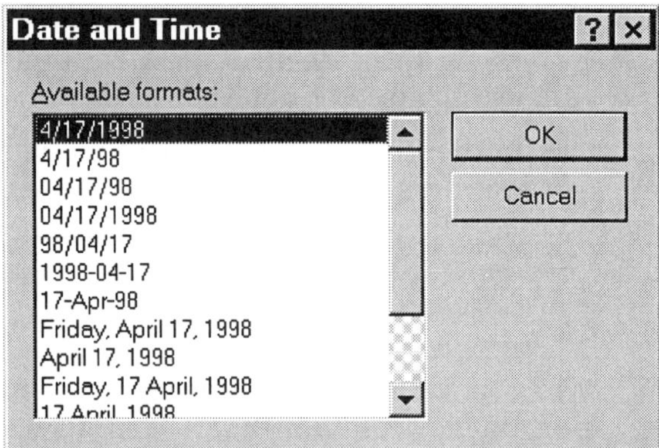

Figure 16 The Date and Time Dialog Box

2. Select the format you want for the date or time and either double-click on it or click on it and choose the OK command button. The date or time selected will be inserted into the document at the insertion point.

Opening Recently-Saved Documents This is a very handy, time-saving feature: To open one of the last four documents saved by WordPad:

1. Open the File menu.
2. Choose that document from the list at the bottom of the menu (see the figure at the right).

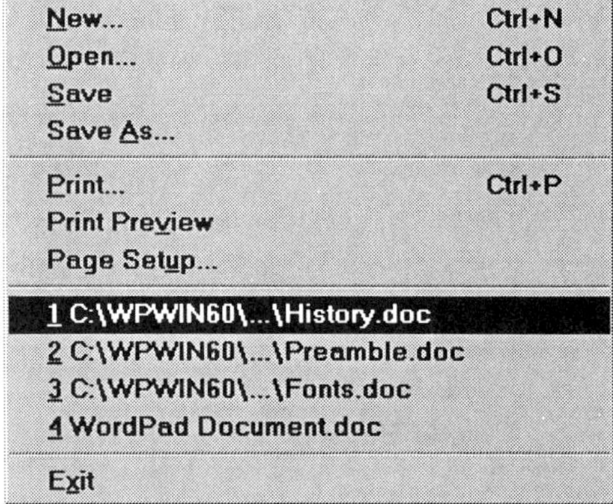

Specifying Units of Measurement By default, all measurements shown on the Ruler and in the Paragraph and Tabs dialog boxes are given in inches. If you want to use another unit of measurement:

1. Choose the Options command from the View menu. The Options dialog box will open.
2. Click on the Options tab in this dialog box and the page shown in Figure 17 will be displayed.

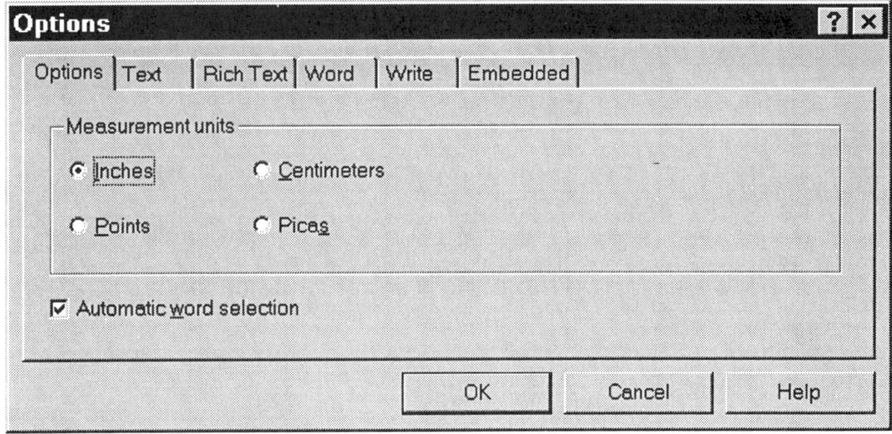

Figure 17 The Options Page of the (View) Options Dialog Box

3. Select the appropriate *Measurement units* option button. (In one inch, there are 2.54 centimeters, 72 points, and 6 picas.)
4. Deselect the *Automatic word selection* check box if you want to be able to select parts of words. Otherwise, leave it selected; it will be easier to use the mouse to select blocks of text.
5. Choose the OK command button to put your changes into effect and close the dialog box.

Try the following exercise on your own.

1. Turn on the computer (if necessary) to start Windows 98.
2. Open WordPad and maximize its window.
3. Insert the Student Disk in its drive and open the document named History.
4. Use the Find and Replace utility to locate the first occurrence of the word *chip* and replace it with *microchip*:
   - Choose the Replace command from the Edit menu.
   - In the *Find what* and *Replace with* boxes, enter *chip* and *microchip*, respectively.
   - Select the *Match whole word only* so you don't locate longer words that contain the letters *chip*, but leave *Match case* deselected so that you do find *Chip* or *chip*.

- Choose the Find Next command button. The first occurrence of the word *chip* will be highlighted.
- Choose the Replace command button. The replacement will be made and the next occurrence of *chip* will be highlighted.
- Choose the Close command button to close the dialog box.

5. Choose the Print Preview item from the File menu and check out the features of this command:
   - Display a single page at a time by clicking on the One Page button. (Notice that its label changes to Two Page.)
   - Page through the document by clicking on the Next Page button twice. Now, page backwards by clicking on the Prev Page button twice.
   - Try the Zoom feature by observing what happens when you click on the Zoom In button twice, then click on the Zoom Out button twice, and finally click (slowly) on the displayed page three times.
   - Click on the Close button to return to the main window.
6. Choose the Options item from the View menu and then click on the Text tab. Click on the *No wrap* option button, deselect the *Format bar* check box, and select the *Ruler* check box. Then, choose the OK button.
7. Choose the New command from the File menu, select Text Document from the list, and choose the OK button. (Respond No to the "save changes?" message.) Notice that, due to the selections made in step 6, the Format bar is hidden and the Ruler is displayed.
8. Type something (without pressing the Enter key) until you see that the line continues past the right margin marker on the Ruler (because word wrap is off).
9. Close WordPad (responding No to the "save changes?" message) and remove the diskette from its drive.

Chapter Summary

Basic Operations in WordPad

To start WordPad	Choose the WordPad item on the Accessories submenu of the Start menu's Programs option.
To select a word of text	Double-click on it.

	To select a line of text	Click in the left margin next to that line.
	To select a paragraph	Triple-click within it *or* double-click in the left margin next to it.
	To select the entire document	Triple-click in the left margin *or* choose Select All from the Edit menu *or* press Ctrl+A.
	To move/copy selected text	Choose Cut/Copy from the Edit menu or press Ctrl+X/Ctrl+C, then paste the text in another location. Or, drag-and-drop the text (holding down the Ctrl key for a copy).
	To undo a change	Choose Undo from the Edit menu *or* press Ctrl+Z.
Changing Fonts in WordPad	To change the typeface	Choose Font from the Format menu and select one from the Font list in the resulting dialog box; *or* select a new typeface from the Format bar's drop-down list.
	To change the font size	Choose Font from the Format menu and select a size from the Size list; *or* select a new size from the Format bar's drop-down list.
	To change the font style	Choose Font from the Format menu and select a style from the Font style list; *or* click on the Format bar's Bold, Italic, or Underline buttons.
	To change the font color	Choose Font from the Format menu and select a color from the Color drop-down list; *or* click on the Format bar's Font color button and then on a color.
Formatting a Document	To specify portrait or landscape orientation	Choose Page Setup from the File menu and select the appropriate option button.
	To set margins	Choose Page Setup from the File menu and enter the settings in the Margin text boxes.
	To change text alignment	Choose Paragraph from the Format menu and select Left, Right, or Center; *or* click on the appropriate Format bar button.
	To change paragraph indentation	Choose Paragraph from the Format menu and enter figures in the text boxes; *or* move the Ruler's indent markers.

	To change tab settings	Choose Tabs from the Format menu and enter desired tab stops; *or* click on the desired positions on the Ruler.
	To create a bulleted list	Choose Bullet Style from the Format menu; *or* click on the Format bar's Bullets button.
Using Graphics in WordPad	To insert a graphic	Paste it from the Clipboard *or* choose Object from the Insert menu.
	To edit a graphic	Double-click on it (if the graphic was created by an OLE-compatible application).
	To select a graphic	Click on it.
	To delete a graphic	Select it and press the Delete key.
	To move/copy a graphic	Move/copy it as if it were a character of text.
	To resize a graphic	Select it and drag a sizing handle.
Finding Text in WordPad	To find text	Choose Find from the Edit menu *or* click on the Toolbar's Find button, and use the resulting dialog box.
	To replace text	Choose Replace from the Edit menu and use the resulting dialog box.
Print Preview	To open the print preview window	Choose Print Preview from the File menu *or* click on the Toolbar's Print Preview button.
	To page through the document	Choose the Next Page or Prev Page command button.
	To zoom in or out	Choose the Zoom In or Zoom Out command button *or* click on a part of the displayed page.
WordPad File Formats	To specify view option defaults for a format	Choose Options from the View menu, click on the appropriate tab, and select the desired options.
	To use a desired file format option	Open a document saved in that file format (by selecting the latter from the Files of type drop-down list in the Open dialog box); *or* choose New from the File menu and select the file format in the resulting dialog box.
	To save a document in a desired file format	Choose Save As from the File menu and select a format from the *Save as type* drop-down list in the resulting dialog box.

Review Exercises

Section 7.1

1. In WordPad, to move the insertion point to the beginning of the current line, press the ___________ key.
2. To select a word in a WordPad document, ___________ the mouse on any letter within it.
3. To undo the last editing change in WordPad, choose Undo from the Edit menu or just press the ___________ keystroke combination.
4. True or false: To move the cursor to the end of a WordPad document, press the End key.
5. True or false: To select an entire WordPad document, move the insertion point into the left margin and double-click the mouse.
6. True or false: You can copy a selected block of text by dragging it to its new location while holding down the Ctrl key.
7. To paste a block of text into a WordPad document, click on the Toolbar button that looks like:

   a.  b.  c.  d.

8. Which of the following keystroke combinations can be used to select an entire WordPad document?

   a. Ctrl+A
   b. Ctrl+V
   c. Ctrl+X
   d. Ctrl+Z

Section 7.2

9. To print type that is about one inch high, use a ___________ point font size.
10. To change the current typeface in WordPad, select one from the Format bar's drop-down list or choose the ___________ command from the Format menu.
11. True or false: If text is selected when you make a font change in WordPad, the font change applies only to the selected text.
12. True or false: The "strikeout" attribute (selected in the Font dialog box) causes the affected text to become unreadable.
13. Which of the following text formatting features is not accessible from WordPad's Format bar?

a. Changing the font size.
b. Changing the font color.
c. Changing the font style to bold, italic, or underline.
d. All the above features are accessible from the Format bar.

14. Which of the following keystroke combinations will not affect the style of currently selected text?

a. Ctrl+A
b. Ctrl+B
c. Ctrl+I
d. Ctrl+U

Section 7.3

15. When a document is printed with the text running parallel to the long side of the page, we say it is in ___________ orientation.

16. If the left-indent for a paragraph is 1.5" and the first-line-indent is 0.5", then the text on the first line of that paragraph will begin ___________ inch(es) to the right of the left margin.

17. The default tab stops for WordPad are set every ___________ inch(es) across the page.

18. You can select an alignment option in the dialog box that opens when you choose the Format menu's ___________ command.

19. True or false: In WordPad, it is not possible to align text in a given paragraph with both the left and right margins.

20. True or false: If you set a tab stop at the beginning of a WordPad document, then (unless you remove it later on) this tab setting will apply to the entire document.

21. True or false: When using WordPad's bullet style feature, you can elect to use either round or square bullets.

22. Which formatting feature is not available in WordPad?

a. Changing tab settings.
b. Changing page margins.
c. Changing line spacing.
d. Changing page orientation.

23. Assuming that no text is currently selected, which of the following format changes applies to all text in a WordPad document?

a. Changing the margins.
b. Changing the tab settings.
c. Changing the text alignment.
d. Changing the paragraph indentation.

24. Which of the following WordPad format settings is not displayed on the Ruler?

a. The right margin for the document.
b. The left indent for the current paragraph.
c. The alignment option for the current paragraph.
d. Custom tab stops for the current paragraph.

Section 7.4

25. To insert a graphic from a disk file into a WordPad document, begin by choosing the ___________ item on the Insert menu.

26. The feature of Windows that allows you to edit a graphic from *within* a WordPad document is called ___________.

27. True or false: You can delete a graphic from a WordPad document by positioning the insertion point just to the right of the graphic and pressing the Backspace key.

28. True or false: Once you have inserted a graphic into a WordPad document, it cannot be resized.

29. Which of the following techniques cannot be used to reposition a graphic at the beginning of a WordPad document?

    a. Using the mouse to drag it there.
    b. Cutting it to the Clipboard and pasting it there.
    c. Choosing the Move command from the Edit menu and then moving the graphic there using the Arrow keys.
    d. All of the above actions can be used to move the graphic.

30. After a graphic is inserted into a WordPad document, you cannot

    a. Enlarge its size.
    b. Move it to another place in the document.
    c. Copy it to another place in the document.
    d. All of the above operations can be performed on a graphic.

Section 7.5

31. If you want to see where page breaks occur in a WordPad document, either print the document or choose the ___________ item from the File menu.

32. To change the units of measurement on the Ruler, begin by choosing the ___________ command from the View menu.

33. True or false: In the Find dialog box, if you type *the* in the *Find what* text box, select the *Match whole word only* check box, and choose the Find Next button, WordPad will search the current document for any word that contains the letters *the*.

34. True or false: To turn word wrap off for the current WordPad document, begin by choosing Options from the View menu.

35. True or false: You can have WordPad automatically insert the current date in a document by clicking on the Toolbar's Date/Time button and making a selection in the resulting dialog box.

36. The Find command on WordPad's Edit menu can be used to

    a. Locate all occurrences of the word *rich* in a document.
    b. Automatically replace the first occurrence of *rich* with *poor* in a document.
    c. Automatically replace all occurrences of *rich* with *poor* in a document.
    d. Perform all of the above tasks.

37. In WordPad's print preview window, you can

    a. Type new text.
    b. Edit existing text.
    c. Format existing text.
    d. Perform none of the above tasks.

38. Which of the following file formats does not preserve *any* of the text formatting features of the document being saved?

    a. Word for Windows format
    b. Rich Text Format
    c. Text format
    d. Windows Write format

Build Your Own Glossary

39. The following words and phrases are important terms that were introduced in this chapter. (They appear within the text in bold type.) Use WordPad to enter a definition for each term, preserving alphabetical order, into the Glossary file on the Student Disk.

Bullet (symbol)	Graphic	Point (unit of measure)
Edit a document	Landscape orientation	Portrait orientation
File format	Notepad	Scalable font
Font	Object linking and embedding (OLE)	Typeface
Format a document		WordPad
Format bar		

Lab Exercises

Work each of the following exercises at your computer. Begin by turning the machine on (if necessary) to start Windows 98 and closing any open windows.

Lab Exercise 1 (Section 7.1)

a. Start WordPad and maximize its window.

b. Type your name and class on separate lines, and skip a line (by pressing the Enter key twice).

c. Type the sentence: This is a test of the copy and paste operations. Then, press the Spacebar to insert a blank space after the period.

d. Select the sentence and the space that follows it. Describe how you accomplished this.

e. Copy the selected text to the Clipboard. What menu command or mouse actions did you use?

f. Paste the text from the Clipboard onto the end of the document. What menu command or mouse actions did you use?

g. Repeat step *f* four times. Try pasting the text without reselecting and recopying it. Did this work?

h. Print the document. (See Section 2.2, if necessary, for information about printing a document.)

i. Save the document if you wish and exit WordPad.

Lab Exercise 2 (Section 7.2)

a. Start WordPad and maximize its window.

b. Insert the Student Disk in its drive and open the document on this disk named Preamble. (See Section 2.2 for information on opening a document.)

c. Display the Format bar (if it's not currently visible) and use it to help determine the two fonts used in the Preamble document. What are they?

d. Break the title into two lines (after "Constitution"), select both lines, and center them. Describe how you centered the lines.

e. Change the font for the entire title to 19-point Arial bold. Do you have to use the Font dialog box to do this?

f. Within the preamble itself:

   - Bold the phrase *We the people.*
   - Italicize the word *Constitution.*
   - Underline the last four words, *United States of America.*

   What keystroke combination can be used to accomplish each of these text enhancements?

g. Skip a line at the bottom of the document and type your name.

h. Print the revised document (see Section 2.2, if necessary).

i. Save the modified document under another name if you wish, exit WordPad, and remove the diskette from its drive.

Lab Exercise 3 (Section 7.2)

a. Start WordPad and maximize its window.

b. Insert the Student Disk in its drive and open the document on this disk named Fonts.

c. Follow the instructions on the screen.

d. Skip a line at the bottom of the document and type your name.

e. Print the revised document.

f. Save the modified document under another name if you wish, exit WordPad, and remove the diskette from its drive.

Lab Exercise 4 (Section 7.3)

a. Start WordPad and maximize its window.

b. Insert the Student Disk in its drive and open the document on this disk named History.

c. Set all margins to 1.25" and the page orientation to landscape.

d. Type your name at the top of the document and skip a line.

e. Center the document's title and right-align the first paragraph.

f. In the second paragraph, set all indents equal to 0.5".

g. In the third paragraph:

- Remove the existing tabs at 0.35" and 0.7".
- Set a tab stop at 1.25".
- Move the insertion point to the beginning of this paragraph and press the Tab key.

h. Print the *first page* of the revised document.

i. Save the modified document under another name if you wish, return the page orientation to portrait, exit WordPad, and remove the diskette from its drive.

Lab Exercise 5 (Section 7.3)

a. Start WordPad and maximize its window.

b. Create a document similar to the one in Figure 18:

- Set all margins to 1.5" and orientation to portrait.
- Center the title in 18-point bold Arial type.
- Use 12-point Arial type for everything else, with bold for the column headings.
- Use the bullet style feature to create the list.
- Set tab stops to create the table columns at 1.5" and every 0.75" after that.

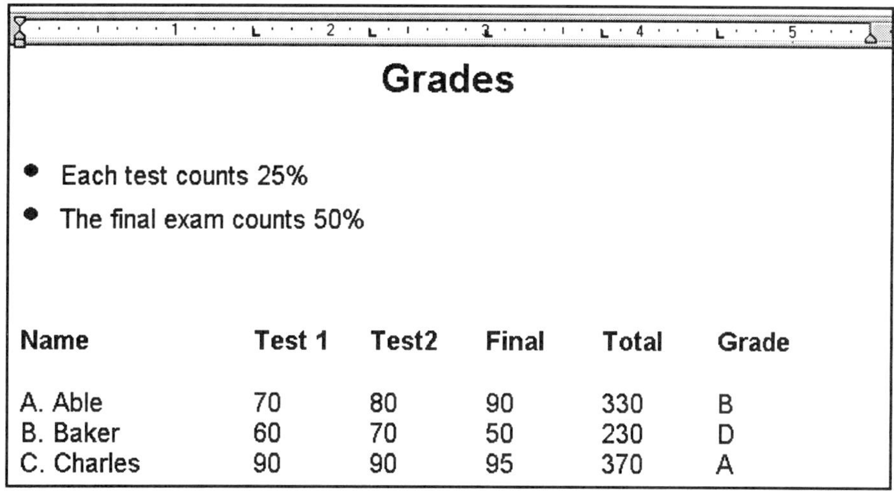

Grades

- Each test counts 25%
- The final exam counts 50%

Name	Test 1	Test2	Final	Total	Grade
A. Able	70	80	90	330	B
B. Baker	60	70	50	230	D
C. Charles	90	90	95	370	A

Figure 18 The Document for Lab Exercise 5

c. At the bottom, skip two lines and type your name.

d. Print the resulting document.

e. Save the document if you wish, exit WordPad, and remove the diskette from its drive.

Lab Exercise 6 (Section 7.4)

a. Start WordPad and maximize its window.

b. Insert the Student Disk in its drive and open the document on this disk named Title-3.

c. Set all margins to 1.25" and the page orientation to portrait, and display the Ruler if it's currently hidden.

d. Reduce the graphic's size so that the width of its "selection box" is about 1.5" (as measured on the Ruler).

e. Create a copy of this smaller graphic, positioned just to the right of the original (on the same line).

f. Position the insertion point between the two graphics and use the Spacebar to "push" the second graphic to the right about 1".

g. Center this configuration of graphics between the margins.

h. Center the document's title and replace the given name, class, and date by your name, your class, and the current date.

i. Skip a line and insert the Shapes graphic on the Student Disk into the document at the insertion point.

j. Print the revised document.

k. Save the modified document under another name if you wish, exit WordPad, and remove the diskette from its drive.

Lab Exercise 7 (Section 7.5)

a. Start WordPad and maximize its window.

b. Insert the Student Disk in its drive and open the document on this disk named History.

c. Set all margins to 1" and the page orientation to portrait.

d. Use the print preview feature to determine the last word on page one of this document. (You may have to zoom in!) What is it?

e. Use WordPad's Find command to locate all occurrences of the words *computer* and *computers.*

- What word should you type in the *Find what* box so that both of these words will be searched for simultaneously?
- How many occurrences of these words were there?
- Were boldfaced words found? Were italicized words found?

f. Use the WordPad Replace command to replace (one-by-one) all occurrences of the word *chip* (but not *Chip*) with *microchip.* Which check boxes in the Replace dialog box did you select?

g. Now find all occurrences of the word *microchip*? How many are there?

h. Determine the file format of the History document. (Open the Options dialog box and note the active page.) What is this format?

i. Click on the Options tab. Which wrap option is in effect?

j. Exit WordPad (responding No to the "save changes?" message) and remove the diskette from its drive.

If You Want to Learn More ...

The notes presented here allow you to delve more deeply into some of the topics covered in this chapter.

Windows' other word processor

Windows also supplies a simple "word processor" called Notepad. This application doesn't have any text formatting capabilities (it is really a *text editor*) and the only file format it recognizes is *Text*. For this reason, Notepad is usually used for certain simple tasks, such as creating and/or editing notes, lists, programs, and system configuration files.

Notepad is discussed in Section 9.2. If you want to try it out, Notepad can be started from the Accessories submenu of the Start menu's Programs option.

What you see is not quite what you get

Strictly speaking, WordPad is *not* a WYSIWYG (what you see is what you get) word processor; for example, it does not show page breaks or margins in its document window. To view on-screen an accurate representation of the way the document will look when you print it, you must use the print preview feature (Section 7.5).

There is a more subtle WYSIWYG problem in WordPad. If the "wrap to ruler" setting is not turned on, line breaks (the right ends of lines on the printed page) will not be accurately shown on the screen. To ensure that this feature is turned on for the current document:

1. Choose Options from the View menu to display the Options dialog box.
2. Select (if necessary) the *Wrap to ruler* option button.
3. Choose the OK command button.

Importing files into WordPad

As you know, WordPad is able to open documents that were saved in other file formats. Unfortunately, this is a mixed blessing. If a document was created in another word processor and saved in Word for Windows, Write, or RTF format, it may very well contain formatting codes (for example, for a header or double-line spacing) that WordPad does not support. In such a case, WordPad will ignore these codes, and the imported document may look quite different from the original.

WordPad should import correctly a document saved in the Text file format. To ensure that it does, check that word wrap is turned off for Text files before opening the document:

1. Choose Options from the View menu and click on the Text tab in the resulting dialog box.
2. Select the *No wrap* option button.
3. Choose the OK command button.

WordPad versus Write (Windows 3.1)

The Windows 98 version of WordPad is virtually identical to the version supplied by Windows 95. However, it differs quite a bit from *Write*, the word processor built into Windows 3.1. For example, Write contains the following features that are not present in WordPad:

- Paragraph alignment with both the left and right margins (*full justification*).
- Double-line spacing and 1½-line spacing, of text.
- Insertion of page breaks and "soft hyphens" (which appear only when needed for line breaks) wherever you want them.
- Subscript and superscript text styles.
- Headers and footers that are automatically placed on every page of a document. This feature also provides automatic page numbering.

On the other hand, the following features appear in WordPad, but not in Write:

- Choice of font color and a strikeout style for text.
- Automatic insertion of bullets and date and time.
- The ability to save and open files in several different formats.
- Print preview.

If you would like to use Write instead of WordPad, you *might* be able to do so if your copy of Windows 98 was upgraded from Windows 3.1. Use the Windows Find utility (Section 4.3) to search for the file Write.exe on your hard disk. If Find locates it, double-click on this file to see if it's really Write or just a shortcut to WordPad.

Where to go from here

Here's where to find some more information about some of the topics discussed in this chapter:

- The process of creating a graphic and copying it to the Clipboard is discussed (for the Paint application) in Chapter 8.
- More information about the subject of object linking and embedding (OLE) can be found in Section 12.5.

CHAPTER 8

Creating Graphics with Paint

Overview

Often, the best way to impart a large amount of information in a small amount of space is to use a **graphic** — a picture, diagram, graph, or other illustrative material. Windows supplies a drawing program called **Paint** to help you create graphics. In this chapter, we will describe how to use this application. You will learn:

1. How to start Paint and select the colors and tools needed to draw a graphic.
2. To use Paint's drawing tools to create lines, curves, and shapes.
3. To place text in a Paint graphic.
4. To erase portions of an existing graphic.
5. To magnify part of a graphic so that you can create or edit fine details.
6. To select part of a graphic and move, copy, flip, rotate, stretch, skew, or resize the resulting "cutout".
7. To set up the printed page and preview it before printing takes place.

8.1 An Introduction to Paint

Creating a *graphic* (a picture) using the Paint application is not unlike creating one using conventional artist's tools. (In fact, some Paint tools have familiar names, such as the Pencil, Brush, and Eraser.) Instead of using an artist's brush to apply paint to a canvas, however, Paint allows you to manipulate the tiny dots of light (*pixels*) that make up the screen image, coloring them as you wish, to create various shapes. In this section, we will provide an introduction to the graphics-creation process.

The Paint Window

To start Paint:

1. Click on the Start button to open the Start menu.
2. Point at the Programs option on this menu and at Accessories on the resulting submenu.
3. On the Accessories submenu, click on the Paint item. The Paint window, shown in Figure 1, will open.

In addition to the usual components, such as title and menu bars, the Paint window is divided into three main parts:

1. The **Tool Box** contains icons that represent the tools you use to create the graphic. The names of these tools are given in Figure 2; we will describe their use later in this chapter. Below the icons is a box (see Figure 1) that displays the options, if any, available for the selected tool. For example, for the Line tool, the **Options Box** (shown at the right) displays the available line widths with the current width highlighted. To select another drawing width, click on it.
2. The **drawing area** (or *work area*) is the window in which you compose the graphic. Often, the graphic is larger than the drawing area, so only part of it is displayed. In such a case, you can view other parts of the graphic by scrolling the window. To minimize scrolling:
   - Maximize the Paint window.
   - Remove the Tool Box, Color Box, and/or Status Bar from the screen by choosing the corresponding command from the View menu. (Each command is a toggle; choosing it again returns the corresponding object to the screen.)

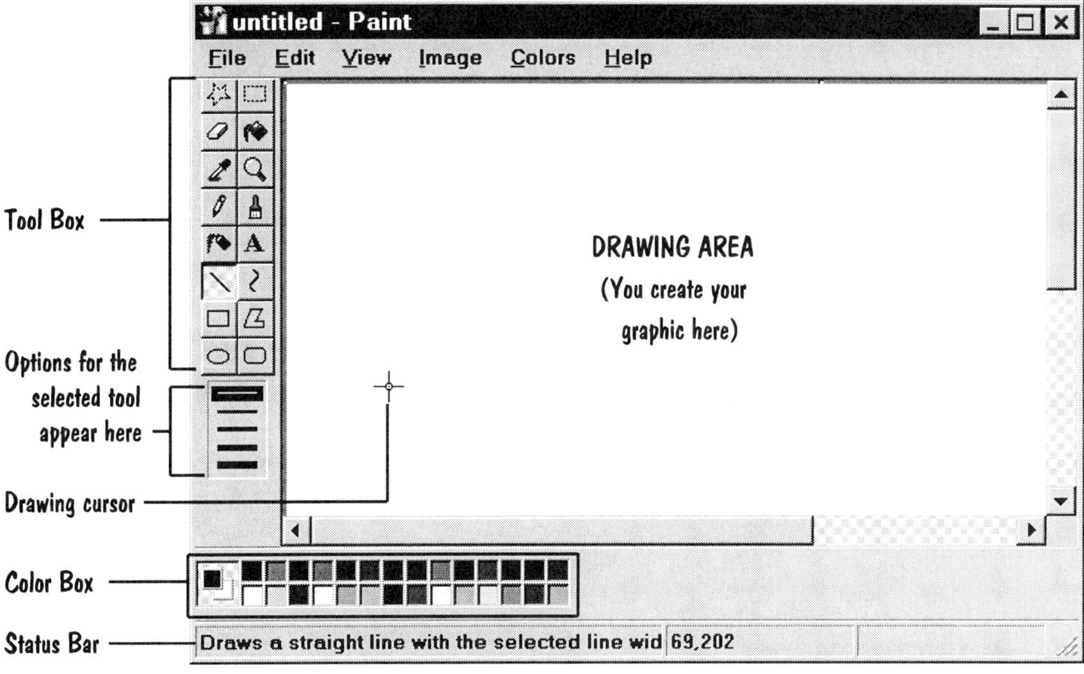

Figure 1 The Paint Window

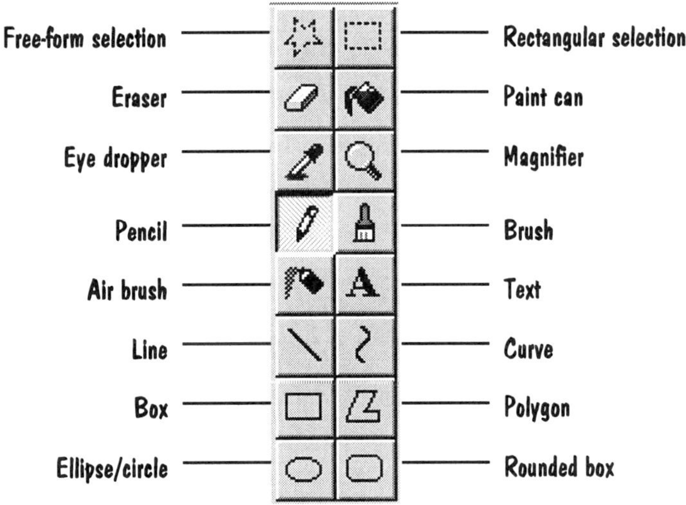

Figure 2 The Paint Tool Box

- To expand the graphic to fill the entire screen (whether or not the Paint window is maximized), choose the View Bitmap command from the View menu. (Unfortunately, you cannot work on your drawing while View Bitmap is in effect.) Clicking anywhere on the screen returns it to "normal".

3. The **Color Box** allows you to select the colors for the object you are about to draw (by clicking on them). It also displays the current foreground and background colors (Figure 3).

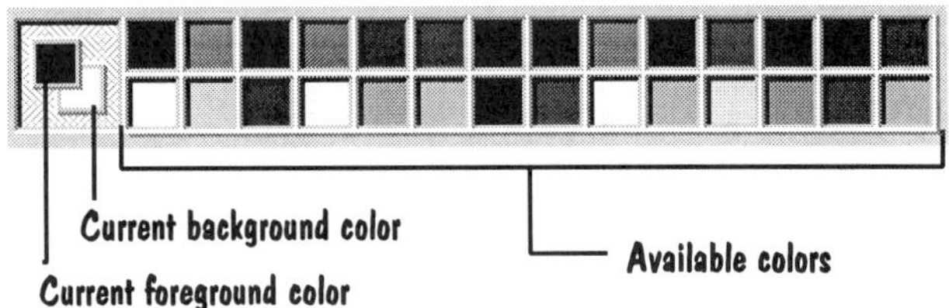

Figure 3 The Color Box

Drawing a Graphic

Using Paint to draw a graphic involves these general steps:

1. Select a **background color**, the color of the drawing area, by *right*-clicking on the desired color in the Color Box. Then, select the Paint Can tool from the Tool Box (by clicking on its icon) and right-click anywhere in the drawing area.
2. For the object you are about to draw:
   - Select a drawing tool by clicking on its icon in the Tool Box. (The selected icon will appear to be "depressed".)
   - Select an option for this tool (when applicable) from the Options Box.
   - Select a **foreground color**, the color with which the object will be drawn, by *left*-clicking on the desired color in the Color Box. In some cases, you may also select a background color, which is used in different ways by different tools; this selection will not affect the color of the drawing area.

Paint makes it easy to select a foreground or background color that matches a color already present in your graphic. To do so, select the **Eye Dropper** tool from the Tool Box, position the

mouse cursor (an "eye dropper") over an object that has the desired color, and select it as the foreground or background color by clicking the left or right button, respectively.

3. Draw the object:
   - Position the cursor at the location in the work area where you want to begin drawing.
   - Drag the cursor to draw the object; release the mouse button when you're done.
4. Repeat steps 2 and 3 until the drawing is complete.

An example To illustrate the drawing process, let's create the graphic image of a signature. (An example of the finished graphic is shown in Figure 4.)

- Leave the foreground and background colors at their default settings: black and white, respectively.

- Select the Brush tool by clicking on its Tool Box icon. The options for Brush are various sizes and styles of "brush tips". Choose the smallest available tip from the Options Box; the one on the right end of the first row.
- Move the cursor (cross hairs) into the work area and position it where you want to begin drawing your first name.
- Drag the cursor to form your first and last names. (To move the

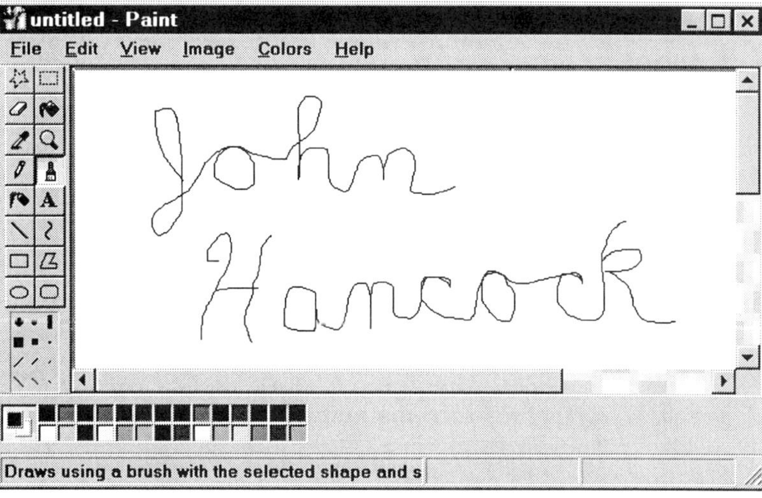

Figure 4 Graphic Image of a Signature

cursor from one place to another without drawing, just release the mouse button, reposition the cursor, and start dragging again.)

It takes some practice to use the Brush tool. If you want to delete the part of the graphic you just drew, choose Undo from the Edit menu or press Ctrl+Z.

NOTE

From Windows' point of view, the graphic you are creating is a "document". It is saved, opened, and printed in the same ways as a WordPad document (see Section 2.2). Moreover, as in WordPad, the last four documents saved in Paint are displayed at the bottom of the File menu. To open one of these files, just click on it.

TUTORIAL

Try the following exercise on your own.

1. Turn on the computer (if necessary) to start Windows 98.
2. Start Paint by selecting it from the Accessories submenu of the Start button, and maximize its window.
3. If the Tool Box or Color Box (see Figure 1) is not visible on the screen, display it by choosing the corresponding item from the View menu.
4. Set the foreground color to red by left-clicking on the red square in the Color box; set the background color to yellow by right-clicking on the yellow square in the Color Box.
5. Color the entire drawing area in the background color: Select the Paint Can tool from the Tool Box (by clicking on its icon); then, right-click inside the drawing area. 
6. Select the Brush tool from the Tool Box. The "brush tip" options will be displayed in the Options Box. 
7. Select the smallest round brush tip by clicking on the right-most icon in the top row of the Options Box.
8. Position the mouse cursor inside the drawing area (it will become a pair of cross hairs) and draw a line across the screen by dragging the cursor horizontally to the right.
9. Delete the line you have just drawn by choosing the Undo command from the Edit menu (or by pressing Ctrl+Z).
10. Experiment with the Brush tool by drawing whatever you want. Now and then, select a different brush tip and foreground color to see their effects. Note the following points:

- To clear the entire picture from the screen, choose the New command from the File menu.
- To print your graphic, choose the Print command from the File menu (see Section 2.2 for information about printing).
- To save your graphic, choose the Save command from the File menu (see Section 2.2 for information on saving a file).

11. Close the Paint window. Respond No to the "save changes?" message unless you want to save your graphic.

8.2 Using the Drawing Tools

Most of the tools in the Paint Tool Box (Figure 2) are used to create the curves, shapes, and text that make up your graphic. We will describe how to use these kinds of tools in this section. Tools that are used in modifying the graphic will be discussed in Section 8.3.

Creating Lines, Curves, and Other Strokes

The Pencil, Brush, Airbrush, Line, and Curve tools are used to form the lines, curves, and other "paint strokes" in the graphic. Each of these tools is used in the same basic way:

The basic technique

1. Select the tool by clicking on its icon in the Tool Box.
2. Select a drawing option (if available) from the Options Box.
3. Select a new foreground or background color, if you want.
4. Position the cursor in the drawing area where you want the paint stroke to begin. (The shape of the cursor depends on the tool selected; it may be cross hairs, a stylized pencil, or a tiny spray can.)
5. If you want to paint with the foreground color, press the left mouse button; to paint with the background color, press the right mouse button.
6. Continuing to depress the mouse button, create the stroke by dragging the cursor to another position in the drawing area.
7. When the stroke is complete, release the mouse button.

Of course, each tool has its own special capabilities; we will discuss them on the following pages.

To some extent, creating graphics with Paint is a trial-and-error process. Occasionally, while creating an object, it will become clear that you are not getting the desired effect. In such a case, to cancel the operation while you are still dragging the cursor, just tap the other mouse button or press the Escape key. Also, remember that you can undo an operation that you have just completed by choosing Undo from the Edit menu. (The last three changes can be undone in reverse order.)

The Pencil Tool The **Pencil** is a basic drawing tool. It is used to draw fine free-form curves, just as if you were using a pencil on paper. There are no options for this tool; all lines drawn with it are one pixel ("dot") wide. The Pencil does have a nice feature, though. If you hold down the Shift key while dragging the cursor, the result will be a straight line that is perfectly horizontal, vertical, or diagonal (inclined at a 45° angle), depending on the direction you move the mouse.

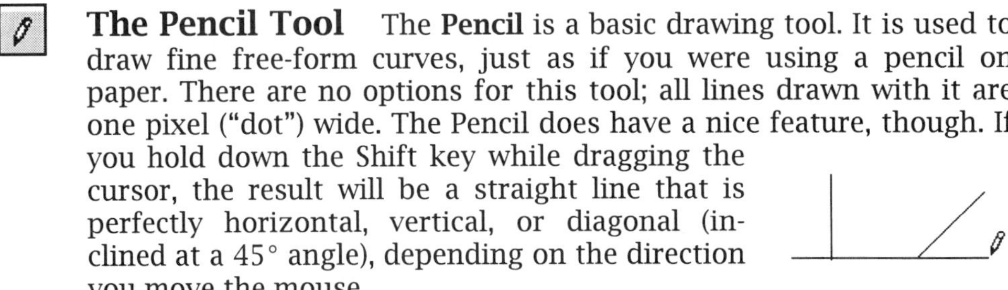

The Brush Tool The **Brush** tool is used like an artist's paint brush; it creates free-form curves using several different brush widths and styles, which are selected from the Options Box. The effect of selecting a few of these options is shown in Figure 5.

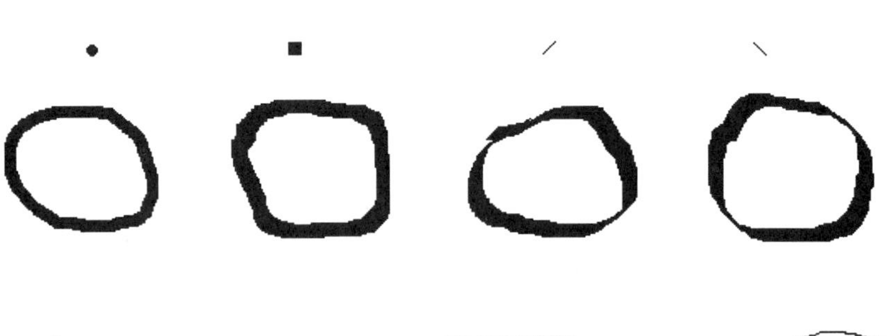

Figure 5 Brush Tip Effects for the Brush Tool

The Airbrush Tool The **Airbrush** tool draws a free-form figure made up of a spray of dots. The faster you move the Airbrush, the finer the spray, as illustrated below:

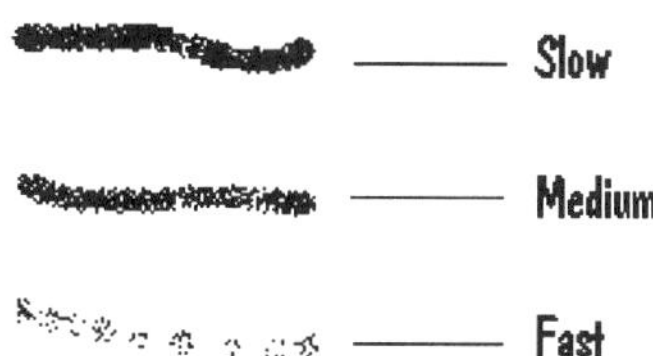

The Options Box for the Airbrush tool, which is shown at the right, allows you to select from among three different spray widths.

The Line Tool The **Line** tool is used to draw straight lines (it can *only* draw straight lines). Several line widths are available, and are selected in the Options Box (shown at the right). Holding down the Shift key while dragging the Line cursor creates perfectly horizontal, vertical, or diagonal (inclined at 45°) lines.

The Curve Tool Although the Pencil and Brush can draw curves, the result is a *free-form* curve. Unless you have a very steady hand, the result may not be as smooth as you might like. The **Curve** tool (which has the same available line widths as the Line tool) draws smooth, uniform curves, but is somewhat tricky to use.

In using the Curve tool, you first construct a line and then deform it into the desired curve by "bending" the line once or twice with the aid of the mouse. To be more specific, after selecting the tool and the appropriate line width and drawing color:

1. Position the cursor (cross hairs) in the drawing area where you want the curve to begin, press the mouse button, drag the cursor to the other endpoint, and release the button. A straight line now connects the curve's two endpoints.
2. Drag the cursor away from the line in the direction you want it to bend it. As you do, a curve will form. Continue to drag the cursor around, until this part of the curve has the desired shape; then release the mouse button. If the curve's appearance is satisfactory, double-click the mouse to complete the operation.
3. If you want the curve to bend in a second direction, drag the cursor in this direction. When the curve has the desired appearance, release the mouse button to anchor the curve in place.

Let's try a specific example. Select the Curve tool from the Tool Box and the second thinnest line width from the Options Box. Now:

- Drag a vertical line that is about two inches in length (as shown in Figure 6a).
- Position the cursor about one-half inch below the top of the line, drag it to the right (Figure 6b), and release the mouse button. Notice that the curve bends to the right as you drag the cursor.
- Position the cursor about one-half inch above the bottom of the current curve, drag the cursor to the left as in Figure 6c, and release the mouse button. Notice that the curve has bent back to the left. When you release the button this time, the curve becomes anchored in place.

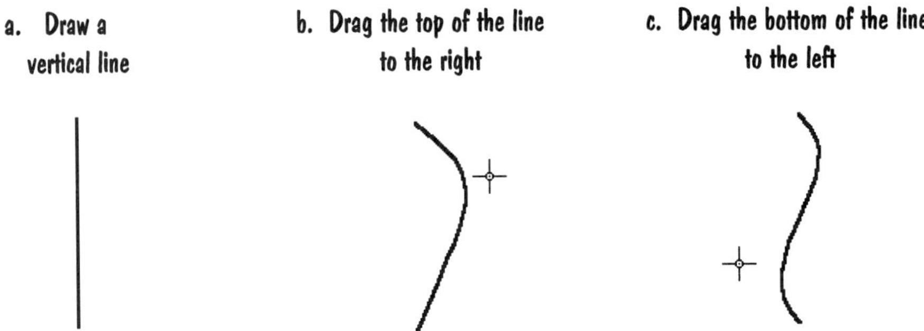

Figure 6 Using the Curve Tool

Creating Geometric Shapes

The Box, Rounded Box, Circle/Ellipse, and Polygon tools are used to create the corresponding shapes. To use one of these tools:

1. Select the tool by clicking on its icon in the Tool Box.
2. From the Options Box (shown at the right), select one of three border/fill options:

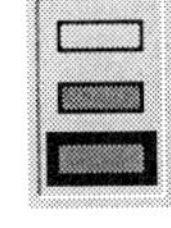

Border/fill options

- *Hollow* — Only the border of the figure will be drawn (see the left box in Figure 7).
- *Filled* — The border will be drawn and the figure will be filled with color (see the center box in Figure 7).
- *Borderless* — The figure will be filled with color, but the border will not be drawn (see the right box in Figure 7).

Figure 7 Hollow, Filled, and Borderless Boxes

3. Select new foreground and background colors (if you want) from the Color Box. These are used to color the figure, as follows:

Drawing colors

   - If you create the figure with the left mouse button, the foreground color is used for the figure's border in the *hollow* and *filled* cases, or for the entire *borderless* shape. The background color is used for the interior in the *filled* option.
   - If you create the figure with the right mouse button, the foreground and background colors have the opposite function.

Border width

4. If the figure is to have a border, choose its width by clicking on the Line tool and selecting from among the five choices shown in the Options Box. (If you do this, you will then have to reselect the tool you want to use to create the geometric shape.)
5. Position the cursor (cross hairs) in the drawing area and draw the figure. The way in which this is done varies a little from tool to tool and will be described below, when each tool is discussed.

The Box Tool The **Box** tool draws rectangles and squares. (Examples of shapes drawn with the Box tool are shown in Figure 7.) To use this tool:

1. Select the Box icon from the Tool Box; then select a border/fill option, drawing colors, and a border width, as described earlier.
2. Position the mouse cursor at one corner of the box-to-be and drag the cursor toward the opposite corner. As you do, the corresponding rectangle will be displayed on the screen. To draw a square box, hold down the Shift key while dragging the cursor.
3. When the box is the correct size, release the mouse button.

The Rounded Box Tool The **Rounded Box** tool draws a rectangle (or square, if you hold down the Shift key while dragging the cursor) with rounded corners. This tool is used in exactly the same way as the Box tool.

The Ellipse/Circle Tool The **Ellipse/Circle** tool is used to draw ellipses and circles. Here are a few examples:

 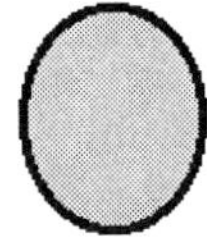 

To use the Ellipse/Circle tool:

1. Select the Ellipse/Circle icon from the Tool Box; then select a border/fill option, drawing colors, and a border width, as described earlier.
2. Picture the ellipse-to-be enclosed in an imaginary box. Now, position the mouse cursor at one corner of this box and drag the cursor toward the opposite corner. As you do, the corresponding ellipse will be displayed on the screen. To draw a circle, hold down the Shift key while dragging the cursor.
3. When the ellipse or circle is the correct size, release the mouse button.

The Polygon Tool The **Polygon** tool helps you draw a many-sided enclosed figure. Here are some examples of the kinds of figures you can draw using the Polygon tool:

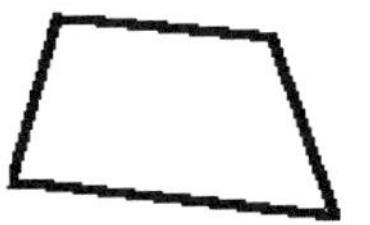   

Although the same border/fill options are available as for the Box tool, the Polygon tool is used in a very different way. Here's how it works:

1. Select the Polygon icon from the Tool Box; then select a border/fill option, drawing colors, and a border width, as described earlier.
2. Position the mouse cursor (cross hairs) at one of the polygon's vertices, drag the cursor to form the first side, and release the mouse button.
3. To construct the rest of the sides, except the last, click the

mouse on each successive vertex. As you do, the side joining the previous vertex to the new one will be displayed.

4. To construct the last side of the polygon (the one that encloses the figure), double-click the mouse on the last vertex. It will automatically be joined to the first vertex by a straight line.

If you want to construct a side that is horizontal, vertical, or inclined at a 45° angle, hold down the Shift key while dragging or clicking.

The Paint Can Tool All the tools we have discussed so far draw objects on the screen. The **Paint Can** does not; it fills an existing enclosed figure with color or changes the color of a previously filled region. To use this tool:

1. Select the Paint Can icon from the Tool Box.
2. In the Color Box, set either the foreground or background color to the desired color.
3. Position the mouse cursor (a tiny paint can) anywhere within the figure to be colored. For small regions, make sure the tip of the "pouring paint" is inside the region.
4. Click a mouse button to color the region. If you click the left mouse button, the figure will be filled with the foreground color; if you click the right mouse button, the background color will be used.

Graphics programs like Paint are not usually used for precision work, such as technical drawing. Nevertheless, Paint supplies a very useful tool for aligning and correctly sizing objects. The Status bar at the bottom of the Paint window constantly displays *cursor coordinates*, (shown on the left in the figure below), which give the precise location of the mouse cursor relative to the upper-left corner of the drawing area. For example, the coordinates shown here indicate that the cursor is 284 pixels from the left border of the drawing area and 161 pixels down from the top border. (The use of cursor coordinates is demonstrated in the Tutorial at the end of this section.)

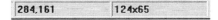

A second set of coordinates is displayed on the Status bar when you are creating a box, rounded box, ellipse/circle, or polygon. They give the width and height of the object being drawn. For example, in the figure above, the current width of the object is 124 pixels and its current height is 65 pixels.

Inserting Text into a Graphic

Although a graphic can often convey a thought without any explanatory text, it sometimes needs a few words to clarify the message. Through the use of the **Text** tool, Paint allows you to place text in a graphic in your choice of color, design, style, and size. To use this tool to insert text:

1. Select the Text icon from the Tool Box.
2. Select a foreground color from the Color Box (by clicking on it) for the color of the text to be inserted. (You should also select a background color from the Color Box if you want the new text displayed on a colored background.)
3. Drag the mouse cursor (cross hairs) to form a box in the drawing area within which you will place the text. Don't be overly concerned about sizing this window to fit the given text; its size (and position) can be adjusted later.
4. Release the mouse button. After a few moments, the Fonts window (which is usually referred to as the *Text Toolbar*) will open somewhere on the screen. (If it doesn't, choose the Text Toolbar item from the View menu.)

The text frame you have created will sprout eight "sizing handles" and an insertion point will appear in its upper-left corner.

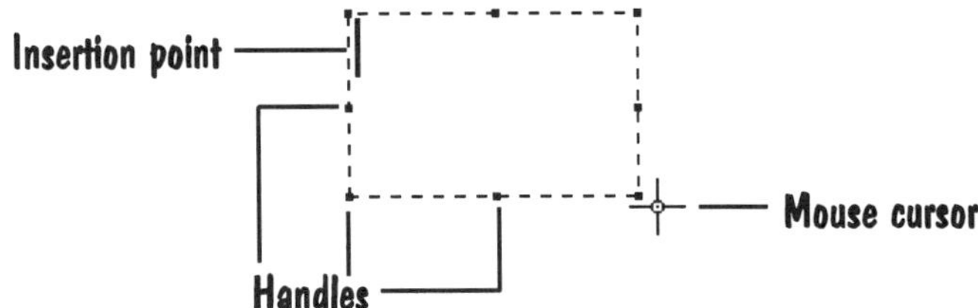

5. Using the Text Toolbar (Fonts window):
   - Select a *typeface* for the text from the first drop-down list. The typeface determines the overall design or "look" of the characters. (The typeface selected in the figure of step 4 is *Arial*.)

- Select a *font size* for the text from the second drop-down list. The font size is (roughly) the height the characters will be on the printed page, measured in *points*, where 72 points equal one inch.
- Select *attributes* for the text (if you want) by clicking on one or more of the buttons. Here are examples of the resulting effects:

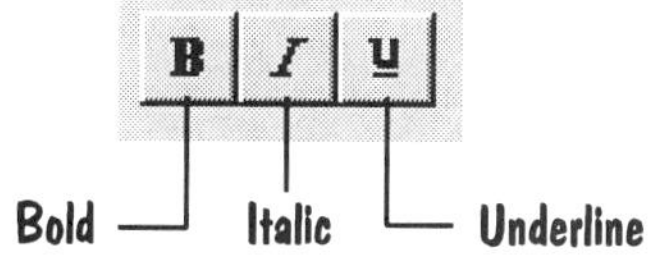

Bold *Italic* <u>Underline</u>

6. From the Options Box, select either *opaque* mode, the top option, or *transparent* mode, which is the one selected in the figure at the right. (As an alternative, you can toggle between these modes by choosing the Draw Opaque command from the Image menu.)

   - If you use opaque mode, the text you type will appear within a frame that is colored in the background color, as shown at the right.

   Text in a frame

   - In transparent mode, the text is displayed without the colored frame.
7. Click inside the text frame and type the desired text. When the text reaches the right frame border, it will wrap to the next line. (The text box will extend, if necessary, in the vertical direction to accommodate the text you are typing.) You can start a new line manually by pressing the Enter key.
8. To complete the text-insertion operation (to "paste down" the text), click anywhere outside the text frame.

Until you paste the text in place (that is, while the frame outline is still visible), it is possible to make changes to the text and its background. You can:

- Modify the text as you would in WordPad (see Section 2.2).
- Change the frame mode — select transparent or opaque.
- Change the color of the text or its background (if any).
- Move the text frame (and enclosed text) by positioning the mouse pointer over any part of the border that is not a handle and dragging the frame to its new location.
- Increase the size of the text frame by dragging one of its han-

dles in the desired direction. For example, to widen the box, drag the middle handle on the right side of the frame to the right. When you release the mouse button, the text will rearrange itself within the new frame (see below).

After the text-insertion operation is complete, the text (and its background, if applicable) becomes a single object in the graphic. At this point, the block of text can be moved (as described in Section 8.4), but none of the other operations listed above can be carried out.

TUTORIAL

Try the following exercise on your own, creating a drawing of the truck shown in Figure 8. Remember: To start over while creating an object, press the Escape key; to undo the last change to the graphic, press Ctrl+Z.

1. Start Windows 98 (if necessary) by turning on the computer.
2. Start Paint by selecting it from the Accessories submenu of the Start button, and maximize its window.
3. Draw the road:

- Select the Line tool from the Tool Box (see Figure 2) by clicking on it and select the second smallest line thickness in the Options Box (see Figure 1) by clicking on it.
- Position the Line cursor in the drawing area about one inch from the lower-left corner, hold down the Shift key (for a horizontal line), and drag the cursor to the right side of the drawing area.

- Select the Airbrush tool from the Tool Box, and select a medium thickness from the Options Box.
- Position the Airbrush cursor just under the left edge of the line you've just drawn and drag the cursor slowly across the screen under this line.

4. Draw the truck tires:

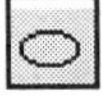

- Select the Ellipse/Circle tool from the Tool Box and the hollow (top) option from the Options Box.
- Draw the rear tire by positioning the cursor about one inch above the road, holding down the Shift key (for a circle), and dragging the cursor down and to the right until the circle touches the road.

Figure 8 Truck Graphic for Tutorial 8.2

- Use the cursor coordinates on the Status bar to help create a front tire of exactly the same size: Position the cursor at the top of the rear tire and note the second cursor coordinate. Then, for the front tire, position the cursor so that its second coordinate has this value, hold down the Shift key, and drag a circle until it touches the road.

5. Draw the truck's trailer:

- Select the Box tool from the Tool Box and the "filled box with border" option (the middle one) from the Options Box.
- Select a foreground of black (by clicking on this color in the Color Box) and a background of light gray (by *right*-clicking on this color in the Color Box).
- Start near the rear wheel and drag a box that makes a rectangle about 2" high and 4" long.

6. Draw the lower (shaded) part of the cab of the truck:

- Select a background color of white from the Color Box.
- Select the Polygon tool from the Tool Box and the "hollow" option from the Options Box.
- Hold down the Shift key (for horizontal, vertical, and diagonal lines) and drag the Polygon cursor from corner to corner of the polygon that makes up the lower cab. At each corner, click the mouse to end the previous line segment before dragging the next one. Double-click on the last corner to close the polygon.

- Fill the polygon with color: Select a foreground color of dark gray from the Color Box, select the Paint Can tool, and click inside your polygon.

- Select a foreground color of black, select the Line tool, hold down the Shift key, and draw the vertical line for the door.

7. Continuing to use the Line tool, draw the four lines that make up the window area of the cab.
8. Insert the text (Sam's Delivery Service) on the truck's trailer using 24-point, boldface type:

   - Select the Text tool from the Tool Box.
   - Drag the cursor to form a box (a text frame) just within the trailer rectangle. When you release the mouse button, the Fonts window will appear.
   - In the Fonts window, select Arial from the first drop-down list, "24" from the second, and click on the Bold button.
   - Click within the text frame and type *Sam's*, *Delivery*, and *Service*, pressing the Enter key after each of the first two words. (If the text doesn't fit, select a smaller font size from the Fonts window.) Now, center each word on the trailer by inserting spaces (using the Spacebar) before that word.
   - Click outside the text frame to complete the operation.
9. Save and/or print this "document", just as you would in WordPad, and exit Paint.

8.3 Editing a Graphic

At some point in the process of creating a graphic, you will probably want to *edit* it — to alter the graphic to correct mistakes or improve its looks. We have already described one way to edit a graphic: You can use the Undo command on the Edit menu to undo the last operation you have carried out. This section discusses other, more specialized editing features of Paint.

Erasing Mistakes

The **Eraser** is the editing tool you're likely to utilize the most. It is used in the same general way as an ordinary eraser, but the Eraser tool is much more powerful:

Basic operation of the Eraser tool

- If you left-drag the Eraser's cursor, it wipes out everything in its path; if you right-drag the cursor, it removes only the current foreground color.
- The area that is erased is replaced with the current background color, which need not be the color of the graphic's background.

More specifically, here's how to use this tool:

1. Select the Eraser tool from the Tool Box by clicking on its icon.
2. Select an eraser size from the Options Box (shown at the right) by clicking on it. The smaller sizes are best for fine work; the larger ones are best at erasing large areas.
3. Set the background color as desired by right-clicking on the corresponding square in the Color Box. (This color will replace the ones erased.)
4. If you only want to erase one specific color, set the foreground to this color by left-clicking on the corresponding square in the Color Box.
5. Position the mouse cursor (a small square) where you want to begin erasing, and drag it across the area to be erased. Remember:
   - Left-dragging the cursor replaces everything in its path with the current background color.
   - Right-dragging the cursor replaces only the current foreground color with the current background color.

An example Figure 9 shows the two ways the Eraser tool can be used. In both erasures, the background color was set to white and the foreground color was set to black. The left erasure was accomplished with a left-drag; it replaces everything with white. The right erasure is the result of a right-drag; only black is replaced with white.

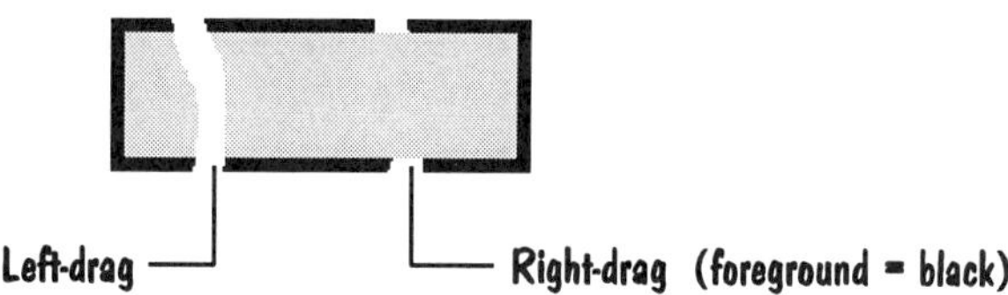

Figure 9 Using the Eraser Tool

Zooming In on the Graphic

At times, you may want to change small details in a graphic. For these occasions, Paint supplies the Zoom command, which allows you to magnify a small part of the graphic so that it fills the Paint window. Once the graphic is suitably enlarged, you can even edit it pixel by pixel. (Recall that *pixels* are the small dots of light that make up the screen image.)

To zoom in on a graphic, point at the Zoom command on the View menu. The resulting submenu has five options. Choosing:

Zoom menu options

- *Normal Size* returns the graphic to its original size if it currently magnified.
- *Large Size* magnifies the image by a factor of four (400 percent). When you choose Large Size, scroll bars may appear in the Paint window so that you can view the entire image. Figure 10b shows the result of applying the Large Size command to the graphic in Figure 10a and then scrolling to display the dog's nose.
- *Custom* opens the following dialog box:

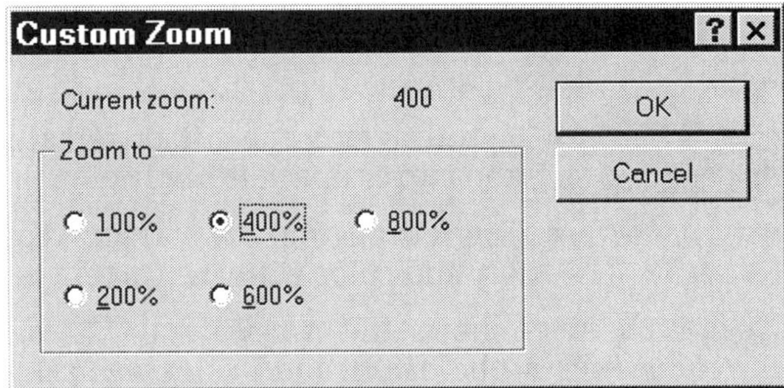

By selecting the appropriate option button and choosing the OK command button, you can magnify the original graphic one, two, four, six, or eight times. (Figure 11a shows the original dog graphic enlarged 600 percent.)

Figure 10a "Normal" Zoom Size

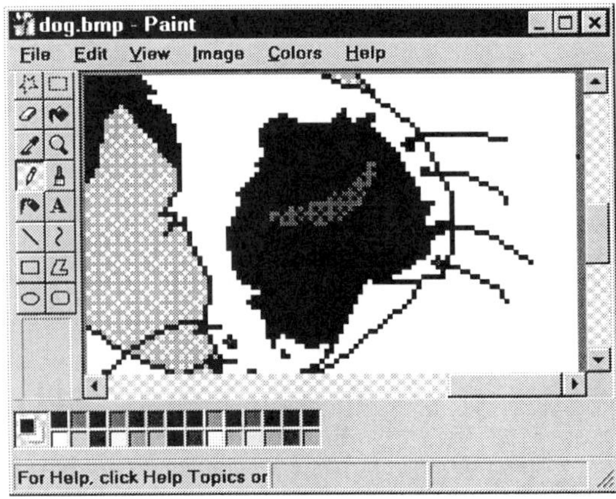

Figure 10b "Large" Zoom Size

- *Show Grid* is a toggle that turns the pixel grid on or off (Figure 11b shows the grid displayed). By magnifying to a relatively large size (600% or 800%) and turning on the grid, you can edit the graphic pixel by pixel, obtaining the finest detail possible.
- *Show Thumbnail* is also a toggle; it turns the Thumbnail window on and off. Displaying this window gives you an overall view of the normal-sized graphic as you work on the close-up. The Thumbnail window can be moved around the screen and resized, if so desired.

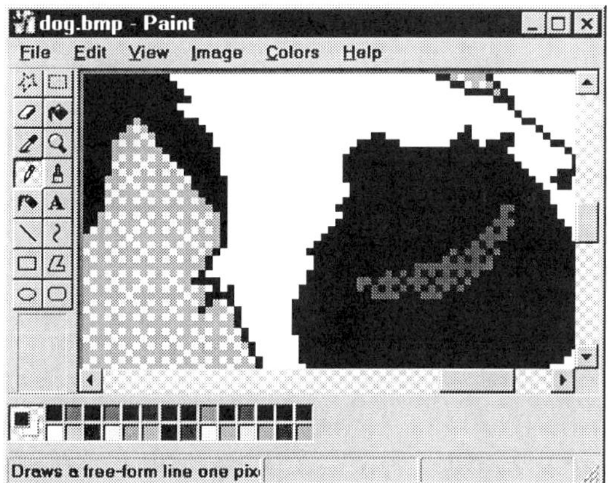

Figure 11a Custom Zoom — 600%

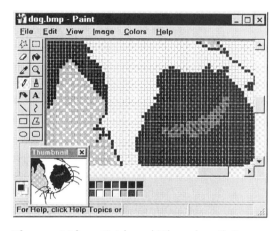

Figure 11b Grid and Thumbnail On

Here is an easy way to edit individual pixels in a graphic:

1. Use the Custom option on the Zoom menu to magnify the image to 600 or 800 percent.
2. Scroll to the part of the image you wish to edit.
3. Select the Pencil tool from the Tool Box.
4. In the Color Box, set the foreground color to the color you want to paint in, set the background color to that of the background area in which you are working.
5. Using the Pencil cursor as a pointer, left-click in any grid square that you want to add to the graphic, and right-click in a grid square if you want to erase it from the graphic.

To edit larger areas, involving a relatively large number of pixels, you may want to use other tools, such as the Brush, Eraser, or Paint Can.

Magnifier tool

The **Magnifier** tool provides another way to zoom in on your graphic. It is a little easier to use, but not as versatile as the Zoom command. To use this tool:

1. Click on the Magnifier icon in the Tool Box.
2. You now have two choices. Either
   - Click on the desired magnification factor in the Options Box (shown at the right). Notice that you can magnify the image two, six, or eight times (but not four times, as with the Zoom command).

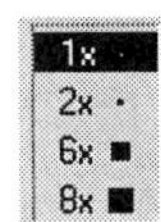

   or

   - Move the mouse cursor into the drawing area. A box containing a magnifying glass icon will appear. Position the box around the part of the graphic you wish to magnify and click the mouse button. (The size of the box and the degree of magnification depend on the last option button selected in the Custom Zoom dialog box.)

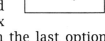

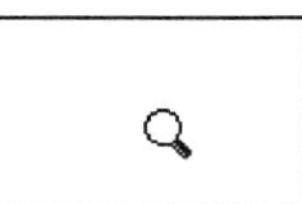

Selecting Part of a Graphic

One of the major advantages of Paint over conventional drawing is its ability to move, copy, and resize any object in the graphic. Before performing one of these operations, you must select the object to be manipulated; in Paint parlance, you must "define a cutout". A **cutout** is a region in the graphic that has been selected using one of Paint's two selection tools:

- The **Rectangular Selection** tool is the easier of the two to use, but it is less versatile. This tool is used when you can place a rectangular box around the object to be selected without including part of another object (see Figure 12a).
- The **Free-form Selection** tool is generally used in situations for

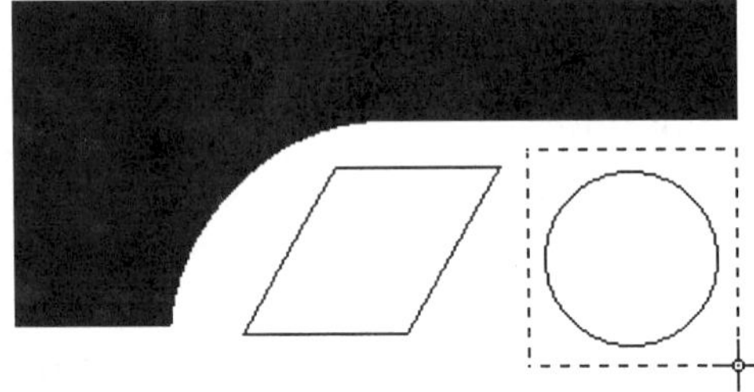

Figure 12a Rectangular Selection

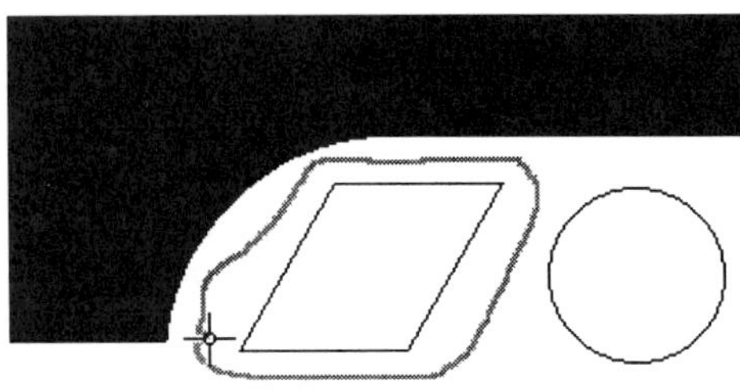

Figure 12b Free-form Selection

which rectangular selection doesn't work; free-form selection creates an irregularly shaped cutout (Figure 12b).

Rectangular selection

To use the Rectangular Selection tool:

1. Select its icon from the Tool Box.
2. From the Options Box, select either *opaque* mode, the top option, or *transparent* mode, which is the one selected in the figure at the right. (As an alternative, you can toggle between these modes by choosing the Draw Opaque command from the Image menu.)

   - If you use opaque mode, the resulting selection will consist of everything within the selected region, both foreground and background colors.
   - In transparent mode, the resulting selection does not include anything colored in the background color. This is the mode that is normally used with cutouts.

   We will provide examples of the two selection modes in Section 8.4, while discussing how cutouts are moved and copied.
3. Position the mouse cursor (cross hairs) at one corner of the cutout, the region that contains the object(s) to be selected.
4. Press the mouse button and drag the cursor to the opposite corner of the cutout. As you drag, a box will move with the cursor, indicating the selected region (see Figure 12a).
5. When the cutout appears as you want, release the mouse button. A "dashed" rectangular box delineates the selected region.

Free-form selection

To use the Free-form Selection tool:

1. Select its icon from the Tool Box.
2. From the Options Box, select either *opaque* mode, the top option, or *transparent* mode, which is the one selected in the figure at the right. (See the description of the two modes under "rectangular selection".) The transparent mode is usually used with free-form selection.

3. Position the mouse cursor in the drawing area where you want to start the cutout, the region that contains the object(s) to be manipulated.
4. Press the mouse button and drag the cursor, creating a free-form curve that defines the cutout (see Figure 12b).
5. Release the mouse button. A "dashed" rectangular box, like the one in rectangular selection, delineates the selected region.

NOTE

Whether you use rectangular or free-form selection:

- To abort the selection process while you are dragging the cursor to define the cutout, press the Escape key.
- To deselect the selected object, which causes the selection box to disappear, click anywhere outside the box.

Deleting a cutout

Here's a simple example of how cutouts are used. Suppose you want to delete an object from a graphic; say, the circle in Figure 12a. Usually the easiest way to do this is to select the circle (that is, define a cutout that includes the circle), as in Figure 12a, and then press the Delete key. The cutout and the object it contains will be replaced by the current background color, so be sure that this color is set properly before pressing the Delete key.

We will discuss many other ways in which cutouts can be manipulated in Section 8.4.

TUTORIAL

Try the following exercise on your own.

1. Start Windows 98 (if necessary) by turning on the computer.
2. Start Paint, maximize its window, and insert the Student Disk in its drive.
3. Open the Truck-2 bitmap image on this disk.
4. Use the Zoom submenu of the View menu to:
   - Choose the Large Size command.
   - Turn off (if necessary) the Show Grid option.
   - Turn on (if necessary) the Show Thumbnail option.
5. Scroll the Paint window so that the front of the truck is visible.
6. Modify the slanted part of the hood, as follows:
   - Erase the slanted line: Select the Eraser tool from the Tool Box, select the smallest size in the Options Box, set the background color to white, and drag the cursor over the line.

   - Using the Curve tool with the second thinnest line option, put a curved line in its place. (See Section 8.2.)
   - Turn on the Show Grid command on the Zoom submenu of the View menu.
   - Fill in the modified area with color: Set the foreground color to dark gray (top row, second from the left), select the Brush tool from the Tool Box and a medium brush tip from the

Options Box, and drag the cursor over the appropriate white squares in the grid to turn them gray.

7. Return the magnification to normal size: Select the Magnifier tool from the Tool Box and click on "1x" in the Options Box. (You can also do this by choosing Normal Size from the Zoom submenu of the View menu.)

8. Delete the word *Sam's* from the side of the truck:
   - Set the background color to light gray.
   - Select the Rectangular Selection tool from the Tool Box.
   - Use the mouse to drag a box around the word to be deleted and then release the mouse button.
   - Press the Delete key.
9. Exit Paint, responding No to the "save changes?" message.

8.4 Manipulating Cutouts

Once you have *defined a cutout* — selected an area in the graphic — using either the Free-form or Rectangular Selection tool (as described in Section 8.3) you can:

- Delete the cutout.
- Cut or copy the cutout to the Clipboard.
- Save the cutout in a graphic file on disk.
- Move, copy, or sweep the cutout to another part of the graphic.
- Resize the cutout.
- Flip, rotate, stretch, or tilt the cutout.

In this section, we will describe how to perform these operations.

Basic Operations on Cutouts

Deleting a cutout As we mentioned in Section 8.3, a convenient way to remove objects from your graphic is to select them (using one of the selection tools), defining a cutout, and then delete the cutout. To delete a cutout, perform any of the following actions:

- Press the Delete key.

- Choose the Clear Selection command from the Edit menu.
- Right-click inside the cutout and choose the Clear Selection command from the resulting pop-up menu.

When you "delete" a cutout, you actually replace it with the current background color, as indicated in the Color Box. Unless you're trying for some special effect, you'll want to make sure that the current background color matches the color behind the cutout. If you forget this fact, you may wonder why the rectangular cutout you just deleted was replaced by, say, a red box on the screen.

Cut, copy, and paste

A cutout, like any other selected information, can be cut or copied to the Clipboard, and then pasted into Paint or another Windows application (see Section 2.3). Recall that when information is *cut* to the Clipboard, it is deleted from the current document, but when it is *copied* to the Clipboard, the current document remains unchanged. Here's how these procedures work in Paint.

- To *cut* a cutout to the Clipboard, choose the Cut command from the Edit menu or right-click inside the cutout and choose the Cut command from the pop-up menu. The cutout will be deleted from the current graphic (and replaced by the current background color).
- To *copy* a cutout to the Clipboard, choose the Copy command from the Edit menu or the right-click pop-up menu.
- To *paste* a cutout from the Clipboard into your Paint graphic, choose the Paste command from the Edit menu or the right-click pop-up menu. The cutout is pasted into the upper-left corner of the drawing area and remains *active*, as indicated by the selection box enclosing it. An active cutout can continue to be manipulated; in particular, it can be moved (as described shortly) to another location in the drawing area.

Once it is selected, a cutout remains active, outlined by the selection box, until it is *pasted down* (anchored in place). To paste down a cutout, perform any of the following actions:

- Click the mouse outside the cutout.
- Define (select) a new cutout.
- Select any tool from the Tool Box.

When a cutout is anchored in place, its selection box disappears.

Saving and retrieving a cutout

Paint allows you to save a cutout as a separate file on disk. It can then be opened at a later time as a graphic of its own or as part of another graphic. In this way, you can create a *library* of graphic components. For example, if you frequently draw pictures of houses, you can create and save types of windows, doors, and other "house components" for use in all your drawings.

To save the active cutout to disk:

1. Choose the Copy To command from the Edit menu or right-click inside the cutout and choose the Copy To command from the pop-up menu. The Copy To dialog box, which is virtually identical to the Save As dialog box (Section 2.2), is displayed.
2. Proceed as you would to save any file to disk.

If you want to *retrieve* a graphic that is stored on disk and place it in your current drawing, you must use the Paste From command. If you use the Open command, the new graphic *replaces* the current one in the drawing area. To insert a graphic file into the current drawing:

1. Choose the Paste From command from the Edit menu. The Paste From dialog box, which is virtually identical to the Open dialog box (Section 2.2), is displayed.
2. Proceed as you would to open any file stored on disk.

The retrieved graphic will be pasted, as an active cutout, into the upper-left corner of the current graphic. You can then move it anywhere in the drawing area, as we will now demonstrate.

Moving, Copying, and Sweeping a Cutout

There are three kinds of operations that *transfer* a cutout from one location in the drawing area to another:

Move

- When you *move* a cutout, it is transferred to the new location and deleted from the original one. (The region occupied by the original cutout takes on the current background color.) To move an active cutout, position the cursor inside the selection box (it will become a four-headed arrow), press the mouse button, drag the cutout to the new location, and release the mouse button.

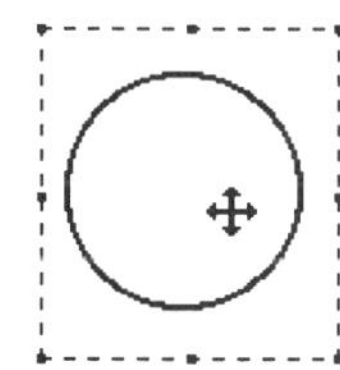

Copy

- To *copy* the active cutout, transferring it to a new location without deleting it from the original one, follow the *move* procedure, but hold down the Ctrl key as you drag the cutout.

Sweep

- To *sweep* the active cutout, transferring it to a new location and leaving a series of copies in its path, follow the *move* procedure but hold down the Shift key as you drag the cutout. The result of sweeping a square (with a black border and gray interior) from one location to another is shown below.

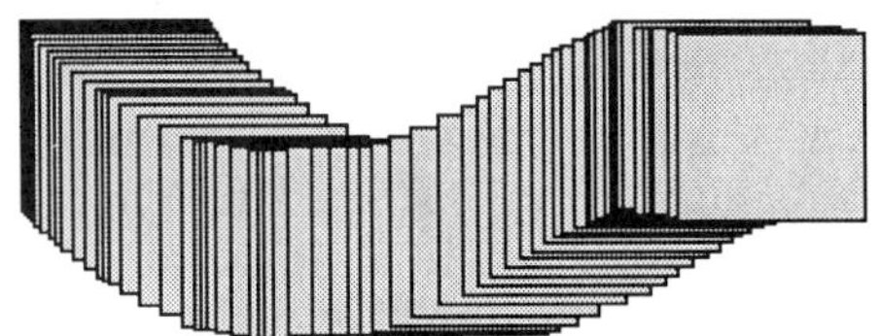

Opaque vs. transparent transfers

When you perform a transfer operation (move, copy, or sweep), the image of the cutout may obscure whatever is beneath it. This is called an *opaque* transfer. When the part of the graphic lying beneath the copy shows through, we call it a *transparent* transfer. Figure 13 illustrates the difference between the two types of transfers. The original figures (circles) are shown on the left. They were selected with the Rectangular Selection tool and copied over the picture of the car on the right. In Figure 13a, the copy is opaque — the copied cutout obscures the car; in Figure 13b, the copy is transparent — the car shows through the copied circle.

a. **Opaque Copying** b. **Transparent Copying**

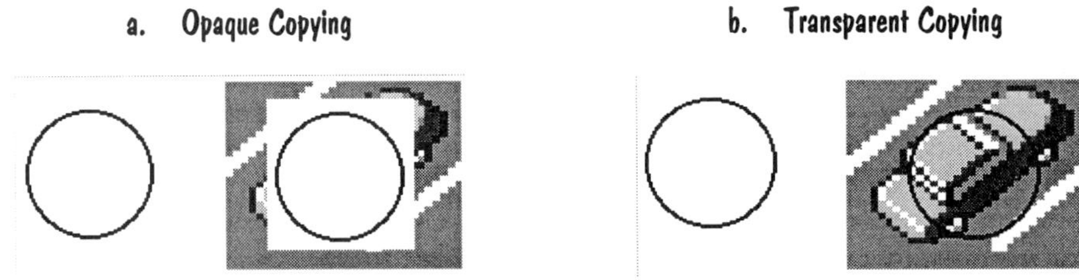

Figure 13 Opaque versus Transparent Transfer

Selecting transparent or opaque mode

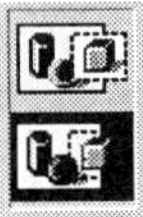

To transfer a cutout opaquely, select the top option from the Options Box before moving, copying, or sweeping the cutout. To transfer a cutout transparently, select the bottom option. Alternatively, you can turn on opaque mode by selecting (placing a check mark on) the Draw Opaque item on the Image menu; to turn on transparent mode, deselect Draw Opaque.

Resizing a Cutout

To change the size of a cutout (and all of the objects contained within it):

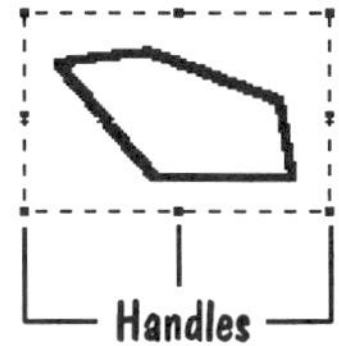

1. Position the mouse pointer over one of the eight *handles*. The pointer will become a two-headed arrow when positioned properly (Figure 14a).
   - Use the middle handle on the top or bottom side to change the height of the cutout without changing its width.
   - Use the middle handle on the left or right side to change the width of the cutout without changing its height.
   - Use a corner handle to change both height and width at the same time.
2. Drag the handle away from the selection box to increase the size of the cutout, or drag it inside the box to decrease its size. An outline of the selection box will move with the cursor to show you the resulting effect (Figure 14b).
3. When the selection box is the desired size, release the mouse button. The cutout will be redrawn in the new size, as shown in Figure 14c. (To abort the process, press the Escape key before releasing the mouse button.)

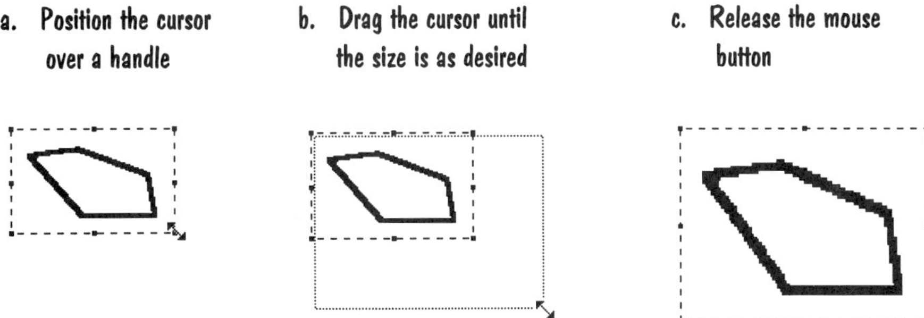

a. Position the cursor over a handle
b. Drag the cursor until the size is as desired
c. Release the mouse button

Figure 14 Resizing a Cutout

When the cutout is resized, the original selection box may take on the current background color, so select an appropriate background color from the Color Box before starting the process.

When the cutout is made larger and opaque mode is in effect, part of the existing graphic may be obscured. If you don't want this to happen, be sure that transparent mode (the bottom option) is selected in the Options Box before beginning the process.

Other Operations on Cutouts

Paint provides several other ways to manipulate cutouts, all of which are accessible from the Image menu (as well as from the right-click pop-up menu).

Flips and Rotations You can *flip* an active cutout from left to right (a *horizontal flip*) or from top to bottom (a *vertical flip*). Here is an example of each type of flip; in an actual graphic, the triangle on the right would *replace* the one on the left.

Flipping a cutout

To flip an active cutout:

1. Choose the Flip/Rotate command from either the Image menu or the menu that pops up when you right-click inside the cutout. The Flip and Rotate dialog box, shown in Figure 15, will be displayed.

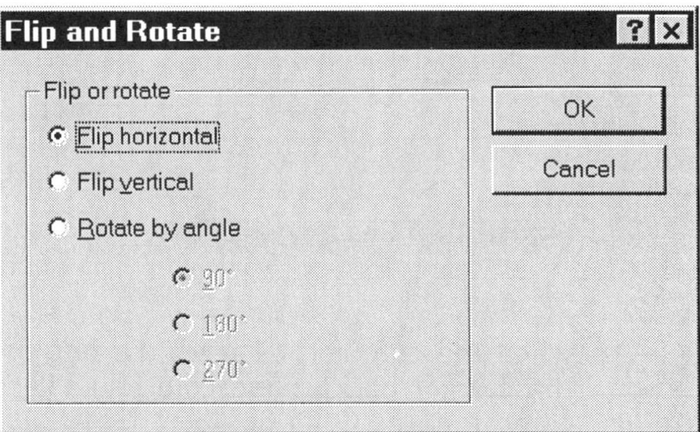

Figure 15 The Flip and Rotate Dialog Box

2. Select the *Flip horizontal* or *Flip vertical* option button, as appropriate.
3. Choose the OK command button.

Rotating a cutout

Paint provides the ability to *rotate* a cutout a quarter turn (90°), a half turn (180°), or a three-quarter turn (270°). Here's an example (as with a flip, the rotated cutout replaces the original):

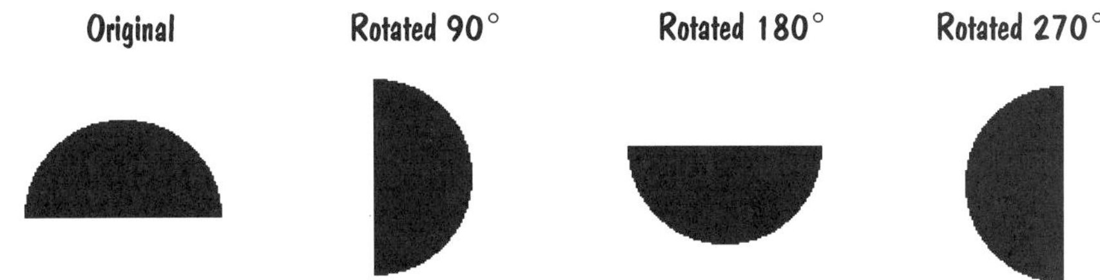

To rotate a cutout:

1. Choose the Flip/Rotate command from either the Image menu or the menu that pops up when you right-click inside the cutout. The Flip and Rotate dialog box, (see Figure 15) will be displayed.
2. Select the *Rotate by angle* option button and then select the option button that gives you the desired amount of rotation. (The rotation takes place in a clockwise direction.)
3. Choose the OK command button.

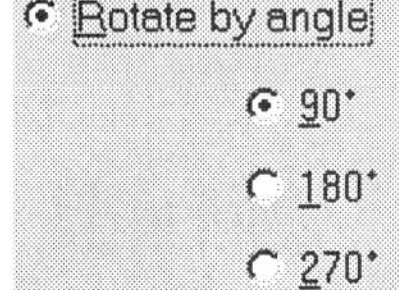

Stretching or Skewing a Cutout *Stretching* a cutout changes its size in either the horizontal or vertical direction. For example, stretching a circle creates an elliptical shape, as shown below:

Stretching a circle

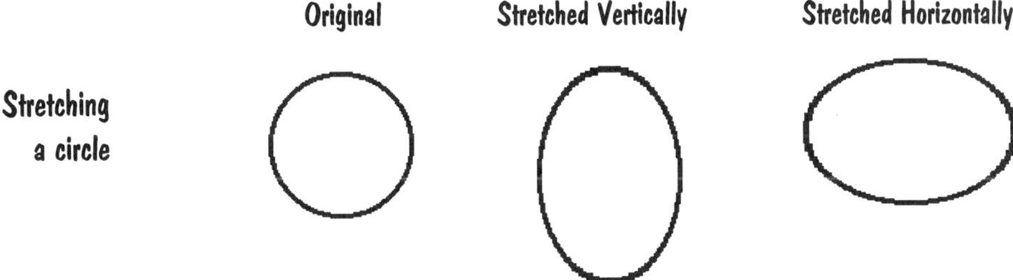

Skewing a cutout tilts it in a horizontal or vertical direction. For example, skewing a square creates a parallelogram, as shown in the figure below:

Skewing a square

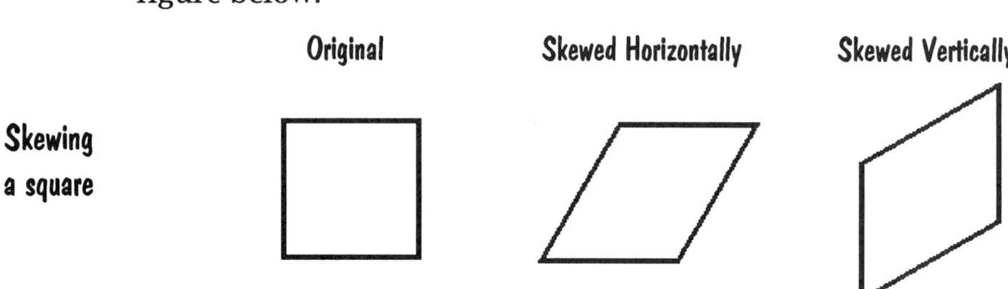

To stretch and/or skew an active cutout:

1. Choose the Stretch/Skew command from either the Image menu or the menu that pops up when you right-click inside the cutout. The dialog box shown in Figure 16 will open.

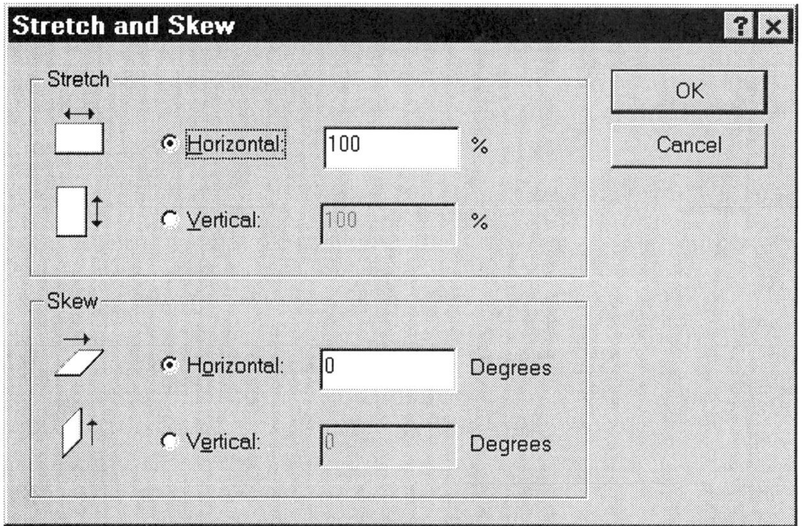

Figure 16 The Stretch and Skew Dialog Box

2. If you want to stretch the cutout, select the Horizontal or Vertical option button in this part of the dialog box and enter a percentage in the corresponding text box. For example, entering "200" in the Horizontal text box will double the cutout's size in that direction; entering "25" will reduce its size by a factor of four. (The circle on the previous page was stretched 150%.)

3. If you want to skew the cutout, select the Horizontal or Vertical option button in this part of the dialog box and enter a number of degrees in the corresponding text box. (You may have to experiment here to get the desired effect.) For example, the square on the previous page was skewed 30°.
4. Choose the OK command button to complete the process.

You can issue the Flip/Rotate and Stretch/Skew commands even if no cutout is active. In this case, the operation applies to the entire graphic!

TUTORIAL

Try the following exercise on your own, creating a drawing of the factory shown in Figure 17.

1. Start Windows 98 (if necessary) by turning on the computer.
2. Set the line width by selecting the Line tool from the Tool Box and, in the Options Box, selecting the second option from the top.
3. Draw the factory building at the bottom of the drawing area: Use the Box tool and the "hollow" (top) option in the Options Box.

Figure 17 Graphic for Tutorial 8.4

4. Draw the smokestack with the Box tool, using the "borderless" (bottom) option and dragging with the *right* mouse button so that the smokestack is colored black.
5. Draw the rightmost window: Use the Box tool with the hollow option for the outside and the Line tool for the crosspieces. (Hold down the Shift key to get the horizontal and vertical lines.)
6. Create the middle window:
   - Select the existing window using the Rectangular Selection tool, position the mouse cursor inside the resulting cutout, hold down the Ctrl key, and drag the cutout's outline to the left of the existing window.
   - Reduce the size of the copy by dragging one of the corner handles toward the center of the new window until it is the proper size; then release the mouse button.
   - Move the new, smaller window into position by placing the mouse cursor inside the cutout and (without holding down Ctrl), dragging it to the proper place.
7. Create the triangular piece above the middle window (the one that was just created) using the Line tool.
8. Copy the middle window and place it to the left of the original (see step 6).
9. With the leftmost window still selected, flip it horizontally so that it faces in the proper direction: Choose the Flip/Rotate command from the Image menu, select the Flip horizontal option button in the resulting dialog box, and choose the OK command button.
10. Select a light gray foreground color and paint the building this color: Choose the Paint Can tool and click on a part of the building that is not a window.
11. Draw the smoke — use the Airbrush tool, with a medium brush width selected from the Options Box.
12. Close Paint, saving the graphic if you want.

8.5 Other Features of Paint

In the first four sections of this chapter, we have discussed how to use the Paint application to create and edit a graphic. In this section, we will introduce a few additional features of Paint. These include:

- Setting page orientation and margins.
- Previewing the way the graphic will look on the printed page.
- Changing image attributes, such as the size of the drawing area.
- Using Paint to create Desktop wallpaper.

Setting Up the Page

Before printing a graphic, you should specify the size of the paper to be used, its orientation, and margins. To select these settings, first choose the Page Setup command from the File menu to open the Page Setup dialog box (Figure 18). Then:

Paper size

- You can specify the size of the paper on which you will be printing by selecting a size from the Paper Size drop-down list.

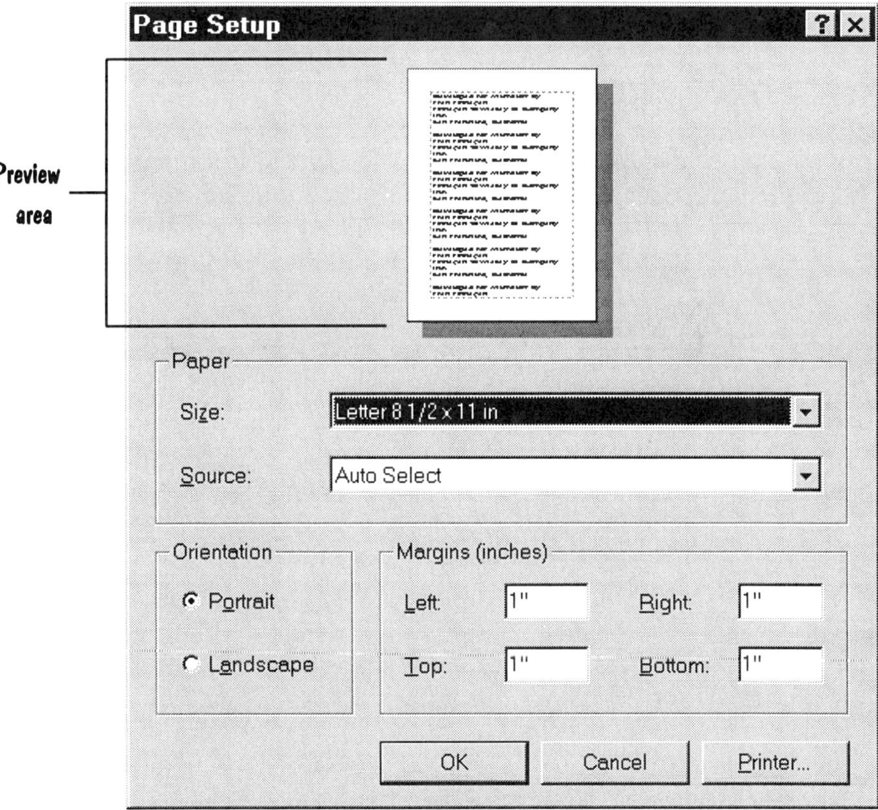

Figure 19 The Page Setup Dialog Box

Margins

- You can specify the top, bottom, left, and right page margins by entering the appropriate numbers in the Margins text boxes. The margin settings determine the size of the blank border around the graphic. For example, by increasing the top and left margins, you can "push" the graphic down and to the right.

Orientation

- You can specify the paper's orientation, either *portrait* or *landscape*, by selecting the corresponding option button. In **portrait** orientation, the graphic is viewed holding the page so that the long side is vertical; in **landscape** orientation, the graphic is viewed with the long side horizontal. The figures at the right further illustrate this concept.

Portrait
Portrait
Portrait
Portrait

Landscape
Landscape
Landscape

When you change a setting, the sample page in the preview area will also change to indicate the effect of the new setting. After you have entered all the needed information, choose the OK button to put the changes into effect.

Print Preview

If you would like to see how the graphic will appear on the printed page before it is actually printed, choose the Print Preview command from the File menu. The **print preview** window will open (Figure 19), not only displaying the graphic as it appears in the drawing area, but also taking into account paper size, orientation, and margins. For example, the graphic in Figure 19 was positioned in the upper-left corner of the drawing area and the page settings were 8½" × 11" paper size, landscape orientation, and margins of 2" left and right, 1" top and bottom.

Zooming in and out

Although you cannot edit the graphic while it is in the print preview window, you can magnify parts of it to see finer detail. In addition to the full-page view shown in Figure 19, there are two "zoom" modes. To *zoom in*, magnifying the graphic:

- Click on the part of the page that you would like to enlarge. (In the preview window, the mouse cursor takes the shape of a magnifying glass, as shown at the right.)

or

- Click on the Zoom In button (at the top of the window). Then, use the scroll bars to display the desired part of the page.

Clicking on the page or the Zoom In button again displays the second Zoom mode, increasing the magnification even more. At this point,

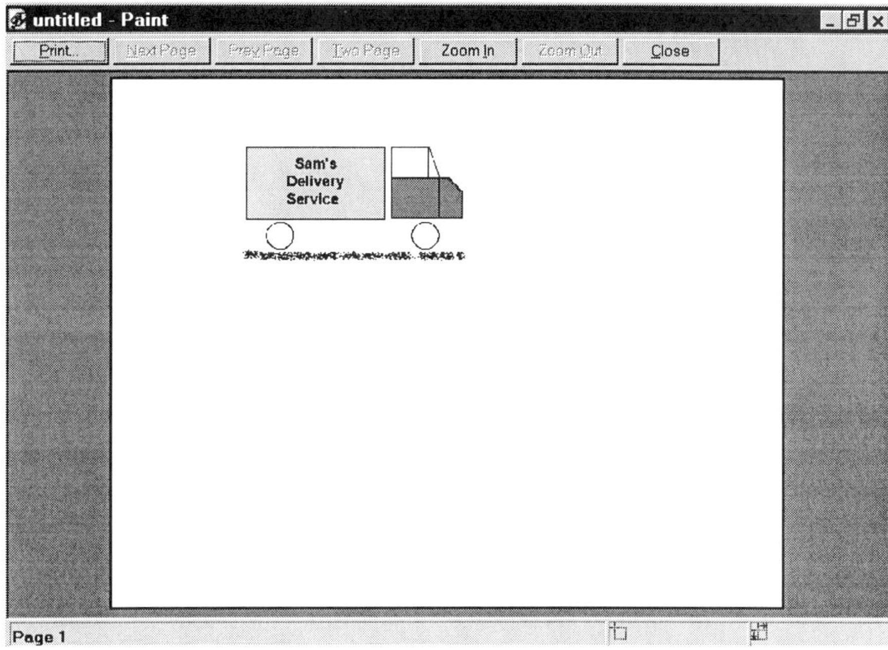

Figure 19 The Print Preview Window

the Zoom In button is dimmed, and clicking again on the page will return the display to the default magnification level. While in one of the two Zoom modes, clicking on the Zoom Out button changes the display to the next lower magnification level.

The relative magnification of the full-page view (on the left) and the two zoom modes is shown below:

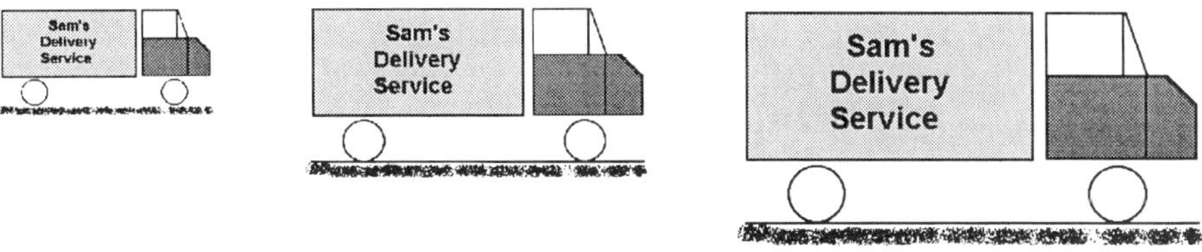

When you are done using the print preview window, either choose the Close button to return to the drawing window or choose the Print button to print the document.

Changing the Size of the Drawing Area

Paint uses a default drawing size that is 6.5" wide and 5" high (on the printed page). When you start Paint, however, the drawing area will be set to the same size it was when you last exited. To return to the default dimensions, or to change to another drawing size:

1. Choose the Attributes command from the Image menu. The dialog box pictured in Figure 20 will be displayed.

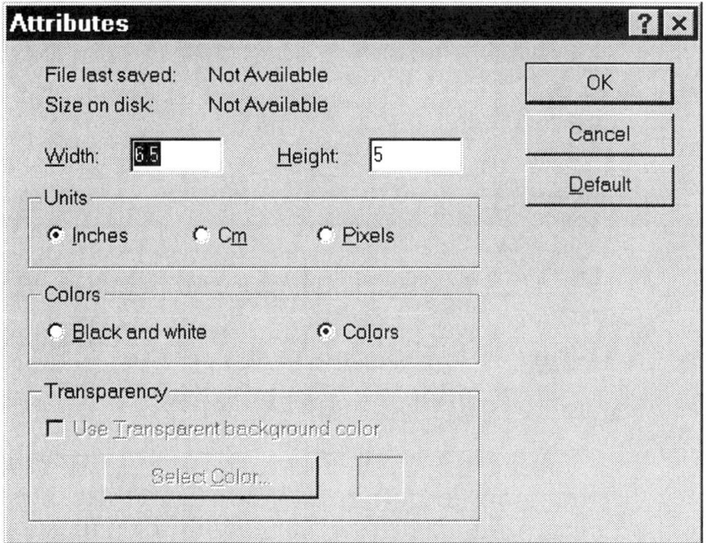

Figure 20 The Image Attributes Dialog Box

2. To return to the default drawing size, choose the Default command button.
3. To set another drawing size, enter the desired dimensions in the Width and Height text boxes. (The units of measurement for the drawing area are determined by which option button is currently selected.)
4. Choose the OK command button to close the dialog box and put the changes into effect.

If the specified dimensions are *larger* than the Paint window can accommodate, scroll bars will appear. (A larger drawing size uses more RAM and it takes more disk space to store the graphic.) If the specified dimensions are *smaller* than the Paint window, a rectangular box will be displayed in its upper-left corner marking off the new drawing area.

NOTE

As you can see, the Attributes dialog box also allows you to:

- Specify units of measurement — inches, centimeters (cm), or pixels — for the drawing size.
- Elect to use patterns of black and white for your palette, instead of colors. Here's how the Color Box will look if you select the *Black and white* option button and then choose the OK command button:

Be aware that if you switch to black and white while creating a graphic, all colors will be changed to patterns and you will not be able to restore its original colors!

Creating Wallpaper

Wallpaper is a graphic image that covers the Desktop. It acts as a background for the icons, windows, and other objects that occupy the Desktop during a typical Windows session. Although wallpaper is normally selected using Control Panel's Display utility (see Section 5.2), you can also specify that a Paint graphic be the current wallpaper. To do so:

1. Use Paint to create or open the graphic.
2. Save it to disk (if the latest version has not already been saved).
3. Choose one of the *Set as Wallpaper* commands from the File menu:
   - If you choose *Set as Wallpaper (Tiled)*, the graphic will be repeated as many times as necessary to cover the entire Desktop.
   - If you choose *Set as Wallpaper (Centered)*, a single copy of the graphic will be centered on the Desktop.

In order to see the new wallpaper, you may have to first minimize all windows. (See Section 5.2 for examples of tiled and centered wallpaper and more information about wallpaper, in general.)

NOTE

When you set a graphic as wallpaper, it not only becomes the current Desktop background, but its file name is also added to the list of wallpapers on the Background page of Control Panel's Display utility (see Section 5.2). Consequently, at any time in the future you can:

- Change this wallpaper to centered, tiled, or stretched.
- Reselect this wallpaper, if another one is currently in use.

Chapter Summary

The Basics of Paint	To start Paint	Choose the Paint item from the Accessories submenu of the Start menu's Programs option.
	To select a foreground color	Click on it in the Color Box.
	To select a background color	Right-click on it in the Color Box.
	To select a Paint tool	Click on its icon in the Tool Box.
	To zoom in on the graphic	Point at Zoom on the View menu and choose a magnification level; *or* use the Magnifier tool to magnify part or all of the graphic.
	To select a part of the graphic	Define a cutout with the Rectangular Selection or Free-form Selection tool.
Paint Tools	Free-form Selection	Defines a cutout by selecting a free-form region.
	Rectangular Selection	Defines a cutout by selecting a box-shaped region.
	Eraser	Erases part of the graphic.
	Paint Can	Fills an enclosed region with color.
	Eye Dropper	Establishes a color in the graphic as the current foreground or background color.
	Magnifier	Magnifies part or all of the graphic.
	Pencil	Draws a free-form figure using a one-pixel-thick curve.
	Brush	Draws a free-form figure using your choice of brush tip.

	Airbrush	Draws a free-form figure made up of a spray of dots.
	Text	Inserts text into the graphic in your choice of font.
	Line	Draws a straight line.
	Curve	Draws a smooth curve.
	Box	Draws a filled or unfilled rectangle.
	Polygon	Draws a filled or unfilled polygon.
	Ellipse/Circle	Draws a filled or unfilled circle or ellipse.
	Rounded Box	Draws a filled or unfilled rectangle with rounded corners.
Operations on Cutouts	To define a cutout	Use the Free-form Selection or Rectangular Selection tool.
	To delete a cutout	Press the Delete key; *or* choose Clear Selection from the Edit or right-click menu.
	To cut, copy, or paste a cutout on the Clipboard	Choose Cut, Copy, or Paste from the Edit or right-click menu.
	To save/retrieve a cutout on disk	Choose Copy To/Paste From from the Edit menu.
	To move/copy/sweep a cutout	Drag the cutout to a new location; hold down the Ctrl key to copy, the Shift key to sweep.
	To resize a cutout	Drag one of the cutout's handles.
	To flip or rotate a cutout	Choose Flip/Rotate from the Image or right-click menu.
	To stretch or skew a cutout	Choose Stretch/Skew from the Image or right-click menu.
Other Features of Paint	To set up the printed page	Choose Page Setup from the File menu; then specify paper size, orientation, and margins in the resulting dialog box.
	To preview the printed page	Choose Print Preview from the File menu.
	To change the size of the drawing area	Choose Attributes from the Image menu and enter a width and height in the resulting dialog box.

Review Exercises

Section 8.1

1. To select red as the foreground color in a Paint graphic, click the ____________ mouse button on that color in the Color Box.
2. To expand Paint's drawing area so that it fills the entire screen, choose the ____________ command from the View menu.
3. True or false: If you select a new background color from the Color Box after drawing a graphic, the background of that graphic will change to the new color.
4. True or false: Paint's Eye Dropper tool can be used to change both the foreground and background colors.
5. To select blue as the foreground color in Paint:

   a. Click the left mouse button on blue in the Color Box.
   b. Double-click the left mouse button on blue in the Color Box.
   c. Click the right mouse button on blue in the Color Box.
   d. Double-click the right mouse button on blue in the Color Box.
6. Which of the following tools is not found in Paint's Tool Box?

   a. Eraser
   b. Pencil
   c. Pen
   d. Brush

Section 8.2

7. To draw a horizontal line with Paint's Line tool, hold down the ____________ key while dragging the cursor.
8. When you use Paint's __________ tool, a spray of dots is produced.
9. When you use Paint's Box tool to create a hollow box (using the left mouse button), it is drawn in the current ____________ color.
10. An existing polygon can be filled with color by using Paint's ____________ tool.
11. True or false: Paint's Brush tool can only produce curves of a single line thickness.
12. True or false: To draw a perfect circle with Paint's Ellipse/Circle tool, hold down the Ctrl key while dragging the cursor.
13. True or false: The Tool Box icon for Paint's Text tool is the capital letter "T".
14. True or false: Paint's Rounded Box tool is used to create a rectangular shape with rounded corners.

15. Which of the following Paint tools cannot draw an "L-shaped" pair of lines?
    a. The Polygon tool
    b. The Line tool
    c. The Pencil tool
    d. The Brush tool
16. To fill an irregularly shaped region in a Paint graphic with color
    a. Double-click on that color in the Color Box.
    b. Use the Filled Box tool.
    c. Use the Paint Can tool.
    d. Use the Airbrush tool.
17. To draw a square using Paint's Box tool, while dragging the cursor, hold down the
    a. Alt key.
    b. Ctrl key.
    c. Shift key.
    d. Spacebar.
18. In the Text tool's Fonts window, you cannot select
    a. The color for the current text.
    b. The typeface for the current text.
    c. The point size for the current text.
    d. A bold and italic style for the current text.

Section 8.3

19. To erase a green circle that is enclosed in a red square using Paint's Eraser tool, set the background color to ___________.
20. You can magnify part of a graphic using Paint's ___________ tool.
21. True or false: To define an irregularly-shaped cutout, use Paint's Free-form Selection tool.
22. True or false: You can use the Custom command (on Paint's Zoom submenu) to magnify the current graphic by any factor you want.
23. To delete the current (active) cutout in Paint, you can
    a. Press the Delete key.
    b. Choose the Clear Selection command from the Edit menu.
    c. Right-click inside the cutout and choose Clear Selection from the resulting pop-up menu.
    d. Carry out any of the above actions.
24. You cannot use the Zoom command (on Paint's View menu) to
    a. Magnify the graphic by 400%.

b. Show the graphic as it will appear on the printed page.
c. Turn the (pixel) grid on or off.
d. Display a thumbnail view of the graphic.

Section 8.4

25. To *sweep* a cutout in Paint, hold down the ___________ key while dragging the cutout.

26. To flip a cutout in Paint from top to bottom, begin by choosing the ___________ command from the Image menu.

27. To save a cutout to disk, choose the Copy To command from Paint's ___________ menu.

28. True or false: To move a cutout transparently in Paint, select the bottom option in the Options Box.

29. True or false: Paint allows you to rotate a cutout by 90°, 180°, or 270°.

30. To paste down (anchor) a cutout in Paint:

    a. Choose Paste from the Edit menu.
    b. Choose Clear Selection from the Edit menu.
    c. Reposition the cursor.
    d. Click outside the cutout.

31. To copy a cutout from one location to another:

    a. Drag it to the new location.
    b. Drag it to the new location while holding down the Ctrl key.
    c. Drag it to the new location while holding down the Shift key.
    d. Drag it to the new location while holding down the Spacebar.

32. Which operation on cutouts is not performed by issuing a menu command?

    a. Resizing
    b. Flipping
    c. Rotating
    d. Skewing

Section 8.5

33. To see how your Paint graphic will look on the printed page before it is actually printed, choose the ___________ command from the File menu.

34. You can replace the colors in a Paint drawing by black-and-white patterns by choosing the ___________ command from the Image menu.

35. True or false: You can edit a Paint graphic while it is displayed in the print preview window.

36. True or false: When you use one of the Set as Wallpaper commands on Paint's File menu, the resulting wallpaper is immediately put into effect.

37. Which of the following operations cannot be carried out using Paint's Page Setup dialog box?

    a. Setting the page margins.
    b. Setting the page orientation.
    c. Placing a header or footer on the page.
    d. Selecting a paper size.

38. Paint's Attributes dialog box can be used to specify the size of

    a. The page margins.
    b. The text font.
    c. The drawing area.
    d. The screen resolution.

Build Your Own Glossary

39. The following words and phrases are important terms that were introduced in this chapter. (They appear within the text in boldface type.) Use WordPad (see Section 2.2) to enter a definition for each term, preserving alphabetical order, into the Glossary file on the Student Disk.

Airbrush tool
Background color
Box tool
Brush tool
Color Box
Curve tool
Cutout
Drawing area
Ellipse/Circle tool
Eraser tool
Eye Dropper tool
Foreground color
Free-form Selection tool
Graphic
Landscape orientation
Line tool
Magnifier tool
Options Box
Paint (application)
Paint Can tool
Pencil tool
Polygon tool
Portrait orientation
Print preview
Rectangular Selection tool
Rounded Box tool
Text tool
Tool Box

Lab Exercises

Work each of the following exercises at your computer. Begin by turning the machine on (if necessary) to start Windows 98 and closing any open windows.

Lab Exercise 1 (Section 8.2)

a. Start Paint and maximize its window.

b. Use the 24-point Arial Bold font to insert the words Greek Flag at the top of the drawing area.

c. Create a drawing that resembles the blue-and-white Greek flag pictured at the right.

d. Insert your name, your class, and the date under the drawing in your choice of font.

e. Save the graphic to a floppy disk under the name Flag and print the graphic.

f. Exit Paint and remove the diskette from its drive.

Lab Exercise 2 (Section 8.2)

a. Start Paint and maximize its window.

b. Create a drawing that resembles the 5¼" floppy disk pictured here. Make it as large as possible, yet ensuring that the entire disk can be viewed without scrolling.

c. Insert your name, your class, and the date on the diskette's label (the rectangle at the top) in an appropriately-sized font.

d. Save the graphic to a floppy disk under the name Floppy and print the graphic.

e. Exit Paint and remove the diskette from its drive.

Lab Exercise 3 (Section 8.3)

a. Start Paint and maximize its window.

b. Insert the Student Disk in its drive and open the Graph1 graphic on this disk.

c. Edit the Graph1 graphic so that the revised version resembles the one pictured at the right, using your class in the title. (Use the 10-point Arial font for all text.)

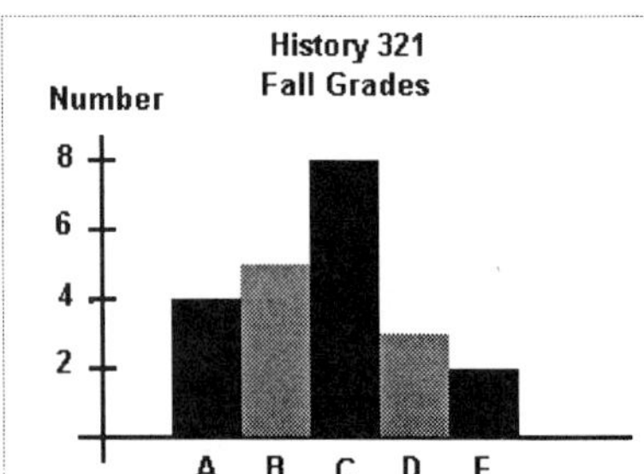

d. Insert your name and the date below the revised graphic in your choice of font.

e. Save the revised graphic to a floppy disk using the filename Graph2 and print the graphic.

f. Exit Paint and remove the diskette from its drive.

Lab Exercise 4 (Section 8.3)

a. Start Paint and maximize its window.

b. Create the Palette graphic shown below. Here are a couple of hints so that your graphic will look right:

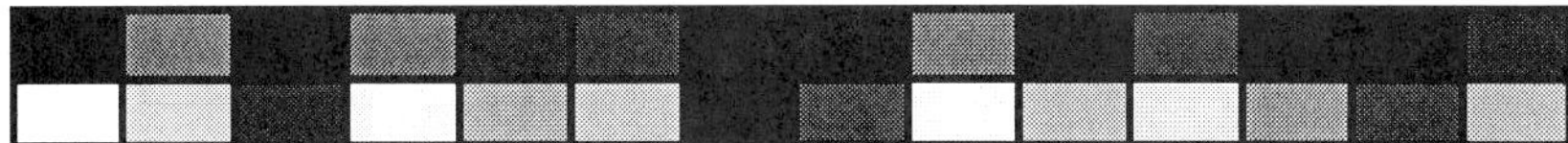

- Use the cursor coordinates on the Status bar to help create even subdivisions in the palette.
- Zoom in at 800% magnification on the line intersections and "clean them up" so that the lines meet perfectly.
- Use the Paint Can tool to fill each compartment with a different color from the Color Box.

c. Insert your name, your class, and the date under the palette in your choice of font.

d. Save the graphic to a floppy disk under the name Palette and print the graphic.

e. Exit Paint and remove the diskette from its drive.

Lab Exercise 5 (Section 8.3)

a. Start Paint and maximize its window.

b. Insert the Student Disk in its drive and open the Factory1 graphic on this disk.

c. Edit the Factory1 graphic, so that the revised version resembles the one pictured in Figure 21 (on the next page), by:

- Using the Eraser tool to erase the triangular part of the two existing windows.
- Using the Box tool to create the new rectangular window and second smokestack.
- Using the Airbrush tool to create the new smoke.

d. Insert your name, your class, and the date to the left of the smokestacks in your choice of font.

e. Save the revised graphic to a floppy disk under the name Factory2 and print the graphic.

f. Exit Paint and remove the diskette from its drive.

Figure 21 Graphic for Lab Exercise 5

Lab Exercise 6 (Section 8.4)

a. Start Paint and maximize its window.

b. Create a drawing that resembles the house shown at the right. Make use of the copy and resize operations to simplify your work.

c. Insert your name, your class, and the date below the graphic in your choice of font.

d. Save the graphic to a floppy disk under the name House and print the graphic.

e. Exit Paint and remove the diskette from its drive.

Lab Exercise 7 (Section 8.4)

a. Start Paint and maximize its window.

b. Create a graphic that resembles the locomotive shown here. Make use of the copy and resize operations to simplify your work.

c. Insert your name, your class, and

the date below the graphic in your choice of font.

d. Save the graphic to a floppy disk under the name Locomotive and print the graphic.

e. Exit Paint and remove the diskette from its drive.

If You Want to Learn More ...

The notes presented here allow you to delve more deeply into some of the topics covered in this chapter.

Editing the colors in the Color Box

As you know, Paint's Color Box displays a palette of 28 colors that can be used for either foreground or background. If you want to use a different color in your graphic, it's easy to replace an existing color with one of your choosing. Here's how:

1. Double-click on the Color Box color to be replaced (or click on it and choose Edit Colors from the Colors menu). The Edit Colors dialog box will open, displaying 48 "basic colors" and any "custom colors" you have defined in the current Paint session. (We will discuss how to define a custom color in the next note.)
2. Click on the color of your choice; it will be enclosed in a box.
3. Choose the OK command button. The selected color will replace the original one in the Color Box.

Defining a custom color

If you want to use a certain color in your graphic and it does not appear in the Color Box or in the basic 48 colors displayed in the Edit Colors dialog box (see the note above), here's how you can create any *custom color* you wish:

1. Choose Edit Colors from the Colors menu to open the Edit Colors dialog box.
2. Choose the Define Custom Colors command button. The Edit Colors dialog box will expand, as shown in Figure 22 on the next page.
3. Click on the desired color in the color spectrum on the right side of the dialog box. The selected color will be displayed on the left side of the Color|Solid box. The right side of this box will display the nearest "solid" (pure) color to it.

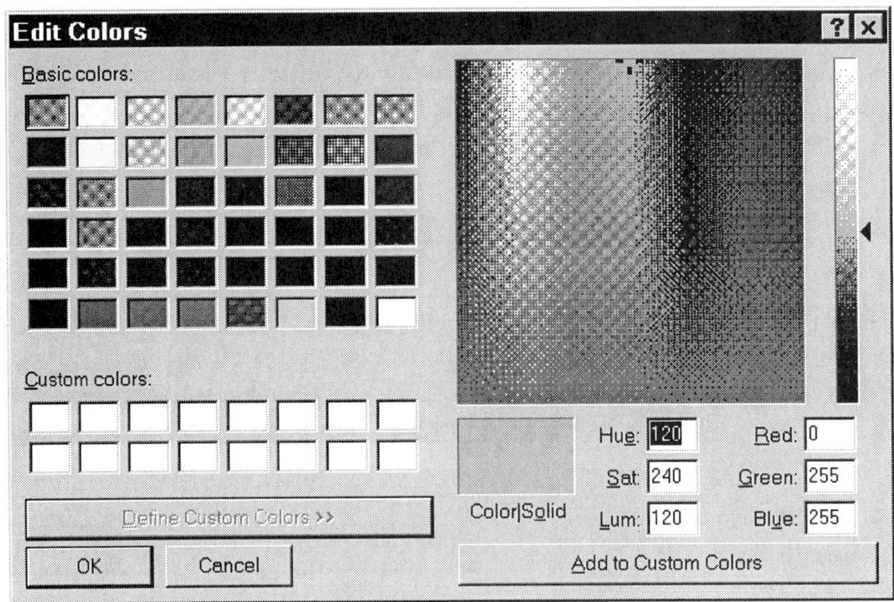

Figure 22 The Edit Colors Dialog Box

4. You can make adjustments to the selected color by changing the entries in the Hue, Sat (saturation), Lum (luminosity), Red, Green, and Blue text boxes, or by dragging the pointer on the "luminosity bar" (on the far right of the dialog box) up or down. The best way to see how these parameters affect the selected color is to experiment with them!
5. If you prefer the nearest pure color (on the right side of the Color|Solid box) to the selected one, double-click on the Color|Solid box.
6. Choose the Add to Custom Colors command button. The new color will fill one of the *Custom colors* boxes.
7. Repeat steps 3 through 6 to create additional custom colors.
8. To place a custom color in the Color Box, replacing the current foreground (or background) color in the palette, click (or right-click) on the desired color and choose the OK command button. Otherwise, choose the Cancel command button.

Moving the Tool or Color Box

As you know, you can increase the size of the work area by removing the Tool Box and/or Color Box from the screen. Unfortunately, you can then no longer select tools and/or colors to be used in your graphic. A more practical way to expand the work area is to "tear off" the Tool Box or Color Box, creating a corresponding "floating" window that sits on top of your graphic and can be moved about the screen.

To tear off the Tool Box or Color Box, creating a floating window:

1. Position the mouse pointer over an empty part of the box.
2. Drag the pointer (and box) to the desired location.

You can now move or close the Tool or Color window in the usual ways — by, respectively, dragging its title bar or clicking on its close button. To return the Tool Box or Color Box to its original, fixed location:

- Position the mouse pointer over an empty part of the box (*not* its title bar) and drag the box to the left edge or bottom-left corner of the screen, respectively.

or

- Double-click on box's title bar.

Comparison of Paint and Paintbrush (Windows 3.1)

The Windows 98 version of Paint is virtually identical to the version supplied with Windows 95. It is also similar to Paintbrush, the Windows 3.1 drawing program. Paint is slightly easier to use than Paintbrush due to the presence of several new features:

- There are two new tools, the Line and Eyedropper. (Paintbrush's Color Eraser has been incorporated into Paint's Eraser and its Paint Roller is now a Paint Can.)
- You can draw figures in either the foreground or background colors (depending on which mouse button you depress).
- Cutouts now have "handles", making it easier to resize them.
- Print preview allows you to see what the printed graphic will look like without actually printing it.

The only significant feature of Paintbrush that is not present in Paint is the former's ability to display headers and footers on the printed page.

CHAPTER 9

Using Other Windows Accessories

Overview

In Chapters 7 and 8, we discussed two of the applications, WordPad and Paint, included with the Windows 98 software package. These applications are sometimes referred to as **accessories** because they appear on the Accessories submenu of the Start menu's Programs option. In this chapter we will describe how to use other Windows accessories. More specifically:

- Section 9.1 introduces a simple, but useful utility called Calculator, which includes two types of on-screen calculators.
- Section 9.2 discusses the Notepad text editor.
- Section 9.3 describes Windows built-in multimedia capabilities.
- Section 9.4 discusses the tools that Windows supplies to help users who have certain physical disabilities.
- Section 9.5 briefly describes the Character Map, Phone Dialer, and Clipboard Viewer utilities.

Since the topics in this chapter are independent of one another, you can read them in any order and skip any you don't need.

9.1 The Windows Calculators

Windows' **Calculator** accessory provides two types of on-screen calculators — a basic *standard* calculator and a more powerful *scientific* calculator. To start Calculator:

1. Click on the Start button to open the Start menu.
2. Point at the Start menu's Programs option and then at Accessories on the resulting submenu.
3. Click on the Calculator item on the Accessories submenu.

Switching between the calculator types

The Calculator window will open, displaying the calculator type (standard or scientific) that was active when you last exited this accessory. To switch from one type to the other, choose Standard or Scientific, as desired, from the View menu.

The Standard Calculator

If you know how to use a conventional calculator, then you'll be able to use Windows' Calculator; it works in a completely analogous way! In standard mode (Figure 1), Calculator contains all the keys usually found on a basic calculator, but instead of pressing a key with your finger, you click on it with the mouse. For example, to multiply 365 by 23:

1. Click on the 3, 6, and 5 buttons. As you do, the corresponding digits appear in the calculator's "display".

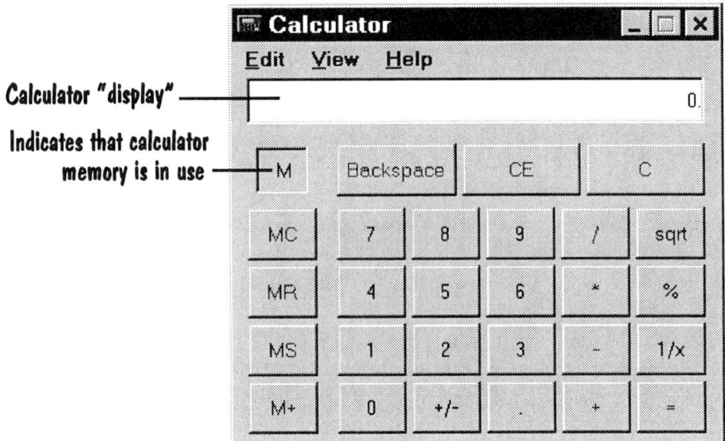

Figure 1 Standard Calculator

2. Click on the multiplication key (*).
3. Click on the 2 and 3 buttons; 23 appears in the display.
4. Click on the equals key (=). The product, 8395, appears in the display.

In addition to the number and operation (/, *, +, -, =) keys, the standard calculator contains all the keys usually found on a basic calculator (and one atypical key, *Backspace*). The following table provides a quick rundown of their functions.

Key	Symbol	Function
Backspace	Back-space	Deletes the last digit entered into the display.
Clear entry	CE	Clears the number in the display.
Clear	C	Clears the entire current computation.
Memory clear	MC	Clears the number stored in memory.
Memory recall	MR	Replaces the displayed number by the one in memory.
Memory store	MS	Stores the displayed number in memory, replacing the currently stored number.
Memory plus	M+	Adds the displayed number to the number in memory.
Plus/minus	+/-	Reverses the sign of the number in the display.
Reciprocal	1/x	Replaces the displayed number by its reciprocal.
Percentage	%	Multiplies the result of a multiplication by 100.
Square root	sqrt	Replaces the displayed number by its square root.

Table 1 Standard Calculator Keys

If you use Calculator a lot, you can speed up data entry by using *keyboard equivalents*. For example, the number keys and operation symbols can be activated by pressing the corresponding keys on the keyboard. (If you use the numeric keypad to do this, make sure the Num Lock light is on; if it isn't, press the Num Lock key.) Here are a few other useful keyboard equivalents; instead of clicking on:

- The Backspace button — press the Backspace key.
- The CE button — press the Delete key.
- The C button — press the Escape key.

To determine other keyboard equivalents, right-click on the key in question and choose *What's This?* from the resulting pop-up menu.

Copy and paste with Calculator

You can transfer numbers between the Calculator display and another application with the aid of the Clipboard:

- To copy the displayed number to the Clipboard, choose the Copy command from the Edit menu.
- To transfer a number from the Clipboard to the Calculator display, choose Paste from the Edit menu.

The Scientific Calculator

In scientific mode (Figure 2), Calculator supplies an impressive array of advanced functions, in addition to all the basic operations provided by standard mode.

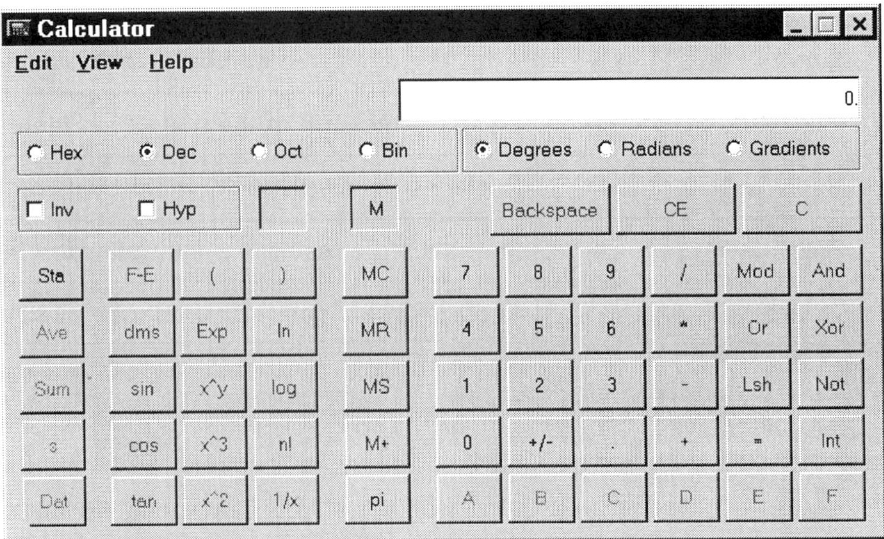

Figure 2 Scientific Calculator

Dealing with Numbers In scientific mode, you can choose to enter and manipulate numbers in four different number systems. Calculator defaults to our everyday *decimal* (base 10) number system. If you want to set Calculator to work in the *hexadecimal* (base 16), *octal* (base 8), or *binary* (base 2) system, select the corresponding option button:

Calculator will only accept numbers that are valid for the selected system. For example, if *Bin* is selected and you try to enter anything but a 0 or 1 into the display, you will hear a "beep" and nothing will happen. At the other extreme, the hexadecimal system uses the digits 0, 1, ..., 9, A, B, C, D, E, and F and the additional "digits" are entered by using the corresponding calculator (or keyboard) keys:

You can use the number system option buttons to convert a number from one system to another. To do so:

1. Select the option button for the system to be converted *from*.
2. Enter the desired number (using its representation in the current system) into the display.
3. Select the system to be converted *to*. The numeral in the display will change to the correct representation in the new system.

Sta
Ave
Sum
s
Dat

Performing Statistical Calculations Calculator can compute the sum, mean (average), and standard deviation of a given set of numbers. To perform one of these operations:

1. Click on the *Sta* button. The Statistics Box window (which is shown at the right) will open.

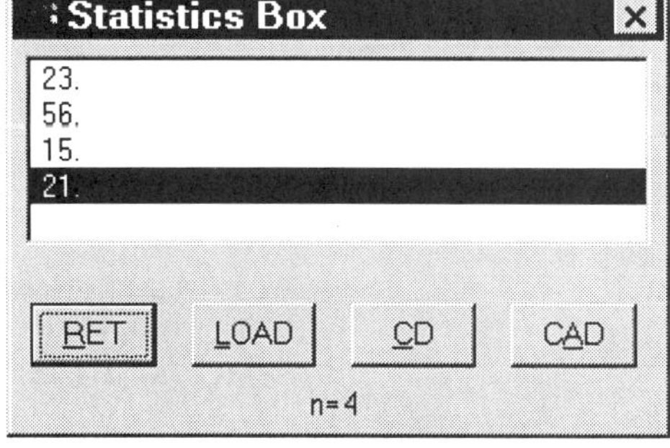

2. Click on the RET (return) button in the Statistics Box to close this window.
3. Enter the data (the numbers with which you want

to work) into the display one at a time, clicking on the *Dat* button after each number is entered. (Each time you click on Dat the displayed number is added to the list in the Statistics Box, even though the latter is hidden from view.)

4. If you wish to review the numbers you have just entered, click on the *Sta* button again. The Statistics Box window will open, displaying the data and the total number (*n* =) of items.
5. To delete a number, select it and click on CD. To clear the window, click on CAD. To replace the number in the Calculator display by the one currently selected in the Statistics Box, click on LOAD.
6. Click on RET to close the Statistics Box. Now, to display:
   - The mean of the data — click on the *Ave* button.
   - The sum of the data — click on the *Sum* button.
   - The standard deviation of the data — click on the *s* button.

Trigonometric Functions Calculator allows you to compute trigonometric and hyperbolic functions and their inverses. Moreover, in working with trig functions, you can elect to have the angle measured in degrees, radians, or gradients by selecting the appropriate option button prior to the calculation.

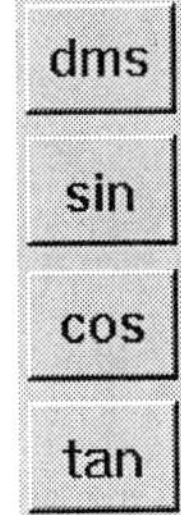

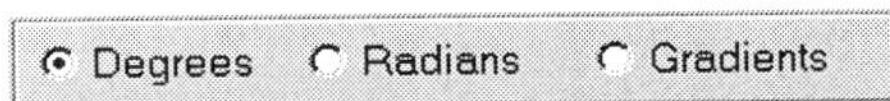

Table 2 gives the functions of the trigonometric keys. Selecting the *Inv* (Inverse) and/or *Hyp* (Hyperbolic) check boxes prior to clicking on one of the trig buttons, modifies its function as described in the table. We will use the following notation with regard to these check boxes:

- Inv+*button* (or Hyp+*button*) means select the *Inv* check box (or *Hyp* check box), then click on the indicated button. For example, Inv+cos means select *Inv*, then click on *cos*.
- Inv+Hyp+*button* means select both check boxes, then click on the indicated button. For example, Inv+Hyp+cos means select *Inv*, select *Hyp*, then click on *cos*.

Key	Function
dms	Converts the displayed angle from decimal degree format to degree-minute-second format. Inv+dms does the reverse.
sin	Calculates the sine of the displayed angle. Inv+sin calculates the inverse sine (arcsin) of the displayed number. Hyp+sin and Inv+Hyp+sin calculate the hyperbolic sine (sinh) and its inverse, respectively.
cos	Calculates the cosine of the displayed angle. Inv+cos calculates the inverse cosine (arccos) of the displayed number. Hyp+cos and Inv+Hyp+cos calculate the hyperbolic cosine (cosh) and its inverse, respectively.
tan	Calculates the tangent of the displayed angle. Inv+tan calculates the inverse tangent (arctan) of the displayed number. Hyp+tan and Inv+Hyp+tan calculate the hyperbolic tangent (tanh) and its inverse, respectively.

Table 2 Calculator's Trig-related Functions

Other Scientific Calculator Functions We conclude this section by briefly discussing the other functions provided in scientific mode.

- *F-E* toggles the display between ordinary (floating point) and scientific (exponential) notation.
- *Exp* allows you to enter numbers using scientific notation.
- The parentheses keys, *(* and *)*, allow you to insert parentheses into a calculation.
- The keys *ln* and *log* calculate the logarithm (base e and 10, respectively) of the displayed number. (Inv+ln and Inv+log calculate e^x and 10^x, respectively, where x is the displayed number.)
- The key *n!* calculates the factorial of the displayed integer.
- The key *x^y* calculates the value of x raised to the y power. (Inv+x^y calculates the yth root of x.)
- The keys *x^2* and *x^3* square and cube, respectively, the displayed number. (Inv+x^2 and Inv+x^3 calculate square and cube roots.)

- The *pi* key inserts the value of π into the display.
- The *Mod* key calculates the remainder in an integer division.
- The *Int* key displays the integer part of a decimal number. (Inv+Int displays the decimal part.)
- *And*, *Or*, *Xor* (exclusive or), *Lsh* (left shift), and *Not* perform the corresponding logical operations on binary numbers.

TUTORIAL

Try the following exercise on your own.

1. Turn on the computer (if necessary) to start Windows 98 and display Calculator by clicking on the Calculator item on the Accessories submenu of the Start menu's Programs option.
2. Switch to the Standard calculator (if necessary) by choosing this item from the View menu.
3. Calculate the value of the expression 21(15 - 3.67):
   - Enter 15 into the calculator's display by clicking on the "1" and "5" calculator buttons.
   - Click on the minus (-) button.
   - Enter 3.67 by clicking on the appropriate buttons.
   - Click on the multiply (*) button.
   - Enter 21 by clicking on the appropriate buttons.
   - Click on the equals (=) button. The answer (237.93) will appear in the display.
4. Clear this calculation by clicking on the C (clear) button.
5. Perform the same calculation as in step 3, but this time use the keys on the computer's keyboard. (Hopefully, your answer will be the same as before.)
6. Clear this calculation.
7. Enter the number 2345. Now, click on the Backspace button to delete the last digit entered (5); then, click on the CE (clear entry) button to clear the resulting number from the display.
8. Determine the reciprocal of the square root of 10, $1/\sqrt{10}$:
   - Enter 10 into the display.
   - Take its square root by clicking on the *sqrt* button.
   - Take the reciprocal of the displayed number by clicking on the *1/x* button. (The answer, 0.316..., will appear in the display.)

9. Use Calculator's memory keys to add the integers from 1 to 5:
   - Enter 1 into the display.
   - Store the displayed number in memory by clicking on the MS button. (An "M" appears in the box above the memory buttons to indicate that the memory is in use.)
   - Enter 2 into the display and add it to the number in memory by clicking on the M+ button.
   - Repeat the previous step for the numbers 3, 4, and 5.
   - Transfer the number currently in memory (the sum of 1, 2, 3, 4, and 5) to the display by clicking on the MR button.
   - Clear Calculator's memory by clicking on the MC button. (The "M" symbol disappears from its box.)
10. Switch to scientific mode by choosing the Scientific item from the View menu. If you are familiar with the use of a conventional scientific calculator, explore this electronic version by performing various calculations. Remember: To get help with a particular button or feature, right-click on it and choose the *What's This?* item from the pop-up menu.
11. Close Calculator by clicking on its close button.

9.2 *The Notepad Text Editor*

Notepad is a very simple type of word processor called a **text editor** because its capabilities are limited to entering and editing (modifying) text. Unlike more sophisticated word processors, such as WordPad, Notepad cannot *format* text (for example, there are no alignment or indentation options) or insert graphics into a document.

Advantages of Notepad

Notepad's major virtue is simplicity; it loads more quickly and takes up less memory than WordPad. Notepad is (arguably) more convenient than WordPad for taking quick notes and editing text files. A **text file**, which is also known as an **ASCII** (pronounced "askey") file, is the simplest and most universal format for storing text. A text file is made up solely of characters you can type on the keyboard; it does not contain any special symbols (such as £ or ©) or formatting codes. Some system files and program files are stored in ASCII format.

Starting Notepad

To start Notepad:

1. Click on the Start button to open the Start menu.
2. Point at the Start menu's Programs option and then at the Accessories item on the resulting submenu.

3. Click on the Notepad item on the Accessories submenu. Notepad will open and display its window, as shown in Figure 3.

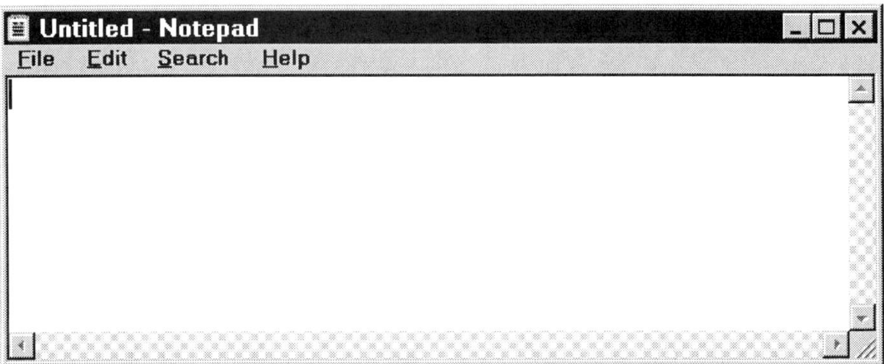

Figure 3 The Notepad Window

Basic Features

At a basic level, Notepad creates, edits, and operates on documents the way you would expect from any Windows-based word processor.

Entering text You enter text into a Notepad document in the same general way as you would in WordPad — just type, and the words appear on the screen. However, when you start Notepad, **word wrap** may be turned off. If so, the text you type will continue on the same line until you press the Enter key. If you turn word wrap on (by choosing this item from the Edit menu), text will wrap to the beginning of the next line when it reaches the right edge of the Notepad window.

Notepad *does* allow you to select a *font* (a design, size, and style) for the text you type, but unlike WordPad, your choice applies to the entire document. To select a font, choose the Set Font command from the Edit menu and, in the resulting dialog box, select a Font, Size, and Style; then choose the OK command button. (See Section 7.2 for information about fonts.)

Editing text Simple editing is done in much the same way as with WordPad; the Backspace and Delete keys work in exactly the same way, as does the Undo command on the Edit menu (see Section 2.2). Moreover, text is selected, cut or copied to the Clipboard, and pasted from the Clipboard in the usual Windows-compliant way (see Section 2.3). Notepad also supplies a quick way to select all the text in a document; just choose the Select All command from the Edit menu. However, Notepad lacks the other, more sophisticated ways of selecting text (described in Section 7.1) that are available in WordPad.

Standard File menu commands

The New, Open, Save, Save As, Print and Exit commands on Notepad's File menu work in the same way as in most Windows applications (see Section 2.2) with one major exception: When you issue the Print command, printing begins immediately; the Print dialog box doesn't open. As a result, you do not have access to some of the usual print features, such as specifying a range of pages to be printed.

Beyond the Basics

Notepad does provide two relatively advanced features: It can locate any specified piece of text within a document and has page layout options to enhance the look of the printed page.

Searching for Text One of Notepad's most useful features when editing a long or complicated document is its ability to search for a specified word or other sequence of characters. To search a Notepad document:

1. Choose the Find command from the Search menu. The Find dialog box (Figure 4) will open.

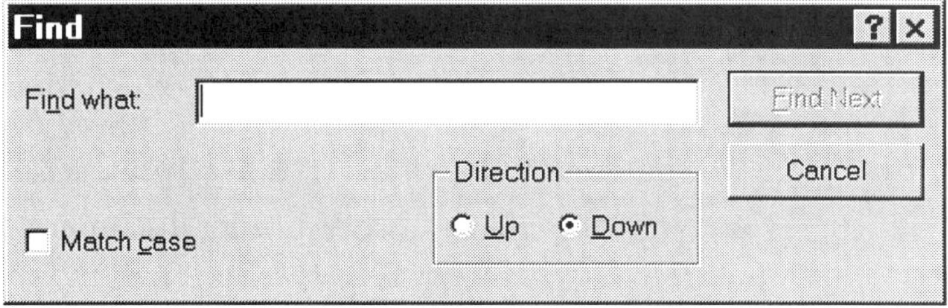

Figure 4 The Find Dialog Box

2. Type the text you are seeking in the *Find what* box. Notepad will search for this sequence of characters, whether or not it is part of a word, an entire word, or spans more than one word. For example, if you enter the win in the *Find what* box, Notepad may locate "the winner" or "the window", but not "a window".

3. Select the *Match case* check box if you want to search for text that has the same combination of upper and lower case letters as that entered in the *Find what* box. For example, if you leave this box *de*selected and search for able, then "able", "Able", and "ABLE" will be located (if they appear in the document); if the check box is selected, then only "able" will be located.
4. The search commences at the insertion point. Select the *Down* option button if you want the search to proceed forward through the document; select the *Up* button to proceed backward.
5. Choose the Find Now command button. Notepad will locate and highlight the next occurrence (in the specified direction) of the *Find what* text. If this text is not found, a message to this effect will be displayed.

You can use Find to locate the last text entered in the *Find what* box even if the Find dialog box is no longer on the screen. To do so, choose the Find Next command from the Search menu or press the F3 function key.

Setting Up the Page Although Notepad provides no choice of alignment or indentation, it does allow you to specify certain page layout options prior to printing. These features are accessed from the Page Setup dialog box (Figure 5), which is opened by choosing the Page Setup command from the File menu.

In the Page Setup dialog box:

- You can specify the size of the paper on which you will be printing and the printer bin from which that paper will be fed by selecting the appropriate items on the Paper Size and Paper Source drop-down lists, respectively.
- You can choose to print your document in either portrait or landscape orientation. In *portrait orientation*, the document's text is printed parallel to the short side of the paper; in *landscape orientation*, the text is printed parallel to its long side. The figures at the right illustrate this concept. To specify page orientation, select the Portrait or Landscape option button. The "page" shown in the Preview area will appear in the selected orientation.

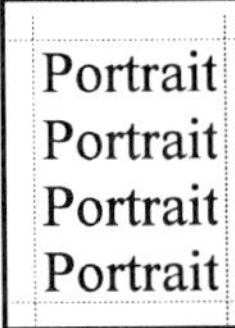

Landscape
Landscape
Landscape

- You can change the margins for the current document by entering the desired margins in

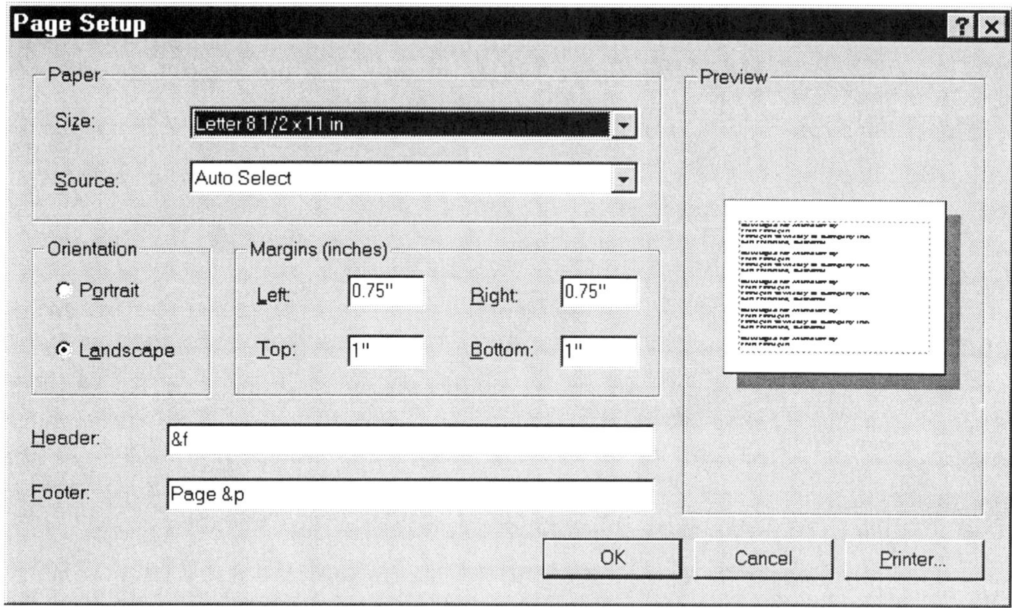

Figure 5 Notepad's Page Setup Dialog Box

the Left, Right, Top, and Bottom text boxes. (The "page" shown in the Preview area will indicate the new margins.)

- You can create headers and footers for the document. A **header** is text that is automatically placed in the top margin of every page of a document. Similarly, a **footer** appears in the bottom margin of every page. To create a header or footer for the current document, type text in the Header or Footer boxes. Your text is printed as entered, except for letters preceded by an ampersand (&) symbol. These codes have the following meaning:

&c	centers the text that follows this code
&d	inserts the current date
&f	inserts the document's file name
&l	aligns the text that follows with the left margin
&p	inserts the current page number
&r	aligns the text that follows with the right margin
&t	inserts the current time

If no alignment code is present, the header or footer text is centered on the line. Thus, in Figure 5: the text in the Header box (&f) will cause the document's file name to be printed at the top center of every page; the Footer text will print the current page number, preceded by the word Page and a blank space, at the bottom center of each page. As another example, the Header text &l&p&cWindows 98&r&d produces a header (when the document is printed) like the following one:

```
1                    Windows 98                    05\01\1998
```

TUTORIAL

Try the following exercise on your own.

1. Turn on the computer (if necessary) to start Windows 98 and open Notepad by clicking on the Notepad item on the Accessories submenu of the Start menu's Programs option.
2. Insert the Student Disk in its drive and open the `History2` document on this diskette. (See Section 2.2 for more information about opening a document.)
3. Maximize the Notepad window.
4. Use Notepad's Find utility to search for all occurrences of the word *computer* in the History2 document:
   - Choose the Find command from the Search menu to open the Find dialog box.
   - Type the word *computer* in the *Find what* box, deselect the *Match case* check box (so that capitalized spellings of *computer* will be found), and select the *Down* option button (so that the search, which begins at the insertion point, will proceed in a forward direction).
   - Choose the Find Next command button. The first occurrence of *computer* will be located and highlighted.
   - Continue to search for additional occurrences of *computer* by repeatedly choosing the Find Next button. When the last occurrence is found, close the resulting message box and choose the Cancel command button to close the dialog box.
5. Prepare the document for printing:
   - Choose the Page Setup command from the File menu to open the corresponding dialog box.
   - Select the Portrait option button.
   - Set the page margins to 1" left and right and 1.5" top and bottom by typing these numbers in the Margins text boxes. (Notice how the Preview "page" reflects these changes.)
   - Place the following text and codes in the Header and Footer boxes so that the indicated text will appear at the top and bottom, respectively, of each page of the printed document (a list of the available codes precedes this tutorial):

Header: `&lHistory &r&d`
(The word "History" aligned with the left margin; the current date aligned right.)
Footer: &c&p
(The current page number, centered.)

- Choose the OK command button.

6. Print the revised document by choosing the Print command from the File menu.
7. Exit Notepad and remove the diskette from its drive.

9.3 Multimedia Utilities

What is multimedia?

Multimedia is a catch-all term that refers to the use of sound, animation, and video to enhance computer software. For example, a multimedia encyclopedia not only contains the usual text and pictures, but also occasional audio and video clips. In order to run multimedia applications, your computer must be equipped with at least a CD-ROM drive, a sound card (occupying one of the slots within the system unit), and speakers. Most desktop PCs sold nowadays come equipped with these components; moreover, they can usually be added fairly easily to most older computers.

In this section, we will discuss several utilities that allow you to create, edit, and/or play back multimedia files of various kinds. These utilities are found on the Entertainment submenu of the Start button's Accessories menu. They include:

- CD Player plays audio compact discs inserted into the computer's CD-ROM drive.
- Sound Recorder records sounds transmitted to the computer through a microphone or other audio source.
- Media Player plays back audio, video, or animation files.
- Volume Control adjusts the volume, balance, and other characteristics of the sound produced by various devices.
- DVD Player, Web TV for Windows, NetShow, and other utilities provide support for special multimedia hardware.

We will also discuss Control Panel's Multimedia utility, which allows you to configure multimedia devices.

CD Player

The **CD Player** utility allows you to play audio compact discs on the computer's CD-ROM drive. To start CD Player:

1. Click on the Start button to open the Start menu.
2. Point at the Programs option, then at the Accessories item, and finally at Entertainment.
3. Choose the CD Player item from the resulting submenu. The CD Player utility will start and open the window shown in Figure 6.

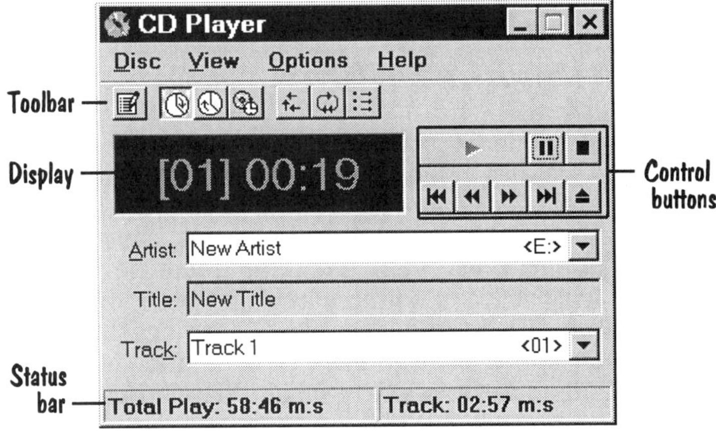

Figure 6 The CD Player Window

Notice that CD Player's interface resembles that of a conventional compact disc player. If you are familiar with the way the latter works, then you should have no trouble using its electronic counterpart.

NOTE

If the toolbar, disc/track information (Artist, Title, and Track), or status bar does not appear in the CD Player window, it can be displayed by choosing the corresponding item from the View menu. The View menu also allows you to change CD Player's display function from Track Time Elapsed (as in Figure 6) to Track Time Remaining or Disc Time Remaining.

Playing a compact disc

To play a compact disc:

1. Start CD Player, as described above.

2. Insert an audio compact disc in the CD-ROM drive.
3. Click on the Play control button.
4. To adjust the volume, choose the Volume item from the View menu and, in the resulting dialog box, drag the appropriate "CD/Aux" slider in the desired direction.
5. To listen to another part of the CD:
   - Click on the Next Track or Previous Track button (Figure 7) to move to this track.
   - Select a track from the Track drop-down list to move to this track.
   - Position the mouse pointer over the Skip Forward or Skip Backward button (Figure 7), press the mouse button, and keep it depressed to advance forward or backward on the disc as much as you like.

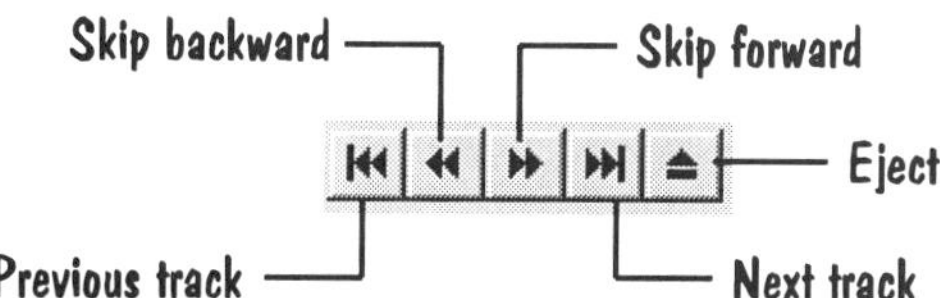

Figure 7 CD Player Control Buttons

6. To pause or stop the playing of the CD, click on the Pause or Stop button, respectively. (Stop is the one on the right.) To resume playing a paused CD, click on the Play button.

7. To eject the compact disc from the CD-ROM player, click on the Eject button (see Figure 7).

NOTE

You may be able to play an audio compact disc without first starting CD Player. Insert the disc into the drive and close the tray. On most computer systems, CD Player will start automatically, minimize itself, and start playing the disc.

Other features of CD Player

In addition to its basic functions, CD Player provides a few niceties:

- The tracks on a disc can be played in a random order. To do so, choose the Random Order item from the Options menu.

- CD Player can automatically play the same disc over and over again; just choose Continuous Play from the Options menu.
- If you choose Intro Play from the Options menu, CD Player will play the first few seconds of each track and then automatically skip to the next track. If you want to listen to an entire track, choose Intro Play again.
- The Play List feature allows you to name a CD, its artist, and even each of its tracks, so that whenever the CD is played, this information will be displayed in the CD Player window. To do this, choose the Edit Play List command from the File menu.

CD Player's toolbar provides easy access to the following functions (from left to right): Edit Play List; Track Time Elapsed, Track Time Remaining, or Disc Time Remaining display functions; Random Order Tracks, Continuous Play, and Intro Play options. As usual, to determine the function of a toolbar button, let the mouse pointer rest over it for a moment or two, and a *tool tip* will appear (as shown here).

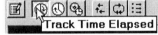

Sound Recorder

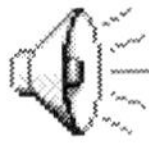

Sound recorder allows you to record sounds input from a microphone, CD-ROM drive, or other device, and save them as a disk file. It also has the capability to edit and play sound files. To start Sound Recorder, choose it from the Entertainment submenu of the Start button's Accessories menu. The window shown in Figure 8 will open.

Recording sounds

To record sounds:

1. Start Sound Recorder, as described above (if it's not already running).
2. Prepare the input device, if necessary; for example, if you're going to record from a compact disc, insert it in the CD-ROM drive and start CD Player.
3. In Sound Recorder, click on the Record button to start recording.
4. When you're done recording, click on the Stop button.
5. To save the recorded sounds to a disk file:
   - Choose the Save As command from the File menu to open the Save As dialog box.

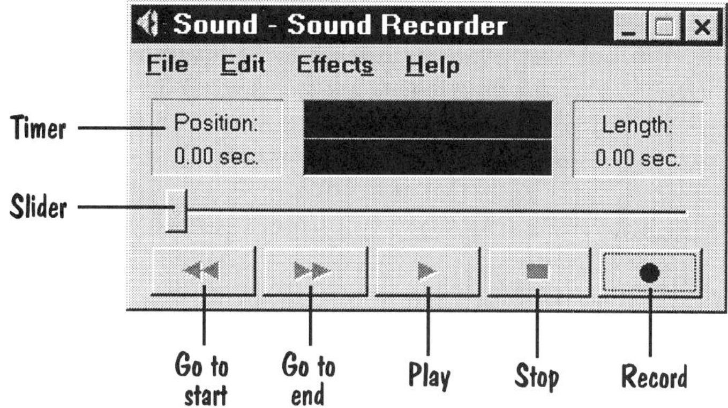

Figure 8 The Sound Recorder Window

- Provide a name for the sound file (as you would in saving any file — see Section 2.2) and choose the Save command button.

Playing sounds You can use Sound Recorder to play the sounds you have just recorded (whether or not they've been saved) or an existing sound file. If you want to play back (or edit) an existing sound file:

1. Choose Open from the File menu. The Open dialog box will be displayed.
2. Select a sound file and choose the Open command button.

To play an open sound file or the sounds you have just recorded (that is, to play back a *sample*), click on the Play button (see Figure 8). The sample will play from the beginning and, as it does, the slider will move to the right and the timer will indicate the elapsed time. To stop the playback before the end of the sample, click on the Stop button (see Figure 8).

Editing sounds You can also use Sound Recorder to *edit* (modify) sounds you have just recorded or an existing sound file. If you want to edit an existing file, open it as described above. Then, in either case:

1. Play the sound sample until you reach the point at which you would like to make the change.
2. Then:
   - You can delete all material prior to, or after, this point by choosing Delete Before Current Position, or Delete After

Current Position, from the Edit menu.

- You can insert or overlay another sound file at this point by choosing Insert File or Mix with File from the Edit menu and selecting the desired file in the corresponding dialog box. When a file is *inserted*, it is spliced into the existing sample at the current position. When a file is *mixed*, it is *overlayed* onto (played together with) the existing sample.
- Paste (as an inserted or mixed sample) the contents of the Windows Clipboard by choosing Paste Insert or Paste Mix, respectively, from the Edit menu.

3. You can also modify the entire sample in the following ways by choosing the corresponding command from the Effects menu:
   - Increase or decrease the volume of the sample.
   - Increase or decrease the speed of the sample.
   - Add an echo effect to the sample.
   - Reverse the sample so that it plays backwards.

NOTE

You can undo all the changes you've made to a sample since the last save (except for the echo effect) by choosing the Revert command from the File menu.

Other Multimedia Accessories

Here, we will briefly discuss a few of the other multimedia utilities that are supplied with Window 98.

Volume Control The **Volume Control** utility allows you to adjust the volume and other characteristics of the sound produced by various devices connected to your computer system. It can be accessed from within certain other multimedia applications (such as CD Player), or from the Desktop. To start Volume Control from the Desktop, either

- Double-click on the "speaker" icon on the Taskbar. (This icon can be added to or removed from the Taskbar by using Control Panel's Multimedia utility, as described later in this section.)

or

- Choose the Volume Control item from the Entertainment submenu of the Start button's Accessories menu.

In either case, the window shown in Figure 9 will open.

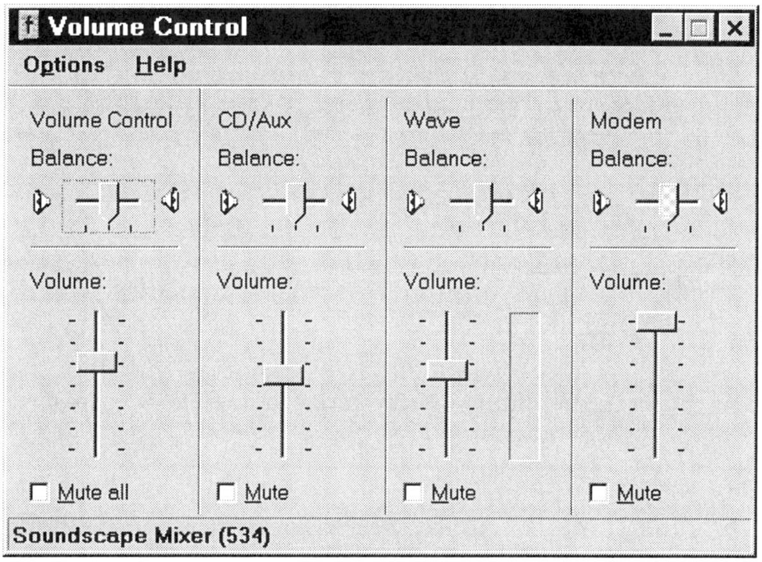

Figure 9 The Volume Control Window

As you can see in Figure 9, several volume controls are displayed. The leftmost one is the master control; it affects all audio devices. The other controls vary depending on system configuration, and affect specific devices. For example, if you want to change the volume of just the CD-ROM's output, use the "CD/Aux" control. (You can change the device controls to be displayed by using the Properties dialog box — choose Properties from the Options menu to open it.)

To use these controls:

- Increase or decrease the volume by dragging the Volume slider up or down.
- Select the Mute check box to shut off all sound produced by the given device (or all sound produced by the system if you select the leftmost Mute check box).
- Adjust the balance by dragging the Balance slider to the left or right.
- Choose the Advanced Controls item from the Options menu (if available) to access additional controls.

If you *single*-click on the Taskbar's speaker icon, a simpler version of the Volume Control window (which is shown at the right) will pop up. Its slider controls the overall system volume; it corresponds to the leftmost slider in Figure 9. This pop-up control provides a quick way to change the volume or to cut it off entirely (by selecting the Mute check box).

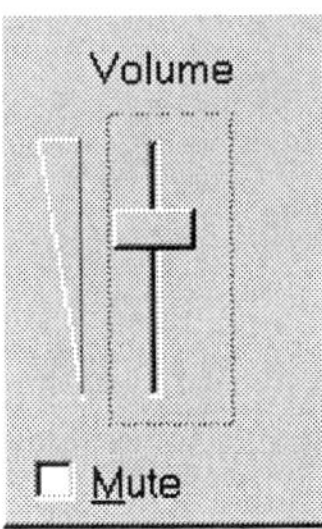

Media Player The **Media Player** utility is a jack-of-all-trades (but master of none), which is used to play back various kinds of multimedia files — sounds, CD music, animation, video, and more. To play a multimedia file:

1. Start Media Player by choosing this item from the Entertainment submenu of the Start button's Accessories menu. The window shown in Figure 10 will open.

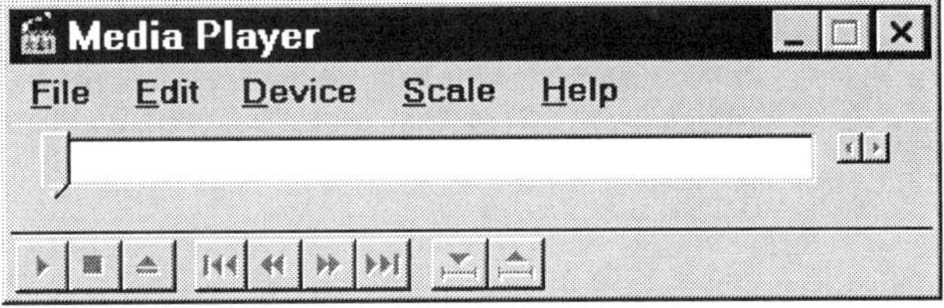

Figure 10 The Media Player Window

2. Choose the type of file you wish to play from the Device menu. In most cases, an Open dialog box will appear, displaying the relevant types of files. For example, fi you choose the Video for Windows item from the Device menu, all files of type "avi" are displayed.

   For options on the Device menu (such as audio or video disc players) that require external media (such as a disc), an Open dialog box will not appear.

3. Either choose the file to be played from the Open dialog box or insert the disc to be played in its drive.
4. Click on the Play button (the leftmost button on the button bar) to play the file or disc. (The other buttons are used in a way similar to that of a CD or tape player; as usual, mouse-pointing at a button displays a tool tip that describes its function.)

Control Panel's Multimedia Utility

The **Multimedia utility** allows you to adjust certain settings for the multimedia devices connected to your system. These may include audio, video, and MIDI (musical instrument digital interface) devices.

To start the Multimedia utility:

Multimedia

1. Open the Control Panel window by clicking on the Start button, pointing at the Settings option, and choosing Control Panel from the resulting submenu.
2. Choose the Multimedia icon in this window. The Multimedia Properties dialog box, shown in Figure 11, will open.

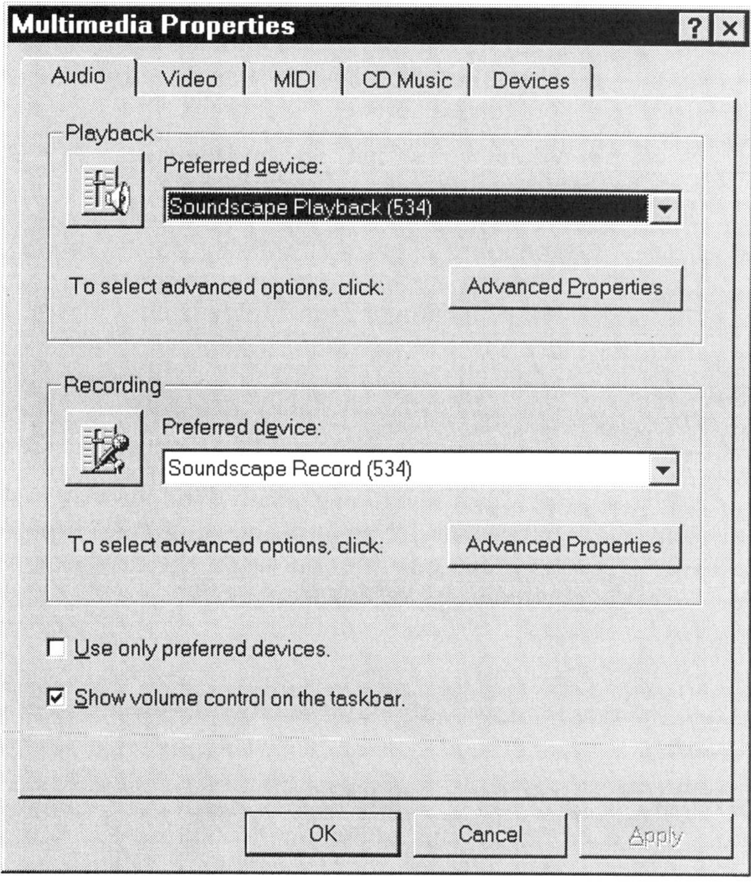

Figure 11 The Multimedia Properties Dialog Box

As you can see, this dialog box contains several pages, each corresponding to some aspect of multimedia. Here's a quick rundown on the options available on each page.

- The Audio page allows you to specify which audio devices connected to your computer will be the default devices for recording and playback, and to specify certain advanced properties for these devices. This page also allows you to display or hide the Taskbar's Volume Control speaker icon.
- The Video page allows you to decide whether to run video clips full-screen or in a window and, if you select the latter, what size window to use.
- The MIDI page lets you select the instrument on which Windows plays MIDI (Musical Instrument Digital Interface) output. If several MIDI instruments are available, you can assign the instruments to different channels.
- The CD Music page lets you specify the drive letter for your CD-ROM drive and set a volume setting for this drive's output.
- When you click on the Devices tab, a list of multimedia categories is displayed on the corresponding page of the dialog box. Clicking on the "+" symbol to the left of a category (or double-clicking on the category name) displays all drivers installed for this type of device. (A *device driver* is a program that translates the various commands from the device into a language that Windows can understand.) Selecting a particular driver and choosing the Properties command button provides information about the driver and allows you to change some of its settings.

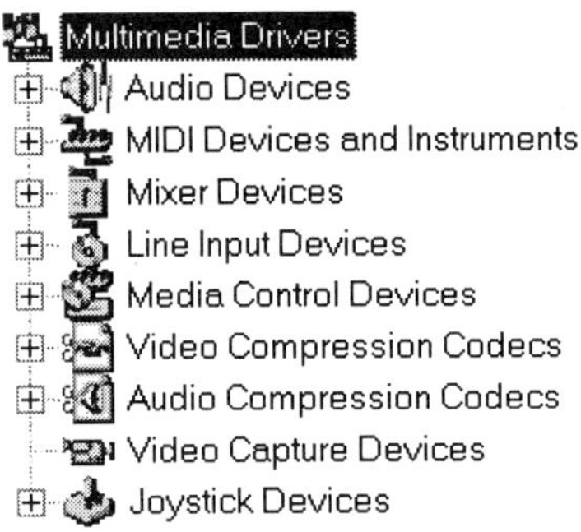

TUTORIAL

Try the following exercise on your own.

1. Turn on the computer (if necessary) to start Windows 98, and close any open windows.
2. Play an audio compact disc in the computer's CD-ROM drive:
   - Start the Windows CD Player utility by choosing the CD Player item from the Entertainment submenu of the Start button's Accessories menu. The CD Player window will open.

- Insert an audio compact disc in its drive.

- Click on the Play button in the CD Player window.
- Adjust the volume by clicking on the Taskbar's speaker icon and dragging the slider on the resulting volume control up or down. (If there is no speaker icon on the Taskbar, open the Volume Control utility from the Start button's Entertainment submenu, and drag the leftmost volume slider.)

- Click on the Next Track button to advance to track 2 of the disc.
- Click on the Stop button.

3. Record part of the audio disc:
   - Start the Sound Recorder utility by choosing this item from the Entertainment submenu of the Start button's Accessories menu. The Sound Recorder window will open.
   - Using the CD Player window, start playing the CD.

   - Start recording by licking on the Record button in the Sound Recorder window.

   - After a few seconds, stop recording.
   - Play back the just-recorded sound sample by clicking on Sound Recorder's Play button.
   - While the sample is playing, experiment with the editing options on Sound Recorder's Effects menu: Increase and decrease the speed and volume, add an echo, and play the sample in reverse.
4. Open the Media Player window by choosing its name from the Entertainment submenu of the Start button's Accessories menu.
5. Use Media Player to play the Windows 98 startup sound:
   - Choose the Sound item from the Device menu.
   - In the resulting dialog box, select "The Microsoft Windows 98 Sound" file (it is in the Media subfolder of the Windows folder) and choose the Open command.
   - In the Media Player window, click on the Play button.
6. Close all windows and remove the compact disc from its drive.

9.4 Enhancing Accessibility

Windows 98 contains several features that make it easier for physically challenged people to use a computer. For example:

- For the visually impaired, portions of the screen can be magnified, text can be made larger and given more contrast, and the mouse pointer can be made easier to follow.

- For the hearing impaired, visual cues can be displayed to accompany system sounds.
- For those who lack full dexterity, certain keystroke combinations can be made easier to manage and mouse movements can be emulated by the keyboard.

These accessibility features can be put into effect by using the Magnifier utility and/or the Accessibility Wizard. We will discuss these utilities in this section.

Microsoft Magnifier

The **Magnifier** utility opens a window on the screen that contains a magnified image of the work you are doing. Magnifier is not only useful for those with impaired vison, but also for all users in certain special situations, such as when reading small text on a laptop's screen.

To start Magnifier:

1. Click on the Start button, point at the Programs option, then point at Accessories and finally at Accessibility on the succeeding submenus.
2. On the Accessibility submenu, click on Magnifier. Two windows will open — the Microsoft Magnifier application window and a magnification window at the top of the screen (Figure 12).
3. To close the Magnifier application window, but leave the magnification window on the screen, choose the OK command in the former.

As you move the mouse or text cursor (depending on how Magnifier is configured), the contents of the magnification window will move with it, providing an enlarged view of the region around the cursor.

Manipulating the magnification window

Although the magnification window (as it appears in Figure 12) does not have a title bar, it can be resized and moved about the screen.

- To resize the window, drag its outer border up or down to make it larger or smaller.
- To move the magnification window, position the cursor inside it (the cursor will take on a "hand" shape), and drag the window to a new location. If you drag the magnification window to another

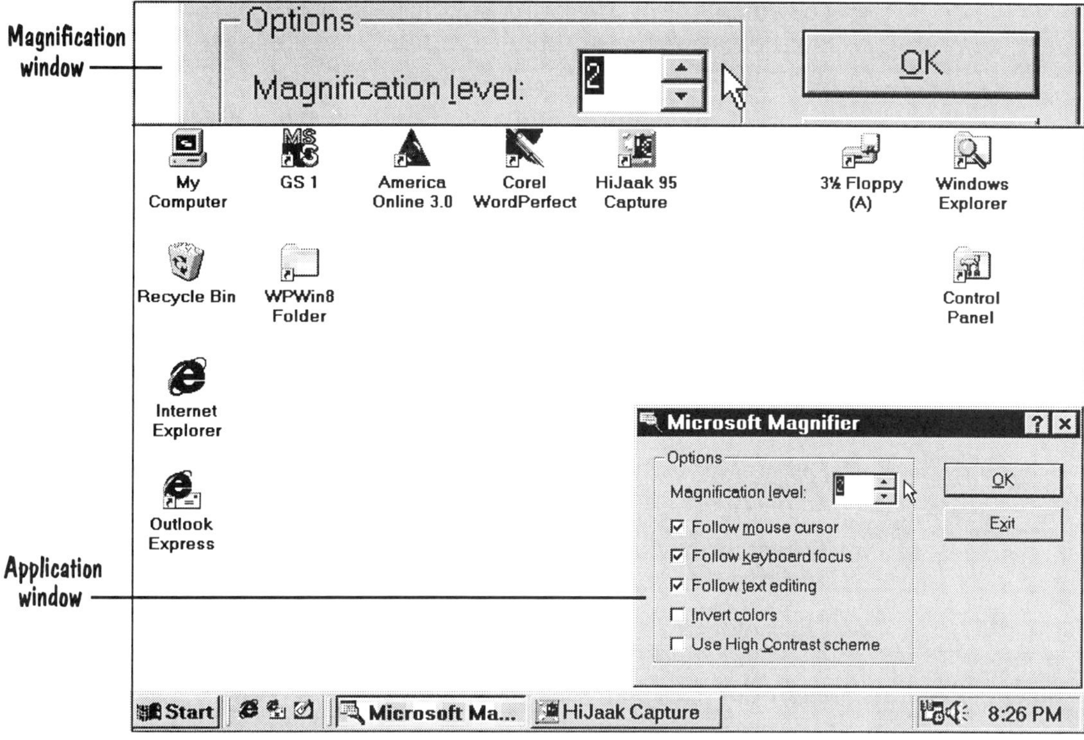

Figure 12 The Windows Desktop with Magnifier Running

edge of the screen, it will align along that edge. If you drag it to the center of the screen it will turn into an ordinary window, oddly titled the Magnifier Stationary Window (Figure 13).

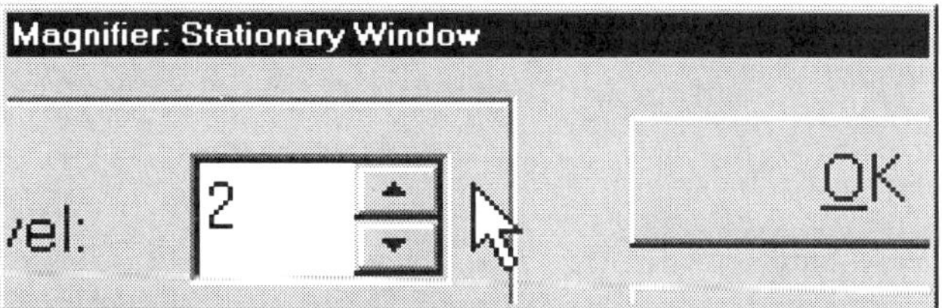

Figure 13 Stationary Magnification Window

Magnifier's stationary window can be moved and resized in the usual ways.

- To redisplay the Magnifier application window, right click on the magnification or stationary window and choose Options from the pop-up menu.
- To close the magnification or stationary window, right-click on it and choose Exit from the pop-up menu.

Setting options Magnifier can be configured from its application window (see Figure 12) in the following ways:

- The magnification level of the magnification window can be changed by using the *Magnification level* text box.
- The contents of the magnification window can be configured to move with the mouse cursor, keyboard cursor movement keys, and/or the insertion point by selecting the *Follow mouse cursor, Follow keyboard focus*, and/or *Follow text editing* check boxes, respectively.
- The colors of the magnification window can be inverted (white becomes black, etc.) by selecting the *Invert colors* check box.
- The colors of the entire screen (not just the magnification window) can be changed to improve visibility by selecting the *Use High Contrast scheme* check box.

The Accessibility Wizard

The **Accessibility Wizard** allows you to specify many different accessibility settings. To start this utility:

1. Click on the Start button, point at the Programs option, then point at Accessories and finally at Accessibility on the succeeding submenus.
2. On the Accessibility submenu, click on Accessibility Wizard, which will start and display its initial screen.

Now, just follow the instructions on each screen. To move to the next screen, choose the Next command button; to return to the previous screen, choose the Back button. To cancel all changes you've made (and close the Wizard), choose the Cancel button. To put the changes into effect, choose the Finish command button on the last screen.

The first couple of Wizard screens allow you to select a larger text size for certain window elements (such as titles and menus), decrease the screen resolution so that all items will appear larger, and/or have Microsoft Magnifier open each time Windows starts.

The next Wizard screen provides a menu of options (Figure 14). Select those check boxes that relate to the kinds of changes you'd like to make; your selections determine which Wizard screens will subsequently appear. (If you choose the Restore Default Settings command button, all settings will return to those in effect when you started Windows 98 for the first time.)

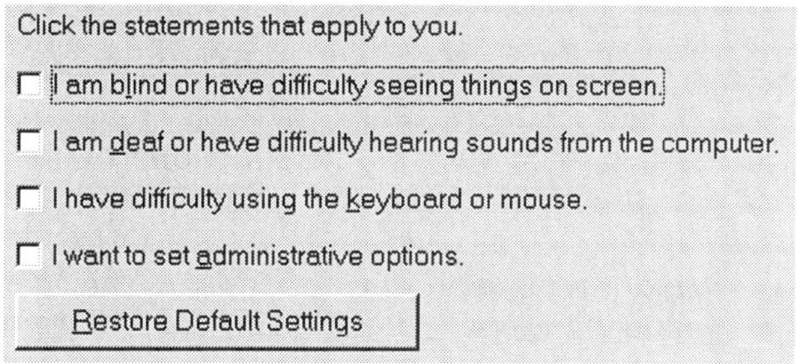

Figure 14 Accessibility Options

Here's a rundown on the kinds of changes you can make.

Options for the visually impaired

If you have difficulty seeing things on screen:

- You can enlarge scroll bars, window borders, and icons.
- You can elect to use a high contrast color scheme.
- You can change the size and color of the mouse pointer and/or put "mouse trails" (see Section 5.4) into effect.

Options for the hearing impaired

If you have difficulty hearing sounds produced by the computer:

- You can have Windows give a visual warning (such as flashing the title bar) whenever the computer's speaker emits a sound (SoundSentry).
- You can enable (put into effect) ShowSounds, which allows certain applications to display captions explaining what type of sound has just been emitted.

Options for those with poor dexterity

If you have difficulty using the keyboard or mouse:

- You can enable the StickyKeys option, which allows you to enter Shift, Ctrl, and Alt keystroke combinations (such as Ctrl+Esc) by pressing one key at a time.

- You can use the BounceKeys (FilterKeys) option to have Windows ignore brief or repeated keystrokes.
- You can enable the ToggleKeys option, which causes Windows to emit a sound when the Num Lock, Scroll Lock, or Caps Lock key is pressed.
- You can enable the MouseKeys option, which allows you to use the keyboard's numeric keypad to move the mouse pointer and simulate clicks. For example, with MouseKeys enabled, pressing the Right Arrow key moves the pointer to the right and pressing the 5 key causes a single click.
- You can reverse the functions of the left and right mouse buttons and change the mouse pointer speed.

Administrative options

Windows allows you to control the Accessibility features in the following ways:

- You can elect to have Windows turn off many of the features if the computer has been idle for a specified period of time.
- You can have the accessibility settings apply to all users or just the current user.
- You can save the accessibility settings to a file.

NOTE

All modifications that can be made by the Accessibility Wizard can be accomplished directly through other Windows utilities:

- Magnifier can be started from the Accessibility submenu of the Start button's Accessories menu, as described earlier in this section.
- Control Panel's Accessibility Options utility can be used to enable Sticky Keys, Filter Keys, Toggle Keys, Show Sounds, Sound Sentry, and MouseKeys, and apply a high contrast color scheme.
- Control Panel's Display utility (see Section 5.3) can be used to change text size and screen colors and resolution.
- Control Panel's Mouse utility (see Section 5.4) can enable pointer trails, change pointer speed, and reverse the functions of the left and right buttons.

TUTORIAL

Try the following exercise on your own.

1. Turn on the computer (if necessary) to start Windows 98 and close any open windows.

2. Start the Microsoft Magnifier utility by choosing the Magnifier item from the Accessibility submenu of the Start button's Accessories menu. A magnification window that shows an enlarged view of the area around the cursor, as well as the Magnifier application window, will open.
3. In the application window, enter a magnification level of 2 in the text box. Also, select the first three check boxes so that the contents of the magnification area will follow both the mouse and text cursor. Notice that as you move the mouse pointer in the application window, that part of the screen is duplicated and enlarged in the magnification window.
4. Choose the OK button to close the Magnifier application window.
5. Create a "floating" magnification window: Position the mouse pointer inside the window and drag it toward the center of the screen. Now, you can resize this window in the usual ways.
6. Close the magnification window by right-clicking inside this window and then choosing the Exit command from the pop-up menu.
7. Start the Accessibility Wizard by choosing this item from the Accessibility submenu of the Start button's Accessories menu.
8. Page through the first few Wizard screens by repeatedly choosing the Next command button, and note the available options. When you reach the Set Wizard Options screen, select the four check boxes so that the Wizard will display all possible options on subsequent screens.
9. Continue paging through the Wizard screens, noting the available accessibility options.
10. When you reach the last screen (on which the Next button is replaced by a Finish button), choose the Cancel command button to exit the Wizard without putting any changes you may have made into effect.

9.5 *Additional Accessories*

In this section, we will briefly discuss a few other Windows 98 utilities started from the Accessories menu. These include Character Map, Phone Dialer, and Clipboard Viewer.

Character Map

Character Map lets you insert special symbols into a document open in another Windows application. To use Character Map:

1. Click on the Start button, point at Programs, then at Accessories, and finally at System Tools. Choose Character Map from the resulting submenu; the window shown in Figure 15 will open.

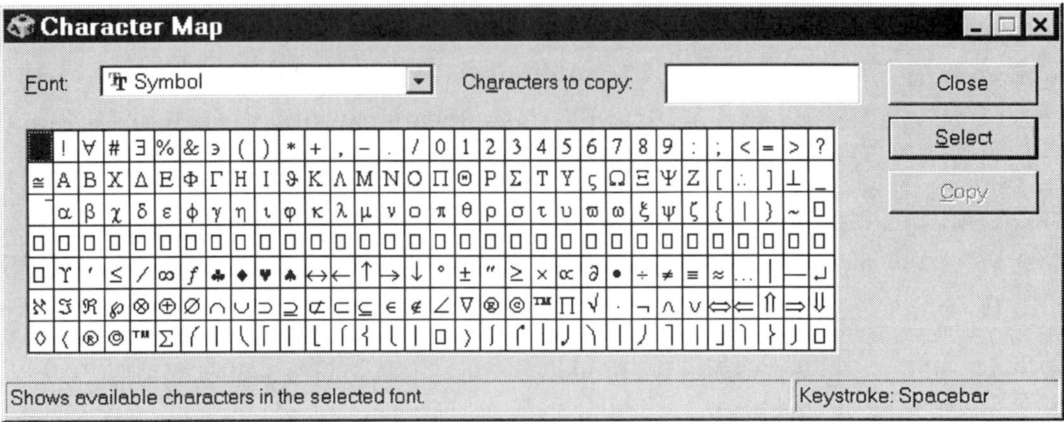

Figure 15 The Character Map Window

2. Select a typeface from the Font drop-down list. The *character set* for the selected font will be displayed in the window.
3. Select a character from those displayed by double-clicking on it (or by clicking on it and choosing the Select command button). The selected character will appear in the *Characters to copy* box.
4. If you want, repeat step 3 to select additional characters.
5. Choose the Copy command button to copy the selected characters to the Clipboard.
6. Switch to the application and document in which you want to insert the characters.
7. In this document, position the insertion point where you want the characters to be inserted, select the same typeface as the one used in Character Map, and choose the Paste command from the Edit menu.

Phone Dialer

If your computer is equipped with a **modem**, a device that translates computer-generated data into signals that can be sent over phone lines, you can use the **Phone Dialer** accessory to place telephone calls. To use Phone Dialer:

1. Click on the Start button, point at Programs, then at Accessories, and finally at Communications.
2. Choose Phone Dialer from the resulting submenu. The window shown in Figure 16 will open.

Figure 16 The Phone Dialer Window

3. Enter the phone number you want to call by mouse-clicking on the appropriate Phone Dialer number buttons or by typing it in the *Number to dial* text box;

or

Select a recently-called number from the *Number to dial* drop-down list.

4. Choose the Dial button to place the call. When it is answered, you will hear the other party through the computer's speaker.

5. To talk to the party you have dialed, use a standard telephone.

Using speed dial Phone Dialer has a "speed dial" feature that allows you to place a call by clicking on one of its eight Speed dial buttons. First, you must *program* these buttons, associating each with a specific telephone number. To do so:

1. Choose the Speed Dial item from the Edit menu. The window shown in Figure 17 will be displayed.

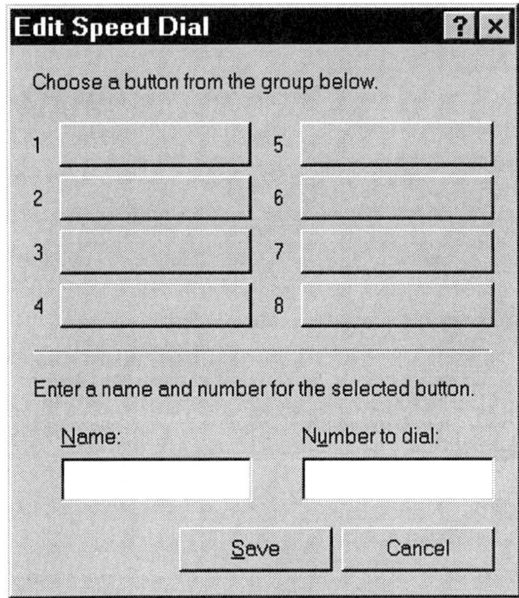

Figure 17 Programming Speed Dial

2. Click on the button that you want to program.
3. Type the name of the person or organization and the telephone number in the *Name* and *Number to dial* boxes, respectively.
4. Repeat steps 2 and 3 for each of the buttons to be programmed.
5. Choose the Save command button to complete the process. The Edit Speed Dial window will close, returning you to Phone Dialer.

Each programmed Phone Dialer button will display the name you have associated with it in the programming process. To dial that party, just click on that button.

To program a single (empty) speed dial button, click on that button; the dialog box shown at the right will open. Now, enter the desired name and number, and choose the Save command button. (If you choose the Save and Dial button, the phone number associated with this button will be dialed as well.)

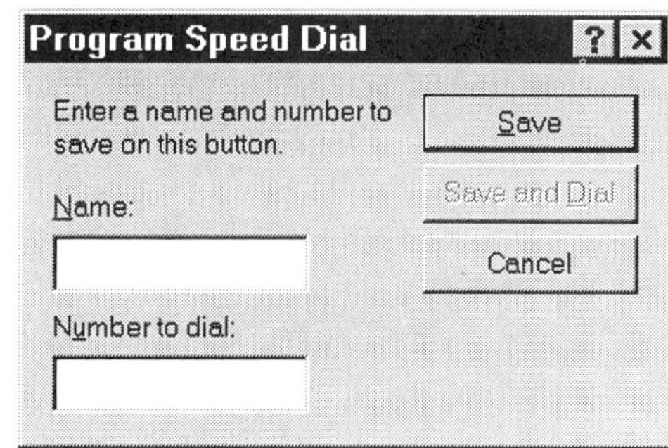

NOTE

Phone Dialer is known as a *communications program* — one which allows you to communicate, via your modem and the phone lines, with another person or computer. Windows supplies several other, more powerful, communications programs. We will discuss these applications in Chapter 11.

Clipboard Viewer

As you know, the Windows Clipboard (Section 2.3) allows you to transfer information from one application to another. Windows 98 provides a utility, **Clipboard Viewer**, to view, and to manipulate to some extent, the contents of the Clipboard. To use Clipboard Viewer:

1. Click on the Start button, point at Programs, then at Accessories, and finally at System Tools.
2. Choose Clipboard Viewer from the resulting submenu. The window shown in Figure 18 will open, displaying the current contents of the Clipboard, if any.

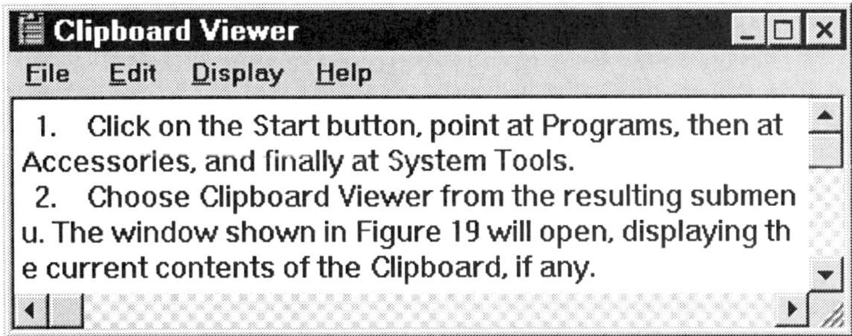

Figure 18 The Clipboard Viewer Window

3. From the Clipboard Viewer window, you can:
   - Save the contents of the Clipboard to a file by choosing the Save command from the File menu and making use of the resulting Save As dialog box in the usual way (see Section 2.2).
   - Open a previously-saved Clipboard file by choosing the Open command from the File menu and making use of the resulting Open dialog box in the usual way (see Section 2.2).
   - Delete the contents of the Clipboard by choosing the Delete command from the Edit menu.

Clipboard Viewer will attempt to display the contents of the Clipboard as best it can. As you can see in Figure 18, the results may not be completely accurate. You may be able to render the Clipboard's contents more accurately by choosing another display format from the Display menu. This is especially true for graphics. If a graphic does not display as it should, try choosing Bitmap or one of the other formats from this menu.

Chapter Summary

Calculator	To start Calculator	Click on Calculator on the Accessories submenu of the Start button's Programs option.
	To select a mode	Choose Standard or Scientific from the View menu.
	To activate a calculator key	Click on it.
Notepad	To start Notepad	Click on Notepad on the Accessories submenu of the Start button's Programs option.
	To enter and edit text	Proceed as in WordPad (see Section 2.2).
	To specify a font for the entire document	Choose the Set Font command from the Edit menu.
	To search for text	Choose Find from the Search menu.
	To set up the printed page	Choose Page Setup from the File menu and specify paper size, orientation, and margins in the resulting dialog box.

	To create a header or footer	Choose Page Setup from the File menu and enter text and codes in the Header and/or Footer text boxes.
Multimedia Utilities	To start a multimedia utility	Click on the desired item on the Entertainment submenu of the Accessories menu.
	CD Player	Plays audio compact discs using controls similar to those of a conventional CD player; can also store and display information (disc title, artist, and track titles) about a disc.
	Sound Recorder	Records, edits, and plays sounds using controls similar to those of an audio tape player.
	Volume Control	Adjusts the volume and other characteristics of the sound produced by the computer.
	Media Player	Plays sound, animation, MIDI, and video files and audio and video discs.
	Control Panel's Multimedia option	Specifies audio, video, MIDI, and CD music settings and configures multimedia device drivers.
Accessibility Utilities	Starting an accessibility utility	Click on the desired item on the Accessibility submenu of the Accessories menu.
	Magnifier	Enlarges a portion of the screen in a magnification window. The user can select the size and location of this window, the magnification level, and the cursors to follow.
	Accessibility Wizard	Makes the computer easier to use for people with certain physical disabilities: For the visually impaired: increases text size, scroll bar size, and icon size; applies a high contrast color scheme; increases mouse pointer size and speed, and enables mouse trails. For the hearing impaired: provides visual cues and captions to accompany certain computer-produced sounds. For those with poor dexterity: alters the action of the keyboard and emulates mouse actions with keyboard commands.
Additional Accessories	Character Map	Started from the System Tools submenu; inserts special characters into Windows documents.

Phone Dialer	Started from the Communications submenu; dials phone numbers.
Clipboard Viewer	Started from the System Tools submenu; displays and manipulates the contents of the Windows Clipboard.

Review Exercises

Section 9.1

1. In the Calculator accessory, you can display a standard or scientific calculator by choosing the corresponding item from the ___________ menu.
2. To clear Calculator's memory, click on the ___________ button.
3. In Scientific mode, to have Calculator find the mean and standard deviation of a collection of numbers, begin by clicking on the ___________ button.
4. True or false: Clicking on Calculator's Backspace button deletes the last digit entered into the display.
5. True or false: It is not possible to copy the number in Calculator's display to the Clipboard.
6. True or false: To calculate the sine of an angle using Calculator's Scientific mode, you must enter the angle in radian measure.
7. If you want to multiply 3.14 by the number in Calculator's memory, enter 3.14 into the display, click on the multiply symbol (*), and then

   a. Click on the MC button.
   b. Click on the MR button.
   c. Click on the MS button.
   d. Click on the M+ button.

8. The default number system used by Calculator when in Scientific mode is:

   a. Binary
   b. Octal
   c. Decimal
   d. Hexadecimal

Section 9.2

9. Notepad is a simple word processor that has no text formatting capabilities and is thus known as a ___________.

10. If ____________ is turned off in Notepad, the text you type remains on the same line until you press the Enter key.

11. A ____________ for a document is text that is automatically placed at the top of every page.

12. True or false: Although Notepad can search a document for a specified word, it cannot automatically replace it with another word of your choice.

13. True or false: To read a page that is printed in portrait orientation, hold it so that the long side is vertical.

14. True or false: In Notepad, you can specify the number of copies of the current document to be printed before the printing process begins.

15. Which of the following operations can be performed by Notepad?

    a. Aligning text with the right margin.
    b. Setting top, bottom, right, and left margins.
    c. Using one font for a document's title and another font for the rest of its text.
    d. Indenting the text in a given paragraph.

16. Which of the following sequences of symbols is used to create a Notepad footer that displays the current page number at the left margin and the current date at the right margin?

    a. &p &d
    b. &l &p &d
    c. &l &p &d &r
    d. &l &p &r &d

Section 9.3

17. The term ____________ refers to applications that contain sophisticated graphics, sound, and/or video components.

18. The ____________ multimedia utility can play both sound files and audio compact discs.

19. True or false: You can program the CD Player utility to display the title and artist of the compact disc in the CD-ROM drive.

20. True or false: To record an audio compact disc, begin by starting Sound Recorder and clicking on its Play button.

21. True or false: Only the master volume control can be accessed using the Taskbar's speaker icon.

22. True or false: The Volume Control utility can change the volume of the CD that you are playing, but not the left-right speaker balance.

23. Which of the following is not a multimedia device?

    a. A sound card
    b. A CD-ROM drive
    c. A modem
    d. A MIDI keyboard

24. Which multimedia utility can be used to *edit* a sound file?

    a. CD Player
    b. Sound Recorder
    c. Volume Control
    d. Media Player

25. Which multimedia utility can be used to *play* a video file?

    a. CD Player
    b. Sound Recorder
    c. Volume Control
    d. Media Player

26. Control Panel's Multimedia option can be used to

    a. Play an audio compact disc.
    b. Display or hide the Taskbar's speaker icon.
    c. Change the sound that is heard when Windows starts.
    d. Perform none of the above actions.

Section 9.4

27. To enlarge a portion of the screen around the cursor (without starting the Accessibility Wizard), use Microsoft's ____________ utility.

28. The Accessibility Wizard's StickyKeys, BounceKeys, and ToggleKeys options are intended for those people who have trouble using the ____________.

29. To close the Accessibility Wizard and put all the options you have selected into effect, choose the ____________ command button on the last Wizard screen.

30. True or false: Magnifier's magnification window must be positioned at the top part of the screen.

31. True or false: The Magnifier application window must remain open as long as its magnification window is displayed.

32. True or false: The purpose of the Accessibility Wizard's ShowSounds and SoundSentry options is to help the hearing-impaired use Windows more effectively.

33. To help the visually-impaired, the Accessibility Wizard can have Windows display

a. High-contrast screens.
b. Thicker scroll bars.
c. A larger mouse pointer.
d. All of the above.

34. To help those people who have trouble using the mouse, the Accessibility Wizard can have Windows

a. Change the double-click speed.
b. Emit a sound whenever the mouse is clicked.
c. Emulate mouse movements with keystrokes.
d. All of the above.

Section 9.5

35. The Windows ____________ accessory enables you to insert special symbols into documents open in another Windows application.

36. The Phone Dialer utility is started from the ____________ submenu of the Accessories menu.

37. True or false: To copy a character from the Character Map utility to the Clipboard, choose the Copy command on the Edit menu.

38. True or false: You can use Clipboard Viewer to alter the contents of the Clipboard.

39. Phone Dialer has the capability to

a. Dial phone numbers.
b. Act like a standard telephone once a call has been answered.
c. Dial a second number while a call is in progress.
d. Perform all of the above tasks.

40. Clipboard Viewer has the capability to

a. Display the contents of the Clipboard in various formats.
b. Delete the contents of the Clipboard.
c. Save the contents of the Clipboard to a disk file.
d. Perform all of the above tasks.

Build Your Own Glossary

41. The following words and phrases are important terms that were introduced in this chapter. (They appear within the text in boldface type.) Use WordPad (see Section 2.2) to enter a definition for each term, preserving alphabetical order, into the Glossary file on the Student Disk.

Accessibility Wizard
Accessories
ASCII
Calculator utility
CD Player utility
Character Map
Clipboard Viewer
Footer
Header
Magnifier utility
Media Player utility
Modem
Multimedia
Notepad
Phone Dialer utility
Sound Recorder utility
Text editor
Text file
Volume Control
Word wrap

Lab Exercises

Work each of the following exercises at your computer. Begin by turning the machine on (if necessary) to start Windows 98 and closing any open windows.

Lab Exercise 1 (Section 9.1)

a. Start Windows Calculator and display the Standard calculator. Can you maximize the Calculator window?

b. What value would you expect for the expression 4 + 5 * 6, 34 or 54? Why? Use Calculator to find its value. What did you get?

c. Enter the number 13 into memory. Which memory key did you use? Did an "M" appear in the box above the memory keys?

d. Add 22 to the number in memory? Which memory key did you use?

e. Now, find 6% of the number in memory. What did you get?

f. Clear both memory and the current calculation. What two keys did you use to accomplish this?

g. Find $1/\sqrt{11}$ and $\sqrt{1/11}$. Did you get the same answer for both expressions?

h. Close Calculator.

Lab Exercise 2 (Section 9.2)

a. Start Notepad and maximize its window.

b. Type your name and class on separate lines, and skip a line (by pressing the Enter key twice).

c. Type the sentence: This is a test of the copy and paste operations. Then, press the Enter key.

d. Select this sentence. Describe how you accomplished this.

e. Copy the selected text to the Clipboard. What menu command or mouse actions did you use?

f. Paste the text from the Clipboard onto the end of the document. What menu command or mouse actions did you use?

g. Repeat step *f* four times. Try pasting the text without reselecting and recopying it. Did this work?

h. Print the document.

i. Save the document (see Section 2.2), if you wish, and exit Notepad.

Lab Exercise 3 (Section 9.2)

a. Start Notepad and maximize its window.

b. Insert the Student Disk in its drive and open the History2 document (see Section 2.2, if necessary).

c. In the Page Setup dialog box:

- Set the orientation to *portrait* and all margins to one inch.
- Create a header that contains your name (left-aligned) and your class (right-aligned).
- Create a footer that displays the date, centered on the line.

d. Open the Find dialog box and enter the word *large* in the *Find what* box. Now, use this utility to determine the number of times the word *large* occurs in the document.

e. At the end of the document, type complete sentences stating the number of times the word *large* occurs and the number of times words containing *large* occur in the document.

f. Print the revised document.

g. Save the document if you wish, exit Notepad, and remove the diskette from its drive.

Lab Exercise 4 (Section 9.3)

a. Start the CD Player utility. On which submenu of the Accessories menu can it be found?

b. Insert an audio compact disc in the CD-ROM drive. Did it automatically start playing? If not, click on CD Player's Play button to start the CD.

c. Adjust the volume up or down from within the CD Player window. Which menu did you open to accomplish this?

d. Move to the next track on the disc. Can this be done with both the Skip Forward and Next Track buttons? What is the difference in the function of these buttons?

e. Change the track/time function of the CD Player's "display". What was the previous function called? What is the new one called?

f. Display the toolbar (if it's not already displayed) and turn on Intro Play. How many seconds of each track is played? (Use the CD Player display to determine this.)

g. Turn on Random Play. Does this feature work with Intro Play? (Again, use the CD Player display to determine which tracks are being played.)

h. Close CD Player and remove the disc from the CD-ROM drive.

Lab Exercise 5 (Section 9.3)

a. Insert an audio compact disc in the CD-ROM drive. Did it start playing automatically? If not, start CD Player and play the disc.

b. Start Sound Recorder. Which of the five control buttons are available (not dimmed)?

c. Record about 10 seconds of the audio CD. Which control buttons are available after you stop recording?

d. Increase the volume in Sound Recorder by 25%. Which menu did you use to accomplish this? Decrease the volume of the CD you're playing to its lowest audible level.

e. Click on Sound Recorder's Play button. What do you hear: the recording, the CD, both, or neither? In CD Player, stop playing the CD.

f. Open the Volume Control utility. How did you do this?

g. One-by-one, from right to left, drag each slider to the maximum volume position, click on the Sound Recorder's Play button, and return the slider to its normal position. Which volume controls affected the volume of the playback?

h. In succession, turn on each of the following effects and play the sound sample: Increase Speed, Decrease Speed, Add Echo, and Reverse. Which of these effects worked?

i. Close CD Player and Sound Recorder and remove the CD from the drive. (Answer No to the "save changes?" message.)

Lab Exercise 6 (Section 9.4)

a. Start WordPad and the Magnifier utility. Does the magnification window align with the top edge of the screen?

b. Drag the magnification window to the top edge of the screen (if necessary) and maximize the WordPad window. Does the magnification window or Magnifier application window cover part of the WordPad window?

c. Using the Magnifier application window:

- Change the magnification level to 1; then to 2. Do you immediately see the changes in the magnification window?
- By experimenting with WordPad, determine (and describe) the results of selecting each of the first three check boxes.
- What color is the Microsoft Magnifier title bar in the magnification window? Now, click on the Invert Colors check box. What color is the title bar now?

d. Close the Magnifier application window without closing the magnification window. How did you do this?

e. Turn the existing magnification window into a "stationary window". How did you do this?

f. Close the magnification window without reopening the Magnifier application window. How did you do this? Close WordPad.

Lab Exercise 7 (Section 9.4)

a. Start the Accessibility Wizard. What is the initial screen called?

b. Don't make any changes on the first two Wizard screens, but on the third screen, select all four check boxes. Now, page through the rest of the Wizard screens and answer the following questions:

- How many choices of icon size are there?
- How many high contrast schemes are available?
- Describe what is meant by the following accessibility features: SoundSentry, ShowSounds, StickyKeys, BounceKeys, and ToggleKeys.
- Once MouseKeys is enabled, what key is used to double-click the mouse? What keys are used to emulate a mouse-drag?
- How many choices of mouse pointer size and color are available?
- What is the Web address for Microsoft's "Accessibility and Disabilities Group" site?

c. Click on the Cancel command button on the last Wizard screen and click on the No button in the resulting message box to close the Accessibility Wizard.

Lab Exercise 8 (Section 9.5)

a. Start Notepad, WordPad, and the Character Map and Clipboard Viewer utilities. On which submenu of the Accessories menu are the last two found?

b. In Character Map, choose the Symbol font from the drop-down list. Are all the "boxes" in the Character Map window filled with characters?

c. Position the mouse pointer over a character and hold down the mouse button. What happened?

d. Select several characters (of your choice), displaying them in the *Characters to copy* box.

e. Choose the Copy command button. What does this action accomplish?

f. Switch to Clipboard Viewer. Are the characters that you copied in Character Map displayed in the Clipboard Viewer window? Do they look the same as in Character Map?

g. Switch to WordPad and display the Format bar, if necessary. What is the current font (as indicated on the Format bar)?

h. Choose the Paste command from the Edit menu. Are the same characters displayed in the WordPad document window as were copied from Character Map? What is the current font now?

i. Switch to Notepad and choose the Paste command from the Edit menu. Are the same characters displayed in the Notepad window as were copied from Character Map?

j. Close all open windows (responding No to the "save changes?" messages).

If You Want to Learn More ...

The notes presented here allow you to delve more deeply into some of the topics covered in this chapter.

Installing missing accessories

If a Windows 98 utility discussed in this chapter (or mentioned in the next note) does not appear on your Accessories menu or on one of its submenus, you can install it from the Windows 98 CD-ROM. To do so:

1. Start Control Panel by choosing this item from the Start menu's Settings option.
2. In the Control Panel window, choose the Add/Remove Programs icon. The Add/Remove Programs Properties dialog box will open.
3. Click on the Windows Setup tab.
4. Insert the Windows 98 CD-ROM in its drive.
5. Select the Accessories, Communications, Multimedia, or System Tools item from the Components list.
6. Choose the Details command button. A list of all available utilities of the type selected in step 5 will appear. (Those that are already installed have a check mark beside their name.)
7. Select the check box next to each of the utilities you want to add.
8. Choose the OK button in the active dialog box.
9. Select another component type from the list, if desired, and repeat steps 6, 7, and 8.

10. Choose the OK button in the Add/Remove Programs Properties dialog box. The relevant files will be copied to the hard disk and the selected utilities will appear on the Accessories menu or one of its submenus.

(See Section 2.4 for more information about adding and removing Windows components.)

Other items on the Accessories submenus

The content of the Accessories menu and its submenus on a given computer depends on several factors: the configuration of the system, whether or not Windows 98 was installed as an upgrade, and which utilities were "manually" added after the original installation. Here are some items that may appear on these menus, but have not yet been discussed in the text:

- *Games*, as you might guess, supplies a few simple computer games for you to play. The content of the Games submenu depends on the same factors (described above) as the Accessories menus.
- The System Tools *Backup*, *Compression Agent*, *Disk Cleanup*, *Disk Defragmenter*, *Drive Converter*, *DriveSpace*, *Maintenance Wizard*, *Resource Meter*, *ScanDisk*, *Scheduled Tasks*, *System Information*, and *System Monitor* will be discussed in Chapter 10.
- *Briefcase*, *Dial-Up Networking*, *Direct Cable Connection*, and *HyperTerminal* are communication utilities, and will be discussed in Chapter 11.
- The Entertainment submenu may contain additional items such as *DVD Player* (which plays movies from DVD discs), *NetShow Player* (which allows you to view and/or listen to TV-like or radio-like broadcasts on the Internet), and *Broadcast Data Services* (which provides enhancements to TV viewing on your computer).

CD Player options

If you enjoy listening to music while working at the computer, CD Player may become your favorite Windows accessory. In Section 9.3, we described some of its features. Here, we will discuss how you can fine-tune the workings of CD Player. First, choose the Preferences item from the Options menu. Then, in the resulting dialog box:

- Deselect the *Stop CD playing on exit* check box if you want to be able to close CD Player, yet still listen to the disc.
- Select the *Save settings on exit* check box to turn on all current settings (such as whether or not Random Play or Intro Play are in

effect) the next time CD Player is started.

- Select the *Show tool tips* check box to display a tool tip when the mouse rests on a toolbar button.
- Enter a new figure in the *Intro play length* box to change the amount of time each track will play in Intro Play mode.
- Select a small or large "display" font using the appropriate option button.

Finally, choose the OK command button to put your preferences into effect.

Control Panel's Accessibility Options utility

As you know, the Accessibility Wizard (Section 9.4) provides ways to make the computer easier to use for people with certain physical disabilities. You can enable all the features supplied by the Wizard, and in most cases exert more control over their implementation, by using Control Panel's Display, Keyboard, Mouse, and Accessibility Options utilities. We have discussed the first three of these utilities in Chapter 5; here's a brief rundown on the last.

To start the Accessibility Options utility, open the Control Panel window (by pointing at Settings on the Start menu and then clicking on Control Panel) and choose the Accessibility Options icon. The resulting dialog box has five tabs:

- The Keyboard page allows you to enable the StickyKeys, FilterKeys (BounceKeys), and ToggleKeys features. Moreover, a Settings command button for each feature allows you to fine tune that feature.
- The Sound page allows you to enable the SoundSentry and ShowSounds features and provides additional settings for the former.
- The Display page allows you to put a high contrast scheme into effect.
- The Mouse page allows you to enable the MouseKeys feature with some additional settings.
- The General page provides the "administrative features" found in the Accessibility Wizard.

Inserting special characters without using Character Map

If you insert certain special characters (such as Greek letters or a copyright or trademark symbol) into your documents frequently, there may be a way to do it without starting Character Map (Section 9.5). In many applications, some special characters can be entered directly from the keyboard. To determine the appropriate keystroke:

1. Start Character Map and select the typeface (from the Font drop-down list) that contains the desired character.
2. Click on the character, highlighting it.
3. The keystroke that will create this character in most Windows applications is displayed in the lower-right corner of the Character Map window.

For example, suppose you want to use the Greek letter α (alpha) and the copyright symbol, ©, in a WordPad document. Both of these characters are contained in the Symbol font (see Figure 15 on page 460). Clicking on α and then © in the Character Map window, we see that the corresponding keystrokes are *a* and Alt+0211, respectively. Thus, in WordPad, to insert one of these characters at the insertion point:

1. Select the Symbol typeface.
2. Then:
   - To insert the character α, type the letter *a*.
   - To insert the character ©, turn on Num Lock, hold down the Alt key, type 0211 on the numeric keypad, and then release the Alt key.

CHAPTER 10

Maintaining Your Computer System

Overview

A computer is a low maintenance machine. A well-made computer system can provide you with years of satisfactory service, even though you do little more than occasionally clean the display screen and mouse roller ball. Nevertheless, from time to time, you may want to add a new device or speed up a sluggish hard disk. This chapter discusses the built-in utilities that Windows 98 provides to help you perform maintenance tasks of this sort. To be more specific:

- Section 10.1 discusses adding new hardware devices to your system.
- Section 10.2 deals with the process of backing up your hard disk.
- Section 10.3 describes various ways to increase your free disk space, including compressing the disk and changing to a new file system (FAT).
- Section 10.4 discusses utilities that fine-tune your disks (Scan-Disk and Disk Defragmenter) and run programs automatically (Maintenance Wizard and Task Scheduler).
- Section 10.5 covers several utilities that provide information about, monitor, and improve the performance of your system.

The sections in this chapter are independent of one another, so they can be covered in any order or skipped entirely, if so desired.

10.1 Adding Hardware

One of the great things about personal computers is that they are "expandable" — you can install new hardware (such as more RAM or a modem) or replace existing components to adapt the machine to your changing needs. Installing a piece of hardware involves two fundamental steps:

1. You must physically connect the device to your computer, via either an external *port* (at the back of the system unit) or an internal connector (inside the system unit).
2. You must change certain settings and/or install special software so that the computer recognizes the device and makes full use of its capabilities.

The second step in this process may or may not involve Windows. For example, if you install additional RAM in your computer, the machine will recognize the change when it runs its start-up tests, and either automatically alter the necessary settings or instruct you to do so using a setup program. On the other hand, if you install a modem, Windows will probably detect the new hardware and either accommodate it automatically or guide you through the process.

In this section, we will discuss the way in which Windows deals with a new piece of hardware once the device has been physically connected to the computer. (Note that the process of adding a printer is discussed in Section 4.5.)

WARNING

Before installing a new piece of hardware, you should always read the instruction manual that accompanies it. The manual will not only include instructions for physically connecting the device to your computer system, but also provide information about configuring it correctly. If the manual suggests a procedure that is different from the ones described in this section, it is usually best to follow the manufacturer's recommendations.

Plug and Play

Plug and Play is an industry-wide standard that makes it easy to install certain hardware devices. To make full use of Plug and Play, both the new device and your computer must support this standard.

To add a Plug and Play device to your system:

1. Physically install the device (with the computer off), following

the manufacturer's instructions.

2. Turn on the computer. During the startup process, a message will appear stating that Windows has detected the device.
3. The Add New Hardware wizard (see below) may start and request that you insert a disk containing the device's *driver* into the drive. (A **driver** is a program that translates signals from the device into a language that Windows can understand.) In any case, Windows will determine the necessary settings and install the relevant software so that the new device will run properly.
4. Click on the Finish button or OK button (depending on the situation) to complete the process. In some cases, Windows may restart itself to put the changes into effect.

The Add New Hardware Utility

If you want to install a device that has not been designed to meet the Plug and Play standard, the process is more difficult. Once you have physically connected the new hardware to the system, turn on the computer and proceed as follows*:

1. Close all open windows and exit any running applications.
2. Start Control Panel. (Click on the Start button, point at the Settings option, and choose Control Panel from the resulting menu.)

3. Choose the Add New Hardware icon, which starts the **Add New Hardware** wizard.
4. In the resulting dialog box, choose the Next command button. A new wizard screen will be displayed telling you that Windows will now search for new Plug and Play devices. Choose the Next button to start the search.
5. After Windows has completed its search for new Plug and Play devices, the next wizard dialog box will appear, and may list a few hardware-related items.
   - If the device you are installing is listed here, select the *Yes, the device is in the list* option button, select that device, and choose the Next button. Windows will now install this device as described in the Plug and Play section above.

*These procedures are generic in nature and do not apply to adding RAM, a disk drive, and certain other hardware. The installation of these devices proceeds quite differently; follow the instructions supplied by the manufacturer.

- If the new device is not listed, select the *No, the device isn't in the list* option button, choose the Next button, and continue with this procedure.

6. In the next wizard dialog box (Figure 1), you have to decide whether or not to have Windows try to detect the new hardware. If you select the Yes option button and click on Next, then:

   - In the next wizard dialog box, choose the Next button, and Windows will search for the new hardware
   - If the search is successful, Windows will display a new wizard dialog box. Choose the Details button to see a list of all devices found, select the ones that you want installed, and choose the Finish button.
   - You may then be asked to insert a certain diskette or CD-ROM in its drive so that the proper device driver can be copied to the hard disk.
   - Windows may then restart the computer to put the changes into effect. The installation process is now complete.

   If Windows informs you that no new hardware was found, it will return you to the window shown in Figure 1.

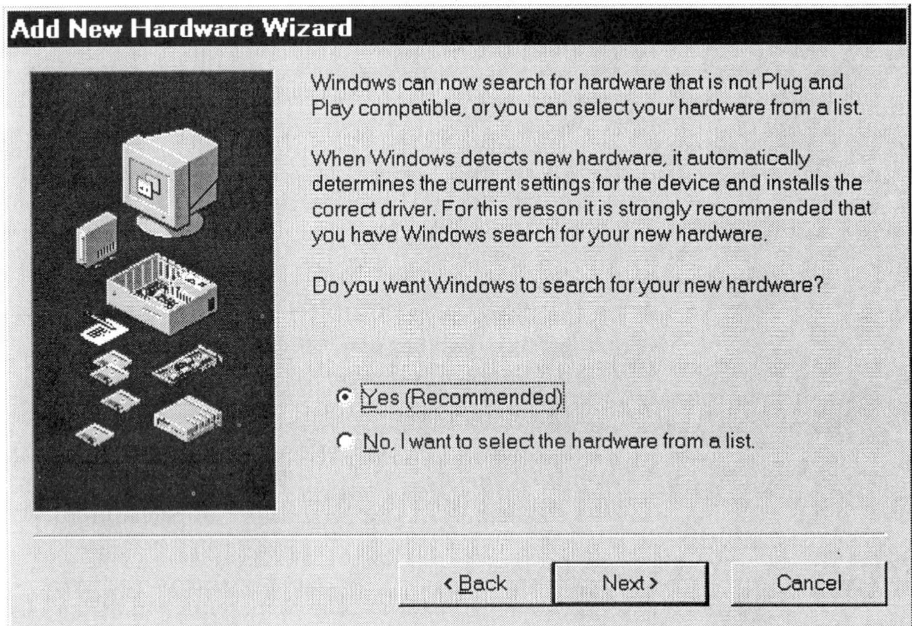

Figure 1 Should Windows Try to Detect the New Hardware?

7. If you select the No option button in Figure 1, you will have to complete the remaining steps in this procedure. Choose the Next command button, and a dialog box, like the one shown in Figure 2, will be displayed.

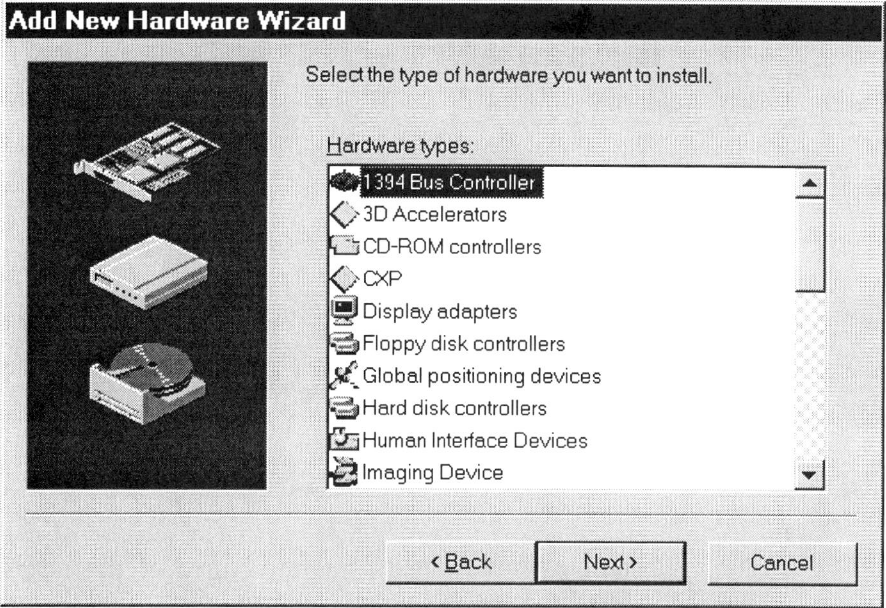

Figure 2 Selecting the Type of Hardware to be Installed

8. Select the type of hardware you are installing and choose the Next command button. A dialog box, like the one shown in Figure 3 (on the next page), will be displayed.

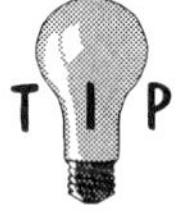

If you are not sure what "type" of hardware you are installing, select *Other devices* from the list and click on the Next button. This selection will display all available hardware choices in the Wizard dialog box, which will be similar to the one shown in Figure 3.

9. If the manufacturer has supplied an installation disk, insert it in its drive, choose the Have Disk command button, enter the appropriate drive in the resulting dialog box, and choose OK.

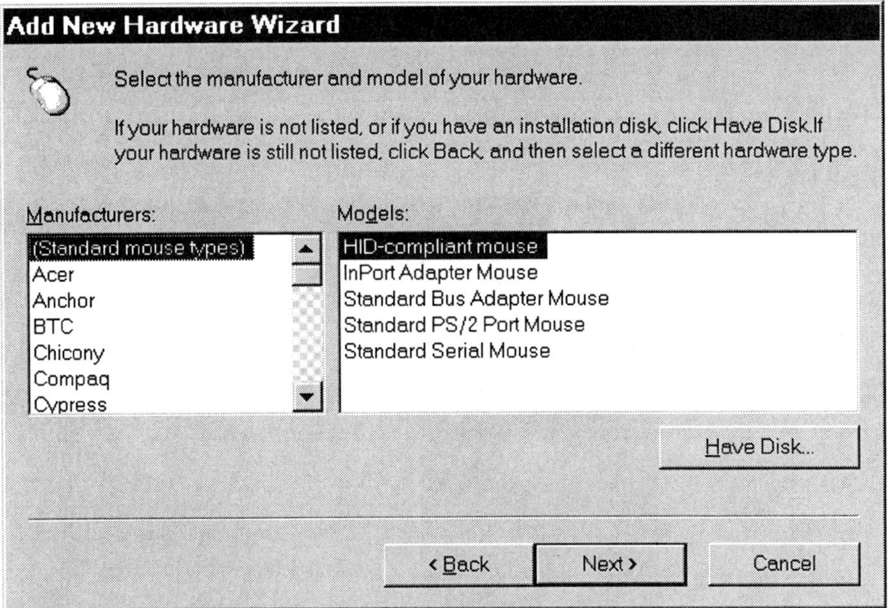

Figure 3 Selecting the Particular Piece of Hardware to be Installed

Otherwise, select the manufacturer of the new hardware in the left box and a list of corresponding models will appear in the right box. Select the appropriate model from this list and choose the Next command button.

10. Depending on the device you are installing:

    - Windows may now display a list of settings for the device to be installed and it may be necessary for you to set certain switches or jumpers on the device to match these settings. If so, make these changes after you are finished with the Add New Hardware Wizard and have turned off your computer.
    - Windows may now ask that you insert a certain diskette or CD-ROM in its drive in order to copy relevant files to your hard disk.
    - Windows may advise you that there is a conflict between the new device and another device. To proceed, choose the Next button, follow the instructions, and see if the *Conflict Troubleshooter* can help. If you have any doubts about your ability to handle this situation, choose the Cancel button

instead and get help from someone who is more experienced in this area.

11. When the process is complete, choose the Finish button (if necessary). You may be asked to restart your computer at this point to put the changes into effect.

TUTORIAL

Try the following exercise on your own. It simulates the configuration of a mouse that you have supposedly just connected to your computer.

1. Turn on the computer (if necessary) to start Windows 98, and close any open windows.
2. Open the Control Panel window (from the Settings option on the Start menu) and choose the Add New Hardware icon. This starts the Add New Hardware wizard.
3. Read the information displayed and then choose the Next command button. In the Next wizard dialog box, click on Next to have Windows search for new Plug and Play devices.
4. We will pretend that your new mouse is not a Plug and Play device, so it does not appear in the list of such devices after the search is complete. Thus, select the No option button and then click on Next.
5. In the next wizard dialog box, select the No option button, telling Windows that you will enter the information about the new device instead of having the system try to detect it automatically. Then, choose the Next button. A list of hardware types will be displayed.
6. Select Mouse from the list and choose the Next button. Two lists, of manufacturers and models, will be displayed.
7. Select Microsoft from the list on the left and one of the Microsoft Serial Mouse choices from the list on the right. (In practice, you would get this information from the device's instruction manual.) Choose the Next button. A dialog box is displayed informing you that Windows can install this hardware.
8. Choose the Cancel button to abort the installation process. The Add New Hardware wizard will close, returning you to Control Panel. (In practice, you would click on Finish and follow the on-screen instructions to complete the process.)
9. Close the Control Panel window.

10.2 Backing Up Your Hard Disk

To **back up** a file on your hard disk means to copy it to another medium; for example, a floppy disk or tape. It is a good idea to back up newly-created or just-modified data files at the end of every session at the computer. Then, if a file becomes damaged or you accidentally erase it at some time in the future, you can easily copy that file from your backup to the hard disk, instead of having to recreate it from scratch.

In addition to daily backups of individual files, many users also make more extensive backups, of key folders or even the entire disk, every once in a while. Then, should a major disaster occur and your hard disk (or a large part of it) become inaccessible, you can recreate its contents.

Starting the Backup Utility

Simple backups can be made using the Copy or Send To commands in Explorer or My Computer (see Chapter 3). For more extensive backups, Windows supplies the **Backup utility**. To start Backup:

1. Click on the Start button, point at Programs on the Start menu, and then at Accessories on the submenu.
2. On the Accessories menu, point at System Tools, and then click on the Backup item on the resulting submenu. Then, depending on how Backup has been set up, either the Backup welcome dialog box (Figure 4) or the main Backup window (Figure 5) will be displayed.

In the Backup welcome dialog box (Figure 4), you have four options:

- Selecting the *Create a new backup job* option button starts the Backup Wizard which guides you through the backup process. We will discuss the Backup Wizard later in this section.
- Selecting the *Open an existing backup job* option button displays the Open Backup Job dialog box, allowing you to select a previously-specified file set and backup location. We will discuss backup jobs later in this section.
- Selecting the *Restore backed up files* option button starts the Restore Wizard, which guides you through the process of transferring backed up files from the backup medium to the hard disk. We will discuss the Restore Wizard later in this section.

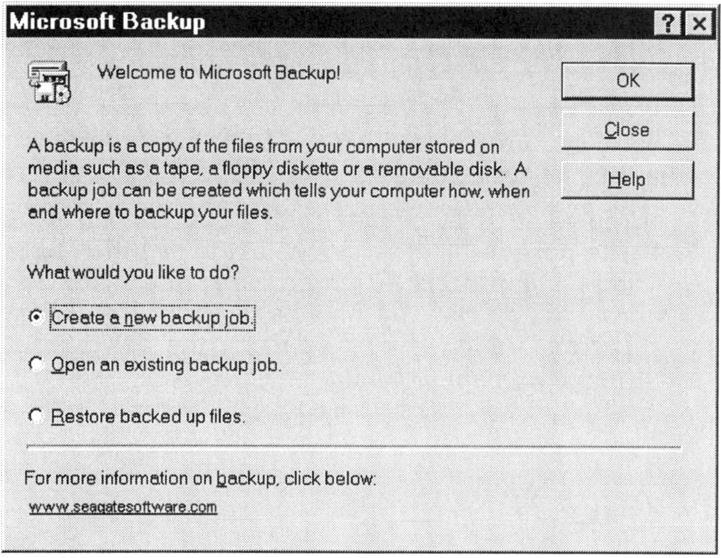

Figure 4 Backup's Welcome Dialog Box

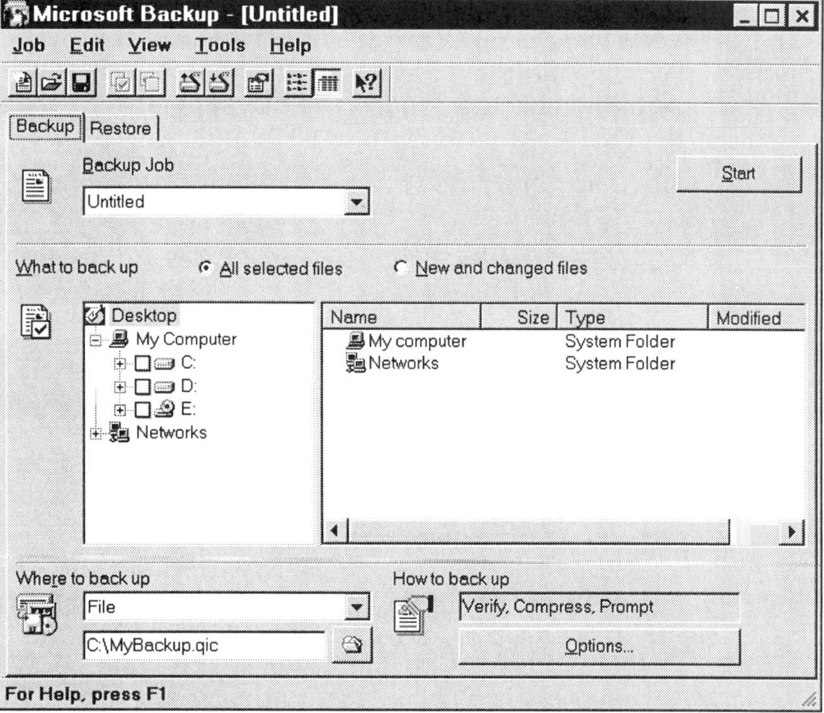

Figure 5 The Main Backup Window

- Choosing the Close command button (or clicking on the title bar's close button) displays the main Backup window (Figure 5).

NOTE

If your Backup window looks somewhat different from the one in Figure 5, be aware that:

- You can display or hide the toolbar, status bar, and "job details" (the portion of the window just above the status bar) by choosing the appropriate item from the View menu.
- You can display the objects in the right window pane in either List or Details view by selecting the desired option from either the View menu or toolbar.

The Backup Procedure

The basic backup procedure consists of three steps:

1. Select the files to be backed up.
2. Select a destination to which they will be backed up.
3. Start the copying process.

Carrying out these steps is easy if you're familiar with Explorer's way of navigating the Windows folder system (see Section 3.2). Here's a detailed description of the backup process:

1. Start the Backup utility and display its main window, as described above.
2. Select the *New and unchanged files* option button if you do not want to back up files that have not changed since the last backup. Otherwise, select the *All selected files* option button.
3. If you want to back up specific files in a given folder, open that folder (by clicking on its icon) and then click on the little boxes to the left of the desired files. If you want to back up an entire folder, click on the box to the left of the folder's icon. In either case, a blue check mark will be displayed in the box when a file or folder has been selected.

   Figure 6 shows the result of opening the Chap-2 folder and clicking on the box to the left of the Chap-2 icon in the folder tree. As a result of the latter action, all files in the contents (right) pane were automatically selected. A gray check mark also appears in the box next to the parent folder (Win 98 Text), indicating that part, but not all, of this folder has been selected.

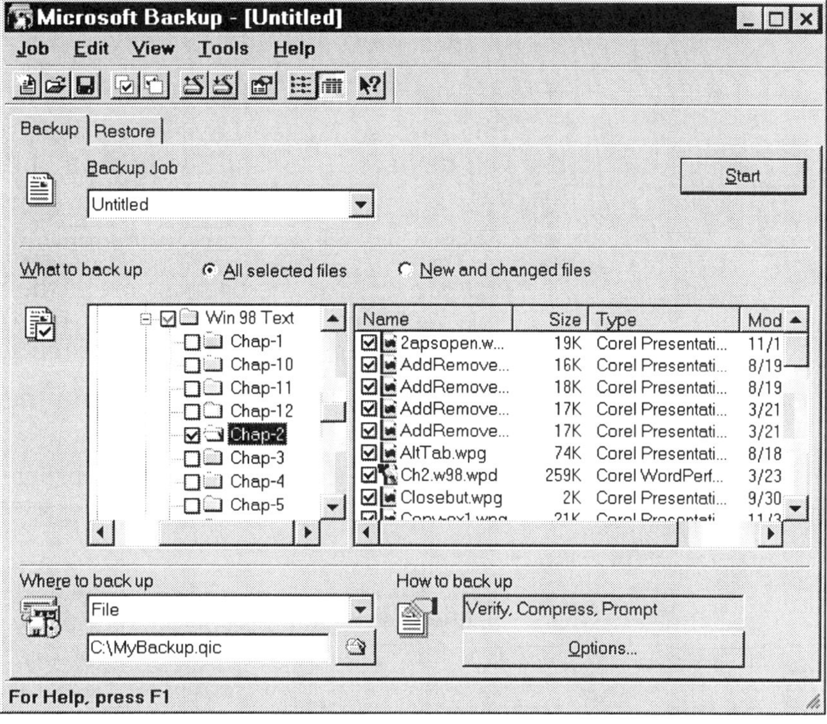

Figure 6 Selecting the “Chap-2" Folder in Backup

4. Select options for the backup process by clicking on the Options command button or choosing the Options item from the Job menu. (We discuss the available options on pages 491 and 492.)
5. To view a count of the number of files selected and the total number of bytes they contain, choose the Selection Information item from the View menu.
6. Insert the *backup media* — a diskette, tape cartridge, or other removable storage medium) in its drive. (If you are backing up to a network drive or other hard drive, skip this step.)
7. Choose the *destination* for the backed up files:

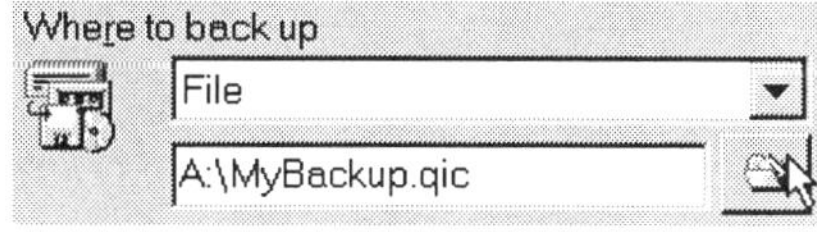

   - Click on the “open folder” icon in the *Where to back up* section of the window.
   - In the resulting dialog box (which is similar to a standard

Open file dialog box), select a drive, folder, and name for the file that will contain the contents of the backup.

- Choose the Open command button.

8. Save this **backup job** — the selected files, the location to which they will be backed up, and the backup options selected — to a disk file:
   - Choose the Save As command from the Job menu
   - Type a name for the backup job in the resulting dialog box. (This name can be, but need not be, the same as the one selected for the destination file in step 7.)
   - Choose the Save command button in the dialog box.
9. Choose the Start command button. The Backup Progress dialog box (Figure 7) will open and show the progress of the operation, as the files are copied, as well as some related information.

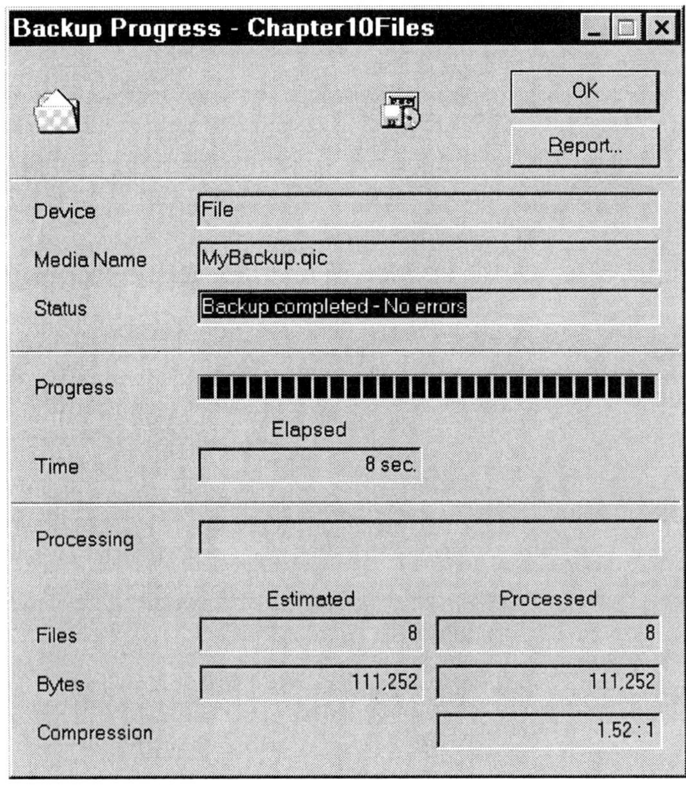

Figure 7 The Backup Progress Dialog Box

10. A message is displayed when the process is complete. Choose the OK button to clear the message box from the screen.
11. Choose the Report command button to view a report of the backup in Notepad. You can print this report by choosing the Print command from Notepad's File menu. Close Notepad when you are done.
12. Close the Backup Progress dialog box and, if so desired, the Backup utility.

Backup Job Options As mentioned in step 5 of the backup procedure described above, you may want to specify certain preferences for the way the backup process will proceed. To do so, choose the Options command button or click on the Options item on the Job menu. The dialog box shown in Figure 8 will open.

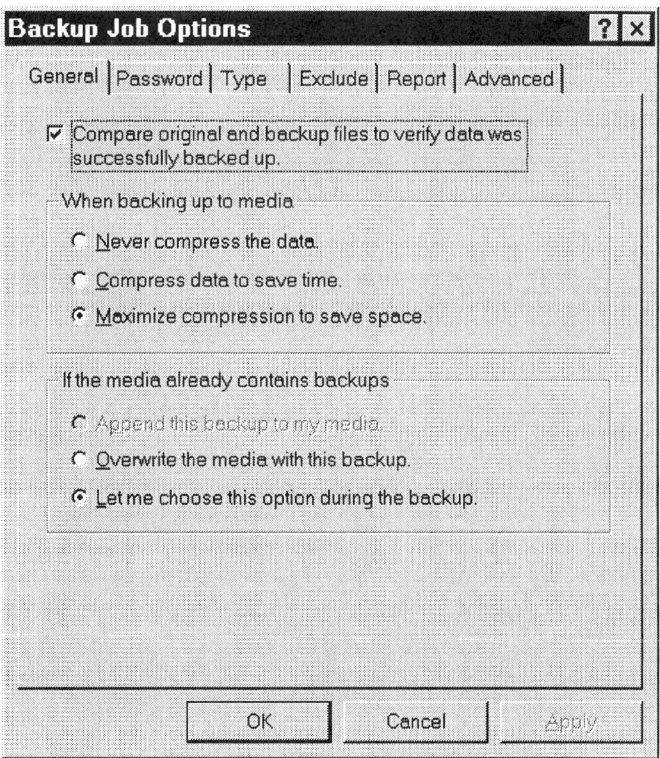

Figure 8 the Backup Job Options Dialog Box

Here's a rundown on the available options. Be aware that, in general, the defaults are reasonable choices, so you need not agonize over which options to select.

On the *General* page (Figure 8):

- Select the top check box to have Backup compare the original and backed up files to insure that the former have been copied properly. The backup will take longer if this option is selected (especially with big backup jobs), but it may provide some peace of mind.
- Select a *level of compression* for the data being backed up. Compressed data requires less space on the backup media, but adds time to the backup process. The top button in this group disables compression. If the middle option is selected, a moderate level of compression will be used, which results in a faster backup that uses more space than the bottom option.
- The bottom group of options tells Windows what to do if an existing backup job on the backup media has the same name as the current job. The overwriting option will destroy the previous backup files. The safest course here is to select the lowest option button, *Let me choose this option during the backup.*

The *Password* page allows you to specify a password that must be used when restoring (retrieving) the backup files.

On the *Type* page, you can choose to back up all selected files or just those that have changed since the last backup. If you select the latter option, you can choose an incremental or differential type of backup. *Incremental* backs up any *changed* file; *differential* backs up all files that have changed since the last *All selected files* backup, even if they have not changed since the last incremental backup.

The *Exclude* page allows you to exclude specified types of files from being backed up.

The *Report* page has options that determine what information is included in the report that is issued when the backup is complete. For long backups, you might want to select the *Perform an unattended backup* check box. This will disable prompts or messages that would normally be issued during the backup, but retain the report issued at the end of the backup.

The *Advanced* page allows for the automatic backup of the Windows Registry (see Section 12.4) whenever a backup is performed. This selection increases the time required for a backup (sometimes considerably), but is a valuable safety measure due to the important system information that the Registry contains.

Using an Existing Backup Job The Backup utility provides a convenient and time-saving way to perform regular backups. If you want to back up a set of files that you have already saved as a backup job (or a set of files that is similar to those in an existing backup job):

1. Start the Backup utility and either
   - Select the *Open an existing backup job* option button in Backup's welcome dialog box (Figure 4).

   or
   - Choose the Open command from the Job menu in the main Backup window (Figure 5).

   In either case, the Open Backup Job dialog box (Figure 9) will be displayed.

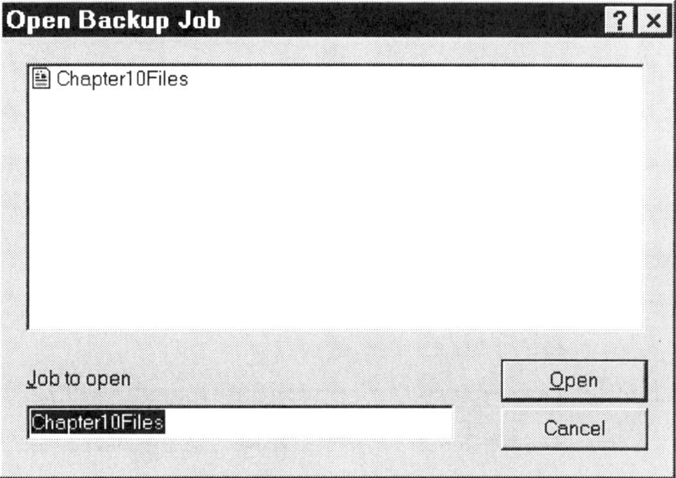

Figure 9 The Open Backup Job Dialog Box

2. Select the appropriate backup job from the list and choose the Open command button.
3. In the main Backup window, make any changes to the files selected, backup options, or backup destination.
4. If you've made changes in step 3, use the Save As command from the Job menu to save the new backup job.
5. Choose the Start command button and proceed with the backup as described earlier in this section.

NOTE

As we mentioned earlier, Windows provides a Backup Wizard to guide you through the backup process. To start the Wizard, either:

- Select the *Create a new backup job* option button and choose the OK command button in Backup's welcome dialog box.

or

- Choose the Backup Wizard command from the Tools menu in the main Backup window.

The Backup Wizard

In typical wizard fashion, the Backup Wizard displays a series of dialog boxes that present options and initiate actions that guide you through the backup procedure described earlier in this section. The Backup Wizard has the advantage that you don't have to remember what to do next, and thus is a useful tool if you don't back up files very often. On the other hand, the Wizard does not provide all the options available in the "manual" backup procedure, nor does it allow you to work with a previous backup job.

Restoring Backed Up Files

Backups are worth their weight in gold when something goes wrong so that the original files become unusable. In such a case, it is an easy matter to **restore** the backups — copy them to their original locations. Here's how the process works:

1. Start Backup and display the main Backup window, as described earlier in this section.
2. Insert the appropriate backup diskette, tape cartridge, or other removable media in its drive. (This is the point at which careful labeling pays off!) Of course, if the backed up files are stored on a hard drive, skip this step.
3. Click on the Restore tab to display the corresponding page of the Backup window (Figure 10). If a message box asks if you want to "refresh this view", click on Yes and follow the prompts.
4. If the proper drive and/or backup file is not displayed in the *Restore from* area of the dialog box, click on the open folder icon. select the proper drive and file in the resulting dialog box, choose the Open command button, and then refresh the view (if necessary) as in step 3.

   A:\Win95Contnets.qic

5. In the *What to restore* pane, open the folder that contains the files or folders that you want to restore. Then, select the check boxes for these objects in the folder tree or contents panes.

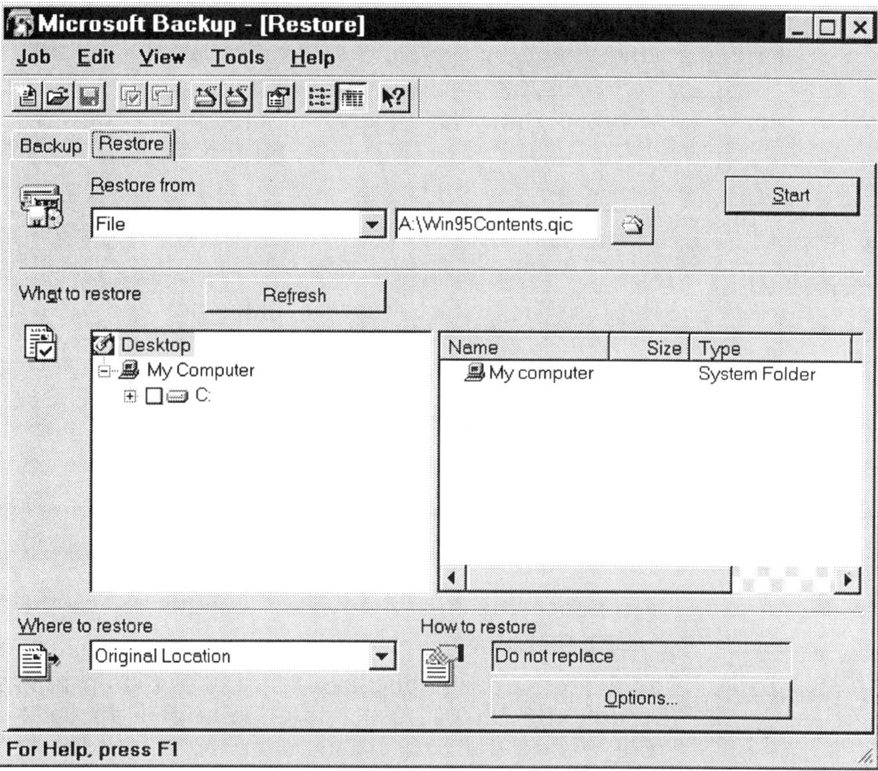

Figure 10 The Restore Page of the Backup Window

6. If you don't want to restore the objects to their original locations on your hard disk, select the Alternate Location item from the *Where to restore* drop down list, click on the open folder icon, select another folder in the resulting dialog box, and choose the OK button.

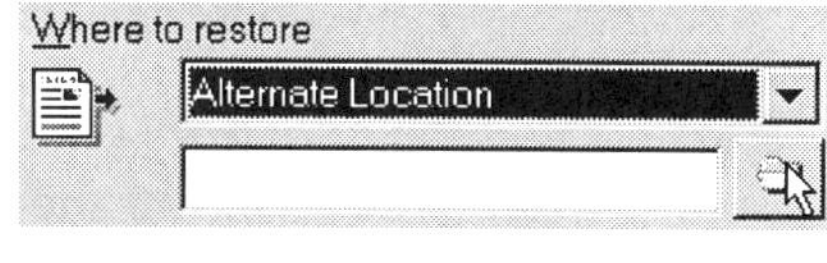

7. Select options for the restore process by clicking on the Options command button or choosing the Options item from the Job menu. The Restore Options dialog box will open, allowing you to select your preferences.

8. Choose the Start button. A dialog box may appear informing you that you must insert the disk or tape that contains the appropriate backup file. If necessary, do so and choose the OK button.

The restore process will begin and a Restore Progress dialog box, similar to the Backup Progress dialog box of Figure 7, will be displayed.

9. When the process is complete, a message to this effect will be displayed. Choose the OK button to clear the message box from the screen.
10. Choose the Report command button to view a report of the restore in Notepad. Close Notepad when you are done.
11. Close the Report Progress dialog box and, if so desired, the Backup utility.

NOTE

Windows 98 supplies a Restore Wizard to guide you through the restore process. To start this Wizard, either:

- Select the *Restore backed up files* option button and choose the OK command button in Backup's welcome dialog box.

or

- Choose the Restore Wizard command from the Tools menu in the main Backup window.

The Restore Wizard

The Restore Wizard displays a series of dialog boxes that guide you through the restore procedure described above. Note that the Restore Wizard does not really simplify this process, but it does lead you through it in a step-by-step manner.

TUTORIAL

Try the following exercise on your own.

1. Turn on the computer (if necessary) to start Windows 98 and open the Backup utility: Click on the Start button, successively point at Programs, Accessories, and System Tools, and finally click on the Backup item on the last submenu.
2. If Backup's "welcome" window appears, choose its Close button.
3. Place a formatted diskette in its drive.
4. Select files to be backed up:
   - In the left (folder tree) pane, open the Programs subfolder of the Start Menu folder: Successively click on the plus (+) symbols next to the C:, Windows, and Start Menu icons; then click on the Programs icon.
   - In the right (contents) pane, select the Accessories subfolder and the Windows Explorer and MS-DOS Prompt shortcuts by clicking on the box to the left of each of these items.

5. Select a destination for the backup:
   - In the *Where to backup* section of the window, click on the open folder icon.
   - In the resulting dialog box, select "3½ Floppy (A:)".from the *Look in* drop-down list, type TestBackup in the *File name* text box, and choose the Open command button.
6. Save this *backup job*: Choose Save As from the Job menu, type BackupTest in the Job Name box, and choose the Save button.
7. Start the backup by choosing the Start command button. (The Backup Progress dialog box will open, as well.)
8. When the process is complete, click on OK in the corresponding message box and close the Backup Progress dialog box.
9. Restore the backed up files to their original locations (which would be necessary if the originals became unusable):
   - Click on the Restore tab in the Backup window. (If you are asked to "refresh the current view", click on No.)
   - Click on the open folder icon in the *Restore from* section and, in the resulting dialog box, select the TestBackup item and choose the OK button.
   - If you are asked to "refresh the current view", click on Yes; if not, click on the Refresh button and then Yes. In either case, choose the OK button in the resulting dialog box.
   - In the folder tree pane, open the Programs subfolder of the Start Menu folder: Successively click on the plus (+) symbols next to the C:, Windows, and Start Menu icons; then click on the Programs icon.
   - Click on the three items in the contents pane.
10. At this point, you would normally choose the Start command button to begin the process. Here, however, just close the Backup window (by choosing Exit from the Job menu) and remove the diskette from its drive.

10.3 Increasing Free Disk Space

Modern hard disks have seemingly limitless capacities, at least when they're new. However, if you use audio, video, or complex graphics files, even the largest of disks will eventually fill up. At this point, you could add another hard disk to your system, but there are easier and cheaper ways to create free disk space.

In this section, we will discuss several techniques, both simple and complex, for increasing your free disk space. Before we begin, here's an easy way to determine how much free space you currently have:

Checking free disk space

1. Start Windows Explorer or My Computer.
2. Right-click on the icon of the disk you want to check (for example, C:) and choose Properties from the pop-up menu. The resulting dialog box (Figure 11) will supply the information.

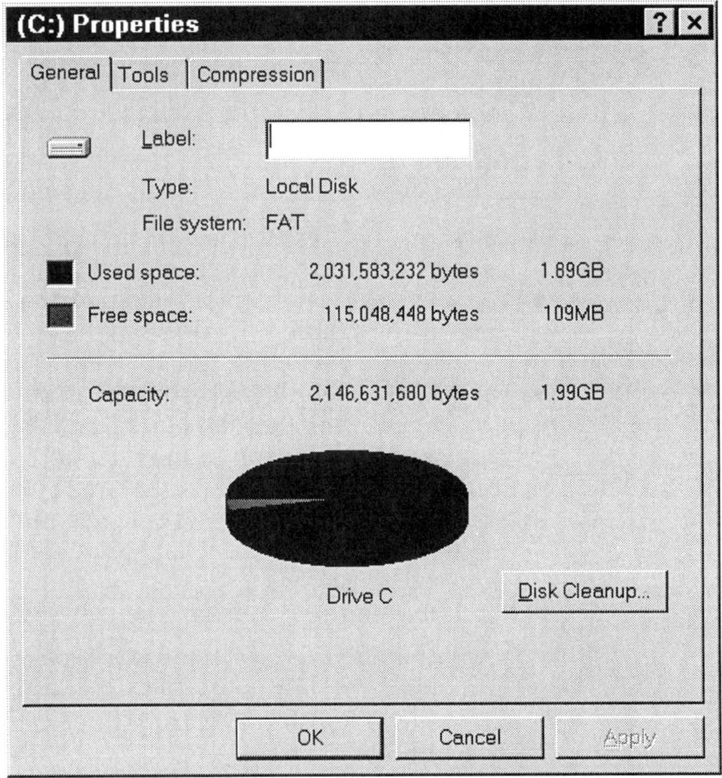

Figure 11 Determining Free Disk Space

Some Basic Techniques

Here are several simple things you can do to free up disk space.

Empty the Recycle Bin The easiest way to increase free space is often overlooked — just empty the Recycle Bin. Recall (from Section 3.4) that when files or folders are deleted, they are not normally removed from disk; they are actually moved to a folder commonly called the Recycle Bin and continue to take up disk space. Thus, the Recycle Bin often contains files that you no longer need. To empty it:

1. Choose the Recycle Bin icon (on the Desktop).
2. After verifying that you no longer need the files contained within this folder, choose the Empty Recycle bin item from the File menu.

Delete Unneeded Files and Applications It is inevitable that, over time, you will amass files and applications that you no longer use, It is an easy matter to delete most of these, but it may take a little time and patience. Here are some tips for carrying out this process:

- Start Control Panel's Add/Remove Programs utility (see Section 2.4) and check the list box for unwanted programs. To remove one of these, select it, choose the Add/Remove command button, and follow the on-screen instructions.
- Start Windows Explorer and look for folders and individual files that you no longer need; then delete them in the usual way. (Don't forget to empty the Recycle Bin after these deletions.) Remember that some applications you may no longer want will not show up in the Add/Remove Programs list (see above), so you will have to delete there folders "manually". Here are a few other places you can look for unneeded files:

  The Temp subfolder of the Windows folder contains temporary files that can usually be safely deleted. The same is true of the Temporary Internet Files subfolder of the Windows folder and the Temp subfolder of the root folder, if the latter folders are present on your computer.

  Font files tend to proliferate quickly. Use Control Panel's Fonts utility (Section 5.5) to delete those you don't want.

  Graphics, sound, and video files often take up a lot of disk space. Check the folders of applications that use these kinds of files to see if you can find candidates for deletion.

Run the Disk Cleanup Utility Windows 98 supplies a utili called **Disk Cleanup** that helps you free up disk space, primarily making it easier for you to delete certain files. To start this utility:

1. Click on the Disk Cleanup item on the System Tools submenu the Start button's Accessories menu. The Select Drive dialog

will be displayed:

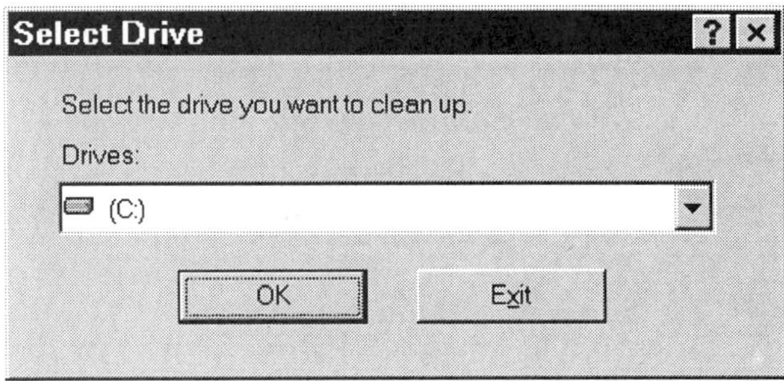

2. Select the drive on which you want to free up space from the drop-down list and choose the OK command button. The Disk Cleanup dialog box (Figure 12) will be displayed.

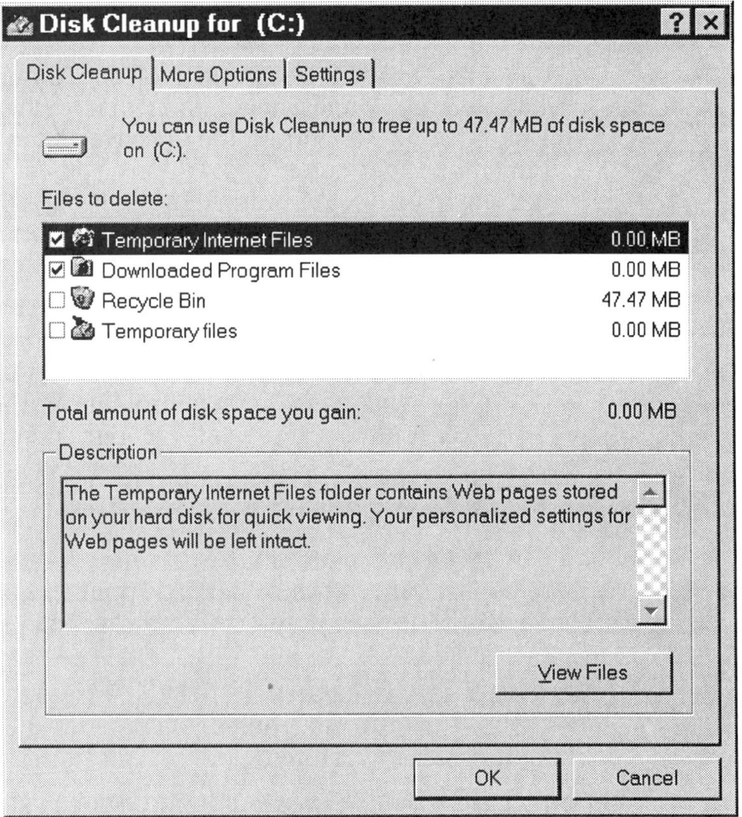

Figure 13 The Disk Cleanup Dialog Box

NOTE

You can also start Disk Cleanup from My Computer or Explorer. To do so, right-click on the desired disk icon (for example, C:), choose Properties from the pop-up menu, and click on the Disk Cleanup command button in the resulting dialog box (see Figure 11). In this case, the Select Drive dialog box is skipped and you are taken directly to the Disk Cleanup dialog box of Figure 12.

Using Disk Cleanup to delete files

To use the Disk Cleanup dialog box (Figure 12) to delete files:

1. In the *Files to delete* check box, select the type of files you'd like to delete (for example, Temporary Internet Files).
2. If you'd like to view the list of files selected in step 1, choose the View Files command button.
3. Choose the OK command button. A dialog box asking you to confirm the deletion will open.
4. Choose the Yes command button to complete the process.

Other features of Disk Cleanup

The other tabs in the Disk Cleanup dialog box (Figure 12) provide access to additional features:

- On the *More Options* page, you can start the Add/Remove Programs utility (see Section 2.4) to remove certain software or start the Drive Converter utility (which we will discuss later in this section) to install a more efficient version of this disk's file allocation table (FAT).
- On the *Settings* page, you can elect to have Disk Cleanup start automatically when an insufficient amount of free disk space is detected.

Compressing a Drive

You can dramatically increase the amount of free space or drive by **compressing** it — encoding the files on the driv way that they take up much less space. Windows built-i utility compresses and "uncompresses" both hard It does this by creating a single large file on the compressed files. The original drive that co *volume* is called the *host drive*. When a file drive, it is automatically compressed; compressed volume, it is automatically performing a read or write operation, a tinguishable from an uncompressed one.

WARNING

Before compressing a drive, you should give the matter considerable thought. Here are a few reasons why you might *not* want to compress a drive:

- Compression will slow access to the drive somewhat.
- Some applications don't work as well on compressed drives.
- Compressed drives cannot be read by other operating systems, such as Windows NT.

It also takes a long time — often several hours — to compress a hard disk, especially if it already contains a lot of files. First, DriveSpace checks the disk for errors and rearranges the data on it (the compressed volume must occupy a single unbroken unit of disk apace). Then, an empty compressed volume is created. Finally, DriveSpace copies each file to this area, compressing it in the process and erasing it from its original location.

The compression process usually goes through without a hitch. Nevertheless, with an operation of this scope and complexity, something may go wrong. To avoid the potential loss of valuable data, it's a very good idea to back up the entire disk (see Section 10.2) before proceeding.

Running DriveSpace To use DriveSpace to compress a disk:

1. Click on the DriveSpace item on the System Tools submenu of the Start button's Accessories menu. This starts the utility and displays the DriveSpace 3 window, which is shown in Figure 13.

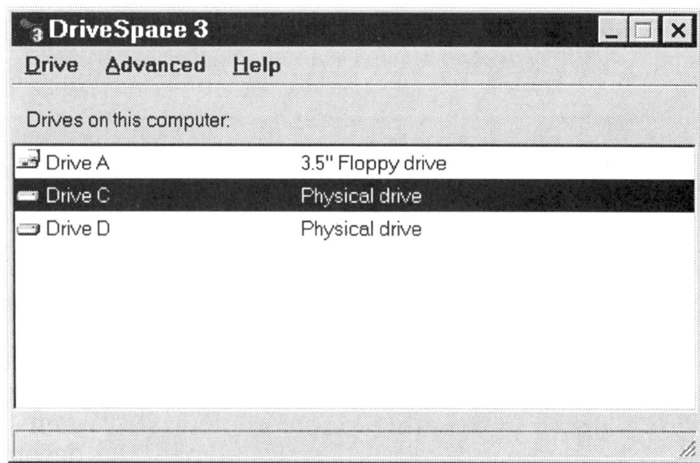

Figure 13 The DriveSpace 3 Window

2. Select the drive to be compressed.
3. Choose the Compress command from the Drive menu. The Compress a Drive dialóg box shown in Figure 14 will open.

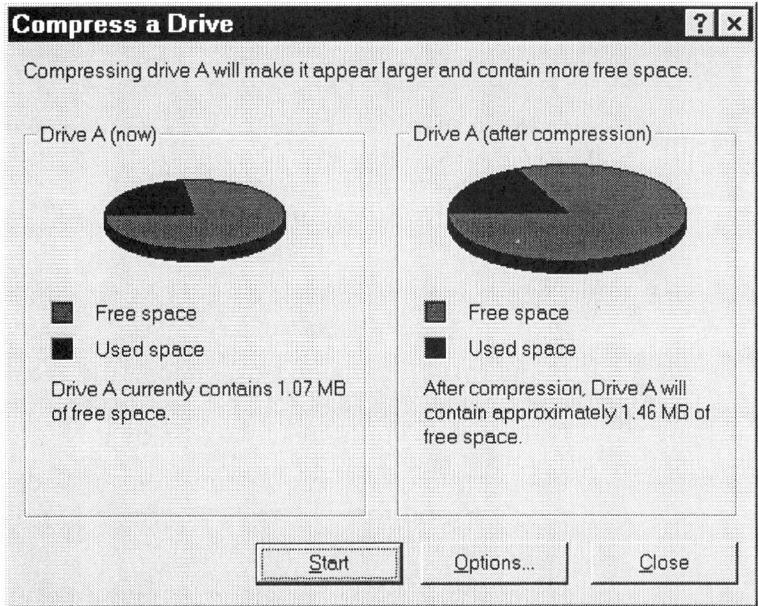

Figure 14 Compressing a Drive Begins Here

4. Choose the Start command button. A dialog box will appear giving you the opportunity to back up your files. If you have not yet backed them up, do so now!
5. Choose the Compress Now command button to begin the compression process. A dialog box will open, showing the progress of this procedure.
6. At the completion of the process, you may be prompted to restart Windows or you may have to close the Compress a Drive dialog box and the DriveSpace 3 window.

NOTE

The compressed volume takes on the drive letter of the original drive and the host drive is assigned a new letter, such as H. By default, the entire disk is compressed, so that no "free" (uncompressed) space remains on the host drive. However, it is sometimes desirable to leave free space on a hard disk to store, for example, important disk utilities should something go wrong with that disk.

Prior to compression, you can specify the amount of "free" space on the compressed drive by choosing the Options command button in the Compress a Drive dialog box. After compression, you can accomplish this by selecting the drive in the DriveSpace 3 window and choosing the Adjust Free Space command from the Drive menu.

Windows 98 provides another utility, **Compression Agent**, to further compress files that have already been compressed by DriveSpace. DriveSpace uses either standard or *HiPack* compression. With Compression Agent, you can use *UltraPack* compression to free the most disk space. To use Compression Agent:

1. Choose the Compression Agent item from the System Tools submenu of the Start button's Accessories menu.
2. In the resulting dialog box, choose the Settings command button and specify the files to be compressed and the desired level of compression in the resulting dialog box.
3. Choose the OK button to close the Settings dialog box and then the Start button in the Compression Agent dialog box. The compression process will begin.
4. When the process is complete, choose the Exit button to close Compression Agent.

Uncompressing a Disk If you want to, you can *uncompress* a compressed drive — decompress all files on it and delete the compressed volume. To do so:

1. Start DriveSpace, as described earlier. The DriveSpace 3 window (Figure 13) will be displayed.
2. Select the desired drive and choose the Uncompress command from the Drive menu. The Uncompress a Drive dialog box (which is similar to the one in Figure 14) will open.
3. Choose the Start command button. The resulting dialog box will give you the opportunity to back up your files. If you have not done this already, do it now!
4. Choose the Uncompress Now command button to begin the process.

   If a dialog box appears asking if you would like to remove the compression driver from memory, choose the Yes button unless you want to use DriveSpace again in this session. (If you do want to use DriveSpace again after choosing Yes, click on the Settings command on the Advanced menu and, in the resulting dialog box, make sure that the *Automatically mount new compressed devices* check box is selected.)

5. The decompressing process will begin; a dialog box will appear showing the progress of the operation.
6. When the operation is complete, close the Uncompress a Drive dialog box and the DriveSpace 3 window.

Trimming the FAT

Still another way to increase your free disk space is to change the file allocation system for a drive. The **file allocation table (FAT)** keeps track of the location of the files on a drive, and is itself stored in a special area of the disk in question. When a new file is created, the operating system consults the FAT for the location of free disk space, assigns the file to some of this space, and records (in the FAT) the file's location.

The file allocation system used for hard disks by DOS, Windows 3.1, and early versions of Windows 95 is called *FAT16*, because 16 bits (two bytes) of disk space are allowed for each entry in the FAT. Although FAT16 works well with relatively small drives (under 512 MB), it has two major deficiencies in these days of large-capacity disks:

Disadvantages of FAT16

- Each disk file, regardless of its size, is assigned a minimum of up to 32 kilobytes of storage. (The minimum storage space allocated, known as a *cluster*, varies with the size of the drive.) This limitation wastes a lot of disk space. For example, most shortcuts have a file size of less than one KB, but will occupy 32 KB of space on a large-capacity drive, wasting the other 31 kilobytes.
- FAT16 limits the maximum size of a drive to two gigabytes. To get around this restriction, disks with capacities greater than two GB are partitioned into several smaller *logical drives*; each *partition* appears to the user as if it were a separate disk in the computer. For example, if My Computer lists drives C: and D: in its window, there is no way of knowing from this information (and no real need to know) if the computer houses two separate hard disks or just a single disk partitioned into two logical drives.

The most recent version of Windows 95 introduced an improved FAT system, known as *FAT32*. This file system is also available with Windows 98. FAT32 does away with the two disadvantages of FAT16 described above: FAT32's minimum storage requirement (cluster size) is only 4 KB for drives up to 8 GB in size and it can address hard disks up to 2000 GB in capacity (!) without the need for partitioning.

Thus, if you have a large number of small files on a large-capacity FAT16 drive, you can substantially increase your free disk space by converting that drive to FAT32. To determine which version of FAT is in use on a given drive:

Checking the FAT version of a drive

1. Start My Computer, right-click on the desired drive icon, and choose Properties from the resulting pop-up menu.

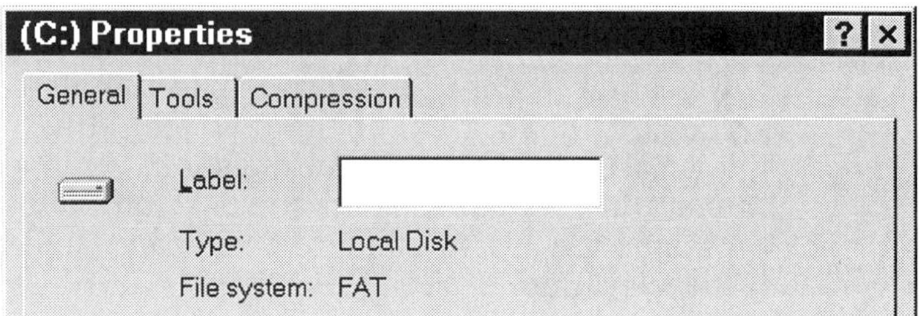

2. In the resulting dialog box, check the entry following *File system.* If it reads FAT, this drive is using FAT16.

WARNING

Before you convert to FAT32, you should be aware that the conversion process is essentially irreversible; to return to FAT16 requires reformatting the drive, which erases all the information stored on it! There are also several *disadvantages* to FAT32:

- FAT32 drives cannot be compressed using the DriveSpace utility.
- FAT32 drives cannot be read by other operating systems, such as Windows NT 4 and OS/2.
- Older disk utilities will not work under FAT32.
- You cannot uninstall Windows 98 from a FAT32 drive.

Also be aware that the process may take several hours, during which time you won't be able to use the computer. If you do decide to convert a drive to FAT32, back up that drive (see Section 10.2) before proceeding.

If you want to convert a drive from FAT16 to FAT32, Windows 98

provides a utility for just this purpose, which is aptly named **Drive Converter**. (Drive Converter can only be used on drives that exceed 512 MB in capacity; in particular, it cannot convert floppy disks to FAT32.) To use this utility:

Using Drive Converter

1. Click on the Drive Converter (FAT32) item on the System Tools submenu of the Start button's Accessories menu. This starts the Drive Converter wizard, which displays an informational screen. Choose the Next command button to display the next wizard screen (Figure 15).

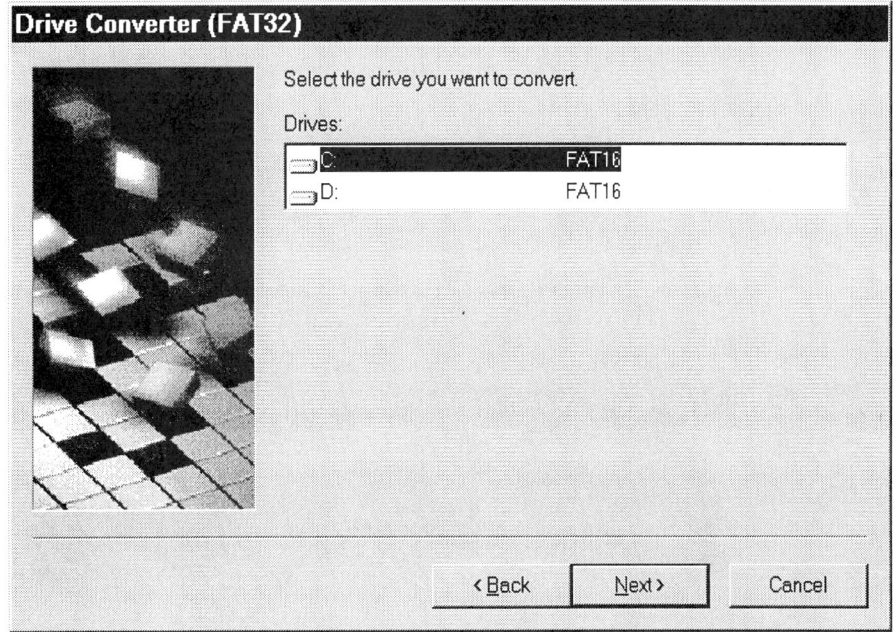

Figure 15 Selecting a Drive in the Drive Converter Wizard

2. Select the drive you want to convert to FAT 32 from the list and choose the Next button.
3. The wizard prepares the drive for conversion by scanning for applications that might not work with FAT32 and suggests that you backup this drive before proceeding. Several warning messages will be displayed in the process.
4. After you confirm that you really do want to proceed, Drive Converter will reboot your system (to a DOS prompt) and perform the conversion.

TUTORIAL

Try the following exercise on your own.

1. Insert the Student Disk in its drive.
2. Try to increase the free space on this disk using the Disk Cleanup utility:
   - Start Disk Cleanup from the System Tools submenu of the Start button's Accessories menu.
   - Select the A: drive in the resulting Select Drive window and choose the OK button.
   - In the Disk Cleanup window, select all check boxes in the *Files to delete* box and choose the OK command button.
   - Choose the Yes command button in the resulting warning dialog box to start the process. (Note that in this particular case, no additional free space will be created on the Student Disk.)
3. Reopen the Disk Cleanup window. Click on the More Options tab and notice that you can start the Add/Remove Programs and Drive Converter utilities from this page, both of which can be used to free up disk space.
4. Click on the Settings tab and note the available options. Then, close the Disk Cleanup utility.
5. Compress the files on the floppy disk:
   - Start the DriveSpace utility from the System Tools submenu of the Start button's Accessories menu.
   - Select the A: drive in the DriveSpace 3 window.
   - Choose the Compress command from the Drive menu.
   - Choose the Start command button in the Compress a Drive dialog box and then the Compress Now button in the resulting dialog box.
   - When the process is complete, close the Compress a Drive dialog box.
6. Uncompress the floppy disk:
   - Select the A: drive in the DriveSpace 3 window.
   - Choose the Uncompress command from the Drive menu.
   - Choose the Start command button in the Uncompress a Drive dialog box and then the Uncompress Now button in the resulting dialog box. (If the Remove Compression dialog box appears, choose the Yes button.)
   - When the process is complete, close the Uncompress a Drive dialog box and the DriveSpace 3 window.
7. Remove the diskette from its drive.

10.4 Fine-tuning Your Hard Disk

In this section, we will discuss several utilities that can help you improve the performance of your hard disk. Like those presented in Sections 10.2 and 10.3, these programs are started from the System Tools submenu of the Start button's Accessories menu. In this section, we will discuss:

- *ScanDisk*, which finds and repairs (when possible) certain disk problems.
- *Disk Defragmenter*, which rearranges the data on a disk so that its files occupy contiguous sectors.

We will also discuss the Maintenance Wizard and Task Scheduler utilities, both of which can be used to automate system maintenance chores.

ScanDisk

Considering their complexity, disk drives and disk drive controllers are amazingly reliable devices. Nevertheless, every once in a while, disk problems cause data to become unusable or to needlessly take up extra space. You should periodically use the **ScanDisk** utility to detect and repair these problems.

Running ScanDisk To have ScanDisk check one of your disks:

1. Click on the ScanDisk item on the System Tools submenu of the Start button's Accessories menu. ScanDisk will start and display the window shown in Figure 16, on the next page.
2. In the ScanDisk window, select the drive you want to check for errors.
3. Select either the *Standard* or the *Thorough* option button. The Standard option checks for errors in the way files and folders have been stored on disk. The Thorough option not only runs these tests, but also checks the physical integrity of the selected disk. Thc Thorough option takes *much* longer and, as a practical matter, need not be run as frequently as the Standard one.
4. If you select the *Automatically fix errors* check box, ScanDisk will not only detect and report any errors, but also attempt to repair them. It is safer to deselect this box. You can always have Scan-Disk try to fix the reported errors later.

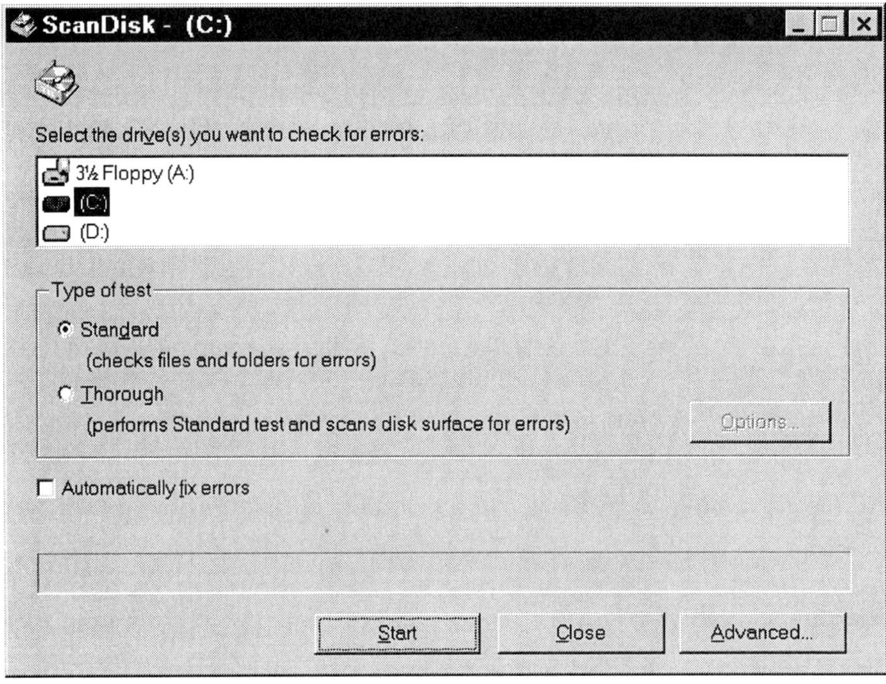

Figure 16 The ScanDisk Window

5. You can select additional options for the ScanDisk run by choosing the Advanced button (for both Standard and Thorough test modes) and the Options button (which is available only if the Thorough mode is selected). There is normally little reason to change most of these options, and we will discuss them below.
6. Choose the Start command button to activate ScanDisk. The progress of the testing process will be indicated at the bottom of the ScanDisk window. (You can abort the process at any time by choosing the Cancel button.) When testing is complete, a message to this effect or a report summarizing ScanDisk's findings will be displayed.
7. Choose the Close command button to exit ScanDisk.

ScanDisk Options As we mentioned earlier, you can select options for ScanDisk testing by choosing either the Advanced or Options (in Thorough test mode only) command buttons. You should be aware that the defaults chosen for these options tend to emphasize safety over speed; think twice before changing them.

Choosing the Advanced button

When you choose the Advanced command button in the ScanDisk window, the dialog box shown in Figure 17 is displayed.

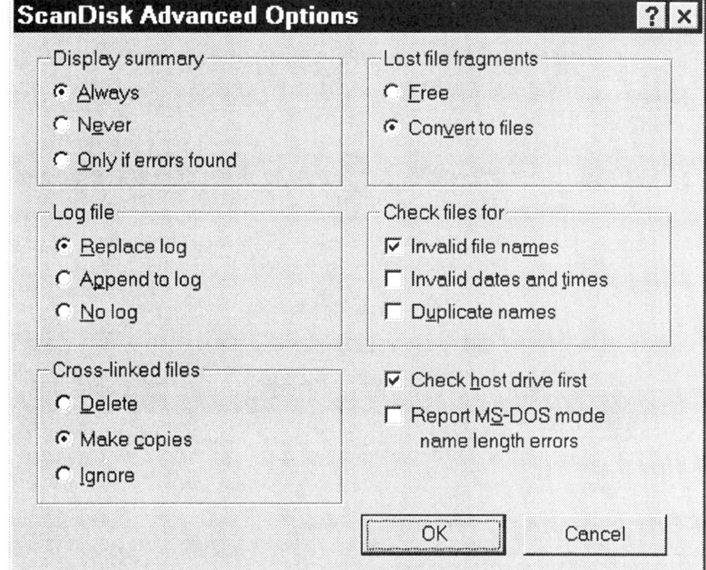

Figure 17 "Advanced" ScanDisk Options

Here's a description of some of these options:

- The *Log file* option buttons determine whether or not a report of the testing is stored on disk (in the Scandisk log file in the C:\ folder) and, if it is, whether it replaces or is appended (added) to the existing file.
- *Cross-linked files* are files that, according to the disk's file allocation table, share the same disk space. If you try to read a cross-linked file, you may be denied access or see "garbage" displayed on the screen. Although cross-linked files can rarely be fixed without losing some data, ScanDisk gives you several options for dealing with them. *Delete* erases the cross-linked files; *Make copies* copies each cross-linked file to a new location (the "safe" alternative), and *Ignore* leaves the problem unfixed. (The last option is actually the best one *if* you have other, more advanced disk-repair software with which to attack this problem.)
- *Lost file fragments* (or *lost clusters*) are parts of the disk that, according to the disk's file allocation table, contain data which

does not belong to any file. The *Free* option deletes these files; the *Convert to files* option is almost always the better choice — you can then try to view the resulting files (which are named File0000, File0001, etc.) to see if they contain useful information.

Choosing the Options button

The Options button in the ScanDisk window provides options for thorough testing only. Choosing this command button displays the dialog box shown in Figure 18.

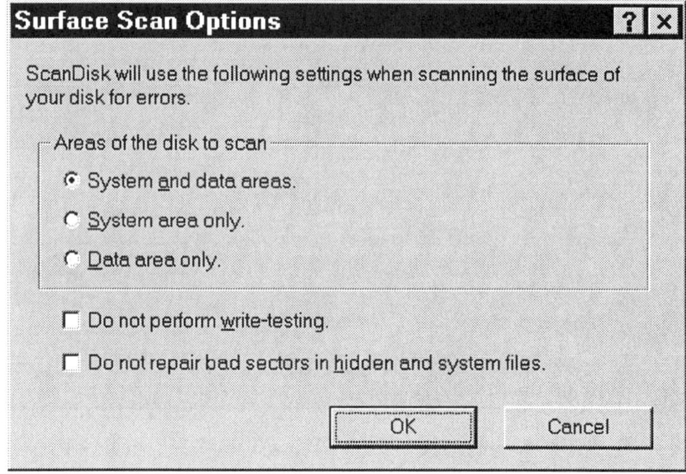

Figure 18 Options for Thorough Testing

Here's a description of these options. (The defaults are set for the most thorough, and most time-consuming, disk testing.)

- *Areas of the disk to scan:* In this context, the disk is divided into two parts — the system area (consisting of operating system files that control startup, file allocation, and the like) and the data area (everything else). Be aware that disk surface errors in the system area can rarely be fixed (at least by ScanDisk).
- By default, ScanDisk tests the surface of a disk by both reading from and writing to every disk location. If you want to speed up the testing process, using a less rigorous test, select the *Do not perform write-testing* check box.
- Hidden and system files are usually used for special purposes. Although it may be possible to move such a file to a new location if the disk area in which it is stored has become damaged, the file may not work in the new location. So, unless you observe

problems in running Windows or an application that seem to be related to the file in question, it may be best to select the *Do not repair bad sectors in hidden and system files* check box.

Disk Defragmenter

When a file is stored on disk, Windows writes it to the first available location. If that area is not large enough to hold the entire file, the file becomes *fragmented* — parts of it are stored in noncontiguous locations. This occurs often and isn't as bad as it sounds. You won't have any trouble accessing the file (the operating system keeps track of where the various parts are stored); it may just take slightly longer to load the file into RAM.

However, if a disk has become highly fragmented, its performance may suffer. The Windows **Disk Defragmenter** utility allows you to **defragment** a hard or removable disk (such as a floppy) — to rearrange its files so that each is stored as a single contiguous unit.

Running Disk Defragmenter To use this utility:

1. Click on the Disk Defragmenter item on the System Tools submenu. This action starts the utility and displays the small window shown in Figure 19.

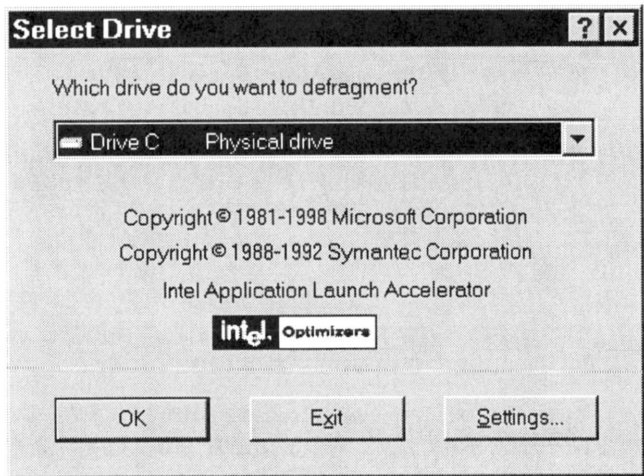

Figure 19 Initial Disk Defragmenter Window

2. Select the drive to be defragmented from the drop-down list.
3. Choose the Settings command button if you want to select options for the defragmentation process. The dialog box shown in Figure 20 will be displayed.

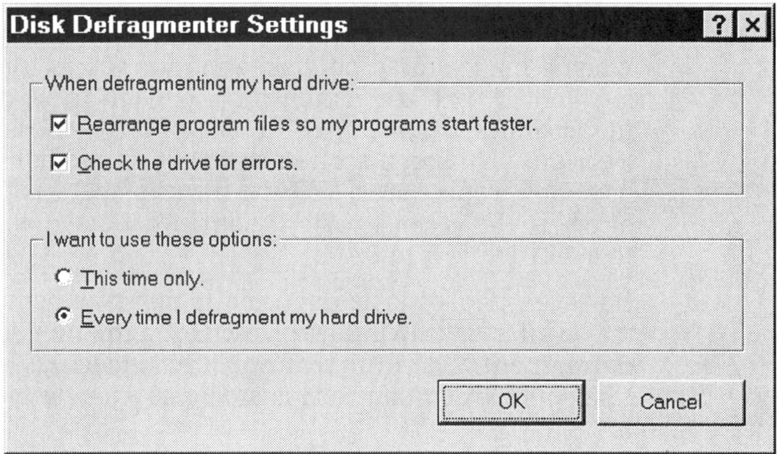

Figure 20 Selecting Preferences for the Defragmentation

- Select the *Rearrange program files so my programs start faster* check box to place program files at the beginning of the disk. This will increase defragmentation time somewhat.
- Select the *Check the drive for errors* check box to run Scan-Disk's "Standard" test prior to defragmentation. This is a good idea, but takes extra time.
- Select the appropriate option button and then choose the OK button to return to the Select Drive dialog box of Figure 19.

4. Choose the OK button in the Select Drive dialog box to begin the defragmentation process. If Disk Defragmenter believes that this drive does not need defragmentation, a dialog box will appear suggesting you cancel the process
5. Once the defragmentation process begins, the dialog box shown in Figure 21 will appear showing the progress of the operation.
   - To halt the process, choose the Stop button.
   - To pause the process temporarily, choose the Pause button (it will be replaced by a Resume button).

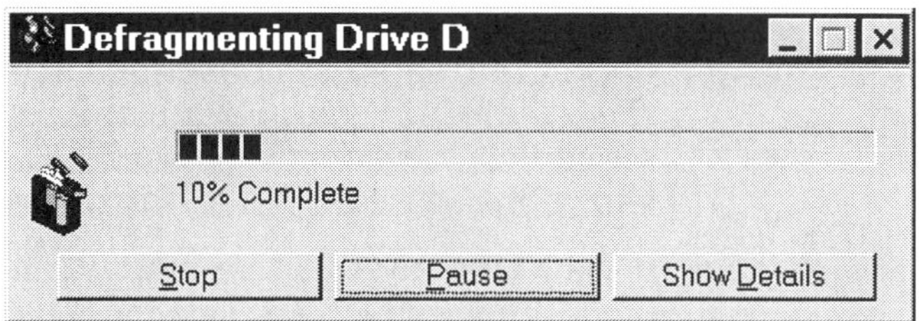

Figure 21 Defragmentation in Progress

- To see a graphical display of the defragmentation process, choose the Show Details command button. In the resulting dialog box, choose the Legend button for an explanation of the symbols displayed. Choose the Hide Details button to return to the dialog box of Figure 21.

6. When the defragmentation process is complete, a dialog box will pop-up asking if you want to close the Disk Defragmenter utility. If you are done defragmenting disks, choose the Yes button.

Automating the Maintenance Process

It is a good idea to run certain maintenance utilities, such as ScanDisk and Disk Defragmenter, on a regular basis. To automate this chore, Windows supplies a Maintenance Wizard and Task Scheduler.

Maintenance Wizard The Windows 98 **Maintenance Wizard** makes it possible to program Disk Cleanup, ScanDisk, and Disk Defragmenter to run automatically on a regularly-scheduled basis. To use this utility to schedule or reschedule these maintenance tasks:

1. Click on the Maintenance Wizard item on the System Tools submenu of the Start button's Accessories menu.

   - If any maintenance tasks have been scheduled to run automatically, the dialog box shown at the right will appear.

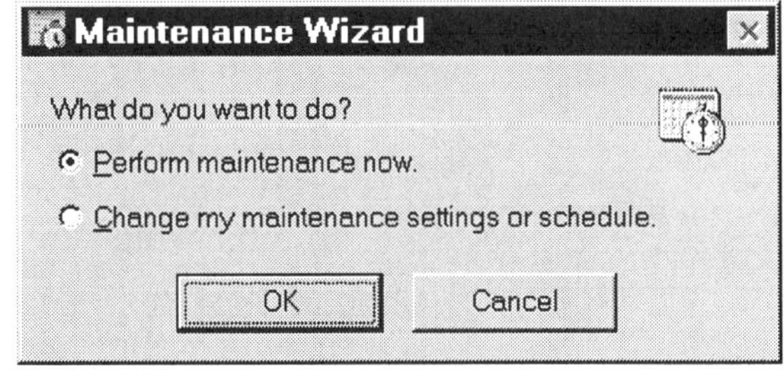

Select the *Change my maintenance settings or schedule* option button and choose the OK command button to start the wizard. (If you activate the other option, the currently scheduled tasks will be run.) The initial wizard screen, shown in Figure 22, will be displayed.

- If your computer has no maintenance tasks currently scheduled, the initial wizard screen (Figure 22) will be displayed.

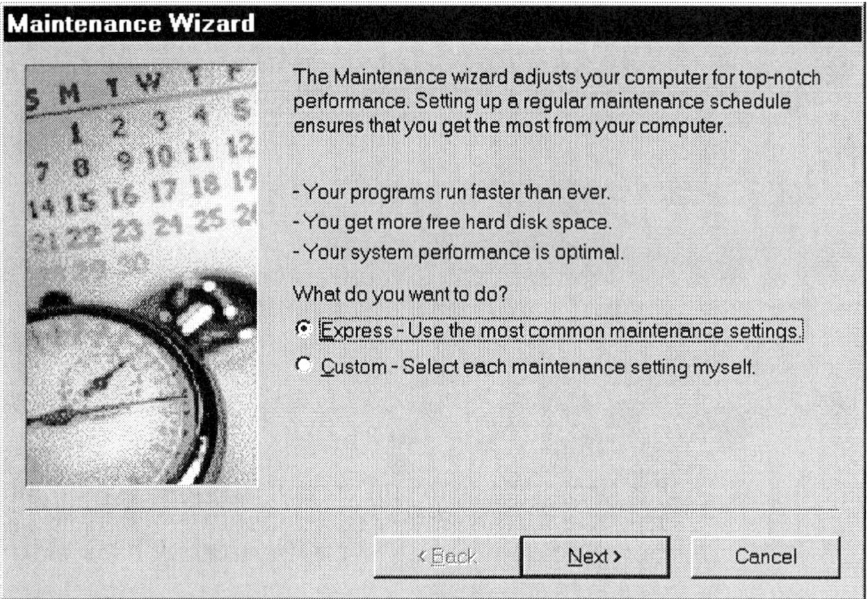

Figure 22 The Initial Maintenance Wizard Screen

2. Select one of the two option buttons:
   - *Express* runs the three maintenance utilities, starting at one of the three times selected on the next screen.
   - *Custom* gives you much more control over the scheduling process; you can choose to run each of the three tasks on any regular basis at any time of day and also configure each utility to some extent. *Custom* also provides a few other options, which are mentioned below.
3. Choose the Next command button to view the next wizard screen, which allows you to select the time of day the scheduled tasks will run. You will be asked to select from among the three

times of day shown at the right. (If tasks are currently scheduled, there will be a fourth choice: to use the current settings.)

When do you want Windows to run maintenance tasks?

- Nights - Midnight to 3:00 AM
- Days - Noon to 3:00 PM
- Evenings - 8:00 PM to 11:00 PM

NOTE

If you selected the *Custom* option on the initial wizard screen, subsequent screens will give you much greater flexibility in selecting running times. Also be aware that your computer must be turned on when a task is scheduled to run; if it isn't, that run will be skipped.

4. Choose the Next command button.
   - Under the *Express* option, you will now view the last wizard screen. It summarizes the settings and also allows you to run the three maintenance tasks right now, if you wish.
   - Under the *Custom* option, you will now view the first of several screens that allow to customize the running of each task, as described below. The last wizard screen under the Custom option, like that of the Express option, summarizes the selected settings and optionally allows you to run the three maintenance tasks right now.
5. Choose the Finish button to close the wizard and put the settings into effect.

Additional wizard options

If you select the Custom, rather than Express, option on the initial wizard screen (Figure 22), four additional screens become available. The first of these, which is displayed when you click on Next on the screen described in step 3 above, allows you to disable any shortcut listed in the StartUp folder (see Section 4.2). If you do so, the corresponding program will no longer open automatically when Windows starts. (You can restore an application's automatic startup by running the wizard again and selecting the appropriate check box.)

The next three screens are similar in structure. Each allows you to customize the running of one of the three maintenance tasks: Disk Defragmenter, ScanDisk, and Disk Cleanup. The screen for the defragmenting task is shown in Figure 23, on the next page.

Here is a description of the options available for the Disk Defragmenter task (see Figure 23).

- Select the Yes option button if you want your disk automatically defragmented on a regular basis.

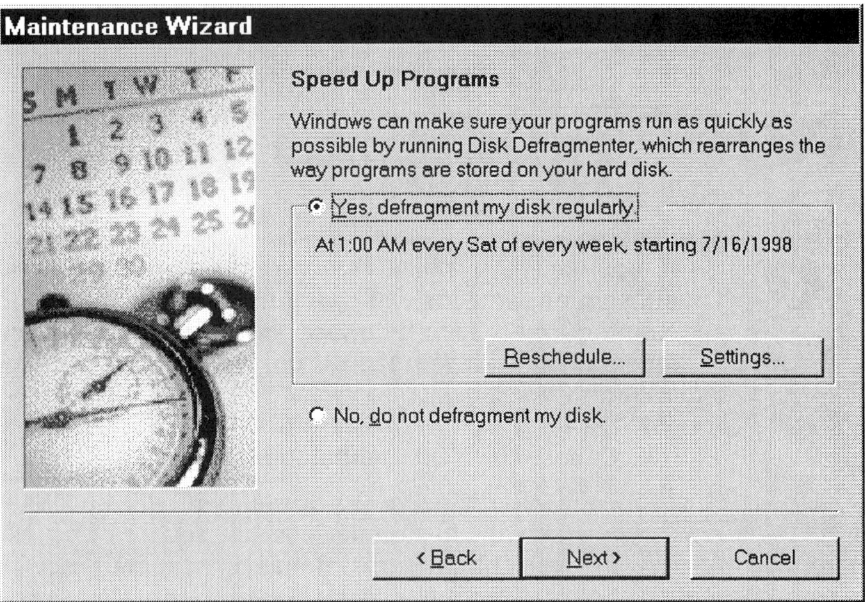

Figure 23 Customizing the Defragmentation Task

- Choose the Reschedule command button to open a dialog box which allows you to specify the day and time that defragmentation will take place and the interval (weekly, monthly, etc.) between runs.
- Choose the Settings command button to open a dialog box that allows you to specify the drives to be defragmented on these runs.

The analogous ScanDisk and Disk Cleanup Maintenance Wizard screens are similar to the one shown in Figure 23 for Disk Defragmenter. In particular, they contain Yes and No option buttons and Reschedule and Settings command buttons. The Reschedule buttons on these screens provide the same options as for Disk Defragmenter; the Settings buttons provide access to the following features:

- On the ScanDisk wizard screen, the Settings button allows you to select the disks to be scanned, whether the Standard or Thorough test is used, and whether or not ScanDisk should automatically fix errors. It also provides access to the advanced options shown in Figure 17 on page 511.
- On the Disk Cleanup wizard screen, the Settings button allows you to select the types of files to be deleted.

Task Scheduler When you use the Maintenance Wizard, you are requesting that certain maintenance tasks be run at certain times. Windows stores this information in a special subfolder of the Windows folder called Tasks (which appears in the My Computer window as *Scheduled Tasks*). Just as Windows consults (*polls*) the StartUp folder — see Section 4.2 — to see if any applications should be opened on system startup, Windows periodically polls the Tasks folder to see if and when other programs should be run.

You can make use of the Tasks folder to schedule any program to start automatically at a specified time. To accomplish this, you must add the proper file to this folder with the aid of the Task Scheduler Wizard. To use this wizard:

1. Open the My Computer window (by choosing its Desktop icon) and choose the Scheduled Tasks icon from within this window. The Scheduled Tasks folder will open, as shown in Figure 24.

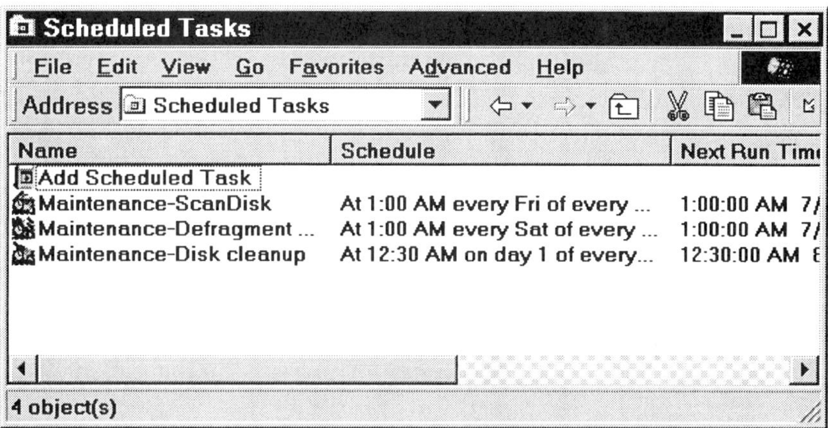

Figure 24 The Scheduled Tasks Folder

2. Choose the Add Scheduled Task item from this folder window. The Scheduled Task Wizard will start and display an informational screen.
3. Choose the Next command button. A list of the applications present on your computer will be displayed. Select the one you want to run automatically.
4. Choose the Next command button. The wizard screen shown in Figure 25 will be displayed.

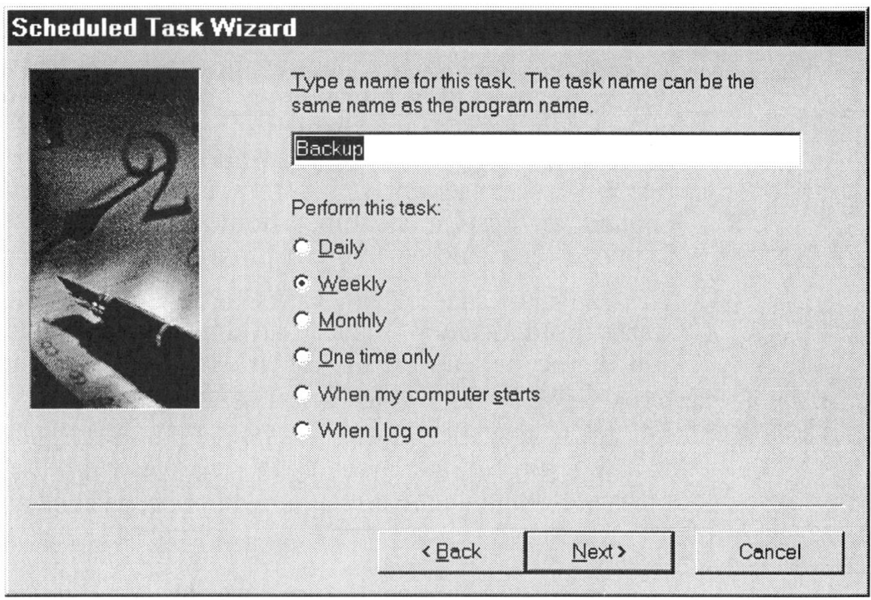

Figure 25 Scheduled Task Wizard — Selecting a Runtime

5. In this dialog box, select a name for the task (this name will appear in the Scheduled Tasks folder window) and when you want this task performed.

   If you select *Daily*, *Weekly*, *Monthly*, or *One time only* and choose the Next command button, the next screen will request further information about the time(s) scheduled. For example, if you selected *Weekly*, the next dialog box will request a day of the week and time of day to run the selected program.

6. Choose the Next command button. The final wizard screen will appear, summarizing your selections. Choose the Finish button to complete the process.

You can also open the Scheduled Tasks folder by double-clicking on its icon, on the Taskbar to the left of the Clock. This icon can be added to [or removed from] the Taskbar by choosing Start [Stop] Using Task Scheduler from the folder window's Advanced menu. Choose Pause from this menu (or from the Taskbar icon's right-click menu) to prevent Task Scheduler from running scheduled jobs. The Taskbar icon will now look like the one at the lower-right. To "unpause" it, choose Continue Task Scheduler from either menu.

TUTORIAL

Try the following exercise on your own.

1. Insert the Student Disk in its drive.
2. Check this floppy disk for errors:
   - Start the ScanDisk utility from the System Tools submenu of the Start button's Accessories menu.
   - Select the A: drive in the ScanDisk window.
   - Select the Standard option button (which checks the disk for file and folder errors, but not for physical flaws). Leave all options (available from the Advanced command button) at their defaults.
   - Choose the Start command button.
   - When testing is complete, close the Results dialog box and the ScanDisk window.
3. Defragment the Student Disk:
   - Start the Disk Defragmenter utility from the System Tools submenu of the Start button's Accessories menu.
   - Select the A: drive from the Select Drive drop-down list and choose the OK command button.
   - In the Disk Defragmenter window, choose the Settings command button; then, deselect the *Check the drive for errors* check box (because you have just used ScanDisk to do this), select the *This time only* option button, and choose the OK command button.
   - In the Disk Defragmenter window, choose the OK button.
   - When the defragmentation starts, choose the Show Details command button and then the Legend button to obtain a graphical view of what is going on.
   - When defragmentation is complete, choose the Yes command button in the message box to close Disk Defragmenter.
4. Use the Maintenance Wizard to schedule a ScanDisk run:
   - Start the Maintenance Wizard from the System Tools submenu of the Start button's Accessories menu. (If a dialog box pops up asking "What do you want to do?", select the *Change my maintenance settings* option button and choose the OK command button.)
   - On the initial wizard screen, select the Custom option and choose the Next button.
   - On the next screen, select the *Nights* option so that the scheduled job will run after midnight and choose Next.
   - Read the "Start Windows More Quickly" screen and choose Next (to leave the startup applications unchanged).

- On the "Speed Up Programs" screen, select *No* so that Disk Defragmenter will not run when the scheduled job does.
- On the "Scan Hard Disk for Errors" screen, select *Yes* and choose the Reschedule button. In the resulting dialog box, select *Once* from the Schedule Task drop-down list, enter yesterday's date, and choose OK. Then, choose Next.
- On the "Delete Unnecessary Files" screen, select *No* to decline to schedule Disk Cleanup, and choose Next.
- On the last wizard screen, choose the Finish button to complete the scheduling process.

5. Open the Scheduled Tasks folder by starting My Computer and choosing the Scheduled Tasks icon from the window. Notice that one of the scheduled tasks is "Maintenance-ScanDisk". Select Details to view the settings. Then, close the Scheduled Tasks window and (if necessary) close My Computer.
6. Remove the diskette from its drive.

10.5 Other System-related Utilities

In this section, we will describe additional system-related tools. These utilities can help you to:

- Monitor the workings of your system.
- Modify certain hardware settings and improve performance.
- Add or configure a modem.

Monitoring Your System

Windows 98 supplies several utilities that help you keep track of *system resources*: the computer's hardware, software, memory usage, and CPU interactions. We will discuss these utilities — System Information, System Monitor, and Resource Meter — on the following pages.

System Information The **System Information** (SI) utility supplies information about many aspects of your computer system and also provides access to a variety of tools for tinkering with it. To open the SI window (Figure 26), choose System Information from the System Tools submenu of the Start button's Accessories menu.

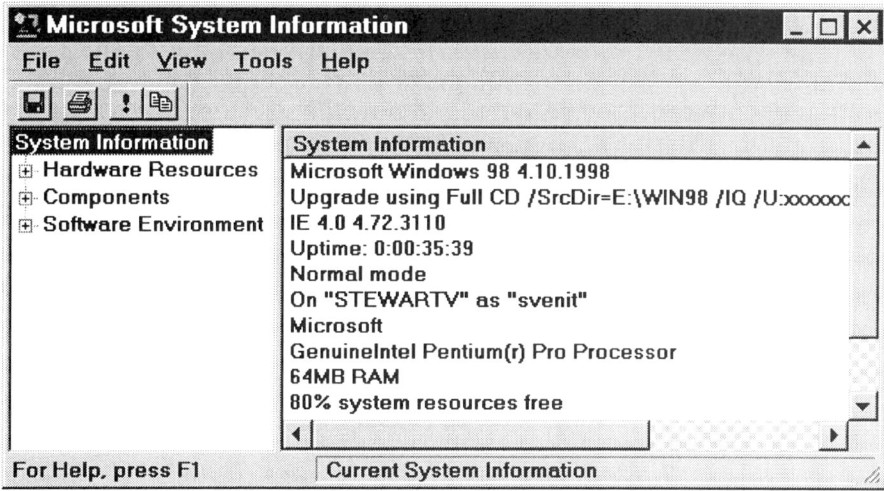

Figure 26 The System Information Window

As you can see, the SI window is divided into two parts. The left pane lists the components of your system. To view the items in a general category, such as Hardware Resources, click on the plus sign preceding it. The right pane then displays information about the selected component.

The top item in the left pane, System Information, cannot be expanded; when selected it displays the information shown in Figure 26. Here's a brief rundown of the information supplied under each of the other three categories listed in the left pane:

- *Hardware Resources* provides details on how the computer's various hardware components are communicating with the CPU. It describes how IRQs (interrupt request lines), DMA (direct memory access) channels, I/O (input/output) ports, and RAM are allocated to these components and shows any potential conflicts resulting from sharing these resources.
- *Components* displays information about how Windows has been configured to handle the system's peripheral devices, such as its display, keyboard, mouse, multimedia components, etc.
- *Software Environment* provides comprehensive information about the device drivers, applications, and other programs that currently reside in RAM, as well as Registry data associated with this software. (See Section 12.4 for information about the Windows Registry.)

The System Information utility can be very useful if you have problems with Windows. If you call Microsoft Technical Support or access its Web site through the Start menu's Help option (see Section 2.5), SI can provide details about your system's configuration that may be useful in attacking the problem. Moreover, this utility also provides access to other utilities that can help troubleshoot and/or fix a problem. These troubleshooting tools are described below.

The Tools menu System Information only displays information about your system's configuration; you cannot change any of these settings from within this utility. However, its Tools menu allows you to start other utilities that can be used to further diagnose problems and, in some cases, fix them. Here are brief descriptions of some of these tools.

- *Dr. Watson* is useful when a system fault (or *crash*) occurs. When you activate it, Dr. Watson records information about the current state of your system and, if a problem is detected, offers a brief diagnosis. You can also add your own comments and save the resulting report to disk.
- *Registry Checker* checks the integrity of your Registry files (see Section 12.4) and replaces them with a backup copy if it finds a problem.
- *System Configuration Utility* is the primary tool for diagnosing startup problems. It can be used to start Windows in several different modes or to enable or disable specific commands in the startup files. (See Section 12.3 for more information about this utility.)
- *System File Checker* can be used to check the integrity of your system files and to replace them with the originals if they have become damaged.
- The *Windows Report Tool* allows you to generate a *bug report* — a memo to Microsoft Technical Support about a problem you've encountered in using Windows.
- The *Update Wizard Uninstall* tool is used to replace a driver that was installed using the Windows Update utility with the former version. (The *Windows Update* utility, which is opened from the Start menu, allows you to access the Microsoft Web site to download recent drivers and other program updates.)

System Monitor **System Monitor** is a sophisticated utility which is useful when troubleshooting a system that has "bogged down" or run out of memory for no apparent reason. It allows you to track the performance of your CPU, RAM, hard disk, and even network resources as you use your system. A typical System Monitor window is shown in Figure 27.

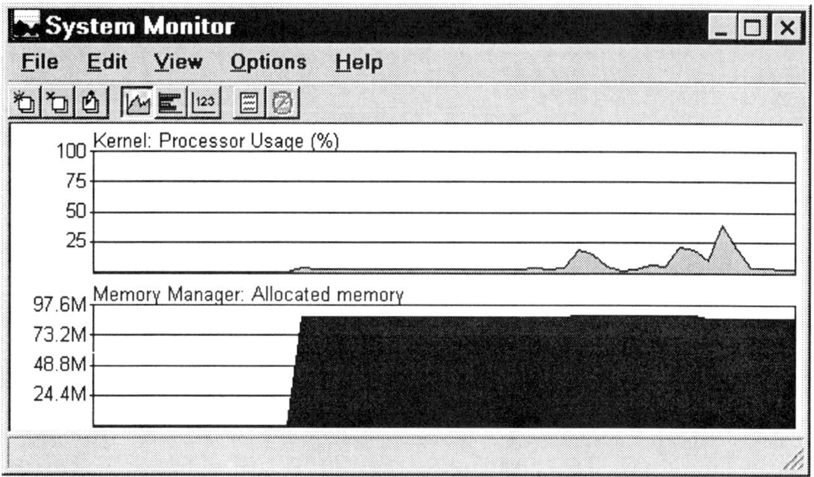

Figure 27 System Monitor in Line Chart View

To use this utility, start it by clicking on the System Monitor item on the System Tools submenu of the Accessories menu. Then:

Charting a system resource

1. Select the kind of chart — line chart, bar chart, or numeric chart — you want to use to display the resources being monitored by choosing the corresponding command from the View menu. (Figure 27 uses line charts to display the selected resources.)
2. Choose the Add Item command from the Edit menu to display the Add Item dialog box (Figure 28, on the next page).
3. Select the *type* of resource to be monitored from the Category list box. Here, Dial-Up Adapter refers to a network connection (see Section 11.2), Disk Cache and File System list hard disk resources, Kernel deals with CPU performance, and Memory Manager involves the use of RAM.
4. Select a resource to be monitored from the Item list box. (To view a description of a selected item, choose the Explain button.)
5. Choose the OK button. A chart, as specified in step 1, of the selected resource will be shown in the System Monitor window. As time passes, the contents of this chart will change to reflect the performance of this resource.

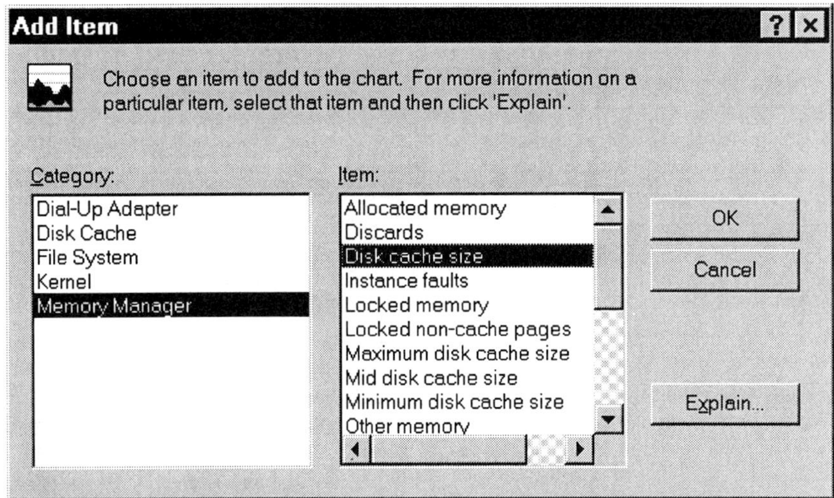

Figure 28 Adding a Chart to the System Monitor Window

6. To keep the System Monitor window on the screen while you are working with Windows or an application, choose Always on Top from the View menu.

Removing a chart

To remove a chart from the System Monitor window, choose the Remove Item command from the Edit menu and, in the resulting dialog box, select the item to be removed and choose the OK button.

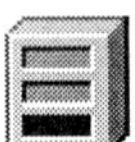

Resource Meter **Resource Meter** is a small utility that keeps track of the resources used by your applications. (In this context, the term *resources* refers to certain reserved areas of memory.) The resources monitored by this utility are:

- *User resources*, which store the objects (such as windows and menus) utilized by the user interface.
- *GDI* (Graphics Device Interface) *resources*, which are the memory involved in drawing objects to the screen.
- *System resources*, which refer to a combination of the User and GDI resources. Thus, the term *free system resources*, which appears in several Windows dialog boxes, describes the space available (given as a percentage) in these two areas of memory.

To use Resource Meter:

1. Start this utility by choosing the Resource Meter item from the System Tools submenu of the Start button's Accessories menu. (If an informational dialog box pops up, choose the OK button to

clear it from the screen.) A small icon, shown at the right, will appear near the right end of the Taskbar to indicate that Resource Meter is running.

2. To obtain a readout of the resources described above, either
   - Point at the Resource Meter icon on the Taskbar to display the percentage of each resource that is currently available.

   or
   - Double-click on the Taskbar icon to open the window shown below. (Click on its OK button to hide this window.)

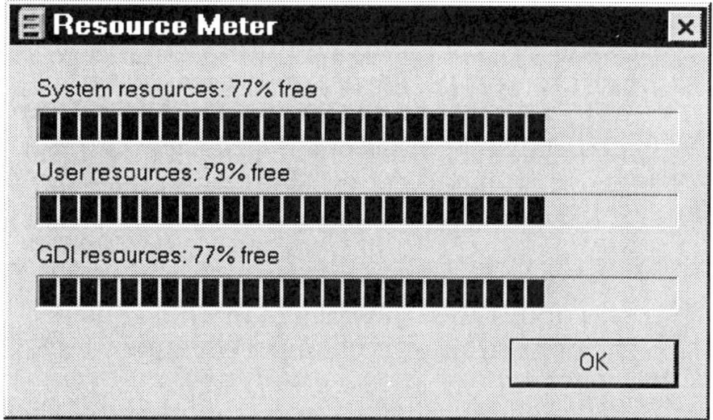

3. To close the Resource Meter utility, right-click on its Taskbar icon and choose Exit from the pop-up menu.

System Properties

The **System Properties** dialog box displays information about the various components of your computer and allows you to make changes in the way that some of them operate. To display System Properties, either

- Open the Control Panel window from the Start menu's Settings option and choose the System icon from the resulting window.

or

Right-click on the Desktop's My Computer icon and choose the Properties item from the resulting pop-up menu.

In either case, the System Properties dialog box will open. The first page of this dialog box displays some general information about the computer system. The other three pages, which are discussed below, allow you to make changes to certain system parameters.

WARNING

The System utility should be treated with respect. Changing certain settings in the System Properties dialog box can sometimes have unfortunate consequences. For example, after making a modification, a piece of hardware may stop working or Windows itself may fail to run. So, do not make any changes here unless you are sure of what you are doing.

The Device Manager Page Clicking on the Device Manager tab in the System Properties dialog box displays a list of the types of hardware connected to your computer. If you want to see the hardware devices within a particular category, click on the plus sign next to the category name. (The diagram above shows the result of clicking on the plus sign next to the CD-ROM icon.)

Now, if you double-click on a particular device (or select it and then choose the Properties command button), a dialog box with information about that device will open. In most cases, you will also be given the opportunity to change certain settings for the device.

The Hardware Profiles Page A **hardware profile** consists of a specified set of device drivers. Normally, the hardware attached to a computer does not change from session to session, so only one hardware profile, created automatically by Windows, is necessary.

In certain special circumstances, however, you may want to use a couple of different hardware configurations on a regular basis. This is sometimes the case with a portable computer. Most of the time, you will probably use the portable's built-in screen, keyboard, and pointing device. However, at times, you may find it more convenient to connect a regular monitor, keyboard, and mouse to the portable. In such a case, you would need different drivers for these components. This set of drivers can be set up as a hardware profile.

To create a new hardware profile:

1. Open the System Properties dialog box as described above and click on the Hardware Profiles tab to display this page.
2. Select an existing profile, choose the Copy command button, type the new profile's name in the resulting dialog box, and choose OK.
3. To enable or disable a specific device for this profile, click on the Device Manager tab and:

- Click on the plus sign next to the desired hardware type and then double-click on the device that you want to enable or disable.
- In the Device Usage area of the resulting dialog box, select the appropriate check box to enable or disable the selected device.
- Choose the OK command button to return to the System Properties dialog box.

4. Choose the OK button in the System Properties dialog box.

If more than one hardware profile has been set up for your computer, when Windows starts, you will be asked which profile you want to use.

The Performance Page When Windows 98 is installed on a computer or a new device is added, Windows tries to set up the hardware so that it operates in an optimal manner. The Performance page of the System Properties dialog box displays information about memory and disk use and allows you to change a few related settings to enhance performance "manually". However, in most cases, it is best not to make changes here; they are more likely to *adversely* affect performance.

There are three command buttons on this page. Choosing the File System button opens the File System Properties dialog box, which allows you to change certain settings for the disk drives connected to your computer, For example:

File System settings

- On the Hard Disk page, you can change the *read-ahead buffer* size allotted to the hard disk. When a hard disk read takes place, Windows will not only copy the requested information to RAM, but also *read-ahead* — transfer the data stored in the next disk sectors, as well. The amount of additional data sent to the hard disk — the read-ahead buffer size — is normally set to "Full", the largest available amount.
- On the CD-ROM page, you can change the *supplemental cache* size allotted to the CD-ROM drive. A *cache* is an area in RAM set aside to temporarily store information read from a hard disk or CD-ROM. Then, if this information is needed again, it can be quickly retrieved from RAM, instead of using the much slower process of reading again from the disk or CD. This setting is normally set to "Large".
- On the Troubleshooting page, you can disable certain performance-enhancing features if they appear to be causing trouble.

Graphics settings Choosing the Graphics command button on the Performance page allows you to adjust the amount of *hardware acceleration* used by Windows. (*Acceleration* is accomplished through routines that speed up the display of new information on the screen.) This setting is normally set to "Full".

Virtual Memory settings **Virtual memory** refers to Windows' practice of using the hard disk as if it were additional RAM. Windows 98 normally determines the amount of hard disk space to be used for this purpose, and it's best to accept this setting. If you want to change it (perhaps to use a different hard disk to hold the *swap file*), choose the Virtual Memory command button on the Performance page.

The Modems Utility

In previous chapters we have discussed most of the Control Panel utilities that can be used to modify hardware settings. These include Printers, Display, Keyboard, Sounds, and Multimedia. Here, we will describe the utility that sets a modem's properties.

Recall that a *modem* is a device that translates computer-generated data into signals that can be sent (usually over phone lines) to another computer. A modem, together with the proper software gives you the potential for computer-to-computer communication. The **Modems** utility helps you to install and/or configure a modem. To start this utility:

1. Open the Control Panel window (from the Settings option on the Start menu).
2. Choose the Modems icon.

The Modems Properties dialog box, shown in Figure 29, will open.

Installing a Modem To use the Modems Properties dialog box to install a new modem:

1. With the computer off, connect the modem to the computer:
   - If the modem is an *internal* type, insert it in a free slot within the system unit.
   - If the modem is an *external* type, attach it to a serial computer port with the appropriate cable and turn it on.
2. Turn on the computer. Windows' Plug and Play routine will probably detect the modem, in which case the rest of the installation process will proceed as described in Section 10.1.

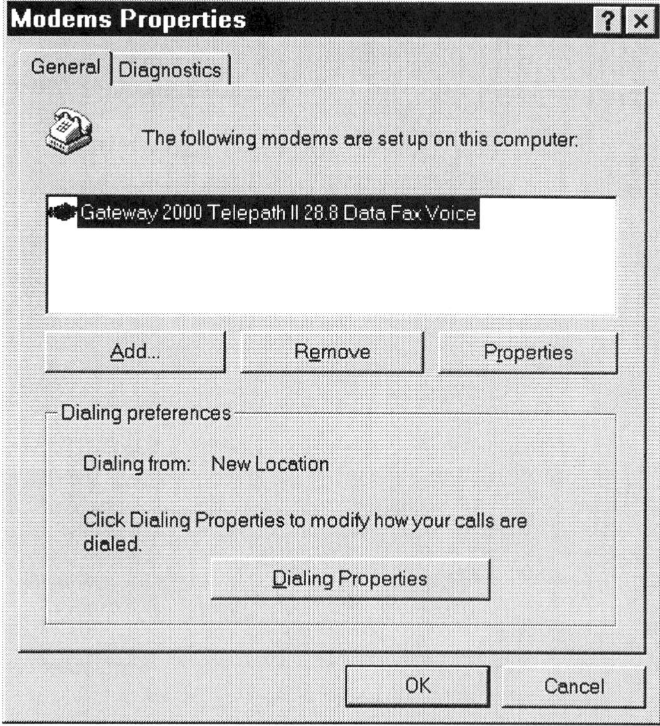

Figure 29 The Modems Properties Dialog Box

If Windows does not detect the new modem on startup, open the Modems Properties dialog box, as described above.

3. Choose the Add command button, which starts the Install New Modem wizard. Follow the instructions, making selections and choosing Next (or Finish), until the process is complete. (It may help if you have the modem's user's manual handy during this procedure.)

Configuring a Modem The Modems utility provides an easy way to configure the modem's driver by setting various parameters for its operation. This information can be entered or changed from the Modems Properties dialog box by choosing either the Properties or Dialing Properties command button (see Figure 29).

Choosing the Properties button opens a dialog box that allows you to change information about the modem itself. This includes:

- The volume level of the modem's speaker.

- The maximum speed, measured in bits per second (bps), at which the modem can connect to a remote computer.
- Default connection parameters — the parity, and number of data and stop bits. (The settings for these parameters must match the requirements of the remote computer and can be changed, if necessary, using communications software when making a particular connection.)
- Certain default calling preferences, such as how much time is allowed to elapse (between dialing a number and making the connection) before the call is canceled.
- Certain advanced settings, such as those that affect the serial port the modem is using.

Choosing the Dialing Properties button opens a dialog box that allows you to express preferences for the way a call is made. For example, you can specify that a certain country code or area code be used when dialing a phone number or that *tone* or *pulse* dialing be used to make the call.

Chapter Summary

Adding New Hardware	If it is Plug and Play compatible	Physically install the device, turn on the computer, and follow the on-screen instructions.
	Using the Add New Hardware utility	Physically install the device, choose Control Panel's Add New Hardware icon, and use the resulting Add New Hardware Wizard.
Backing Up Your Hard Disk	To start the Backup utility	Choose the Backup item from the System Tools submenu of the Accessories menu.
	To back up files	On the Backup page of the Backup window, select the files to be backed up, select a destination, and start the process.
	To restore backed up files	Click on the Restore tab in the Backup window, select the appropriate backup job, and start the process.
Increasing Free Disk Space	To start one of these utilities	Choose the appropriate item from the System Tools submenu of the Accessories menu.

	Disk Cleanup	Automatically deletes selected types of files.
	DriveSpace	Compresses (or uncompresses) a drive.
	Drive Converter	Converts a FAT16 drive to FAT32.
Other Disk Maintenance Utilities	To start one of these utilities	Choose the appropriate item from the System Tools submenu of the Accessories menu.
	ScanDisk	Checks a drive for errors and, if you want, tries to fix them.
	Disk Defragmenter	Rearranges data on a drive so that each file is stored in one contiguous region.
	Maintenance Wizard	Allows you to schedule maintenance tasks to run automatically at future times. (These tasks are stored in the Scheduled Tasks folder.)
Monitoring Your System	To start one of these utilities	Choose the appropriate item from the System Tools submenu of the Accessories menu.
	System Information	Displays information about almost every aspect of your system; provides access to several tools for diagnosing problems.
	System Monitor	Monitors disk, memory, and CPU performance as you work on the computer.
	Resource Meter	Monitors memory allocated for the user-interface and display purposes.
Control Panel Utilities	To start one of these utilities	Open the Control Panel window from the Start button's Settings option and choose the appropriate icon from this window.
	System	Displays computer system information, changes device driver and performance settings, and creates hardware profiles.
	Modems	Installs and configures modems.

Review Exercises

Section 10.1

1. The term ___________ refers to an industry-wide standard that makes the installation of certain hardware devices easier.

2. Configuring a new hardware device can be accomplished from Control Panel's ___________ utility.

3. True or false: A (device) driver is a program that translates the signals from the device into a language that Windows can understand.

4. True or false: When you use the Add New Hardware Wizard to configure a newly-installed device, it is recommended that you first let Windows try to detect the new hardware.

5. Before you use the Add New Hardware utility to help install a new device, you should

    a. Physically connect the device to your computer.
    b. Open Control Panel and then restart Windows.
    c. Start the Add/Remove Programs utility.
    d. Make sure that the device's driver is installed.

6. The Add New Hardware Wizard

    a. May automatically appear when Windows starts if a new device has been installed in your computer.
    b. Must be used to install a Plug and Play device.
    c. Only works with Plug and Play devices.
    d. Has all of the above characteristics.

Section 10.2

7. The Backup utility is found on the ___________ submenu of the Start button's Accessories menu.

8. To ___________ a backed up file means to copy it from the backup medium to its original location.

9. True or false: In Backup, a box containing a *gray* check mark next to a folder icon in the *What to back up* window signifies that some, but not all, of the files in that folder have been selected.

10. True or false: The Backup utility provides access to "wizards" that will guide you through either the backup or the restore process.

11. The Backup utility cannot back up a file on the hard disk to

    a. A tape cartridge, even if your computer is equipped with a tape drive.
    b. A floppy disk.
    c. Another location on the hard disk.
    d. None of the above is correct.

12. The Backup utility cannot be used to

    a. Back up files and folders from the hard disk to a floppy.

b. Restore backed up files from a floppy to the hard disk.
c. Move (copy and delete) files from the hard disk to a floppy.
d. Compare a backed up file to the original.

Section 10.3

13. The ___________ utility, which is found on the Start button's System Tools submenu, can be used to delete some unneeded files from your hard disk.

14. When you ___________ a drive, one large file is created that stores the entire contents of that drive.

15. The ___________ for a drive keeps track of the location of all files on that drive.

16. True or false: You can increase your free disk space by emptying the Recycle Bin if it contains previously-deleted files.

17. True or false: when you use DriveSpace to compress a drive, the process is irreversible; that drive cannot be decompressed.

18. True or false: The Drive Converter utility converts the selected drive's file allocation table to the FAT16 file system.

19. Which of the following utilities does not have the capability to increase the amount of free space on a hard disk:

    a. Disk Cleanup
    b. Disk Defragmenter
    c. Drive Converter
    d. DriveSpace

20. If you convert your primary hard disk to the FAT32 file system:

    a. The computer will no longer be able to read your old diskettes.
    b. All the applications on that disk must be reinstalled.
    c. You will not be able to uninstall Windows 98.
    d. None of the above will be a problem.

Section 10.4

21. If you want to locate and delete lost file fragments, use the Windows ___________ utility.

22. A disk file is said to be ___________ if it is stored in two or more nonadjacent locations on disk.

23. If you want to use the Maintenance Wizard to schedule Disk Cleanup but not ScanDisk, you must select the ___________ option on the initial wizard screen.

24. To see which maintenance tasks are scheduled to run automatically on your system, open the My Computer window and choose the ___________ folder icon.

25. True or false: The ScanDisk utility can be set up to detect errors, but not to try to fix them.
26. True or false: Disk Defragmenter tells you the degree to which the selected disk is fragmented before starting the defragmentation process.
27. True or false: If you use the Maintenance Wizard to schedule tasks, you must select from one of three specified times of day to run these tasks.
28. True or false: In order to run a program listed in the Scheduled Tasks folder, the computer must be on at the specified time.
29. To use the ScanDisk utility to check for physical flaws on the surface of a disk:
    a. Choose the Advanced command button.
    b. Select the Standard option button.
    c. Select the Thorough option button.
    d. ScanDisk cannot perform this test.
30. When Disk Defragmenter is running, to see a graphical display of the defragmentation process
    a. Choose the Settings button.
    b. Choose the Pause button.
    c. Choose the Show Details button.
    d. Choose the Legend button.

Section 10.5

31. To keep track of the extent to which the CPU is being utilized as an application runs, use the ____________ utility.
32. To keep track of free User (user-interface) and GDI (graphics device interface) resources, use the ____________ utility.
33. If you frequently use a laptop computer with an auxiliary monitor, you should set up a ____________ that tells Windows, on system startup, to load the proper driver for this device.
34. A ____________ is a portion of RAM set aside to temporarily store information read from a hard disk or CD-ROM so that, if the information is needed again, it can be quickly retrieved.
35. True or false: The System Information utility provides access to tools that can diagnose system problems.
36. True or false: The System Information utility can display information about system software, but not about hardware devices.
37. True or false: The term *virtual memory* refers to RAM that has been added to your computer after the initial purchase.

38. True or false: Only Plug and Play modems can be added to a system that is running Windows 98.

39. Which of the following tasks cannot be accomplished using the Modems utility?

    a. Install a driver for a newly-connected modem.
    b. Set the maximum connection speed for your modem.
    c. Set up an "address book" of phone numbers that can be dialed from your modem.
    d. Specify that pulse dialing be used by your modem.

40. You can fine-tune your computer's hard disk and CD-ROM performance using Control Panel's

    a. System utility.
    b. System Monitor utility.
    c. Resource Meter utility.
    d. Hardware Profiles utility.

Build Your Own Glossary

41. The following words and phrases are important terms that were introduced in this chapter. (They appear within the text in boldface type.) Use WordPad (see Section 2.2) to enter a definition for each term, preserving alphabetical order, into the Glossary file on the Student Disk.

Add New Hardware utility
Back up a file
Backup job
Backup utility
Compress a drive
Compression Agent
Defragment a disk
Disk Cleanup utility
Disk Defragmenter
Drive Converter utility
Driver
DriveSpace utility
File allocation table (FAT)
Hardware profile
Maintenance Wizard
Modems utility
Plug and Play
Resource Meter utility
Restore a backup
ScanDisk utility
Scheduled Tasks folder
System Information utility
System Monitor utility
System Properties
Virtual memory

Lab Exercises

Work each of the following exercises at your computer. Begin by turning the machine on (if necessary) to start Windows 98 and close any open windows. If you want to produce a written record of your answers, review the material on WordPad and capturing screens in Sections 2.2 and 2.3.

Lab Exercise 1 (Section 10.1)

a. Open the Control Panel window and start the Add New Hardware utility. What is the name of the resulting dialog box?

b. Choose the Next command button twice. After the wizard has checked for Plug and Play devices, select the No option button and choose Next on the next two screens.

c. You are going to simulate setting up a printer that has just been connected to your computer, so select Printer from the hardware types list and choose the Next button. What is the name of the first manufacturer listed in the resulting dialog box?

d. Suppose that the Printer is made by Epson and its model designation is "LQ-850". Select the appropriate items from the Manufacturers and Printers lists. What is the exact name of the item in the Printers list?

e. Choose the Next button to display the "ports" page. Which computer port is highlighted? Which abbreviation, COM or LPT, refers to a parallel port?

f. Choose the Next button. Select, if necessary, the No option button so that the new printer does not become the default one. What *is* the name of your default printer?

g. Choose the Next button and then the Cancel button.

h. Close the Control Panel window.

Lab Exercise 2 (Section 10.2)

a. Start the Backup utility. Did the "welcome" dialog box appear? If so, close it to display the main Backup window.

b. Insert the Student Disk in its drive (we will assume this drive is A:) and back up a file to this disk, as follows:

- In the left window, open the Windows folder.
- In the right window, select the Faq.txt file to be backed up. Does a check mark appear in the box next to the Windows folder icon in the left window? If so, what color is it?
- Specify A:\MyBackup as the destination for the backup. Describe how you accomplished this?
- Try to start the backup. What message was displayed?
- Save the backup job, calling it MyBackup.
- Start the backup. How long did it take?

c. Restore the backed up file to its original location. Describe how you accomplished this.

d. Start Windows Explorer and locate the MyBackup file on the A: drive. What size is it? Delete this file.

e. Close Explorer and Backup and remove the diskette from its drive.

Lab Exercise 3 (Section 10.3)

a. Use My Computer to determine how much free space there is on the C: drive. How did you accomplish this? How much free space is there?

b. Open the Recycle Bin. According to the status bar, how much disk space is occupied by the files in the Recycle Bin? Close this folder.

c. Start the Disk Cleanup utility. On what submenu of the Start button is it located?

d. Select the C: drive. According to Disk Cleanup, how much disk space is being used by the Recycle Bin? How much space in total would be gained by running Disk Cleanup?

e. Insert the Student Disk in its drive and select this drive in Disk Cleanup. What types of files can be "cleaned up" on the Student Disk?

f. Close Disk Cleanup and remove the diskette from its drive.

g. Use My Computer to determine the file allocation system used by the C: drive. How did you accomplish this? Is the file system FAT16 or FAT32?

h. Close My Computer.

Lab Exercise 4 (Section 10.3)

a. Insert the Student Disk in its drive and start the DriveSpace utility. What drives are listed in the DriveSpace 3 window?

b. Select the A: drive and choose the Compress command from the Drive menu. What error message is displayed? Clear this message from the screen.

c. Remove the Student Disk from its drive. Then, insert a new, formatted diskette in the drive, make sure that the A: drive is still selected, and choose the Compress command. What is the name of the resulting dialog box?

d. Start the compression process. When it is complete, how much space is indicated as free on the compressed drive?

e. Close the Compress a Drive dialog box. What drives are listed in the DriveSpace 3 window now?

f. Uncompress the disk in the A: drive. List the steps you used to accomplish this. (If you are asked whether to "remove compression", click on Yes.)

g. Close the DriveSpace 3 window and remove the diskette from its drive.

Lab Exercise 5 (Section 10.4)

a. Start the ScanDisk utility.

b. Insert the Student Disk in its drive and select this drive in the ScanDisk window.

c. Select the Thorough test mode, but elect not to perform write-testing or to repair bad sectors in hidden or system files. In which dialog box are the last two options found?

d. Elect not to print a "log file" but to check files for invalid dates and times. Also, make sure that a summary is displayed whether or not there are errors. In which dialog box did you select these options?

e. Start the ScanDisk tests. (They will take a few minutes to complete.) Were any errors found? If so, what are they?

f. Use the summary to answer the following questions:

   - What is the total disk space for this disk?
   - How many bytes of space are there in bad sectors?
   - How many files are there are on this disk?

g. Close the Results dialog box, the ScanDisk window, and remove the Student Disk from its drive.

Lab Exercise 6 (Section 10.4)

a. Start the Disk Defragmenter utility.

b. Insert the Student Disk in its drive, select this drive from the drop-down list, and choose the OK button to begin the defragmentation process. What is the resulting dialog box called?

c. Choose the Show Details button, then the Legend button. Use the Defrag Legend window to answer the following questions. (You can choose the Pause button to give yourself more time to find the answers.)

   - What color is used to represent free disk space?
   - Are any parts of the disk marked as "bad (damaged) area"?
   - What does each box in the display represent?

d. Resume the defragmentation, if necessary. When defragmentation is complete, is a summary report produced?

e. Close Disk Defragmenter and remove the diskette from its drive.

Lab Exercise 7 (Section 10.5)

a. Start the System Information (SI) utility. Determine (from the information displayed) the version number of Windows 98 that is installed on your system.

b. Use SI to answer the following questions about your system:

- What device is using DMA channel 2?
- What device is using IRQ 7?
- What type of mouse and keyboard are installed?
- Is Task Scheduler (mstask.exe) one of the Startup Programs?

c. Close SI and open the System Monitor utility.

d. Remove all the currently displayed charts and specify that all charts be of Line Graph type. What menu(s) did you use to accomplish these tasks?

e. Add the following charts to the System Monitor display: "Kernel: Processor Usage" and "Memory manager: Other Memory". With the help of the Explain command button, describe each resource.

f. Edit the Processor Usage chart to change the color to black. What other attribute of Processor Usage can be edited? *Optional*: Reduce the System Monitor window to a relatively small size and capture it.

g. Close System Monitor and start Resource Meter. If a dialog box is displayed, clear it from the screen. What is the only evidence that Resource Meter is now running?

h. Use Resource Meter to display the percentage of free User, GDI, and System resources. What are these figures?

i. Start the WordPad and Paint applications. What are the percentages of free resources now? What is the easiest way to increase free resources?

j. Close Resource Meter. How did you do this?

k. Close the other open windows.

Lab Exercise 8 (Section 10.5)

a. Open the Control Panel window and start the Modems utility. How many pages are there in the resulting dialog box?

b. If your computer is equipped with a modem, use this utility to answer the following questions:

- What is the name and maximum speed for this modem?
- What are the current settings for data bits, parity, and stop bits?
- Is the modem using tone dialing or pulse dialing?

c. Close the Modems utility.

d. Start the System utility, opening the System Properties dialog box. Use the latter to answer the following questions:

- What kind of processor and how much RAM does your computer have?
- What type of display adapter and monitor does it have?
- What are the names of the available hardware profiles?
- Is the hard disk making maximum use of the read-ahead buffer?
- Is the CD-ROM drive set for "Quad-speed or higher"?
- Are virtual memory settings specified or is Windows managing them automatically?

e. Close the System Properties dialog box and the Control Panel window.

If You Want to Learn More ...

The notes presented here allow you to delve more deeply into some of the topics covered in this chapter.

A simple backup technique

As we mentioned in Section 10.2, it really is important to back up files, especially your data files. If a *program* file becomes inaccessible or is accidentally deleted, it can usually be reinstalled from the original distribution disks. But, documents (and all the hours of work you put into creating them) may be irretrievable if disaster strikes.

Unfortunately, the Windows Backup utility is somewhat cumbersome for small backups; enough so that it might discourage daily use. Here's an easier way to back up your data files. First, you need to do some one-time preparation:

1. Create a folder on your hard disk (see Section 3.4) to hold the documents you generate from each application you use.

2. Create a Desktop shortcut (see Section 3.4) for each of these folders and rename them appropriately.

3. Use the shortcuts to successively open each folder's window. In the folder window, select the Details view option and order the files by date, with the most recent ones at the top (to do so, click on the *Modified* button).

Now, whenever you choose one of these shortcuts, the documents you've just created will appear at the top of the folder window. To back up these documents:

1. Insert an appropriately labeled diskette in its drive.
2. Select the files to be backed up.
3. Right-click on one of the selected files, point at the Send To command on the pop-up menu, and then choose the appropriate drive from the submenu. The selected files will be copied to the floppy.

Try to get in the habit of using this technique at the end of every session in which you create or modify documents.

Checking System and Registry files

As we mentioned in Section 10.5, the System Information (SI) utility provides access to other utilities that you can use to diagnose (and sometimes repair) problems with your computer system. These diagnostic utilities, which are started from SI's Tools menu, are fairly sophisticated but not so difficult to use, and can be life-savers when certain problems arise.

TROUBLESHOOTING

Two of the most valuable diagnostic/repair utilities are System File Checker and Registry Checker:

- System File Checker scans your *system files* (those with a System attribute — see Section 4.6) to see if any have been damaged, changed, or deleted. You can use its Settings command button to specify the folders opened by System File Checker and to select other options for its use. If it finds errors, you can also request that System File Checker restore the original file or files from the Windows CD-ROM.
- Registry Checker scans the Windows Registry for errors. (The Registry — covered in Section 12.4 — is a database of information about your system that is crucial to the operation of Windows.) If it finds any errors, this utility will automatically replace the current copy of the Registry with a backup.

Dr. Watson

Another useful System Information Tools menu utility is Dr. Watson, which tracks system errors and *crashes* (unexpected termination of a program or Windows itself). The information it gathers can help Microsoft Technical Support to diagnose a system problem. To use Dr. Watson:

TROUBLESHOOTING

1. Choose the Dr. Watson item from System Information's Tools menu. The Dr. Watson icon will appear on the right

end of the Taskbar, next to the Clock.

2. To create a "snapshot" of the current state of your system, double-click on the Dr. Watson Taskbar icon. Dr. Watson will record a picture of the computer's current software environment and open the following window on the screen:

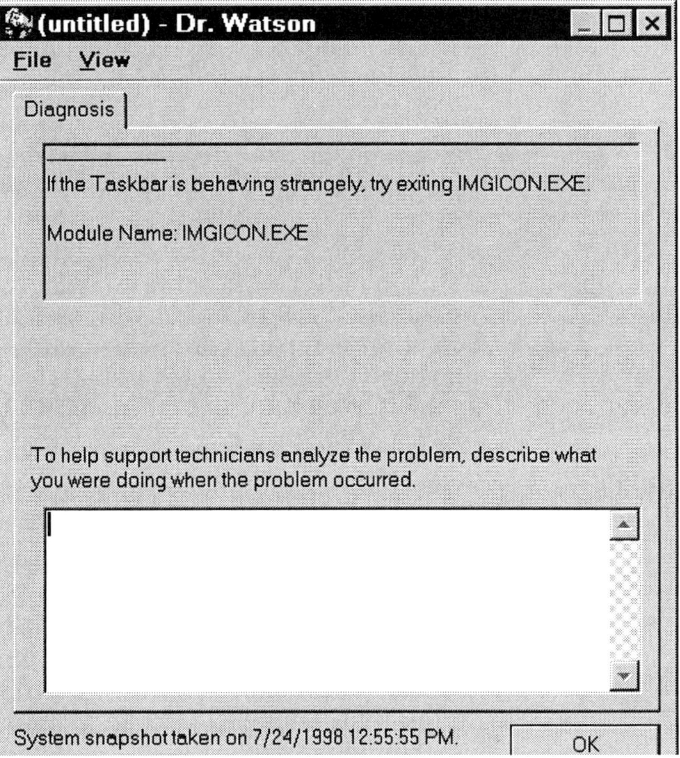

Notice that the Dr. Watson window contains a brief diagnosis of the problem.

3. In the window's text box, type a description of what actions led to the error.
4. Choose the Save command from the File menu, and save the report to disk. If you decide to contact Microsoft Technical Support, this report could be helpful in diagnosing the problem.
5. Close Dr. Watson by choosing th Exit command from the File menu or by right-clicking on the Taskbar icon and choosing Exit from the pop-up menu.

Improving performance

As we mentioned in Section 10.5, it's usually best to leave the System utility's Performance settings at their defaults. Here are two special cases in which you might want to make a change:

- If your system has an older single- or double-speed CD-ROM drive, you might be able to improve its performance by telling Windows that it's a quad-speed drive. To do so:

  1. Click on the Performance tab in the System Properties dialog box and choose the File System command button.
  2. In the resulting dialog box, click on the CD-ROM tab and select *Quad-speed or higher* from the drop-down list.
  3. Choose the OK button and close the System utility.

  Windows will now assign a larger amount of cache memory to the CD-ROM drive.

- If your system has two hard disk drives, you might improve performance by using the faster of these disks (especially if it has more free disk space) for the Windows swap file. To do so:

  1. Click on the Performance tab in the System Properties dialog box and then choose the Virtual Memory command button.
  2. In the resulting dialog box, select the *Let me specify my own virtual memory settings* option button and then select the faster drive from the *Hard disk* drop-down list.
  3. Choose the OK command button (a warning message will appear; respond "No" if you're not sure you want to do this) and close the System Properties dialog box.

  Of course, if you experience any difficulties with a new setting, return it to the default.

Printing a system resource report

Control Panel's System utility allows you to print a "system resource report"; a comprehensive listing of your computer system's components and their settings. This report contains information about the computer's processor, IRQ (interrupt request lines) and I/O (input/output) settings, memory usage, hardware devices, and installed device drivers. To print the report:

1. Open the System utility and click on the Device Manager tab.
2. Choose the Print command button and, in the Print dialog box, select the *All devices and system summary* option button.
3. Choose the OK command button.

Be aware that the report might be more than ten pages long!

CHAPTER 11

Networking and Communications

Communication in our society is increasingly characterized by the electronic exchange of information. When this exchange occurs by linking computers together, the connection is usually made possible by networking. A **network** is a communication system that moves information from one computer to another. This chapter introduces the concepts of networking and computer-to-computer communications and describes some of the ways in which Windows helps make them possible. To be more specific, you will learn about:

1. Different types of networks and the equipment needed to create a local area network.
2. Establishing a Dial-Up Networking connection.
3. Using the HyperTerminal application for computer-to-computer communication.
4. Windows features that are specific to portable computing, such as docking station detection and the use of the Briefcase to manage transported files.
5. The deferred printing option.

11.1 An Introduction to Networking

Networking can exist on a small scale or a large scale. In any case, a network enables computer users to communicate with each other and to share resources, such as files and printers. In this section, we will discuss some network terminology and how to access a network.

Network Types and Connections

Some definitions are necessary before we can explore networking in more detail. First we will discuss different types of networks and how they function.

- A **local area network** (or **LAN**) is a network on a small scale. A LAN might span one company site, a campus, or a small office. A LAN usually requires a *server*, which is a computer that manages the network, and server software (sometimes called a *scheduler*) that manages and allocates the network resources.
- A **peer-to-peer network** is a small LAN that allows individual computers to communicate and share resources without using a server.
- As our society becomes a global community, more and more of us will be using networks to send and receive electronic mail and "surf" the Internet. These kinds of communication use a **wide area network** (a **WAN**), which connects computers in distant locations, even across continents.

Advantages of networking

Regardless of the network type, networking provides several benefits related to the cost and convenience of computing. To be specific:

- System resources can be shared on a network, minimizing the cost of hardware and software. For example, the confusion that might result from client scheduling done through several different offices can be eliminated by accessing a single database. Moreover, with a LAN, these offices could also make use of the same printer to create copies of the appointment schedule for everyone concerned.
- Communications among those connected to a network are greatly enhanced. In particular, networking provides access to e-mail and other information sharing (see Chapter 6).

Physical connections

The computers and other equipment in a network system are usually physically connected to one another by means of network cable or other wire. Telephone lines are often used for connections because that wire is already installed in most buildings. Large capacity phone lines called *trunk lines*, or T1s, are used for high traffic areas, but are expensive. *ISDN* lines (Integrated Services Digital Network), which allow high-speed digital telephone access at a relatively low cost, are becoming more common in both homes and offices. *Fiber optic* lines are sometimes used instead of ordinary copper phone wire because they enable a higher quality transmission of the network connection.

As we transmit more and more information over networks, the rate at which the data are exchanged becomes increasingly important. The table below provides a comparison of the time it takes to transfer a given block of data at several different transfer rates, measured in *bits per second.*

Rate in bits per second	Time necessary for a given data transfer
9,600 bps	9.6 hours
56,000 bps	1.6 hours
1,000,000 bps	6.87 minutes
(T1) 1,540,000 bps	3.6 minutes
10,000,000 bps	41.25 seconds
(T3) 45,000,000 bps	0.92 seconds
1,000,000,000 bps	0.4 seconds

Depending on the hardware configuration, a local area network sends data at a rate ranging from 1 to 10 mps (megabits per second). Of course, the faster that data are transmitted, the more effective is the networking process.

Network Hardware

When the decision is made to share resources through networking, the following additional hardware may be necessary:

- A network **server** is a computer designated to run the network operating system. The network operating system controls the multitasking and scheduling of resources. **Multitasking** is the ability to perform more than a single task concurrently, which (for example) allows the server to answer user requests while managing the network resources. A server is usually a high performance machine because of its heavy workload.

- A **workstation** is a computer that can operate as a stand-alone machine or can be connected to the network; it is the computer on which a user performs tasks. A workstation must have *client* software installed, which allows communication between the workstation and the server and also with the shared resources. (The workstation is the *client*; the server is the *host*.)
- **Network cabling** consists of wire and connectors. A wireless network (or *virtual network*) works with transmitters and receivers, and does not require traditional cabling.
- A **network interface card (NIC)** is an adapter card (a circuit board) that installs in the workstation's system unit. The NIC connects the network cabling to the computer and, with the aid of the proper software, sets up the workstation for network use.
- **Network hubs** join together the cabling from computers and peripheral hardware and act as network traffic controllers. Hubs also assist in reducing "noise" and strengthening the line signal.

A typical network configuration is shown below.

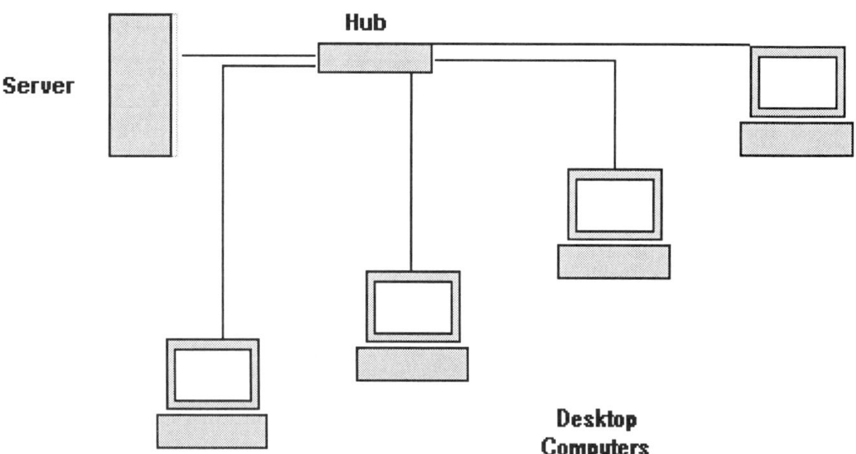

Accessing a Network

Windows 98 establishes access to both traditional server-based networks and peer-to-peer networks with a login and a password. A *login* is a unique name given to a user of the network; a *password* is a secret word or phrase that only the user knows. Both elements are required to gain access to the network system.

Most networks are set up to provide access to users only through the login and password system, which provides security for the network files against improper or illegal use. The *network administrator*, the person in charge of setting up and maintaining the network, controls the user logins and passwords for the system. This information must be set up for specific users prior to their connecting (or *logging on*) to the network. Before turning off the computer, the user normally *logs out* (or *logs off*) of the system. The process for logging on and off of a particular network system will vary, depending upon what network software is being used.

An example of logging in

In the following procedure, we will use the Novell NetWare software as an illustration of how to log in to a network system. Be aware that your network may act differently from this example, although entering the login and password is always a part of the process.

To access the network:

1. Click on the Start button, point at the Programs option, and choose Novell from the resulting submenu. Now, click on NetWare Login on the Novell submenu. A dialog box similar to the one shown in Figure 1 will open.

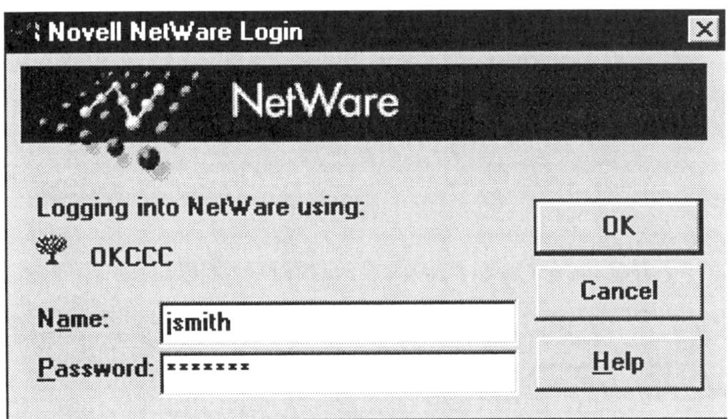

Figure 1 A Sample Login Dialog Box

2. Type your login name in the Name text box.
3. Press Tab, or click in the Password text box, and then type your password. For security reasons, the characters you type will usually display as asterisks.

4. Choose the OK command button. A window (like the one in Figure 2) will open, indicating whether the attempt to log in was successful or not. Choose the Close command button to return to the Windows Desktop.

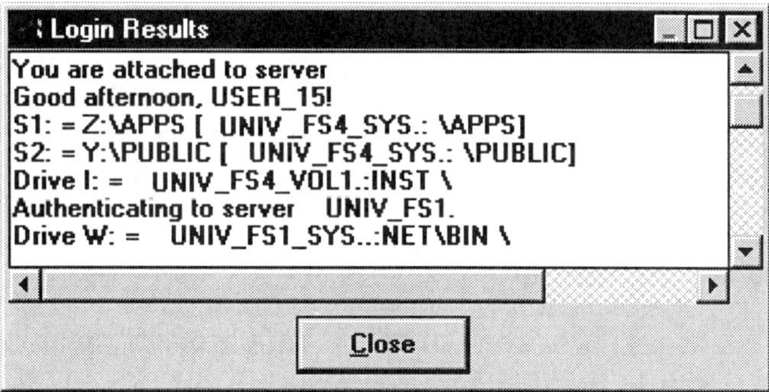

Figure 2 The Login Results

Logging off

After using the network system, its log out procedure should be executed. This procedure is a sequence of steps that differ for each network. Some networks require that you run a logout routine; others log you out of the system automatically when you shut down Windows. In the latter case, if you want to log out but continue to use Windows, choose the Start menu's Log Off command (just above Shut Down).

The Network Neighborhood

The **Network Neighborhood** is a Windows folder that is normally represented by an icon on the Desktop if the computer is connected to a network. Network Neighborhood provides a window in which you can browse and access folders and other resources on the network.

Choosing the Desktop's Network Neighborhood icon opens a window like the one shown in Figure 3, displaying the resources of the network. This window is similar to a My Computer (or any folder) window. To open (display the contents of) any of the available resources, just choose its icon (click on it in Web style mode or double-click on it in Classic style mode).

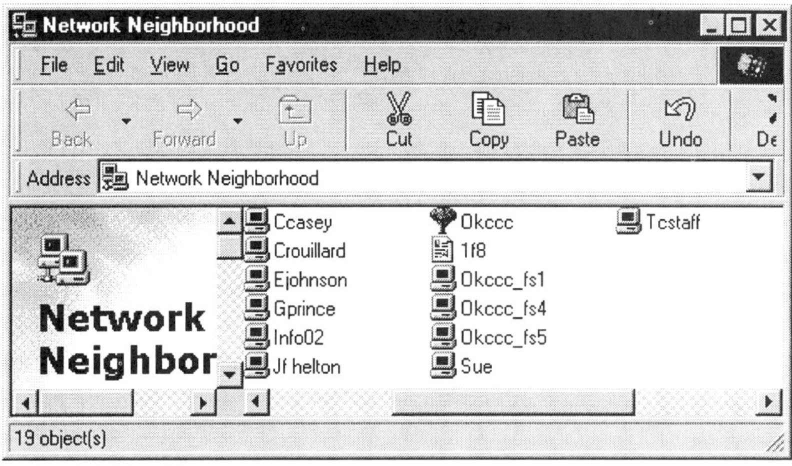

Figure 3 The Network Neighborhood Window

Mapped network drives

Some network resources (such as drives or folders) may be displayed in the Network Neighborhood as a drive letter (such as H:). We call such a drive a **mapped network drive**. Mapped drives are usually created by the network administrator for the purpose of providing easy access to frequently used network resources. A mapped drive can also be accessed from Windows Explorer, My Computer, or any folder window. If a network drive has not been mapped, you will not be able to access it from your computer.

The Network Utility

Control Panel's **Network utility** identifies network hardware and *drivers* (programs that allow Windows to communicate with various devices) and allows certain settings for these resources to be modified. (The network administrator usually determines these settings.) For instance, the Network utility is used to configure the network driver on your workstation, enabling the network to communicate with your specific computer.

To start the Network utility, choose its icon in the Control Panel window. A dialog box similar to the one shown in Figure 4 (on the next page) will be displayed.

There are three pages in the Network utility dialog box. Here is a rundown on the content of these pages.

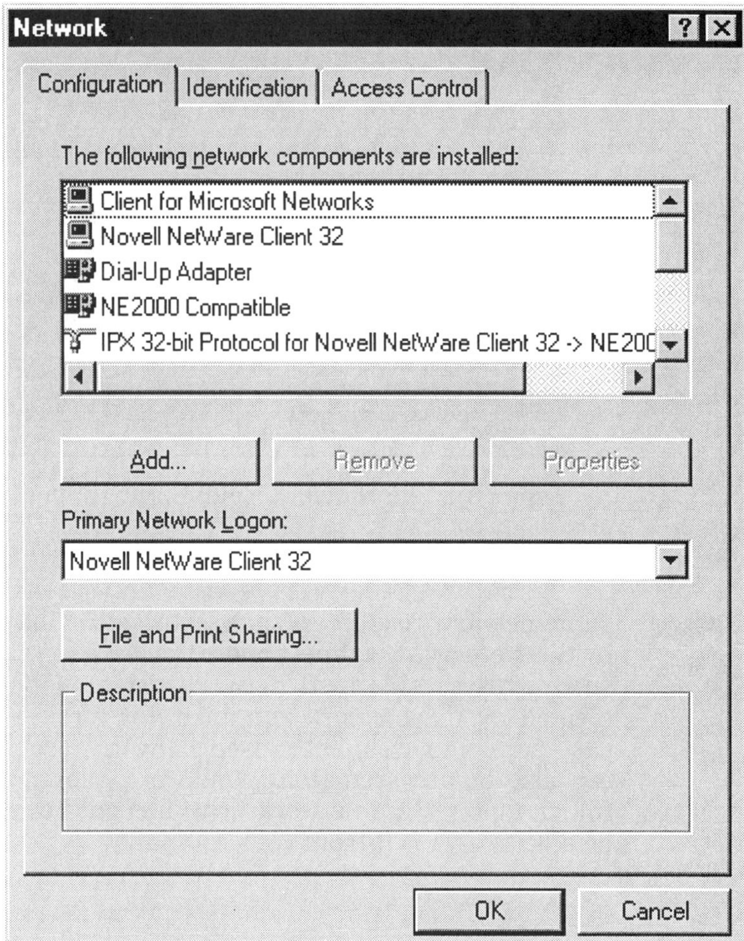

Figure 4 Control Panel's Network Utility

- The first page, Configuration, adds or removes the network components that are needed for communications. This page also activates File and Print Sharing, which allows you to share files and printers with other users on the network.
- The Identification page contains text boxes (see the figure below) for naming and describing your computer and workgroup. These descriptions determine how you (or your computer) will be known by other users on the network. For example, the name given a computer identifies it in the Network Neighborhood and the Windows Find utility (see Section 4.3).

Computer name: User 1

Workgroup: Computer class

Computer Description: User 1 Computer

The workgroup with which a computer is identified limits the display of and access to files and other resources to users included in that workgroup.

- The Access Control page (Figure 5) provides two levels of access control that can be designated for files and/or printers on a network:

  Share-level access control lets you set a password for each shared printer or file; other network users must supply that password before using a resource.

  User-level access control provides the ability to select specific users with whom your files and/or printer(s) will be shared; these specific users will not need a password to gain access to the designated resources.

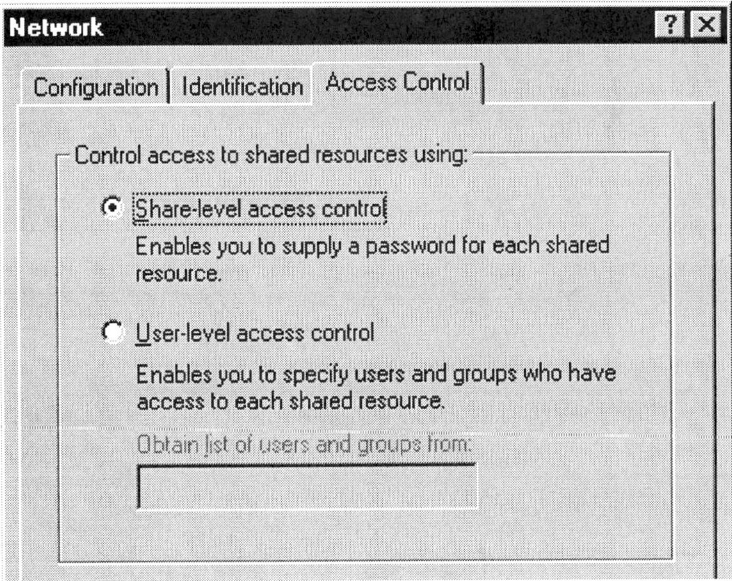

Figure 5 Network Utility — Access Control Page

11.2 Dial-Up Networking

Dial-Up Networking is a built-in Windows application that allows connection to another computer, a network system, or an online service. Dial-Up Networking provides **remote network access** to another computer system, using a modem and a telephone line, without formally networking the two computers. With remote access, the computers do not require traditional network hardware and cabling and do not have to be located close to one another. The remote dial-up system functions as if it were a regular network connection, but does not process information as quickly.

With a dial-up connection, in order for one computer to share the resources of another, the latter must be configured as a network server. For example, if you want to use a home computer to dial in and connect to your networked office computer, both machines must have modems and the Dial-Up Networking program must be installed and configured on the home computer. Then, once connected, you have complete network computing capabilities from home, such as printing to a network printer, accessing a customer database, or using shared files.

When two computers are linked with a dial-up networking connection, one machine is called the *host* and the other the *guest*. The host computer allows the guest to access its information.

Installing the Dial-Up Networking Files

You can easily determine if Dial-Up Networking has been installed on your system. Dial-Up Networking is present if

- It is listed on the Communications submenu of the Start button's Accessories menu.

or

- Its icon appears in the My Computer window.

If Dial-Up Networking does not appear on your computer, to install the appropriate files:

1. Open the Control Panel window from the Start button's Settings option.
2. Choose the Add/Remove Programs icon, which opens the Add/Remove Programs Properties dialog box.
3. Click on the Windows Setup tab, which displays the corresponding page of the dialog box.

4. Select the Communications item from the Components list box and choose the Details command button. A list of communications options will be displayed. If the Dial-Up Networking option is not selected, click on its check box.
5. Choose the OK command button. The Network dialog box (see Section 11.1) will open, displaying its Identification page. Enter a name for your computer and the workgroup to which it belongs in the appropriate text boxes. Then, choose the Close command button.

   You may be asked to insert the Windows 98 CD-ROM in its drive. If so, follow the on-screen instructions.
6. When the process is complete, Windows will display a message advising you that the computer must be restarted to use Dial-Up Networking. Choose the OK command button and restart the computer.

Using the Make New Connection Wizard

Once the Dial-Up Networking files have been installed, Windows needs to know about the computer (or computers) with which you want to connect. The setup process for a remote connection is handled by the New Connection Wizard, which prompts you for information about the remote computer, creates a connection "definition", and stores these settings in a file in the Dial-Up Networking folder.

The following procedure gives the specifics of the process of creating a new connection.

1. Open the Dial-Up Networking folder window by either
   - Starting My Computer and choosing the Dial-Up Networking folder icon in the My Computer window.

   or
   - Clicking on the Dial-Up Networking item on the Communications submenu of the Start button's Accessories menu.
2. Choose the Make New Connection icon in the Dial-Up Networking window. The Make New Connection wizard will start.

3. Place the cursor in the first text box (see Figure 6) and type the name of the computer you wish to access with the remote connection (for example, The Office Computer).

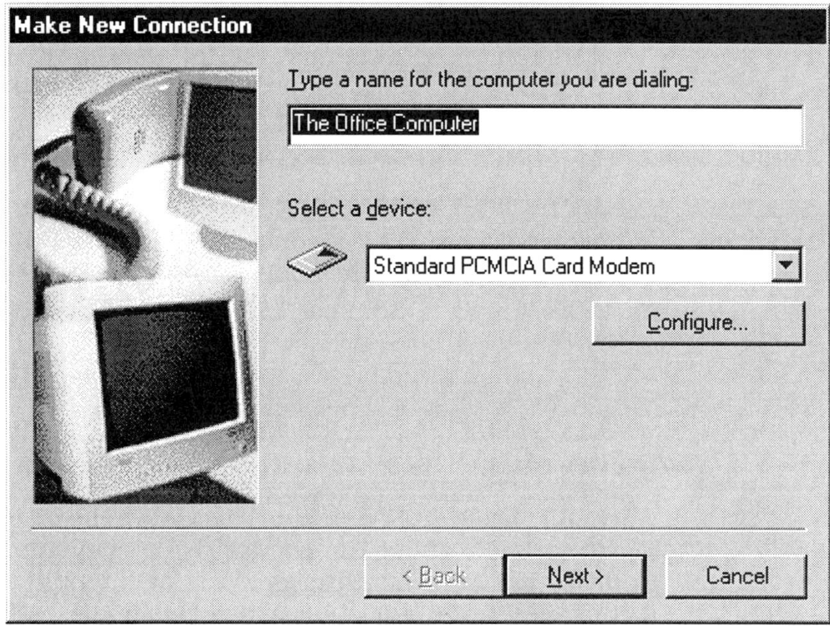

Figure 6 The Make New Connection Wizard

4. Choose the Next command button and enter the phone number for the remote computer. If the number is a local one, don't enter the area code.
5. Choose the Next button to display the next screen, which will inform you that the process is complete.
6. Choose the Finish command button; then the Close button. The connection you created will be displayed in the Dial-Up Networking window as an icon, as shown at the right.

If you are connecting to a remote network, you need to let Windows know the server type for that computer system. To do so, in the Dial-Up Networking window, right-click on the icon for the connection and then click on Properties on the pop-up menu. The Properties dialog box for the connection icon will be displayed. Now, click on the Server Type command button to display a list of servers (see the figure below) and select the type of dial-up server that matches the operating system of the remote computer.

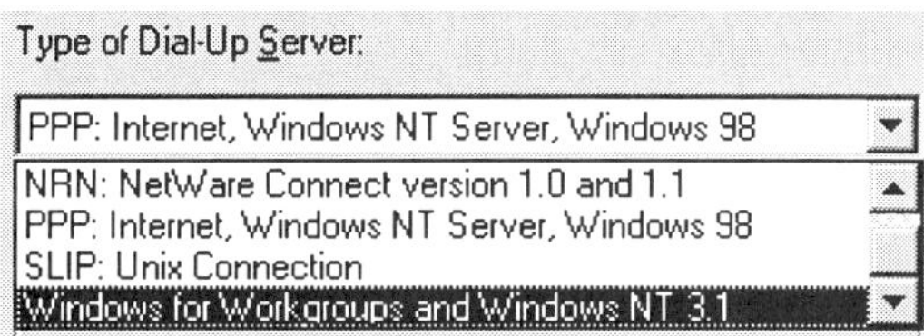

Now, choose the OK command button to return to the Properties dialog box and choose the OK button again to accept the settings change.

Using a Remote Connection

After you have set up a connection file for a remote computer, as described above, to connect to this computer:

1. Open the Dial-Up Networking window by either
   - Starting My Computer and choosing the Dial-Up Networking folder icon in the My Computer window.

   or
   - Clicking on the Dial-Up Networking item on the Communications submenu of the Start button's Accessories menu.
2. Choose the icon for the desired connection in the Dial-Up Networking window. The Connect To dialog box will open.
3. Choose the Connect command button to begin the dialing process. When the connection is made, a window may open, within which you can read information transmitted by the remote computer and type responses or execute commands. This process is discussed in Section 11.3, under the heading "Communicating with the Host Computer".

11.3 HyperTerminal

In the first two sections of this chapter, we discussed computer-to-computer communications made possible through a local area network or with a modem and the Windows Dial-Up Networking utility. In this section, we will describe another way to connect to a remote computer — by using Windows built-in **HyperTerminal** program. HyperTerminal is a type of application known as *communications software*, which allows you to establish a modem connection with a computer at a remote site (the *host* computer) and to exchange data with it.

Starting HyperTerminal

To start HyperTerminal:

1. Open the Communications submenu of the Start button's Accessories menu.
2. Click on the HyperTerminal item on this submenu, which opens the HyperTerminal folder (Figure 7). This folder contains previously established connection files (such as MCI Mail in Figure 7) as well as the HyperTerminal program file, Hypertrm.exe.

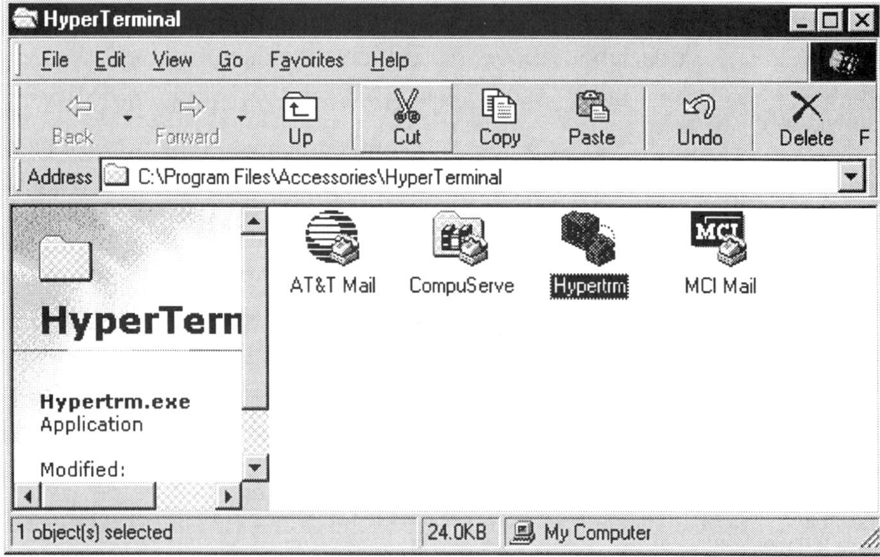

Figure 7 The HyperTerminal Folder

3. If you want to
   - Connect to a host computer for which a connection file has already been created (and which appears in the HyperTerminal folder window), choose its icon.
   - Create a new connection, choose the Hypertrm icon.

We will describe how to make a new connection and how to use an existing one in the remainder of this section. Once a communications link is established, you can exchange information, view data, and/or transfer files between your computer and the host system.

Creating a New Connection

If you want to connect to a remote computer whose icon does not appear in the HyperTerminal folder window, proceed as follows:

1. Start the HyperTerminal program by choosing the *Hypertrm* icon in the HyperTerminal folder window as described above. The Connection Description dialog box, which is shown in Figure 8, will open. (If you are already in a HyperTerminal session, choosing New Connection on the File menu will open this dialog box.)

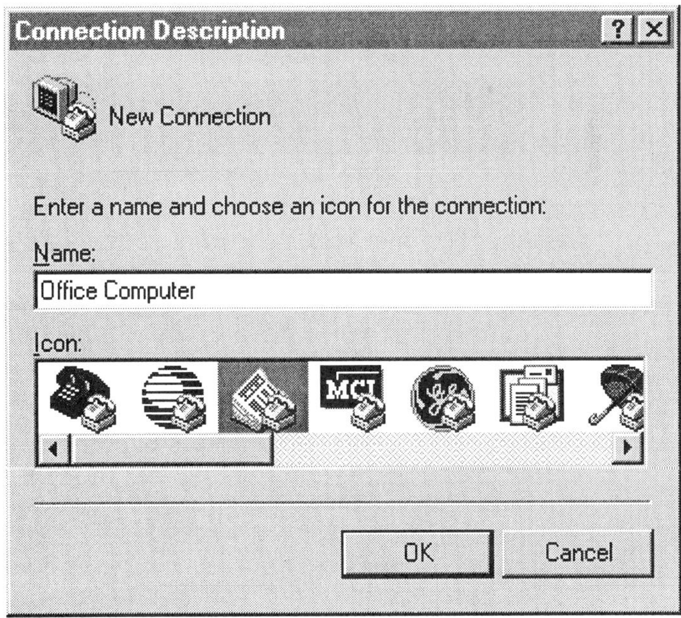

Figure 8 Naming the Connection

2. In the Name text box, type the name you want to assign to the connection and select an icon to represent it. (The name and icon will appear in the HyperTerminal folder window if you save this connection.)
3. Choose the OK command button. The Connect To dialog box, shown in Figure 9, will open.

Figure 9 The Connect To Dialog Box

4. Choose the Country code for the country from which you are calling. Then enter the area code, if necessary, in the Area code text box and the phone number for the remote computer in the Phone number text box. (This is the number that HyperTerminal dials when you activate the connection.) Spaces, parentheses, and hyphens are ignored. Thus, (213) 555-1212 and 2135551212 will dial the same number.

   If you want the modem to pause in the dialing process (perhaps to wait for the dial tone on an "outside line"), place a comma at this point in the phone number. Typically, each comma inserts a two-second pause. For example, 9,,5551212 inserts a four-second pause after the 9 is dialed.
5. Make sure that the modem you are using is listed in the *Connect using* drop-down list. (The default setting is most likely correct.)

6. Choose the OK command button. The Connect dialog box (Figure 10) will open.

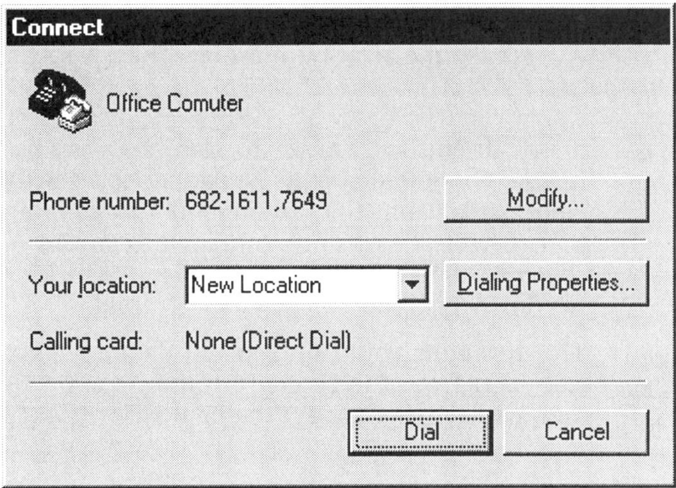

Figure 10 The Connect Dialog Box

7. Choose the Dial command button to dial the phone number of the remote computer (as specified in the Connect To dialog box). Through your computer's speakers, you will hear the number being dialed, followed by the sounds of the modems "handshaking", and (if all goes well) the connection will be established and a communications window will open.

If all does not go well — if the attempted connection fails — check to make sure that you have the correct phone number. If that's not the problem, you may have to change some configuration settings (or *parameters*) for the connection. Fortunately, most parameters can usually be left at their *default* values — those suggested by Windows. The others are normally prominently listed in your modem's user guide or in documentation available from the organization that runs the host system.

To change the parameters for a connection:

1. Open the Connect dialog box (Figure 10) for that connection and choose the Modify command button, which opens the connection's Properties dialog box. Make sure that the correct modem is listed in the *Connect using* box; if not, select this modem.

2. Choose the Configure button and, in the resulting dialog box, try the following "fixes". On the General page, select a lower baud rate (9600 almost always works). On the Connection page (if you don't have the necessary information), change the data bits setting from 7 to 8 (or vice-versa), change the parity. and increase the stop bit number. Then, choose the OK button.

Saving the new connection If you intend to connect to this host computer at some time in the future, you should save the connection settings by choosing the Save command from the File menu. (Remember: The connection was named when it was created.) The resulting file will be stored in the HyperTerminal folder and its icon will be displayed in the folder window when you start HyperTerminal.

Opening a connection file The next time you want to call this host computer, choose its connection icon from the HyperTerminal window. HyperTerminal will start and display the Connect dialog box for that connection.

Communicating with the Host Computer

When you establish a new or existing connection by choosing the Dial command button in HyperTerminal's Connect dialog box (see Figure 10), the HyperTerminal communications window will open. A typical communications window is shown in Figure 11.

The HyperTerminal communications window allows you to read text transmitted by the host computer and to type responses and execute commands from your keyboard. For example, if you have connected to a password-protected network, such as a university or college computer system, you will be asked to enter your username and password. Respond by typing each and pressing the Enter key.

After you have logged onto the host computer, you will have access to specific applications and/or data on this system. Access is often provided in the form of menus or queries sent by the host and displayed in the HyperTerminal window. Some systems also allow you to type commands to access information. These, too, appear in the window as you type them.

HyperTerminal stores all text sent and received in a special area of RAM called the *scroll buffer*. If you have sent and/or received more text than can fit in the window, you can review text that is not visible by using the scroll bars to move through the scroll buffer.

Printing text Text can be *printed* in two ways:

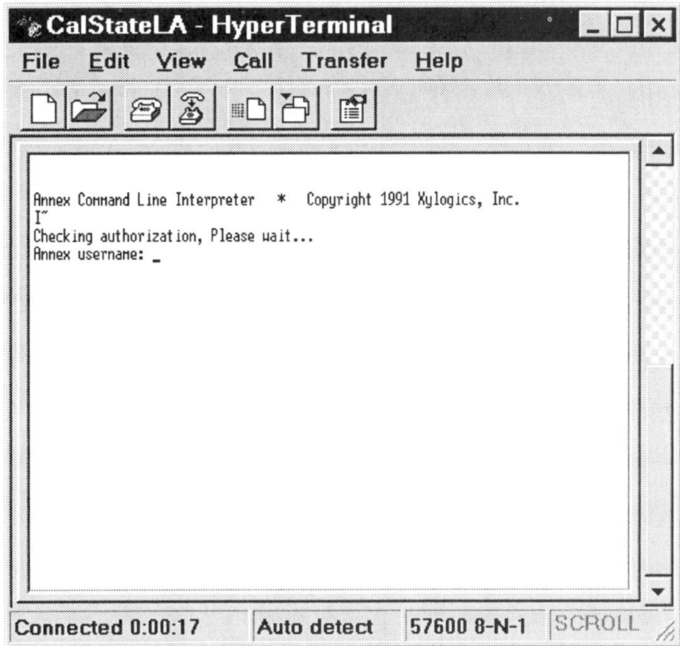

Figure 11 HyperTerminal Communications Window

- You can print incoming text as you receive it by choosing Capture to Printer from the Transfer menu. The Capture to Printer option remains in effect until you choose it again. A check mark next to this menu item indicates that it is in effect.
- You can print any or all text in the scroll buffer by copying it to the Clipboard, pasting it into a word processor such as WordPad, and then printing it from this application. (The Select All item on the Edit menu may be useful here; it selects all the text currently in the scroll buffer.)

Transferring Files

You can send (*upload*) files to the host computer or receive (*download*) files from it. HyperTerminal can send or receive two types of files:

- In a *text file transfer*, the file must consist entirely of *ASCII characters*; roughly speaking, those that can be typed at the keyboard. Text files cannot contain any other symbols or formatting commands, such as you might find in a spreadsheet or word processing file.

- In a *binary file transfer*, the symbols in the file are transmitted as a sequence of bits — zeros and ones. Any file, including a text file, can be transmitted as a binary file.

Sending a File Before sending a file, you must decide which of the two forms of file transfer to use. Since text file transmission is faster, you should use it whenever you can; for example, for electronic mail and word processing files in ASCII form (those with no special formatting codes). Non-ASCII data files and graphics must be sent in binary form. If you try to transmit a binary file using a text transfer method, an error message will be displayed or the transmission will be garbled.

To send a file to the host computer:

1. Prepare the host computer (usually by selecting an option from a menu) to receive your file. Sending a *text* file is usually treated the same way as typing the text at the keyboard, so this step may not be necessary for text files.
2. Choose either Send Text File or Send File (for binary files), as appropriate, from the Transfer menu. The corresponding dialog box will open. For example, if you choose Send File, the dialog box shown in Figure 12 is displayed. (The Send Text File dialog box is almost identical to an Open dialog box — see Section 2.2.)

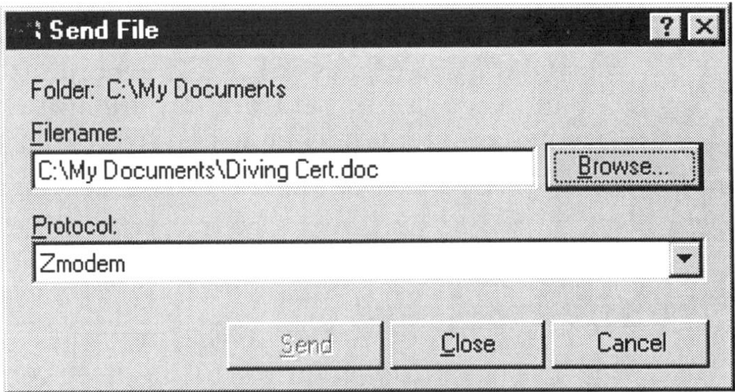

Figure 12 The Send File Dialog Box

3. In the Send File dialog box, enter the file's path name (see Sec-

tion 3.1) in the Filename text box or choose the Browse command button and select the file from the Browse dialog box (see Section 3.5).

4. Select the *protocol* required by the host computer for the transfer from the Protocol drop-down list. If no protocol is specified by the host, use the *Zmodem* default.

5. Choose the Close command button and the file will be transferred. (On some systems, it may be necessary to issue a command in the HyperTerminal window to initiate the transfer.)

NOTE

For a text file transfer, steps 3 through 5 of the above procedure are replaced by a process similar to opening a file on your own computer: In the Send Text File dialog box, select the drive and folder in which the file is stored from the *Look in* drop-down list. Then, double-click on the appropriate file name or select it and choose the Open button to send the file. (Step 4 of the above procedure, selecting a protocol, is not necessary in a text file transfer.)

Receiving a File To receive a file from the host computer:

1. Give the host computer the required command (it varies from host to host) to start transmission.

2. Choose Receive File from the Transfer menu. The resulting dialog box, which is shown in Figure 13, will open.

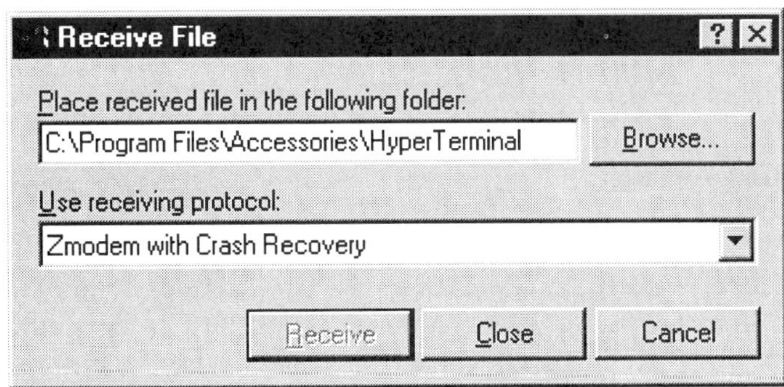

Figure 13 The Receive File Dialog Box

3. Select the drive and folder in which to save the incoming file and the *protocol* the host computer is using to send the file.

4. Choose the Receive command button.

Terminating Your Session

When you are done working with the host computer:

1. Execute the host's *log-off* procedure. This usually consists of choosing an exit command from the main menu or typing a word such as exit at a command prompt.
2. If necessary, break the connection by choosing Disconnect from the Call menu.
3. Close the HyperTerminal communications window.

11.4 Portable Computing

Portable (or **laptop**) **computers** are smaller versions of the desktop models, providing powerful computing while away from the home or office. Using a laptop allows you to remotely access a network or another computer, thus taking advantage of full work-group functions; you can work on the remote connection just as if you were using a desktop computer connected to the network. Moreover, Windows has built-in user-friendly laptop tools that make portable use easier than ever.

Windows delivers laptop support in several ways:

Windows' support for laptops

- Users get the most out of a portable's hardware with less hassle because Windows automatically loads the necessary configuration files during installation.
- Windows tools provide assistance with the transfer of information between the laptop and a desktop computer.
- Dial-Up Networking can establish a connection to a LAN (local area network) at a remote site, provided that the LAN has a terminal server enabled. When used in this way, Dial-Up Networking acts as the laptop's network card. This feature gives the portable e-mail and Web browsing capability.
- *Deferred printing* allows a laptop user to leave the printer at home; files can be "printed" to disk and later be sent automatically to the printer of choice.

Laptop users tend to use their portable computers for the same tasks as their desktop machines (word processing, spreadsheets, electronic mail, and so on). Although the computing tasks may be the same, the desktop and mobile computing environments are quite different. Nonetheless, portable computer users can take advantage of most of the Windows features that we have discussed in this chapter. For example, laptop users can create a network connection using Dial-Up Networking (Section 11.2) to access their desktop workstation or communicate with another computer with the aid of the HyperTerminal software (Section 11.3).

In this section, we will explore other Windows features that make portable computing a more pleasant experience. To be more specific, we will discuss the following topics:

- Docking detection
- The Direct Cable Connection utility
- The Briefcase utility
- Deferred printing

Docking Detection

A **docking station** connects a portable computer, through communications ports, to a network or *peripheral hardware*, such as a monitor, CD-ROM drive, or other storage device. Because the system hardware changes when a laptop is connected to a docking station, the machine must be reconfigured to work properly.

Windows 98 enables a user to perform docking and undocking operations without turning off the equipment, a process known as *hot docking*. Windows provides the flexibility of multiple *hardware profiles* (see Section 10.5), each defining a different hardware configuration. (If more than one profile exists, Windows prompts the user, when booting the computer, to choose the desired profile.) For example, the screen resolution for the docked monitor on the desktop may be higher than the laptop's built-in LCD panel, and Windows adjusts for this change via the appropriate hardware profile.

Direct Cable Connection

The simplest way to connect a laptop to a desktop computer (or, for that matter, to connect *any* two computers) is with Windows' **Direct**

Cable Connection (DCC) utility. (The machines are usually physically connected by a serial or parallel cable.) While connected, the laptop has access to the shared resources on the desktop computer and to any network to which that computer is connected. Transmitting files between a desktop and a portable computer with DCC provides a reasonably fast transfer and is much less expensive than using a docking station.

When two computers are connected with Direct Cable Connection, one machine is labeled the *host* and the other the *guest*. The guest computer can access all folders on the host, but the host cannot access folders on the guest.

Before using Direct Cable Connection, you must first determine if this software has been installed on your computer. To do so, open the Communications submenu of the Start button's Accessories menu. If Direct Cable Connection does not appear on the Communications submenu, then you must install it.

To install the Direct Cable Connection utility:

Installing DCC

1. Open the Control Panel window from the Start menu's Settings option.
2. In the Control Panel window, choose the Add/Remove Programs icon. The Add/Remove Programs Properties dialog box will be displayed.
3. Click on the Windows Setup tab to view that page of the dialog box.
4. Select Communication from the Components list and then click on the Details command button.
5. In the resulting dialog box, select Direct Cable Connection and choose the OK command button. Windows may prompt you to insert the original Windows disks or CD so that the appropriate files can be copied to your hard disk. If so, follow the on-screen instructions.

Connecting Two Computers To link two computers with Direct Cable Connection, first physically connect the serial or parallel ports of the machines using the proper cable. Next, you must configure the host computer by carrying out the following procedure:

1. Choose the Direct Cable Connection item from the Communications submenu of the Start button's Accessories menu. The Direct Cable Connection wizard will start and display its first screen, as shown in Figure 14.

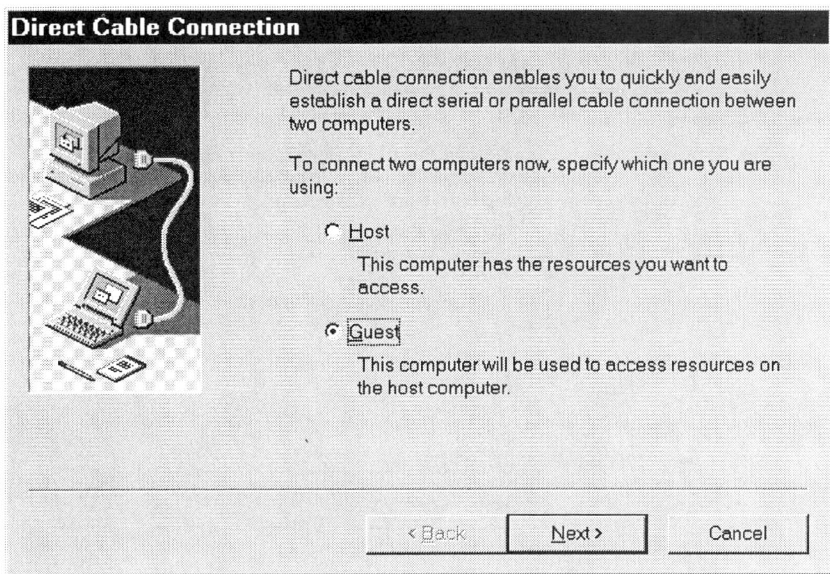

Figure 14 The Direct Cable Connection Wizard

2. Specify whether the computer you are using is to be the *host* or *guest* by selecting the appropriate option button. (Remember: The guest can make use of the host's files, but not vice-versa.) Then choose the Next command button; the wizard checks the communications ports on your computer and then displays another screen.
3. Select the communications port you are using for the connection and choose the Next command button.
4. The next wizard screen may prompt you to activate File and Print Sharing between the two computers. If so, click on the File and Print Sharing command button, which will open the Network dialog box (Figure 15, on the next page).
5. Choose the File and Print Sharing command button in this dialog box, which opens the File and Print Sharing dialog box (Figure 16, on the next page).
6. In this dialog box, select either or both of the options to allow file sharing and/or printer sharing between the two computers. Then choose the OK command button. The Network dialog box (Figure 15) will be redisplayed; choose the OK command button to close it.

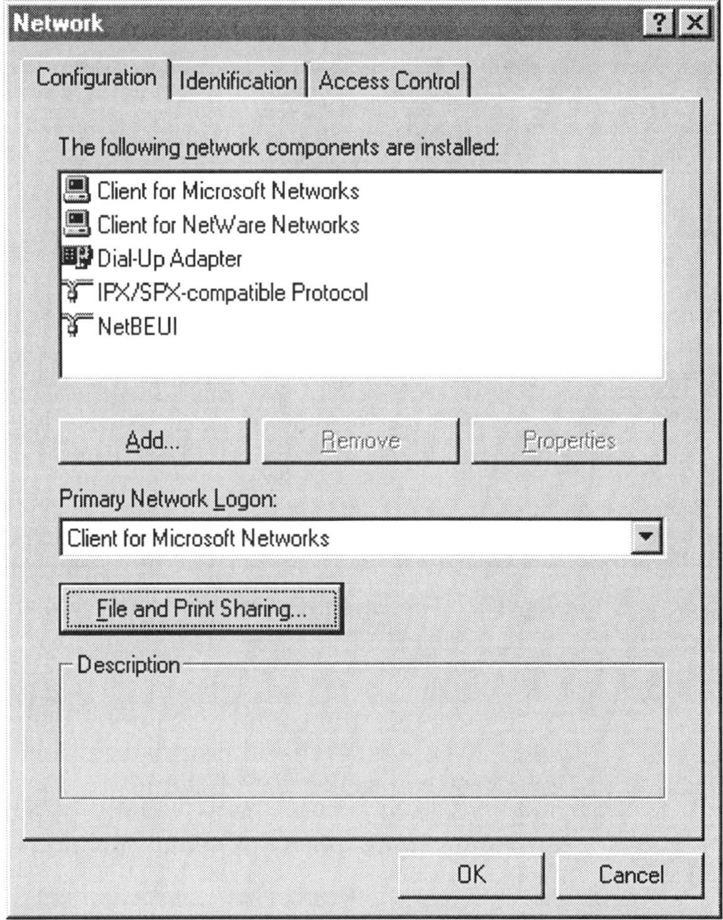

Figure 15 The Network Dialog Box

File and Print Sharing

I want to be able to give others access to my files.

I want to be able to allow others to print to my printer(s).

OK Cancel

Figure 16 The File and Print Sharing Dialog Box

7. From within the Direct Cable Connection wizard, choose the Next command button. When configuring the host computer, a wizard screen will be displayed that allows you to select a password, if desired. This password can be used to restrict access to files and printers on the host computer to authorized users. To enable password protection:
   - Select the Password Protection check box and choose the Set Password command button.
   - In the resulting dialog box, type the desired password twice (in the Password and Confirm password text boxes).
   - Choose the OK command button.
8. After setting the password, or if you decide not to use a password, choose the Finish command button.

Finally, repeat this procedure to set up the Direct Cable Connection on the other computer.

Using a Direct Cable Connection To allow the guest computer to share the host's resources, you must start DCC on both computers. To do so:

1. On the host computer, click on the Direct Cable Connection item on the Communications submenu of the Start button's Accessories menu.
2. In the resulting dialog box, choose the Listen command button.
3. On the guest computer, click on the Direct Cable Connection item on the Communications submenu of the Start button's Accessories menu.
4. In the resulting dialog box, choose the Connect command button.

The guest computer is now able to access resources on the host. The host's drives will appear in Explorer and folder windows on the guest and its printers will appear in the guest's Printers folder.

The Briefcase Utility

When one person works with both a portable and desktop computer, typically there are copies of the same files on both machines. After working on the portable, some of the files may need to be updated to the desktop computer, and vice-versa. Keeping that information organized is a difficult and on-going task. Moreover, if you lose data by inadvertently overwriting a new file with an old version, it can be an exasperating experience!

Windows built-in **Briefcase** utility takes care of updating the files, whether the newer files are on the laptop or the desktop computer, with a process called *synchronization*. Synchronization keeps track of the original locations of the files. The Briefcase identifies which files have been modified and which ones haven't, and older files are updated to the newest version. Briefcase will update the files on the desktop or laptop computer automatically, preventing confusion.

If the Briefcase icon appears on the Desktop, then this utility has already been installed. If the icon does not appear, it must be created before the program can be used.

Creating a My Briefcase icon on the Desktop

If you believe that Briefcase is installed, but its icon isn't on the Desktop, create the Briefcase folder using the following procedure:

1. Right-click on an empty area of the Desktop and point at the New option on the pop-up menu to open its submenu.
2. If the Briefcase item is listed on the submenu, then Briefcase has been installed.
3. Choose the Briefcase item. A new icon, called My Briefcase, will appear on the Desktop.

If a Briefcase option did not appear on the submenu in the previous procedure, you need to install the Briefcase utility. To do so, proceed as with Direct Cable Connection, as described earlier in this section.

Using the Briefcase Once the Briefcase icon has been created on the Desktop, files to be used on the laptop must be copied into the Briefcase on the portable computer. While the portable is connected to the desktop computer by a Direct Cable Connection:

1. From the desktop computer, open My Computer or Windows Explorer and locate the files to be copied.
2. Copy these files to the My Briefcase icon on the Desktop (of the main computer) using the following technique:
   - Select the files to be copied to the Briefcase, right-click on one of them, and point at the Send To command on the pop-up menu.
   - Choose the My Briefcase item on the resulting submenu.
3. Using the direct cable connection, copy the Briefcase to the portable computer. Briefcase makes a copy of each file and records information about its original location on the desktop

computer. The Briefcase file is called a *sync copy* (or synchronization copy).

When you copy a *folder* into the Briefcase, a sync copy of the entire contents of the folder is made, including all files and any existing subfolders.

4. While working on the portable computer, don't copy the files out of the Briefcase. Instead, to access a file, open the Briefcase window (by choosing its Desktop icon) and open the file by choosing its icon from within that window.
5. When you have finished working with the files on the portable, reconnect to the main computer.
6. Open the Briefcase on the portable computer by choosing its Desktop icon.
7. Choose the Update All command on the Briefcase menu to automatically replace the unmodified files on the main computer with the modified files in your Briefcase. To update individual files, select those files in the Briefcase window and choose the Update Selection command from the Edit menu.
8. A dialog box will open (Figure 17, on the next page), listing the files that Briefcase suggests be updated, including the file date and time of last modification and the file's original location.
9. Choose the Update command button to revise the files.

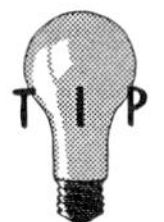

Use the Briefcase to update files between a networked computer's local drive and the network drive. This is helpful, for example, when you are working on the local desktop computer, but want to back up your files to the network.

After copying files to Briefcase, take care not to move the original files on the desktop computer. The Briefcase keeps track of the original file location, but there is no built-in tracking system for moved files. If you *do* move a file on the desktop computer, the file is no longer associated with the sync copy of that file in the Briefcase. Even if you move the file back to its original location, the file will not be updated correctly. This problem must be corrected with manual synchronization.

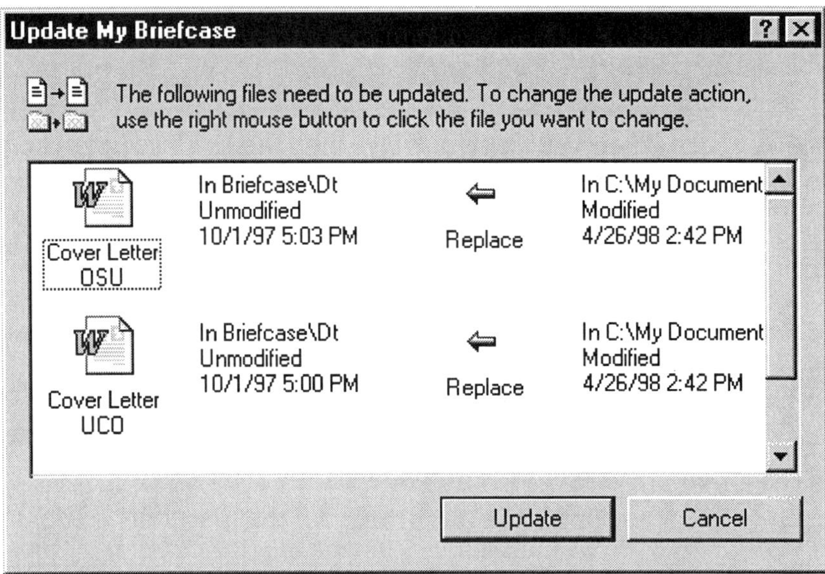

Figure 17 The Briefcase Update Dialog Box

Manual Synchronization If Briefcase cannot find the original files, and is therefore unable to update them, *manual file synchronization* may solve the problem. This procedure allows you to recreate a sync copy in the Briefcase by manually copying the most current file to the appropriate location, either the drive or the Briefcase.

To manually synchronize a file, first decide if you want to use the original file on the desktop computer or the copy of the file in the Briefcase as the most recently updated file. Then:

- If you choose to use the original file, delete the copy of that file in the Briefcase and copy the original file to the Briefcase.
- If you choose to use the copy of the file in the Briefcase, move that file from the Briefcase to a new location on your hard disk and copy the file to the Briefcase.

Deferred Printing

Deferred printing is a feature that holds and manages print jobs that you create while not connected to a local or networked printer. Deferred printing establishes a *print queue* that saves print information until the printer is available. Thus, you can send files to a printer that is not connected to your computer and, when convenient, connect the printer to your computer and activate the deferred printing queue to print these files.

Deferred printing is especially useful for portable computers. It allows you to "print" documents while traveling with a laptop, queuing them to print all at once when you return. Upon connecting the laptop to a printer, the document will print automatically if that printer supports Plug and Play technology (see Section 10.1). Otherwise, you must manually start the printing process.

NOTE

The automatic printing of queued jobs works only if the reconnected printer is the same as the one to which the documents were "printed" in the first place.

How to defer printing

To defer printing when using a portable computer or network printer:

1. Click on the Start button, point to the Settings option, and choose Printers from the resulting submenu. The Printers folder will open.
2. Select the printer that you want to use by clicking on its icon. It will appear highlighted.
3. Choose the Work Offline command from the File menu, which places a check mark next to this menu item, indicating that the Work Offline feature is active. The printer itself will remain inactive and the printer icon will appear dimmed, indicating that it is unavailable.

To defer printing with a local printer:

1. From within the Printers folder, select that printer's icon and choose the Pause Printing option from the File menu. (A check mark will appear there.)
2. Close the Printers folder.

How to reactivate deferred jobs

To reactivate deferred print jobs (if Plug and Play does not reactivate them automatically):

1. Click on the Start button, point to the Settings option, and choose Printers from the resulting submenu. The Printers folder will open.

2. Select the offline printer that you want to use. (Printers that are offline will be dimmed.)
3.
   - When using a portable computer or network printer, choose the Work Offline option from the File menu to remove the check mark next to this item.
   - When using a local printer from a desktop computer, choose the Pause Printing option from the File menu to remove the check mark.
4. Close the Printers folder by choosing its close button. The deferred print jobs will begin to print.

Chapter Summary

Networking	To access a network	Click on the Start button, point at the Programs option, and choose your network program. Then, enter the login and password when prompted.
	To browse and access network resources	Open the Network Neighborhood folder by choosing its Desktop icon.
	To configure the network options	Open Control Panel and choose the Network icon; the Network utility will open, allowing you to change settings.
Dial-Up Networking	To create a Dial-Up Networking connection	In My Computer, open the Dial-Up Networking folder; *or* click on Dial-Up Networking on the Communications submenu of the Start button's Accessories menu. Then, choose the Make New Connection icon and make use of the New Connection Wizard.
	To use a Dial-Up Networking connection	In the Dial-Up Networking folder, choose the desired connection and choose the Dial button in the resulting dialog box.
HyperTerminal	To start HyperTerminal	Choose the HyperTerminal item from the Communications submenu of the Start button's Accessories menu.
	To configure a connection	Choose the HyperTerminal icon; then, name the connection, select an icon, and enter the phone number of the host computer.

	To connect to the host computer	Choose the connection icon from the HyperTerminal window. Then, choose the Dial button and log onto the host computer.
	To transfer files	To send a file, choose the Send Text File or Send File option from the Transfer menu. To receive a file, choose the Receive File option from the Transfer menu.
	To disconnect from the host computer	Execute the host computer's log off procedure and break the connection by choosing Disconnect from the Call menu.
Portable Computing	Direct Cable Connection	To connect two computers, choose the Direct Cable Connection item from the Communications submenu of the Start button's Accessories menu; decide whether the computer will be the host or guest; identify the communications port to be used; and activate the desired File and Print Sharing options.
	The Briefcase	To create a Briefcase icon on the Desktop, right-click on the Desktop, point at the New option, and choose Briefcase. To work with files in the Briefcase, copy the files from the main computer to the Briefcase folder on the Desktop; then copy the Briefcase folder to the portable computer or to a floppy disk. Edit the files from within the Briefcase folder. To update the files from the Briefcase, copy the Briefcase back to the main computer *or* connect to the main computer; then, open the Briefcase folder and choose the Update All option from the Briefcase menu and choose the Update command button.
	Deferred printing	To defer printing, choose Printers from the Start button's Settings option, select the desired printer, and choose the Work Offline option from the File menu. To print the deferred jobs: If the printer supports Plug and Play, simply connect the printer to the computer; if not, open the Printers folder, select the desired (dimmed) printer, and choose Work Offline from the File menu.

Review Exercises

Section 11.1

1. A small scale network is called a ____________.
2. A large scale network is called a ____________.
3. A computer designated to run the network operating system is called a ____________.
4. NIC is a type of network hardware best described as
   a. A commonly used cable type.
   b. A hub, which assists in strengthening the line signal and controlling the network traffic.
   c. A card that fits in the computer, connecting it to the network cabling.
   d. A wireless network (or *virtual network*), which works with infrared transmitters and receivers and does not require traditional cabling.
5. To establish a connection with the network, each user must initiate a(n)
   a. Logout procedure.
   b. Login procedure.
   c. Server procedure.
   d. Exit procedure.
6. The Network Neighborhood displays the resources to which you have access
   a. On the network.
   b. In My Computer.
   c. In Explorer.
   d. On the Desktop.

Section 11.2

7. ____________ is a Windows utility that provides the user with remote access to another computer system, using a modem and a telephone line.
8. Once connected via Dial-Up Networking, you will have complete ____________ capabilities, such as printing to a network printer, accessing a customer database, and using shared files.
9. True or false: The remote dial-up system functions as if it were a network interface card, except that it does not process information as quickly.
10. True or false: The Make New Connection wizard can assist you in setting up a phone connection to a fax machine.
11. True or false: A modem is a hardware device that sends and

receives the appropriate codes through telephone lines from one computer to another.

12. When you are using remote access and are connected to an office computer, the latter is called the
    a. Guest.
    b. Server.
    c. Host.
    d. Link.

13. When you are using remote access and are connected to an office computer, the computer you are dialing in on is called the
    a. Guest.
    b. Server.
    c. Host.
    d. Link.

14. The process of setting up a Dial-Up Networking connection definition is handled by
    a. Peripheral hardware.
    b. The Make New Connection wizard.
    c. The Next command button.
    d. Direct Cable Connection.

Section 11.3

15. The HyperTerminal application is found on the ___________ submenu of the Start button's Accessories menu.

16. To create a new connection, choose the ___________ icon in the HyperTerminal window.

17. True or false: HyperTerminal stores all text sent and received in a special area of RAM called the scroll buffer.

18. True or false: In a text file transfer, the file can contain non-ASCII symbols and formatting commands.

19. With HyperTerminal, you can
    a. Send e-mail.
    b. Send and receive files.
    c. Defer print jobs.
    d. All of the above.

20. When entering the phone number for the host computer, which character inserts a "pause"?
    a. Period
    b. Comma
    c. Question mark
    d. Quotation mark

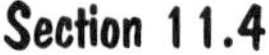

21. A portable computer, also known as a ___________, is a small version of a desktop model.

22. A ___________ physically connects a portable computer, through its communication ports, to a network or peripheral hardware.

23. A portable and desktop computer that are physically connected to each other by a cable can be logically connected using the Windows ___________ utility.

24. True or false: When a computer is reconnected to a printer that supports Plug and Play, deferred print jobs will automatically be sent to that printer.

25. True or false: The Windows deferred printing feature is available only for portable computers.

26. True of false: To make use of the Briefcase utility, the My Briefcase icon must be present on the Desktop.

27. The Briefcase program takes care of updating files with a process known as

    a. Synchronization.
    b. Annihilation.
    c. Transportation.
    d. Communication.

28. Deferred printing is a feature that holds print jobs in

    a. The Briefcase.
    b. The Print dialog box.
    c. A print queue.
    d. The Recycle Bin.

Build Your Own Glossary

29. The following words and phrases are important terms that were introduced in this chapter. (They appear within the text in boldface type.) Use WordPad (see Section 2.2) to enter a definition for each term, preserving alphabetical order, into the Glossary file on the Student Disk.

Briefcase utility
Deferred printing
Dial-Up Networking
Direct Cable Connection
Docking station
Hub
HyperTerminal
Laptop computer
Local Area Network (LAN)
Mapped network drive
Multitasking
Network
Network cabling
Network interface card (NIC)
Network utility
Network Neighborhood
Peer-to-peer network
Portable computer
Remote network access
Server
Wide area network (WAN)
Workstation

Lab Exercises

Work each of the following exercises at your computer. Begin by turning the machine on (if necessary) to start Windows 98 and closing any open windows.

Lab Exercise 1 (Section 11.1)

a. Click on the Start button and point at the Programs option. On the resulting submenu, what network options are listed?

b. Click on an empty area of the Desktop to close the Start menu.

c. Choose the Network Neighborhood icon on the Desktop, which opens the Network Neighborhood window. Describe the contents of the window. Close the Network Neighborhood window.

d. Open the Control Panel window and start the Network utility, which opens the Network dialog box. Which network options are installed?

e. Click on the Identification tab to display that page of the dialog box. Are the computer and workgroup named? If so, what are their names?

f. Choose the Cancel command button to close the Network dialog box.

g. Close the Control Panel window.

Lab Exercise 2 (Section 11.2)

(This exercise requires that Dial-Up Networking and a modem be installed on your computer.)

a. Start My Computer.

b. Open the Dial-Up Networking folder by choosing its icon in the My Computer window. What icons appear in the Dial-Up Networking folder window?

c. Start the Make New Connection wizard by choosing this icon. Use the following information to create the connection:

- Name your connection"*your name's* Connection".
- Enter your home phone number as the dial-up number.

d. *Optional:* Capture the Dial-Up Networking window with your icon visible, and paste it into WordPad. Print the resulting document. (See Section 2.3 for the procedure for capturing screens.)

e. Delete your connection icon from the Dial-Up Networking folder and close all open windows.

Lab Exercise 3 (Section 11.3)

(You must have a modem installed on your computer system to complete the following exercise.)

a. Open the HyperTerminal window.

b. Turn on the Capture to Printer option. On which menu does it appear?

c. In the HyperTerminal window, choose the MCI Mail connection icon. (This connection is installed by default by Windows 98.) What is the name of the dialog box that is displayed?

d. Choose the Dial command button to initiate the connection and open the communications window. What is displayed in this window?

e. If prompted to enter a user name, type your name and press Enter. For a password, any word will do. Since you do not have an account with MCI Mail, the sign-on information will be rejected. What message, if any, is displayed?

f. Turn off the Capture to Printer feature. How did you accomplish this?

g. Click on HyperTerminal's close button. A dialog box will open. What message does it display? Choose the Yes command button to terminate the connection.

h. Close the HyperTerminal window.

Lab Exercise 4 (Section 11.4)

a. Insert the Student Disk in its drive and open My Computer.

b. Display the contents of the Student Disk.

c. Right-click on the file called Preamble and point to the Send To option; then choose the My Briefcase item from the resulting submenu. In the Briefcase window, what is the status of the Preamble file? Where does Briefcase indicate that the sync copy exists?

d. Open the Preamble file from the Briefcase window. Insert a blank line at the top of the document and type your name. Then, save and close the file.

e. In the Briefcase window, choose the Update All option from the Briefcase menu. Which file(s) are listed in the window? Update the Preamble document to your Student Disk.

f. Close the Briefcase and My Computer windows and remove the diskette from its drive.

Lab Exercise 5 (Section 11.4)

a. Open the Printers folder.

b. Select the printer that is connected to your computer. What is it called?

c. Open the File menu. Which option is available for deferring printing on this printer? Choose this option.

d. Open the File menu again. What change has occurred in the appearance of the option of step *c*?

e. Use the Escape key to deactivate the File menu without changing any options.

f. Start WordPad and maximize its window (if necessary).

g. Insert the Student Disk in its drive and open one of the text documents. Choose the Print command and exit WordPad. Does the file print?

h. In the Printers window, select your printer (if necessary). Open the File menu and activate printing by choosing either the Work Offline or the Pause Printing option. Close the Printers window. What happened when you did this?

i. Close all open windows and remove the Student Disk from its drive.

If You Want to Learn More ...

The notes presented here allow you to delve more deeply into some of the topics covered in this chapter.

Sharing files, folders, and printers

As you have seen in this chapter, one of the advantages of a network is that its resources can be shared among those connected to the network. To share resources, however, it is not enough to *designate* them for sharing with the Network utility; you must tell Windows exactly which resources are to be shared. To do so:

1. Right-click on the icon of a file, folder, or printer to be shared and choose the Sharing item from the pop-up menu. The Properties dialog box for the selected object will open.
2. Click on the Share tab to display this page of the dialog box.
3. On the Share page, designate how you want to share this resource by providing it with a network name and specifying that

others either have read-only rights, full rights, or must use a password to use the resource. For example, sharing printers or project folders within a project workgroup on the network allows just those workgroup members to use those resources.

Using the network drives for backup locations

To protect your data from loss due to hardware failure, you can use the network drive as a location for your backups. Network drives are usually backed up frequently by the network administrator. Take advantage of this routine by copying your critical files to your designated area on the network drive. Then, if your computer fails or if you lose data for any other reason, the relevant files can be retrieved from the network drive.

Be aware that if you keep critical files on the network drive, you should also keep copies of these files on your own computer. Then, if the network server goes down (out of service), you can continue working even though you can't access the network.

CHAPTER 12

Additional Topics

This chapter contains an assortment of Windows 98 topics. Some, such as those dealing with DOS and OLE, expand on material that was briefly covered earlier in the text. Others, for example the section on the Windows Registry, contain information of a relatively advanced nature. To be more specific:

- Section 12.1 discusses certain special aspects of running DOS programs, such as the mark/copy/paste operation, changing the display font, and running a DOS session using MS-DOS Prompt.
- Section 12.2 continues the discussion of DOS applications, concentrating on a DOS program's property sheets.
- Section 12.3 describes various options that affect the way Windows starts up, including those available in special configuration files.
- Section 12.4 introduces the Registry and discusses how it can be used to further customize Windows.
- Section 12.5 covers object linking and embedding (OLE), which allows you to easily create and edit documents that contain information produced by multiple applications.

The first three sections in this chapter contain DOS-related material and should be covered in the order presented, but Sections 12.4 and 12.5 are independent of this material and of each other.

12.1 Running DOS Programs

A program that was designed to run under the DOS operating system, but not under Windows, is known as a **DOS application**. Although Windows-based software has many advantages over DOS programs (see the Introduction), the latter often run faster and make more efficient use of computer resources. For this reason, some graphics-intensive contemporary computer games are designed as DOS applications.

DOS programs are normally started in the same manner as Windows applications (see Section 2.1). You can run several DOS and Windows applications at the same time and switch among them using the techniques described in Section 2.3. In addition, Windows 98 provides special features for DOS applications that make them easier to use. We will discuss these features in this section.

Running DOS Applications under Windows

Unlike Windows applications, which always run inside a window on the Desktop, DOS programs can be run in two modes — in a window or *full-screen*; in the latter case the application occupies the entire Desktop, as shown in Figure 1.

Figure 1 A DOS Application Running Full-screen

Switching screen modes

To switch from one mode to the other, press the Alt+Enter keystroke combination. When the program of Figure 1 is switched to window mode, the result is shown in Figure 2. Notice that the application window contains a title bar (complete with minimize, maximize, and close buttons) and a toolbar. (The toolbar can be toggled on and off by clicking on the Control icon, which opens the Control menu, and then choosing the Toolbar command.) We will only consider window mode in the remainder of this section because the special features described below cannot be accessed in full-screen mode.

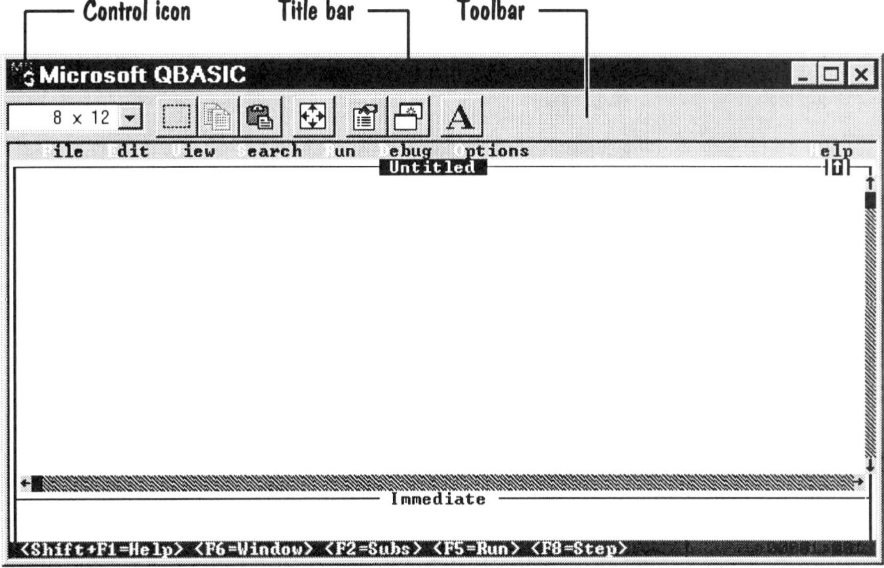

Figure 2 A DOS Application Running in a Window

Mark, Copy, and Paste Text in a DOS window can be selected and copied to the Windows Clipboard, and information on the Clipboard can be pasted into the current document. (See Section 2.3 for general information about these operations.)

Selecting text

To select (or *mark*) text in a document in a DOS window:

1. Click on the toolbar's Mark button (see the figure at the right).
   or
   Click on the Control icon (or right-click on the title bar) to display the Control menu, point at the Edit

item, and choose the Mark command on the resulting submenu.

2. Use the mouse or keyboard to position the cursor at the beginning of the block of text to be selected and either mouse-drag the cursor to the end of the block, or hold down the Shift key and move the cursor to the end of the block.

The selected block of text will become highlighted.

Copying text To copy a selected block of text to the Clipboard, take any of the following actions:

- Press the Enter key.
- Click on the toolbar's Copy button.
- Click on the Control icon to display the Control menu, point at the Edit item, and choose Copy from the resulting submenu.

Pasting text To paste text from the Clipboard into a document:

1. Position the cursor where you want to paste the text.
2. Click on the toolbar's Paste button.
   or
   Click on the Control icon (or right-click on the title bar) to display the Control menu, point at Edit, and choose the Paste command from the resulting submenu.

Selecting a Font You can change the size of the font used to display the text in a DOS window by:

1. Opening the drop-down list on the toolbar (the result is shown at the right).
2. Selecting (clicking on) one of the listed sizes.

8 x 12
8 x 12
8 x 13
8 x 14
9 x 15
10 x 16
10 x 18
10 x 20
11 x 18

The various font sizes are given in *pixels*; for example, the current font in Figure 2 is 8 pixels wide and 12 pixels high. Be aware that:

- Selecting a larger font size means that the text will be easier to read, but less text will fit in a given window. Selecting a smaller font has the opposite effect.
- Selecting the Auto item from the top of the list sizes the text so that a full DOS "screen" automatically fits the current window. If you resize the window, the font will resize accordingly.

NOTE

You can also change the size of the display font by clicking on the toolbar's Font button (shown at the right). Doing so opens the Font page of the Properties dialog box. The same

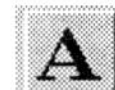

font choices are available here as on the toolbar drop-down list, but when you select a font in this dialog box, its preview windows show the resulting window size and font size.

Other Toolbar Buttons Three other buttons reside on the toolbar (Figure 3). Here are their functions:

- Clicking on the Full Screen button switches the DOS application from the current window mode to full-screen mode.
- Clicking on the Properties button displays the application's Properties dialog box. This dialog box allows you to fine-tune the way the application runs under Windows. We will discuss its options in Section 12.2.
- The Background button determines whether or not the DOS program will continue to process data when you switch to another application. If the button appears to be "depressed" (indented), background processing will take place.

Full Screen Properties Background

Figure 3 Other Toolbar Buttons

Running a DOS Session

If you are familiar with the DOS operating system, you may want to issue commands or run programs from the DOS prompt from time to time. You can do this — run a **DOS session** — without shutting down Windows 98 by starting the MS-DOS Prompt program. **MS-DOS Prompt** allows you to view directories, copy files, start programs, and so on, just as if you were actually running DOS.

Starting MS-DOS Prompt

To start MS-DOS Prompt:

1. Click on the Start button to display the Start menu.
2. Point at the Programs option to open its submenu.
3. Click on the MS-DOS Prompt item on this submenu. The window shown in Figure 4 (on the next page), sometimes referred to as a *DOS box*, will open.

The DOS box provides all the features (described in the first part of this section) afforded to any DOS program running in a window. Using the toolbar or Control menu, you can mark, copy, and paste text within the window, change the display font, switch between

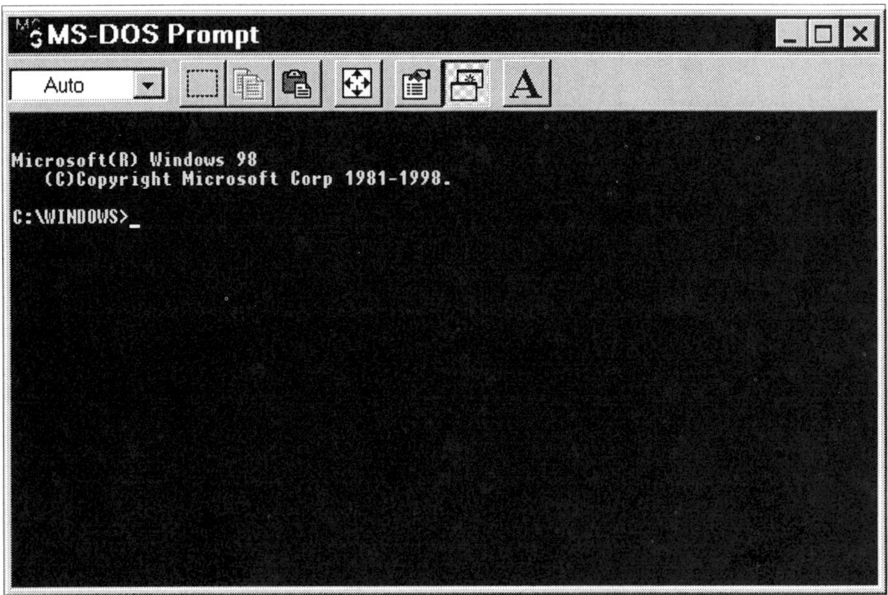

Figure 4 The MS-DOS Prompt Window

window and full-screen mode, and change certain properties. Moreover, from the DOS prompt, which is `C:\WINDOWS>` in Figure 4, you can issue any available DOS command (see Appendix B).

Exiting MS-DOS Prompt

To exit MS-DOS Prompt, close the program that's running (if necessary), and then take any of the following actions:

- Type `exit` at the DOS prompt and press the Enter key.
- Click on the window's close button.
- Double-click on the Control icon.
- Click on the Control icon to open the Control menu and choose the Close command.

NOTE

Here are two basic ways to run DOS by itself, outside of Windows 98 — before startup and after shut down.

- To run DOS before Windows starts up, turn on your computer and press (and hold down) the Ctrl key after the memory test is complete. A menu of startup options will appear. Now, select the menu item entitled "Command prompt only" and press the Enter key. The version of DOS embedded in Windows 98 will start up.

This technique is normally only used in special cases; for example, if Windows refuses to start and you would like to run DOS-based diagnostic software.

- To run DOS after Windows 98 shuts down, while in Windows, choose the Shut Down command from the Start menu. Then, select the *Restart in MS-DOS mode* option button in the resulting dialog box and choose the OK command button. DOS will start after the computer reboots. This technique for running DOS may be useful if one of your DOS applications will not run under Windows; it may run in **MS-DOS mode** — after Windows has shut down.

There are a few other, somewhat more complicated, ways to run DOS outside of Windows. We will discuss them in Section 12.3 and in the *If You Want to Learn More* section at the end of this chapter.

TUTORIAL

Try the following exercise on your own.

1. Turn on the computer (if necessary) to start Windows 98 and insert the Student Disk in its drive.
2. Start the Dosprog application on this diskette by choosing the Run option from the Start menu, typing a:dosprog in the resulting dialog box, and choosing the OK command button.
3. Dosprog will open, and should be running in a window. Press Alt+Enter to run it full screen and then Alt+Enter again to return it to window mode.
4. Maximize the program's window, if necessary. If the toolbar is not displayed near the top of the window, display it by clicking on the Control icon on the left end of the menu bar and selecting the Toolbar item from the resulting Control menu.
5. Successively select fonts from the drop-down list on the left end of the toolbar or from the dialog box that opens when you click on the toolbar's Font button. Note the effect of your selections on the Dosprog window. Then, return to the Auto font. A
6. Exit Dosprog by following the on-screen instructions and then close its window, if necessary, by clicking on its close button.
7. Start a DOS session by opening the MS-DOS Prompt window: Choose the MS-DOS Prompt item from the Programs submenu of the Start menu.
8. Maximize the MS-DOS Prompt window, if necessary.

9. At the DOS prompt, probably `C:\Windows>`, type DIR and press the Enter key to get a listing of the Windows directory (folder).
10. Select (mark) the words *Windows 98* on the screen:
    - Open the Control menu (see step 4), point at the Edit item, and choose Mark from the sub-menu; *or*, click on the toolbar's Mark button.
    - Highlight *Windows 98* by dragging the cursor (a white square) over it or by positioning the cursor at the beginning of the phrase, holding down the Shift key, and moving the cursor to the end of the phrase.

11. Copy the selected words to the Clipboard by pressing Enter, choosing Copy from the Edit submenu of the Control menu, or by clicking on the toolbar's Copy button.
12. Paste the phrase *Window 98* at the DOS prompt by choosing Paste from the Edit submenu of the Control menu or by clicking on the toolbar's Paste button.
13. Exit MS-DOS Prompt by clicking on its close button or by typing `exit` at the DOS prompt. Remove the diskette from its drive.

12.2 Property Settings for DOS Programs

Windows applications, by definition, follow certain rules governing their peaceful coexistence with other programs sharing the Desktop. A DOS program, on the other hand, assumes that it has sole possession of the computer's resources (its memory, display, hard disk, etc.). Most of the time, this doesn't cause problems; most DOS applications run well under Windows. However, on occasion, you may have to change the way a DOS program uses system resources in order for it to run more efficiently (or even run at all!) under Windows. This section discusses how you can make such changes.

Displaying a DOS Program's Property Sheets

As you have probably realized by now, just about everything in Windows or controlled by Windows has "properties": files, folders, shortcuts, printers, the display, the mouse, and so on. A DOS application has properties as well. These properties help determine the way it runs under Windows.

You can view a DOS program's properties in two ways:

Viewing a DOS program's properties

- Run the DOS program in a window and display its toolbar, if necessary (see Section 12.1); then, click on the toolbar's Properties button (shown at the right). 

or

- Right-click on the DOS program's icon (in Explorer or a folder window), and choose Properties from the pop-up menu.

In either case, the program's Properties dialog box* (or, its *property sheets*), will be displayed (Figure 5).

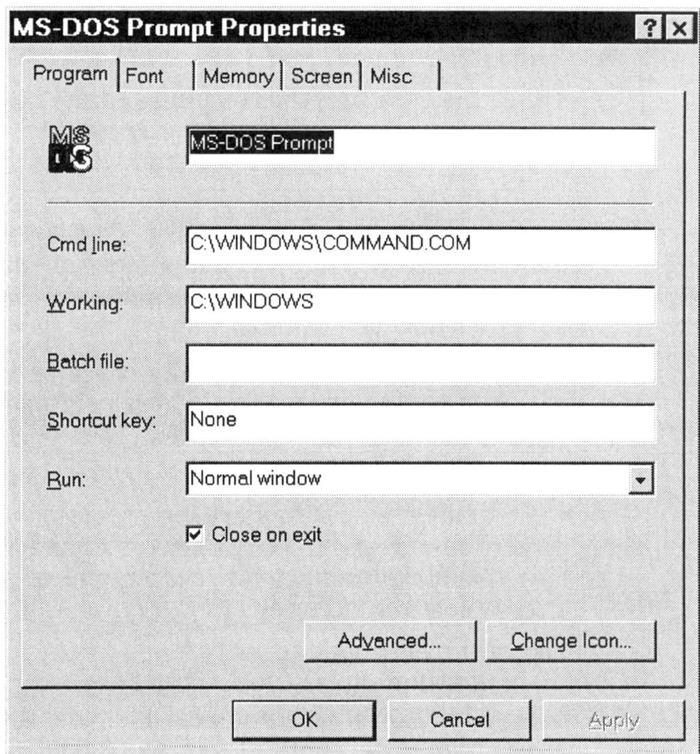

Figure 5 A Typical DOS Properties Dialog Box

*In Windows 3.1, the function of the Properties dialog box was carried out by the PIF Editor utility.

NOTE

The dialog box shown in Figure 5 was displayed by starting MS-DOS Prompt and clicking on its toolbar's Properties button. If you display the Properties dialog box by right-clicking on a DOS program's icon, that dialog box will contain one additional page. This page gives general information about the DOS program (or the shortcut to it).

TIP

Often the easiest way to locate a DOS program icon is to start the Windows Find utility (see Section 4.3). This technique may be the *only* way in some cases, because certain DOS icons are hidden in Explorer, My Computer, and folder windows. To aid your search, be aware that DOS program shortcuts usually have a *pif* extension (*pif* stands for "program information file").

Basic Properties

Some of the DOS program settings in the Properties dialog box affect the program in a fundamental way. We will discuss these settings here; others are more advanced, and will be discussed later.

On the Program Page The Program page of the Properties dialog box (see Figure 5) contains most of the basic properties. (It is similar to a shortcut's property sheet, which is discussed in Section 4.6.) Here's how you can make use of this page:

- If your DOS program usually saves and opens files in a folder other than the one from which it is started, enter this folder's path name in the *Working* text box. This folder will become the default for save, open, and certain other commands.
- To make it easier to start the program, you can place a shortcut to it on one of the Start button menus (see Section 4.2) and then define a *shortcut key* for it. Once you do, pressing this keystroke combination anywhere in Windows will start (or switch to) the application.

  To define a shortcut key, click in the *Shortcut key* text box; then type the keystroke combination you want to use to start the program. The shortcut key will take precedence over the keystroke's normal function in the active program, so choose a shortcut key that is not likely to be used in applications. Typically, a shortcut key begins with some combination of Ctrl, Alt, and Shift; for example, Ctrl+Alt+D. To enter this keystroke into the *Shortcut key* text box, hold down the Ctrl and Alt keys and type D.

- The *Run* drop-down list determines how the window will look when the program is started — minimized, maximized, or "normal" (the way it looked at the last exit).
- Select the *Close on exit* check box if you want the program's window to close when you execute the exit command. If this check box is not selected, exiting the program will terminate it, but its window will remain on the screen and the word *Finished* will be displayed on the title bar. In this case, to remove the program's window from the screen, click on the close button or press Alt+F4.
- Choose the Change Icon command button to change the icon that represents this program. A dialog box will open, allowing you to select a new icon.

On the Screen Page If you click on the Screen tab, the DOS program's Properties dialog box will look as shown in Figure 6. Here are some features found on this page:

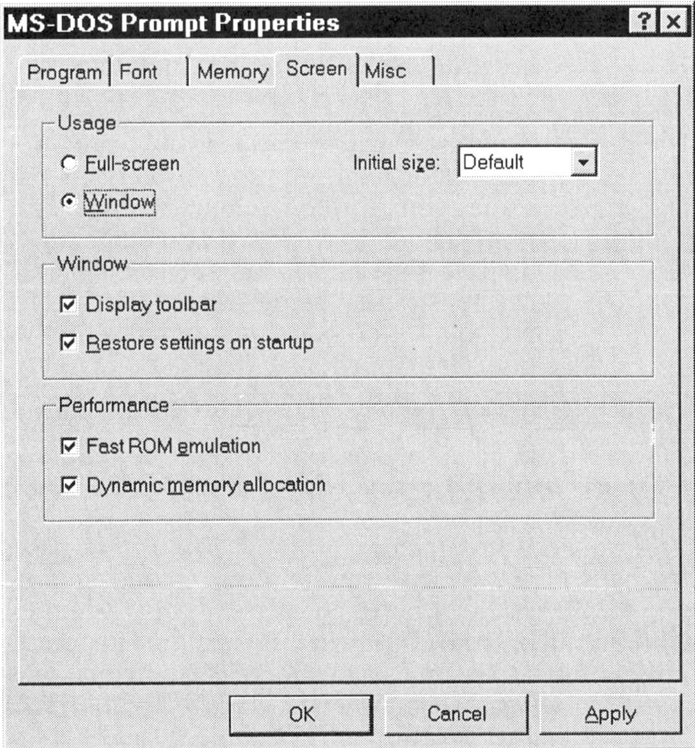

Figure 6 DOS Properties Dialog Box — Screen Page

- As you know, a DOS program can be run in a window or full-screen. To set the startup mode, select the appropriate option button. The program may run slightly faster full-screen, but the special features described in Section 12.1 can only be accessed in window mode.
- The *Display toolbar* check box allows you to specify whether or not the toolbar will be displayed on program startup.
- The *Restore settings on startup* check box determines the startup settings for such parameters as display font and window size. If the box is selected, the default settings are used; if not, the settings in effect when the program was last exited are used.

On the Font Page You can use this page of a DOS program's Properties dialog box to set the default display font for the program. (See Section 12.1 for information about DOS display fonts.)

On the Misc Page The Misc (Miscellaneous) page of a DOS program's Properties dialog box is shown in Figure 7. Here are the basic features found on this page:

- If you want your screen saver to work while running the DOS program, be sure the corresponding check box is selected. If the screen saver seems to cause a problem, deselect this check box.
- If certain shortcut keys used by your DOS program don't seem to be working, you can probably correct the situation by deselecting a check box in the *Windows shortcut keys* area. For example, say that the Alt+Tab keystroke combination in your DOS program invokes a paragraph indent. To enable this function, the Alt+Tab check box must be deselected on the Misc page. If it isn't, pressing this keystroke combination will switch to another application. (See Appendix A for a list of common Windows shortcuts.)

Types of Memory Used by DOS Programs

Recall that memory (RAM, ROM, or disk-based) is measured in *bytes*, where each byte can hold one character of information. One *kilobyte* (KB) is 1,024 bytes and one *megabyte* (MB) is 1,024 KB, or about one million bytes. (See the Introduction for more information about this topic.) To access memory, each byte is assigned an *address* — a number designating its storage location. (An address is really the "logical" location of a byte; physically, it resides on chips on the motherboard or on a circuit board plugged into the motherboard.)

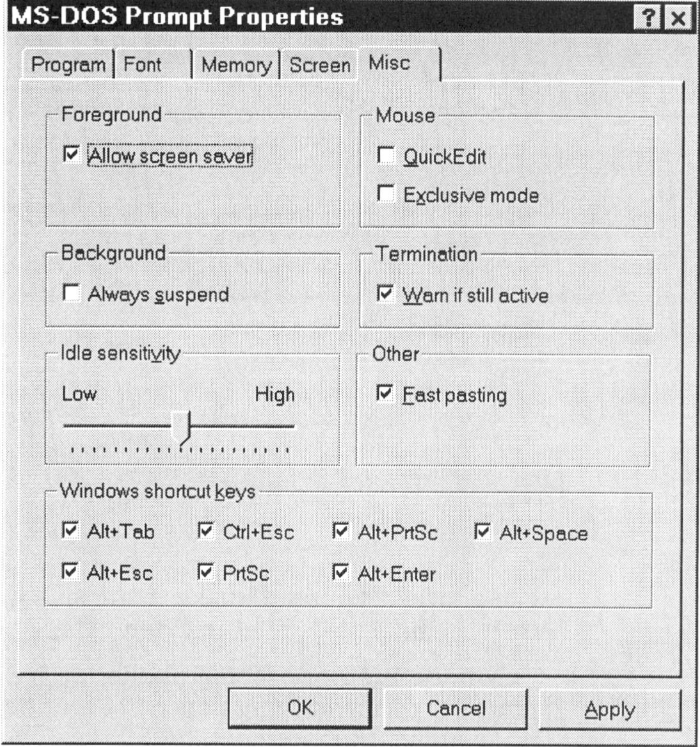

Figure 7 DOS Properties Dialog Box — Misc Page

Memory is sometimes classified according to its storage location or the way it is used. (Figure 8, on the next page, illustrates this in a pictorial fashion.)

- **Conventional memory** refers to the first 640 KB of RAM. All programs running under DOS must reside, at least partly, in this address space.
- **Upper memory** has addresses ranging from 640 KB to one MB. This region was originally reserved for memory used by hardware devices (such as the video adapter) and ROM. Nowadays, a piece of system software called a *memory manager* can make use of unused portions of upper memory to store small programs, such as device drivers, and for other special purposes.
- **Extended memory (XMS)** is the term used to describe all memory in locations above one MB. An *extended memory manager* allows programs to use this memory without conflicting with

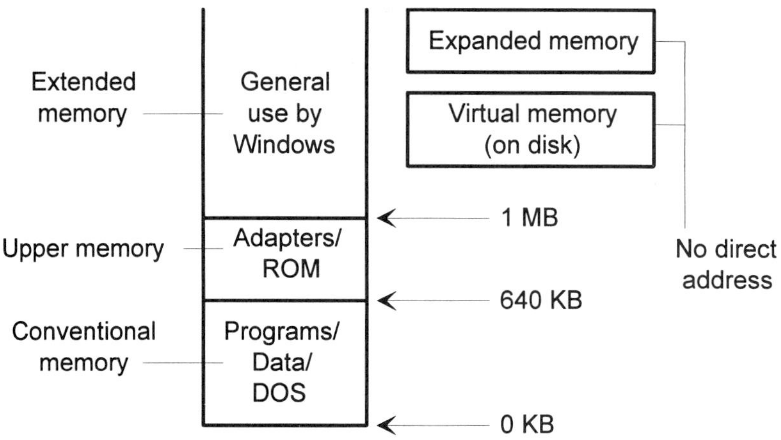

Figure 8 Types of Memory

one another. Windows makes extensive use of extended memory with the help of its built-in extended memory manager.

- **Expanded memory (EMS)**, unlike the types just described, does not refer to memory in a specific location. Rather, it is a system of memory management, developed before Windows became popular, that allows DOS programs to access more RAM than found in conventional memory. Windows and Windows-based applications do not use expanded memory, but Windows can provide expanded memory to DOS programs through a built-in *expanded memory manager.*
- **Virtual memory** is hard disk space that is used by the computer system as if it were additional RAM. Windows makes use of virtual memory through the use of a *swap file*, which allows it to run more applications simultaneously than the amount of available RAM would otherwise permit (see Section 10.5).

The Memory page

The Memory Page of a DOS program's Properties dialog box (Figure 9) allows you to control to some extent the way Windows supplies conventional, extended, and expanded memory for the program. The *Auto* entry on the various drop-down lists, the default selection, usually means that Windows will supply as much memory of each type as the DOS program requests.

- There is little reason to change the default *Auto* selection for *Conventional memory.* Even if the full 640 KB is allotted to a DOS program, conventional memory can still be supplied to other

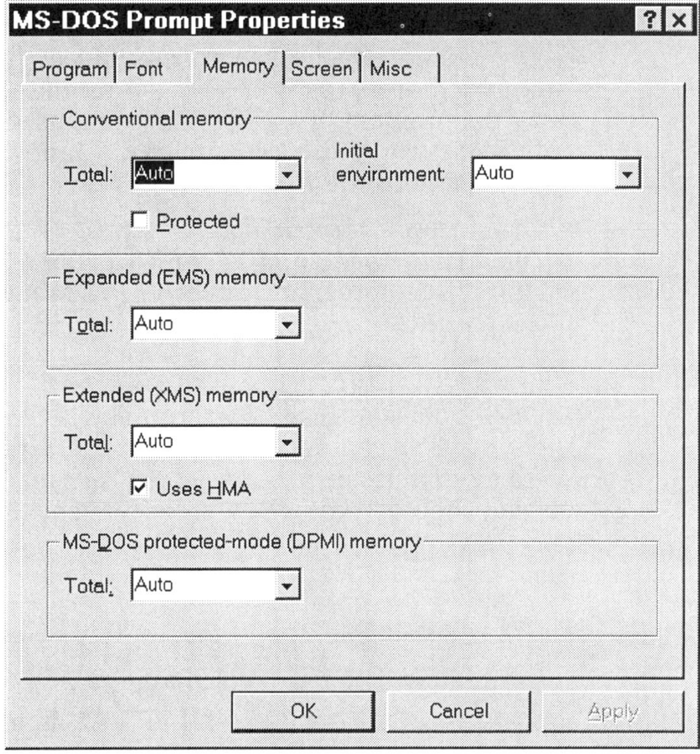

Figure 9 DOS Properties Dialog Box — Memory Page

applications because each DOS program runs in its own "virtual machine", as if it alone had control of the entire computer.

- It's usually a good idea to select the *Protected* check box to reduce the possibility that Windows will crash if the DOS program performs an "illegal" operation. (This selection may slow down the program a little, however.)
- In the *Initial environment* box, *Auto* supplies the amount of memory specified in the Config.sys system file (see Section 12.3). If the program will not start, check its user guide to see how much memory is required for environmental variables. Then, select this figure from the *Initial environment* drop-down list. (The numbers here are bytes, not kilobytes!)
- Some DOS programs will take all available RAM for use as expanded memory. In this case, set the *Expanded (EMS) memory* selection to a fixed figure; check the program's user guide. (The EMS setting will not be available if there is an entry in Config.sys

that prevents programs from using this type of memory.)

- The *Uses HMA* check box determines whether or not the **High Memory Area**, the first 64 KB of extended memory, can be used by the program. If the HMA is being used by Windows for other purposes, or if the DOS program cannot make use of the HMA, this selection will be ignored.
- DPMI, *DOS Protected Mode Interface*, is a Microsoft specification concerning the use of extended memory. Leave this setting on Auto. If the program cannot use DPM memory, this setting will be ignored.

NOTE

The DOS Properties dialog box contains a few settings that we have not discussed in this section. You can use Windows' context-sensitive help to determine the function of any setting — just right-click on its label and choose *What's This?* from the resulting pop-up menu.

TUTORIAL

Try the following exercise on your own.

1. Turn on the computer (if necessary) to start Windows 98.
2. Start MS-DOS Prompt from the Start menu's Programs submenu and switch to window mode, if necessary, by pressing Alt+Enter.
3. Click on the toolbar's Properties icon to open the Properties dialog box.

4. Note the current settings for the following parameters:
   - *Shortcut key* and *Run* on the Program page
   - *Usage* and *Display toolbar* on the Screen page
   - *Alt+Enter* shortcut key on the Misc page
5. Specify the settings shown for the indicated parameters:
   - *Shortcut key* (Program page) — Ctrl+Alt+D (Hold down Ctrl and Alt while typing D in the text box.)
   - *Run* (Program page) — Maximized
   - *Usage* (Screen page) — Window
   - *Display toolbar* (Screen page) — set (Select its check box.)
   - *Alt+Enter* (Misc page) — clear (Deselect its check box.)
6. Choose the OK command button to put the changes into effect.
7. Close MS-DOS Prompt by clicking on its close button.
8. Start MS-DOS Prompt by pressing Ctrl+Alt+D, which is possible due to its *shortcut key* setting. Notice that on startup, MS-DOS

Prompt is running in a maximized window and its toolbar is displayed because of the settings specified in step 5.

9. Press Alt+Enter. Notice that nothing happens. This shortcut key should have caused a switch to full-screen mode, but it was disabled in step 5.
10. Open the Properties dialog box by clicking on its toolbar button.
11. Choose the Change Icon button on the Program page. Scroll through the available icons in the resulting dialog box; then, choose the Cancel button to close it.
12. In the Properties dialog box, return all parameters to their original settings as noted in step 4. (If the original setting for *Shortcut key* was "None", click in this text box on the Program page and press the Backspace key to reset it.)
13. Choose the OK command button to close the Properties dialog box and then close MS-DOS Prompt.

12.3 Startup Options and Configuration Files

Normally, when you turn on your computer, you sit back, wait for a minute or so, and the Windows Desktop appears on your screen. However, in that "minute or so", a lot is going on behind the scenes. Moreover, if so desired, Windows makes it possible for you to change not only some of the things that occur during this period of time, but also the end result (for example, whether a Windows or a DOS start-up screen is displayed). In this section, we will discuss the startup process (or **boot process**) in detail, including the configuration files that are accessed at this time.

The Boot Process

With the default settings in place (the way Windows is normally installed), this is what occurs after you turn on your computer:

1. The computer's read-only memory (ROM) performs a few quick self-tests and starts a small program called Io.sys, whose main job is to start Windows 98. At this time, your screen display may show the results of the testing process and display a list of the installed hardware.

2. Windows[*] now reads the commands located in three **configuration files**, in the order indicated here:
   - **Msdos.sys** determines the startup configuration for Windows 98 (such as whether Windows starts, DOS starts, or a menu of options is displayed), loads a memory manager that is needed to start Windows, and sets defaults for certain system parameters.
   - **Config.sys** contains commands that configure your system's hardware so that Windows and other software can use it.
   - **Autoexec.bat** contains commands that store startup information for DOS, establish the automatic search path, and perform other tasks that are to be carried out when the system starts up.

   We will discuss the functions of these files in more detail, as well as how to edit them, later in this section.
3. The Windows 98 logo screen, and possibly the contents of Config.sys and Autoexec.bat, are displayed on the screen. Then, an "enter password" dialog box may open and, after you have entered the proper information, the Windows Desktop appears.

Startup Options

The scenario described above is the default boot process. You can alter this process:

- For just the current session, by pressing (and holding down) the Ctrl key until a menu of options is displayed.

or

- For future sessions, by editing the Msdos.sys file.

We will discuss each of these techniques below.

Using the Startup Menu If you hold down the Ctrl key while Windows is starting (after the ROM-based self-tests are performed), a menu of startup options, which are described in Table 1, will be displayed. To activate an option, select it and press Enter. (If you don't select an option, a normal Windows startup will take place.)

---

[*]Some say that DOS is actually in control of the computer at this point, but since DOS is now an integral part of Windows, rather than a separate operating system, this is really a moot point.

	Option	Effect on Startup
1	Normal	Starts Windows 98 as described above.
2	Logged (Bootlog.txt)	Same as Option 1, but creates a file (Bootlog .txt, in the root folder of the C: drive) that supplies details of the boot process.
3	Safe Mode	Starts Windows 98 in *safe mode*. — a basic configuration in which only generic device drivers are loaded.
4	Step-by-Step Configuration	Starts Windows 98 *interactively*, allowing you to specify the details of the startup configuration (including whether or not to execute each command in Config.sys and Autoexec .bat).
5	Command Prompt Only	Starts DOS 7.1, the version of DOS embedded in Windows 98.
6	Safe Mode Command Prompt	Starts DOS 7.1 in safe mode.
7	Previous Version of MS-DOS	Starts the previous version of DOS, the one that was running when Windows 98 was installed.

Table 1 The Windows 98 Startup Menu

The Startup menu (see Table 1) is activated automatically when Windows detects something wrong in the boot process. In this case, you can proceed in several ways to try to rectify matters:

- First, try the *Normal* option. Windows will try to start again, and often does so successfully.
- Instead, select *Logged*. Here, too, Windows 98 will attempt to boot up. If it doesn't, you (or a more experienced Windows user) can examine the Bootlog.txt text file and try to determine the part of the startup process that is causing trouble.
- Start Windows in *Safe Mode*. (This will take a few minutes.) Safe mode bypasses the Config.sys and Autoexec.bat files and ignores certain other startup information, such as Windows Registry entries. (We will discuss the Registry in Section 12.4.) Once in safe mode, you can examine the configuration files or run diag-

nostic software to try to locate the problem.

- If you believe the problem lies in the Config.sys or Autoexec.bat file (perhaps because you have just installed hardware or software that has changed one of these files), select the *Step-by-Step Confirmation* option and disable the suspect line of the appropriate file.

Editing the Msdos.sys File To alter the Windows 98 boot process on a more permanent basis, you will have to edit the Msdos .sys configuration file.

WARNING

It is not difficult to edit Msdos.sys, but you should do so with care because a misstep here could prevent your system from booting up. Thus, before you edit Msdos.sys:

- Be sure you have an emergency startup disk, a diskette that can be used to boot the system should something go wrong (see Section 2.4).
- Copy the current Msdos.sys file and rename the copy (say, Msdos .old) before editing the original.

To edit the Msdos.sys file to provide a customized boot process:

1. Msdos.sys is a hidden file, so "unhide it" if necessary:
   - Start Explorer or My Computer and choose Folder Options from the View menu to open the corresponding dialog box.
   - Click on the View tab and select the *Show all files* option button (under the *Hidden files* heading).
   - Choose the OK command button.
2. Open Notepad (Section 9.2) from the Accessories submenu of the Start menu's Programs option.
3. Choose the Open command from Notepad's File menu, select All Files from the *Files of type* drop-down list, open the root folder of the boot drive (probably C:), and choose the Msdos.sys file. Figure 10 shows the result of these actions.
4. In the [Options] section of Msdos.sys, change, delete, or insert lines to get the desired effect on the boot process. If an available option does not appear in the file, then the default value is used. Here are some examples:
   - BootGUI=1 (the default value) boots Windows 98;

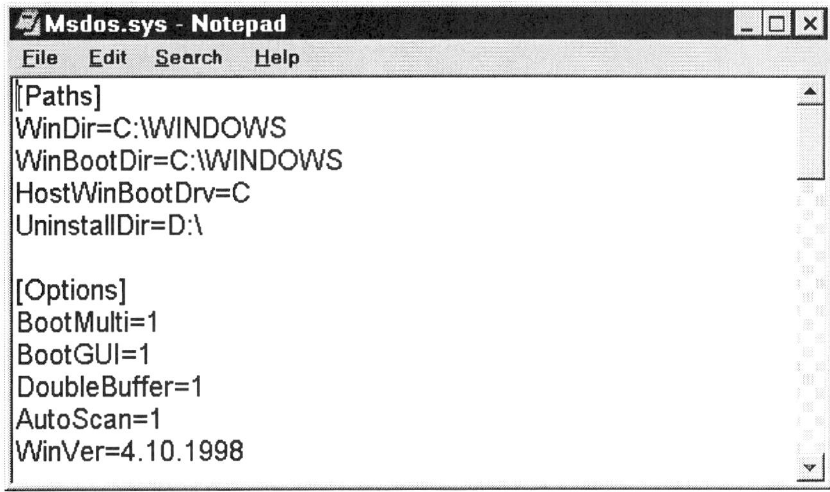

Figure 10 The Msdos.sys File Open in Notepad

BootGUI=0 boots DOS 7.1. Moreover, if this setting is in effect, activating one of the first four options on the Startup menu will boot DOS, not Windows.

- BootMenu=0 (the default value) boots without displaying the Startup menu.
  BootMenu=1 displays the Startup menu on every startup.
- BootKeys=1 (the default value) enables (allows the use of) the startup shortcut keys. Pressing one of these keys (see Appendix A) while Windows is starting activates a Startup menu option.
  BootKeys=0 disables the startup shortcut keys.

5. Choose Save from the File menu to save your changes; or, if you don't want to save them, exit Notepad, responding "No" to the warning message.

WARNING

In the procedure above, we used Notepad to edit Msdos.sys. Other text editors could be used instead. However, you must remember that Msdos.sys, Config.sys, and Autoexec.bat are *text files* and may not include any characters or codes that can't be typed at the keyboard. So, if you use another program to edit one of these files, make sure it saves files in Text format. Otherwise, the file will probably become unreadable, which in turn could cause major problems.

The [Paths] section of the Msdos.sys file tells Windows which folders contain certain key information. Editing one of these lines could have disastrous consequences.

The Config.sys and Autoexec.bat Files

The Config.sys and Autoexec.bat files date back to the first version of DOS and are included in Windows 98 to ensure compatibility with DOS, Windows 3.1, and their applications. Both files are stored in the root folder of the boot drive (probably C:). However, these files are not needed to run Windows 98 and may not be present on your system.

Config.sys and Autoexec.bat, like Msdos.sys, are text files. They consist of a series of lines, each of which represents a command to be executed on system startup, and are edited in the same way as Msdos.sys, described earlier in this section.

The Config.sys File Config.sys is short for *configure system*, which describes, in a nutshell, the purpose of this file. Here are a few of the more common commands found in the Config.sys file (Figure 11 shows a typical one):

Some typical Config.sys commands

- When a line begins with the letters *rem* (for "remark"), it is not executed by the computer. ("Remming out" a line is a good way to delete a command; it makes it easy to restore it if you change your mind later on.)
- The DEVICE and DEVICEHIGH commands load device drivers into RAM. (The latter command loads into upper memory, the region between 640 KB and 1 MB — see Section 12.2.) For example, the line in Figure 11

  ```
  DEVICE=C:\DOS\MTMCDAI.SYS /D:MTMIDE01
  ```

  loads the CD-ROM driver (MTMCDAI.SYS), which is stored in the DOS folder on the C: drive, into memory.
- The DOS=HIGH command specifies that DOS will use the *high memory area* (HMA) — the first 64 KB of extended memory (see Section 12.2).

NOTE

In looking at Figure 11, you might notice that Config.sys does not load any mouse, keyboard, monitor, or other drivers. Efficient "32-bit" versions of these drivers are all loaded by Windows into extended memory. As a result, they do not take up any valuable conventional or upper memory.

```
rem - By Windows 98 Network - DEVICE=C:\WINDOWS\SETVER.EXE
DEVICE=C:\WINDOWS\HIMEM.SYS
DOS=HIGH
rem ---------------- MTM ATAPI CD-ROM ----------------
[COMMON]
DEVICE=C:\DOS\MTMCDAI.SYS /D:MTMIDE01
rem ---------------- MTM ATAPI CD-ROM ----------------
DEVICEHIGH=C:\WINDOWS\COMMAND\DRVSPACE.SYS /MOVE
```

Figure 11 A Typical Config.sys File

Although some DOS programs can make use of expanded or extended memory, all DOS programs must run, whether in a DOS session or in MS-DOS mode, in conventional memory. It is thus sometimes necessary to make every possible scrap of conventional memory available to certain DOS programs.

For DOS programs running under Windows (in a DOS session) available conventional memory is usually maximized automatically. However, for DOS programs running after Windows has shut down (in MS-DOS mode), you have to use Config.sys to optimize conventional memory. To do so, as many drivers and *memory resident programs* (TSRs) as possible must be loaded into upper memory. Fortunately, this can be done for you, relatively easily, by running the MemMaker program, which is located in the Windows folder, or another optimization program.

The Autoexec.bat File Autoexec.bat is short for *automatically-executed batch.* A **batch file** is a program that contains a list of commands that are executed when it is run. Autoexec.bat is a batch file that is run at system startup unless you specify otherwise (by, for example, holding down the Shift key as Windows starts up).

Autoexec.bat may contain almost any command that can be typed at the DOS prompt. A typical Autoexec.bat file is shown in Figure 12 (on the next page). Here's an explanation of the commands displayed there:

Annotation of Figure 12

- As with the Config.sys file, a line beginning with *rem* is ignored by Windows when it processes the file.
- The ECHO OFF command suppresses the display of the commands that follow it. An @ symbol at the beginning of a line suppresses the display of just that line. Thus, in Figure 12, all

```
rem - By Windows Setup
rem - C:\WINDOWS\COMMAND\MSCDEX.EXE /D:MTMIDE01 /M:10
@ECHO OFF
PROMPT $p$g
PATH C:\WINDOWS;C:\WINDOWS\COMMAND;C:\DOS;D:\TBV5
SET TEMP=C:\DOS
```

Figure 12 A Typical Autoexec.bat File

commands preceding ECHO OFF will be displayed on the screen as Windows starts, but this command and those that follow it won't be displayed.

- The PROMPT command determines the way the DOS prompt will be displayed. Here, "$P" causes the current drive and directory to be displayed and "$G" displays a greater than (>) symbol, as in `C:\WINDOWS>`. (This type of prompt is actually set as the default by Msdos.sys.)
- The PATH command tells DOS where to search for a program whose name is typed at the DOS prompt. The search begins with the current directory and then continues, if necessary, with the directories listed in PATH commands, in the order listed. (Msdos .sys also contains PATH commands.)
- The SET command defines an *environmental variable*, which acts as an alias for a directory (folder) or collection of parameters. For example, the last line in Figure 12 allows programs to refer to the variable TEMP when they want to access a certain directory, which on this system happens to be C:\DOS.

For quick, detailed help with any Config.sys or Autoexec.bat command, type the word *help*, followed by the command name at a DOS prompt, and press the Enter key. For example, for help with the SET command, type `help set` and press Enter.

NOTE

Windows 3.1 used two additional configuration files, Win.ini and System.ini. Both files are usually also present in Windows 98, mostly for compatibility purposes. At installation, all relevant information in these files was placed in the Registry database (see Section 12.4). As a result, Windows 98 ignores almost all the information that appears in Win.ini and System.ini.

The System Configuration Utility

The **System Configuration utility** is a powerful startup troubleshooter. This tool allows you to easily modify the startup configuration, which can help locate problems that seem to occur during the boot process.

To start the System Configuration utility:

1. Open the System Information utility from the System Tools submenu of the Start button's Accessories menu.
2. Choose the System Configuration Utility item from its Tools menu. The window shown in Figure 13 will open.

Before you make any changes to the configuration files, back them up! Then, if your modifications make matters worse, you can always return to the previous version and start over. To back up the files,

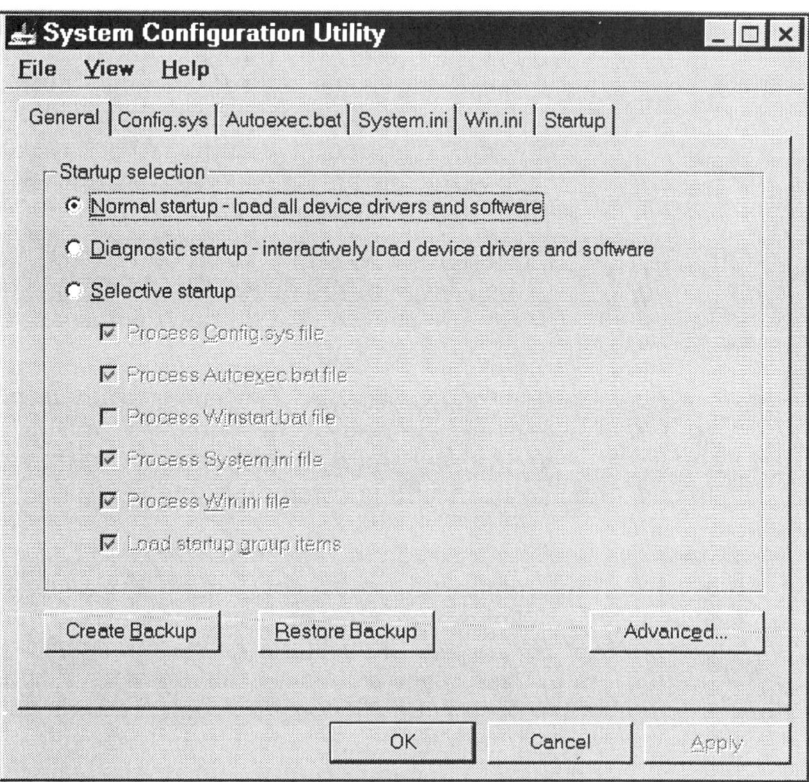

Figure 13 The System Configuration Utility

choose the Create Backup command button on the System Configuration utility's General page (see Figure 13) and click on the OK button in the resulting dialog box. (The backups will be named Autoexec.pss, Config.pss, etc.) To copy the backed up originals over the current versions, choose the Restore Backup command button.

Using the System Configuration Utility If Windows fails to perform a normal startup, you may be able to use the System Configuration utility together with a process of elimination to diagnose the problem. First, if necessary, start Windows in Safe Mode as described earlier in this section. Then, open the System Configuration utility and take the following steps:

1. On the General page (see Figure 13), select the *Selective startup* option button.
2. Select the Process Config.sys file and Process Autoexec.bat file check boxes, deselect the others, and choose the OK command button. Windows will try to restart in a basic configuration.
3. If Windows does *not* run successfully, the problem probably lies in one of these two configuration files. Use the Config.sys and Autoexec.bat pages of the System Configuration Utility dialog box to disable their commands (by deselecting the corresponding check boxes) one at a time. After each command is disabled, choose the OK button to restart Windows. Continue this process until the problem is found.
4. If Windows *does* run properly after step 2 is taken, then, on the General page of the dialog box, select one of the remaining check boxes and choose OK. Windows will again try to restart using the new configuration.
5. If Windows does restart successfully, repeat step 4 for another startup component. If Windows fails to restart, click on the appropriate dialog box tab and try to find the problem by successively disabling commands and using the process of elimination.

NOTE

The *Diagnostic startup* option on the General page allows you to boot Windows in a "clean" (generic) environment. To do so, select this option, choose OK, select *Step-by-step configuration* from the Startup menu, and elect to bypass the Config.sys and Autoexec.bat files. If this fails to cure the startup problems, then you could try the sophisticated options made available by choosing System Configuration's Advanced command button but, realistically speaking, it's probably time to contact Microsoft's Technical Support.

12.4 The Windows Registry

Windows 3.1 used special files (such as System.ini and Win.ini) to store information about the hardware and software configuration of the computer system, and about user-specified preferences for the look and feel of its interface. These files are still present in newer versions of Windows, but their main function here is to provide compatibility with older applications. Almost all the configuration information needed by Windows 98 is stored in files that are collectively known as the **Registry**.

The Structure of the Registry

The Registry consists primarily of two files located in the Windows folder on your hard disk:

Registry files

- The file System.dat contains information about the hardware and software present on your computer: the installed devices, drivers, ports, applications, and so on.
- The file User.dat contains information about user preferences such as Desktop icons, Start button menu items, wallpaper, screen colors, and the like. If more than one user profile has been set up (see Section 5.5), then there will be more than one User.dat file.

Keys and value entries

When you view the Registry (as described later in this section), it is represented as a single object with a tree-like structure. This structure is analogous to that of the Windows file system. However, instead of folders, there are *keys*, and instead of files, there are *value entries.* A **key** describes the settings present in that section of the Registry; a **value entry** gives the name and value of a setting. As in the Windows file system, an entry in the Registry is located by means of a path name. For example, the entry that determines the size of Desktop icons is My Computer\HKEY_CURRENT_USER\Control Panel\Desktop\WindowMetrics\Shell Icon Size. Here, Shell Icon Size is the value entry and all the rest of the names are keys; each key (except My Computer) is a subkey of the ones to its left.

The root of the Registry tree is called My Computer. There are six main keys (sometimes called *root keys*) that appear as subkeys of it. (See Figure 14, on the next page, for a pictorial representation of the relationship.) Here is a general description of the contents of each root key:

- HKEY_USERS contains information about user-specific preferences for the "default user" (as defined in the User Profiles section of the Passwords utility; see Section 5.5), the "current user" (the one currently logged on), and possibly other users. (If no users were added by means of User Profiles, then the default user is the only subkey here.) This data is obtained from the User.dat configuration file and includes information about Control Panel settings, the Desktop setup, network connections, installed applications, and many other user-specified preferences.

- HKEY_CURRENT_USER is identical to a subkey of HKEY_USERS. It contains the part of this key that applies to the user that is currently logged on to the computer.
- HKEY_LOCAL_MACHINE contains all information about the hardware and software present on your computer (except for the preference selections made by its users). This data is obtained from the System.dat configuration file.
- HKEY_CURRENT_CONFIG is identical to a subkey of the HKEY_LOCAL_MACHINE key; it contains information pertaining to the currently selected *hardware profile.* Hardware profiles are established in Control Panel's System utility (see Section 10.5); they create different hardware configurations for a single computer so that, for example, it can be easily switched from use as a standalone laptop to one that is connected to a network or docking station.
- HKEY_DYN_DATA contains current information about the status of devices and software that have been loaded during the current Windows session. (DYN stands for *dynamic.*) This key is the same as a subkey of HKEY_LOCAL_MACHINE and has an important role in the workings of Plug and Play devices (see Section 10.1).
- HKEY_CLASSES_ROOT primarily contains information relating to file associations (see Section 4.4) and object linking and embedding (see Section 12.5). This key is identical to a subkey of HKEY_LOCAL_MACHINE.

Editing the Registry

Whenever you make changes to settings in Control Panel, on a property sheet, or in certain other Windows locations, these modifications are reflected in the Registry. Thus, when you make such changes, you are, in effect, editing the Registry. It is also possible, and sometimes desirable, to edit the Registry directly. However, the Registry files, System.dat and User.dat, are not text files and cannot therefore be modified using Notepad or another text editor. To edit these files, you must use the Windows 98 **Registry Editor**.

WARNING

Using the Registry Editor improperly can have unfortunate consequences; Windows may not load when you restart your computer, or if it does load, it may not work properly. For this reason, you should understand how the Registry is backed up and restored, and also exercise care when modifying it. We will discuss backing up and restoring the Registry later in this section.

The Registry Editor is a program with file name Regedit.exe that resides in the Windows folder. To start the Registry Editor, either

- Choose the Regedit icon in Windows Explorer or My Computer.

or

- Choose the Run option from the Start menu, type Regedit in the resulting dialog box, and choose the OK command button.

In either case, the window shown in Figure 14 will open.

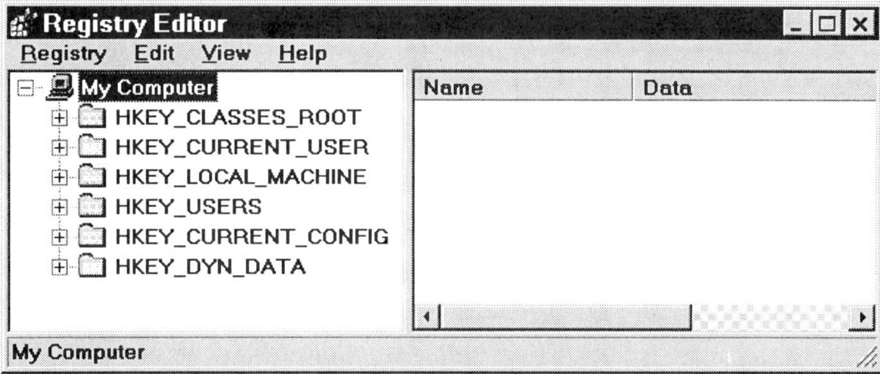

Figure 14 The Registry Window Showing the Six Main Keys

NOTE

If you are running Windows 98 in a computer lab and/or on a network, you may not be able to start the Registry Editor. It may have been removed by the lab coordinator or system administrator to protect the integrity of the system.

The general Registry editing procedure

Here is an outline of the general procedure for editing an entry in the Registry:

1. Start the Registry Editor, as described above.
2. Expand branches of the Registry tree (by clicking on the plus symbol next to certain keys in the left pane) until the desired key appears.
3. Click on this key to display its contents (all the value entries contained within it) in the right pane.
4. Double-click on the desired entry's name and enter its new value in the resulting dialog box.
5. Close the Registry Editor by choosing Exit from the File menu.

Some changes to the Registry are put into effect when you restart Windows; others take place immediately.

An example

As you can see, the procedure just given is not very specific. We can better illustrate how to use the Registry Editor by walking through an example: Suppose you want to change the color of the text used to represent "dimmed" or "grayed-out" menu entries. Proceeding in what seems to be a logical way (once you've read Section 5.3), you open Control Panel's Display utility and click on the Appearance tab. However (as you can see if you work this example), there is no selection in the Item drop-down list for grayed-out items and clicking on *Disabled* in the sample window's menu bar doesn't help either. In other words, the color of grayed-out text cannot be changed from Control Panel.

Nevertheless, you *can* change the color of grayed-out text using the Registry. First, you have to determine the red-green-blue (RGB) composition of the color you want to use. This can be done by using the Display utility:

1. Click on the Color button on the Appearance page and, when the color palette is displayed, choose the *Other* command button. This action opens the Color dialog box.
2. In the color spectrum area of this dialog box, click on the desired color and make a note of the values displayed in the Red, Green, and Blue text boxes. (If these values don't change when you click in the color spectrum, first click on the vertical luminosity bar, then in the color spectrum.)

Now close the Display utility and start the Registry Editor, as described earlier in this section, and proceed as follows:

1. Since the entry you want to change is a user preference, click on

the plus symbol next to HKEY_CURRENT_USER to display its subkeys.

2. Notice (in Figure 15) that one of the subkeys of HKEY_CURRENT _USER is Control Panel, so expand this branch (by clicking on its plus symbol).
3. Finally, a Colors subkey appears; click on its name or icon to display its value entries. The result is shown in Figure 15. (Notice that the Status bar, at the bottom of the Registry window, contains the path for the Colors key.)

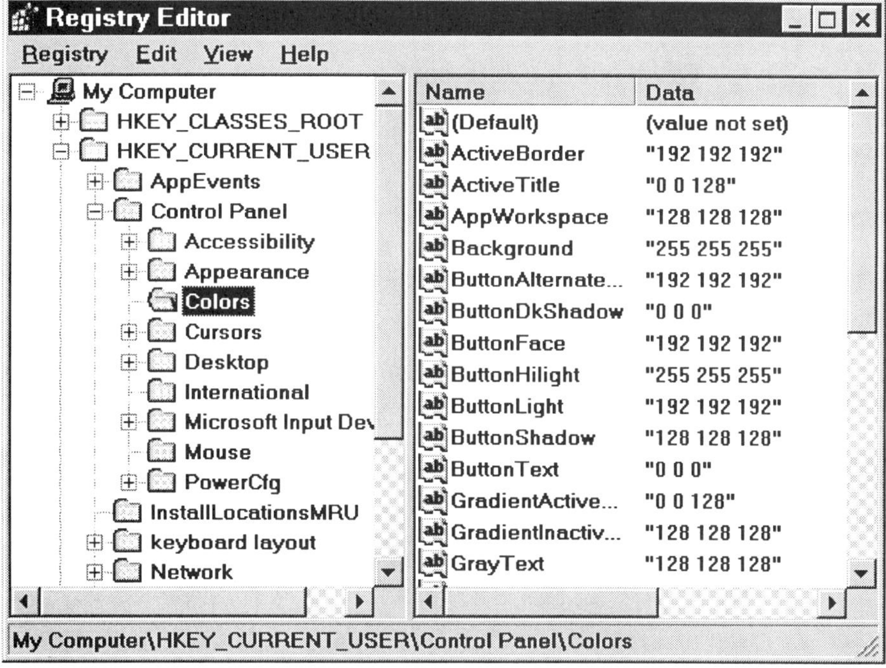

Figure 15 The Registry Window after Clicking on the Colors Key

4. Double-click, in the right pane, on the value entry named Gray Text. (Notice that its current value, its RGB composition, is "128 128 128".) A dialog box will open, as shown in Figure 16 (on the next page), allowing you to modify the value of this entry.
5. Enter the desired red, green, and blue figures in the *Value data* text box and choose the OK command button.
6. Close the Registry Editor.

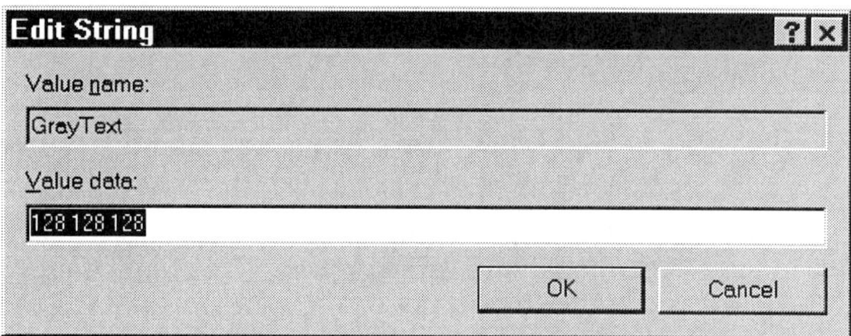

Figure 16 The Editing Dialog Box

Regedit's Find utility

Often the hardest part of using the Registry Editor is locating the desired key or value entry. Fortunately, Regedit supplies a *Find utility* to help you in this respect. We will use another example to illustrate the use of the Find utility.

Suppose you would like to rename the Recycle Bin. But, when you right-click on its icon, the resulting pop-up menu has no Rename command. Obviously, Microsoft does not really want you to rename the Recycle Bin, but you can do so using the Registry Editor. The problem here is that it could take hours to locate the appropriate key in the Registry Editor window. Using Find, however, it's a snap:

1. In the Registry Editor, choose the Find command from the Edit menu. The Find window, shown in Figure 17, will open.

Figure 17 The Registry Editor's Find Window

2. Enter the words Recycle Bin in the *Find what* text box.

3. Select the *Match whole string only* check box so that we do not turn up other items that contain the words *Recycle Bin.* (There is usually little point in changing the selected status of the other check boxes.)

3. Choose the Find Next command button. When the words Recycle Bin are found, the Registry Editor will locate and open the appropriate key. The result of the search is shown in Figure 18.

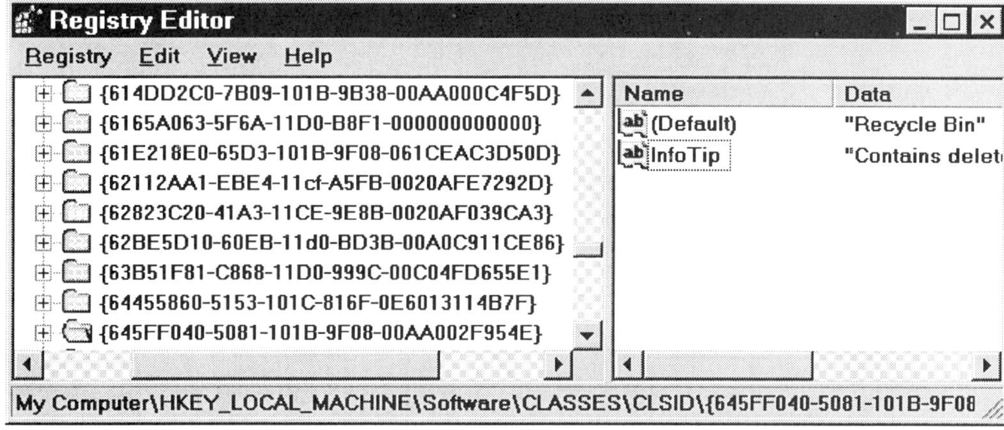

Figure 18 The Result of the Search for *Recycle Bin*

4. Now, double-click on the word *Default* in the right-pane, enter a new name in the resulting dialog box, choose the OK button, and exit the Registry Editor.

NOTE

The long strings of characters in the left pane of Figure 18 are known as *Class IDs*. Every object in Windows has a unique Class ID number, or CLSID. (The reason why a CLSID is so long is that it is assigned randomly and the length of the string virtually assures its uniqueness.) A good way to find the CLSID for a particular object is to use Regedit's Find utility, just as we did here.

The item *Info Tip* in the right pane of the window in Figure 18 is the tool tip that is displayed when you rest the mouse pointer on the Desktop's Recycle Bin icon. As you can see from this example, the Registry Editor also provides a means of changing the text displayed by an icon's tool tip.

Backing Up and Restoring the Registry

As we mentioned earlier in this section, if you're going to use the Registry Editor, then it is important to know how the Registry is backed up and restored.

Automatic Backups and Restores Windows automatically backs up the Registry (the System.dat and User.dat files, as well as Win.ini and System.ini) every time it successfully starts. Moreover, if while starting up, Windows discovers that the Registry is corrupted, it postpones the backup process and automatically *restores* the Registry files, replacing them by the backups created in the last successful startup.

Manual Backups and Restores If you want, you can backup or restore the Registry at any time. This is done with the aid of the **Registry Checker**, which actually consists of two files — the Windows-based ScanRegW, which is used for backups, and the DOS-based ScanReg, which is used for restores.

Manual backups To manually back up the Registry:

1. Start the System Information utility from the System Tools submenu of the Start button's Accessories menu.
2. Choose the Registry Checker item from this utility's Tools menu. Registry Checker will start, scan the Registry for errors, and report the results.
3. To back up the Registry, choose the Yes command button; otherwise choose the No button.
4. If you do back up the Registry, when the process is complete, choose the OK button.

NOTE

You can also back up the Registry by running the ScanRegW program. To do so, either enter this filename in the Run dialog box and press Enter or choose its icon from the Windows folder in Explorer or My Computer.

Manual restores To manually restore the Registry, you must run the ScanReg program in MS-DOS mode. To be more specific:

1. Restart the computer in MS-DOS mode from the Shut Down Windows dialog box.

2. At the DOS prompt, type `scanreg/restore`.
3. From the listed files, select the latest "good backup" — the most recent file date for which the word *Started* appears.
4. Press the Enter key and the restore will take place.

Exporting and Importing the Registry As you know, the Registry files System.dat and User.dat are not text files. However, if you want, you can create a text version of all or part of either file. This process is called *exporting the Registry*. The exported files can be modified using an ordinary text editor, such as Notepad, and then *imported* into the Registry — their data can be incorporated into System.dat and User.dat.

Exporting the Registry

To export the Registry:

1. Start the Registry Editor, as described earlier in this section.
2. Choose the Export Registry File item from the Registry menu; the corresponding dialog box, shown in Figure 19, will open.

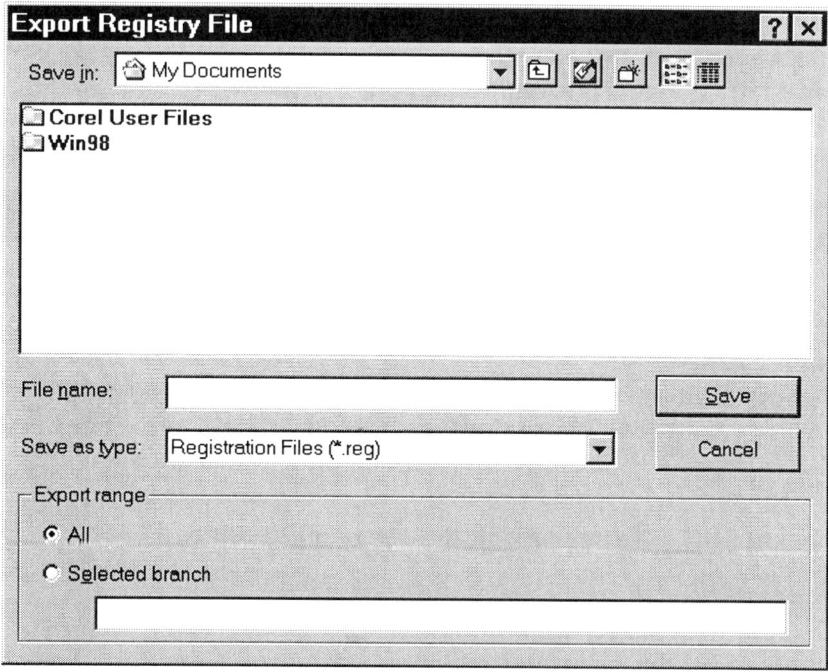

Figure 19 The Export Registry File Dialog Box

3. Select a folder in which to save the exported text file, just as if you were working in a Save dialog box.
4. If you only want to export a branch of the Registry, click on the *Selected branch* option button and enter the path name that defines this branch in the text box.
5. Enter a file name for the exported Registry file in the *File name* text box. (Windows will automatically add a *reg* extension to your name.)
6. Choose the Save command button.

NOTE

An exported Registry file may be too large to open in Notepad. (The size of the entire Registry, converted to a text file, will probably exceed one megabyte.) In that case, you can use WordPad to edit it. A *reg* file is automatically opened and saved by WordPad as a text file.

The Registry looks quite different when viewed as a text file. Figure 20 shows a small portion of an exported Registry file opened in WordPad. Notice that:

- Registry keys are described by enclosing their path name in square brackets.
- Entry names are enclosed in double-quotes.
- Entry data values are either enclosed in double-quotes (if they are strings) or preceded by *dword* or *hex* (if they are decimal or binary values).

Importing the Registry

If you want to copy an exported (text) Registry file over the corresponding portion of the Registry, replacing the latter in the process, you must *import the Registry*. To do so:

1. Start the Registry Editor.
2. Choose Import Registry File from the Registry menu, which displays the corresponding dialog box (Figure 21).
3. Select the appropriate *reg* file in the resulting dialog box or type its name in the *File name* text box.
4. Choose the Open command button.

Notice that the export/import procedures provide another way to back up and restore the Registry. However, this technique requires the use of the Registry Editor, which would not be accessible if Windows refused to start.

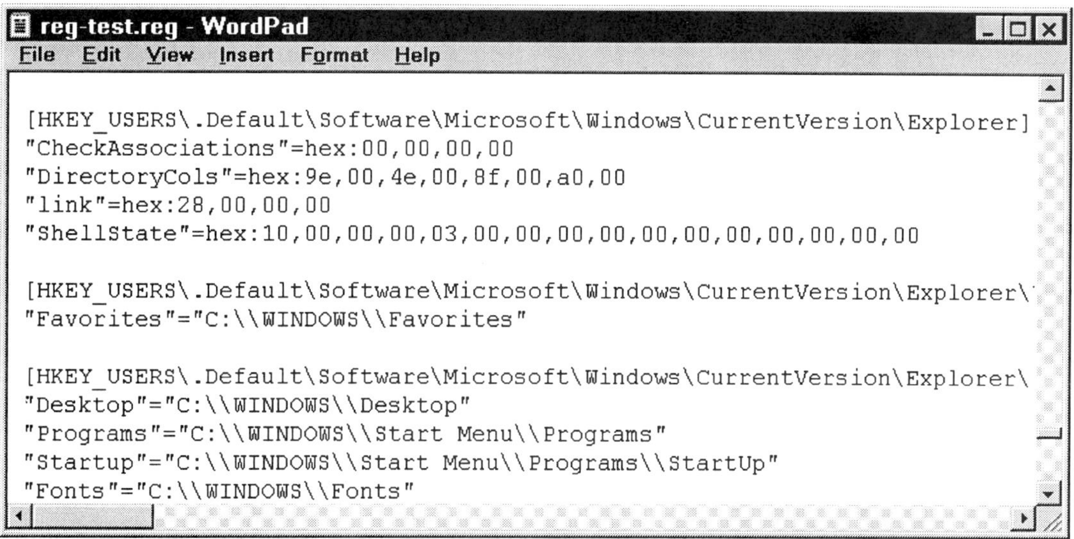

Figure 20 An Exported Registry File Opened in WordPad

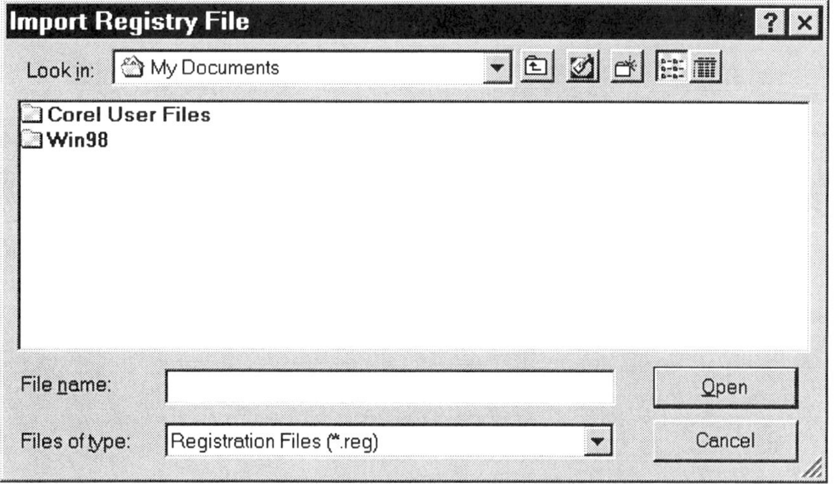

Figure 21 The Import Registry File Dialog Box

If you want, you can import the Registry from Windows Explorer or My Computer. To do so, start either one and:

1. Open the folder that contains the appropriate *reg* file.

2. Right-click on the file's icon and choose Merge from the resulting pop-up menu. (Here, *Merge* has the same meaning as *Import*.)

Help! As you must realize by now, the Registry is large and complex. Fortunately, Microsoft has seen to it that you can make almost all the modifications you'd want to Windows 98 without having to use the Registry Editor. On the other hand, if you would like more information about this subject, see Chapter 31 of the *Windows 98 Resource Kit*, published by Microsoft Press, or the electronic version of this book, accessed by opening the RK98Book.chm file located in the tools\reskit\help folder on the Windows 98 CD-ROM. (The Registry Editor's own help files contain little information about the Registry.)

TUTORIAL

Try the following exercise on your own. It simulates making changes to a couple of Registry entries.

1. Turn on the computer (if necessary) to start Windows 98.
2. Start the Registry Editor: Choose the Run option from the Start menu, enter Regedit in the Open text box, and choose the OK command button.
3. Use the Registry Editor to change the active window's title bar color to black:
   - In the left pane, click on the plus symbols next to HKEY_CURRENT_USER and Control Panel to expand this key and subkey.
   - Click on the Colors icon (in the left pane) to display, in the right pane, the value entries for this key.
   - In the right pane, select the Active Title entry name and then change its value to "0 0 0", the red-green-blue values for black: Double-click on the entry name, enter the text "0 0 0", without the quotation marks, in the resulting dialog box, and choose the OK command button.
4. Use the Registry Editor to change the name of the object currently called *Recycle Bin* to *Trash Bin*:
   - Find a reference to the Recycle Bin object by using the Find dialog box: Choose the Find command from the Edit menu, enter *Recycle Bin* in the *Find what* text box, select the *Match whole string only* text box, and choose the Find Next command button.

- Windows will eventfully display the value entry for the Recycle Bin in the right pane. Notice, from the status bar, that it is contained in the \Software\CLASSES\CLSID subkey of HKEY_LOCAL_MACHINE. The long number at the end of the path name is the class ID number for the Windows object currently named *Recycle Bin*.
- Double-click (in the right pane) on the word *Default*, enter *Trash Bin* in the resulting dialog box, and choose the OK command button.

5. Close the Registry Editor window without putting your changes into effect by clicking on the close button. (Had you wanted to put the changes into effect, you would have chosen Exit from the Registry menu and then restarted Windows.)

12.5 Object Linking and Embedding

The Windows Clipboard (Section 2.3) provides an easy way to transfer information from one document to another. However, once that information has been placed in the target document, it may not be so easy to edit it. For example, if you want to make changes to a picture in a word processing document, you might have to start the application that created the picture, open the appropriate file, make the desired changes, and reinsert the picture into the document after deleting the original. Windows' *object linking and embedding* feature provides a more versatile way to transfer information — one that allows it to be easily edited should the need arise. In this section, we will discuss the embedding, linking, and editing processes.

What is OLE?

Object linking and embedding (or **OLE**) allows you to transfer information, which in this context is called an **object**, from one document (the *source*) to another (the *destination*) in such a way that the transferred object retains a link with the application that created it. Using OLE, you can produce a **compound document** — one that contains pieces of information created using diverse applications — and then, if necessary, easily modify the document's various components. For example, you can create a letter within a word processor that contains easy-to-edit graphics, spreadsheet data, and even sound or video clips produced by other applications.

Not all Windows applications can make use of linking and embedding. If an application can *create* embeddable and linkable objects, it is called an **OLE server**. If it can *receive* these objects, it is called an **OLE client** or **container**. For example, Paint (Chapter 8) is an OLE server; WordPad (Chapter 7) is an OLE client. Some Windows applications can act as both servers and clients.

The difference between linking and embedding

Although embedding and linking are usually mentioned together, they are actually two different processes:

- When you **embed** an object, a copy of it is inserted into the destination document. Then, if you edit the embedded object, the copy is modified, not the original; in other words, the editing process does not change the source document.
- To **linking** an object, it must be saved as a separate file. Then, when you link it to a document, an image of the object and information about it (for example, in which file it can be found) is inserted into the destination document. If you edit a linked object, the original file in which the object resides (the *source file*) is modified, and when the link is *updated*, so is the image of the object in the destination document.

Embedding and linking have the same end: they both transfer an object from one document to another and provide easy editing of the image. So, which should you use? Broadly speaking:

- If an object is likely to be used in just one destination document, you should *embed* it there. An embedded object is a little easier to edit than a linked one and the resulting file is a little smaller.
- If you plan to use the same object in several documents, you should *link* it to them. Then, to edit the object's image in all the destination documents, you need only modify it once — in the source file.

Note that embedding is the more common process and is usually the default for the insertion operation.

How to Embed or Link an Object

There are several ways to embed and/or link an object. You can:

- Select the object in the OLE server, copy it to the Clipboard, and paste it into the destination document. This method only works for embedding the object, unless the object is a file.

- Copy a file to the Clipboard (say, from Explorer) and paste it into the destination document. This method works for both linking and embedding.
- Use the Insert Object command in the OLE client to embed or link an object created by another application.
- Drag-and-drop the object from the OLE server into the destination document as an embedded object.

We will now explain how each of these methods works.

Embedding an Object using Select, Copy, and Paste The procedure described in Section 2.3 for using the Clipboard to transfer information between documents will often *embed* an object created in an OLE server into a client document. Here's how it works:

1. In the OLE server application, select the object in the source document that you want to embed.
2. Choose Copy from the Edit menu to place the object on the Clipboard.
3. Switch to the OLE client application and position the cursor in the destination document where you want to insert the object.
4. Now, either
    - Choose Paste from the Edit menu. This action will normally embed the object, displaying it at the cursor, and you can skip the rest of this procedure.

    or

    - Choose the Paste Special item from the Edit menu if you want more control over the insertion process. A dialog box, like the one shown in Figure 22 (on the next page), will be displayed and you must complete the rest of this procedure.
5. Select the *Paste* option button (if it's not already selected).
6. In the *As* window, select a format in which to embed the object. It is usually best to use the default (highlighted) option. Other formats, such as *Picture* and *Device Independent Bitmap* in Figure 22, will insert the object without embedding it. The text in the *Result* area of the dialog box provides a short explanation of the consequences of choosing the currently selected format.
7. Select the Display As Icon check box if you want to insert an icon representing the object, instead of the image of the object, into the destination document. (Choosing the icon in the document will then display the object.)

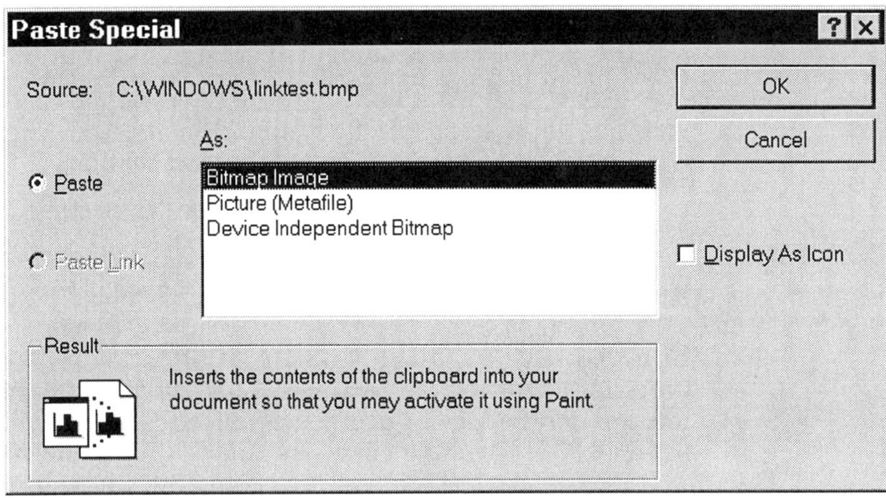

Figure 22 A Typical Paste Special Dialog Box

8. Choose the OK command button to embed the object, displaying it at the cursor.

Inserting a File using Copy and Paste You can use the procedure just described to embed *or* link an object saved in a separate file into an OLE client document. To be more specific:

1. Select the desired file in Windows Explorer or My Computer.
2. Copy the selected file to the Clipboard by choosing Copy from the File menu or the right-click pop-up menu.
3. Switch to the OLE client application and position the cursor in the destination document where you want to insert the object.
4. Now, either
   - Choose the Paste item on the Edit menu, which normally embeds the object.

   or
   - Choose the Paste Special item on the Edit menu to open a dialog box like the one in Figure 22, select the *Paste* option button (for embedding) or the *Paste Link* option button*, and

*Some OLE clients have a separate *Paste Link* command on their Edit menu to be used to insert a linked object. If this is the case, and you want to link the object, choose this command instead of Paste Special.

choose the OK command button. (In this situation, the Paste Link option will not be grayed out, as it is in Figure 22.)

5. The object contained in the file will be inserted into the client document and its image, or an icon representing it, will be displayed at the cursor.

Using the Insert Menu to Embed or Link When you embed or link an object using the copy and paste technique, as described above, the process begins in the server application. It is also usually possible to initiate the process from within the OLE client through the use of an Insert Object command. This method is especially easy if the object is stored on disk. Here's how it works:

1. Place the cursor in the destination document (of the OLE client) where you want the object to appear.
2. Choose the Object item from the Insert menu. The Insert Object dialog box, shown in Figure 23, will open.

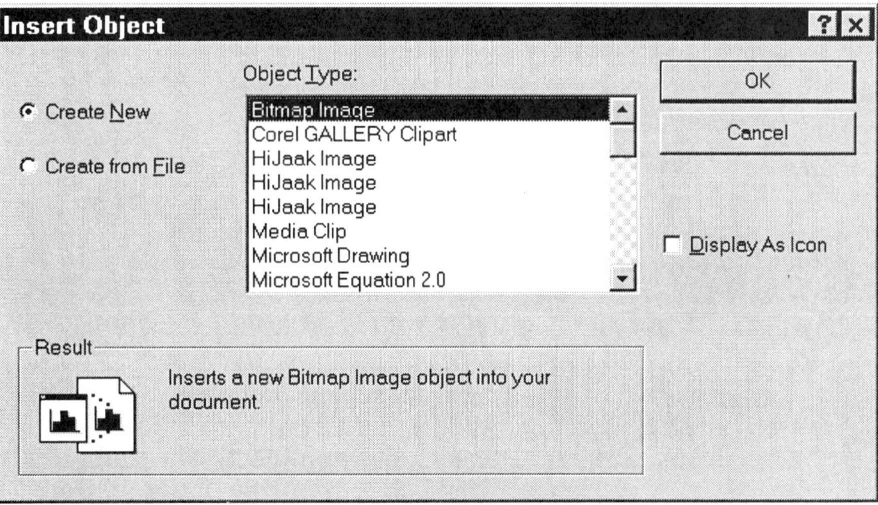

Figure 23 The Insert Object Dialog Box

3. If you want to create the object (using another application), select the Object Type corresponding to that application and then choose the OK command button. A box will open (at the cursor) in the destination document, in which you can create the object using the selected application's tools. When you are done,

click the mouse anywhere outside of the box and the object will be *embedded* in the document.

As an example, if you open the Insert Object dialog box in WordPad, select Bitmap Image, and choose OK, the Paint application will open, and the WordPad window will look as pictured in Figure 24. (Although the title bar says "WordPad", the menus and available tools are those of Paint.)

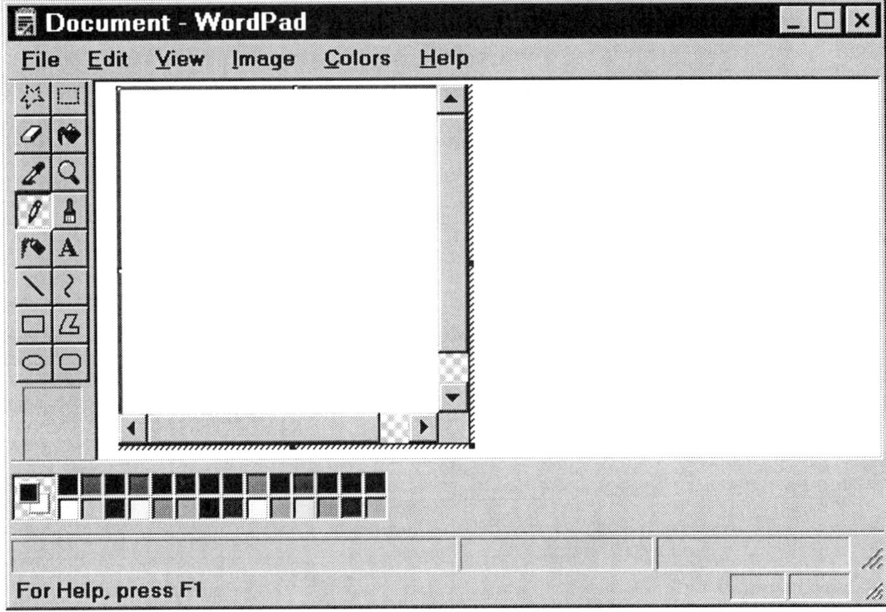

Figure 24 Working with Paint Inside the WordPad Window

4. If, instead of creating an object, you want to retrieve one from disk, select the *Create from File* option button. The Object Type list in the Insert Object dialog box will be replaced by the following display:

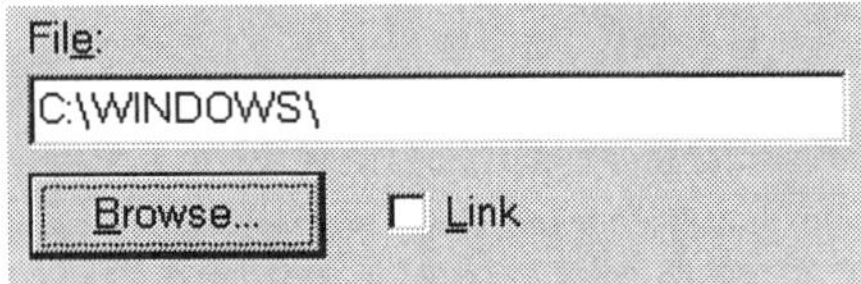

Now, either type the path name for the desired file in the *File* text box or choose the Browse button to locate the desired file by browsing folders. Then, choose the OK command button, and the object will be *embedded* in the client document at the cursor. If you want to *link* the object to the document, select the Link check box before choosing OK.

Using Drag-and-Drop This technique can only be used to embed an object and only works for some applications. All you need to do to carry out this technique is:

1. In the OLE server, select the object to be embedded.
2. Drag the object to the destination document and drop it (release the mouse button) where you want it inserted.

As an example, here's how you can insert a sound effect into a WordPad document. Start Explorer and arrange its window so that it and the WordPad window are both visible on the screen. Now, open the Windows folder, select the Chimes file, and drag it into the document; it will be displayed there as a icon, as shown at the right. The sound file is now embedded in the document. If you want to play the sound associated with the icon, just choose that icon.

Editing an Embedded or Linked Object

Once an object is embedded in or linked to a document, it can be edited from within that document. Linked objects can also be edited from within the OLE server, which normally changes the corresponding images in all linked documents.

Editing an Embedded Object If an object has been embedded in a OLE client document, the editing process starts within the client application and the changes made affect only that document, not the source material. To edit an embedded object:

1. Within the OLE client, open the document, if necessary, and select the object to be edited.
2. Double-click on the selected object. The server application will open within the client's window; the window size will remain the same, but a "box" will frame the object and the menus, menu items, and toolbars will change to reflect those of the server application.

As an example, Figure 25b shows the effect of double-clicking on the bitmap graphic embedded in the WordPad document shown in Figure 25a. Notice that the content of the document window has not changed, but that Paint's Tool Box, Color Box, menu bar, and status bar are now displayed.

3. Use the server application to modify the object.
4. Click anywhere outside the framed box (but within the client window) to complete the process.

Figure 25a An Embedded Object

Figure 25b Double-clicking the Object

NOTE

Double-clicking on an icon that represents a sound file or video clip will play the corresponding sound or video. To edit these objects, you must use the technique described in the TIP below.

Because the sizes of the image and window do not change when you double-click on an embedded object (see Figure 25), it may be awkward to modify the object. If you prefer, you can edit the selected embedded object in a separate server window. To do so:

1. Right-click on the object, which displays a menu.

2. Point at the last item on this menu (for example, "Bitmap Image Object") and choose the Open command from the resulting submenu. (Choosing the Edit command from this menu has the same effect as double-clicking on the object.) The server application will start and open the object within it.
3. Modify the object as desired.
4. Choose the Exit and Return command from the server's File menu to complete the process.

This technique also gives you the opportunity to save the modified object in a separate file. To do so, choose the Save Copy As command from the server's File menu before returning to the client application.

Editing a Linked Object The process for editing a linked object differs slightly from the one described above for embedded objects. To edit a linked object:

1. Within the OLE client, open the document, if necessary, and select the object to be edited.
2. Either
   - Double-click on the selected object.

   or
   - Open the Edit menu or the right-click menu, point at the last item on it, and choose either Edit or Open from the resulting submenu.

   In either case, the server application will open in its own window.
3. Modify the object.
4. Save the modified file by choosing the Save command from the server's File menu.
5. Close the server application and save the changes in the client application.

The Links dialog box

If you carry out the procedure just described for editing a linked object, the linked document will, by default, be updated automatically to reflect these changes. However, you can change this default and control the linking process in other ways by choosing the Links command on the client's Edit menu, which opens the dialog box shown in Figure 26 on the next page.

In the Links dialog box, you can perform the following actions:

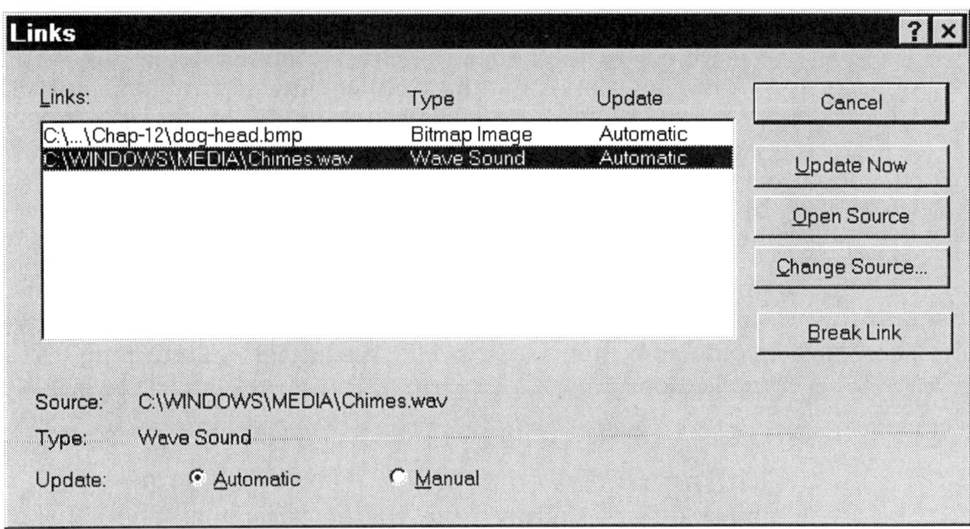

Figure 26 The Links Dialog Box

- You can elect to update the client document when you want to, not necessarily whenever the source file changes. To do so, select the *Manual Update* option button.
- When manual updating is in effect, changes to the source file can be transferred to the client document by choosing the Update Now command button. (The Update Now button has another function — see the TIP given below.)
- Choosing the Open Source command button will open the source file within the application that created it. Choosing the Change Source command button will display a dialog box that allows you to link the selected object to another file.
- To end the association between the image of the object in the client document and the source file, choose the Break Link command. If you do, changes to the source file will no longer affect the object in the client document.

A linked object can be edited without first opening the client application. This technique is especially useful when several documents contain a link to a given source file. Here's how it works:

1. Open the server application and the source file.
2. Make the desired modifications, save the source file under the same name, and close the server application.

3. Open the client application and the linked document.
4. Choose Links from the Edit menu, which opens the Links dialog box, and select the appropriate linked object from the displayed list.
5. Choose the Update Now command button and then the Close button. The changes made to the source file will now be reflected in the linked document.
6. From the client's File menu, save the changes to the linked document.

TUTORIAL

Try the following exercise on your own.

1. Turn on the computer (if necessary) to start Windows 98.
2. Open WordPad and Paint (both reside on the Accessories submenu of the Start menu's Programs option) and insert the Student Disk into its drive.
3. In Paint, an OLE server application, open the Dog-head file on the Student Disk.
4. Choose the Select All command from the Edit menu and then choose Copy from the Edit menu to place the graphic on the Clipboard. Then, close Paint.
5. In WordPad (an OLE client), *embed* the object currently on the Clipboard in the WordPad document: Choose the Paste Special item from the Edit menu, select the Paste option button and the Bitmap Image type (if necessary), and choose the OK command button.
6. In WordPad, deselect the graphic by clicking to the right of it, and press the Enter key twice to move the insertion point.
7. Now link the Dog-head graphic to the WordPad document using another insertion technique: Choose the Object command from the Insert menu and, in the resulting dialog box, select the Create from File option button and the Link check box. Then, type `A:\dog-head` in the *File* text box and choose the OK command button.
8. Edit the linked graphic: Double-click on it to start Paint (the OLE server), make any changes you like to the dog's head, and save the resulting graphic in Paint. Then, close Paint. The changes you made will be reflected in the WordPad document.
9. In WordPad, deselect the linked graphic and select the embedded one by clicking on the latter.

10. Edit the embedded graphic: Double-click on it (which starts Paint within the WordPad window and frames the graphic in a "box"), make any changes you wish, and then click anywhere (in the document window) outside of the box to return to WordPad's menus and toolbars.
11. Close WordPad, responding No to the "Save Changes?" message, and remove the diskette from its drive.

Chapter Summary

Running DOS Programs in a Window	To switch between window and full-screen modes	Press Alt+Enter; *or*, in window mode, click on the toolbar's Full Screen button.
	To open the Control menu	Click on the Control menu icon or press Alt+Spacebar.
	To select, copy, or paste text	Click on the Mark, Copy, or Paste toolbar button; *or* open the Control menu's Edit submenu and choose the Mark, Copy, or Paste command.
	To change the display font	Select a font from the toolbar's drop-down menu or click on the toolbar's Font button.
Running a DOS Session	To start MS-DOS Prompt	Choose the MS-DOS Prompt item from the Programs submenu of the Start menu.
	To exit MS-DOS Prompt	Type `exit` at a DOS prompt and press Enter; *or* click on the close button.
DOS Program Property Sheets	To open a DOS program's Properties dialog box	Right-click on the program's icon or shortcut and choose Properties from the pop-up menu; *or* click on the program's Properties toolbar button.
	Program page options	Specify the default startup folder, define a shortcut key, and specify the type of window used at startup and whether the window closes when exiting from the program.
	Font page options	Specify the font used on program startup.
	Memory page options	Specify the amount of conventional, extended, and expanded memory made available to the program.

	Screen page options	Specify whether the program starts in a window or full-screen, and whether the toolbar is displayed on startup.
	Misc page options	Specify whether a screen saver and certain shortcut keys can be used with the program.
Types of Memory	Conventional memory (0 KB - 640 KB)	Stores programs and data while they are in use.
	Upper memory (640 KB - 1 MB)	Stores ROM and adapter memory; also used by memory managers to provide additional RAM and expanded memory.
	Extended memory (Above 1 MB)	Used by Windows to provide additional memory for programs and DOS.
	Expanded memory	Used by an expanded memory manager to provide additional RAM for DOS programs.
	Virtual memory	Hard disk space used by Windows as if it were additional RAM.
Startup Options	To change the default Windows 98 startup	Edit the Msdos.sys file.
	To access the Windows 98 Startup menu	Press the Ctrl key while Windows 98 is starting; select Diagnostic startup in the System Configuration utility; *or* edit the Msdos.sys file.
	Startup menu options	See Table 1 in Section 12.3.
	To start up DOS instead of Windows	Select a DOS option from the Startup menu or set BootGUI=0 in the Msdos.sys file.
Configuration Files	Msdos.sys	Determines the startup configuration for Windows 98, loads a memory manager necessary for startup, and sets various system parameters.
	Config.sys	Contains commands that load memory managers and device drivers which configure the system's memory and hardware.
	Autoexec.bat	Contains commands that store startup information, establish the automatic search path, and perform other tasks to be carried out at system startup.
The Registry	Purpose of the Registry	Stores all the configuration information (concerning system hardware and user preferences) needed by Windows 98.

	Structure of the Registry	Contained primarily in the System.dat and User.dat files, which when viewed by the user, appear as a tree-like structure with six main branches (keys) containing subkeys and value entries.
	To edit the Registry	Make changes in Control Panel, a property sheet, or certain other Windows folders; *or* use the Registry Editor.
	To start the Registry Editor	Open the Regedit file from the Start menu's Run option, Explorer, or My Computer.
	To use the Registry Editor	Locate the required subkey in the left pane, double-click on the desired entry name in the right pane, and make the change in the resulting dialog box.
	To manually back up or restore the Registry	Use the Registry Checker to back up; start the ScanReg program in MS-DOS mode to restore.
	To import/export the Registry (as a text file)	Choose the Import Registry File/Export Registry File command from the Registry Editor's Registry menu.
Object Linking and Embedding	Embedded objects vs. linked objects	Embedded objects are copies of the source material; editing them does not affect the latter. Linked objects contain pointers to the source *file*; to edit them, you edit the latter.
	To embed an object	Copy the object or object's file to the Clipboard and paste it into the desired document; *or* use the Object command on the Insert menu; *or* drag-and-drop the object from the source file onto the destination.
	To edit an embedded object	Double-click on the object, make the changes in the resulting "box", and click outside that box.
	To link an object	Copy the object's file to the Clipboard and paste it into the desired document; *or* use the Object command on the Insert menu.
	To edit a linked object	Double-click on the object, make the changes in the new window, and save the source document to disk.

Review Exercises

Section 12.1

1. Under Windows 98, DOS applications can be run in a window or ____________.
2. To display the Control menu for a DOS program that is running in a window, click on the ____________, which appears on the title bar.
3. You can change the display font for a DOS program that is running in a window by selecting a new one from the drop-down list that appears on the ____________.
4. True or false: You can switch a DOS program between window and full-screen modes by pressing the Alt+Tab key.
5. True or false: Text displayed in a DOS program document cannot be copied to the Windows Clipboard.
6. True or false: To start a DOS session, choose the MS-DOS Prompt item from the Programs submenu of the Start menu.
7. To end a DOS session, you should close any open DOS programs, and then
   a. Turn off the computer.
   b. Type `exit` at the DOS prompt.
   c. Close Explorer.
   d. Restart the computer in MS-DOS mode.
8. You can run a DOS application by
   a. Double-clicking on its program file in Explorer.
   b. Starting a DOS session, typing its program file's name at the DOS prompt, and pressing the Enter key.
   c. Restarting the computer in MS-DOS mode, typing its program file's name at the DOS prompt, and pressing the Enter key.
   d. Performing any of the above actions.

Section 12.2

9. You can display a DOS program's property sheets by clicking on the Properties button on its ____________.
10. If you want a DOS program's window to close when you exit that program, select the *Close on exit* check box on the ____________ page of its Properties dialog box.
11. ____________ memory, or XMS, is the term used to describe all memory in locations above one MB.
12. True or false: Using a DOS program's Properties dialog box, you can set that program to open in full-screen mode, if you want.

13. True or false: A shortcut key used to start a DOS program must begin with Ctrl or Ctrl+Alt.
14. True or false: Virtual memory is hard disk space that is used by the computer system as if it were additional RAM.
15. The type of memory that occupies addresses from 0 to 640 KB is called
    a. Conventional memory.
    b. Upper memory.
    c. Expanded memory.
    d. Extended memory.
16. You cannot use the Memory page of the Properties dialog box to limit the amount of
    a. Conventional memory used by a DOS program.
    b. Expanded memory used by a DOS program.
    c. Extended memory used by a DOS program.
    d. Virtual memory used by a DOS program.

Section 12.3

17. The actions that a computer takes when starting up are collectively called the startup, or ___________, process.
18. If you want to alter your computer's default startup process, press the ___________ key while Windows is starting.
19. The two DOS configuration files that are no longer required by Windows 98, but which are usually accessed during startup, are ___________ and ___________.
20. True or false: The System Configuration utility allows you to start Windows without processing the Autoexec.bat file.
21. True or false: You can specify whether the computer will start in DOS or start in Windows in future sessions by placing the appropriate command in the Config.sys file.
22. True or false: The PATH command tells DOS where to search for a program whose name is typed at the DOS prompt.
23. The command DOS=HIGH in a Config.sys file
    a. Allows DOS to provide access to upper memory blocks.
    b. Loads device drivers into upper memory.
    c. Loads DOS into upper memory.
    d. Loads DOS into the HMA (in extended memory).
24. If you don't want a particular command in an Autoexec.bat file to be executed when the file is accessed
    a. Begin the line with the @ symbol.

b. Begin the line with *ECHO OFF.*
c. Begin the line with *rem.*
d. Begin the line with *SET.*

Section 12.4

25. The Registry primarily consists of the data files ___________ and ___________.
26. To edit the Registry "manually", you must start the Registry Editor, which has the file name ___________.
27. The left pane of the Registry Editor window resembles Windows Explorer's folder tree pane, but the items listed there are called ___________, not folders.
28. True or false: When you make changes to Control Panel settings, these changes are entered in the Registry.
29. True or false: Registry keys, entry names, and entry data can all be located using the Registry Editor's Find utility.
30. True or false: The Registry files are automatically backed up every time Windows starts successfully.
31. The root key of the Registry that contains information about your Desktop color preferences is called:

    a. HKEY_USERS
    b. HKEY_CLASSES_ROOT
    c. HKEY_LOCAL_MACHINE
    d. HKEY_CURRENT_CONFIG

32. Using the Registry Editor to create a text file containing the contents of the Registry is called

    a. Saving the Registry.
    b. Importing the Registry.
    c. Exporting the Registry.
    d. None of the above.

Section 12.5

33. The application that creates an embeddable or linkable object is called the OLE ___________.
34. When you edit a(n) ___________ object, only the copy of that object in the client document is changed; the original object in the server is not.
35. You can link an object to an OLE client document by choosing the __________ command from the client's Insert menu.
36. You can embed the object currently on the Clipboard in an OLE client document by choosing the Paste or ___________ command from the client's Edit menu.

37. True or false: Modifying and saving the source file to which an object has been linked never affects the object in the client document.

38. True or false: With OLE, you can edit embedded objects, but not linked objects, in the client document window.

39. True or false: If you drag-and-drop a sound file from Explorer into WordPad, that file becomes linked to the WordPad document.

40. True or false: The Links dialog box allows you to end the association of a linked object with its source file.

41. In editing a linked object

    a. The process must be started from within the client application.
    b. The original source file need not be changed.
    c. The source file is opened in a separate window.
    d. The linked object can be transformed into an embedded one.

42. In editing an embedded object

    a. The process must be started within the client application.
    b. The original source file must be modified.
    c. The OLE server cannot be opened in a separate window.
    d. The object can be transformed into a linked one.

Build Your Own Glossary

43. The following words and phrases are important terms that were introduced in this chapter. (They appear within the text in boldface type.) Use WordPad (see Section 2.2) to enter a definition for each term, preserving alphabetical order, into the Glossary file on the Student Disk.

Autoexec.bat file
Batch file
Boot process
Compound document
Configuration file
Config.sys file
Conventional memory
Device driver
DOS application
DOS session
Embed an object
Expanded memory (EMS)
Extended memory (XMS)
High memory area (HMA)
Key (in Registry)
Link an object
MS-DOS mode
MS-DOS Prompt
Msdos.sys file
Object (in OLE)
Object linking and embedding (OLE)
OLE client
OLE container
OLE server
Registry
Registry Checker
Registry Editor
System Configuration utility
Upper memory
Value entry (in Registry)
Virtual memory

Lab Exercises

Work each of the following exercises at your computer. Begin by turning the machine on (if necessary) to start Windows 98 and closing any open windows.

Lab Exercise 1 (Section 12.1)

a. Start the DOS program called Edit by using the Run command on the Start menu. What is the name of this program according to its title bar?

b. Switch to window mode, if necessary, maximize the window, and select the "8 × 12" display font. Does the Edit window occupy the entire screen (except, of course, for the Taskbar)?

c. Select the Auto font and maximize the window. Does it occupy the entire screen now?

d. Type your name and class on the first line and press the Enter key. Then, mark your name, copy it to the Clipboard, and paste it onto the second line. What shape did the cursor become when you clicked on the Mark command or button?

e. Restore the Edit window. Did the text shrink in size? *Optional*: Resize the window so that it is as small as possible and copy it to your homework document.

f. Close Edit, responding No to the "Save" message. What actions did you have to take to exit this application?

g. Start MS-DOS Prompt, type Edit at the DOS prompt, and press the Enter key to open this program again.

h. Try to exit MS-DOS Prompt by clicking on its close button. What message appeared?

i. Close the message box (by clicking on No), close the Edit program, and exit MS-DOS Prompt. How did you accomplish the latter?

Lab Exercise 2 (Section 12.2)

a. Start Explorer and open the \Windows\Command folder.

b. Locate the Edit program and open its Properties dialog box without starting the program. Which dialog box page is active?

c. In the Properties dialog box, note the current settings for the following properties and change each (if necessary) as indicated:

- Select a maximized window.
- Deselect *Close on exit*.

- Select the "8 × 12" font.
- Select window mode on startup.
- Deselect *Display toolbar*.

Choose the OK command button to put your changes into effect.

c. Start Edit from the Explorer window. When Edit starts:

- Is the window maximized? (Is there a restore button?)
- What display font is being used?

d. Display the toolbar. How did you do this?

e. Open Edit's Properties dialog box without leaving the program. How did you do this?

f. Return all properties except "closc on exit" to their original settings and choose the OK command button.

g. Exit the Edit program. Did its window close automatically? If not, click on its close button.

h. Close Explorer.

Lab Exercise 3 (Section 12.3)

a. Display the Windows 98 Startup menu by restarting your computer and pressing the appropriate key on startup. Which key did you press?

b. On the Startup menu, select the "Start DOS in safe mode" option. What text is displayed for the DOS prompt?

c. Type `ver` (for *version*) at the DOS prompt and press the Enter key. What text was displayed?

d. Press the Ctrl+Alt+Del keystroke combination to restart the computer, display the Startup menu, and activate the step-by-step configuration option. What's the first question you are asked? (Answer "yes" to all questions.)

e. From the Shut Down Windows dialog box, restart the computer in MS-DOS mode.

f. At the DOS prompt, type `ver` and press the Enter key. What text is displayed now?

g. Type `win` and press the Enter key to return to Windows.

Lab Exercise 4 (Section 12.3)

a. Open the Notepad application from the Accessories submenu of the Start menu's Programs option and maximize its window.

b. Successively open the following files, all of which reside in the root directory of your computer's boot drive (probably, C:). For each file, explain as many of the commands as you can.

- Msdos.sys
- Config.sys
- Autoexec.bat

c. Close Notepad when you are done.

Lab Exercise 5 (Section 12.4)

a. Start the Registry Editor. How did you do this?

b. Expand the HKEY_CURRENT_USER branch (by clicking on its plus symbol). What are its subkeys?

c. Expand branches of HKEY_CURRENT_USER until you find the Desktop subkey; then, click on it. What is its path name (as stated on the status bar)? List three of its value entries.

d. Open the HKEY_CURRENT_USER\Control Panel\Colors key. Note the current value of the Active Title entry and then change it to "0 0 0" (black). What is the name of the dialog box in which the change is actually made?

e. Press the F5 function key to refresh the Registry. Did its title bar color change to black?

f. Return the Active Title entry to its original setting.

g. Use the Find utility to search for Recycle Bin. Use the results of the search to determine its Class ID number. What is it?

h. Close the Registry Editor by clicking on its close button.

Lab Exercise 6 (Section 12.5)

a. Start WordPad.

b. Insert the Student Disk in its drive and *embed* the Shapes graphic on this diskette into the WordPad document. What command did you use to do this? Click to the right of the graphic to deselect it and press the Enter key.

c. Start Explorer, open the Windows\Media folder, and drag-and-drop the Tada sound file into WordPad at the insertion point. Is this file embedded in, or linked to, the WordPad document?

d. Double-click on the Shapes graphic to edit it. What application has control of the editing process? (Hint: Open the Help menu.)

e. Terminate the editing process, returning control to WordPad. How did you do this?

f. Double-click on the icon in the WordPad document that represents the Tada file. What happened?

g. Right-click on the Tada icon to edit it. What command did you employ on the pop-up menu? What application started?

h. Close WordPad, responding No to the "Save changes?" message, close Explorer, and remove the diskette from its drive.

Lab Exercise 7 (Section 12.5)

a. Start WordPad.

b. Insert the Student Disk in its drive and *link* the Shapes graphic on this diskette to the WordPad document. What command did you use to do this? Click to the right of the graphic to deselect it and press the Enter key.

c. Start Explorer, open the Windows\Media folder, and use the Clipboard to "paste link" the Tada sound file at the insertion point in the WordPad document. What WordPad command did you use to perform this task?

d. Double-click on the Shapes graphic to edit it. What application was started to carry out the editing process? Did a separate window open for this application?

e. Terminate the editing process, returning to WordPad. How did you do this?

f. Double-click on the icon in the WordPad document that represents the Tada file. What happened?

g. Right-click on the Tada icon to edit it. What command did you employ on the pop-up menu? What application started?

h. Close WordPad, responding No to the "Save changes?" message, close Explorer, and remove the diskette from its drive.

If You Want to Learn More ...

The notes presented here allow you to delve more deeply into some of the topics covered in this chapter.

Running DOS Programs in MS-DOS Mode

Most DOS programs will run just fine under Windows. However, occasionally, a DOS program will run only if it has sole control of the computer. In this case, you should run the program, after Windows has shut down — in *MS-DOS mode*.

As you know from Section 12.1, you can enter MS-DOS mode from the Shut Down Windows dialog box by activating the *Restart in MS-DOS mode* option. It is also possible to give a *particular* DOS program sole control of the computer whenever it is run (and automatically return control to Windows when it is exited) using the following technique:

1. Open the DOS program's Properties dialog box (as described in Section 12.2).
2. On the Program page, choose the Advanced command button.
3. In the resulting dialog box, select the *MS-DOS mode* check box. (It's also a good idea to select the *Warn before entering MS-DOS mode* check box, which gives you a chance to change your mind about shutting down Windows.)
4. Choose the OK command button to close this dialog box; then choose the OK button again to close the Properties dialog box.

Now, when this program is started, Windows will shut down all open applications, shut itself down, and relinquish control to DOS, which starts the DOS program.

More on MS-DOS mode

When you specify, via its property sheets, that a particular program is to run in MS-DOS mode (see the note above), you can set up a system configuration that will be used with this program alone. To do so:

1. Open the program's Properties dialog box, click (if necessary) on the Program tab, and choose the Advanced command button to open the Advanced Program Settings dialog box.
2. Select the *Specify a new MS-DOS configuration* option button. (This option becomes available when the *MS-DOS mode* check box is selected.)
3. Enter the commands in the CONFIG.SYS and AUTOEXEC.BAT list boxes that this program will need at startup to successfully run in MS-DOS mode. (Windows displays, in these check boxes, the commands that *it* believes the program will need.)
4. Choose the OK command button to exit this dialog box and then choose it again in the Properties dialog box.

When running a recalcitrant DOS program in MS-DOS mode, it is often necessary to maximize the amount of conventional memory available to this program. The following commands, placed in the CONFIG.SYS list box in the Advanced Program Settings dialog box, should help in this respect:

```
DEVICE=C:\WINDOWS\HIMEM.SYS /TESTMEM:OFF
DEVICE=C:\WINDOWS\EMM386.EXE NOEMS
DOS=HIGH
DOS=UMB
DEVICEHIGH= . . .
     .
     .
     .
```

(The last few lines represent DEVICEHIGH commands that load the necessary device drivers into upper memory.)

More about Msdos.sys options

In Section 12.3, we discussed a few of the commands that you can place (using a text editor like Notepad) in the [Options] part of the Msdos.sys configuration file to modify the way Windows 98 starts up. Here's a more complete list:

- `BootMulti=1` allows you to boot the previous version of DOS or Windows (if there is one) by selecting the appropriate Startup menu option.
- `BootWin=0` boots the previous version of DOS (and possibly, Windows 3.1).
- `BootGUI=0` together with `BootWin=1` (the default) automatically boots DOS 7.1.
- `BootMenu=1` automatically displays the Startup menu on every startup.
- `BootKeys=0` disables the startup shortcut keys (see Appendix A).
- `BootMenuDelay=`*n* specifies the number of seconds, *n*, the Startup menu will remain on the screen before the first menu option is automatically put into effect.
- `Logo=0` turns off the display of the Windows 98 logo screen during startup.

Playing with the Registry Editor

In Section 12.4, we demonstrated a couple of changes you can make using the Registry Editor that can't be made from anywhere else in Windows. Here are a few more:

- You can change the size of the icons on your Desktop by opening the HKEY_CURRENT_USER\Control Panel\Desktop\Window Metrics key and double-clicking on Shell Icon Size in the right pane. This entry's value gives the height and width of the Desktop icons in pixels.

- When a window is minimized to its Taskbar button or is restored from the button, it may seem to zoom in or out in the process. This feature can be turned off from the Display Properties dialog box. To use the Registry to accomplish this:

  1. Open the HKEY_CURRENT_USER\Control Panel\Desktop\WindowMetrics key.
  2. If there is a MinAnimate value entry, change its value to "0". Otherwise, carry out the rest of this procedure.
  3. Right-click on an empty part of the right pane, point at the New item on the pop-up menu, and choose String Value from the submenu. A new value entry will appear in the right pane.
  4. Rename the new value entry *MinAnimate* and press the Enter key.
  5. In the resulting dialog box, enter the number 0 and choose the OK command button.

  To turn on the zooming effect, set MinAnimate equal to "1".

- When you create a Desktop shortcut, its icon contains a small arrow in the lower-left corner to indicate that it's a shortcut. To eliminate these arrows:

  1. Open the HKEY_CLASSES_ROOT\lnkfile key.
  2. Right-click on the IsShortcut item and choose Rename from the pop-up menu.
  3. Rename the IsShortcut item anything else; for example, NoArrowShortcut.

  To eliminate the small arrow of a Desktop icon that represents a shortcut to a DOS program, you will have to repeat this procedure, but this time, begin by opening the HKEY_CLASSES_ROOT\piffile key.

APPENDIX 

General Shortcut Keys

As befits software running under a graphical user interface, Windows and its applications make extensive use of the mouse. Nevertheless, some operations can be performed more quickly using keystrokes (or keystroke combinations), which Windows refers to as *shortcut keys*. In this appendix, we will list some important shortcut keys and their functions. Other shortcut keys (for example, those for WordPad) are described at the appropriate place in the text.

On the Desktop

Alt+Enter	Displays the properties sheet for the selected item.
Alt+Esc	Cycles through the Taskbar buttons.
Alt+Print Screen	Copies the active window to the Clipboard (anywhere in Windows).
Arrow key	Selects the closest icon to the highlighted one in the specified direction.
Ctrl+Esc	Displays the Start menu.
Del	Sends the selected item to the Recycle Bin.
Enter	Opens the selected item.
F1	Starts Windows Help.

F2	Prepares the selected item for renaming.
F3	Opens the Find dialog box.
Print Screen	Copies the entire screen to the Clipboard (anywhere in Windows).
Shift+Del	Deletes the selected item without sending it to the Recycle Bin.
Shift+F10	Opens the selected item's right-click menu.
Tab	Moves the focus to the Start button.

In a Dialog Box

Alt+Down Arrow	Opens a drop-down list (if it has the focus).
Alt+F4	Closes the dialog box, putting all changes into effect.
Alt+Spacebar	Opens the System (Control) menu.
Arrow keys	Cycles through a group of option buttons or check boxes (if one of them has the focus).
Ctrl+Tab	Cycles forward through the dialog box tabs.
Ctrl+Shift+Tab	Cycles backward through the dialog box tabs.
Escape	Closes the dialog box, canceling all changes.
Tab	Moves the selection cursor (focus) from item to item.
Shift+Tab	Moves the selection cursor from item to item in the reverse direction.
Spacebar	Selects or deselects a check box (if it has the focus).

In Most Windows Applications

Alt	Moves the focus to the application's menu bar. (Or, closes all open menus and deactivates the menu bar.)
Alt+*underlined letter*	Opens the corresponding menu.
Alt+F4	Closes the application.

Alt+Spacebar	Opens the System (Control) menu.
Alt+Tab	Switches among the running applications.
Ctrl+C	Copies the selected data to the Clipboard.
Ctrl+V	Pastes the contents of the Clipboard.
Ctrl+X	Cuts the selected data to the Clipboard.
Escape	Closes an open menu or dialog box.
F1	Starts Help for the application.
F10	Moves the focus to the application's menu bar. (Or, closes all open menus and deactivates the menu bar.)
Shift+F10	Opens the selected item's right-click menu.

In Explorer and My Computer

Alt+Enter	Displays the properties sheet for the selected object.
Backspace	Opens the parent folder.
Ctrl+A	Selects all objects.
Ctrl+Z	Undoes the last action.
Del	Sends the selected objects to the Recycle Bin.
Right/Left Arrow	Expands/collapses the selected folder (Explorer only).
Plus/Minus (on numeric keypad)	Expands/collapses the selected folder (Explorer only).
Asterisk (on numeric keypad)	Expands all folders (Explorer only).
F2	Prepares the selected object for renaming.
F3	Opens the Find dialog box.
F4	Displays the Address box drop-down list.
F5	Refreshes the display.
F6	Switches among the left and right panes and the Address box (Explorer only).
Shift+Del	Deletes the selected objects without sending them to the Recycle Bin.

Shift+F10	Opens the right-click menu for the selected object.

When Starting Up The following keys apply when Windows 98 is starting, after the ROM-based tests take place (see Section 12.3).

Ctrl	Displays the Startup menu.
F4	Starts the previously installed version of DOS (if possible).
F5	Starts Windows 98 in safe mode.
Shift+F5	Starts DOS 7.1 in safe mode.
F8	Starts Windows 98, allowing you to configure the startup "step-by-step".

For "Windows Keyboards" The following shortcut keys only apply to keyboards (such as the Microsoft *Natural Keyboard*) that contain a "Windows key", which we designate here by Win.

Win+E	Starts Explorer.
Win+F	Opens the Find dialog box to search for files.
Win+Ctrl+F	Opens the Find dialog box to search for computers.
Win+F1	Starts Windows Help.
Win+M	Minimizes all open windows.
Win+Shift+M	Undoes the Minimize All command.
Win+R	Opens the Run dialog box.
Win+Tab	Cycles through the Taskbar buttons.

APPENDIX B

DOS Commands in Windows 98

One of the major advantages of Windows over DOS is that you don't have to memorize esoteric commands to start programs, to copy, rename, or delete files, or to perform other routine tasks. However, there are situations in which DOS commands will do a job better than Windows. For example, DOS is superior for:

- Copying, renaming, deleting, or changing the attributes of certain *sets* of files, such as those with the same extension.
- Printing a listing of the files within a given folder.
- Creating a *batch file*, one made up of a sequence of commands that is executed when the file is opened.

In this appendix, we will list the commands supported by DOS 7.1, the version embedded in Windows 98, and discuss how some of them can help you perform tasks like the ones listed above.

DOS Commands

The table that follows lists the commands recognized by DOS 7.1 (except for batch file commands, which are given later in this appendix.) To execute one of the commands in this table, type it at a DOS prompt and press the Enter key. (Most of these commands can be executed at any DOS prompt, but some require MS-DOS mode.)

Command	Function
APPEND	Allows programs to open data files in specified directories as if they were in the current directory*.
ATTRIB	Sets or clears file attributes.
BREAK	Allows the use of Ctrl+C to halt program execution at any time.
CD	Changes the current directory. (Same as CHDIR.)
CHCP	Displays or sets the number of the active code page.
CHDIR	Changes the current directory. (Same as CD.)
CHKDSK	Checks a disk for errors and displays a status report.
CLS	Clears the screen.
COMMAND	Starts the command processor, COMMAND.COM.
COPY	Copies files (see also XCOPY, XCOPY32).
CSCRIPT	Starts the Microsoft Scripting Host.
CTTY	Changes the terminal device used to control your computer.
CVT	Changes a drive's file system from FAT16 to FAT32 (see Section 10.3).
DATE	Displays and/or changes the date on the computer's internal clock.
DBLSPACE	Configures a DoubleSpace compressed drive.
DEBUG	Starts the Debug program editor.
DEFRAG	Runs a DOS-based defragmentation program (see Section 10.4).
DEL	Deletes files from disk. (Same as ERASE.)
DELTREE	Deletes a directory and its subdirectories.

*In this appendix, we will use the word *directory*, the DOS terminology, instead of its Windows 98 alias, *folder*.

DIR	Displays information about the contents of a directory.
DISKCOMP	Compares the contents of two floppy disks.
DISKCOPY	Copies an entire floppy disk.
DOSKEY	Reuses or edits previously-issued DOS commands.
DOSSHELL	Starts MS-DOS Shell, a menu-driven DOS interface.
ECHO	Turns the echoing of DOS commands on or off.
EDIT	Edits text files.
EMM386	Turns a DOS-based expanded memory manager (see Section 12.3) on or off.
ERASE	Deletes files from disk. (Same as DEL.)
EXIT	Closes the command processor, COMMAND.COM.
EXPAND	Decompresses compressed files.
EXTRACT	Decompresses CAB files (used in Windows 98 setup) .
FASTHELP	Displays a summary of DOS commands.
FASTOPEN	Opens frequently-used files and directories more quickly.
FC	Compares the contents of files.
FDISK	Partitions a disk.
FIND	Searches a file for specified text.
FORMAT	Formats a hard or floppy disk.
GRAPHICS	Loads (into RAM) a program that can print graphics.
HELP	Starts the DOS help system or displays help for a given command.
IEXTRACT	Extracts particular files from backup files.
INTERLNK	Connects two computers through their serial or parallel ports for the purpose of sharing files or printers.
INTERSVR	Copies files on one linked computer to another.

KEYB	Sets up a computer for use with a specified language.
LABEL	Creates, changes, or deletes a disk's volume label.
LH	Loads a program into upper memory. (Same as LOADHIGH.)
LOADFIX	Loads and runs a program in a specified memory address space.
LOADHIGH	Loads a program into upper memory. (Same as LH.)
MD	Creates a directory. (Same as MKDIR.)
MEM	Displays information about current memory use.
MEMMAKER	Starts the MemMaker program, which optimizes the memory available to DOS programs.
MKDIR	Creates a directory. (Same as MD.)
MODE	Configures ports and devices and changes other system settings.
MORE	Displays output to the screen one screen at a time.
MOVE	Moves (and optionally renames) files.
MSAV	Scans drives for computer viruses.
MSBACKUP	Backs up and restores files, directories, and disks.
MSD	Provides technical information about your computer system.
NLSFUNC	Loads country-specific information to provide language support.
PATH	Specifies or displays the path for executable files.
PAUSE	Suspends processing of a batch file.
POWER	Turns power management on or off.
PRINT	Prints the contents of a text file on a printer.
PROMPT	Specifies the form of the DOS prompt.
QBASIC	Starts the Microsoft QBasic programming environment for creating DOS programs.
RD	Deletes a directory. (Same as RMDIR.)

REN	Renames files. (Same as RENAME.)
RENAME	Renames files. (Same as REN.)
REPLACE	Replaces files.
RMDIR	Deletes a directory. (Same as RD.)
SET	Creates DOS environmental variables.
SETVER	Sets the version number for DOS to a required value.
SHARE	Allocates storage space and locking capability for DOS files.
SORT	Sorts an input list.
START	Runs a Windows (or DOS) application from the DOS prompt.
SUBST	Associates a specified path with a drive letter.
SYS	Copies DOS system files and the command processor to a disk.
TIME	Displays and/or change s the time on the computer's internal clock.
TREE	Displays the structure of the directories on a disk.
TYPE	Displays the contents of a text file on the screen.
UNDELETE	Restores a deleted file.
UNFORMAT	Recovers from an accidental format.
VER	Displays the version number of DOS or Windows.
VERIFY	Verifies that your files are written correctly to disk.
VOL	Displays a disk's volume label.
VSAFE	Loads a program that scans your drives for computer viruses.
XCOPY	Copies files and directories (an extended version of COPY).
XCOPY32	Copies files and directories (a version of XCOPY for use with long file names).

Parameters and switches

Every DOS command has a specific form, or *syntax*, which must be followed exactly or the command will not be processed. The syntax for most commands includes optional parameters and/or switches.

- A command *parameter* generally gives the name of the file, directory, or drive to which the command applies.
- A command *switch*, which is preceded by a slash (/) symbol, specifies that a certain option will or will not be in effect when the command is executed.

For example, when the DIR command is issued without any parameters or switches, the contents of the current directory are displayed. Here are some examples of how this command is modified by adding parameters and/or switches:

`DIR a:` (with parameter "a:")

Displays the contents of the (root directory of the) disk in the a: drive; the listing will scroll until the end is reached.

`DIR c:\dos /p` (with parameter "c:\dos" and switch "/p")

Displays the contents of the c:\dos directory, pausing after each full screen until you press a key.

`DIR /w /p` (with switches "/p" and "/w")

Displays the contents of the current directory in "wide" format (which allows you to see more files at once), pausing after each full screen until you press a key.

DOS Help

Due to their complexity and the need for exact syntax, DOS commands are not easy to master. Fortunately, help is always just a few keystrokes away. To obtain online help, at the DOS prompt type any of the following commands and press the Enter key:

- The **HELP** command starts MS-DOS Help and displays a list of all available commands. To access information about a particular command, scroll until that command is displayed, and then click on it or press the Enter key. The resulting help screen displays the function of the command, its syntax, and the available parameters and switches.
- Use **HELP *command*** (for example: `Help DIR`) to display the help entry for the specified command directly, without going through the general Help system (described above). The information supplied is the same as that obtained via general Help.
- Use ***command* /?** (for example: `DIR /?`) to obtain concise help about the specified command.

Using Wildcards with DOS Commands

In Section 4.3, we discussed the use of *wildcards* — symbols that represent one or more characters of any kind — with the Windows Find utility. In fact, wildcards have limited range in Windows 98; they can only be used in the Find window and the Save and Open dialog boxes. In DOS, however, they are an important factor in increasing the power of many commands, and sometimes allow you to perform certain tasks more efficiently than in Windows.

DOS wildcards DOS (like Windows) uses two wildcards:

? represents any single character.

* represents any combination of any number of characters.

For example, in the current directory:

.	represents all files, with or without an extension.
*.ltr	represents all files with extension *ltr*.
S*	represents all files beginning with *S* and having no extension.
S?m	represents all files with a three-character filename beginning with *S*, ending with *m*, and having no extension.
?d*.*	represents all files with second character *d*.

Using wildcards Used with certain DOS commands, wildcards allow you to process sets of files, all at once. For example, here are some things that DOS does, with the aid of wildcards, more easily than Windows:

- To display only those files in the current directory with extension *bak*, use:

  ```
  DIR *.bak
  ```

- To rename all files in the current directory, changing their existing extension *bak* to the extension *old*, use:

  ```
  REN *.bak *.old
  ```

- To set read-only and hidden attributes for all files in the current directory with filename *outline* (regardless of their extension), use:

  ```
  ATTRIB +r +h outline.*
  ```

Wildcards are also useful with the DEL command in deleting sets of files and with the COPY, XCOPY, and XCOPY32 commands in copying sets of files.

Special DOS Commands

As you have just seen, with the help of wildcards, DOS can perform certain tasks more efficiently than Windows. There are also certain DOS commands that can perform tasks that Windows cannot do at all! For example:

Printing a directory listing

- You can print a hard copy of the contents of a directory by "redirecting" the output of the DIR command to the printer. For example, the command

  ```
  DIR > PRN
  ```

  sends a listing of all files in the current directory to the printer; and the command

  ```
  DIR \windows\*.bak > PRN
  ```

  prints all files in the windows directory with extension *bak*.

Creating a file containing a directory listing

- You can create a text file that contains all files in a specified directory (or all files satisfying a wildcard string) by redirecting the output of the DIR command to a file. For example,

  ```
  DIR > DIR.TXT
  ```

  creates a text file (in the current directory) that contains a listing of the current directory.

Recovering a deleted file

- You can recover files that have been deleted from a hard or floppy disk by using the UNDELETE command. This is especially important when using DOS because files deleted from the DOS prompt are not sent to the Recycle Bin. Nonetheless, the UNDELETE command works with files deleted from disk by any means, including those removed from the Recycle Bin. Issuing the UNDELETE command starts the Undelete utility, which provides instructions for its use. (This command must be run in MS-DOS mode — after Windows is shut down.)

Comparing files

- You can compare the content of two files by using the FC command. For example,

  ```
  FC study.dat study.bak
  ```

  compares the data in the files study.dat and study.bak and issues a report.

Batch Files

A *batch file* is a program that consists of DOS commands. A batch file is usually created in a text editor, such as Windows' Notepad or DOS' Edit, and must be saved as a text (ASCII) file with a *bat* extension. As an example, Autoexec.bat is a batch file that is normally executed automatically when Windows or DOS is started.

Executing a batch file

You can execute a batch file in the same ways you would start any DOS program; for example:

- Type its filename (without the extension) at the DOS prompt.
- Choose its icon in Windows Explorer or any folder window.
- Choose a shortcut icon to the batch file.
- Use the Run option on the Start menu.

Batch files can also be executed from within many applications, but the way this is accomplished varies considerably; check the application's documentation.

Batch files are often used to automate oft-repeated tasks such as logging on to a network or setting up a modem link to another computer. As an example, the batch file

```
CD \DATA
\WP60\WP
CD \
```

changes the default directory to DATA, starts the program in the WP60 directory named WP and, after this application terminates, changes the default to the root directory.

Most DOS commands may be used in a batch file. The following table lists those whose primary use is in creating batch files.

Command	Function
CALL	Executes another batch file and then returns to the current one.
CHOICE	Prompts the user to select from a specified set of options.
ECHO	Turns the display of commands ON or OFF during execution.
FOR...IN...DO	Creates a loop that repeats a set of commands.
GOTO	Causes a specific labeled command to be executed next.

IF	Causes a branch to a specific block of code.
REM	Inserts a "remark", which is ignored by the computer, into the code.
@	Turns off the display of the current line during execution.

APPENDIX C

Answers to Odd-Numbered Review Exercises

Introduction

1. hardware
3. eight
5. tape *or* CD-ROM *or* Zip
7. true
9. false
11. false
13. false
15. d
17. a
19. operating system
21. graphical user interface
23. false
25. true
27. c
29. ENIAC
31. 1975
33. Apple Macintosh
35. false
37. false
39. b
41. b

Chapter 1

1. icon
3. false
5. left mouse button
7. dialog box
9. false
11. false
13. c
15. title bar
17. right border / left border
19. true
21. a

23. A: System menu icon B: Title bar
    C: Minimize button D: Maximize button
25. OK *or* Close
27. check box
29. true
31. c
33. Start
35. true
37. c

Chapter 2

1. Ctrl+Esc
3. Close (*or* Exit)
5. true
7. c
9. Accessories
11. open
13. true
15. true
17. a
19. Taskbar
21. Clipboard
23. true
25. c
27. install
29. true
31. c
33. Start
35. book
37. true
39. true
41. c

Chapter 3

1. file
3. true
5. b
7. contents (*or* right)
9. Details
11. true
13. d
15. Ctrl (Control)
17. Send To
19. true
21. a
23. Recycle Bin (*or* Recycled)
25. box
27. false
29. d
31. double-click
33. true
35. d
37. right-clicking
39. true
41. b

Chapter 4

1. top
3. tiled
5. true
7. false
9. d
11. shortcut
13. Start Menu Programs
15. false
17. d
19. Named
21. double-click
23. true

25. c
27. registered
29. false
31. d
33. spool
35. queue
37. true
39. false
41. a
43. sheet
45. true
47. a

Chapter 5

1. Settings
3. true
5. b
7. Display
9. screen saver
11. false
13. b
15. Appearance
17. true
19. true
21. a
23. Keyboard
25. false
27. d
29. Date/Time
31. Sounds
33. false
35. d

Chapter 6

1. network/online service/ISP
3. browser
5. false
7. true
9. b
11. Favorite
13. Address box
15. false
17. d
19. engine
21. false
23. d
25. e-mail
27. Insert File
29. true
31. d
33. Forms
35. true
37. false
39. b
41. Channel
43. Manage Subscriptions
45. false
47. true
49. b
51. d

Chapter 7

1. Home
3. Ctrl+Z
5. false
7. c
9. 72
11. true
13. d
15. landscape
17. one-half
19. true
21. false
23. a

25. Object
27. true
29. c
31. Print Preview
33. false
35. true
37. d

Chapter 8

1. left
3. false
5. a
7. Shift
9. foreground
11. false
13. false
15. a
17. c
19. red
21. true
23. d
25. Shift
27. Edit
29. true
31. b
33. Print Preview
35. false
37. c

Chapter 9

1. View
3. Sta
5. false
7. b
9. text editor
11. header
13. true
15. b
17. multimedia
19. true
21. false
23. c
25. d
27. Magnifier
29. Finish
31. false
33. d
35. Character Map
37. false
39. a

Chapter 10

1. Plug and Play
3. true
5. a
7. System Tools
9. true
11. d
13. Disk Cleanup
15. file allocation table *or* FAT
17. false
19. b
21. ScanDisk
23. Custom
25. false
27. false
29. c
31. System Monitor
33. hardware profile
35. true
37. false
39. c

Chapter 11

1. local area network (*or* LAN)
3. server
5. b
7. Dial-Up Networking
9. true
11. true
13. a
15. Communications
17. true
19. b
21. laptop
23. Direct Cable Connection
25. false
27. a

Chapter 12

1. full-screen
3. toolbar
5. false
7. b
9. toolbar
11. Extended
13. false
15. a
17. boot
19. Config.sys/Autoexec.bat
21. false
23. d
25. System.dat/User.dat
27. keys
29. true
31. a
33. server
35. Object
37. false
39. false
41. c

Index

A

B

C

E

F

M

N

O

Q

R

S

T

U

V

W

X

Y

Z